INSTRUCTIONAL DESIGN FOR
CLASSROOM TEACHING AND
LEARNING

Kevin B. Zook, *Messiah College*

©2001 • 464 pages • Paperback • 0-395-85702-

EXPLORE

OUR MULTIMEDIA SUPPLEMENTS

HOUGHTON MIFFLIN'S
TEACHER EDUCATION WEB SITE

Go to **college.hmco.com** to access Houghton Mifflin's **Teacher
Education web site,** which provides resources for beginning
and experienced professionals in education.

The **Ticket Booth** contains
- text pages
- links to the catalog
- exam copy orders

Concept Carts have information on five key learning themes
- cooperative learning
- constructivism
- inclusive classrooms
- learning environments
- technology as a tool

Trains link to other HMCo Teacher Education web sites
developed especially to support new and practicing teachers.

NEW VIDEO POLICY

Houghton Mifflin offers a library of more than 20 videos
from Films for the Humanities to qualified adopters. Contact
your local sales representative for details.

Instructional Design
for Classroom Teaching
and Learning

Kevin B. Zook
Messiah College

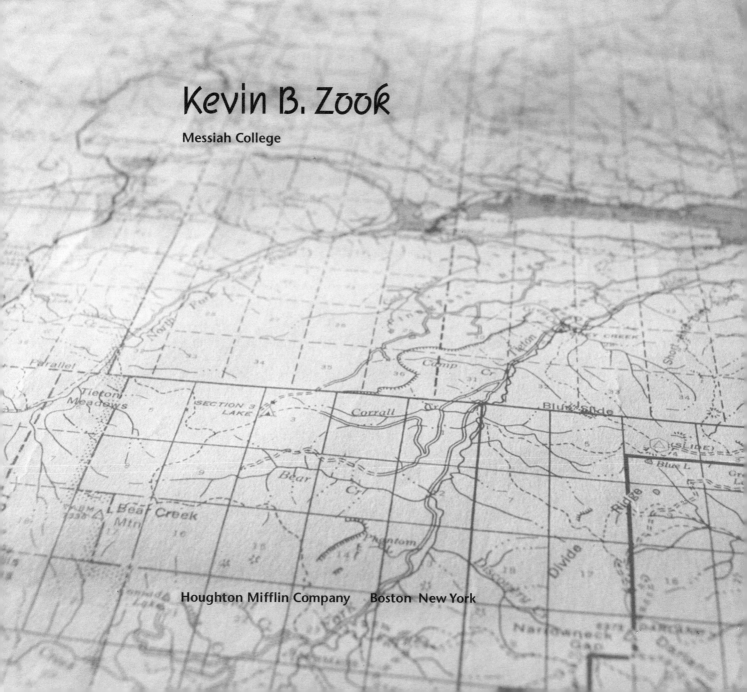

Houghton Mifflin Company   Boston New York

To Amy

Thanks for doing the work that matters the most.

Senior Sponsoring Editor: Loretta Wolozin
Development Editor: Lisa Mafrici
Editorial Assistant: Sarah Rodriguez
Project Editor: Florence Kilgo
Editorial Assistants: Jennifer O'Neill, Cecilia Molinari
Senior Production/Design Coordinator: Jill Haber
Senior Manufacturing Coordinator: Priscilla Bailey
Marketing Manager: Jay Hu

Cover design by Diana Coe/Ko Design
Cover illustration by Bong-Tae Kim. Hansun Gallery, Seoul, Korea
Photo credits: John Nordell/Index Stock Imagery, p. 1; Michael Zide, pp. 8, 37, 89, 147, 214, and 374; Spencer Grant/Index Stock Imagery, pp. 101 and 195; Susie Fitzhugh, pp. 112, 273, 311, and 350; Joel Gordon, p. 180; Jean-Claude Lejeune, p. 247; Ron Chapple/FPG International, p. 369.

Printed in the U.S.A.

Library of Congress Catalog Number: 00-104961

ISBN: 0-395-85702-3

1 2 3 4 5 6 7 8 9– SUB –03 02 01 00 99

Brief Contents

Part One   Where Are We Going?
Developing and Analyzing Learning Goals 1

 1 Teachers Are Instructional Designers 2
 2 Writing Instructional Goals for Learning Outcomes 22
 3 Analyzing Instructional Content 59

Part Two   What Will We Do When We Get There?
Assessing the Achievement of Learning Goals 101

 4 Principles of Classroom Assessment 102
 5 Classroom Assessment Strategies 129
 6 Preparing and Using Instructional Objectives 166

Part Three   How Will We Get There?
Developing Instructional Strategies for Learning
Goals 195

 7 Instructional Strategies for Verbal Information Outcomes 196
 8 Instructional Strategies for Concept-Learning Outcomes 235
 9 Instructional Strategies for Rule, Principle, and Cognitive Strategy
Learning Outcomes 262
10 Sequencing Instructional Events 289
11 Designing Instructional Units 334

Part Four   Points of Departure
Personalizing the Instructional Design Process 369

12 Instructional Design in the Classroom 370

Contents

Preface xvii

Part One

Where Are We Going?
Developing and Analyzing Learning Goals 1

1 Teachers Are Instructional Designers 2

Instructional Design: Beginning at the End 3

The Ends Determine the Means 4

Basic Principles of Instructional Design 5

Planning a Camping Trip 5
Selecting a Destination 5   Preparing for the Trip 6
Three Fundamental Questions of Trip Planning 7
Design-Teaching: Where Are We Going? 7
A Process and Product View of Learning 7   Describing Learned
Capabilities with Instructional Goals 10   Specifying and Analyzing
the Content to be Learned 11
Design-Teaching: What Will We Do When We Get There? 12
Preparing Instructional Objectives 12   Assessment Validity and
Reliability 12   Using Multiple Assessment Strategies 13
Design-Teaching: How Will We Get There? 13
Planning an Instructional Strategy 14   Resolving Learning
Difficulties 15

**Putting the Pieces Together:
A Systems Approach to Instructional Design 15**

Features of Instructional Systems 16
Specifying Instructional Goals 17   Identifying and Analyzing
Content 17   Preparing Assessment Procedures 18   Designing
an Instructional Strategy 18   Implementing Instruction and
Assessment 18   Diagnosing and Remediating Learner
Difficulties 19
Supporting Learner Diversity Through Systematic
Instructional Design 19
LOOKING BACK   LOOKING AHEAD   20
RESOURCES FOR FURTHER REFLECTION AND EXPLORATION   20
Print Resources 20   WWW Resources 21

2 Writing Instructional Goals for Learning Outcomes   22

Instructional Goals   23

Features of Instructional Goals   24
Effects of Instructional Goals on Assessment and Teaching   24

Learning Outcomes   26

Declarative Knowledge   27
Procedural Knowledge   27
Affective Knowledge   29

Gagne's Five Learning Outcomes   29

Verbal Information   29
  Labels   30   Facts   30   Organized Facts   32   Verbal Chains   32
  Capability Verbs for Verbal Information Goals   32
Intellectual Skills   33
  Discriminations   35   Concepts   36   Rules and Principles   38
  Problem Solving   40
Cognitive Strategies   41
Intellectual Skills and Cognitive Strategies: A Bigger Picture   42
Motor Skills   45
Attitudes   47

Using Instructional Goals to Focus Classroom Teaching   48

Deriving Instructional Goals from Subject Matter   50
Deriving Instructional Goals from Professional Standards   50
Diverse Instructional Goals for Diverse Learners   51

Instructional Design Case Analyses   52

Case 1: Ms. Nelson   52
Case 2: Mrs. Torres   56
Case 3: Mr. Hoffman   56
  LOOKING BACK   LOOKING AHEAD   57
  RESOURCES FOR FURTHER REFLECTION AND EXPLORATION
  Print Resources   58   WWW Resources   58

3 Analyzing Instructional Content   59

Solving Instructional Problems   60

Understanding: The Key to Problem Solving   60
Content Analysis: A Search for Understanding   61
Using Content Analysis for Instructional Decision Making   61
  Planning Instruction   62   Delivering Instruction   63   Diagnosing
  Learning Difficulties   63

Selecting a Content Analysis Procedure   64
   Organizational Relationships   64   Chronological Relationships   64
   Learning Relationships   64

Cluster Analysis   65

Performing a Cluster Analysis   65
   What Is the Verbal Information to Be Learned?   66   What Are
   Some Conceptual Categories That We Can Use to Cluster the
   Information?   66   How Are the Conceptual Categories Related to
   Each Other?   68   How Can We Visualize the Organizational
   Structure?   69

Value of Cluster Analysis for Learning and Teaching   70

Deciding When to Perform a Cluster Analysis   71
   Case Analysis: Cluster Analysis in the Classroom   72

Hierarchical Analysis   74

Performing a Hierarchical Analysis   74
   What Is the Intellectual Skill to Be Learned?   75   What Are
   the Prerequisite Skills That Comprise the Intellectual Skill to
   Be Learned?   75   What Are the Prerequisite Intellectual Skills to Be
   Learned for Each Instructional Subgoal?   75   How Far Down the
   Learning Hierarchy Do We Go?   76   How Can We Organize and
   Display the Results of a Hierarchical Analysis?   76

Hierarchical Analysis for Concepts   78
   Identifying Concept Features   79   Correlational Concept
   Features   80   Organizing Concept Features   81

Hierarchical Analysis for Rules and Principles   82
   Identifying Subordinate Concepts   82
   Case Analysis: Hierarchical Analysis in the Classroom   84

Procedural Analysis   87

Performing a Procedural Analysis   87
   What Are the Major Steps in the Procedure?   87   What Is the
   Instructional Subgoal for Each Step?   87   What Are the Subordinate
   Skills for Each Subgoal?   88   Are There Any More Subordinate Skills?
   89   How Do We Display the Results of a Procedural Analysis?   89
   Case Analysis: Procedural Analysis for an Intellectual Skill   91
   Case Analysis: Procedural Analysis for a Cognitive Strategy   93

Combining Content Analysis Procedures   95

How Learning Outcomes Interact   95

Analyzing Attitude Instructional Goals   96
   Analyzing the Affective Component   96   Analyzing the Cognitive
   Component   96   Analyzing the Behavior Component   97

Some Final Thoughts About Content Analysis   98

LOOKING BACK   LOOKING AHEAD   99
RESOURCES FOR FURTHER REFLECTION AND EXPLORATION
Print Resources   99

Part Two   What Will We Do When We Get There?
Assessing the Achievement of Learning Goals 101

4 Principles of Classroom Assessment 102

The Role of Assessment in Instructional Decision Making 103

Evaluating Learners 103
Assessing Learners 104
   Principles of Assessment 104   Classroom Testing 106
Measuring Learners 107
   Quantitative and Qualitative Assessment Data 107   Advantages of
   Quantitative Assessment 108

Major Types of Instructional Decisions 110

Preinstructional Evaluation 110
Formative Evaluation 111
Summative Evaluation 112
Diagnostic Evaluation 113

Validity and Reliability 115

Validity and Reliability: Basic Definitions 115
   Validity 115   Reliability 116   Relationships Between Reliability
   and Validity 116
Maximizing Assessment Validity 117
   Content Consistency 117   Action Consistency 118
Strategies for Enhancing Assessment Validity 120
   Begin with Clear Instructional Goals 120   Prepare Assessment
   Blueprints 120   Ask Other People to Evaluate Performance
   Opportunities 121
Maximizing Assessment Reliability 122
   Reliability and Measurement Error 122   Learner Characteristics 126

Why Bother with Assessment? 127

LOOKING BACK   LOOKING AHEAD 127
RESOURCES FOR FURTHER REFLECTION AND EXPLORATION
Print Resources 128   WWW Resources 128

5 Classroom Assessment Strategies 129

Selecting an Assessment Item Format 130

Commonly Used Test Item Formats 130
   Cognitive Test Items 131   Performance Test Items 133   Attitude
   Assessments 133

Criteria for Selecting Test Item Formats   133
Validity   133   Reliability   135   Response Production   135   Ease of
Developing the Stimulus   135   Ease of Developing Scoring Criteria
136   Ease of Scoring   136   Ease of Administering   136   Range of
Instructional Goals   136

Developing Cognitive Assessment Items   137

Guidelines for Developing Objectively Scored Cognitive Items   137
Multiple-Choice Items   137   True-False Items   139   Matching   140
Completion   141

Guidelines for Developing Subjectively Scored Cognitive Items   142
Writing Short-Answer and Essay Items   142   Scoring Short-Answer
and Essay Items   143

Developing Performance and Attitude Assessments   144

Rules and Procedures for Developing Performance Items   145
Types of Performance Items   145   Constructing Performance
Items   145   Scoring Performance Items   148   The Value of
Analytical Scoring   150   Using Portfolios as Performance
Assessment   150

Assessing Attitudes   151
Focusing on Voluntary Behaviors   151   Direct and Indirect
Approaches to Attitude Assessment   154   Constructing Thurstone
Scales   155   Constructing Likert Scales   156   Constructing
Semantic Differential Scales   157
Case Analyses: Selecting and Preparing Assessment Tools in the Classroom   159
LOOKING BACK LOOKING AHEAD   164
RESOURCES FOR FURTHER REFLECTION AND EXPLORATION
Print Resources   164   Software Resources   165   WWW Resources   165

6 Preparing and Using Instructional Objectives   166

Expressing Educational Outcomes   167

Educational Goals   168
Instructional Goals   168
Instructional Objectives   169

Developing Instructional Objectives   171

Understanding Different Terms   171
Understanding Different Formats   171
Performance: What Will Learners Do?   173
Context: Under What Conditions Will Learners Perform?   174
Describing Cues to Stimulate Performance   176   Describing
Resources to Enable Performance   178   Describing Complexity of
Context to Restrict Performance   178
Quality: How Will Learner Performance be Evaluated?   178
Accuracy or Precision   180   Number of Correct Responses
or Errors   180   Time Limits   181   Consistency with an Established
or Stated Standard   181   Concrete Consequences or Outcomes   182

Determining Mastery Criteria   183
Learner Characteristics   183   Task Characteristics   183
Consequences of Misclassification   184   Summary and a Final Word
on Form   185

Instructional Objectives for Learning Outcomes   186

Instructional Objectives for Verbal Information Outcomes   186
Instructional Objectives for Intellectual Skill Outcomes:
Concepts   188
Instructional Objectives for Rules, Principles, and
Cognitive Strategies   189
Instructional Objectives for Motor Skill Outcomes   191
Instructional Objectives for Attitude Outcomes   191
LOOKING BACK   LOOKING AHEAD   193
RESOURCES FOR FURTHER REFLECTION AND EXPLORATION
Print Resources   193

Part Three   How Will We Get There?
Developing Instructional Strategies for Learning Goals   195

7   Instructional Strategies for Verbal
Information Outcomes   196

Internal and External Conditions of Learning   197

Instructional Events and Learning Processes   197
Internal and External Conditions of Learning   198
Conditions of Learning for Major Learning Outcomes   199
The Instructional Strategy: The Teacher's Game Plan   201
Information   201   Engagement   201   Practice   202

Verbal Information: Internal Conditions of Learning   203

Learners Are Information Processors   203
An Information Processing Model of Learning   204
Memory Structures   205   Control Processes   205   Executive
Control   206
Schemas: The Building Blocks of Long-Term Memory   207
Meaningful Encoding: Elaboration Processes   209
Meaningful Encoding: Organization Processes   211

Verbal Information: External Conditions of Learning   212

Helping Learners Attend to Verbal Information   213
Highlighting Strategies   213   Questioning Strategies   213
Distinctiveness Strategies   214
Helping Learners Activate Prior Knowledge   216
Direct Cues and Reminders   216   Instructional Analogies   216
Advance Organizers   217   Concrete Experiences   219

Helping Learners Encode Information: Supporting Generative
Learning 220
Verbal Elaboration and Imagery 220 Self-Generated Analogies 220
Self-Summaries and Self-Questioning 221

Manufacturing Meaning: Using Mnemonic Devices 221
Rhyme-Based Mnemonics 221 Word-Based Mnemonics 222
Image-Based Mnemonics 223

Helping Learners Encode Information: Supporting Organization 224
Outlines, Charts, and Tables 224 Concept Maps 225 Schematic
Diagrams 225

Practice: Helping Learners Construct and Strengthen
Retrieval Routes 226
Case Analysis: Designing an Instructional Strategy for Verbal
Information Learning 227

LOOKING BACK LOOKING AHEAD 232

RESOURCES FOR FURTHER REFLECTION AND EXPLORATION
Print Resources 233 CD-ROM Resources 233 WWW Resources 234

8 Instructional Strategies for Concept-Learning Outcomes 235

Intellectual Skills: General Learning Processes 236

Representing Procedural Knowledge 237
Productions: Units of Procedural Knowledge 237 Production
Systems: Condition-Action Rules for Complex Skills 238

Acquiring Conditionalized Procedural Knowledge 240
Cognitive Stage of Skill Learning 240 Associative Stage of Skill
Learning 240 Autonomous Stage of Skill Learning 241

Concepts: Internal Conditions of Learning 242

Prerequisite Concepts and Discriminations 242
Verbal Labels for Prerequisite Concepts 243
The Generalization Process 244
The Discrimination Process 247

Concepts: External Conditions of Learning 249

Concept Learning: The Cognitive Stage 249
Concept Learning: The Associative Stage 252
Supporting Concept Generalization 252 Supporting Concept
Discrimination 253 Providing Informative Feedback 254

Concept Learning: The Autonomous Stage 255
Case Analysis: Designing an Instructional Strategy for Concept Learning 256

LOOKING BACK LOOKING AHEAD 259

RESOURCES FOR FURTHER REFLECTION AND EXPLORATION
Print Resources 260 WWW Resources 260

9 Instructional Strategies for Rule, Principle, and Cognitive Strategy Learning Outcomes 262

Rules and Principles: Internal Conditions of Learning 263

Prerequisite Concepts 264
The Generalization Process 265
The Discrimination Process 266

Learning Rules and Principles: External Conditions 267

Rule and Principle Learning: The Cognitive Stage 267
Rule and Principle Learning: The Associative Stage 269
Supporting the Generalization Process 270 Supporting the
Discrimination Process 270 Providing Practice and Feedback 271
Rule and Principle Learning: The Autonomous Stage 272
Case Analysis: Designing an Instructional Strategy for Rule Learning 273
Case Analysis: Designing an Instructional Strategy for Principle Learning 279
Case Analysis: Designing an Instructional Strategy for Cognitive
Strategy Learning 283
LOOKING BACK   LOOKING AHEAD 286
RESOURCES FOR FURTHER REFLECTION AND EXPLORATION
Print Resources 287   WWW and CD-ROM Resources 287

10 Sequencing Instructional Events 289

An Introduction to Instructional Sequencing 290

What Is an Instructional Sequence? 290
Gagne's Events of Instruction 291
Planning External Instructional Events 293
Learner Characteristics 293 Instructional Media 295 Learning
Outcome 295

Preparation: Planning for the Preinstructional Phase 296

Attention: The Gateway to Learning 296
Using Variability to Support Attention 296 Using Humor to
Support Attention 297 Using Concreteness to Support
Attention 298 Using Cognitive Conflict to Support Attention 299
Using Inquiry to Support Attention 299 Using Active Participation
to Support Attention 299
Expectancy: Establishing a Reason for Learning 300
Informing Learners of Objectives 300 Activating Learner
Motivation 302 Using Keller's ARCS Model to Support
Motivation 302
Retrieval to Working Memory: What Do Learners Already Know? 304
Relevant Prior Knowledge and Learning Outcomes 305 Supporting
Retrieval to Working Memory 305
Case Analysis: Planning Preinstructional Events 307

Construction: Planning for the Instructional Phase   309

Selective Perception: Focusing on the Meaning That Matters   309
Selective Perception and Learning Outcomes   310   Selective
Perception and Learner Schemas: A Developmental Perspective   310
Strategies to Support Selective Perception   312

Encoding: Constructing Personal Meaning   314
Encoding for Different Learning Outcomes   314   Supporting
Encoding Through Learning Strategies   314
Case Analysis: Planning Instructional Events for a Verbal Information Goal   316
Case Analysis: Planning Instructional Events for an Intellectual Skill Goal   317

Finishing Touches: Planning for the Postinstructional Phase   318

Responding: Applying New Skills and Recalling New Facts   318
Practice for Learning Outcomes   318   Principles of Effective
Practice   319

Reinforcement: Confirmation of Learning   321
Feedback for Different Learning Outcomes   322   Delivering Feedback:
Sources and Strategies   323   Principles of Effective Feedback   324

Cueing Retrieval: Teaching for Transfer   326
Transfer for Different Learning Outcomes   326   Effects of
Situated Cognition on Transfer   327   Supporting Retention and
Transfer   327

A Brief Word About Summative Assessment   329
Case Analysis: Planning Postinstructional Events for a Verbal Information Goal   330
Case Analysis: Planning Postinstructional Events for a Cognitive Strategy Goal   331

LOOKING BACK   LOOKING AHEAD   331

RESOURCES FOR FURTHER REFLECTION AND EXPLORATION
Print Resources   332   WWW Resources   333

11 Designing Instructional Units   334

A Rationale for Unit Planning   335

Benefits of Designing Instructional Units   336
Major Components of Instructional Units   337

Designing a Unit Plan   338

Selecting a Central Theme or Topic   338
Identifying Educational Goals and Instructional Goals   339
Identifying Organizing Themes   343
Selecting and Analyzing Essential Content   343
Preparing Assessment Procedures   344
Sequencing Goals and Allocating Time   346
Clustering Instructional Goals   346   Developing a Block Plan   348
Selecting Learning Activities and Resources   349
Organizing Instructional Resources   349   Planning Culminating
Activities   350
Case Analysis: Unit Planning in the Classroom   352

Designing Thematic Units   362

Using Thematic Units to Support a Seamless Curriculum   362

Planning a Thematic Unit   364
Identifying an Integrating Theme   364   Identifying Goals, Content, and Objectives   365   Identifying Instructional Resources   365

LOOKING BACK   **LOOKING AHEAD**   366

RESOURCES FOR FURTHER REFLECTION AND EXPLORATION
Print Resources   367   WWW Resources   368

Part Four   **Points of Departure**
Personalizing the Instructional Design Process   369

12   **Instructional Design in the Classroom**   370

Systematic Instructional Design: A Classroom Perspective   371

Impediments to *Design-Teaching*   371
Classroom-Level Impediments to *Design-Teaching*   371   School-Level Impediments to *Design-Teaching*   373   Personal Impediments to *Design-Teaching*   373

So Why Be a *Design-Teacher?*   374

Questions, Answers, and Points of Departure   375

LOOKING BACK   **LOOKING AHEAD**   380

RESOURCES FOR FURTHER REFLECTION AND EXPLORATION
Print Resources   380

GLOSSARY   383

REFERENCES   391

INDEX   407

Preface

Educational reform seems to be on everyone's minds these days. Open any popular magazine or newspaper and you will find anecdotal articles decrying the inability of U.S. high school graduates to name the capital of some foreign country, write complete sentences, or solve real-world math problems. Open nearly any journal in the field of education and you will find a smorgasbord of strategies for reforming our nation's system of schooling: national standards, critical thinking curricula, cooperative learning, constructivist teaching methods, whole-language reading programs, outcome-based education, school vouchers, magnet schools, merit pay for teachers, more rigorous teacher preparation programs, and on and on it goes.

I have been watching these calls for reform with interest since about 1982, the year I graduated from college with a degree in elementary education and one year before "A Nation at Risk" got the nation's collective attention. After nearly twenty years of the reform movement spawned by "A Nation at Risk" and a spate of other national reports, the reform drumbeat continues at a steady cadence as educators and politicians search for the magic elixir to cure whatever ails our schools. Understandably, reforming something as complex as schooling is no small undertaking. There simply are too many intertwined variables with which to tinker, intractable bureaucracies to restructure, and entrenched public opinions to sway.

Purpose and Assumptions of the Book

Although I understand and respect the social, economic, and political realities within which schools operate, I believe that the quality of student learning is primarily a function of the quality of *instruction* that students experience while they are at school, and instructional quality is arguably one of the few variables that educators can actually control to some degree. When teachers close the doors of their classrooms and actually get to the business of teaching, they have tremendous opportunities to create effective learning environments. Against the backdrop of perpetual calls for school reform and the potential power of instructional quality, I offer *Instructional Design for Classroom Teaching and Learning*.

A Book for Teachers

My primary goal in writing this book is to empower those closest to the teaching-learning enterprise, classroom teachers, to think strategically and systematically about designing, implementing, and evaluating instruction to maximize the likelihood that all students will learn effectively and master significant learning outcomes. The book is firmly grounded in the field of systematic instructional design, an approach to teaching that has yielded impressive results in business, industry, and military educational settings for several decades but, curiously, has had virtually no significant impact on K-12 schooling. Indeed, as I have talked with classroom teachers about principles of instructional design at in-service seminars and conferences, I have been at once encouraged by the number who say to me that the ideas make a lot of sense and disheartened by the number who also admit that they are hearing those sensible ideas for the very first time. With this book, I attempt to bridge the gap between the world of instructional designers and classroom teachers because I believe the former have much to offer the latter.

Three major assumptions have guided my development of this book. First, I believe that K-12 classroom teachers—especially those who are beginners—can enhance their effectiveness significantly by understanding and applying a systems approach to their instructional planning and delivery. Teachers should understand how the various parts of an instructional *system* (e.g., goals, content, objectives, assessment, learning activities, diagnosis, remediation) work together in an interconnected, integrated way to influence student learning. They should be skilled in applying the principles and procedures that are specific to each part of the process, and they should be able to put the parts together in ways that serve the learning needs of their students.

Second, I believe that teachers need to be *empowered* to design instructional events for themselves. By providing beginning and experienced teachers with the principles and conceptual tools to think for themselves about instructional design, they can be equipped to make better decisions concerning the needs of their own particular learners in their own specific classrooms. As informed teachers become the focal point of classroom thinking, decision-making, and problem-solving processes, both their professional satisfaction and status will be enhanced.

Third, I believe that instructional design is the thoughtful application of *educational psychology*. Systems approaches to instructional design simply provide general strategies (or heuristics) to help structure and guide our thinking as we apply principles of learning, motivation, assessment, individual differences, and so on—the stuff of educational psychology. Throughout the book, I have consistently drawn from the current theoretical and empirical knowledge base generated by educational psychologists to help readers understand the rationale for specific instructional design actions, decisions, and procedures.

Audience

The primary audience for this book is upper-level undergraduate students who are preparing to become classroom teachers. The book would work well as the text for a "Principles of Instruction" course for either elementary or secondary pre-service teachers. The systems model presented in the book is equally applicable to both elementary and secondary teaching. Throughout the book, I demonstrate the model's relevance to teachers of all levels by providing a mix of examples from a wide variety of grade levels and content areas.

A secondary audience for the book includes graduate students who are preparing for positions of instructional leadership within schools. Administrators, school psychologists, school counselors, curriculum specialists, and other educational professionals should be grounded in principles of systematic instructional design so they are in the best possible position to support teachers' efforts in the classroom. For this audience, the book could work well as the text for an introductory graduate course such as "Instructional Design" or "Instructional Systems" that is geared toward the special needs and characteristics of school learning environments.

Content and Organization

The book is organized around a generalized systems model of instructional design. I introduce readers to the model in three major phases, or chunks, that correspond to three questions travelers should ask when planning a trip: (a) Where are we going? (b) What will we do when we get there? and (c) How will we get there? In the first part of the book, we address the first question by exploring principles and procedures for establishing clear teaching goals. After providing an overview of the entire systems model (Chapter 1), we then examine the characteristics of major learning outcomes and the process of developing appropriate instructional goals for each (Chapter 2). The first part concludes with an introduction to specific procedures teachers can use to analyze and understand the content of their instruction (Chapter 3).

In the second part of the book, we devote three chapters to the critical topic of assessment: What will we do when we get there? Assessment is presented as a tool to assist teachers in making important decisions about their students' learning (Chapter 4) and as a vital issue to think about *before* planning learning activities and materials. In Chapter 5, I introduce readers to the wide variety of objective, subjective, and performance assessment tools that are available to them, emphasizing that developing any assessment strategy is a thinking process that must ultimately produce information that is as valid and reliable as possible. After laying this foundation, I demonstrate in Chapter 6 how to write instructional objectives so that they function as useful guides in helping teachers prepare to assess and evaluate student learning.

The third part of the book focuses on the third question: How will we get there? How can teachers prepare instructional events that have the potential to move students toward achieving the goals and objectives that they have specified? Throughout this section, we focus on the internal learning processes that teachers must support to facilitate the acquisition of verbal information (Chapter 7), concepts (Chapter 8), and rules, principles, and cognitive strategies (Chapter 9). In Chapter 10, we examine the use of basic cognitive processes to guide the general sequence of events in any lesson. The third section concludes with an instructional design perspective on unit planning, with special emphasis on designing thematic units (Chapter 11).

In the last part of the book, I encourage readers to think about how they will actually apply systematic instructional design within the complex classroom environment (Chapter 12). Acknowledging that applying a systems model in the classroom is often challenging, I offer some practical advice on adapting the approach to specific teaching situations and personalizing the model as a "point of departure" to inform thinking, decision making and problem solving.

Learning Supports and Supplementary Materials

While developing this book, I have been keenly aware of the need to "practice what I am preaching." I have tried to model for readers instructional design principles by building in a variety of pedagogical features to support active processing and learning.

Voice and Structure.   I have structured each chapter as a very personal, informal conversation with readers. Each chapter begins with a personal anecdote that serves as a meaningful advance organizer to introduce the chapter's major themes and principles. Following the advance organizer, I focus attention on a list of specific instructional goals. The instructional goals describe for readers what they should be able to do to *demonstrate* their learning from each chapter.

In-Text Supports.   Each chapter has a generous number of **learning supports** such as multiple classroom examples (and, where appropriate, nonexamples) to make concepts and principles meaningful; schematic diagrams to help readers visualize and understand how major concepts are interrelated; and various in-text activities to help maintain reader attention and interest and to provide opportunities for readers to become actively involved in processing the material. **Key terms** are bold-faced to signal readers of their importance. These terms are defined immediately in the text as readers encounter them and also in a comprehensive end-of-book glossary. Each chapter ends with a set of **additional resources** to encourage readers to continue exploring major ideas. These resources include recommended readings from print sources such as journal articles, books, and book chapters and nonprint sources such as internet web sites, computer software, and CD-ROMs that pertain to the chapter's themes.

Extended Case Analyses.   To help readers grasp the meaning of *systematic* instructional design, I have built classroom case analyses into nearly every chapter. Early in the book, readers are introduced to three hypothetical classroom teachers who represent different grade levels and subject matter. As I describe important concepts, principles, and procedures, I then have the three case analysis teachers model their application. The three teachers actually "think aloud," providing readers with the opportunity not only to observe their actions (what they do), but to experience vicariously the underlying thinking and decision-making processes (why they do it). By following the same three teachers throughout the book, readers experience first-hand how the various parts of the instructional design process actually fit together in a systematic, integrated way.

Student Exercise Guide.   Above all, I want readers to come away from this book with the ability to *do* instructional design—not just to know something about it. Achieving this goal, of course, requires opportunities for practice—opportunities for readers to get their hands dirty. The *Student Exercise Guide* that accompanies the book provides practice exercises to give readers the chance to begin applying skills and transforming their "knowing about" to "knowing how to." Each exercise is referenced in the text (and with a special icon) at the point where it is most relevant, and readers are encouraged to try each exercise before moving on to new material. At the end of each chapter, one particular exercise is provided to check readers' achievement of the instructional goals that were presented at the beginning of the chapter. This feature models the systematic instructional design principle of establishing clear instructional goals; engaging learners with subject matter, examples, and activities to help them achieve the goals; and then assessing learners by finding out if they can actually demonstrate the capabilities described by the goals. I hope that the various learning supports I have built into the book are useful in bringing instructional design to life and engaging readers actively.

Acknowledgments

Throughout this project, I have incurred enormous debts of gratitude to some wonderful people. Loretta Wolozin, Senior Sponsoring Editor for Education at Houghton Mifflin, shared my vision for the project from the very beginning, and I appreciate the instrumental role she played in making this opportunity possible. I gratefully acknowledge the fine guidance of Lisa Mafrici, Development Editor, whose encouraging words and gentle reminders of impending deadlines helped keep the project moving and on track. Many thanks, also, to Sarah Rodriguez, Julie Lane, Florence Kilgo and Jean Zielinski DeMayo for shepherding the manuscript through various stages of development, production, and marketing. In addition, I wish to thank the following individuals for providing constructive feedback, insights, and suggestions during the development of the manuscript:

John V. Gallagher, Rowan University of New Jersey
Marti Julian, University of Virginia
Brenda C. Litchfield, University of South Alabama
Peggy G. Perkins, University of Nevada, Las Vegas
W. Michael Reed, New York University
Michael A. Rossi, Jr., Centenary College
Willi Savenye, Arizona State University
Martin Tessmer, University of Southern Alabama
John Wedman, University of Missouri–Columbia

This book is a cumulative reflection of many people who have graciously contributed to my personal and professional life over the years. I am profoundly grateful to the Education Department at Messiah College for its significant role in laying a firm foundation for continued personal and professional development. In particular, I gratefully acknowledge the extraordinary work of Edward Kuhlman, who broadened my vision and inspired me to enter the field of educational psychology, and Shirley Carroll, who carefully nurtured my teaching aspirations and always challenged me to stretch myself. I remain deeply indebted to Frank Di Vesta, my graduate mentor at Penn State, whose generous, scholarly influence continues to sharpen my teaching, thinking, and writing. I am also grateful to J. William Moore, long-time Chair of the Education Department at Bucknell University, for giving me the opportunity to explore the field of instructional design and for helping to plant some of the seeds that germinated and took root in this book. Thanks to members of the Education Department at Bucknell, who demonstrated their interest and support in many concrete ways. In particular, Joe Murray, Judith Schaut, Katharyn Nottis, Robert Midkiff, Abe Feuerstein, Russell Dennis, and Sue Ellen Henry all made useful contributions to the project by reading drafts, providing feedback, digging up obscure references, loaning resources, chatting about ideas, and offering encouraging words along the way. Many thanks, also, to Will George of the Bucknell Computer Center for his good-natured, expert assistance with unexpected and untimely computer problems. Finally, to numerous family members and friends who innocently asked on more than one occasion, "So how's the book coming?" I am happy to say simply, it's finished—thanks for asking!

K. Z.

Instructional Design
for Classroom Teaching
and Learning

Where Are We Going?
Developing and Analyzing Learning Goals

The first part of this book focuses on the importance of establishing clear learning goals to guide your thinking and decision-making as a classroom teacher. The first chapter introduces you to a general "systems" approach to designing instruction. This systems model provides an overall sense of direction for designing effective instruction. The next two chapters will help you recognize different types of learning outcomes, write appropriate instructional goals for those outcomes, and analyze the content associated with the outcomes. You will discover how specific instructional goals and carefully analyzed content help to provide a clear destination for your classroom teaching.

1

Teachers Are Instructional Designers

I am a teacher. Over the past fifteen years, I have had the good fortune to teach kindergarten children, elementary-age children, early adolescents, undergraduate college students, and graduate students. Through my varied teaching experiences, I have come to understand and appreciate just how complex and demanding classroom teaching can be at *any* level. With a finite amount of time, energy, and resources, teachers are expected to meet the needs of large numbers of learners who represent an infinite variety of individual personalities, aptitudes, interests, motivations, cultural perspectives, and past experiences. The following description of teaching vividly captures the problems and complexities that teachers experience daily:

> The classroom, located within the larger school organization, is a crowded setting in which the teacher has to manage twenty-five or more students of approximately the same age who involuntarily spend—depending upon their grade level—anywhere from one to five hours daily in a room. Amidst continual communication with individual students and groups (up to 1,000 interactions a day in an elementary classroom), the teacher is expected to maintain control, teach a prescribed content, capture student interest in that content, match levels of instruction to differences among students, and show tangible evidence that students have performed satisfactorily. (Cuban, 1986, pp. 57–58)

I don't know about you, but just reading that description makes me tired. Regardless of our students' age levels and the subject matter that we attempt to help our students understand, teaching is complex, hard, and tiring work because we are interacting with other human beings who are themselves extremely complex. The needs and complexities of students force us to play many interrelated roles in the classroom. Stop for a moment and think about all the different roles that you have observed in your own teachers. Make a list of all the words that you associate with the word *teacher*. Then compare your list to mine in Table 1.1.

INSTRUCTIONAL GOALS FOR CHAPTER 1

After reading and thinking about this chapter, you should be able to . . .

1. Explain the meaning of design, instruction, and instructional design.

2. Describe the features of *design-teachers*.

3. State three critical questions that guide the instructional design process, and explain how the three questions are interrelated.

4. Explain and illustrate the meaning of learning, including internal and external processes and products.

5. Describe the two essential features of a system.

6. Describe and illustrate the major components and interrelationships of an instructional system.

7. Explain how systematic instructional design can help teachers meet the needs of diverse learners.

Table 1.1 What Is a Teacher?	
Counselor	Learner
Coach	Organizer
Motivator	Collaborator
Judge	Model
Friend	Explorer
Referee	Listener
Nurse	Custodian
Confidant	Artist
Advocate	**Instructional designer**
Evaluator	

Do you notice any differences between your list and mine? I suspect that our lists are probably very similar, with the possible exception of the last item on my list: teachers are *instructional designers*. An **instructional designer** is one who carefully and thoughtfully creates learning experiences for others. With all the complexities of teaching and the diverse roles that teachers must play, it is often easy to overlook instructional design as the central responsibility of teaching. Instructional design is the central activity of teaching because teachers are charged with the difficult task of helping others learn through their instruction.

This book is about the process of designing instruction to help students learn in school classrooms. Getting other people to learn is not as easy as it may seem, especially in a complex environment. Therefore, in this first chapter, I introduce a particular instructional design strategy to help structure and focus your thinking about classroom teaching and learning. Before continuing, look closely at the specific goals listed at the beginning of the chapter that you will achieve through your reading.

Instructional Design: Beginning at the End

What does it mean to *design instruction*? Designing instruction is the same as designing anything else—say, a car, a building, or a computer system. Engineers design new cars to achieve specific safety goals or performance features that will appeal to car buyers. Architects design buildings (e.g., family residence, office building, department store) to perform specific functions for people. Programmers design computer systems to help people process information efficiently so that they can achieve their productivity goals.

As you can see, people design cars, buildings, and computer systems to achieve specific *goals*. **Design** refers to the actions, processes, or procedures that are intended to accomplish a particular outcome or goal. The design process begins by clearly specifying the goals to be achieved. Then all subsequent actions and decisions focus on those goals. Eventually the resulting product or outcome is evaluated by assessing how well it achieves the intended goals. Does the car provide a smooth, quiet ride? Do people like the car enough to buy it? Does the house have enough bedrooms and bathrooms for the family who will live in it? Does the computer system have enough memory and operating space to run the word processing or statistical software? Notice that these evaluation questions can be answered by directly observing the performance of the product. Very little speculation, intuition, or subjective judgment is necessary to determine if the product performs according to its original design goals.

When teachers design instruction, they carefully and thoughtfully prepare the classroom environment to help their learners achieve clearly specified learning outcomes. Instructional designers begin the planning process by clearly identifying the learning outcomes that their learners will be able to demonstrate at the end of the teaching-learning process. By specifying the end result of instruction, teachers are then able to make critical decisions regarding appropriate materials, teaching methods, sequencing of content, time allocation, and evaluation procedures. As with cars, buildings, and computer systems, teachers can assess the effectiveness of their instruction by directly observing the capabilities of their learners. If learners can demonstrate that they have achieved the goals for which the instruction was designed, then teachers have evidence that their instruction was indeed effective.

The Ends Determine the Means

The instructional designer's focus on the final learning outcome is similar to a traveler's focus on a final destination. Perhaps you recall the following well-known interchange between a traveler and her "travel agent" from *Alice in Wonderland*:

Alice: Would you tell me, please, which way I ought to go from here?

Cat: That depends a good deal on where you want to get to.

Alice: I don't much care where.

Cat: Then it doesn't matter which way you go.

Alice: So long as I get somewhere!

Cat: Oh, you're sure to do that, if you only walk long enough.

The point of this interchange is that decision making (in any context) depends first on identifying clear goals. Once we identify our goals, all remaining decisions, activities, and processes should point us in the direction of achieving those goals. Similarly, instructional decision making for classroom teachers depends first on identifying clear learning goals. Until we know where we want to get to, deciding which way we ought to go will be difficult and possibly ineffective.

Let's pretend that Alice grows up to become a teacher who is seeking advice from an instructional designer. The conversation might go something like this:

Alice: Would you tell me, please, how I should teach my lesson?

Designer: That depends a good deal on what you want your learners to be able to do as a result of your lesson.

Alice: I really don't know. I have some topics to discuss and some activities to try, but I'm not really sure what I want my students to learn from them.

Designer: Then it doesn't matter how you teach your lesson.

Alice: So long as they learn something!

Designer: Oh, it's possible that they could learn something from your lesson. It's hard to tell, though, exactly what that might be.

I have designed this book to help you design effective learning experiences for students in your classroom. By applying instructional design principles to your own teaching, you will not have to follow in Alice's footsteps, trying random activities that lack focus and purpose and leave learning to chance. In contrast to Alice's activity-based approach, instructional designers make important teaching decisions based on the learning outcomes they want their learners to achieve. As the conversation between Alice and the designer illustrates, until clear learning outcomes are identified, we have no firm basis for classroom decision making. Throughout this book, I use a special term, *design-teacher*, to refer to teachers who take this goal-directed approach to classroom instruction. **Design-teachers** approach the complex task of teaching with clear learning goals that guide their specific decisions, actions, and interactions with learners in the classroom.

Basic Principles of Instructional Design

As we begin this exploration of *design-teaching*, I want you to understand several basic principles of instructional design so that we have a common foundation and vocabulary for the remainder of the book. Before we examine the principles in the context of instructional design, I want you to construct a mental set (or schema) that will provide you with a meaningful framework within which to understand, interpret, and apply them. I have decided to create this advance organizer for you because it will help you to achieve some of the chapter's learning goals. I will have more to say about learning goals later in the chapter. For now, let's go camping!

Planning a Camping Trip

The Zook family sat around the kitchen table on a cold, snowy January evening. Our minds were not focused on the cold and the snow, but rather on the warmth, sunshine, and camping opportunities of the upcoming summer. Because we knew from experience that successful camping trips are the result of careful planning, we began making a list of all the decisions that we would need to make and questions that we would need to answer to prepare for our adventure:

- How many miles will we travel?
- What travel route should we take?
- How much travel time should we allow?
- What are the sights we will see?
- Will there be any sightseeing opportunities along the way?
- How many days will we camp?
- What campground will we use?
- What activities will be available?
- What equipment will we need to take along?
- What types of clothes should we pack?
- How much food will we need to pack?

Now that we had a set of useful questions to guide our planning, it was time for some answers and decisions. We quickly discovered, however, that the answers to some questions depended on the answers to other questions. For example, thinking about the types of clothes and equipment we would need to take along was difficult without knowing the types of activities that would be available to us. Furthermore, it quickly became apparent that we had neglected a fundamental question that we would need to address before we could answer any of the other questions: Where exactly would we be going? As you can see from Table 1.2, our important trip planning questions were impossible to answer without specifying a final destination.

Selecting a Destination   As we thought about destinations, we agreed on two possibilities: to return to a familiar location, Shenandoah National Park in

Table 1.2
Zook Family Camping Decisions

Possible Destination	Not Specified	Shenandoah National Park	Cape Hatteras National Seashore
Sights to see	?	Dark Hollow f\Falls, black bears	Ocracoke lighthouse
Activities	?	Hiking, fly-fishing, pony rides	Swimming, beach
Campground	?	Big meadows	Ocracoke
Length of stay	?	5 days	3 days
Travel route	?	Interstates 81, 66	Interstates 83, 95, 64
Distance from home	?	225 miles	535 miles
Travel time	?	Approximately 5 hours	Approximately 10 hours
Sights enroute	?	Luray Caverns	Kitty Hawk
Food supply needed	?	For 5 days; keep out of tent because of bears!	For 3 days
Clothes needed	?	Sweatshirts for cool weather	Swimwear for hot weather
Equipment needed	?	Fly rod, hiking shoes	Sunscreen, beach toys

Virginia, or try a new location, the Cape Hatteras National Seashore in North Carolina. Now that we had identified two possible final destinations, we could return to answering our questions (see Table 1.2). We knew from experience that Shenandoah, with its scenic waterfalls, hiking trails, trout streams, pony rides, and black bears, would be fun. Thus, once we specified where we were going (Shenandoah National Park), we were able to describe what we expected to be able to do (hiking, fishing, pony riding, bear sighting) when we reached our destination.

■ **Preparing for the Trip** With our clear destination and specific expectations, we also could begin to think about the process of preparing for the trip to the park (see Table 1.2). Using a map, we determined that we would travel approximately 225 miles—about a five-hour drive on Interstates 81 and 66. Knowing that we could easily make the trip in one day, we decided that we would be able to stay at our campground for five days, with one day for the return drive. Therefore, we would need to pack enough food for five days.

To be prepared for the park's activities and the mountain environment, we would need to take with us a combination of warm-weather and cool-weather clothes. Daytime hiking would require lightweight shorts and T-shirts, as well as sturdy hiking shoes for the steep, rocky trails. Cooler evenings around the campfire would require heavier clothing, such as jeans and sweatshirts. I planned to take my fly rod to take advantage of the excellent fishing for native brook trout in the park's mountain streams. Finally, with Luray Caverns located near our travel route and plenty of extra travel time, we decided that we would be able to spare a couple of hours on the way to the campground to visit that attraction. Thus, our specific destination and clear expectations allowed us to make decisions about how we would travel to and prepare for Shenandoah.

Three Fundamental Questions of Trip Planning

Notice that our decision making focused on three major categories of questions (Mager, 1984): (1) Where are we going? (2) What will we do when we get there? and (3) How will we get there? As illustrated in Figure 1.1, these three major questions are interrelated. The answers to one set of questions provided information with which to address the questions in the other two categories. Notice also that the fundamental question on which all our decision making ultimately depended was the destination question: Where are we going? The critical importance of specifying the final destination in planning our camping trip is illustrated in Table 1.2. Notice that when we focused our attention on a different destination, Cape Hatteras, all of our decisions changed in ways that were consistent with and appropriate for that particular goal.

Design-Teaching: Where Are We Going?

Design-teaching is like planning a trip. As *design-teachers*, we address the three basic questions of trip planning in our instructional planning:

1. Where are we going?
2. What will we do when we get there?
3. How will we get there?

The ultimate "destination" for our teaching is that students will learn something (remember Alice?), but what exactly does it mean to learn?

■ **A Process and Product View of Learning** Although learning can take several different forms, as we will see in the next chapter, the underlying features remain constant. Educational psychologists often define learning as a relatively stable change in behavior that is produced by experience (Gagne, 1985; Ormrod, 1995). I prefer an expanded definition that focuses attention on the inner cognitive processes that make the outward behavior possible: **learning** is a relatively stable change in outward capability that is constructed internally from experiences with the world.

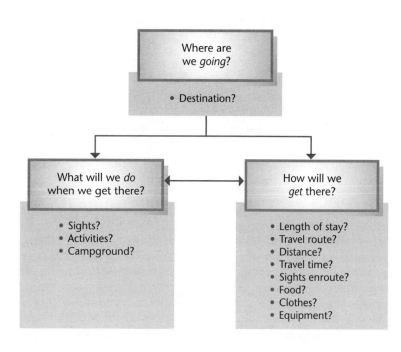

Figure 1.1
Three Categories of Questions in Trip Planning

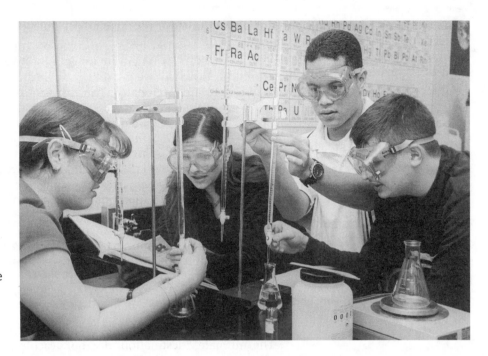

When students demonstrate new capabilities, they provide external evidence of the internal products and processes of learning.

Notice from this definition that some aspects of learning are external and observable, and some aspects are internal and unobservable because they occur within learners' minds. Notice also that some aspects of learning are *processes*, or events, and some aspects are *products*, or outcomes. Crossing the external-internal and process-product dimensions, we see that every learning episode really comprises four critical elements:

1. External processes
2. External products
3. Internal processes
4. Internal products

The **external processes** of learning refer to our experiences with the world—that is, how we interact with objects, people, events, and ideas from the environment. These interactions provide the "input" for the construction process and can take many different forms: reading information from a book, participating in a computer simulation, observing a model perform a skill, listening to oral instructions, watching a videotape, working cooperatively with a group to solve a problem, and so on. Whether such external processes produce learning ultimately depends on the **internal processes** that we use to perceive, interpret, and think about them. These constructive mental actions are hidden from direct observation.

Internal learning processes transform our experiences into forms of knowledge that we represent mentally—the **internal products** of learning. Learning products are the factual information, intellectual skills, motor skills, and attitudes that we store in long-term memory. If we have constructed some type of new knowledge, we should be able to demonstrate a corresponding capability. Let's refer to this outward manifestation of learning as the **external product**. If, for example, you learn the concept of racial prejudice, you should then be able to demonstrate that internal learning product by classifying a wide range of specific social situations as examples and nonexamples of racial prejudice.

Learning is fundamentally an unobservable, internal, mental construction. However, the evidence of learning is some type of external capability. We have no choice but to examine the external products of learning because the internal processes and products are not open for us to observe directly. Consider the following learning scenarios. For each scenario, try to identify the four critical elements of learning. Then compare your analysis with the features in Table 1.3.

▶ A three-year-old boy, Lamont, attempts to pick up the family pet, a large, temperamental cat named Whiskers, by its tail. He hears a loud screech and feels pain as Whiskers's sharp claws scratch his bare arm. Lamont's grandmother first tends to her grandson's scratches and tears. When both Lamont and Whiskers appear to have recovered from the ordeal, she demonstrates to Lamont how to pick up the cat by placing her arms around its body. She then guides Lamont's arms to the right places as she helps him pick up Whiskers. Later in the day, Lamont approaches Whiskers. Avoiding the animal's tail, he gently picks up the cat by wrapping his arms carefully around its body.

▶ Meagan, a fourth-grade girl, watches as her teacher, Mr. Ramirez, demonstrates how to round numerals to the nearest ten. Mr. Ramirez writes the numeral "34" on the board. He then asks the class what multiples of ten are immediately lower and higher than 34. Meagan and her classmates respond that 30 is lower and 40 is higher. "Great!" responds Mr. Ramirez. He then asks if 34 is closer to 30 or to 40. The entire class responds, "30!" Mr. Ramirez places a circle around the "30" on the board, stating that 34 rounded to the nearest multiple of ten is 30. He repeats the process for several additional examples and hands out a practice sheet that contains fifteen numerals for the students to round to the nearest ten. The next day, Mr. Ramirez writes the numeral "47" on the board and calls Meagan up to the front of the classroom to round the numeral to the nearest ten. She writes "40" below the numeral and "50" above it. Then she circles the "50" and says, "Forty-seven rounded to the nearest ten is fifty."

▶ A high school social studies class watches a videotape on the destruction of the world's rain forests, the depletion of natural resources, and other environmental problems. In addition to making viewers aware of the problems, the tape presents a variety of practical steps that ordinary people can take to help alleviate them: recycling, writing letters to political leaders, and so on. Following the tape, the teacher, Ms. Berg, places students into small groups to develop a strategy for implementing one of the practical activities presented in the tape. After completing the assignment, one group voluntarily decides to follow through with its strategy by initiating a community recycling program. Over the next several months, the students, outside school and without Ms. Berg's prompting, work with community leaders to design and implement their program.

As you can see from Table 1.3, the four basic elements of learning operate consistently across a wide variety of learning environments, people, subject matter, and materials. Although *design-teachers* attend carefully to all four components to guide their instruction, the two *product* components provide particular guidance in addressing the critical destination question: Where are we going? Because the proof of learning is provided by the capabilities learners can demonstrate (external products), we need to establish a clear destination for our teaching by describing what those capabilities will look like. For the Zook family camping trip, the clear destination was either Shenandoah National Park or Cape Hatteras National Seashore. For the three learning scenarios we just analyzed, the destinations were picking up a cat, rounding numerals to the nearest ten, and choosing to implement a community recycling

Table 1.3
Processes and Products of Learning

Feature	Boy and Cat	Rounding Numerals	Recycling Project
External process	• Boy pulls cat's tail. • Boy experiences pain from cat's scratching. • Boy watches as grandmother picks up cat. • Boy practices picking up cat with grand-mother's guidance.	• Girl watches teacher's demonstration. • Girl responds to teacher's questions. • Girl practices round-ing. • Girl receives feedback from teacher. • Girl receives praise from teacher.	• Students view video-tape on environmen-tal problems and solu-tions. • Students work in groups to design solu-tion strategies. • Groups present strate-gies to class. • Groups receive feed-back from class.
External product	• Boy avoids picking cat up by tail. • Boy wraps arms around cat's body.	• Girl rounds numeral to nearest ten at board.	• Group chooses to im-plement recycling strategy.
Internal process	• Punishment (cat's scratch and screech are unpleasant conse-quences of boy's be-havior). • Internalizing model's actions. • Positive reinforcement (picking up cat with-out scratches is a pleasant consequence of boy's behavior).	• Understanding round-ing rule. • Application of round-ing rule.	• Understanding envi-ronmental problems. • Application of recy-cling principles. • Identification with models. • Adopting models' concerns and strate-gies.
Internal product	• Knowledge—avoid unpleasant outcome by picking up cat's body. • Skill—picking up ani-mals gently.	• Skill—rule for round-ing numerals to near-est ten.	• Positive attitude to-ward recycling. • Knowledge of envi-ronmental problems. • Skills—principles of recycling.

program. Notice that each of these three external products of learning is ex-pressed as an observable action on the part of the learner. "Picking up," "rounding," and "choosing to implement" are all observable capabilities that provide clear evidence of learning.

■ **Describing Learned Capabilities with Instructional Goals** Instruc-tional designers often refer to the external products of learning as instructional goals (Dick & Carey, 1996; Gagne, Briggs, & Wager, 1992). **Instructional goals** describe the capabilities that learners should be able to demonstrate as a result of instruction. We examine instructional goals more closely in Chapter 2. For now, let's simply recognize that *design-teachers* need to address the critical destination question (Where are we going?) by establishing instructional goals that will provide clear evidence that learning has occurred and that instruction has been effective (see Figure 1.2).

Of course, we recognize that learners' observable capabilities, or their demonstration of instructional goals, reflect the internal products of learning, such as new factual knowledge, skills, or attitudes. Therefore, we need to clarify our final teaching destination even further by specifying the internal products of learning that enable, or make possible, our students' external capabilities. *Just getting an outward performance to occur is not good enough.* We want to ensure that the performance is possible because our learners possess underlying knowledge that they will be able to remember and apply far into the future— well beyond our teaching and our classroom. For our three learning scenarios, the internal products of learning are *factual knowledge* that cats scratch when you pick them up by their tails and the *skill* of picking up animals gently, the *skill* of rounding numerals to the nearest ten, and a *positive attitude* toward recycling, supported by knowledge of environmental problems and recycling principles.

■ **Specifying and Analyzing the Content to Be Learned**   The actual knowledge, skill, or attitude to be acquired by learners represents the content of teaching. *Design-teachers* specify clearly the content that learners must acquire to demonstrate the capability described by the instructional goal. Specifying the content of instruction then makes it possible for us to identify additional knowledge or skill that our learners may need to acquire before they can achieve the instructional goal. For example, before Meagan can acquire the ability to round numerals to the nearest ten (instructional goal), she needs to understand that numerals are rounded to the nearest ten by determining if they are closer to the next highest or next lowest multiple of ten, with the agreed-on convention that numerals exactly halfway are rounded up to the next highest multiple (the rule for rounding).

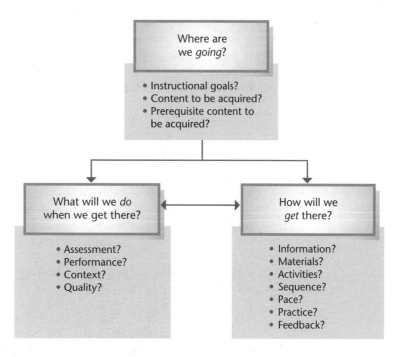

Figure 1.2
Three Categories of Questions in Instructional Planning

Now that we are aware of the rule, we can easily see that Meagan is probably going to have difficulty understanding and acquiring the rule if she does not possess lower-level skills such as counting by multiples of ten and identifying the ten's place in numerals. In this book, we refer to the process of identifying prerequisite knowledge and skill as **content analysis**. We examine specific principles and procedures related to content analysis in Chapter 3. For now, let's recognize that *design-teachers* need to analyze the content of their instruction to clarify further their teaching destinations (see Figure 1.2).

LET'S SUMMARIZE

Where are we going? As illustrated in Figure 1.2, *design-teachers* address this fundamental question by determining (1) clear instructional goals that describe the learned capability that students will be able to demonstrate as a result of instruction (*external product*); (2) the specific content that students will need to acquire to enable their performance of the instructional goals (*internal product*), and (3) any prerequisite content that they need to understand first (*internal product*). Armed with a clear destination, the Zook family was able to make informed decisions about the details of our camping trip. Armed with a clear destination, *design-teachers* are able to make informed decisions about the details of classroom teaching. Let's examine now the other two major trip planning questions and see how a clear destination works to our advantage.

Design-Teaching: What Will We Do When We Get There?

Recall that the Zook family expected to participate in several specific activities (hiking, fishing, bear sighting) when we arrived at our destination, Shenandoah National Park. In fact, the success of the trip really depended on how many of these activities we experienced and how much we enjoyed them. Although the park provided us a clear destination, simply arriving there was not the purpose of the trip. The purpose was to arrive and then *do* lots of things that we would enjoy. Engaging in those activities would provide evidence that we actually had arrived.

Similarly, when we design instruction, we need to establish clear expectations of the types of ways in which students will demonstrate their learned capabilities, providing evidence that they have, in fact, arrived at the destination (the instructional goal). For example, how will we know that Lamont can pick up animals gently, that Meagan can round numerals to the nearest ten, and that Ms. Berg's students will choose to implement recycling principles?

■ **Preparing Instructional Objectives**   Detailed descriptions of how learners will demonstrate their achievement of instructional goals are called **instructional objectives**. Instructional objectives describe how we will *assess* learners' achievement of instructional goals following instruction. As I explain in detail in Chapter 6, an assessment strategy should possess three critical elements (see Figure 1.2): performance, context, and quality. For example, to assess Meagan's ability to round numerals to the nearest ten (*instructional goal*), we could provide a two-digit numeral written on the chalkboard (*context*); have her write the next higher and lower multiple of ten and circle the multiple to which the original numeral is closer (*performance*); and judge her performance to be acceptable if she writes the correct multiples of ten and circles the correct multiple (*quality*).

■ **Assessment Validity and Reliability**   Now we have a statement that describes exactly how to assess students' rounding skills. Notice that the assessment strategy is consistent with the type of learning expressed by the instructional goal. The instructional goal states that learners should be able to *apply* a skill, rounding numerals to the nearest ten. The instructional objective builds on the instructional goal by describing *how* the skill will be applied. The degree to which instructional objectives are consistent with their corresponding instructional goals is referred to as assessment **validity**. We examine validity, an important characteristic of all educational assessment, in Chapter 4.

A second important characteristic of all educational assessment is *reliability*. Meagan's success with our instructional objective does not necessarily mean that she has in fact acquired the skill of rounding to the nearest ten. After all, the objective provides for only *one* performance opportunity. Perhaps she simply made a good guess on the single assessment opportunity we provided. If we were to provide a different two-digit numeral for rounding, Meagan's guessing perhaps would not be accurate. Thus, with only a single performance opportunity, we might get different, and inconsistent, results, depending on the specific numeral we provide. We would be more confident that Meagan's success reflects acquisition of the skill if she is able to perform correctly on a larger number of two-digit numerals (perhaps ten rather than just one). **Reliability** refers to the degree of confidence in our assessment data to provide dependable reflections of our learners' abilities. We examine this important assessment concept more closely in Chapter 4.

■ **Using Multiple Assessment Strategies**   Finally, let's recognize that having learners write and circle multiples of ten on the chalkboard is only one way of assessing their achievement of the instructional goal. This particular data collection procedure is not necessarily even the best assessment strategy. For example, if I were a fourth-grade teacher with twenty-eight children in my class, I would be reluctant to use an assessment strategy that involved individual learners working at the board one at a time. The procedure is time-consuming and, as we already have noted, not likely to produce reliable results. I could obtain more reliable data by giving each learner a worksheet with ten two-digit numerals to be rounded to the nearest ten.

The specific medium (e.g., chalkboard, worksheet, or computer program) used to assess learners' achievement of instructional goals is far less important than making sure that the results of the assessment strategy are as valid and reliable as possible. Nevertheless, as we will see in Chapter 5, we can improve the quality of our assessments by being aware of the variety of specific formats and procedures that are available. With diverse learning goals to assess and students who are themselves quite diverse, we need to be able to use a wide variety of assessment tools.

LET'S SUMMARIZE

What will we do when we get there? Knowing that we would visit Shenandoah National Park, we expected to be able to hike, fish, ride ponies, and sight bears at that destination. If, at the end of our camping trip, we have not experienced those activities, we might question whether we really did arrive at our destination. Similarly, as illustrated in Figure 1.2, *design-teachers* transform clear instructional goals into detailed expectations for what their learners should be able to do if, in fact, those goals have been achieved. The resulting instructional objectives describe how we will collect concrete evidence that our learners have learned and our instruction has been effective. Now that we have established a set of criteria for assessing the achievement of our learning destination, we are ready to begin planning and preparing for the actual trip.

Design-Teaching: How Will We Get There?

Recall that the Zooks were able to plan the details of the camping trip to Shenandoah by focusing on the characteristics of that destination. With a clear destination, we were able to make critical decisions regarding travel strategies, what to take along, and what to leave behind. For example, we decided to travel on Interstates 81 and 66 because they offered the most direct routes to our destination. From our home in central Pennsylvania, we have easy access to other interstate highways such as I-80, I-76, and I-95. However, we disregarded these alternative routes because they clearly did not support the achievement of our particular destination. All of these routes go somewhere (remember Alice?), but they do not lead to Shenandoah—at least not directly.

With respect to the resources that we would need to take, we packed equipment related to Shenandoah's features: hiking shoes, shorts, T-shirts, jeans, fly rod. We decided that we could safely leave behind our ice skates, winter coats, the piano, and the television set because we had absolutely no need for them. These were relatively easy decisions. However, other items were more difficult to categorize as essential or nonessential. For example, should we take our children's bicycles along? Making room in the car for the bicycles would require leaving behind items that we already had designated as essential. Therefore, we decided to leave the bikes at home, although we could have developed a rationale (and possibly car space) for taking them with us. Thus, our clear destination easily helped us make the obvious black-and-white decisions (no winter coats) and helped us think logically about the less obvious gray-area decisions (should we take the bicycles?).

■ **Planning an Instructional Strategy** An instructional strategy is the plan we develop to help learners achieve the instructional goal. The decisions we make when planning an instructional strategy are similar to travel decision making. The value of specific instructional materials, methods, and learning activities is determined by their usefulness in helping learners achieve our specified instructional goals. We need to design materials and learning activities (external processes) that support the *internal* learning processes that learners must engage in to acquire the internal learning products that will make their performance of the instructional objective (external product) possible.

To illustrate, let's continue to analyze the "rounding numerals to the nearest ten" scenario. If we want learners to be able to round numerals to the nearest ten following instruction (*external product*), then we need to prepare materials and learning activities (*external processes*) that will help them understand, remember, and apply that particular intellectual skill (*internal product*). To acquire the internal product, our learners will need to engage in particular types of cognitive processes (*internal processes*) that effectively promote the acquisition of the skill.

The internal processes that help learners acquire intellectual skills such as rounding numerals, punctuating sentences, identifying deciduous trees, and analyzing poetry are different from those required for learning factual information, such as the names of state capitals, symbols for elements on the periodic table, the names of the planets of the solar system, and the names of the bones in the human body. Because learner processing needs vary with the type of internal learning product desired, our instructional strategies (external processes) must also vary so that our teaching efforts do indeed help learners achieve our instructional goals. In the last part of the book, we examine the different types of cognitive processing that are required for achieving different learning outcomes such as verbal information (Chapter 7), concepts (Chapter 8), and rules, principles, and cognitive strategies (Chapter 9).

Are students guaranteed to acquire the rounding skill with an appropriate instructional strategy? Unfortunately, even with the best-designed instructional strategy, there is no guarantee that all learners will achieve the instructional goals. Students bring diverse cultural perspectives, special needs, background knowledge, prior skills, motivation levels, and so on into the classroom. Students are much too diverse and complex to expect any instructional strategy to be equally effective for everyone. Therefore, it is extremely important to collect direct evidence that learning has occurred by implementing the assessment strategy (instructional objective) that we already have designed. If learners are successful with the assessment, then we have concrete evidence that the instructional strategy was appropriate. If learners are not successful, then we have concrete evidence that our instructional strategy—however well designed we thought it to be—was not effective.

■ **Resolving Learning Difficulties**   When we identify learners who have not met our objectives, we need to ask an additional question: *Why* didn't we get there? If the Zook family ends up in Washington, D.C., rather than Shenandoah National Park, we will realize that we have made a wrong turn. By analyzing our carefully planned travel routes and figuring out exactly where we are, we will be able to develop some possible explanations for being off course (e.g., it was that wrong turn onto Interstate 70 in Hagerstown). After pinpointing the cause of the problem, we can retrace our path and try our original travel strategy again or devise an alternative route to reach the destination from our (mis)location. Because Washington, D.C., was not our planned destination, we will not be satisfied to stay there, although that city may be a fine destination for another trip at another time.

Similarly, as *design-teachers* we should not be satisfied to leave our learners stranded, not having achieved the learning outcomes that we thought were important for them. We first make an effort to understand (or diagnose) why particular learners have not been successful. Once we have a valid **diagnosis** of the problem, we can plan and implement potentially effective teaching strategies to move these learners closer to the original learning destination. This reteaching process is known as **remediation**.

For example, Meagan may not be able to round numerals to the nearest ten for the assessment because she does not yet understand place-value concepts well enough to identify the appropriate numerals to manipulate. Through careful follow-up questioning, observing, and data collection, Mr. Ramirez may be able to pinpoint the precise causes of Meagan's misunderstanding and plan additional (or alternative) learning activities to remediate (or correct) the identified weaknesses. Following remediation of the subordinate skills, Mr. Ramirez can return to rounding procedures with Meagan because the final destination is too important to disregard.

LET'S SUMMARIZE

I have been comparing *design-teaching* and trip planning activities to help you acquire a meaningful awareness and understanding of basic principles of systematic instructional design. Through the remainder of the book, I elaborate further on these principles. For now, I hope you understand and agree that *design-teaching*, like trip planning, is a complex activity that requires us to think carefully about many interrelated variables: instructional goals, content to be learned, prerequisite content, assessment procedures, teaching strategies, problem diagnosis, and problem remediation. When we make teaching decisions by integrating these important instructional variables, we design an *instructional system*. In the next section, we identify the features of instructional systems and examine the model of systematic instructional design that we will focus on for the remainder of the book.

Putting the Pieces Together: A Systems Approach to Instructional Design

A *system* is an integrated collection of component parts that work together to produce a particular outcome or to achieve a desired goal. For example, my computer system is made up of the following interrelated parts:

keyboard, mouse, hard drive, disk drive, video monitor, printer. All of these parts work together to help me process information. The heating system in my house has several parts: oil tank, furnace, heat ducts, thermostat. They all work together to keep my house warm. Our family camping trip represents a "travel system" comprising several interrelated parts: destination, activities, food, equipment, clothes, travel routes. All of these parts work together to help us arrive at our destination and have a good time while there.

As you can see, each of these three systems is designed to achieve a particular goal. The effectiveness of each system can be judged by how well its goal is achieved. For example, my computer system is not effective if I cannot print a document that I saved on my hard drive; my heating system is not effective if the temperature falls below the level I have set on the thermostat. Clearly just having all the parts there is not good enough; they have to produce the desired *result*. Furthermore, the effectiveness of the entire system depends on the *relationships* among the individual parts. So, for example, oil moves from the storage tank to my furnace as the furnace needs it; the furnace burns oil when the thermostat tells it to burn oil; heat is delivered to rooms in my house only if the ducts are connected to the furnace and each room. In a system, action at one component part influences action at one or more related parts.

Features of Instructional Systems

An **instructional system** is made up of several critical components that work together to produce learning. Over the years, instructional designers have developed numerous models of instructional systems (see Andrews & Goodson, 1980; Seels & Glasgow, 1998; Tennyson, 1997). Some of these systems models are quite complex (e.g., Dick, 1997; Dick & Carey, 1996), and others are relatively simple (e.g., Kemp, Morrison, & Ross, 1994). It is well beyond the scope of this book to describe all the systems models that are available. Instead, my goal is to help you develop a meaningful awareness and understanding of the major features that are common to most models.

Regardless of their complexity, all systems models address the three fundamental questions of instructional design (and trip planning): (1) Where are we going? (2) What will we do when we get there? and (3) How will we get there? A diagram of the general systems model that we will explore together is provided in Figure 1.3. Notice that the system comprises several action components that relate to our three questions:

1. *Where are we going?*

   Specify instructional goal.

   Identify and analyze content.

2. *What will we do when we get there?*

   Prepare assessment procedure.

3. *How will we get there?*

   Design instructional strategy.

   Implement instructional strategy and assessment procedure.

   Diagnose and remediate learner difficulties.

Most important, each action component is related to one or more other action components. Thus, any decisions or actions that occur at a particular point in the system are related to preceding, as well as subsequent, actions and decisions, exactly as illustrated by camping, heating, and computer systems. Let's examine how our model would guide us in designing an instructional system. Since you are already familiar with the rounding skills scenario, we will continue to use it for our example.

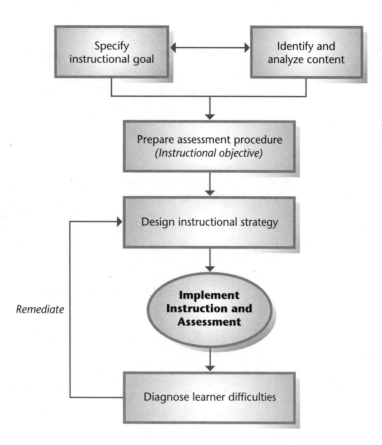

**Figure 1.3
A Systems Model of
Instructional Design**

■ **Specifying Instructional Goals**   The first step is to decide what capability we want our learners to be able to demonstrate as a result of our teaching. We want them, of course, to understand the rule for rounding numerals to the nearest ten, but since it is impossible to measure understanding directly, we need to change it to some type of performance that we can observe and evaluate. If students can apply the rounding rule (external product), we will be able to infer that they understand it. Thus our *instructional goal* is the following: *Learners will be able to apply the rule for rounding numerals to the nearest ten.*

■ **Identifying and Analyzing Content**   Now we ask, What is the *content* that our learners need to acquire (internal product) so that they can round any numeral to the nearest ten? We can state the rounding rule as follows: *When rounding any numeral to the nearest ten, examine the digit in the one's place to determine if the numeral is closer to the next higher multiple of ten (greater than five) or the next lower multiple of ten (less than five); if the numeral is exactly halfway between the next lower and higher multiple of ten (exactly five), round it up to the higher multiple.* Understanding, remembering, and applying this rounding rule will enable learners to perform the instructional goal. This rule, however, comprises subordinate concepts that learners must first understand and be able to apply: ten's place, one's place, digit, multiple of ten, higher, lower. By analyzing the rule into these subordinate concepts, we make ourselves aware of additional content that some or all learners may need to acquire before we can expect them to be successful in learning the rule.

Notice the two-headed arrow that connects the first two general phases of the systems model of instructional design (see Figure 1.3). The two-directional relationship between these components is a reminder that instructional goals and content can be considered in either order. Sometimes, as in the rounding example, we will first be able to state a clear instructional goal and then determine the content that learners will need to acquire to demonstrate the capability. Sometimes, however, we will be able to identify content first (e.g., principles of photosynthesis, the concept of democracy, alliteration as a figure of speech) and then determine an appropriate set of instructional goals. As *design-teachers*, do we begin instructional planning by thinking about instructional goals or content? In fact, the order does not matter. Both are essential and need to be considered so that we know where we are going.

■ **Preparing Assessment Procedures**   Although the instructional goal provides a statement of learner performance following instruction, it does not describe in detail *how* the performance will occur. We need to decide how we will actually assess our learners' ability to round numerals to the nearest ten. So that the assessment is valid for both the instructional goal and the specified content, we need to create an opportunity for learners to round numerals to the nearest ten. That is, they must be able to *do* it, not just talk about it or explain it. We could provide learners with twenty numerals (half of them two-digit numerals and half three-digit numerals) written on a sheet. We will tell them orally to write the next higher multiple of ten above each numeral and the next lower multiple of ten below each numeral. Learners will then circle the multiple of ten to which the numeral should be rounded. When we evaluate the results, we expect at least eighteen of the twenty numerals to be rounded correctly. This detailed description of an assessment procedure provides an *instructional objective* for our teaching. Not only do we know how we are going to assess our learners, we also have an even clearer target to help us make decisions about our instructional strategy.

■ **Designing an Instructional Strategy**   How should we teach rounding to the nearest ten? According to the systems model (see Figure 1.3), the instructional strategy we design depends on the instructional goal to be achieved, as assessed by the instructional objective, and the content to be acquired. Hence, our learners need to construct a meaningful representation of a rule that they can apply as a skill (internal product). To learn a rule, students must do the following:

1. Become aware of the rule.
2. Understand the subordinate concepts that comprise the rule.
3. Understand the range of examples to which the rule applies.
4. Understand the range of nonexamples to which the rule does not apply.
5. Practice applying the rule.
6. Receive feedback on their performance.

These conditions reflect learners' *internal* learning processes. The specific instructional methods that we choose or design will be effective (as assessed by the instructional objective) only to the extent that they support learners' internal learning processes.

■ **Implementing Instruction and Assessment**   Now we put our teaching plans to the test. We implement the learning activities that we designed to support our learners' internal processing needs for rule acquisition. Following the review of subordinate concepts, demonstrations of the rule, practice exercises, and other learning activities that we planned, we come to the moment of truth: Was our teaching *effective*? Can learners actually round numerals to the nearest ten? To answer these questions, we implement our assessment procedures (instructional objective) to collect concrete evidence.

■ **Diagnosing and Remediating Learner Difficulties**   If all of our learners round at least eighteen of the twenty numerals correctly (criteria stated in the instructional objective), we will infer that they have achieved the instructional goal, and therefore our instruction has been effective. If one of our learners— let's call her Ling—does not achieve this criterion, we need to find out why so we can reteach or remediate. Perhaps the pattern of incorrect responses on the sheet will provide clues. Examining Ling's paper, we may see that she frequently does not write the correct multiples of ten above and below the numeral to be rounded. We may suspect, therefore, that perhaps she has not mastered the prerequisite skill of counting in multiples of ten.

Referring back to the content analysis, we see that this is an important subordinate skill for rounding to the nearest ten. We can verify our diagnosis by asking Ling to count in multiples of ten from various numerals that we provide. As expected, she makes frequent errors. Therefore, we design an instructional strategy to help her acquire the skill of counting in multiples of ten. When we have concrete evidence that Ling has mastered the subordinate skill, we can return to the original instructional goal: applying the rounding rule.

LET'S SUMMARIZE

Systematic instructional design is a *thinking* process. As you can see from the preceding example, *design-teachers* make plans and decisions that are related to each component of the systems model of instructional design (see Figure 1.3). Most important, the example demonstrates how our thinking and action within any one component of the model are integrated with our thinking and action within all other components. By applying this systematic thinking process, *design-teachers* increase the potential effectiveness of their classroom instruction, thereby maximizing the learning of their students.

Supporting Learner Diversity Through Systematic Instructional Design

One of the variables that adds significantly to the complexity of classroom teaching is learner diversity. Teachers are increasingly being held accountable for the learning of students who reflect racial, cultural, gender, linguistic, physical, intellectual, and social-emotional differences. A systematic approach to instructional design can be a powerful tool to help you meet the needs of all your learners in three major ways. First, the precision with which a systems model encourages you to think about each instructional decision and action can heighten your awareness of the impact those decisions and actions may have on different types of learners, resulting in your ability to detect when modifications and adaptations may be necessary.

Second, the goal-directed focus of systematic instructional design helps you plan and evaluate learning experiences for students who have specific learning needs. Federal legislation such as Public Law 94-142 (Individuals with Disabilities Education Act–IDEA), passed in 1975 and reauthorized in 1997 as Public Law 105-17, requires public school teachers to plan appropriate instructional programs for students with specific learning needs, handicapping conditions, and disabilities. These laws are based on the general philosophy of **inclusion**: the effort to provide learning experiences for children with special needs in regular classrooms with their normally functioning peers. To assist such children, you will be expected to establish attainable learning outcomes, plan effective learning activities to help them achieve those outcomes, and provide concrete evidence that the outcomes are achieved. Systems models of instructional design are particularly well suited to support this type of goal-directed teaching.

Finally, using a systems model to guide your instructional decision making can help you make adaptations for individual learners and ensure that they are achieving important learning goals. Modifying learning goals, content, assessment strategies, and teaching methods on the basis of individual differences can do students a grave disservice if the modifications are simply intended to make your work easier, more efficient, or less demanding. For example, giving students who do not speak English an alternative activity may keep them busy and occupied while you work with English-speaking students, but will it help them acquire a new capability that helps them learn and develop in ways comparable to your English-speaking students? A goal-directed focus to the teaching-learning process increases the probability that you will ask yourself this critical question and, more important, that you will always attempt to answer it affirmatively. Systematic instructional design is arguably one of the best safeguards against leaving any learners behind.

LOOKING BACK LOOKING AHEAD

In this introductory chapter, we have explored instructional design as a systematic thinking process. We have seen that the entire instructional design process is focused on helping learners achieve important instructional goals. *Design-teachers* help their learners achieve instructional goals by addressing three interrelated questions in their instructional planning and implementation: (1) Where are we going? (2) What will we do when we get there? and (3) How will we get there? When we address these questions in an orderly, integrated manner, we create an instructional system that can be implemented in classroom teaching. The quality of an instructional system is determined by how well it helps students learn, as specified by our instructional goals. *Design-teachers* make decisions about content, materials, learning activities, and assessment by considering their relationship to the instructional goals to be achieved by learners.

This chapter was written to help you achieve the instructional goals that you saw at the beginning of the chapter. Let's see if you can demonstrate your achievement of the instructional goals by completing Exercise 1.1, which you will find in your *Student Exercise Guide*. If you can demonstrate all of the capabilities described by the chapter's instructional goals, you will have acquired a foundation of basic concepts and principles that should help you learn a lot from the chapters to follow.

Now that we have established the importance of thinking systematically about instructional design, let's begin to explore instructional design principles and procedures in greater detail. You will notice that the book is organized according to the three major questions of instructional design and trip planning. In the next two chapters, we continue examining in detail the first fundamental question: Where are we going? We have an interesting journey ahead of us. Let's go!

RESOURCES FOR FURTHER REFLECTION AND EXPLORATION

Print Resources

Dick, W., & Carey, L. (1996). *The systematic design of instruction* (4th ed.). New York: HarperCollins.

This classic text presents a detailed description of the well-known Dick and Carey systems model of instructional design. Although the book is not written specifically for classroom teachers, you can get a comprehensive overview of the principles and procedures of systematic instructional design for any learning context.

Dick, W., & Reiser, R. A. (1989). *Planning effective instruction*. Englewood Cliffs, NJ: Prentice Hall.

The authors of this short book demonstrate how to apply a systems approach to classroom instruction. The model they present is an adaptation of the more complex Dick and Carey model and is similar to the systems model presented in the first chapter of this book.

Educational Technology Research and Development (ETR&D). Washington, DC: Association for Educational Communications and Technology.

ETR&D is a leading scholarly journal in the field of instructional design. You may be interested in scanning some issues to get an idea of the types of theoretical issues that concern instructional designers, examples of instructional design applications in a variety of learning contexts, and research studies that investigate various questions related to the instructional design process.

World Wide Web Resources

You can expand your perspective on the field of instructional design by exploring the following web sites:

http://connect.barry.edu/ect607/references.html

Numerous links to instructional design topics such as professional organizations, journals and magazines, readings, and instructional design models.

http://www.cudenver.edu/~mryder/itc/idmodels.html

Links to a wide variety of instructional design models and perspectives. Maintained by the School of Education, University of Colorado, Denver.

http://www.coe.sdsu.edu/eet/

Encyclopedia of Educational Technology, Education Department, San Diego State University. Links and documents related to instructional design processes, organized by general phase: analysis, design, development, implementation, evaluation. Also includes information on cognition and learning.

http://www.wisc.edu/learntech/grp/id.htm

Provides links to a wide variety of instructional design topics on the web. Maintained by Learning Technology and Distance Education, University of Wisconsin, Madison.

2

Writing Instructional Goals for Learning Outcomes

At the beginning of my first year of teaching, I decided to develop a several-week unit on trees for my eighth-grade life science class. Without a textbook or curriculum guide, I set out to teach my students about trees. I began accumulating books, pamphlets, pictures, posters, and other materials related to the topic. I began to investigate field trip possibilities. I explored the school grounds, identifying all the trees and thinking about how I might use these real examples in my teaching. I collected ideas for demonstrations and learning activities that would actively involve my students. I created a list of tree topics that my students could learn about: parts of trees, tree and plant classification, tree identification, human uses for trees, how trees contribute to ecosystems, how tree leaves change colors in the fall, and so on. I thought about other areas of the curriculum (math, social studies, reading) that I could integrate with trees.

After accumulating a lot of tree-related information, resources, and teaching ideas, I was ready to chart my course for the unit. I still recall feeling quite overwhelmed by the amount of material and the wide variety of teaching strategies and learning activities that I could potentially use with my students. How could I possibly hope to cover all the information that I had collected? How could I squeeze all the activities and materials into the tree unit?

Although I had accumulated a wealth of information, activities, and resources, I was not ready to begin teaching because I had not yet established a clear destina-

INSTRUCTIONAL GOALS FOR CHAPTER 2

After reading and thinking about this chapter, you should be able to. . .

1. Describe the purpose and essential features of instructional goals.

2. Recognize appropriately written instructional goals.

3. Explain the differences between declarative, procedural, and affective knowledge, and identify examples of each.

4. State the characteristics of five major types of learning outcomes (verbal information, intellectual skills,

cognitive strategies, motor skills, attitudes), and identify examples of each.

5. State the characteristics of four types of intellectual skills (discriminations, concepts, rules and principles, problem solving), and identify examples of each.

6. Explain and apply Gagne's hierarchy of intellectual skills.

7. Write instructional goals that are valid for specific learning outcomes.

tion. I had a list of topics to cover but had not yet decided what capabilities I wanted my students to be able to demonstrate as a result of learning about those topics. *Design-teachers* begin the instructional design process by transforming general topics into clear instructional goals that reflect specific learning outcomes. This clear destination then helps us design appropriate assessment strategies (What will we do when we get there?) and potentially effective instructional strategies (How will we get there?).

In this chapter, we focus on the major types of learning that learning theorists have identified. We also examine principles for developing instructional goals that are appropriate for each type of learning outcome. I have designed this chapter to help you achieve the specific instructional goals listed on the preceding page. These goals are not just topics to "cover"; they represent learning outcomes that you should be able to demonstrate as the result of reading the chapter and participating in the accompanying exercises.

Instructional Goals

When I walk into a classroom to teach, I usually have three major goals in mind:

1. I want my students to leave the classroom *knowing* some things that they did not know before.
2. I want them to *understand* some things that they did not understand before.
3. I want them to *value and appreciate* the new things that they have come to know about and understand.

For example, I wanted my students to come away from the tree unit knowing the names of the vein patterns in tree leaves and the identifying features of specific species of trees. I wanted them to understand how water and nutrients are transported through a tree's circulatory system, how trees manufacture their food, and how tree leaves turn different colors in the fall. I wanted them to appreciate the role that trees play in various ecosystems and in our lives. I wanted them to think that trees are really interesting and valuable.

Knowing, understanding, and appreciating certainly are worthy educational goals for classroom teaching. However, they do not function adequately as instructional goals because they represent internal knowledge and feelings rather than external, observable capabilities that we can assess. Although we recognize that learning happens internally, we have to rely on external evidence to infer that learning has actually taken place (Perkins & Unger, 1999). **Instructional goals** express the observable actions (external product) that we will accept as evidence that learners have indeed acquired new knowledge, understanding, and appreciation. The ultimate goal of instruction is meaningful learning. Performing a new capability is evidence of learning. Instructional goals describe what that new capability will be.

To demonstrate the inadequacy of knowing, understanding, and appreciating as instructional goals, let's examine the following vague learning outcome: understand fractions. If you are teaching a class of third-grade children about fractions, you certainly want them to understand fractions when you are finished. But what exactly does it mean "to understand fractions"? Before reading further, make a list of all the ways that a person could demonstrate an understanding of fractions. When you have completed your list, compare it to my list in Table 2.1.

Notice from our lists that the vague learning outcome "understand fractions" can be transformed into a variety of different external capabilities. "Understanding fractions" is not a useful *instructional* goal because it can mean so

Table 2.1
Multiple Instructional Goals for the Outcome "Understand Fractions"

Action	Content
Write	fractions for parts of objects.
Generate	equivalent fractions.
Write	fractions for parts of sets.
Reduce	fractions to lowest terms.
Identify	numerators and denominators.
Compare	proper, improper, and mixed fractions.
Add	proper, improper, and mixed fractions.
Subtract	proper, improper, and mixed fractions.
Multiply	proper, improper, and mixed fractions.
Divide	proper, improper, and mixed fractions.
Solve	story problems involving fractions.
Convert	fractions to their decimal equivalents.

many different things to different people. Hence, if we want to help learners understand fractions, we need to specify which capability (or capabilities) we really mean. Only then will we have clear direction for assessment and instruction.

Features of Instructional Goals

As you were working on your list, you probably noticed that you were changing "understand fractions" in two ways. First, you needed to change *understand* to verbs that represent observable actions: *reduce, identify, compare, add, subtract, multiply, divide* (see Table 2.1). As you made your verbs more precise, you probably found that you also needed to make the objects of your verbs more precise. The objects of your action verbs represent the content that learners will be processing, acquiring, and acting on: numerator, denominator, lowest terms, proper fraction, improper fraction, mixed fraction, and so on.

From this illustration, we see that useful instructional goals possess two major features: observable *action* and clear *content*. Notice in Table 2.1 how each potential instructional goal can be separated into these two components. To provide the clearest possible destination, both components of instructional goals need to be as precise as possible. For example, although "understand fractions" can be sharpened by changing *understand* to *compare*, the instructional goal "compare fractions" still is too broad to be useful because *fractions* is too general. Are we expecting learners to be able to compare proper, improper, and mixed fractions as the result of our teaching? If so, we should specify those three content areas to ensure that we assess for all three and provide appropriate learning activities. If we expect our learners, because of their age, grade level, or developmental characteristics, to compare only proper fractions, we should specify that particular content to ensure that we design appropriate assessment and learning activities.

Effects of Instructional Goals on Assessment and Teaching

As demonstrated in Table 2.2, we can express any general learning outcome as an instructional goal, regardless of learner age, grade level, or subject matter. Notice that each instructional goal has an action word (in boldface type) that describes what learners will be able to do following instruction. The action words that we use in our instructional goals provide two types of direction for *design-teaching*. First, the verb establishes our approach to assessment. If, for ex-

Table 2.2
Instructional Goals for Different Grade Levels and School Subjects

School Subject	Grade Level	General Outcome	Instructional Goal
Mathematics	Third grade	Know multiplication facts.	**State** multiplication facts.
	Fifth grade	Be exposed to geometry.	**Identify** right triangles.
	Eighth grade	Be familiar with a compass.	**Draw** circles with a compass.
	Tenth grade	Understand quadratic equations.	**Solve** quadratic equations.
Social studies	Second grade	Know about communities.	**State** the characteristics of communities.
	Sixth grade	Understand latitude and longitude.	**Determine** latitude and longitude coordinates for map locations.
	Eleventh grade	Know about study strategies.	**Construct** concept maps.
Reading	Kindergarten	Know letters of the alphabet.	**Differentiate** between "b" and "d."
	Third grade	Develop keyboarding skills.	**Type** a paragraph on the computer.
	Fourth grade	Appreciate poetry.	**Write** haiku poems.
	Seventh grade	Use study strategies.	**Generate** outlines for textbook chapters.
Science	First grade	Understand plant growth.	**Describe** the necessary conditions for plants to grow.
	Fourth grade	Be familiar with rocks.	**Identify** sedimentary rocks.
	Sixth grade	Value the earth's resources.	**Choose** to recycle.
	Ninth grade	Appreciate ecological relationships.	**Apply** the nitrogen cycle.
	Eleventh grade	Understand the scientific method.	**Design** an experiment.
English	Third grade	Know about adverbs.	**Identify** adverbs.
	Eighth grade	Understand sentence structure	**Diagram** sentences.
	Twelfth grade	Appreciate Shakespeare.	**Choose** to read a Shakespearean play.
Physical Education	Seventh grade	Acquire basketball skills.	**Dribble** a basketball.
Music	First grade	Be familiar with major and minor keys.	**Discriminate** between major and minor triads.
	Ninth grade	Appreciate baroque music.	**Choose** to listen to recordings of Bach concertos.
Art	Second grade	Understand colors.	**Discriminate** between shades of red.

ample, our instructional goal is for learners to be able to *generate outlines for textbook chapters,* then we eventually will need to assess their learning by providing them with an opportunity to demonstrate that they can generate outlines for textbook chapters. If we want our learners to be able to *apply the nitrogen cycle,* we eventually will need to assess their learning by providing them with opportunities to demonstrate that they can apply the nitrogen cycle.

Second, the action word establishes direction for our teaching. If, for example, we want our learners to be able to *generate outlines,* we will need to help them understand the basic rules of outlining. Furthermore, we will need to provide ample practice and feedback opportunities so that they can acquire those rules as skills. Similarly, for our learners to *apply the nitrogen cycle,* they will need to construct a meaningful understanding of the scientific principles that govern the cycle. As with outlining, we also will need to provide opportunities for learners to practice applying the nitrogen cycle as a skill to a wide variety of ecological situations.

As you can see, *design-teachers* need to think carefully about the specific verbs they use in writing instructional goals because of the significant implications for both assessment and teaching. Although we can use a wide variety of verbs in instructional goals, the most useful verbs are those that relate clearly to the underlying type of learning that makes the outward behavior possible. Consider, for example, this instructional goal: *learners will be able to write organized paragraphs.* Although this is an appropriately written instructional goal, we could strengthen it by including a verb that calls attention to the type of learning that must occur. Because the ability to write an organized paragraph is enabled by applying a rule, including this information in our instructional goal will make it more useful as a destination for teaching and assessment: *learners will be able to <u>apply the rule</u> for writing organized paragraphs.*

In the preceding example, the verb *apply* serves as a *capability verb* (Gagne, Briggs, & Wager, 1992). A **capability verb** describes an outward performance that is consistent with the internal product of learning that we are trying to develop within learners. Although there are an unlimited number of specific instructional goals that learners can achieve, we can reduce all of them to a smaller number of learning outcomes that have appropriate capability verbs. To develop useful instructional goals, we need to be aware of these basic learning outcomes and their corresponding capability verbs.

Learning Outcomes

et's return to the list of instructional goals presented in Table 2.2. At first glance, it would appear that we have generated twenty-three different instructional goals, each requiring its own special methods and procedures for teaching, learning, and assessment. However, if we examine each instructional goal for the underlying learning that is implied, we find categories of learning outcomes that cut across irrelevant variables such as grade level and subject area.

A **learning outcome** is a set of learned performances that have common learning processes, teaching strategies, and assessment procedures (Gagne, 1984, 1985). For example, the ability to identify right triangles (fifth-grade mathematics), sedimentary rocks (fourth-grade science), adverbs (third-grade English), chemical reactions (high school chemistry), and personification (high school English) all suggest a common internal product of learning. This internal product involves understanding, remembering, and applying the features that must be present for an object or event to be identified as a right triangle, sedimentary rock, adverb, chemical reaction, or personification. Although teaching learners to identify members of each of those categories will look a bit different on the surface, the same general approach to teaching and assessment will be required for all three because we are developing the ability to place new objects and events into categories with common features. As you will see later in this chapter, these categories are called *concepts*. Thus, what appear to be three different instructional goals actually represent one major type of learning outcome with common requirements for teaching, learning, and assessment.

How many different learning outcomes are actually in the list of instructional goals in Table 2.2? As demonstrated in Table 2.3, we can classify all of these instructional goals (plus some that I have added) according to three general types of knowledge that learners acquire:

1. Declarative
2. Procedural
3. Affective

Each of these types of acquired knowledge is stored, or represented, differently in our memories and possesses distinctive features that enable the performance of similar instructional goals. For example, notice that all of the declarative knowledge goals involve stating factual information, all of the procedural knowledge goals involve the performance of skills, and all of the affective knowledge goals reflect personal choices based on feelings and emotions.

Declarative Knowledge

The two types of knowledge that we usually focus on in school learning are *declarative* and *procedural* (Anderson, 1976, 1980). **Declarative knowledge** is factual information that we store in long-term memory so that we can recall and express it when desired. When learners acquire this type of knowledge, they are able to *declare* it as evidence of their learning. For this reason, declarative knowledge often is referred to as *knowing that* something is the case (Gagne, Yekovich, & Yekovich, 1993). For example, I can demonstrate that I possess declarative knowledge of multiplication facts by declaring that $2 \times 3 = 6$, $3 \times 4 = 12$, $4 \times 6 = 24$, and so on. I can declare that the chemical symbol for sodium is Na; the third president of the United States was Thomas Jefferson; the scapula is the bone commonly known as the shoulder blade; and all plants need adequate amounts of sunlight, warmth, moisture, and nutrients to grow.

Most cognitive psychologists currently agree that we store declarative knowledge in memory as propositions. A **proposition** is a complete idea unit that can be judged as true or false (Anderson, 1980; Gagne, Yekovich, & Yekovich, 1993). All of the declarative knowledge that we hold in our long-term memories is linked together in a huge web, or network, of interrelated propositions (Anderson, 1995; Hayes-Roth & Thorndyke, 1979; Norman, 1982).

Procedural Knowledge

In contrast, **procedural knowledge** takes the form of skills that we can apply to perform mental and physical tasks. When learners acquire this type of knowledge, they are able to perform a *procedure* as evidence of their learning. For example, I can demonstrate that I possess procedural knowledge of right triangles by identifying them when I encounter them in the real world. I can perform the mental tasks of writing haiku poems, diagramming sentences, constructing concept maps, and discriminating between major and minor triads as evidence of my procedural knowledge. I can also perform the physical tasks of drawing circles with a compass and dribbling a basketball as evidence of procedural knowledge. As is evident from these examples, procedural knowledge is *how-to* knowledge (Gagne, Yekovich, & Yekovich, 1993).

Because procedural knowledge helps us produce new behavior, many cognitive psychologists believe that we store this type of knowledge in memory as

Table 2.3
Instructional Goals Classified by Declarative, Procedural, and Affective Knowledge

Declarative Knowledge	*Procedural Knowledge*	*Affective Knowledge*
• State the symbols for the elements on the periodic table. • Name all the bones of the human body. • Write the symbol for pi. • State multiplication facts. • Name the capital of each state. • State the Pythagorean theorem. • State the characteristics of communities. • Describe the necessary conditions for plants to grow. • Explain differences between baroque and classical music. • Count from 1 to 10 in Spanish. • Recite the preamble to the U.S. Constitution. • Recite Robert Frost's "Stopping by Woods."	• Differentiate between "b" and "d." • Discriminate shades of red. • Differentiate between major and minor triads. • Identify right triangles. • Identify sedimentary rocks. • Identify adverbs. • Demonstrate the rule for simplifying quadratic equations. • Determine latitude and longitude coordinates. • Write haiku poems. • Apply sentence diagramming rules. • Apply the nitrogen cycle. • Demonstrate the principle of checks and balances. • Originate concept maps. • Originate outlines for textbook chapters. • Originate an experiment. • Execute a layup. • Execute the Virginia reel. • Type a paragraph.	• Choose to recycle. • Choose to read a Shakespearean play. • Choose to listen to recordings of Bach concertos. • Choose not to smoke. • Choose to cooperate in small groups. • Choose not to abuse alcohol. • Choose to vote in elections. • Choose to say "please" and "thank you."

productions. A **production** is a rule that triggers an action (either mental or physical) when certain conditions are met (Anderson, 1980; Gagne, Yekovich, & Yekovich, 1993). For example, when I see a three-sided shape that has one right angle (*conditions*), I classify it as a right triangle (*action*).

As *design-teachers*, we must be able to distinguish clearly between declarative and procedural instructional goals because the implications for teaching and assessment are significant. For example, if a high school English teacher wants her students to be able to recognize examples of personification, a procedural knowledge learning outcome, she must help them acquire a production for applying the skill. Just remembering and stating the definition of personification, a declarative knowledge outcome, does not guarantee that students will be able to recognize examples of personification in their reading. If the teacher is serious about her students' acquiring procedural knowledge, she will need to include opportunities for them to practice the skill in her teaching. Furthermore, she will need to assess her students by having them apply the skill to new examples, not just state the definition or repeat examples they have memorized.

Both declarative and procedural knowledge are valuable learning outcomes and have important roles in school curricula. Neither one is superior or inferior to the other; they are simply different. As *design-teachers*, we must write instructional goals that are consistent with the types of knowledge we wish our learners to acquire. Then we must align all of our subsequent instructional and assessment activities with those types of knowledge.

Affective Knowledge

Now let's look at the third column of Table 2.3. All of the instructional goals in this column involve personal choices that are influenced by our feelings or emotions. If I have positive feelings toward recycling, I am more likely to make the effort to throw my empty soda can into a recycling bin. If I have negative feelings toward smoking, I am less likely to take up the habit. If Bach concertos really turn me on, I will be inclined to listen to them whenever I can. **Affect** is a psychological term that refers to our feelings and emotions. **Affective knowledge**, therefore, is emotional knowledge that influences what we choose to do.

Although much of our learners' school-learned affective knowledge is acquired unintentionally (e.g., I hate math; I love to read; I can't wait for recess!), we as teachers sometimes attempt to develop this type of knowledge intentionally. For example, instructional programs may be designed to promote students' positive emotional commitments to character values such as justice, respect, loyalty, and caring for others (Chaskin & Rauner, 1995; Lickona, 1999; Noddings, 1995). Instructional programs that are designed to prevent substance abuse usually attempt to develop students' emotional commitment to avoiding alcohol and other drugs.

Gagne's Five Learning Outcomes

Declarative, procedural, and affective knowledge are three broad learning outcomes that provide direction for developing instructional goals. Building on these three general types of knowledge, Robert Gagne (1984, 1985) recommends five outcomes that *design-teachers* can use to classify all types of learning:

1. Verbal information
2. Intellectual skills
3. Cognitive strategies
4. Motor skills
5. Attitudes

Figure 2.1 shows how Gagne's five categories are related to the three general outcomes that we have been examining. As you can see from the figure, verbal information is equivalent to declarative knowledge, and attitudes are equivalent to affective knowledge. In Gagne's classification system, procedural knowledge can take the form of intellectual skills, cognitive strategies, or motor skills. In Table 2.4, I show you how we can classify the sample instructional goals from Table 2.3 according to these five learning outcomes. Let's take a closer look at each of Gagne's five learning outcomes and their implications for writing instructional goals, teaching, and assessment.

Verbal Information

Verbal information is declarative knowledge: information that students store in long-term memory so that they can recall and state it when needed. According to Gagne (1985), verbal information takes four major forms: labels, facts, organized facts, and verbal chains. You will find sample instructional goals for each of these forms in Table 2.4.

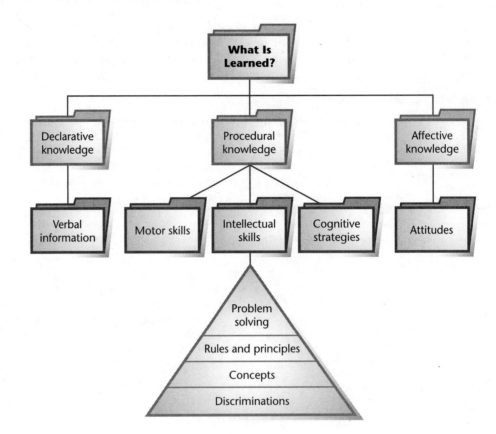

**Figure 2.1
Gagne's Five Learning
Outcomes Related to
Three Types of
Knowledge**

■ **Labels** Labels are names or symbols that we associate with objects or events so that we can refer to them easily. For example, when we wish to refer to the man from Virginia who led American troops during the Revolutionary War, lived at Mount Vernon, and served as the first U.S. president, we can use the convenient name label, "George Washington." "Jupiter" is the name label that we use to talk about the fifth planet from the sun in the solar system. *"Hola"* is a Spanish name label that means "hello" in English. A chemist who wants to refer to sodium in a chemical equation can use the symbol "Na." Symbols provide time-saving, shorthand ways to refer to objects or events without using complete words—for example:

%	Percent
π	Pi (mathematics)
?	Question mark
♯	Sharp (music)

■ **Facts** Facts are ideas that we store in memory so that we can recall them and express them as complete sentences. Here are three facts that I have stored in my long-term memory:

▶ The Declaration of Independence was signed in 1776.

▶ Chlorophyll is the substance in plants that gives them their green color.

▶ In a right triangle, the sum of the squares of the two shorter sides is equal to the square of the longest side.

We store facts as meaningful ideas, or propositions, in long-term memory, not as sentences. Any sentence that we might use to express a fact is simply a way to communicate the stored idea to other people. For example, we could

Table 2.4
Instructional Goals Classified by Gagne's Five Learning Outcomes

Declarative Knowledge	Procedural Knowledge	Affective Knowledge
Verbal information	**Intellectual skills**	**Attitudes**
Labels	*Discriminations*	• Choose to recycle.
• State the symbols for the elements on the periodic table.	• Differentiate between "b" and "d."	• Choose to read a Shakespearean play.
• Name all the bones of the human body.	• Discriminate among shades of red.	• Choose to listen to recordings of Bach concertos.
• Write the symbol for pi.	• Differentiate between major and minor triads.	• Choose not to smoke.
Facts	*Concepts*	• Choose to cooperate in small groups.
• State multiplication facts.	• Identify right triangles.	• Choose not to abuse alcohol.
• Name the capital of each state.	• Identify sedimentary rocks.	• Choose to vote in elections.
• State the Pythagorean theorem.	• Identify adverbs.	• Choose to say "please" and "thank you."
Organized facts	*Rules and principles*	
• State the characteristics of communities.	• Demonstrate the rule for simplifying quadratic equations.	
• Describe the necessary conditions for plants to grow.	• Determine latitude and longitude coordinates.	
• Explain differences between baroque and classical music.	• Write haiku poems.	
Verbal chains	• Apply sentence diagramming rules.	
• Count from 1 to 10 in Spanish.	• Apply the nitrogen cycle.	
• Recite the preamble to the U.S. Constitution.	• Demonstrate the principle of checks and balances.	
• Recite Robert Frost's "Stopping by Woods."	**Cognitive strategies**	
	• Originate concept maps.	
	• Originate outlines for textbook chapters.	
	• Originate an experiment.	
	Motor skills	
	• Execute a layup.	
	• Execute the Virginia reel.	
	• Type a paragraph.	

use any of the following sentences to express the proposition about the signing of the Declaration of Independence in 1776:

▶ The Declaration of Independence was signed in 1776.

▶ In 1776, the Declaration of Independence was signed.

▶ The document that was signed in 1776 was the Declaration of Independence.

▶ The year in which the Declaration of Independence was signed was 1776.

▶ Signed in 1776, the Declaration of Independence . . .

▶ The signing of the Declaration of Independence took place in 1776.

As you can see, the fact that is being expressed is independent of the particular sentence structure that we might use to state it. The declarative knowledge that makes stating the fact possible is stored as a meaningful proposition in long-term memory. Teaching facts as verbal information involves helping students understand and store propositions, not just having them memorize sentences by rote.

■ **Organized Facts**   We often want learners to be able to remember and express **organized facts**, a collection of propositions connected in a meaningful way. For example, as one of the outcomes of my tree unit, I wanted my students to be able to explain how trees manufacture their food. Biologists use the name label *photosynthesis* to refer to this process. Here are several organized facts about photosynthesis:

▶ The food-making process in green plants is called photosynthesis.

▶ The green plant combines carbon dioxide and water to make glucose.

▶ The plant takes carbon dioxide in through the stomata in its leaves.

▶ The plant takes in water from the soil through its root system.

▶ The energy needed for photosynthesis comes from sunlight.

Together these propositions represent a set of organized facts. To learn organized facts, students must understand and remember each individual fact, as well as understand and remember how each fact relates to other facts. As we noted in the discussion of fact learning, the learner must store in memory the propositions, or meanings, not the specific sentences.

■ **Verbal Chains**   The fourth form that verbal information may take is verbal chaining. A **verbal chain** is a series of words or sentences that is stored in memory verbatim, that is, word for word. Examples of this type of learning are reciting the Pledge of Allegiance, reciting a poem, reciting the alphabet, stating the names of all fifty states alphabetically, and listing the names of U.S. presidents chronologically. In each of these examples, a sequence of words is stored in memory, recalled, and expressed as a verbatim chain.

We learn verbal chains differently from facts and organized facts because there are no underlying meaningful propositions to store in memory. Students must simply associate the links in the chain with each other in the correct order. Whereas facts and organized facts can be expressed in numerous ways, there is only one way to express a verbal chain: either all the words and sentences are stated in the correct order, or they are not. This type of rote, verbatim learning does not necessarily depend on meaningful understanding. For example, I'll bet you were able to recite every word of the Pledge of Allegiance and every letter of the alphabet long before you had any notion of what you were talking about. A great challenge for us as *design-teachers* is to ensure that students are not learning verbal chains when they should be constructing meaningful ideas.

■ **Capability Verbs for Verbal Information Goals**   For all four types of verbal information, students can demonstrate their learning by stating the declarative knowledge that they have stored in memory. Therefore, when we write instructional goals that reflect learners' acquisition of some form of verbal information, we can use *state* as the action word. When we use *state* as the capability verb, we begin to clarify our destination in two ways. First, with respect to assessment, we now know that we will need to provide learners with an opportunity to state the verbal information that they should have acquired through our instruction. Second, with respect to teaching, we now know that we will need to help learners store the verbal information in their long-term memories so that they will be able to remember, recall, and state it.

Notice that each of the verbal information goals in Table 2.4 is expressed using *state* as the capability verb. Although *state* is the capability verb of choice for verbal information instructional goals, we can use other verbs to communicate the same meaning, as the following pairs of examples illustrate:

State the symbol for pi.	*Write* the symbol for *pi*.
State the necessary conditions for plants to grow.	*Describe* the necessary conditions for plants to grow.
State the Spanish numerals from 1 to 10.	*Count* from 1 to 10 in Spanish.
State Robert Frost's "Stopping by Woods."	*Recite* Robert Frost's "Stopping by Woods."

Depending on the exact nature of the verbal information we want learners to acquire, we may wish to write the corresponding instructional goal using any of the following verbs as acceptable substitutes for *state*: *name, describe, recite, list, write, explain.*

Although verbal information instructional goals are extremely important for learners to achieve, there are many types of procedural knowledge that we want them to acquire as well. We turn our attention now to three general types of skills that are common in school learning: intellectual skills, cognitive strategies, and motor skills. Of these three types of procedural knowledge, intellectual skills are by far most frequently the focus of our classroom teaching and learning.

Intellectual Skills

Have you solved any problems lately? If so, you have applied a large number of powerful abilities known as intellectual skills. Before offering a definition for the term *intellectual skill*, I first want to describe three problems that I solved recently and demonstrate the critical role of intellectual skills in my thinking about those problem situations.

I was doing some landscaping at my home by placing landscaping timbers around the driveway. At the corner of the driveway, I decided to create a triangle in which we could plant a tree and shrubs (see Figure 2.2). After deciding how long I wanted each leg of the triangle to be (eight feet each), I was able to determine the length of the third side by applying the Pythagorean theorem: for any right triangle, the sum of the squares of the two shorter sides is equal to the square of the longest side (the hypotenuse).

The second problem involved a sticking door in my house. During the winter, the door swung freely; during the summer, it stuck. To understand this

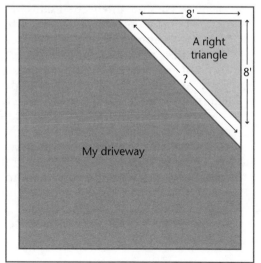

Step 1: $a^2 + b^2 = c^2$

Step 2: $8^2 + 8^2 = c^2$

Step 3: $64 + 64 = c^2$

Step 4: $128 = c^2$

Step 5: $11.31 = c$

Figure 2.2
Applying the Pythagorean Theorem to a Landscaping Problem

problem, I remembered and applied the following physics principle: warm things expand, and cold things contract. I decided to solve the problem by planing the sides of the door and sanding the frame during the summer so that I would remove just the right amount of wood to stop its sticking.

The third problem occurred just a few minutes ago as I was writing the paragraph that you just read. At the end of the last sentence, I needed to select which form of the pronoun *it* to use before the word *sticking* (*it* or *its*). As you can see, I chose *its* because of a rule I applied: pronouns that come before gerunds must be in the possessive case (a gerund is a noun that is formed by adding *-ing* to the end of a verb).

Here are the three specific intellectual skills that helped me think about and solve the preceding problems:

1. $a^2 + b^2 = c^2$ (the Pythagorean theorem).
2. Warm things expand; cold things contract.
3. Pronouns that come before gerunds must be possessive.

At first glance, it may appear that these three statements are simply facts that I have memorized as declarative knowledge. However, I was able to do far more with these propositions than just state them. I was able to *apply* them to my particular problem situation. I was able to use them in my thinking, reasoning, and decision making. As you can see, intellectual skills are powerful tools for thinking and problem solving.

Intellectual skills are generalizations that we symbolize mentally and use to interact with the environment. Let's see how this definition applies to the three intellectual skills that I used in my problem solving. First, intellectual skills are *generalizations*. This means that they represent predictable relationships among two or more variables. This feature gives us the power to apply the skill to an infinite number of specific situations or instances. For example, the relationships among the three sides of a right triangle always conform to the Pythagorean theorem. Therefore, use of the theorem can be extended (or generalized) to an infinite number of situations involving the lengths of the sides of specific right triangles. In contrast, verbal information does not generalize. For example, there is only one way that Jefferson was our third president. Jefferson was a specific person who was president at a specific time. There is only one way that "Jupiter" can be the name of the fifth planet from the sun. There is only one planet that is in the fifth position from the sun. There is only one way to recite the preamble to the U.S. Constitution.

The second important feature of intellectual skills is that we *symbolize them mentally*. We store intellectual skills in our long-term memories as productions. In each of my problem situations, I first needed to recall the relevant rule or principle from memory and then execute it to produce a new thought or action within my mind. Although I expressed the new thoughts and actions using physical abilities such as speaking and writing, the primary work took place in my mind. *Mental skills* and *cognitive skills* are two other common names for intellectual skills that reflect their mental nature.

The third feature of intellectual skills is that they help us to *interact with the environment*. For each of my three problems, I applied an internal intellectual skill to help me think about a situation that was occurring in my environment: landscaping, sticking doors, writing. Intellectual skills do not just reside in our heads. We activate and apply them to an infinite number of objects, events, people, and situations that we encounter daily. Although we symbolize intellectual skills mentally, they allow us to make contact with the world around us, providing understanding, guidance, and direction in our thinking and decision making.

Although all intellectual skills share the three critical features noted above, they take different forms that allow us to think about the environment in different ways. According to Gagne (1985), there are four categories of intellectual skills:

1. Discriminations
2. Concepts
3. Rules and principles
4. Problem solving

Let's look at some characteristics, capability verbs, and sample instructional goals for each.

■ **Discriminations**   No doubt you have entered a cool, air-conditioned building after being outside in hot, humid weather and noticed the different air temperature immediately. Your ability to notice the change in temperature is an example of the intellectual skill known as discrimination. **Discriminations** are the ability to detect differences in perceptual stimuli. Perceptual stimuli are the sights, sounds, tastes, smells, and touches that we experience (or perceive) through our five senses. Discriminations help us to differentiate among perceptual stimuli such as the following:

Sight:	straight line versus curved line	"b" versus "d" versus "p"
Sound:	short "a" versus long "a"	piano versus harpsichord
Taste:	peach versus apricot	sour versus bitter
Smell:	gasoline versus alcohol	coffee versus tea
Touch:	hot versus cold	smooth versus rough

For each of these pairs of stimuli, we demonstrate our discrimination ability when we recognize that specific instances are either different or the same.

Because we acquire many of our discriminations through informal experience, we rarely need to teach discrimination skills directly in school. However, some parts of the school curriculum are built on important discriminations that young children may not develop through informal experience. For example, early decoding skills in reading depend on the ability to discriminate between the funny-looking symbols of the alphabet such as "b," "d," and "p." Once young children (or perhaps illiterate adults who are learning to read) learn to discriminate these three similar-looking letters, they should be able to generalize the skill to all the specific instances of "b," "d," and "p" that they encounter, regardless of size, font style, or position with a word:

b	*b*	b	big	lab	label	*b*	b	b
d	*d*	d	dig	lad	ladle	*d*	d	d
p	*p*	p	pig	lap	lapel	*p*	p	p

When we determine that learners need to acquire a basic discrimination skill, we write an instructional goal that reflects the internal capability of differentiating among perceptual stimuli. The best capability verbs to use for such instructional goals are *discriminate* and *differentiate*. I have used these two verbs to write the discrimination instructional goals in Table 2.4. As you can see, I followed each verb with a description of the stimuli that learners need to be able to discriminate (e.g., "b" and "d," shades of red, major and minor triads). Although *discriminate* and *differentiate* are the capability verbs of choice for discrimination instructional goals, we can use other verbs to communicate the same meaning, as the following pairs of examples illustrate:

Differentiate between "b" and "d."	*Recognize the difference* between "b" and "d."
Discriminate among shades of red.	*Tell the difference* among shades of red.
Discriminate between major and minor triads.	*Indicate differences* between major and minor triads.

Differentiating between two perceptual stimuli does not necessarily mean that we can identify them. For example, you may be able to discriminate various shades of red without being able to classify the colors as scarlet, maroon, fuchsia, crimson, claret, cerise, carmine, or vermilion. The ability to classify objects and events represents a second major type of intellectual skill learning outcome: concepts.

Concepts   We are constantly classifying objects and events in our environment. To illustrate this point, stop reading now and go outside for a quick five-minute walk.

When you return, make a list of all the things you saw during your walk. While you went out for your walk, I went out too. Here is a partial list of all the objects and events I saw:

car	tree	grass	Frisbee throwing
truck	window	shrub	painting
street sign	person	bench	people conversing
rain	sidewalk	street light	road repairing
building	parking lot	squirrel	walking
brick	white line	bird	driving a car

Each object and event on our lists represents a classification category, or *concept*, that we carry around inside our heads. A **concept** is a category of objects or events that share common features. When we acquire a concept, we acquire the ability to respond to objects or events as a single class, or category, because they share the same general characteristics (Gagne, 1985). We usually also acquire a verbal label for the concept so that we can communicate about the category with others. For example, on my walk I saw several four-legged, bushy-tailed, gray, furry creatures that scurried about on the ground and in trees. I was able to look at each of these creatures and make the same classifying response: "That's a squirrel." Despite their individual differences (e.g., size, markings, location, activity), I classified all the gray, furry creatures as "squirrels" because they all possessed the features that I expected to find in my concept of "squirrel."

The concepts that we acquire to classify objects and events in the world around us span a broad continuum, from very simple (e.g., red) to quite complex and abstract (e.g., democracy, truth). Concepts on this simple-to-complex continuum usually can be separated into two groups: concrete and defined (Gagne, 1985; Ormrod, 1995). **Concrete concepts** have common features that we can easily perceive through one or more of our five senses. For example, "squirrel" is a concrete concept because I can easily visualize four legs, a bushy tail, and tree climbing. In contrast, **defined concepts** are abstract categories that do not have easily perceived features. An example of a defined concept is "friend." It is impossible to classify a person as a friend by appearance alone. To make a "friend" classification, we need to know something about how two or more people relate to each other at an unobservable psychological level. Other examples of defined concepts are socialism, noun, predator, and community.

When we design instruction for concept learning, we want learners to be able to apply the concept as a skill. This means that they should be able to classify new instances as either belonging to the category or not belonging to the

Concepts are mental categories that we use to classify the events, objects, and ideas we experience. What concepts are these children applying in this sorting activity?

category. Instances that can be classified as members of the category are called *positive instances*, or *examples*. Instances that cannot be classified as members of the category are called *negative instances*, or *nonexamples*. If, for example, I am teaching the concept of right triangle, I want my learners to be able to recognize, or identify, any positive instances of right triangles that they encounter in the world around them, as well as identify any nonexamples they experience (see Figure 2.3).

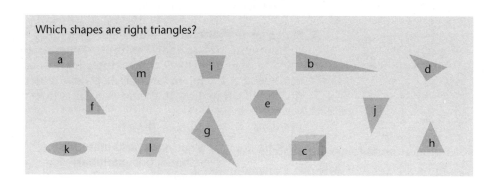

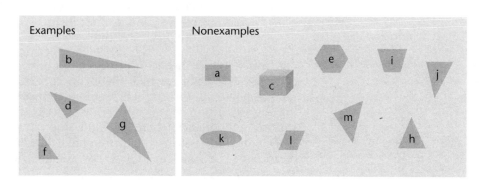

**Figure 2.3
Identifying Examples
and Nonexamples of
Right Triangles**

Instructional goals for concept learning outcomes should reflect the internal capability of identifying positive instances of the concept category. Therefore, the capability verb that best expresses the outcome of concept learning is *identify*. As illustrated in Figure 2.3, we demonstrate that we can apply a concept by identifying new specific instances as examples or nonexamples. Notice how I have used *identify* as the capability verb for the concept instructional goals in Table 2.4. In each case, I follow the capability verb (*identify*) with the name of the concept category (*right triangle, sedimentary rock, adverb*). Although *identify* usually serves as an appropriate capability verb for concept learning, some others express the same learning outcome, as the following sets of instructional goals illustrate:

Identify right triangles.	*Classify* right triangles.
	Recognize right triangles.
	Categorize shapes as right triangles.
	Differentiate between examples and nonexamples of right triangles.
Identify adverbs.	*Classify* adverbs.
	Recognize adverbs.
	Categorize words as adverbs.
	Differentiate between positive and negative instances of adverbs.

As you can see from the examples, we can write an instructional goal for a concept learning outcome in several different ways, as long as we express the essential capability of concept learning, that is, the ability to use the concept to identify members and nonmembers according to the features that define membership in the category.

The concepts that we have stored in our memories aid our thinking by providing categories that we can apply to classify our experiences. My procedural knowledge of the right triangle concept allowed me to identify a right triangle in my landscaping problem situation. Then I was able to activate related knowledge of right triangles, including the Pythagorean theorem. Generalizations such as the Pythagorean theorem are examples of yet another major type of intellectual skill: rules and principles.

◼ **Rules and Principles**   Rules and principles express generalizable relationships among two or more concepts. Whereas **rules** express concept relationships that guide behavior, **principles** express concept relationships that help us understand, explain, and predict. Let's return to two of my problem situations to illustrate how rules and principles help us think:

Problem	Rule or Principle	Concepts
Sticking door	*Principle*: Warm materials expand; cold materials contract.	Warm, cold, expansion, contraction, material
Pronoun case	*Rule*: Pronouns that come before gerunds must be in the possessive case.	Pronoun, gerund, before, possessive case

Notice that each rule or principle is a meaningful combination of several concepts. The ways in which these concepts relate to each other produce the unique, powerful thinking skill represented by each rule or principle. By applying the expansion-contraction principle, I could explain why the door was sticking and predict when it would stop sticking. Although this principle helped me understand, explain, and predict, it did not actually tell me what to do to solve the problem. In contrast, the gerund-pronoun rule reminded me that I needed to make the pronoun possessive. The rule gave me direct guidance that influenced my writing behavior: change *it* to *its*.

Sometimes rules provide a series of specific steps to take to reach particular goals (e.g., rounding numbers to the nearest ten, looking up a word in a dictionary, loading a piece of software into a computer). Rules that provide this type of step-by-step guidance are called **procedural rules**, or **algorithms**. Algorithms are particularly powerful intellectual skills because they always work—provided, of course, that we apply them correctly and in the right situations.

The typical school curriculum is loaded with rules and principles for students to acquire as intellectual skills. Here is a brief sampling of some of the possibilities:

Rules

- Adverbs are formed by adding -ly to adjectives.
- "I" before "e" except after "c" or when sounding like "a" as in *neighbor* and *weigh.*
- Say "please" after making a request.
- Indent the first line of a new paragraph.
- Round numerals to the next highest multiple of ten if the digit in the one's place is 5 or greater.
- Summarize a passage by identifying main ideas and deleting details.

Principles

- Distance traveled is equivalent to the time spent traveling multiplied by the rate of travel (distance = rate × time).
- Shorter vibrating strings produce higher pitches; longer strings produce lower pitches.
- Climates are warmer the closer they are to the earth's equator.
- If supply exceeds demand, prices drop; if demand exceeds supply, prices increase.
- The stages of insect metamorphosis are egg, larva, pupa, adult.
- Each branch of the federal government imposes checks on the other two branches and is balanced (limited) by the other two branches.

Notice that I have stated the preceding rules and principles as verbal information only to communicate them. The ability to state a rule or principle as verbal information does not guarantee that learners will be able to apply the rule or principle as an intellectual skill. For example, knowing that climates are warmer the closer they are to the earth's equator is not the same learned capability as knowing how to predict the climates of specific locations such as Puerto Rico and Pennsylvania. Therefore, when we design instruction for rules and principles, we must be careful to write instructional goals that reflect procedural knowledge outcomes.

We demonstrate procedural knowledge of rules and principles when we are able to apply them to new instances. We might expect our learners to be able to solve a new problem or reach a goal by applying a newly learned rule or principle, as I illustrated with my three problem situations. Another way to assess learners is to provide them with a new instance and have them demonstrate how the rule or principle works. For example, we could give learners a real or fictitious issue involving the federal government and ask them to demonstrate how the principle of checks and balances operates. Therefore, when writing instructional goals for rules and principles, we usually employ *apply* and *demonstrate* as capability verbs (see Table 2.4).

We can also use capability verbs that express the actual goal that would be achieved by applying the rule or principle. For example, if learners can *apply* the rules for writing haiku poems, then they should be able to *write* haiku poems. If students can *demonstrate* the rule for simplifying quadratic equations, then they should be able to *simplify* quadratic equations. Thus, we can emphasize either the learned capability or the result of applying the learned capability when we write instructional goals for rules and principles, as illustrated by the following pairs of examples:

Apply the rules for writing   *Write* haiku poems.
haiku poems.

Demonstrate the rule for simplifying   *Simplify* quadratic equations.
quadratic equations.

Rules and principles are extremely powerful intellectual skills because they can help us produce new actions in an infinite number of specific thinking and problem-solving situations. However, there is more to problem solving than simply applying a previously learned rule or principle. Let's explore the characteristics of problem solving as a learning outcome.

■ **Problem Solving**   Above all else, most teachers want their students to become effective problem solvers—people who can produce new and creative solutions to the problems that they will encounter daily throughout their lives. Unfortunately, developing students' problem-solving abilities is a difficult, frustrating, and elusive educational goal (Glaser, 1984; Mayer, 1987). Problem-solving capability is a difficult learning outcome to achieve because it requires a complex orchestration of declarative, procedural, and even affective knowledge.

Broadly defined, a **problem** is any situation in which we identify a goal (or goals) that we need to achieve but have no clear set of procedures for achieving (Gagne, Yekovich, & Yekovich, 1993; Newell & Simon, 1972). In other words, we know where we want to be but are not exactly sure how to get there. From this definition, we can construct a complementary view of **problem solving** as the set of thinking processes and actions that we take to move us closer to a goal that we want to achieve. Problem-solving activity closes the gap between our understanding of where we are (our initial state) and our understanding of where we want to be (our goal state).

When I solved my landscaping problem, in addition to achieving my immediate goal (how long should the hypotenuse timber be?), I also may have learned something new: a higher-order rule that I should be able to apply again in the future when I find myself in a similar situation. **Higher-order rules** are combinations of rules and principles that we sequence and apply as intellectual skills to guide our problem-solving thinking and behavior (Gagne, 1985). Higher-order rules that we construct during problem-solving experiences may become intellectual skills that guide our behavior in future problem-solving situations. Of course, we can neither acquire nor apply higher-order rules if we have not already acquired the lower-level rules and principles as intellectual skills.

If our learners have acquired a higher-order rule, then they should be able to use it to solve new problems that have a similar structure. Therefore, the capability verb for problem-solving instructional goals is *solve*. Writing instructional goals for problem-solving outcomes, however, is difficult because we cannot possibly anticipate all the combinations and sequences of domain-specific rules and principles that our students will need when they leave our classrooms and encounter a wide variety of problems. All of the rules and principles that were listed earlier in the chapter are examples of domain-specific skills. A **domain-specific** rule or principle is a skill that can be applied within a well-defined content area such as physics, algebra, English, or mathematics (Chi, Glaser, & Farr, 1988).

If, for the purpose of teaching, we identify a specific type of problem solving for which to design instruction and then teach our students how to solve those specific problems, then the problem situation ceases to be a problem. All we have accomplished is teaching learners how to apply a set of domain-specific rules and principles to a specific type of situation so that when they encounter that situation, they will know what to do. Recall, however, that we defined problem solving as an activity that helps us achieve a goal when we are not certain how to proceed.

How can we possibly design instruction for problem solving when, by definition, a problem occurs only when we do not know exactly what rules and principles to apply? We acquire higher-order rules as the result of solving new problems. Therefore, we can best prepare learners for future problem-solving experiences by designing instruction that teaches them how to apply a wide variety of domain-specific rules and principles as intellectual skills (Carey, 1985; Carey & Smith, 1993; Case, 1993). For this reason, you will notice that I have not included any problem-solving instructional goals in Table 2.4, even though problem solving is a type of intellectual skill. When we help learners acquire domain-specific rules and principles as generalizable intellectual skills, we build the foundation that they will need to create the unique higher-order rules that will be applicable to their various personal problem situations.

In addition to teaching domain-specific rules and principles, we can develop our learners' problem-solving skills by helping them acquire the ability to manage their thinking and behavior. When we design instruction to teach learners how to manage their own thinking, we are developing yet another major learned capability: what Gagne (1985) calls *cognitive strategies*.

Cognitive Strategies

Cognitive strategies are mental plans that we apply to manage our thinking and behavior during problem solving or learning. They help us regulate the flow of information, consider pieces of information systematically, access relevant prior knowledge and skills from long-term memory, combine pieces of information in creative and effective ways, and so on. Cognitive strategies do not accomplish our thinking. Productive thinking occurs only when we apply intellectual skills. Cognitive strategies are like ready-made higher-order rules. They help us select and activate specific intellectual skills that may be relevant to our goals. They also provide guidance as we apply the skills and use the results in our thinking.

Cognitive strategies are useful when we engage in two types of goal-directed behavior: problem solving and learning. Problem-solving strategies, or **heuristics**, are general plans that help us coordinate our declarative and procedural knowledge to originate a solution to achieve a goal within our environment. Problem-solving heuristics that we might teach students include Polya's (1957) well-known four-step process (understand, plan, carry out, think back) and the scientific method (observe, question, hypothesize, collect data, analyze data, draw conclusions). We can also teach heuristics for creating analogies, brainstorming, breaking problems into smaller subproblems, and other general approaches to problem solving. The systems model of instructional design that we are exploring in this book is an example of a cognitive strategy to guide your thinking when you are faced with the problem of helping others learn.

Learning strategies are general procedures that help us manage the flow of new information so that we can store it effectively in long-term memory. These types of strategies help us to originate a personal, meaningful understanding of new information so that we can retain and recall it. Some common learning strategies that can help us process information more meaningfully are outlining, concept mapping (networking, webbing), summarizing, elaborative note taking, creating analogies, and applying mnemonic aids (Grabowski, 1996).

Sometimes we teach the *SQ3R* reading strategy (survey, question, read, recite, review) to help learners process text material more actively. To apply the strategy effectively, however, the reader must be able to apply specific rules and principles to accomplish each phase of the five-step procedure. Again, I must emphasize that although cognitive strategies can help *guide* our learning and problem-solving behavior, they do not *produce* learning and problem solving for us.

Instructional goals for cognitive strategies need to reflect the creative, original, problem-solving behavior that they facilitate. If learners do acquire a cognitive strategy as the result of instruction, they should be able to apply the strategy as procedural knowledge to create new, or original, knowledge. Thus, Gagne's suggested capability verb for cognitive strategy learning outcomes is *originate*. Notice how I have used this verb to write the sample instructional goals in Table 2.4. As with rules and principles, we can also write cognitive strategy goals that express the actual goal that would be achieved by applying the strategy, as illustrated by the following sets of examples:

Originate outlines for textbook chapters.

Construct outlines for textbook chapters.
Develop outlines for textbook chapters.
Create outlines for textbook chapters.

Originate an experiment.

Develop an experiment.
Create an experiment.
Design an experiment.

Intellectual Skills and Cognitive Strategies: A Bigger Picture

The vast majority of the instructional goals that you will develop to guide your classroom teaching will represent intellectual skill and cognitive strategy learning outcomes. Therefore, I want to elaborate further on the relationships among these important learning outcomes before moving on to the remaining two learned capabilities, motor skills and attitudes. Let's return once again to my driveway landscaping problem.

As I have already illustrated, I solved my problem by inventing and applying a higher-order rule. As noted in Figure 2.4, I used the cognitive strategy of diagramming and labeling to guide me in creating this higher-order rule. However, before I could create and apply my higher-order rule, I needed to be able to apply each individual subordinate rule and principle. For example, I needed to be able to apply the Pythagorean principle as a skill. Because rules and principles represent regular relationships among concepts, I needed to learn how to apply each individual subordinate concept (right triangle, sum, square, leg, hypotenuse) before I could learn how to apply each relevant rule and principle. Finally, notice that *right triangle*, *leg*, and *hypotenuse* are concrete concepts, requiring some basic discriminations before I could acquire them (see Figure 2.4).

To summarize (follow along with Figure 2.4), successful problem solving requires the application of previously learned rules and principles. Learning rules and principles requires the application of previously learned concepts that make up those rules and principles. Learning new concrete concepts requires the application of previously learned discriminations. As you can see, we acquire each type of intellectual skill by building on less complex skills that we already have mastered. Thus, the four types of intellectual skills form a learning hierarchy that often is referred to as *Gagne's hierarchy of intellectual skills* (Gagne, 1985; Gagne, Briggs, & Wager, 1992). A hierarchy is like a pyramid in that lower levels of the structure provide a solid foundation for building

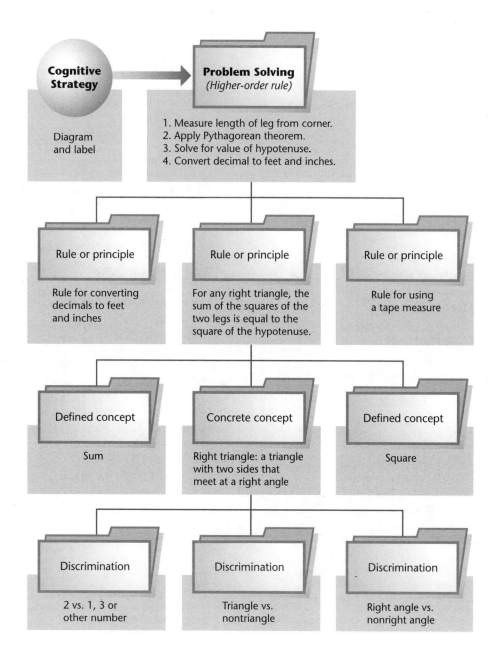

Figure 2.4
Applying Gagne's
Hierarchy of
Intellectual Skills to a
Mathematics Principle

higher, more complex levels. For this reason, I have represented Gagne's hierarchy of intellectual skills as a pyramid in Figure 2.1.

I do not want you to think that the intellectual skill hierarchy applies only to mathematics, so let's analyze a science principle to illustrate Gagne's hierarchy. Figure 2.5 shows how the hierarchy of skills relates to my sticking door problem. I was able to apply the expansion-contraction principle in a new, original way because I had learned it as a skill. Learning the principle as a skill was possible because I had learned the subordinate concepts and discriminations as skills.

Now it's your turn to apply Gagne's hierarchy to the pronoun-gerund rule, one of many important grammatical rules that help us to solve the problem of meaningful written communication. Using Figure 2.6 as a model, draw a pyramid and label each level of intellectual skill in Gagne's hierarchy. Place the phrase "communicate meaning through writing" at the top of the hierarchy;

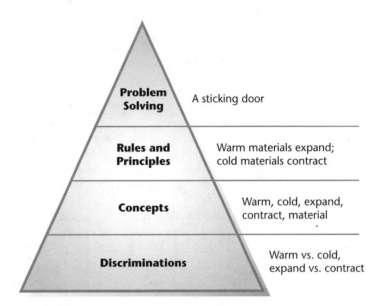

**Figure 2.5
Applying Gagne's
Hierarchy to a
Science Principle**

that is your problem-solving goal. Place the pronoun-gerund rule at the next level, as well as two or three additional rules or principles you are aware of that are relevant to effective writing. At the next level, indicate the specific concepts that make up those rules and principles. Finally, at the lowest level, indicate the specific discriminations that are related to any concrete concepts you identified. When you are finished with your hierarchy, look at Table 2.5 to see how I approached the analysis.

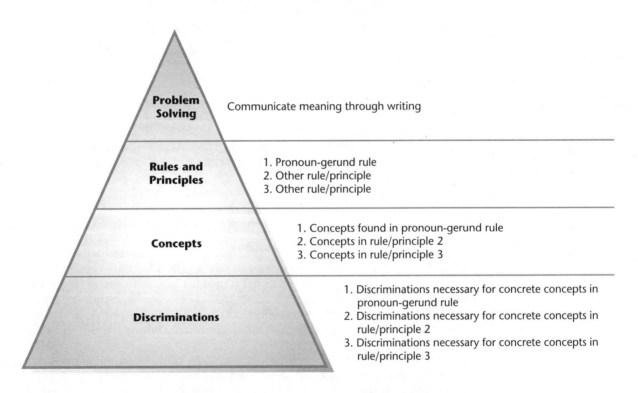

**Figure 2.6
Applying Gagne's Hierarchy to Rules and Principles of Writing**

Table 2.5
Applying Gagne's Hierarchy of Intellectual Skills to Writing Rules

Levels of Intellectual Skill	Examples of Intellectual Skills	Examples of Intellectual Skills	Examples of Intellectual Skills
Problem solving	Goal: meaningful written communication		
Rules and principles	Pronouns that come before gerunds must be in the possessive case.	Capitalize the first word of every sentence.	Each sentence in a paragraph must support the topic sentence of the paragraph.
Concepts	Pronoun, gerund, possessive case, before	Capital letter, word, sentence, first	Sentence, paragraph, topic sentence, support
Discriminations	Before versus after	Capital versus lowercase, first versus other positions	None (no concrete concepts)

The implications of Gagne's hierarchy for instructional design are significant. First, whenever we write instructional goals that reflect intellectual skill outcomes, we need to consider all the lower-level intellectual skills that learners already should have acquired. By moving *down* the hierarchy, we can identify lower-level instructional goals that we may need to address before we can teach toward higher-level intellectual skills. Second, when we design and deliver instruction, we need to begin with the foundational lower-level skills and move *up* the hierarchy toward the higher-level skills. We apply these two important implications extensively when we explore principles of content analysis in the next chapter. Third, the relationships expressed in Gagne's hierarchy are valid as long as lower-level skills are actually acquired as skills, that is, as *procedural* knowledge. If we do not help learners acquire discriminations, concepts, and rules and principles as intellectual skills that they can apply as procedural knowledge, then their potential to be effective problem solvers beyond our classrooms will be severely limited.

Thus far, we have been examining procedural knowledge that we apply mentally, or cognitively. Although we may use physical actions such as speaking, writing, pointing, sorting, or drawing to display the results of our applying intellectual skills and cognitive strategies, these outward actions are not the primary focus of our learned cognitive capabilities. Sometimes, however, we need to design classroom instruction to develop learners' physical capabilities, or motor skills. Motor skills are the third type of procedural knowledge (see Figure 2.1) and yet another of Gagne's major learning outcomes to consider in developing instructional goals.

Motor Skills

Recently I was talking with my youngest daughter, Rebekah, on the night before her first day of first grade. Jokingly, I asked her if she had learned enough in kindergarten to qualify her for the rigors of first grade. She replied earnestly and proudly, "Of course, I'm ready for first grade, Daddy. I can write my name now!" Rebekah's response reminded me that writing our names, a capability that we perform effortlessly as adults, is a major accomplishment for young children. Not only did she learn to state the sequence of letters that comprise her name (verbal information), she also learned to produce the funny-looking marks that represent those letters in the English language. To produce the marks, she had to learn how to coordinate several physical actions: holding a pencil or other writing instrument, positioning her upper body, holding the paper still with her nonwriting hand, and moving her arm and wrist to make combinations of vertical, horizontal, diagonal, and curved lines of varying sizes. Yes, writing her name is quite an accomplishment.

When young children perform the physical act of writing their names, they demonstrate that they have acquired a *motor skill*. A **motor skill** is a series of smooth, coordinated, well-timed muscular movements performed to accomplish a goal (Gagne, 1985). When we perform a motor skill, we use our skeletal muscles to move specific parts of our bodies. For example, to shoot a layup in basketball, you dribble toward the basket, jump toward the basket, extend your shooting hand upward, bounce the ball against the backboard so that it ricochets through the hoop, and land on your feet.

It sounds easy on paper, but if you have ever attempted to shoot a layup, you know that putting all of those bodily movements together takes a lot of practice. Sure, you can perform each movement in a halting, choppy, uneven, uncoordinated way and still manage to get the ball through the hoop but you will not have demonstrated the correct bodily form for a layup. Conversely, you may demonstrate a perfectly executed, smooth, coordinated layup and still miss the shot. Performing a motor skill therefore involves more than just achieving the goal of the bodily movement (e.g., getting the ball through the hoop, getting the letters on the piece of paper). It encompasses performing the series of muscular movements with the appropriate form, timing, and level of coordination.

Although we demonstrate motor skills by exhibiting bodily movements, we use thinking processes to guide our physical actions. Through mental activity, we plan, monitor, modify, and evaluate our motor performances. For example, I am using my typing skills to produce the words for this chapter. As I move my fingers to press buttons on the keyboard (motor skill), I am constantly *thinking* about the sequences of letters that I want to appear on my computer screen. I frequently stop to think about what I want to say, and then my fingers go to work to turn my thoughts into words. Sometimes a word on the screen doesn't look rigggght (oops!) and I have to move my fingers toward the Backspace or Delete key. As you can see, there is a constant interaction between motor skills and intellectual skills. For this reason, some instructional designers prefer the term **psychomotor** to refer to motor skills (e.g., Dick & Carey, 1996; Smith & Ragan, 1993). The *psycho-* part of the term reminds us that thinking skills support the performance of motor skills and therefore should be included in motor skills instruction.

When motor skills are the focus of instruction, we need to write instructional goals that reflect performance of the skills as procedural knowledge. Learners provide evidence that they have acquired a motor skill by actually carrying out the skill, or *executing* it. Therefore, Gagne recommends that we use *execute* as the capability verb for motor skill instructional goals. Notice how I have used *execute* in writing the first two sample instructional goals for motor skills in Table 2.4. We also can write motor skills instructional goals using specific behavior verbs as long as we clearly represent the capability of executing physical movement, as the following sets of examples illustrate:

Execute a layup.	*Shoot* a layup.
Execute a soccer kick.	*Kick* a soccer ball.
Execute the Virginia reel.	*Dance* the Virginia reel. *Perform* the Virginia reel.
Execute paragraph keyboarding.	*Type* a paragraph. *Produce* a typed paragraph.

The intellectual skills, cognitive strategies, and motor skills that we learn throughout our lifetimes give us the potential for producing an impressive array of adaptive behaviors. However, knowing how to perform a skill does not necessarily mean that we will want to perform it. For example, although I know how to apply the algorithm for three-digit division, I do not particularly enjoy demonstrating that skill. In fact, I intensely dislike doing three-digit division by hand and reach for a calculator (if I can) when I have to apply that rule to solve a problem. I also avoid changing the oil in my car, sanding drywall plaster, and making the bed, even though I know how to execute these motor skills and could perform each of them if I had to. In contrast, not only do I know how to play a trumpet, design and carry out a research study, and fly-fish, I enjoy performing these skills and actively seek opportunities to do so. What accounts for the discrepancy between what I am able to do and what I am willing to do? For answers to this question, let's examine the fifth and final major learning outcome: attitudes.

Attitudes

If you had the power and freedom to be doing any activity at this very moment, what would you choose to do? Let your mind wander and list three or four specific activities that you would love to be doing at this moment. Here is my list:

- Fly-fishing for trout in a clear mountain stream
- Teaching an educational psychology class
- Listening to a Haydn symphony
- Pruning my fruit trees, grape vines, and blackberry bushes

I possess the declarative and procedural knowledge that is necessary to perform these activities. I also possess a positive emotional regard for these activities so that I would voluntarily choose to do them if given the opportunity. I am sure that you can say the same of the activities on your personal list. When we make voluntary choices to engage in specific activities, those behavior choices demonstrate our *attitudes* toward those activities. Gagne (1985) defines **attitudes** as "internal states that influence the individual's choices of personal action" (p. 219).

The internal catalyst for our action choices is affect (feeling or emotion). When I close my eyes and think about the four attitude objects on my list (fly-fishing, teaching, Haydn symphonies, pruning fruit trees), I feel a positive sense of affect. That is, I experience good feelings toward those objects. Those good feelings in turn motivate me to engage in activities that involve those particular objects. In contrast, when I think about three-digit division, sanding drywall plaster, and making the bed, I experience negative affect—bad feelings toward those activities that motivate me to avoid them. Attitudes primarily represent affective knowledge (see Figure 2.1) because our emotional reactions to objects, events, and activities influence our choices to approach or avoid them.

You will constantly be teaching attitudes to your learners, whether you realize it or not. Your students will develop positive or negative attitudes toward school, learning, and subject matter largely because of the ways in which you model your own positive or negative attitudes. However, you sometimes will want to make deliberate efforts to develop or change your students' attitudes. For example, you may want to develop positive attitudes toward recycling, Shakespeare, Bach, cooperation, civic responsibility, and politeness. You may want to develop negative attitudes toward smoking, abusing alcohol and other drugs, vandalism, and dishonesty. For such attitudinal outcomes, you will need to write instructional goals that describe the capability that you should expect your learners to exhibit if indeed they do acquire those positive or negative attitudes.

For positive attitudes, you should expect your learners to exhibit *approach behaviors* that engage them directly with the attitude object (e.g., initiating a community recycling program, attending a Bach concert, going to the polls to vote). For negative attitudes, you will expect learners to exhibit *avoidance behaviors* that keep them away from the attitude object or help them to refrain from specific activities (e.g., turning down the offer of an alcoholic drink, not purchasing a pack of cigarettes, resisting peer pressure to perform acts of vandalism). Learners may demonstrate their attitudes through a range of possible approach and avoidance behaviors (Krathwohl, Bloom, & Masia, 1964). Sometimes, for example, people demonstrate attitude change when they are simply willing to listen to, or receive, new emotional information concerning an attitude object (e.g., choose to listen to a presentation on the benefits of recycling).

To provide convincing evidence that they have acquired a positive or negative attitude, your learners should freely choose their approach or avoidance behaviors. If, for example, you require your students to read an additional play by Shakespeare outside class, you cannot assume that they necessarily have a positive attitude toward doing so, even if they comply with the requirement. Therefore, the capability verb that Gagne recommends for attitudinal instructional goals is *choose*. When we use *choose* as the capability verb, we remind ourselves that we are striving for an affective outcome that will be strong enough to influence our learners' voluntary action choices. Notice in Table 2.4 how I have used *choose* to write several attitudinal instructional goals. In writing such goals, we need to make professional judgments about the types of voluntary behaviors that will provide convincing evidence of attitude learning. For example, the instructional goal *choose to vote in elections* is only one type of voluntary behavior that we could use to infer that learners have a positive attitude toward civic responsibility. Here are some other possibilities:

▶ Choose to read the local newspaper to stay abreast of current events.

▶ Choose to give donations to local charities.

▶ Choose to donate time to community service organizations.

▶ Choose to attend and participate in town meetings.

LET'S SUMMARIZE

An instructional goal describes what students should be able to do to demonstrate their internal learning. The capabilities that learners are able to exhibit should permit us to infer whether they have acquired the intended learning outcome. Therefore, we should write our instructional goals so that they clearly reflect the learning outcomes that we intend to develop in our learners. Using the capability verbs that Gagne suggests (see Table 2.6) will help us to focus not only on the observable external evidence that learners should be able to demonstrate, but also on the internal products of learning that make the external performance possible.

Using Instructional Goals to Focus Classroom Teaching

Learning outcomes have significant implications for two critical components of the instructional design process: assessment and instruction. When you are aware of the type of learning outcome that your learners need to acquire, you will be better able to design assessment procedures that are appropriate (or valid) for that particular outcome. Appropriate assessment procedures that are valid for the intended learning outcome have the potential to produce

Table 2.6
Summary of Learning Outcomes

Outcome	Definition	Capability Verb	Sample Instructional Goals
1. Verbal information	Factual knowledge stored in memory and recalled when desired	*State*	State the colors of the light spectrum. Recite the preamble to the U.S. Constitution.
2. Intellectual skills	Generalizations, symbolized mentally, used to interact with the real world	Capability verbs for specific types of intellectual skills:	Instructional goals for specific types of intellectual skills follow:
Problem solving	Higher-order rule, used to achieve a goal	*Solve*	Solve mathematics problems involving percent. Solve problems involving interpersonal conflict.
Rules and principles	Concept relationships, used to guide behavior, make predictions, and solve problems	*Apply* *Demonstrate*	Apply the rule for using apostrophes to show possession. Demonstrate the principle of checks and balances.
Concepts	Categories for classifying objects and events based on common features	*Identify* *Classify*	Identify triangles, rectangles, and trapezoids. Classify sedimentary, igneous, and metamorphic rocks.
Discriminations	Perceptual differences	*Differentiate*	Differentiate between the sound of /p/ and /b/. Differentiate between sour and bitter tastes.
3. Cognitive strategies	Processes used to control learning or problem-solving activity	*Originate*	Originate a concept map for a text chapter. Originate a plan for conserving energy.
4. Motor skills	Purposeful movement of skeletal muscles	*Execute*	Execute a tennis serve. Execute the tying of a double overhand knot.
5. Attitudes	Internal states that influence personal choices of action	*Choose*	Choose to exercise daily. Choose to drive safely.

useful information for you to evaluate your students' learning and your teaching effectiveness.

The second reason for classifying instructional goals according to their learning outcomes is that it helps you design appropriate (or valid) instructional events. In short, *different learning outcomes have different requirements for learning* (Gagne, 1984, 1985; Ragan & Smith, 1996). Therefore, your teaching strategies should vary accordingly to maximize the likelihood that your students will in fact achieve the learning outcomes represented by your instructional goals. For example, if an instructional goal represents a concept learning outcome, then you will need to include instructional events that are potentially effective in promoting concept learning. If you are designing instruction for an attitudinal outcome, you will need to include instructional activities that effectively promote attitude formation or attitude change.

Obviously instructional goals cannot help us focus our classroom teaching until we actually specify them. How do we identify our instructional goals? Where do they come from? Instructional goals can come from a variety of sources. School curriculum guides, state departments of education, publications from professional organizations, textbooks, and other instructional materials may offer instructional goals for teachers. Usually, however, *design-teachers* are in the best possible position to determine what their classroom instructional goals should be and which of the five learning outcomes those goals represent because they have a good understanding of both their learners and the subject matter to be taught.

Deriving Instructional Goals from Subject Matter

Writing and classifying instructional goals encourages us to think carefully about what we want to accomplish with our teaching. The subject matter that we intend to teach does not determine the type of learning outcome that we are trying to achieve. To illustrate this important principle, let's return to a piece of subject matter that I wanted to include in my tree unit: deciduous trees.

What learning outcome does *deciduous trees* represent? Is it verbal information? A concept? A rule or principle? An attitude? As a topic, *deciduous trees* does not clearly represent any learning outcome. I need to specify what I want learners to be able to do as a result of learning about deciduous trees before I can classify their learning. What do I want them to be able to do? I can write at least five different instructional goals for the topic of deciduous trees:

1. State the features of deciduous trees. (*verbal information*)
2. State the names of several deciduous tree species. (*verbal information*)
3. Identify deciduous trees. (*intellectual skill, concepts*)
4. Demonstrate how the leaves of deciduous trees change color in autumn. (*intellectual skill, principle*)
5. Choose to recycle paper products to conserve deciduous trees. (*attitude*)

As you can see, subject matter alone does not determine the learning outcome. What we expect learners to be able to *do* with the subject matter determines the learning outcome that will become our focus for teaching.

Deriving Instructional Goals from Professional Standards

Design-teachers can look to professional educational organizations for assistance in developing instructional goals. For example, the National Council of Teachers of Mathematics (NCTM) has developed a set of curriculum standards to guide mathematics instruction (NCTM, 1989). Here, for example, is a learning goal found in Standard 6, Number Sense and Numeration: *Students can understand our numeration system by relating counting, grouping, and place-value concepts.* Although this statement is much too broad and vague to function as an effective instructional goal, a teacher could certainly use it for general guidance. A *design-teacher* could transform this general standard into several focused instructional goals such as the following:

1. Students will be able to count in multiples of 10, 100, and 1,000. (*intellectual skill, rule*)

2. Students will be able to name place values in order to the millions place. (*verbal information*)

3. Students will be able to determine the value of each digit in a four-digit numeral. (*intellectual skill, rule*)

Similarly, the National Council for the Social Studies (NCSS) suggests standards for social studies instruction that are organized around ten thematic strands (NCSS, 1998). For the first strand, culture, NCSS recommends that social studies programs include experiences that provide for the study of culture and cultural diversity. A *design-teacher* could operationalize this broad guideline by writing specific instructional goals such as the following:

1. Students will be able to demonstrate how environmental conditions influence the cultures of Native American people. (*intellectual skill principle*)

2. Students will be able to name and describe the major European ethnic groups that immigrated to the United States in the early 1900s. (*verbal information*)

3. Students will choose to read the works of Hispanic authors. (*attitude*).

State departments of education often provide curriculum standards that specify learning goals for teachers. For example, in its K–12 Social Studies and History Standards, the state of Nebraska recommends that students should be able to do the following:

▶ Identify the elected representative bodies responsible for making local, state, and federal laws (grades K–1).

▶ Describe Nebraska's history from territory to statehood (grades 2–4).

▶ Identify natural, human, and capital resources; describe their distribution; and explain their significance, such as location of contemporary and selected historical economic and land-use regions (grades 9–12).

As you can see from the second goal (describing Nebraska's history), instructional goals sometimes reflect the unique characteristics or values of a particular geographic location or group of people. Ultimately the instructional goals and learning outcomes we develop to guide our classroom teaching reflect our *values*: what we believe to be important and in the best interest of our students. Of course, the values of families, communities, state and federal educational agencies, and professional organizations also influence the instructional goals we select. Exploring the social, political, and organizational principles underlying curriculum development is well beyond the scope of this book. Regardless of the processes and values used by professional organizations, states, and communities to determine significant learning outcomes, you as a *design-teacher* will still need to make sure that those outcomes are stated as clear instructional goals so that you have focus and direction for your classroom teaching.

Diverse Instructional Goals for Diverse Learners

Well-written instructional goals provide a focus for classroom teaching. However, that does not necessarily mean that all students must always achieve exactly the same goals. There may be times when it is appropriate to create different instructional goals for different groups of learners, depending on their unique characteristics and learning needs. Consider, for example, a situation in which a student with cerebral palsy, confined to a wheelchair, is included in a regular high school biology classroom. For this learner, the psychomotor instructional goal *prepare a microscope slide* may be impossible to achieve because of the student's severe motor impairment and lack of physical coordination. However, the related goal, *state the procedure for preparing a microscope slide,* may be possible to achieve because the capability falls within the student's range of physical abilities. Alternatively, the student could be expected *to recognize the correct procedure for preparing a microscope slide.* This instructional goal implies that the student will observe others as they prepare microscope slides and indicate if the skill has been performed correctly or incorrectly.

Clearly *design-teachers* need to be aware of their students' diverse characteristics and learning needs so that they can make informed decisions about appropriate instructional goals. For example, if some of your students have not yet acquired prerequisite skills for a higher-level learning outcome, you should first establish instructional goals for them that focus on those lower-level skills. For students who have mastered the prerequisite skills, an instructional goal focusing on the higher-level skill is appropriate. Eventually, of course, you want all of your students to attain the highest level of skill learning possible. You just may need to make adjustments in the speed with which your learners achieve those skills. In short, you will need to modify and adapt your instructional goals for groups or individuals to maximize the learning of all your students.

Before we conclude this chapter, let's examine three classroom scenarios that I will use to illustrate the systems approach to instructional design. To help you see how all the component parts of the instructional design process work together, I will return to these three scenarios in each chapter to illustrate key principles and procedures. Here I demonstrate how three *design-teachers* identify and classify instructional goals to provide clear destinations for their teaching.

INSTRUCTIONAL DESIGN CASE ANALYSES

Case 1: Ms. Nelson

Ms. Nelson is beginning her first year as a fifth-grade teacher. For several weeks before the start of school, she begins to familiarize herself with the school district's curriculum. She discovers that the district's curriculum guide provides an outline of topics in each subject that teachers are expected to "cover" with their students during the school year. As she reviews the fifth-grade science section, one particular topic catches her eye: geology.

Ms. Nelson has a keen personal interest in geology. Ever since she was a little girl, she has enjoyed studying rocks, minerals, and fossils and even has developed her own personal collection, which is quite extensive. "Terrific!" she thinks to herself. "I'll be able to teach a topic that really excites me!" Returning to the curriculum guide, she sees that several subtopics are listed for geology: rocks, minerals, fossils, earth history, and so on. Ms. Nelson wonders how she can provide her students with in-depth instruction on all of these topics, especially with all the other science subjects outlined in the curriculum guide. She realizes that she will need to identify clearly the specific knowledge and skills that her students should acquire in their study of geology. Although she knows that she cannot possibly teach them everything about geology in a few weeks, she can help them acquire the knowledge and skills that are appropriate for their developmental level and will provide them with a good foundation for continued learning in later grades.

"What do I want my students to know about geology?" she asks herself. Ms. Nelson begins to answer her question by skimming the geology chapters in the fifth-grade science textbook that the district has adopted. She also reviews some of the geology-related materials that she has collected over the years and visits several geology-related web sites on the Internet. Finally, she begins to list some learning goals for the geology unit that she will teach. She believes that her students should have the following capabilities:

1. Be familiar with several common minerals that are found in our region.
2. Understand the properties of minerals that are used to identify them.
3. Understand how mineral crystals grow.
4. Appreciate how useful minerals are to our everyday lives.
5. Visit the rock, mineral, and fossil exhibits at a nearby museum.
6. Understand how minerals form rocks.
7. Know what the three major types of rocks are and understand how they are formed.
8. Be familiar with several common rocks that are found in our region.
9. Know how the rock cycle operates.
10. Understand how fossils form.
11. Be familiar with several common types of fossils that are found in our region.
12. Make fossil models with clay.
13. Know the characteristics of the major geologic periods in the earth's history.

As Ms. Nelson reviews her ambitious list, she realizes that many of her goals are not instructional goals because they do not describe what her students should be able to *do* to demonstrate their learning. How, for example, will she know that her students "understand" how mineral crystals grow? How will she know that her learners are "familiar with" common rocks that are found in the region? How will she know that they "know" the characteristics of the earth's geologic periods? Ms. Nelson returns to her list and thinks carefully about the type of learning outcome she hopes to achieve with each learning goal and the observable evidence of learning that she wants her students to be able to demonstrate. Her thinking results in a set of clear instructional goals and learning outcomes, summarized in Table 2.7. Here are brief descriptions of the thinking processes she used to transform some of her general goals into powerful instructional goals:

General goal 1: Be familiar with several common minerals that are found in our region. In this region, students are likely to see natural examples of quartz, azurite, garnet, feldspar, and mica. I want them to recognize these minerals when they encounter them in the environment. To recognize these minerals, they will need to acquire each as a concept that they can apply as an intellectual skill. Here, then, is my instructional goal: *Students will be able to identify examples of quartz, azurite, garnet, feldspar, and mica (intellectual skill, concepts).*

Notice how Ms. Nelson replaces the vague term *be familiar with* with the capability verb *identify*, which is appropriate for concept application. She also improves the goal by replacing the vague content, *several common minerals*, with the names of the specific minerals that she wants students to be able to identify.

General goal 3: Understand how mineral crystals grow. There are several principles that help us explain how minerals grow and the shapes and sizes that they attain. One such principle that I think my fifth graders could under-

Table 2.7
Changing General Goals to Instructional Goals for Science Teaching

General Goal	Instructional Goal	Learning Outcome
1. Be familiar with several common minerals that are found in our region.	Identify examples of quartz, azurite, garnet, feldspar, and mica.	Intellectual skill: Concepts
2. Understand the properties of minerals that are used to identify them.	Apply hardness, streak, luster, and color tests to identifying minerals.	Intellectual skill: Rules
3. Understand how mineral crystals grow.	Demonstrate how the rate of cooling influences the size of a mineral crystal.	Intellectual skill: Principle
4. Appreciate how useful minerals are to our everyday lives.	State common uses for minerals.	Verbal information
5. Visit the rock, mineral, and fossil exhibits at a nearby museum.	*Omit as an instructional goal; use as a learning activity.*	
6. Understand how minerals form rocks.	Explain how minerals form rocks.	Verbal information
7. Know what the three major types of rocks are and understand how they are formed.	State the three types of rock and describe how each is formed.	Verbal information
	Identify sedimentary, igneous, and metamorphic rocks.	Intellectual skill: Concepts
8. Be familiar with several common rocks that are found in our region.	Identify examples of limestone, shale, schist, conglomerate, and slate.	Intellectual skill: Concepts
9. Know how the rock cycle operates.	Demonstrate how the rock cycle operates.	Intellectual skill: Principle
10. Understand how fossils form.	Identify the molds and casts of fossils.	Intellectual skill: Concepts
11. Be familiar with several common types of fossils that are found in our region.	Classify fossils as brachiopods, trilobites, gastropods, and crinoids.	Intellectual skill: Concepts
12. Make fossil models with clay.	*Omit as an instructional goal; use as a learning activity.*	
13. Know the characteristics of the major geologic periods in the earth's history.	State the names of the three major eras in the earth's history and several important characteristics of each.	Verbal information

stand is the relationship between how fast a mineral solution cools and the resulting size of the mineral crystals that form. Specifically, I want them to know that when solutions cool more quickly, they produce smaller mineral crystals; when they cool more slowly, larger crystals form. I don't want them just to memorize this proposition as declarative knowledge. I want them to be able to apply this principle as an intellectual skill, so that they will be able to use the principle whenever they are thinking about problems that involve the sizes of crystals that are formed from cooling solutions. Here, then, is my instructional goal: *Students will be able to demonstrate how the rate of cooling influences the size of a mineral crystal (intellectual skill, principle).*

Notice that Ms. Nelson replaces *understand* with an observable capability verb, *demonstrate*. Demonstrating how a principle applies to new instances is a valid way for her students to show that they have learned the principle as a generalizable intellectual skill. Ms. Nelson also improves her instructional goal by specifying the principle of mineral growth that she wants her students to be able to apply. Although there are other principles of crystal growth, she is choosing to focus her instruction on this particular principle.

General goals 5 and 12: Visit the rock, mineral, and fossil exhibits at a nearby museum; make fossil models with clay.   These two goals seem to be different from the others. Rather than describing what my students should be able to do as a *result* of my instruction, they describe activities that I may be able to use *in* my instruction. A field trip to a museum and making fossil models could be very useful learning activities to help my fifth graders achieve my instructional goals. However, these activities are not in themselves instructional goals. I need to remember that my instructional goals should describe the learned capabilities that my students will be taking away with them from my classroom. They should not describe what my students will be doing in my classroom to acquire the learned capabilities. Later in the instructional design process, I may consider using a field trip and the clay activity to help my students achieve some of my other instructional goals. For now, however, I will eliminate them from my list of instructional goals.

General goal 13: Know the characteristics of the major geologic periods in the earth's history.   The major periods that I want my students to know about are the Precambrian, Paleozoic, Mesozoic, and Cenozoic eras. For each period, I will develop a list of features that I will help my students understand and remember. The four names are examples of labels that my learners should be able to recall and state as verbal information. Each era has a set of characteristics that students can store in long-term memory as propositions. As evidence that my learners actually have stored each era's propositions in long-term memory, I will expect them to be able to recall and state the appropriate propositions for each era. Here, then, is my instructional goal: *Students will be able to state the names of the four major eras in the earth's history and several important characteristics of each (verbal information).*

Notice that Ms. Nelson transforms the vague verb *know* into a capability verb, *state*, that is appropriate for a verbal information learning outcome. She also clarifies the content of the goal by specifying that there are four eras that students will be able to describe.

Case 2: Mrs. Torres

As a veteran teacher of twenty-three years, Mrs. Torres is thoroughly familiar with the first-grade mathematics curriculum and the characteristics of first-grade children. However, ready for a change and a new professional challenge, she has just moved to a third-grade classroom for the start of a new school year. The school district does not have a formal curriculum guide. Instead, teachers are expected to follow their textbooks to determine subject matter and instructional goals. As a *design-teacher,* Mrs. Torres has been reviewing her textbooks to identify the instructional goals that her third graders should achieve. One of the topics that appears near the beginning of her mathematics textbook is rounding numbers to the nearest ten and hundred. Mrs. Torres thinks to herself . . .

TEACHER'S THINKING AND PLANNING Rounding is an important skill for my students to acquire. Rounding skills will help my students in estimating, problem solving, and thinking mathematically—important learning outcomes identified by the National Council of Teachers of Mathematics. Therefore, my third graders should learn about rounding as an intellectual skill so that they will be prepared to round any number, in any situation, to the nearest ten or hundred. Because the procedural rules, or algorithms, for rounding to the nearest ten or hundred generalize to any number, they represent intellectual skills. I want my third graders to do more than just talk about rounding as verbal information. I want them to be able to demonstrate their rounding skills as procedural knowledge. Here, then, is my instructional goal: *Students will be able to apply the rules for rounding numbers to the nearest ten and hundred (intellectual skill, rules).*

Mrs. Torres demonstrates how she transformed a broad mathematics topic (rounding) into an instructional goal. She could have omitted the capability verb *apply* and written the following instructional goal: *Learners will round numbers to the nearest ten and hundred.* Although this would have been an acceptable instructional goal, including the phrase *apply the rules for rounding* creates a more powerful instructional goal because it reminds her that rules are the internal learning product her students need to acquire.

Case 3: Mr. Hoffman

Mr. Hoffman is a middle school social studies teacher. His school district's curriculum committee has just recommended a district-wide initiative to develop students' strategic learning abilities. In addition to teaching subject matter, teachers are now expected to help their students acquire learning strategies. In short, the district wants its students to learn how to learn. Rather than creating special classes to teach learning strategies, the committee has recommended that teachers integrate strategy learning with their content-related instruction. Thus, along with acquiring content-related verbal information, intellectual skills, motor skills, and attitudes, students will learn how to construct summaries, create analogies, apply mnemonic strategies, construct concept maps, apply generative note-taking strategies, and so on. Because the committee has recommended that students learn concept mapping strategies at the middle school level, Mr. Hoffman finds himself wondering how he will address this learning goal in his eighth-grade social studies class. . .

TEACHER'S THINKING AND PLANNING

I know a little about concept mapping from a graduate course in educational psychology that I took recently. If I remember correctly, concept mapping is a learning strategy that is based on schema theory and generative learning models. When we store new information in long-term memory, we need to link it in a meaningful way to the network of ideas we already have stored there. In the strategy known as concept mapping, students show on paper the important links or relationships among new concepts that they are learning about. They also create (or generate) links that connect the new concepts to ideas that they already have firmly embedded in their schemas. By engaging in the cognitive effort to generate these links, learners enhance their understanding of new ideas and construct meaningful retrieval pathways that will help them recall the information when they want to use it.

Concept mapping is an example of procedural knowledge because my students need to know how to do it. My students will need to learn the step-by-step procedure for creating concept maps. They will need to be able to generalize the procedure to an infinite number of reading or study situations in which the strategy could be useful—and not just social studies. When my students create concept maps, they will be making diagrams that show the unique, personal meaning that they are constructing from their reading. The meaning that they construct will be the result of a complex interaction between the information that appears on the page and the ideas they already have stored in their schemas. Therefore, concept maps represent my students' original creations to help them solve the problem of understanding and learning from reading materials. Here, then, is my instructional goal: *Students will be able to originate concept maps for social studies textbook chapters (cognitive strategy).*

Mr. Hoffman recognizes that concept mapping is a cognitive strategy that can strengthen the understanding that his learners construct from their reading. Therefore, he deliberately uses the capability verb *originate* so that he focuses on the ultimate problem-solving goal of concept mapping rather than just the rule-based mechanics of the concept mapping procedure. Because he is expected to integrate concept mapping with his social studies teaching, Mr. Hoffman focuses his instructional goal on social studies textbook chapters.

LOOKING BACK LOOKING AHEAD

In this chapter, we have begun to address the first fundamental instructional design question: Where are we going? *Design-teachers* answer this question by writing precise instructional goals that indicate the capabilities that their learners should be able to demonstrate as the result of instruction. The capabilities described by our instructional goals enable us to make inferences about the internal learning products that our learners should acquire from our teaching. These learning products, or outcomes, take five major forms: verbal information, intellectual skills, cognitive strategies, motor skills, and attitudes. We should identify the type of learning outcomes that we are trying to develop in our learners and then write our instructional goals using capability verbs that are appropriate to represent those outcomes.

By now, you have read a lot of information that is related to our instructional goals for this chapter. However, this does not necessarily mean that you can demonstrate all the capabilities described by the goals. Some of the instructional goals represent procedural knowledge learning outcomes that will require you to practice and receive feedback. In your *Student Exercise Guide,* I have provided three exercises for this purpose. In Exercise 2.1, you can practice recognizing appropriately written instructional goals. Exercise 2.2 provides an opportunity to practice classifying instructional goals according to the learning outcomes they represent. In Exercise 2.3, you can try your hand at writing instructional goals that are valid for specific learning outcomes. Finally, if you have processed the chapter in a meaningful way, participated in all the demonstrations and activities, and completed the three practice exercises successfully, you should be ready to demonstrate your achievement of the instructional goals for the chapter by completing Exercise 2.4.

Your mastery of the declarative and procedural knowledge presented in this chapter should prepare you for the next leg of our instructional design journey. In the next chapter, we examine procedures that *design-teachers* can use to gain a full understanding of the declarative, procedural, and affective knowledge that they will help their learners acquire. By developing a thorough understanding of the content reflected in their instructional goals, *design-teachers* prepare themselves for effective decision making throughout the remainder of the instructional design process.

RESOURCES FOR FURTHER REFLECTION AND EXPLORATION

Print Resources

Gagne, R. M. (1985). *The conditions of learning* (4th ed.). Philadelphia: Holt, Rinehart and Winston.

A classic work that describes each of Robert Gagne's major learning outcomes in detail and outlines important implications for instruction and assessment.

Gagne, R. M., Briggs, L. J., & Wager, W. W. (1992). *Principles of instructional design* (4th ed.). New York: Harcourt Brace Jovanovich.

An approach to systematic instructional design that builds on Robert Gagne's major learning outcomes.

Smith, P. L., & Ragan, T. J. (1993). *Instructional design.* New York: Merrill.

A thorough description of the instructional design process from the perspective of Robert Gagne's major learning outcomes.

World Wide Web Resources

http://nde4.nde.state.ne.us//SS/ssstandards.html

Provides Nebraska's K–12 social studies and history standards.

http://www.ncss.org/

Web site of the National Council for the Social Studies. Provides link to national social studies curriculum standards.

http://www.nctm.org/

Web site of the National Council of Teachers of Mathematics. Provides link to national mathematics teaching standards.

http://www.ncte.org/standards/

Web site of the National Council of Teachers of English. Provides Standards for the English Language Arts.

3

Analyzing Instructional Content

I remember when my three daughters began taking violin lessons. Needless to say, the girls' violin teacher did not start them out with a Mozart violin concerto. Their first lesson began with some basic information about the parts of the violin such as the strings, tuning pegs, scroll, bridge, and frog. They also learned how to hold the violin and bow and how to produce sounds on each of the four strings. After mastering these basics, they learned in subsequent lessons how to produce new notes with left-hand fingerings, identify the names of notes on the treble clef, and produce rhythms from musical notations. They gradually acquired the ability to play recognizable songs by building on the basic information and skills they acquired early in their violin learning experiences.

My daughters' violin learning experiences illustrate the importance of carefully sequenced instruction. Developing complex learning outcomes is a slow, gradual process as learners combine their prior knowledge and new experiences in increasingly sophisticated ways. As *design-teachers*, we strengthen the quality of our instruction by identifying the supporting information and skills that learners need to master so that eventually they will be able to achieve our instructional goals. The supporting information and skills that we identify will then help us make critical decisions about which lower-level skills to include in our instruction and how we should sequence those skills.

To determine all the supporting information and skills to consider in sequencing instruction, instructional designers have developed a number of procedures that *design-teachers* can apply to clarify the content of teaching. We refer to this set of procedures as *content analysis.* I have designed this chapter to help you acquire content analysis skills. You should be able to demonstrate the instructional goals listed below as the result of your interacting with the chapter.

INSTRUCTIONAL GOALS FOR CHAPTER 3

After reading and thinking about this chapter, you should be able to . . .

1. Explain the general purpose of content analysis.

2. Explain and demonstrate the value of content analysis for instructional planning, instructional delivery, and diagnosis of learning problems.

3. State and apply the rules for performing a cluster analysis.

4. State and apply the rules for performing a hierarchical analysis.

5. State and apply the rules for performing a procedural analysis.

6. Explain the theoretical rationale for cluster, procedural, and hierarchical analyses.

7. State and apply the rules for combining content analysis procedures for attitudinal instructional goals.

Solving Instructional Problems

nstructional design is fundamentally a problem-solving process (Jonassen, Hannum, & Tessmer, 1989). Once we establish a set of instructional goals, there is no readily apparent, guaranteed algorithm that sets out exactly what to do to reach our goals. Success in achieving our instructional goals depends on how well we think, make decisions, and act throughout the instructional design process. As with all other complex problem-solving tasks, successful goal attainment depends on the ability to construct an accurate understanding of the problem situation and consider all relevant variables systematically.

Understanding: The Key to Problem Solving

The initial understanding of the problem that we construct in our minds is our **problem representation** (Mayer, 1992; Newell & Simon, 1972). The quality of our problem representation—how accurately we understand the problem-solving task—has a profound influence on how easily and effectively we attain a solution. To illustrate the powerful effects of problem representation on your own problem-solving behavior, try to solve the nine-dot problem illustrated in Figure 3.1. Your task is to connect all nine dots with no more than four straight lines and *without lifting your pencil from the paper.* (If you are familiar with this problem, just play along and try to remember some of the difficulties you experienced the first time you tried it.) When you are convinced that there is no way to do it (or if you do find a way), check the solution that I provide in Figure 3.2.

If you found it difficult to solve the nine-dot problem, what was your reaction when you looked at the solution in Figure 3.2? You may have thought to yourself, "Well why didn't he *tell* us that it's okay to go outside the box?" Actually, I never said that you *couldn't* go outside the box. The nine-dot problem is difficult for most people because they perceive the square shape formed by the dots and then incorrectly assume that they have to stay inside the square. This false assumption, a self-imposed constraint, becomes part of their problem representation. Their faulty problem representation then makes it impossible to solve the problem.

The nine-dot problem illustrates that problem solvers often create their own impediments to effective problem solving. When we construct a problem representation, we may perceive the problem only one way (*It's a box*), add unnecessary constraints (*I have to stay inside the box*), and fail to consider all possible variables (*Is it okay to use the same dot more than once?*). If problem represen-

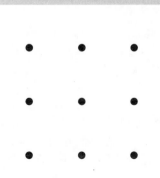

Figure 3.1
The Nine-Dot Problem

tation plays a critical role in a relatively simple problem such as the nine-dot problem, imagine how important it is in the complex problem-solving domain of instructional design.

Content Analysis: A Search for Understanding

The first critical step in instructional problem solving is understanding clearly the nature of the problem. As we saw in the preceding chapter, every instructional goal requires learners to construct an understanding of *content*, regardless of whether that content represents declarative, procedural, or affective knowledge. Therefore, the *design-teacher*'s problem representation needs to include a thorough, accurate understanding of the content that learners must acquire to perform each instructional goal. Instructional designers have developed numerous procedures that we can use to enhance our understanding of instructional content. I refer to these procedures collectively as *content analysis*.

Content analysis is a broad term that refers to the principles and procedures that instructional designers use to gain a thorough understanding of the subject matter that learners are to acquire. When we apply content analysis procedures, we break down the declarative, procedural, or affective knowledge to be learned into its component, or supporting, parts and specify how those parts are related to each other. Instructional designers often refer to this process as **task analysis** (Gagne, 1985; Jonassen et al., 1989; Kemp, Morrison, & Ross, 1994).

Some designers consider content analysis to be one set of procedures within the broader category of task analysis (Jonassen et al., 1989; Rothwell & Kazanas, 1992). However, I prefer to use *content analysis* as the broader, more inclusive category because all learned tasks require the acquisition of declarative, procedural, or affective content. In contrast, not all learned content can be expressed as a specific task to be performed. For example, my ability to apply the expansion-contraction principle that we discussed in Chapter 2 does not take the form of any particular task that can be described clearly in a step-by-step sequence of actions. The term *content analysis* focuses attention on the internal product of learning, the acquired *content* that makes possible the performance of a variety of outward tasks.

Through content analysis procedures, we seek to understand the content related to our instructional goals so that we will be in a better position to help learners understand and acquire it. Content analysis procedures are strategies to help us think deeply about the performance that we expect learners to demonstrate as the result of instruction. They are not cookbook recipes to follow mindlessly, but rather a set of powerful tools for developing an accurate, meaningful problem representation that will help us to function as flexible, creative, and effective *design-teachers*. Although I do introduce some specific procedures to use in analyzing content, content analysis is, above all else, a *thinking* process.

Using Content Analysis for Instructional Decision Making

Analyzing instructional content enables us to think more clearly about three aspects of instructional decision making: (1) planning instruction, (2) delivering instruction, and (3) diagnosing learning difficulties. To illustrate each of these types of decisions, let's do a simple content analysis for the following instructional goal: *Learners will be able to apply the commutative property of addition.* To be able to perform this instructional goal, my learners need to understand the commutative principle, so let's begin the content analysis by stating this principle clearly: *The order of the addends in an addition sentence does not change the sum.*

Recall from Chapter 2 that principles are made up of concepts that must be previously acquired as skills. Therefore, we need to identify the commutative

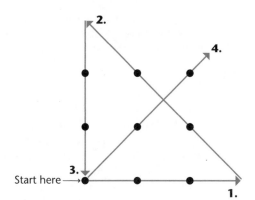

Figure 3.2
Solving the Nine-Dot
Problem in Figure 3.1

principle's component concepts: *order, addend, addition sentence,* and *sum.* Of course, these are concepts only if learners can *apply* them as skills to classify and categorize new instances. Lower-level skills that make possible the learning of higher-level skills are called **prerequisite skills** or **subordinate skills.** For the commutative principle, the component concepts—order, addend, sum, and addition sentence—are *prerequisite* skills because learners need to have acquired them before they can learn the principle. They are *subordinate* skills because they represent a lower, less complex level of skill than the principle to be learned.

Let's examine how the results of content analysis can help guide decision making in the areas of planning, delivering, and diagnosing.

■ **Planning Instruction**   Instructional planning usually focuses on two fundamental questions:

1. What will I teach?

2. In what order will I teach it?

Curriculum guides and textbook series often refer to these complementary issues as decisions about *scope* (answering the first question) and *sequence* (answering the second question) (Doll, 1996; Oliva, 1997; Posner & Rudnitsky, 1997).

Let's consider the first question—What will I teach?—for the instructional goal: *Apply the commutative property of addition.* The initial results of content analysis indicate the specific principle to teach: *The order of the addends in an addition sentence does not change the sum.* However, the content analysis also alerts me to several component concepts that learners need to have acquired as skills before they can learn the principle. With respect to sequence, I now know that I may need to focus on one or more of these prerequisite concepts and devise ways to help my learners understand and apply them as skills before moving on to the commutative principle. If my students cannot identify addends and sums, the principle will not make sense to them. If they cannot recognize addition situations, they will not be able to apply the principle correctly.

Sometimes we know enough about our learners' prior information and skills to make sequencing decisions. Often, however, we need to collect additional data as concrete evidence of the prior information and skills that learners already possess, a process known as **preassessment.** The results of a content analysis can guide the preassessment process. My instruction for the commutative principle instructional goal will be more effective if learners already possess the subordinate concepts uncovered by the content analysis. By preassessing my learners, I can find out which of the subordinate skills they already possess and which they do not. If the data I collect through the preassessment process indicate that all of my learners can apply the subordinate concepts, then we can move ahead to the principle. However, if my data indicate that one or more of my learners cannot apply the subordinate skills, then I need to consider strategies for helping those leaners develop the skills first.

As you can see, the results of content analysis are extremely useful in guiding planning decisions. Armed with the supporting information and skills identified through content analysis procedures, we can make more informed decisions about what to teach, the order in which to teach it, and how to preassess.

■ Delivering Instruction

Content analysis also influences the way we design and implement our instructional strategy. Recall from Chapter 1 (and see Figure 1.3) that the instructional strategy describes the specific activities, materials, and communications that we will use to help learners achieve our instructional goals. Activities, materials, and communications that help learners process the critical content to be learned and emphasize the relationship of that content to supporting information and subordinate skills are likely to be more effective than those that do not.

In my instructional strategy for teaching the commutative principle, I need to do something to make learners aware of the major principle identified in the content analysis: *The order of the addends in an addition sentence does not change the sum.* I also need to do something to help my learners understand the principle. The examples and illustrations that I use in my teaching of the commutative principle must represent that principle accurately and meaningfully. Every time we illustrate a principle with a specific example (or instance), we instantiate the subordinate concepts that make up the principle.

For example, to instantiate the commutative property of addition, I could use the following instance: $3 + 5 = 8$; $5 + 3 = 8$. To make the principle meaningful, I need to be prepared to show how this particular instance corresponds to the subordinate concepts within the principle. For these two *addition sentences*, changing the *order* of the *addends* ($3 + 5$ or $5 + 3$) does not change the *sum* (8). The subordinate concepts to instantiate and emphasize with this specific example are those that were identified through content analysis.

Content analysis also can help us to be more sensitive to learners' diverse needs and perspectives as we teach. When we teach information or skills that we already have mastered, it is very easy to forget what it was like to learn the content for the first time and to ignore some of the prerequisite skills that have become automatic for us. We often project our expert perspective onto our learners and place unreasonable expectations on them. If, for example, I tell my students that the order of the addends doesn't change the sum, will they understand what I am talking about? This statement may make perfect sense to me but sound like gibberish to students who have not yet mastered the concepts of addend and sum.

As *design-teachers*, we constantly need to take a fresh look at the content of our teaching, examining it not from our own "I-already-know-this-stuff" perspective, but from our learners' "this-stuff-is-new-to-me" perspective. Such awareness of the aspects of subject matter that are most critical in the teaching-learning process has been termed *pedagogical* content knowledge (Shulman, 1986). Pedagogical content knowledge includes the teacher's knowledge of the content features that may be potentially difficult to understand, given the prior knowledge and skills that learners possess. Content analysis is a thinking process that can help us become aware of these features.

■ Diagnosing Learning Difficulties

A third major benefit of content analysis is guidance in problem diagnosis. Despite careful planning and well-executed implementation, we have no guarantee that all learners will be able to demonstrate the capability described by our instructional goal. When this happens (and it *will* happen), we need to try to figure out why some (or all) of our learners had difficulty. If we can pinpoint the root of the problem, we will be in a better position to design an effective remediation strategy (see Figure 1.3). This process is similar to the diagnostic procedures that physicians use. Before prescribing medications and treatments, physicians try to identify (or diagnose) the internal reasons for their patients' outward symptoms. Similarly, we can use content analysis results to suggest possible limitations in students' prior knowledge that may be hindering their learning.

The greater the diversity of your students, the more critical problem diagnosis and content analysis become. Students who bring varying levels of prior knowledge and skills, different cultural perspectives, and special needs to the classroom achieve instructional goals with different levels of success despite our best teaching efforts. Thorough content analyses provide a wide variety of subject matter perspectives that we can use to generate and test diagnostic hypotheses.

Selecting a Content Analysis Procedure

Within the field of instructional design, specific content analysis procedures abound. Jonassen et al. (1989), for example, describe twenty-seven different approaches to task analysis. Despite the diversity of approaches and the confusion created by the use of non-agreed-on terminology, I believe that three major content analysis procedures meet all classroom *design-teaching* needs: (1) cluster analysis, (2) procedural analysis, and (3) hierarchical analysis. Each is useful for analyzing particular types of content relationships. Three major types of content relationships are relevant to knowledge acquisition: organizational, chronological, and learning. These approaches are summarized in Table 3.1.

■ **Organizational Relationships**   We find organizational relationships primarily within verbal information. We can group specific facts into higher-level (or superordinate) categories that, in turn, may be combined with other superordinate categories to form still higher-level categories. For example, we can combine the names and features of specific tree species into superordinate family categories such as maples, oaks, pines, and spruces. We can further categorize maples and oaks as deciduous trees (superordinate) and pines and spruces as coniferous trees (superordinate). To determine the superordinate categories that learners can use to organize verbal information, we use *cluster analysis* procedures (Dick & Carey, 1996). When we perform a **cluster analysis**, we organize separate pieces of factual information into groupings (or clusters) of information that represent meaningful subordinate and superordinate relationships. (We examine cluster analysis in more detail in the next section.)

■ **Chronological Relationships**   Chronological relationships describe sequences of mental or physical actions that learners must acquire to perform the instructional goal. For example, the rule for rounding numbers to the nearest ten is an algorithm that is performed in a step-by-step (or chronological) sequence of mental actions. Similarly, serving a tennis ball is a motor skill that is accomplished by executing a series of physical movements in a prescribed chronological order. When the performance of an instructional goal involves a chronologically sequenced series of steps, we can use **procedural analysis** (Gagne, Briggs, & Wager, 1992; Jonassen et al., 1989) to help us understand the content that learners must acquire (see Table 3.1).

■ **Learning Relationships**   There are many intellectual skills that we do not apply according to a chronological series of steps. For example, identifying monocot and dicot plants (concepts) is not governed by any particular procedure. Monocots possess one-part seeds and parallel leaf veins; dicots have two-part seeds and branching leaf veins. Therefore, learning to recognize monocots and dicots will be difficult for learners who have not already learned how to

Table 3.1
Three Approaches to Content Analysis

Content Relationships	Content Analysis	Typical Learning Outcomes
Organizational	Cluster	Verbal information
Chronological	Procedural	Intellectual skills (algorithms), motor skills, cognitive strategies, behavior component of attitudes
Learning	Hierarchical	Intellectual skills, cognitive component of motor skills, cognitive strategies, cognitive component of attitudes

apply the following subordinate concepts: one, two, parallel, branching, leaf veins. We find these types of learning relationships among intellectual skills and their lower-level (or subordinate) prerequisite skills. Recall from Chapter 2 that such learning relationships often conform to a hierarchy of intellectual skills. Hence, we can use **hierarchical analysis** (Dick & Carey, 1996; Gagne et al., 1992; Jonassen et al., 1989) to identify subordinate, prerequisite skills that learners need to possess before they are ready to acquire a higher-level skill (see Table 3.1).

LET'S SUMMARIZE

Cluster, procedural, and hierarchical analysis are three tools that *design-teachers* can use to identify organizational, chronological, and learning relationships within the content they plan to teach. By first thinking about the nature of the content represented by instructional goals, we can select an appropriate approach to content analysis. In the remainder of this chapter, we examine how to perform each type of analysis.

Cluster Analysis

The purpose of a cluster analysis is to create an organizational structure for the factual information that we want our learners to be able to recall (Dick & Carey, 1996). Clearly, then, cluster analysis procedures are most appropriate for verbal information instructional goals. First, let's examine how to use cluster analysis to understand the content of our verbal information instructional goals. Then we explore some of the theoretical and empirical foundations that support the use of cluster analysis.

Performing a Cluster Analysis

Let's imagine that we are designing instruction for the following verbal information goal: *Learners will state the names, locations, and uses of major skeletal muscles of the human body.* This goal could be part of a seventh-grade life-science unit on the skeletal-muscular system of the human body. We can analyze the verbal information related to the goal by applying the following cluster analysis procedure:

1. Specify the verbal information to be learned.
2. Induce superordinate conceptual categories.
3. Organize superordinate categories to show subordinate-superordinate relations.

4. Create a meaningful visual display of superordinate categories and subordinate facts.

■ **What Is the Verbal Information to Be Learned?**   We begin the cluster analysis process by specifying the verbal information that we want our learners to acquire (in the example, the names of the muscles that students should be able to state). We will select a manageable number of the 639 muscles in the human body for our seventh graders—say, eighteen muscles, along with their locations and functions (see Table 3.2).

■ **What Are Some Conceptual Categories That We Can Use to Cluster the Information?**   The next step is to identify some concepts that can help us organize the eighteen muscles. One way to categorize muscles is according to

Table 3.2
Skeletal Muscles Selected for the Verbal Information Instructional Goal
Instructional Goal: *Learners will state the names, locations, and uses of major muscles of the human body.*

Muscle Name	Location	Use
Biceps	Upper arm (front)	Raises forearm
Quadriceps	Thigh (front)	Straightens knee
Gluteus minimus	Hip	Pulls thigh outward
Sartorius	Thigh (side)	Flexes thigh
Hamstring	Thigh (back)	Bends knee
Adductor longus	Hip	Pulls thigh inward
Flexor carpi radialis	Forearm (front)	Bends wrist
Pectineus	Hip	Pulls thigh inward
Triceps	Upper arm (back)	Lowers forearm
Extensor carpi radialis	Forearm (back)	Straightens wrist
Rhomboids	Upper ribs	Lowers shoulder
Sternomastoid	Neck	Pulls head forward
Gastrocnemius	Lower leg (calf)	Extends foot
Deltoid	Shoulders	Raises upper arm
Abductor pollicis brevis	Hand	Pulls thumb away from hand
Abductor hallucis	Foot	Abducts big toe
Gluteus maximus	Buttocks	Extends thigh
Pectoralis major	Chest	Pulls arm toward chest

the types of skeletal movements they produce when they contract. We can organize all eighteen muscles by classifying them as flexors, extensors, abductors, or adductors (see Table 3.3). Each of these four clusters of information is a grouping of specific propositions within a meaningful concept that will call learners' attention to the common features of the muscles represented by their conceptual category. For example, although the hamstring, flexor carpi radialis, sternomas-

Table 3.3
Cluster Analysis for a Verbal Information Instructional Goal
Instructional Goal: *Learners will state the names, locations, and uses of major muscles of the human body.*

Muscle Function	Muscle Name	Location	Use
Flexors: Muscles that bend joints			
Upper body	Sternomastoid	Neck	Pulls head forward
	Biceps	Upper arm (front)	Raises forearm
	Flexor carpi radialis	Forearm (front)	Bends wrist
Lower body	Sartorius	Thigh (side)	Flexes thigh
	Hamstring	Thigh (back)	Bends knee
Extensors: Muscles that straighten joints			
Upper body	Triceps	Upper arm (back)	Lowers forearm
	Extensor carpi radialis	Forearm (back)	Straightens wrist
Lower body	Gluteus maximus	Buttocks	Extends thigh
	Quadriceps	Thigh (front)	Straightens knee
	Gastrocnemius	Lower leg (calf)	Extends foot
Abductors: Muscles that move limbs away from the body			
Upper body	Deltoid	Shoulders	Raises upper arm
	Abductor pollicis brevis	Hand	Pulls thumb away from hand
Lower body	Gluteus minimus	Hip	Pulls thigh outward
	Abductor hallucis	Foot	Abducts big toe
Adductors: Muscles that move limbs toward the body			
Upper body	Pectoralis major	Chest	Pulls arm toward chest
	Rhomboids	Upper ribs	Lowers shoulder
Lower body	Adductor longus	Hip	Pulls thigh inward
	Pectineus	Hip	Pulls thigh inward

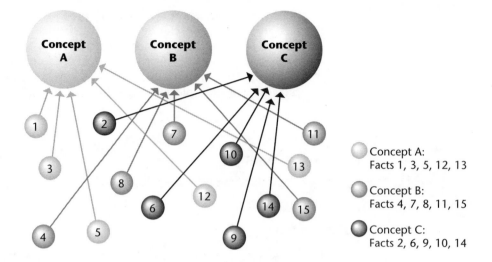

**Figure 3.3
Cluster Analysis is an
Inductive Thinking
Process**

toid, biceps, and sartorius are specific muscles that vary greatly in size, location, and the parts of the body they move, they all perform the same basic function: bending joints when they contract. Therefore, they are all flexors.

Cluster analysis is an inductive thinking process, as illustrated in Figure 3.3. When we think inductively, we find higher-level (or superordinate) patterns among specific examples. The superordinate concepts that we induce for a cluster analysis help to bring an organizational structure to seemingly unrelated pieces of declarative knowledge. Flexor, extensor, abductor, and adductor are four superordinate concepts that we abstracted (or induced) from the common features of specific muscles. These four conceptual categories will provide a useful organizational structure for our learners because they must be able to recall the function of each of the eighteen muscles.

Let's take another look at the four muscle clusters to see whether we can induce any additional superordinate categories to bring even more useful organization to each group of muscles. As you can see from Table 3.3, each muscle can be classified according to the general body region where it is located: upper body or lower body. These two conceptual categories should be useful to learners because they must be able to recall the location of each muscle.

■ **How Are the Conceptual Categories Related to Each Other?** For the third step of the cluster analysis process, we need to determine the subordinate-superordinate relationships that organize the verbal information to be learned. Thus far, we have eighteen facts about skeletal muscles that can be organized by two sets of superordinate concepts: related to muscle function (flexor, extensor, abductor, adductor) or muscle location (upper body, lower body). Clearly, the eighteen muscle names are subordinate to both sets of superordinate concepts. But what about the two sets of superordinate concepts? Should muscle location be subordinate to function, or should function be subordinate to location? This question requires a judgment call.

As you can see from Table 3.3, we will use the four muscle function categories as our major superordinate concepts. Within each of these four concepts, upper body and lower body are subordinate concepts. These two concepts then serve as superordinate concepts for two or three specific muscles. The location concepts, then, are both superordinate and subordinate categories within the organizational structure (see Figure 3.4). This illustration should help you to realize that concepts are neither inherently subordinate nor

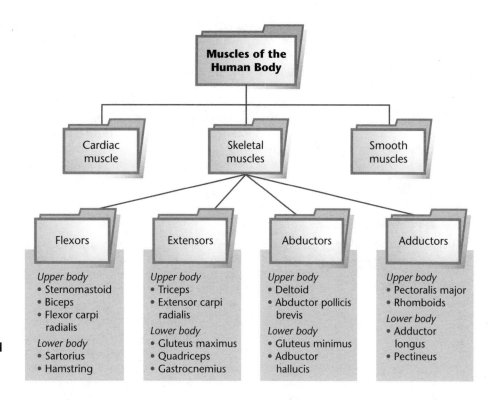

**Figure 3.4
Concept Map for Verbal
Information Cluster
Analysis**

superordinate. In other words, whether a concept functions as a superordinate or subordinate category within an organized declarative knowledge structure depends on its relationship to other concepts and facts.

■ **How Can We Visualize the Organizational Structure?**   For the last step of the cluster analysis process, we transform the subordinate-superordinate relationships that we have induced into a visual format that clearly shows those relationships. Instructional designers usually rely on three major formats: tables, outlines, and concept maps. In a table format, the superordinate categories are column or row headings, with specific pieces of verbal information placed within the appropriate cells that result from crossing columns and rows, as illustrated in Table 3.3.

Outlines are a second convenient format for displaying a cluster analysis. Here is a partial outline for the skeletal muscle cluster analysis:

I. Flexors
   A. Upper-body flexors
      1. Sternomastoid
         A. Located in neck
         B. Pulls head forward
      2. Biceps
         A. Located on front of upper arm
         B. Raises forearm at elbow joint
   B. Lower-body flexors
      1. Sartorius
         A. Located on side of the thigh
         B. Flexes thigh up toward waist
      2. Hamstring
         A. Located in the back of the thigh
         B. Bends knee to raise lower leg

A third way to display a cluster analysis is by creating a concept map, or web, as illustrated in Figure 3.4. Here the superordinate-subordinate relationships are indicated by the positions of concepts in the map. For example, "skeletal muscles" is a superordinate concept with four subordinate concepts: flexors, extensors, abductors, and adductors. Therefore, I have placed "skeletal muscles" *above* each of the four subordinate muscle functions. Because each of the functions is superordinate to the names of specific muscles, organized by body region, they appear above those clusters.

Which visual format is best to display the results of a cluster analysis? None is the best; all three are potentially useful. Because content analysis is a thinking process for the purpose of understanding the instructional problem, you should choose the format that you believe will best serve this purpose.

Value of Cluster Analysis for Learning and Teaching

Cluster analysis seems like a lot of work and effort, but there is a good reason to use it. Eventually, we will reach the point in the instructional design process when we develop strategies for teaching verbal information so that learners can remember it. In psychological terms, this means that we need to help learners store the information in their long-term memories. We store information in long-term memory by relating it in meaningful ways to the preexisting knowledge that is already stored there. Psychological evidence suggests that our long-term memories are composed of **schemas**: organized networks of ideas that are related to each other (Bransford, Vye, Adams, & Perfetto, 1989; Gagne, Yekovich, & Yekovich, 1993; Kellogg, 1995; Mayer, 1992; Norman, 1982; Rumelhart & Ortony, 1977; Schank & Abelson, 1977). Our schemas often exhibit the type of subordinate-superordinate relationships that we identify through cluster analysis. Thus, linking new verbal information meaningfully to preexisting knowledge occurs when learners can relate the information to superordinate categories within their schemas.

Organization is a powerful instructional variable that influences how learners acquire and retrieve declarative knowledge. For example, research studies have demonstrated that people tend to recall pieces of information in organized categories, even when the information is presented to them in a random, unorganized way (Bousfield, 1953; Bransford & Franks, 1971; Reitman & Rueter, 1980; Tulving & Pearlstone, 1966). When learners actively organize new information for themselves (through concept mapping or networking, for example), they are able to recall more of it (Boothby & Alvermann, 1984; Holley, Dansereau, McDonald, Garland, & Collins, 1979; Moore & Readence, 1984). Learners also recall more information when instructional materials provide a clear organizing structure for them (Glynn & Di Vesta, 1977; Hawk, 1986; Thorndyke, 1977).

The results of numerous empirical studies suggest a clear principle for us as *design-teachers*: Learners acquire verbal information more effectively when it is organized. The conceptual categories and subordinate-superordinate relationships that we identify through cluster analysis provide learners with retrieval cues (Gagne et al., 1993; Kellogg, 1995) and retrieval routes (Weinstein & Mayer, 1986) to help them recall and state verbal information.

Organizing verbal information for learners will help them only if they understand the categories used (Di Vesta, 1987). This means that we may need to design instruction for the superordinate concepts that we identify through cluster analysis to ensure that those categories are meaningfully embedded within our learners' schemas. Returning to the muscle example, although "upper body" and "lower body" are superordinate concepts with which our students already will be familiar, we will almost surely need to help them acquire the four muscle function concepts (flexor, extensor, abductor, adductor) as intellectual skills before those concepts can serve as meaningful organizational categories.

Table 3.4
Partial Cluster Analysis for Basic Addition and Subtraction Facts
Instructional Goal: *Learners will state basic addition and subtraction facts for sums and minuends from one through ten.*

Fact Family	Sum or Minuend					
	1	2	3	4	5	6
Addition	$0 + 1 = 1$ $1 + 0 = 1$	$0 + 2 = 2$ $2 + 0 = 2$	$0 + 3 = 3$ $3 + 0 = 3$	$0 + 4 = 4$ $4 + 0 = 4$	$0 + 5 = 5$ $5 + 0 = 5$	$0 + 6 = 6$ $6 + 0 = 6$
Subtraction	$1 - 1 = 0$ $1 - 0 = 1$	$2 - 2 = 0$ $2 - 0 = 2$	$3 - 3 = 0$ $3 - 0 = 3$	$4 - 4 = 0$ $4 - 0 = 4$	$5 - 5 = 0$ $5 - 0 = 5$	$6 - 6 = 0$ $6 - 0 = 6$
Addition		$1 + 1 = 2$	$1 + 2 = 3$ $2 + 1 = 3$	$1 + 3 = 4$ $3 + 1 = 4$	$1 + 4 = 5$ $4 + 1 = 5$	$1 + 5 = 6$ $5 + 1 = 6$
Subtraction		$2 - 1 = 1$	$3 - 2 = 1$ $3 - 1 = 2$	$4 - 3 = 1$ $4 - 1 = 3$	$5 - 4 = 1$ $5 - 1 = 4$	$6 - 5 = 1$ $6 - 1 = 5$
Addition				$2 + 2 = 4$	$2 + 3 = 5$ $3 + 2 = 5$	$2 + 4 = 6$ $4 + 2 = 6$
Subtraction				$4 - 2 = 2$	$5 - 3 = 2$ $5 - 2 = 3$	$6 - 4 = 2$ $6 - 2 = 4$
Addition						$3 + 3 = 6$
Subtraction						$6 - 3 = 3$

Deciding When to Perform a Cluster Analysis

Cluster analysis is a useful problem representation tool when an instructional goal describes a set of propositions for learners to acquire. It is impossible to find meaningful clusters when the focus of instruction is a single or limited number of propositions. Let's say that the instructional goal is, *State the chemical symbol for potassium.* This goal would not lend itself to a cluster analysis because there is only one proposition to learn: the chemical symbol for potassium (K). However, if we were to expand the instructional goal to include other related propositions—*State the chemical symbols for elements on the periodic table*—we could then cluster them according to nine meaningful superordinate categories: alkali metals, alkaline earth metals, transition metals, metalloids, halogens, chalcogens, noble gases, lanthanoids, and actinoids.

Whenever possible, we should write verbal information instructional goals to represent age-appropriate sets of declarative knowledge that we will be able to organize through cluster analysis. By designing instruction for organized sets of factual information, we help our learners develop well-organized schemas and encourage them to see relationships among propositions that they might otherwise have stored in long-term memory as isolated bits of information. For example, rather than teaching basic addition and subtraction facts as unrelated propositions, a first- or second-grade teacher could cluster them according to fact families, as illustrated in Table 3.4. These clusters of math facts encourage learners to organize their declarative knowledge according to powerful mathematical principles (commutative property of addition, inverse relationship between addition and subtraction) and number concepts (sums, minuends). The cluster analysis in Table 3.4 provides an organizational structure within which to teach basic addition and subtraction facts for several months or the entire school year.

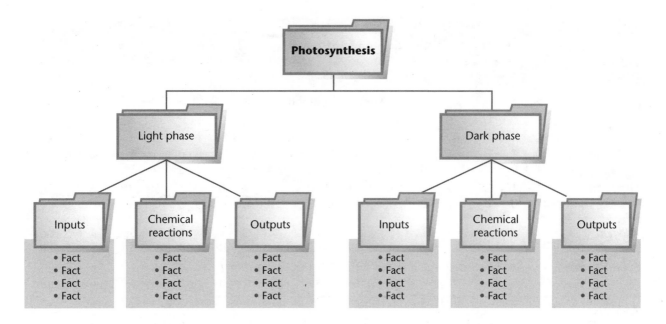

Figure 3.5
Partial Cluster Analysis for Facts About Photosynthesis

Some propositions that we want our learners to acquire may come "prepackaged" as organized facts. Consider this goal: *Explain how green plants manufacture their food by means of photosynthesis.* It implies a set of facts that are already meaningfully related to each other. As we scrutinize the list of specific photosynthesis facts that we may want learners to remember, we can group them according to whether they occur during the *light phase* or the *dark phase*. Furthermore, within each phase, some facts describe *inputs* to the process, some describe *outputs* from the process, and still others describe *chemical reactions*. Take a look at Figure 3.5 for a cluster analysis based on these superordinate concepts.

Before you try some cluster analyses of your own, think about one more example. You may recall that Ms. Nelson from Chapter 2 identified a verbal information goal as one of the learning outcomes for her geology unit: *State the names of the four major eras in the earth's history and several important characteristics of each.* Let's listen to Ms. Nelson think out loud as she develops a cluster analysis for this instructional goal . . .

CASE ANALYSIS

Cluster Analysis in the Classroom

TEACHER'S THINKING AND PLANNING

What is the actual declarative knowledge that my students will need to acquire to perform my instructional goal? I'll begin by specifying the *names* of the four eras: Precambrian, Paleozoic, Mesozoic, and Cenozoic. Now what are the *characteristics* of each era that I want them to be able to state? I'll start making a list:

1. During the Precambrian era, bacteria and algae were present.

2. Humans appeared during the Cenozoic era.

3. The Rocky Mountains were formed near the end of the Mesozoic era.

4. The Cambrian and Ordivician periods occurred during the Paleozoic era.

5. *Mesozoic* means "middle life."

6. Ferns and evergreen plants appeared during the Paleozoic era.

7. Periods of glaciation and recurring ice ages have characterized the Cenozoic era.

8. The Precambrian era began about 4,500 million years ago.

9. The Mesozoic era began about 225 million years ago.

10. Dinosaurs and other reptiles dominated the earth during the Mesozoic era.

Now that I have ten facts listed, let's see if I can start finding some patterns that I can use to organize the information. Of course, I can use the era names as superordinate categories, but what about organizing the characteristics within each era? Are there superordinate concepts that are common across all four eras? Facts 2 and 10 both relate to animal life. Perhaps I could use *animal life* as

Table 3.5
Cluster Analysis for Facts About the Earth's History
Instructional Goal: *Learners will state the names of the four major eras in the earth's history and several important characteristics of each.*

	Precambrian Era	Paleozoic Era	Mesozoic Era	Cenozoic Era
Meaning		Ancient life	Middle life	Recent life
Beginning time	4,500 million years ago	600 million years ago	225 million years ago	65 million years ago
Periods	• Hadean • Archean • Proterozoic	• Cambrian • Ordivician • Silurian • Devonian • Carboniferous • Permian	• Triassic • Jurassic • Cretaceous	• Tertiary • Quarternary
Earth features	• Crust increased • Large oceans formed	• Appalachian Mountains formed • Shallow seas covered land • Forests of fern plants (produced coal)	• Inland seas dried up • Rocky Mountains formed near end	• Volcano activity • Recurring ice ages (glaciation)
Plant life	• Algae • Simple one-celled organisms	• Ferns • Evergreens	• Flowering plants • Plants with seeds	• Present-day plants
Animal life	• Bacteria • Simple one-celled organisms	• Invertebrates: trilobites, snails, insects, jellyfish • Vertebrates: fish, amphibians, reptiles	• Dinosaurs and other reptiles dominated • Turtles, crocodiles, snakes, lizards • Early mammals	• Mammal populations increased • Larger mammals appeared • Humans appeared

a superordinate category and then make sure that I have facts related to animal life for the Precambrian and Paleozoic eras as well. Facts 8 and 9 refer to approximate beginning times for two eras, so I'll use *beginning time* as a category for all four eras. Facts 1 and 6 relate to *plant life*, so I can use that as a category. Facts 3 and 7 relate to geologic features of the earth (mountains, oceans, glaciation), so I could use *geologic features* as a category too.

Now that I have induced several superordinate categories, I'll cross them with each of the four eras [see Table 3.5 on the preceding page]. This gives me an organizational table that has twenty-four cells for specific propositions. I'll record the specific era characteristics that I want my students to be able to state within each cell. The cells also give me some guidance as I add some propositions to my original list.

With the cluster analysis that results from her thinking, Ms. Nelson will be able to design instructional and assessment strategies that focus on meaningfully organized verbal information rather than a large quantity of unorganized, unrelated facts.

Now that you have observed several demonstrations of the cluster analysis process, I invite you to give it a try. Exercises 3.1 and 3.2 in the *Student Exercise Guide* give you an opportunity to practice performing cluster analyses. When you have completed the cluster analysis exercises, you will be ready to tackle the next major type of content analysis: hierarchical analysis.

Hierarchical Analysis

We use hierarchical analysis to identify prerequisite (or subordinate) skills that learners must possess before they can learn how to apply the intellectual skill described by the instructional goal (Dick & Carey, 1996; Gagne, 1985; Gagne et al., 1992; Jonassen et al., 1989; Reigeluth, 1999). Let's examine the general sequence of steps in performing a hierarchical analysis and then apply the process to some specific examples.

Performing a Hierarchical Analysis

To illustrate the general process of hierarchical analysis, I want you to experience the challenge of trying to understand an intellectual skill that is new to you. In fact, I am going to make this skill so new that it will be impossible for you to understand it. I want you to acquire the "giz-yiz" principle. Therefore, my instructional goal is for you to be able to *apply the giz-yiz principle*.

Before I can design instruction effectively for this instructional goal, I need to be sure that I have a thorough, accurate understanding of the giz-yiz principle and its subordinate skills. Therefore, I need to perform a hierarchical content analysis by applying the following six steps:

1. State the intellectual skill to be learned for the instructional goal as declarative knowledge.
2. Identify prerequisite skills, and write each as an instructional subgoal.
3. State the intellectual skill to be learned for each subgoal as declarative knowledge.

4. Identify prerequisite skills for each intellectual skill, and write each as an instructional subgoal.

5. Continue breaking down subordinate skills into prerequisite skills until it is not useful to continue.

6. Create a visual display that clearly shows hierarchical skill relationships.

■ **What Is the Intellectual Skill to Be Learned?**   What do you need to know to apply the giz-yiz principle? Obviously, you need to know what the giz-yiz principle is: *The larger the giz, the smaller the yiz.* If you acquire the ability to generalize this principle to an infinite number of gizzes and yizzes so that you can predict and explain their relative sizes, then you will be able to perform the instructional goal. Because your ability to apply the giz-yiz principle is my ultimate instructional goal, I will refer to it as the **target goal**, and I will refer to the giz-yiz principle as my **target principle**.

■ **What Are the Prerequisite Skills That Comprise the Intellectual Skill to Be Learned?**   Knowing *what* the giz-yiz principle is does not mean that you can *apply* it because you need additional skills. You cannot possibly apply the principle if you cannot identify gizzes and yizzes and cannot recognize when things are getting larger or smaller. *Giz, yiz, larger,* and *smaller* are four subordinate concepts that appear within the giz-yiz principle.

According to Gagne's hierarchy, unless you have acquired these concepts as skills, you will not be able to acquire the target principle as an intellectual skill. Therefore, after identifying the four subordinate concepts that comprise the giz-yiz principle, I need to express each of them as a prerequisite skill to be learned—that is, as an *instructional subgoal*. An **instructional subgoal** is exactly the same as an instructional goal (clear action plus clear content). The only difference between the two concepts is that we write instructional subgoals for subordinate skills and instructional goals for target skills.

Therefore, the second step in my hierarchical analysis is to identify the four subordinate concepts that make up the giz-yiz principle and express each subordinate concept as an instructional subgoal:

1. Classify size changes as *larger.*
2. Classify size changes as *smaller.*
3. Identify *gizzes.*
4. Identify *yizzes.*

■ **What Are the Prerequisite Intellectual Skills to Be Learned for Each Instructional Subgoal?**   To be able to identify gizzes and yizzes, you need to know what their characteristics are:

Giz: A gump that has three gleeps and two gabs.
Yiz: A yerbid yorp that yings yiffly.

Now that you know their features, can you identify gizzes and yizzes? Why not? Identifying gizzes is still impossible if you cannot recognize gumps, gleeps, and gabs, and identifying yizzes will be impossible if you cannot recognize yorps, yerbidity, yinging, and yiffly-ness. As you can see, the features of the target principle's subordinate concepts are also composed of concepts that must be learned as skills. Now I have another level of subordinate concepts that I need to express as instructional subgoals—for example:

1. Identify gumps.
2. Identify gleeps.
3. Identify yorps.
4. Recognize yinging.

■ **How Far Down the Learning Hierarchy Do We Go?**   Obviously you will not be able to identify gleeps and yorps unless you know their features and can apply these features as intellectual skills. So I could (and should) repeat the procedure to reveal yet another level of subordinate concepts for which I will need to write valid instructional subgoals.

Deciding when to stop breaking down intellectual skills into subordinate concepts and discriminations is a matter of professional judgment. If we continue the process indefinitely, we eventually reach a ridiculously low level of prerequisite skill that has little relevance to our instructional problem solving. However, if we terminate the process too early, we run the risk of failing to uncover critical prerequisite skills, resulting in a restricted problem representation that could undermine our instructional problem solving. (Remember the nine-dot problem.)

Although there are no rigid rules concerning how many levels of subordinate skills to generate for a hierarchical analysis, I recommend that you follow two guiding principles:

1. *Consider your learners' developmental levels and diverse characteristics and abilities.* For example, if your learners are middle school students, you can probably assume that they have acquired basic number concepts such as "two" or "three." In contrast, if your learners are kindergarten or first-grade children, you probably should not assume that all of them have mastered basic number concepts and therefore should analyze such concepts further. Also, the more diverse your students are with respect to cultural differences, prior knowledge, and special needs, the further you should proceed down the learning hierarchy. You will need to be very familiar with your students' characteristics so you will be able to decide how far to proceed with your analyses.

2. *When in doubt, always err on the side of going too far rather than not going far enough.* Your problem-solving effectiveness can only be strengthened by examining all relevant variables—in this case, all relevant prerequisite skills. You will be in a better position to teach effectively if you are aware of *more* prerequisite skills than you think may be necessary. Furthermore, the more subordinate skills you identify, the more sources of difficulty you will be able to consider when diagnosing students' learning problems.

■ **How Can We Organize and Display the Results of a Hierarchical Analysis?**   One of the most common and effective ways to display a hierarchical analysis is to create a hierarchical diagram, as illustrated in Figure 3.6 (Dick & Carey, 1996; Gagne, 1985; Gagne, Briggs, & Wager, 1992). Such diagrams have three important features.

First, notice the relative *positions* of the skills. In a learning hierarchy, we place subordinate skills beneath the higher-level skills that they support and connect them with a line. If a skill appears below another skill, it means that learning the higher-level skill depends on prior learning of the lower-level skill. In Figure 3.6 I placed *identify gizzes* below *apply the giz-yiz principle* to show that learning to recognize gizzes must occur before learning to apply the higher-level principle can occur. Skills that appear beside each other, with no connecting lines, are not related to each other hierarchically.

Second, notice that *arrows* clarify the learning relationships represented in the diagram. Arrows show clearly the direction that learning must take for learners to be successful in acquiring the target skill. For example, the arrow between *identify yizzes* and *apply the giz-yiz principle* shows clearly that the ability to recognize yizzes leads to (or makes possible) the ability to apply the target principle. The arrows between the subordinate skills for the features of yizzes show that those lower-level skills lead to acquiring the higher-level skill of identifying yizzes.

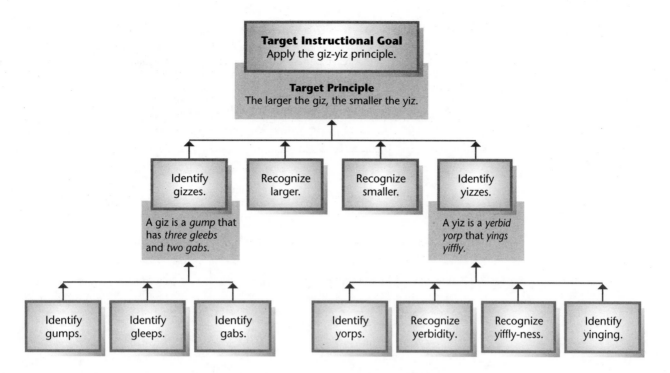

Figure 3.6
Hierarchical Analysis for the Giz-Yiz Principle

Finally, all the skills in the hierarchy are expressed as *instructional goals* with observable actions and clear content. Everything in Chapter 2 about writing clear instructional goals that are valid for learning outcomes applies here as well. This practice is extremely important because it emphasizes that the subordinate skills are exactly that: prerequisite *skills* that must be learned as procedural knowledge. They are not just topics for learners to "know about" or "be familiar with." Expressing subordinate rules, principles, concepts, and discriminations as instructional goals shows us what students need to be able to *do* to enable them to move toward achieving the target instructional goal. If we decide that we need to preassess or design instruction for any of the subordinate skills in the hierarchy, the clear action and content of the instructional subgoals will help give us direction and focus in carrying out those actions effectively.

Notice that some statements in Figure 3.6 are *not* instructional goals. These are verbal information statements of principles and concept definitions. For example, before I could identify the subordinate concepts in the giz-yiz principle, I had to state the giz-yiz principle. I placed this statement close to the intellectual skill it supports (*apply the giz-yiz principle*), expressed only as verbal information. I did the same for the definitions of *giz* and *yiz*. By placing the verbal information statements beside the skills that they support, we are able to see clearly how to derive the next level of subordinate skill.

LET'S SUMMARIZE

When learners must acquire an intellectual skill to achieve an instructional goal, we need to analyze that target skill and identify its prerequisite subordinate skills. Throughout the analysis process, we repeatedly ask a fundamental question: What would the learner have to know how to do in order to perform this task (the instructional goal) with a minimal amount of instruction (Gagne,

Question to Repeat for Each Goal and Subgoal:
What would the learner have to know how to *do* in
order to perform this task (*the instructional goal*)
with a minimal amount of instruction?

Figure 3.7
General Process of
Hierarchical Analysis

1985)? The phrase "minimal amount of instruction" simply means that we want to identify all the prerequisite skills that learners must have acquired first, so that in our instruction for the target skill, we can focus on that particular skill rather than having to backtrack and teach those prerequisite skills. By asking this question for each subordinate skill that we identify, we create successively lower levels of prerequisite skills that are related to each other hierarchically. I have illustrated the general process of hierarchical analysis in Figure 3.7.

Now that you have a general understanding of the hierarchical analysis procedure and appreciate the value of engaging in this type of thinking, let's apply the process to some intellectual skills that you might actually teach in your classroom.

Hierarchical Analysis for Concepts

When the content of the target instructional goal is a concept to be learned, we begin analyzing the learning hierarchy at the concept level. Let's work through a specific concept example to illustrate the process.

In the previous section, I forced you to become a complete novice by presenting a nonsense principle for you to think about because I wanted you to understand the importance of analyzing skills into their subordinate skills. In this section, I move to the opposite extreme and illustrate the analysis process with a concept that you already understand extremely well: rectangle. I have chosen such an easy concept because I want you to understand the content well enough that you can focus your thinking on the process of concept analysis. Furthermore, as I hope you realized from the giz-yiz principle, it is impossible to analyze content that we ourselves do not understand.

The target instructional goal is for learners to *identify rectangles*. Thus, the target skill is the *concept* of rectangle because concepts are the learned capability that enable us to classify objects and events in our environment. We begin the analysis process by asking the fundamental question: What would learners have to know how to do in order to perform this task (identify rectangles) with a minimal amount of instruction? Here is the answer: They need to be able to recognize the *features* of rectangles—that is, what makes a rectangle a rectangle.

■ **Identifying Concept Features**   I sometimes think of concepts as clubs. Clubs have strict rules for membership. The rules clearly include members in the group and exclude nonmembers from the group. Here we need to look at the rules for membership in the "rectangle club." What critical features (or attributes) do all rectangles possess that enable us to group them together as members of the same category? What is the definition of rectangle that generalizes to all possible rectangles?

Let's tackle these questions by looking at the rectangles in Figure 3.8 to determine what features they all have in common. Here are the common features that I see:

▶ All are two-dimensional (flat) shapes.
▶ All are made of straight lines.
▶ All have four lines.
▶ All have four right angles.

The features that all positive instances of a concept possess are called **relevant features** because their presence is essential for membership. If any of these features is violated, the object is excluded from the "rectangle club." **Irrelevant features** are those that vary from example to example and therefore have no bearing on membership. The rectangles in Figure 3.8 have different sizes (c and g), shadings (a and e), rotations (d and i), and lengths of parallel side pairs (c and e). These differences are irrelevant features because specific rectangles can vary on these features and still belong to the "rectangle club." In other words, no rectangle will be thrown out of the club because it is too big or small, has a particular shade or color, is rotated diagonally, or has pairs of parallel sides that are the same length.

Now that we have distinguished between relevant and irrelevant concept features, let's take a closer look at the relevant features. Although the first three relevant features (two-dimensional, straight lines, and four lines) are true for all rectangles, these features are true for other shapes as well. For example,

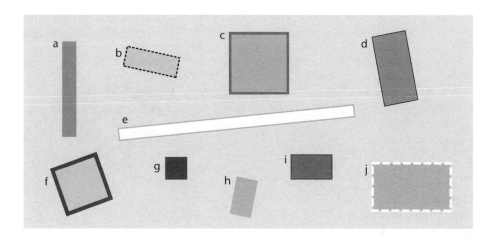

**Figure 3.8
Members of the
Rectangle Club**

trapezoids are two-dimensional, four-sided shapes too. As you can see, these features describe characteristics of rectangles but do not clearly limit the concept so that only rectangles are included. Therefore, let's refer to these characteristics as *describing features*. **Describing features** are relevant features (they must be present) that do not necessarily distinguish examples from nonexamples. In other words, they are necessary but not sufficient to determine concept membership.

When we add the fourth rectangle feature (four right angles) to the three describing features, we limit concept membership to rectangles only. It is impossible for any object other than a rectangle to possess all four features. Because the fourth feature rules out any nonrectangles, it is a feature that *defines* the category. **Defining features** are relevant features that restrict concept membership only to positive instances. Defining features are also known as *critical features, criterial features* (Ormrod, 1995), or *critical attributes* (Tennyson & Park, 1980).

When we analyze concepts into their subordinate features, we need to include both their describing and defining features. Eventually learners will need to be able to apply all of the describing and defining features to classify members of the concept. As I just illustrated, learning only the describing features leads to concepts that are too broad (e.g., trapezoids are rectangles). And learning only the defining features also leads to concepts that are too broad. For example, learning only that rectangles have four right angles does not exclude the shape in Figure 3.9 from the "rectangle club."

■ **Correlational Concept Features**   Now let's turn our attention to the *irrelevant* features. There is no need to include irrelevant concept features in a hierarchical analysis because they vary so widely and unpredictably from member to member. However, there is a special type of irrelevant feature that we do need to consider. Look at rectangles b and c in Figure 3.8. Rectangle b looks like a typical rectangle, with one pair of opposite sides being a bit longer than the other pair. Rectangle c looks more like a square because all the sides have the same length. A lot of people mistakenly believe that squares and rectangles are different shapes. In fact, squares are simply a special type of rectangle. Squares meet all the criteria for membership in the "rectangle club," but they just happen to have pairs of opposite sides that have the same length. The reason that many people believe that a square is not a rectangle is that they do not have a feature that people often associate with rectangles: pairs of opposite sides with different lengths. Most of the rectangles that we experience have one dimension that is a bit longer than the other. Therefore, many people believe that this is a defining feature for the category. In fact, it is an *irrelevant* feature.

Features that are frequently associated with members of a concept but technically are not required for membership are called **correlational features** (Ormrod, 1995). When we analyze concepts into their subordinate features, we

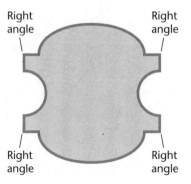

Figure 3.9
This Shape Has Four Right Angles, But Is It a Rectangle?

should search carefully for any correlational features and consider including them in the skill hierarchy. For learners to resist the temptation to include correlational features as defining features, they must be able to identify those features. Eventually, in our teaching for the concept, we will need to call students' attention to correlational features and help them understand that these features are irrelevant, even though they appear frequently.

■ **Organizing Concept Features**   To perform a hierarchical concept analysis, we first identify clearly all of the features that learners need to have acquired as prerequisite skills. Here is a definition of *rectangle* that reveals those skills: A rectangle [*concept*] is a two-dimensional shape with four straight-line sides [*describing features*] that has four right angles [*defining feature*]; rectangles do not need to have pairs of opposite sides with different lengths [*correlational feature*]. This definition will not be useful to learners unless they can apply each of the features as subordinate skills. Therefore, in our learning hierarchy, we express the features as instructional subgoals (see Figure 3.10). Each feature of rectangles is a subordinate concept that learners must be able to generalize to all possible instances of rectangles. Hence, each instructional subgoal reflects a concept learning outcome.

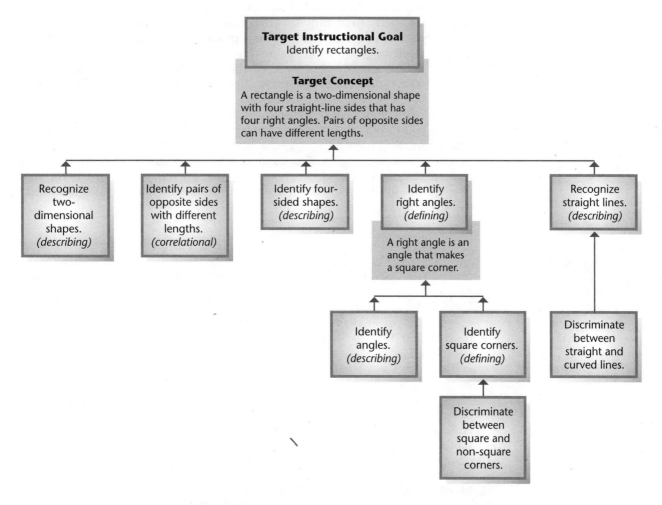

Figure 3.10
Hierarchical Analysis for the Concept of Rectangle

Is the hierarchical analysis complete? No. Because each feature is a subordinate concept, we are right back where we started—only this time, we have five concepts to analyze. What do learners need to know how to do in order to identify examples of each one of these five subordinate concepts? The answer to that question depends on the features of those five concepts. We need to judge the utility of breaking down these concepts further, given the characteristics of our learners. For example, for third- or fourth-grade children, identifying four-sided shapes, recognizing straight lines, and identifying pairs of opposite sides with different lengths should not be difficult. However, recognizing two-dimensional shapes and identifying right angles could be skills that many third and fourth graders may not possess. Therefore, it may be useful to analyze these two concepts further. As an example, notice the subordinate skills for identifying right angles that I have included in Figure 3.10. As for the target concept (rectangles), we begin with an accurate definition of *right angle* to uncover the subordinate concepts.

Before concluding the hierarchical analysis for the concept of rectangle, you should be aware of one final important point. Notice that I have identified discrimination-level skills for two of the subordinate concepts in Figure 3.10. Straight lines and square corners are concrete concepts that depend on the prior learning of basic discriminations, as described by Gagne's hierarchy of intellectual skills. Learning to recognize straight lines depends on the ability to tell the difference between straight lines and curved lines. Similarly, before learners can acquire the ability to identify square corners, they need to be able to discriminate between square corners and corners that are not square. By including these very low-level discriminations in the hierarchical analysis, I am not implying that we will necessarily need to teach these prerequisite skills. We are simply making ourselves aware of the preconditions that must be met before we can expect our learners to be successful in achieving the target instructional goal.

Before moving on to consider hierarchical analysis for rules and principles, I invite you to practice analyzing concepts into their subordinate skills. Exercise 3.3 in the *Student Exercise Guide* provides the opportunity to identify the describing, defining, correlational, and irrelevant features of some concepts that are commonly found in school curricula. Then, in Exercise 3.4, you can practice transforming those concept features into hierarchical diagrams that show learning relationships.

Hierarchical Analysis for Rules and Principles

If the target instructional goal requires students to acquire a concept, we begin with a definition of the concept and work down the learning hierarchy. If, however, the target instructional goal requires the learning of a rule or principle, we begin the analysis process by first stating the rule or principle that learners must acquire and then working down the hierarchy. This is the process that I illustrated with the giz-yiz principle. Let's reexamine the procedure for rules and principles, this time with a meaningful rule from an actual school curriculum.

Imagine that we are designing instruction to develop sixth-grade learners' writing skills. To enhance the clarity of their writing, we establish this target instructional goal for students: *Apply the rule for punctuating compound sentences with commas.* To perform this capability, learners need to acquire a rule as procedural knowledge. Here it is, stated as clearly as possible in a way that is appropriate for sixth-grade students: *Insert a <u>comma before</u> a <u>coordinating conjunction</u> that connects <u>two main clauses.</u>*

■ **Identifying Subordinate Concepts**   I have underlined the five subordinate concepts that appear in the rule. What will learners have to know how to do in order to perform the target goal with a minimal amount of instruction? According to Gagne's hierarchy of intellectual skills, they must already know

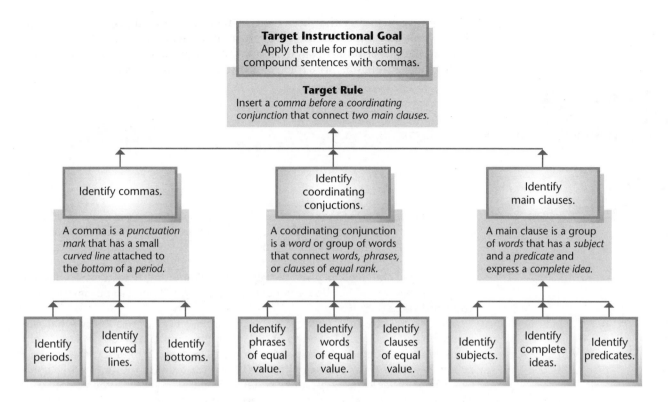

Figure 3.11
Hierarchical Analysis of the Rule for Punctuating Compound Sentences with Commas

how to apply each of the five concepts that comprise the rule (identify commas; identify coordinating conjunctions; identify main clauses; and so on).

The three subordinate concepts that are most critical for learners are *comma*, *coordinating conjunction*, and *main clause* (see Figure 3.11). Although *before* and *two* are important prerequisite concepts, we probably can assume that sixth graders already have mastered them. We continue the analysis by defining each subordinate concept so that the describing, defining, and correlational features are clear. As you can see, from this point on we are simply applying the procedures already described for concept analysis. Notice in Figure 3.11 that I have defined each of the three subordinate concepts and have expressed each feature as a prerequisite skill. Of course, we could analyze each of these prerequisite skills further, depending on students' developmental levels and prior knowledge.

LET'S SUMMARIZE

We analyze a rule or principle by (1) clearly stating the rule or principle, (2) identifying the subordinate concepts contained in the rule or principle, and (3) analyzing the subordinate concepts into *their* subordinate concepts. The resulting hierarchical diagram strengthens our problem representation by providing a learning map that shows the sequence of skills learners must acquire en route to achieving the target instructional goal—the final destination. By carefully studying the "road map," we can determine if learners are ready to receive instruction for the target instructional goal. Hierarchical analysis is a thinking process that provides information to help us think about instruction.

Before concluding the discussion of hierarchical analysis, I want you to think about one more example. We return, once again, to Ms. Nelson and observe as she performs a hierarchical analysis for an instructional goal that involves the learning of a principle. Let's listen as she thinks out loud . . .

CASE ANALYSIS

Hierarchical Analysis in the Classroom

TEACHER'S THINKING AND PLANNING

I want my fifth-grade students to be able to *demonstrate how the rate of cooling influences the size of a mineral crystal*. I should perform a hierarchical content analysis because the learning outcome that this instructional goal represents is a principle, an intellectual skill. I definitely want my students to be able to apply the cooling principle as a skill. Therefore, it would be wise for me to uncover the subordinate concepts that they will need to possess as prerequisite skills.

Before my students can apply the principle, they have to know what the principle is. Of course, *I* need to know what the principle is too, so I can help them learn to apply it. I'll begin the analysis process by stating the cooling principle as clearly and meaningfully as I can for my fifth graders: *When solutions cool quickly, they produce smaller mineral crystals; when they cool slowly, larger mineral crystals form*. Now I'll go back and try to locate the most important subordinate concepts by underlining them: *When solutions cool quickly, they produce smaller mineral crystals; when they cool slowly, larger mineral crystals form*.

What would my learners have to know how to do in order to perform my instructional goal with a minimal amount of instruction? They would already have to be able to apply each of the subordinate concepts that I have underlined. I am pretty sure my fifth graders already understand simple concepts such as *cooling, quick, slow, small*, and *large*. So although I will include them in my diagram [see Figure 3.12], I won't analyze them any further. I am not as confident that my students already understand *solution, mineral*, and *crystal* as concepts. Therefore, in addition to including them in my diagram, I should analyze them further.

I need to remember to express these subordinate concepts as *skills*. For concepts, the skill is being able to identify, recognize, or classify examples of the category. Let's see if I can write an instructional subgoal for each concept that is valid for this type of learning outcome:

Subordinate Concept	Instructional Subgoal
Cooling	Recognize cooling.
Quick, slow	Classify speeds as quick and slow.
Small, large	Classify sizes as small and large.
Mineral	Identify minerals.
Solution	Classify substances as solutions.
Crystal	Identify crystals.

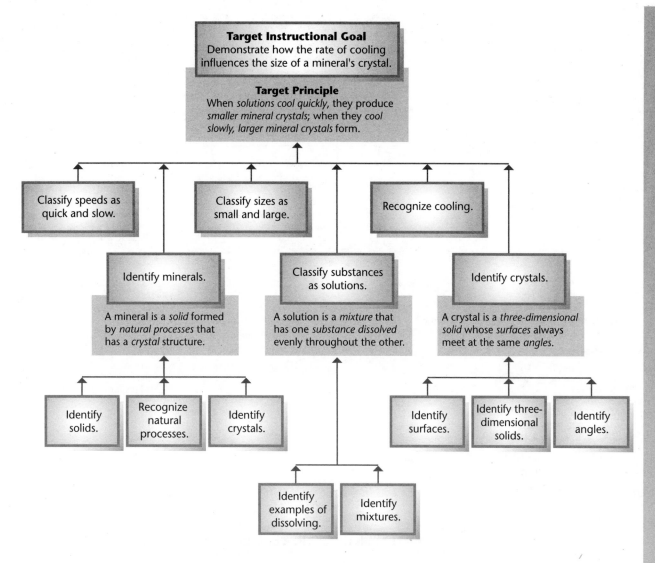

Figure 3.12
Hierarchical Analysis of the Crystal Cooling Principle

Now I'll place each subgoal in the diagram beneath the target instructional goal. I'll use arrows from each of the subgoals to the target goal to remind me that my students need to achieve the subgoals before I can expect them to understand and apply the principle [see Figure 3.12]. If they cannot apply the subordinate concepts as skills, they will simply be memorizing the principle as declarative knowledge, and that is not the learning outcome I want.

Next, I will define the three subordinate concepts that I judged to be most critical for my learners: *mineral, solution,* and *crystal.* The features that I identify will become subordinate skills for those concepts [see Figure 3.12]. Now I have even more skills to analyze! How far should I go with this process?

Since I am planning to teach the concept of mineral in this geology unit, I have already completed a hierarchical analysis for it, so I will not continue with another analysis here. This analysis is an important reminder, however, that I will need to focus on the concept of mineral early in the unit, before teaching the target principle. I also notice that one of the subordinate concepts for mineral is *crystal,* and that particular concept is also a major subordinate concept

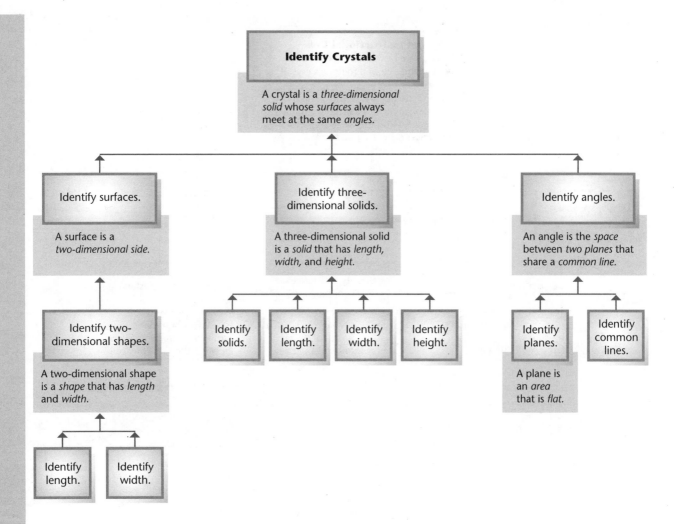

Figure 3.13
Hierarchical Analysis for the Concept of Crystal

for the target principle. Because it appears twice in my analysis, *crystal* seems to be a significant subordinate concept that I should focus on early in the unit. To be sure that I am prepared to teach *crystal* as a concept, I will analyze its subordinate features further [see Figure 3.13]. The concepts *solid* and *solution* and their subordinate concepts (*substance, dissolving, mixture*) are part of an earlier unit on matter. Therefore, I will not analyze these skills further.

Ms. Nelson's hierarchical diagram shows the skills that her learners need to acquire before the target principle will be meaningful to them. Of course, she does not necessarily have to teach all of these subskills, although she may need to teach some of them. Now it is your turn. Exercise 3.5 in the *Student Exercise Guide* provides you with an opportunity to begin proceduralizing your declarative knowledge of hierarchical analysis. When you are confident that you can apply hierarchical analysis to rules and principles, we will move on to the third major type of content analysis: procedural analysis.

Procedural Analysis

S ome instructional goals represent the performance of a series of mental or physical actions that must be executed in a prescribed chronological sequence. For these types of goals, we use procedural analysis to gain a better understanding of instructional content (Dick & Carey, 1996; Jonassen et al., 1989). Here are the major steps for performing a procedural analysis:

1. Identify the sequence of major actions or steps required to perform the instructional goal.
2. Express each action as an instructional subgoal.
3. Identify subordinate procedures, rules, principles, or concepts for each subgoal.
4. Express each skill as an instructional subgoal.
5. Continue with appropriate procedural or hierarchical analyses.
6. Diagram the chronological and hierarchical relationships.

Performing a Procedural Analysis

Let's illustrate the procedural analysis process by applying it to a motor skill. Because motor skills involve the execution of observable physical actions, they are usually easier to analyze than intellectual skills. Although you can tie your own shoes automatically, without thinking much about it, can you specify the steps in the procedure so that you could explain and demonstrate them to someone else? Try it. On a sheet of paper, describe as clearly as you can the step-by-step procedure that you use to tie your shoes. (When I tried to do this, I found that I needed to tie one of my shoes several times and pay close attention to what I was doing. I highly recommend this strategy to you.)

When you have recorded your own shoe-tying steps, compare them to my list in Table 3.6. How can such a simple skill be so complicated? Let's remember that the skill is simple for us *now,* after thousands of practice trials; it was *not* simple when we first learned it. As I stated earlier in this chapter, one of the great values of content analysis is that it forces us to examine content in fresh ways that can make us more sensitive to the diverse perspectives that learners bring to the classroom.

■ **What Are the Major Steps in the Procedure?**   Now that we are aware of the shoe-tying process, we need to identify the major steps or phases in the procedure. As for the hierarchical analysis procedure, we ask the fundamental question: What would our learners have to know how to do to perform the target instructional goal with a minimal amount of instruction? Dick and Carey (1996) recommend answering this question by identifying five to twelve major steps. For example, we can reduce the twelve-step shoe-tying procedure to the five major phases listed in the second column of Table 3.6. These phases eventually will provide an overall plan to guide learners as they begin executing the skill (Fitts & Posner, 1967; Romiszowski, 1999).

■ **What Is the Instructional Subgoal for Each Step?**   Each of the five shoe-tying phases represents a skill that a learner must be able to perform as *part* of the total procedure. Therefore, we refer to these component abilities as **part-skills** (Gagne, 1985). Because learners must acquire each part-skill as procedural knowledge before mastering the total skill, we need to express each one as an action that learners can demonstrate—an instructional subgoal. Notice in Table 3.6 that I have used clear action verbs (*cross, wrap, form, tighten*) and content to express each phase as an instructional subgoal. Because each

Table 3.6
How to Tie Shoes: A Step-by-Step Procedure for Right-Handers

Sequence of Steps	Major Phases	Instructional Subgoals
1. Grasp the ends of the two strings. 2. Move string a from left to right in front of string b, while simultaneously moving string b from right to left behind string a.	A. String crossing	A. *Cross* strings (*execute* string crossing)
3. Wrap string a around string b one time. 4. Grasp the ends of both strings and pull tight.	B. String wrapping	B. *Wrap* strings (*execute* string wrapping)
5. Form a loop with string a. 6. Grasp the loop at the bottom between the right thumb and forefinger.	C. Formation of first loop	C. *Form* first loop (*execute* first loop formation)
7. Circle the bottom of the loop with string b in a clockwise direction. 8. With the left thumb, push string b through the hole made by the right forefinger. 9. Release the right thumb and forefinger from the first loop.	D. Formation of second loop	D. *Form* second loop (*execute* second loop formation)
10. Grasp the new loop made by string b with the right thumb and forefinger. 11. Grasp the first loop made by string a with the left thumb and forefinger. 12. Pull both loops tight at the same time.	E. Tightening the knot	E. *Tighten* knot (*execute* knot tightening)

Note: String a is the string on the left side of the shoe at the beginning of the procedure. String b is the string on the right.

subgoal in this particular example represents a motor skill, I also could have used *execute* as the capability verb for each.

■ **What Are the Subordinate Skills for Each Subgoal?** Now we examine each instructional subgoal and ask the fundamental question for each one: *What would our learners have to know how to do to perform each instructional subgoal with a minimal amount of instruction?* For each of the major phases in the shoe-tying example, the answer to that question yields another procedure. In

Teachers can use the sequence of actions identified in a procedural analysis to organize and guide their classroom instruction.

other words, there is a string-crossing procedure, a string-wrapping procedure, loop-formation procedures, and a knot-tightening procedure. We repeat the first step of the procedural analysis process by stating clearly the sequence of actions that learners must acquire to perform each instructional subgoal. In the first column of Table 3.6, you will find a two- or three-step subprocedure for each instructional subgoal. Notice that I have already stated each of the steps as an instructional subgoal.

■ **Are There Any More Subordinate Skills?**   We now have a detailed list of twelve instructional subgoals organized by five major instructional subgoals. That seems as if it should be enough for the analysis. But what about each of the twelve subgoals? Yes, we need to ask the question again: *What would our learners have to know how to do . . . ?* When we answer the question for each subgoal, we may create even more detailed subprocedures.

However, we also may discover prerequisite intellectual skills that do not represent a sequence of steps. For example, Step 2 involves moving strings from left to right and right to left. It also involves placing strings in front of and behind another string. Therefore, learners must understand *left, right, front,* and *behind* as concepts that they can apply as procedural knowledge. They do not necessarily need to understand the verbal labels (*left, right, front, behind*), but they do need to be able to apply the underlying concepts as skills.

We include supporting intellectual skills in a procedural analysis by applying the hierarchical analysis rules described in the preceding section. First, we write each intellectual skill as an instructional subgoal that is valid for the type of learning outcome it represents. Then we analyze the skill further to uncover its subordinate concepts and discriminations.

■ **How Do We Display the Results of a Procedural Analysis?**   As with hierarchical and cluster analyses, diagrams are an effective means of organizing and displaying the results of a procedural analysis. To show chronological relationships, we place instructional subgoals in sequential order from left to right and clearly indicate the order that they are performed using arrows. As illustrated in Figure 3.14, we begin with the instructional subgoals for the major

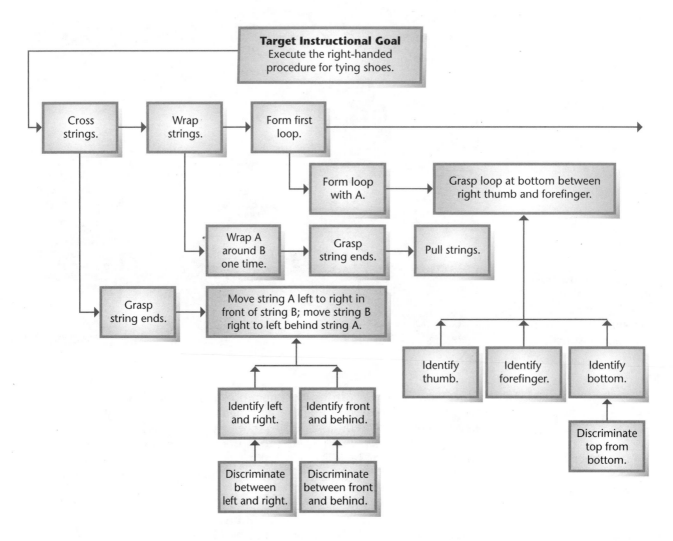

Figure 3.14
Procedural Analysis for Tying Shoes

phases and then show how the subprocedures support those subgoals. Notice that I have included hierarchical analyses of supporting concepts such as *clockwise, bottom, thumb,* and *forefinger.*

The horizontal arrows that show the chronological order of performance do *not* indicate hierarchical learning relationships. Just because an action occurs before another action when the procedure is performed does not mean that it needs to be learned first. For example, learning to form a loop does not depend on the ability to cross or wrap strings. Although crossing and wrapping strings occur before loop formation in the performance sequence, these skills would not have to be learned in that particular order. When we construct a procedural analysis, we make ourselves aware of the sequence of steps (or part-skills) that learners will need to acquire to perform the target instructional goal. Eventually we will need to make decisions about how to group and order those skills for the purposes of learning and instruction.

Motor skills are not the only learning outcomes that involve procedures. Intellectual skills and cognitive strategies may also take the form of action sequences, although the actions are often more difficult to identify because they are cognitive and less easily observed than physical actions. Let's see how to perform procedural analyses for these types of cognitive capabilities.

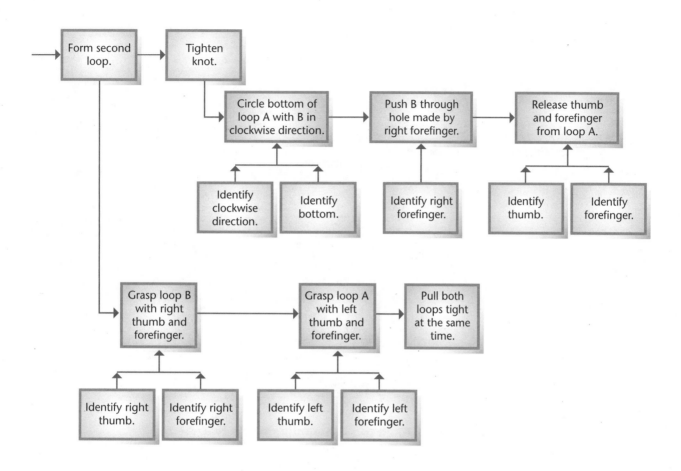

Procedural Analysis for an Intellectual Skill

In Chapter 2, Mrs. Torres developed the following instructional goal: *Learners will be able to apply the rules for rounding numbers to the nearest ten and hundred.* Let's listen as she thinks to herself about the rules for rounding to the nearest ten . . .

TEACHER'S
THINKING AND
PLANNING

If I want my third graders to be able to round any number to the nearest ten, what will they actually need to know about rounding? There seems to be a sequence of steps—an algorithm—that they will need to apply. Maybe if I round a few numbers to the nearest ten, it will help me identify the major steps. I'll try the number 43.

The question in rounding to the nearest ten is whether 43 is closer to the next lower multiple of ten (40) or the next higher multiple of ten (50). There

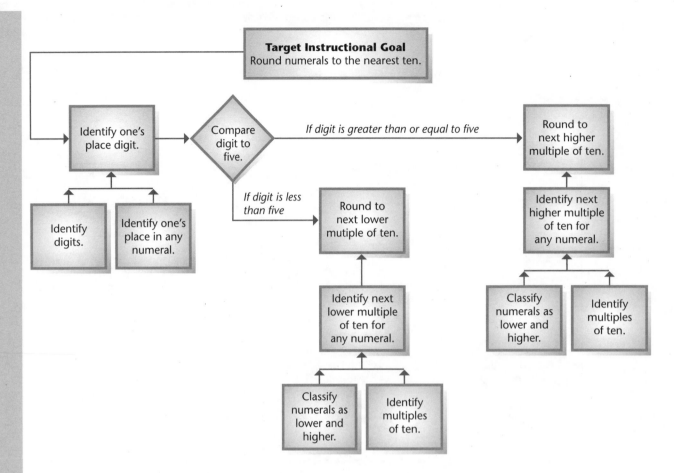

Figure 3.15
Procedural Analysis for Rounding to the Nearest Ten

are ten units between 40 and 50. Five is the halfway point. According to convention, if the number is less than halfway (5) I round down to the next lower multiple of ten (40). If the number is halfway or more, I round up to the next higher multiple of ten (50). The deciding factor, then, is the value of the digit in the one's place, because that tells me where the number is in relation to the halfway point.

Okay. I think I've got it. Here's the procedure for rounding to the nearest ten:

1. Identify the digit in the one's place.

2. Compare the one's-place digit to 5.

3. If the digit is less than 5, round down to the next lower multiple of ten.

4. If the digit is 5 or greater, round up to the next higher multiple of ten.

Before analyzing further, I will diagram these four major steps [see Figure 3.15]. Now I need to examine each step to uncover any subordinate procedures or prerequisite skills. The first step, identifying the one's place digit, will be difficult for my students to learn if they cannot already recognize digits and locate the one's place in any numeral. Therefore, I will place these two subordinate skills below the first step [see Figure 3.15]. Because I am certain my students already can perform these two subgoals, I will not analyze them further.

For each of the two rounding steps, my students will need to be able to identify multiples of ten that are either higher or lower than the present multiple of ten, so I will place these skills below each of the rounding steps. However, performing these skills depends on the ability to classify numerals as lower and higher and to identify multiples of ten, so I'll place these two subordinate skills below the step for identifying multiples of ten [see Figure 3.15].

My diagram tells me that students are going to have difficulty learning to round to the nearest ten if they lack basic number concepts such as *one's place* and *multiple of ten*. My hierarchical analysis suggests that a review of these concepts before teaching the rounding algorithm could be helpful. I will also need to be prepared to provide extra help and support for the handful of students who may still be having some difficulty with these concepts.

Procedural Analysis for a Cognitive Strategy

In Chapter 2, Mr. Hoffman developed the following instructional goal for his seventh graders: *Originate concept maps for textbook chapters.* By helping his students achieve this instructional goal, Mr. Hoffman intends to develop their ability to apply concept mapping as a powerful cognitive strategy that will influence how they process text information. Let's listen as he analyzes the content of his instructional goal . . .

TEACHER'S THINKING AND PLANNING

Although I have seen concept maps developed by others, I have never constructed one myself, so I am not sure of the procedure to teach my students. I'll check some basic educational psychology texts for examples that I can analyze. I'll also read some books [e.g., Novak & Gowin, 1984] and journal articles [e.g., Lambiotte, Dansereau, Cross, & Reynolds, 1989; Novak & Musonda, 1991] that describe concept mapping procedures.

Once I've expanded my knowledge of concept mapping, I think I can describe the basic procedure in four major steps. I'll place these steps in sequential order from left to right on a sheet of paper [see Figure 3.16]. Now what will my students need to know how to do in order to learn each of these subordinate skills? Well, obviously for the first step, they need to understand *concept* and *major*. I'll place these subordinate concepts below the first step and analyze the concept further by defining it. Two features of *concept*, general category and specific example, are subordinate concepts that my learners will need to be able to apply before they can identify concepts, so I will place them below *identify concepts* [see Figure 3.16].

For the second step, I need to analyze *inclusive concepts*. For the third step (arrange concepts in hierarchical diagram), I see a subprocedure made up of three basic steps. Within these three steps, I need to analyze *superordinate concept*, *subordinate concept*, and *linking word*. For the final step, my students will need to be able to identify cross-links as concepts that they can apply, so I will place this prerequisite skill below *create cross-links*.

Although it took a lot of work and thinking, I am glad that I performed this procedural analysis. From my diagram, I can see that I will need to do more than just teach the four steps. I will also need to design instruction for

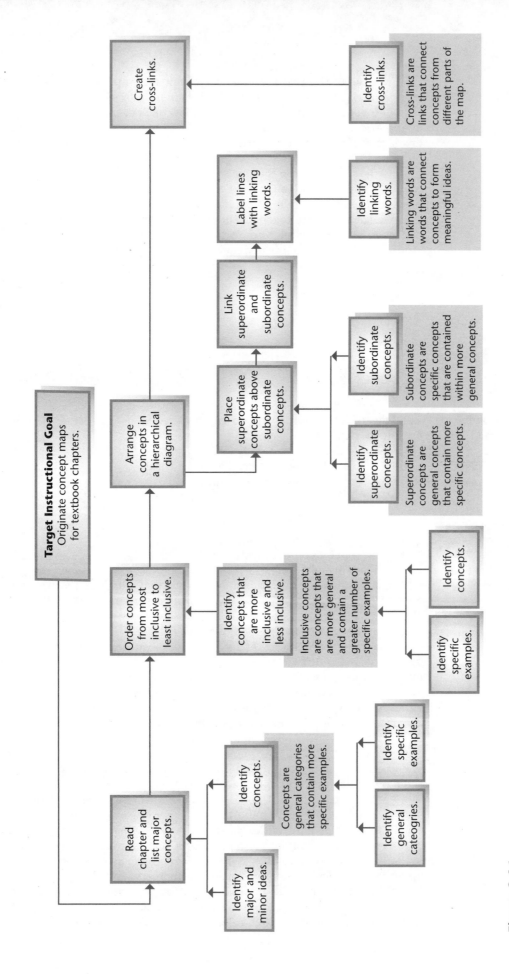

Figure 3.16
Procedural Analysis for Concept Mapping

some very important prerequisite skills. If my students cannot apply these skills, they will be learning the concept mapping procedure as a set of meaningless steps, and that is unacceptable. They need to be able to apply this cognitive strategy in a meaningful way that influences how they process the information they read.

Now that you have seen several demonstrations of the procedural analysis process, it is time for you to give it a try. I have designed Exercise 3.6 in the *Student Exercise Guide* for you to practice applying your procedural analysis skills. When you have completed the exercise successfully, you will be ready to move on to the last major content analysis topic of this chapter: combining content analysis procedures.

Combining Content Analysis Procedures

We have been examining three major approaches to content analysis: cluster, hierarchical, and procedural. I described and demonstrated each approach separately so that you could concentrate on the critical features of each. However, we often need to combine two or more analysis procedures to acquire a complete understanding of instructional content because learning outcomes often interact with each other (Dick & Carey, 1996). Let's examine some of the ways in which learning outcomes interact and the resulting analysis combinations that we need to apply to construct a thorough problem representation.

How Learning Outcomes Interact

Complex learning outcomes often reflect interactions among verbal information, procedural skills (e.g., intellectual algorithms, cognitive strategies, motor skills), and nonprocedural skills (e.g., principles, concepts). Therefore, content analysis procedures should reflect these interactions. For example, intellectual skills such as rules and principles are supported by the ability to recall and state them as declarative knowledge. We begin a hierarchical analysis of a rule or principle by stating the rule or principle as clearly as possible (see Figures 3.11 and 3.12), and we begin a hierarchical concept analysis by stating the concept's features as declarative knowledge (see Figures 3.10 and 3.13). Although stating rules, principles, or concept definitions as verbal information is not the same as applying them as intellectual skills, the ability to recall such declarative knowledge from long-term memory supports skill application.

We also have seen that intellectual skill, motor skill, and cognitive strategy procedures are supported by nonprocedural rules, principles, and concepts. All of the procedural analyses that we examined in the preceding section required hierarchical analysis of subordinate concepts (see Figures 3.14 through 3.16). Furthermore, we began each procedural analysis with a clear statement of the performance steps as verbal information. Certainly learners who can recall and state the steps of a procedure are more likely to be able to perform it. Declarative knowledge often guides our application of procedural knowledge (Gagne et al., 1993).

When we analyze the content associated with our instructional goals, we often need to combine cluster, hierarchical, and procedural analyses to gain a complete problem representation. Although the specific analysis procedures will be determined by the content itself, generally the more complex the instructional content is, the more complex the analysis process becomes. Because attitude instructional goals represent the greatest complexity of all the major learning outcomes, we almost always need to combine all three approaches when we analyze them.

Analyzing Attitude Instructional Goals

Attitudinal instructional goals describe the actions that learners will choose to perform (*behavior*) as a reflection of positive or negative emotion (*affect*) toward an attitude object and knowledge and skill related to that attitude object (*cognition*). Together these components form an **attitude system** (Zimbardo & Leippe, 1991). We analyze the content of attitudinal instructional goals by considering three attitude system components: affect, cognition, and behavior (Breckler, 1984; Kamradt & Kamradt, 1999; Martin & Reigeluth, 1999). Let's illustrate the process of combining the three content analysis procedures by analyzing a typical school-related attitude.

We may wish to develop our learners' positive attitudes toward maintaining personal physical fitness (see Figure 3.17). We will be able to infer that our learners possess this positive attitude if they *choose to plan and implement a personal physical fitness strategy* (our instructional goal). Because the instruction that we design for this goal must focus on each of the three interrelated components of attitudes, we need to develop a clear, thorough understanding (or problem representation) of each critical area.

■ **Analyzing the Affective Component** To analyze the affective component, we need to identify the attitude object and the emotional reaction, or feeling, that the attitude object should arouse in learners. For the instructional goal, the attitude object is a *personal fitness strategy*. To motivate learners' approach behavior toward this attitude object, they need to have a *positive* feeling toward it. We could label this positive feeling with a variety of words that describe positive affect (see Figure 3.17): *fondness, passion, excitement,* and so on.

■ **Analyzing the Cognitive Component** The answers to two questions will yield a clear understanding of the attitude's *cognitive* component:

1. Why should our learners have a positive emotional regard for planning and implementing a fitness strategy?
2. What declarative and procedural knowledge must they possess to plan and implement a fitness strategy?

First, with respect to supporting declarative knowledge, attitude-related behaviors are often supported by our understanding of the reasons for performing them. In other words, we can usually state (verbal information) the positive consequences, or advantages, of engaging in the behavior and the negative consequences, or disadvantages, of not engaging in the behavior. For example, learners may be more likely to plan and implement a personal fitness strategy if they understand some of the benefits of doing so. Conversely, understanding some of the risks of not maintaining personal fitness can also be motivating.

So that we will know if learners understand these positive and negative consequences, we need an instructional goal to help make the internal learning (understanding) observable: *Learners will be able to state the benefits of personal physical fitness and the risks of not maintaining fitness.* This is a verbal information instructional subgoal that supports the target attitudinal instructional goal. Because the content that learners must acquire to perform this subgoal is a set of

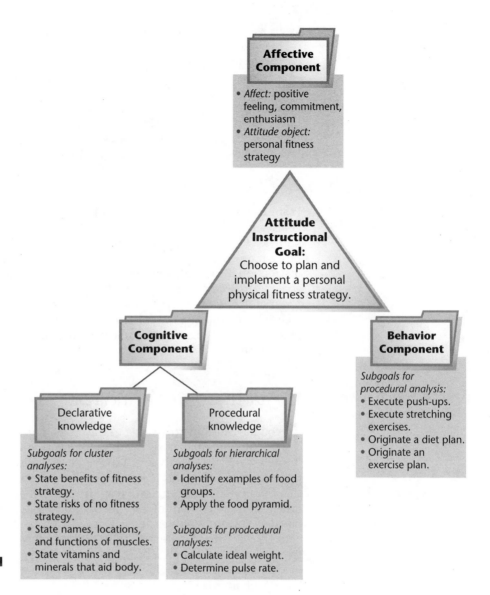

Figure 3.17
Content Analysis for an Attitudinal Instructional Goal

propositions to be acquired as declarative knowledge, we should apply cluster analysis procedures to analyze the content further. Some superordinate categories that we might generate to organize the set of propositions include the following: *benefits, risks, long-term, short-term, appearance, sickness and disease,* and *energy level.* We could also identify additional verbal information subgoals that we believe would help support our learners' attitudes (see Figure 3.17).

We also should try to identify supporting intellectual skills (see Figure 3.17). For example, demonstrating how the food pyramid operates (*principle*) and identifying examples of food group categories (*concepts*) are intellectual skills that would support students' eating habits. Of course, we would analyze the content of these instructional subgoals by means of hierarchical analysis procedures. Intellectual procedures such as calculating one's ideal body weight and determining one's pulse rate during exercise reflect rules that we would understand better by performing procedural analyses.

■ **Analyzing the Behavior Component**   Ultimately learners will need to engage in voluntary behaviors that are consistent with the target attitude. Here again we may need to design instruction to equip learners with supporting skills (see Figure 3.17). Creating a personal fitness plan is an example of applying a cognitive strategy. Therefore, we first need to specify the steps in the strategy (*procedural analysis*) and their supporting intellectual skills (*hierarchical analysis*). If learners' fitness strategies include physical exercises and activities (e.g., aerobic exercises, weight training, stretching exercises), we may need to teach them how to perform these types of motor skills. We should specify the supporting motor skills as instructional subgoals (e.g., execute push-ups, execute body stretching exercises) and submit them to thorough procedural analyses.

LET'S SUMMARIZE

From the preceding explanation, I hope you see that attitudinal instructional goals reflect complex combinations of declarative, procedural, and affective knowledge. Therefore, we often need to combine all three content analysis procedures to construct an adequate problem representation. We first specify instructional subgoals that we judge to be relevant to the target instructional goal. Then we analyze the content of each subgoal by applying the most appropriate content analysis procedure (cluster, hierarchical, or procedural). Exercise 3.7 in the *Student Exercise Guide* provides you with an opportunity to practice combining content analysis procedures for some attitudinal instructional goals.

Some Final Thoughts About Content Analysis

If you have been participating in the chapter exercises, you probably are thinking that content analysis is a difficult, time-consuming process. You are absolutely correct. Nevertheless, I urge you to invest as much time and effort as possible in learning and practicing the content analysis processes examined in this chapter. Your students will reap the benefits of your efforts because you will understand the content of your instruction more thoroughly and be better prepared to solve the sequencing, preassessment, and diagnosis problems that inevitably will arise. Content analysis will not automatically improve your effectiveness as a classroom teacher. However, if you apply content analysis principles in a thoughtful, meaningful way, your ability to think about many instructional issues will improve.

From my personal experiences in teaching content analysis to beginning teachers, I have encountered two recurring difficulties. First, people who are just learning to do content analysis often mistakenly believe that there is a single, correct, final product that they must achieve. In fact, as Dick and Carey (1996) caution, there is no official, correct form for any content analysis. Five different *design-teachers* could analyze the same instructional goal and produce five slightly different analyses. I encourage you, therefore, not to get hung up on trying to create perfect, correct content analyses. Focus instead on applying the principles and procedures as carefully and systematically as you can so that your thinking is fully engaged and you come away from the process with a thorough, meaningful understanding of the content relationships that will influence the quality of your students' learning.

The second difficulty that beginners often encounter is their own limited domain-specific content knowledge. We cannot possibly analyze declarative, procedural, and affective knowledge that we ourselves do not possess or understand. I am not suggesting that you must know "everything about everything" to be an effective *design-teacher*. I *am* suggesting, however, that you make the effort to augment your existing content knowledge when you become aware of the need to do so.

When you find that you do not possess the domain-specific knowledge you need to perform a cluster, hierarchical, or procedural analysis, there is just one thing to do: use all the resources available to you (including other people) to get it. Teachers who possess extensive amounts of well-organized content knowledge make better instructional decisions than those who do not (Stein, Baxter, & Leinhardt, 1990). Content analysis is a set of thinking tools that you can use to expand your knowledge base and support student learning more effectively in your classroom.

LOOKING BACK　　LOOKING AHEAD

Instructional design is a complex problem-solving activity. The effectiveness of any problem-solving activity depends on the quality of our problem representation—that is, how well we understand the nature of the problem. In this chapter, we have explored content analysis as a thinking tool to enhance the quality of our problem representation for instructional problem solving. Content analysis is a thinking process that helps *design-teachers* identify content relationships that influence how learners acquire declarative, procedural, and affective knowledge. When we make the effort to apply content analysis processes to instructional content, we improve our ability to think systematically about important instructional issues such as planning, delivery, and problem diagnosis.

We now have completed the first leg of our instructional design journey. In the first three chapters, we have explored principles and procedures to help us construct answers to the first fundamental question of *design-teaching* (and trip planning): *Where are we going?* In the next part of the book, we focus on the second major question: *What will we do when we get there?* But before we continue our journey, you should be able to perform the instructional goals for this chapter. Exercise 3.8 in the *Student Exercise Guide* gives you the opportunity to do just that.

RESOURCES FOR FURTHER REFLECTION AND EXPLORATION

Print Resources

Dick, W., & Carey, L. (1996). *The systematic design of instruction* (4th ed.). New York: HarperCollins.

Provides detailed descriptions and thorough examples of the three content analysis procedures presented in this chapter.

Jonassen, D. H., Hannum, W. H., & Tessmer, M. (1989). *Handbook of task analysis procedures.* New York: Praeger.

A thorough, comprehensive description of numerous approaches to content analysis.

What Will We Do When We Get There?

Assessing the Achievement of Learning Goals

In Part Two, we explore principles and procedures that *design-teachers* can use to assess learning. Strategies that teachers design to collect assessment data are called *instructional objectives*. Before you can develop effective instructional objectives, however, you need to understand fundamental principles and qualities of all assessment data such as validity and reliability, the focus of Chapter 4. You also should have a good understanding of the variety of specific assessment formats and how to construct them, the topic of Chapter 5. Finally, after developing these foundational principles and procedures, we put them all together with a discussion of instructional objectives in Chapter 6.

4

Principles of Classroom Assessment

Most students do not like exams. When I was a student, I didn't care much for them either. I have often fantasized about how pleasant classroom teaching would be if we were to stop giving tests. Eliminating tests would alleviate students' anxieties about their performance and decrease the amount of time and effort they spend studying and preparing for them. It would also save teachers countless hours of test preparation and scoring, leaving more time for teaching. Eliminating tests would spare both teachers and students the emotional anguish of arguing over points, grades, and "correct" answers.

Does my fantasy sound good to you too? All right then; let's do it: *no more tests!* When I announce this new policy tomorrow to students in my educational psychology class, many of them probably will be very happy because we were to have a unit exam next week. Now that we have abolished classroom testing, we can just forget about it.

But we are coming to the end of a unit, so I suppose I should try to evaluate my teaching and my students' learning. I wonder: Have my students learned anything about motivation, the topic of the unit? To answer that question, perhaps I should look again at some of my instructional goals for the unit. Here are three of my goals: Learners will be able to . . .

1. Explain the difference between intrinsic and extrinsic forms of motivation and recognize examples of each.
2. Describe and demonstrate three major phases in classical conditioning.
3. Identify examples of positive and negative reinforcement.

INSTRUCTIONAL GOALS FOR CHAPTER 4

After reading and thinking about this chapter, you should be able to . .

1. State definitions for the following terms and identify examples of each: *evaluation, assessment,* and *measurement.*

2. Explain the purposes of the following types of instructional evaluation: preinstructional, formative, summative, and diagnostic.

3. Recognize examples of preinstructional, formative, summative, and diagnostic assessment.

4. State and describe the two characteristics that all types of assessment data must possess: reliability and validity.

5. Explain and demonstrate how assessment reliability and validity are related.

6. Describe and demonstrate threats to assessment validity and reliability.

7. Describe and demonstrate strategies for maximizing assessment validity and reliability.

Although I am quite sure my students have learned something about motivation, can I be confident that their learning is consistent with these instructional goals? Can I assume that my students are able to demonstrate the learning outcomes described by the instructional goals because they came to class, took notes, and appeared interested? Can I assume that they achieved the instructional goals just because I think I used some effective teaching strategies?

Fortunately, because I stated my instructional goals as observable outcomes, I do not have to rely on my personal assumptions to judge the quality of teaching and learning in my classroom. I can collect observable evidence to help me decide if students have achieved the goals. For example, I can find out if students are able to *identify examples of positive and negative reinforcement* (Goal 3) by creating some scenarios that we did not use in class and asking them to find the examples of positive and negative reinforcement. Being able to recognize examples in these new scenarios will help me to determine whether my students have acquired the concepts of positive and negative reinforcement as intellectual skills.

I will take the same approach to all of the unit's instructional goals so that I can collect observable evidence of my students' learning. But hold on! This is starting to look like testing, and we already agreed that abolishing tests would make classroom teaching and learning pleasanter. Perhaps testing is more vital to the teaching and learning process than we thought. Because learning is an internal, unobservable process, I have no way of knowing if my teaching has facilitated learning for my students unless I devise ways for them to show me what they can do. That is what classroom testing is all about: providing opportunities for students to demonstrate their learning.

For now, it may be wise to rescind the no-testing decree until we've had a chance to think a bit more about testing and its usefulness to us as *design-teachers*. That is the purpose of this chapter. The instructional goals that I want you to be able to demonstrate when you are finished participating in the chapter are listed at the bottom of the preceding page.

The Role of Assessment in Instructional Decision Making

At the end of the motivation unit in my educational psychology class, I needed to answer two important questions:

1. How well did my learners achieve the unit's instructional goals?
2. How effective was my instruction?

The first question is simply another way of formulating one of our major trip planning questions: Did we arrive at our destination? The second question is clearly related to the first. If my learners did indeed achieve the unit's instructional goals, I can conclude that the instructional strategies I designed to use in my teaching were effective in producing learning. If some or many of my learners could not perform the instructional goals, then I must conclude that my teaching was not effective—at least not for everyone.

Evaluating Learners

The answers that I construct for both questions have the potential to help me make important instructional decisions—for example:

▶ How well have students learned the content of the unit?

▶ Should some students receive additional help?

▶ Are students prepared to move on to learn about related course content or to take further course work that builds on the unit?

▶ Should I reteach some parts of the unit?

▶ Should I change some of my teaching strategies the next time I teach this unit?

Unfortunately, there are no easy, absolute answers to these questions. Each of them requires careful thinking and professional judgment. Each decision requires an *evaluation* of either my learners' performance or my effectiveness as a *design-teacher*. **Evaluation** is the process of making judgments about the value, importance, quality, or worth of the characteristics that we observe in people (Oosterhof, 1990). Such judgments are always subjective.

Let's suppose that I give a fifty-item unit exam to my educational psychology class. If some students answer forty (80 percent) of the questions correctly, is that performance good enough for me to conclude that they have achieved the instructional goals? Or should students answer all fifty (100 percent) of the questions correctly to demonstrate mastery? Or would a score of forty-five (90 percent) be an appropriate level of achievement? You may be surprised to know that there are no official, agreed-on criteria for making these types of decisions concerning student learning. Different *design-teachers* establish different criteria based on knowledge of their learners, instructional goals, and the broader content domains that their instructional goals reflect.

How, then, do we judge the quality of our students' learning? This is a difficult question because learning is an internal process that cannot be observed directly. We could evaluate students by relying on our intuition about what they have learned. After all, if we design our instructional materials carefully and implement them skillfully in the classroom, then our students should learn what we want them to learn. If students are looking attentive and interested, then they probably are learning what we want them to learn.

Drawing such obvious conclusions about learners appears to be a matter of simple observation and intuition. For example, look at the two configurations of circles in Figure 4.1. It is obvious from simple observation and intuition that the center circle in part B is larger than the center circle of part A—or is it? People often perceive the center circle of configuration A to be larger than that of configuration B, although they are exactly the same size. Were you fooled? Optical illusions such as this one demonstrate that our personal, intuitive perceptions of reality are not always correct, even when things appear to be obvious to us. Now if we humans are susceptible to errors in judgment when viewing observable phenomena, imagine the potential for error when we try to evaluate unobservable phenomena such as learning. We need to be very careful about using subjective intuitions to make important evaluation decisions about learners because things are not always as they appear to us.

Assessing Learners

How might we improve our ability to evaluate student learning? Let's address this question by continuing to think about the circles in the optical illusion. To evaluate circle size, we could cut out one circle and place it on top of the other. Or we could cut a strip of paper equal to the diameter of one circle and hold it up to the diameter of the second circle. Although two people could easily disagree on the relative sizes of the circles just by looking at the two configurations, they are far less likely to disagree if they both see that one cut-out circle can be placed perfectly on the other. They are even more likely to reach agreement if they also see that a single strip of paper matches the diameters of both circles.

■ **Principles of Assessment**   The circle example from Figure 4.1 suggests three important principles that can assist with the evaluation process. First, confidence in our subjective evaluations increases when we collect additional information that is relevant to the decision we need to make. This activity is the process of **assessment**. When we assess, we collect information for the pur-

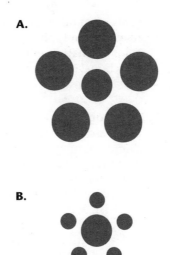

Figure 4.1
Which Center Circle Is Larger?

pose of making decisions (Salvia & Ysseldyke, 1998). We go beyond our current, incomplete knowledge of a situation and actively seek new information to provide illumination and perspective that is not currently available to us. For example, cutting out a circle or creating a strip of paper to compare diameters represents an active attempt to structure a situation to improve how we look at the sizes of the circles. In both cases, we are doing more than just continuing to stare at the circles as they are to arrive at a decision.

Second, the more additional information we collect through the assessment process, the greater our decision-making confidence will be. Certainly, placing one cut-out circle on the other to demonstrate their equivalent sizes is fairly convincing; implementing the strip-of-paper technique provides a second piece of confirmatory information that would be hard to dispute. If we want an airtight case, we could go on to create additional information-gathering strategies. With each new consistent piece of independent evidence, our evaluation becomes more trustworthy.

The third principle concerns the type of information we collect through the assessment process. Placing a cut-out circle on top of the other and placing a strip of paper on each circle's diameter are assessments that minimize the need for subjective interpretation. **Subjective data** are observations that two or more people are likely to interpret differently. In contrast, pieces of observable information that two or more different people are likely to interpret in the same way are called **objective data**. Objective data improve our decision-making ability by helping to control for the personal biases and situational features that can easily distort any perception of reality.

Assessment data are neither inherently subjective nor objective. These terms reflect the extreme poles of a continuum in which degrees of subjectivity and objectivity reflect how easily different people would agree on their interpretations of data. For example, the observation that the center circles in Figure 4.1 are the same size is closer to the subjective end of the continuum, because it would be difficult to get two or more different people to agree that the circles are the same size due to the effects of the optical illusion. In contrast, the observation that one circle fits perfectly on top of another is closer to the objective end of the continuum, because two or more people would easily agree that the two shapes match.

Returning to my educational psychology class, I could evaluate my students at the end of the motivation unit by collecting additional objective data that clearly relate to their ability to perform the unit's instructional goals. I could provide a set of opportunities for them to demonstrate that they can apply the unit's concepts and principles and can state the unit's verbal information. By providing multiple opportunities to perform each instructional goal, I can collect trustworthy data and increase my decision-making confidence.

■ **Classroom Testing**   The sets of opportunities that teachers develop to assess their learners' achievement of instructional goals are usually called tests. A **test** is an assessment tool designed to collect objective data for use in the evaluation process. Salvia and Ysseldyke (1998) define a test as "a predetermined set of questions or tasks for which predetermined types of behavioral responses are sought." This definition suggests three important principles.

First, a test is a set of questions or tasks created to evoke an outward performance that is consistent with an internal learning outcome. As long as there is a clear relationship between the observable performance and the learning outcome being assessed, the specific questions or tasks can take a variety of forms. When people think about tests, they often picture sheets of multiple-choice, true-false, or fill-in-the-blank questions to be answered in writing. Although *design-teachers* may choose to use such paper-and-pencil tests to assess some learning outcomes, there are many other approaches to testing. Consider the following possibilities:

▶ Delivering a speech in front of an audience to demonstrate application of persuasive speaking principles.

▶ Shooting a series of basketball foul shots in a gymnasium to demonstrate the execution of foul-shooting skills.

▶ Constructing a time line of Civil War events to demonstrate the ability to state Civil War verbal information.

Delivering a speech, shooting foul shots, and constructing a time line are all examples of tests, provided that we intend to use the resulting performances to evaluate learners. Whenever we collect performance data about learners for the purpose of evaluation, we are testing.

The second principle suggested by Salvia and Ysseldyke's definition is that testing must be done with a purpose. Predetermined questions, tasks, and behavioral responses are possible only when we have clearly identified the internal learned capability that we are trying to evaluate. For example, for me to evaluate my educational psychology students' procedural knowledge of positive and negative reinforcement as concepts, I need to devise questions or tasks in which they actually identify examples of each category. I must be able to use the students' responses to infer the quality of their conceptual understanding.

Finally, Salvia and Ysseldyke's definition emphasizes the importance of using testing to produce observable behavioral responses from learners. The rationale for this principle is similar to the rationale for writing instructional goals that we discussed in Chapter 2. Although learning is an unobservable internal process, we can infer its presence (or absence) only through some sort of observable evidence. An observable behavioral response provides a greater degree of objective data than does an unobservable internal process. If, for example, I design my positive and negative reinforcement assessments carefully, two or more different evaluators should be able to interpret my students' behavioral responses similarly. However, we must be very careful with this point. Just because we design tests that elicit observable behaviors from learners does not necessarily mean that we can always evaluate those behaviors objectively. In contrast to subjective intuition, observable behaviors have greater potential to be interpreted objectively because they are open to public inspection and scrutiny.

Measuring Learners

We can increase the objectivity of our assessment data by describing them with numbers. For example, if you place a metric ruler on the diameter of each center circle in Figure 4.1, you will find that each measures 0.8 centimeters. From this objective fact, you can easily make a confident inference regarding their relative sizes. Notice that we arrive at the same decision (the circles are the same size) as when we used the cut-out-circle and strip-of-paper assessment strategies. The only difference is the type of assessment data being collected.

■ **Quantitative and Qualitative Assessment Data**   When we collect numeric data, we are engaging in **quantitative assessment**. The word *quantitative* refers to the use of numbers to describe characteristics that are relevant to the evaluation we need to make. Another term for quantitative assessment is *measurement*. **Measurement** is the process of assigning numbers to learner characteristics so that the numbers indicate the degree to which the characteristic is present (Nitko, 1996). Just as we can assess the size of a circle by measuring its diameter on a metric scale, we can assess the learning of students by placing their observable performance on some type of numeric scale. For example, if some students in my educational psychology class successfully identify examples of positive and negative reinforcement on eight of ten test items, I could place their performance on a ten-point numeric scale and report the data as 8/10 correct, or 80 percent on a 100-point scale. Of course, as with all other assessment data, I will still need to make a subjective evaluation regarding the value of scoring at 80 percent. Assessment data, even when quantified with numbers, simply describe learner characteristics. They are not evaluations.

We can measure (or quantify) any human characteristic as long as we have an appropriate measuring stick or scale. A test with many questions or opportunities to perform a task conveniently places learner performance on a numeric scale. A fifty-item test, for example, provides a fifty-point measuring stick to measure the degree to which students possess the learned capabilities represented by the items.

Even tests that do not produce pencil-and-paper responses can yield measurements of learning. To illustrate, look again at the three examples of testing I mentioned earlier:

Test	Measurement Scale
Delivering a speech in front of an audience to demonstrate application of persuasive speaking principles	Using a set of five-point scales to rate how well each student applies specific persuasive speaking principles
Shooting a series of basketball foul shots in a gymnasium to demonstrate the execution of foul-shooting skills	Counting the number of successful foul shots made in twelve trials *or* Using a set of three-point scales to rate how well each student demonstrates the critical features of good foul-shot form
Constructing a time line of Civil War events to demonstrate the ability to state Civil War verbal information	Counting the number of Civil War events correctly recalled and placed in sequence on the time line

As you can see from these three examples, we can describe any test performance quantitatively as long as we determine carefully what aspects of learners' behavioral responses to quantify and develop appropriate measurement scales. (We explore principles and procedures related to developing such measurement scales in the next chapter.)

Quantitative assessment is not the only way to collect data about learners. When we collect data that are not in numeric form, we are engaging in **qualitative assessment**. Returning once again to the optical illusion in Figure 4.1, placing one circle on another and holding up a strip of paper to each circle's diameter both represent qualitative assessment strategies because the data they produce are not numbers. Qualitative data usually take the form of personal, anecdotal interpretations of our experiences, as illustrated by the following examples:

Decision	Quantitative Data	Qualitative Data
Should I go on a diet to lose weight?	I weigh 195 pounds, 10 pounds over my ideal weight.	My pants are getting really tight!
Should we place a traffic light at an intersection?	Every thirty minutes, an average of 237 vehicles pass through the intersection.	The intersection is really busy. I almost had an accident there yesterday!
What size shoes should I buy?	My foot is 11 inches long.	A 10 1/2 size shoe feels too tight, and an 11 1/2 size shoe feels too loose.
Has a learner acquired the concepts of positive and negative reinforcement as intellectual skills?	The learner correctly identified nine of ten examples of positive and negative reinforcement.	The learner confidently and correctly explained why a scenario represented negative reinforcement.

■ **Advantages of Quantitative Assessment**   Both quantitative and qualitative assessments are useful in decision making. Each has the potential to enhance and clarify the other, as illustrated in the preceding examples. However, quantitative data have four advantages that generally make them more useful and trustworthy than qualitative data.

First, the effort that we exert to place learner performance on a meaningful scale usually *forces us to think more carefully and deeply about the characteristic we are attempting to evaluate.* For example, to create ten scenarios for learners to apply the concepts of positive and negative reinforcement, I must make sure that each item does in fact relate clearly to one of those two concepts. This effort helps to ensure that I can confidently use the resulting scores to make evaluation decisions about their ability to apply the two concepts.

Second, quantitative data are *less likely to be biased by subjective interpretation.* Although another teacher and I might disagree on the quality of a student's explanation of positive and negative reinforcement, we are far less likely to disagree that the student answered nine of ten questions correctly—assuming, of course, that we first agree that each question is an appropriate example or nonexample of the concepts being assessed. Quantitative data are not perfectly objective just because they are numbers. They do, however, usually lie nearer the objective end of the continuum than the subjective end.

A third advantage of quantitative data is the *precision that they offer in communication and evaluation*. Saying that a learner obtained a score of 95 percent on a test communicates performance more precisely than saying, "She did really well." The added precision of quantitative data also helps us make more informed evaluations. I will be more confident that a learner who scores 95 percent on a well-designed test has mastered the instructional goals than a learner who scores 80 percent, even if the lower-scoring student has done exceptionally well compared to how she usually scores.

Finally, quantitative data are valuable because we often *can manipulate them further to gain a more thorough understanding of learner performance*. Let's suppose a student in my educational psychology class scores 65 percent on the motivation unit exam. Does this score accurately reflect the quality of learning for the entire class and the effectiveness of my instruction? To answer this question, I can examine the entire set of scores and perform some basic statistical operations. If the average (or mean) of all the students' scores is 65 percent, with only one high score of 70 percent and several low scores of 50 percent, I might conclude that my instruction was quite ineffective—for everyone. If, however, the average is 95 percent, with several perfect scores of 100 percent and only one low score of 65 percent, I probably will conclude that my instruction was highly effective—for *almost* everyone—and I should view the 65 percent score as an atypical data point and try to find out why that student had so much difficulty. Qualitative data do not permit such precise statistical manipulation.

LET'S SUMMARIZE

We have been exploring fundamental principles of testing from the broader perspective of evaluation, assessment, and measurement. As I have depicted in Figure 4.2, these three concepts are interrelated. Broadly defined, testing is a tool to make learning outcomes observable so that we can assess them. We assess because we have important decisions, or evaluations, to make. In the next section, we apply the concepts of evaluation, assessment, and measurement to the major types of instructional decisions that concern us as *design-teachers*. Before moving on to this topic, I invite you to practice identifying the examples of evaluation, assessment, and measurement that you will find in Exercise 4.1 in the *Student Exercise Guide*.

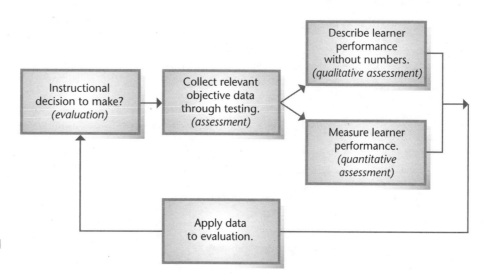

**Figure 4.2
A Model of Instructional
Decision Making**

Major Types of Instructional Decisions

Through testing procedures, we collect information that assists in making important instructional decisions. Determining how well learners have achieved instructional goals is our most important instructional decision. However, testing also can provide information to help answer a variety of instructional questions such as the following:

▶ At what level in a skill hierarchy should I begin designing instruction?

▶ Do my students possess adequate prerequisite skills to achieve the terminal instructional goal?

▶ Are my instructional materials making sense to my students?

▶ Which students are catching on to the new material quickly, and which students need more time?

▶ Should I provide my students with more opportunities to practice the new skill before checking to see if they can perform the instructional goal?

▶ Why did some of my students have difficulty performing the instructional goal?

The preceding list of questions suggests that assessment is not just something that happens at the end of a unit or lesson to determine how much students have learned. Assessment is a pervasive process that permeates all aspects of classroom teaching and learning. *Design-teachers* usually have four major types of instructional decisions to make: preinstructional evaluation, formative evaluation, summative evaluation, and diagnostic evaluation. These evaluations and their characteristics are summarized in Table 4.1. Let's examine how *design-teachers* collect assessment data to help them make each type of decision.

Preinstructional Evaluation

We must make some important decisions before we can teach effectively. **Preinstructional evaluation** is the process of determining learners' readiness for instruction. Learners are ready for instruction if they possess the prerequisite knowledge on which their new learning will build. For example, learners who cannot state (verbal information) basic single-digit addition facts will have dif-

Table 4.1
Four Major Types of Instructional Decisions

Type of Evaluation	Purpose	Question to Answer	Timing
Preinstructional	Determine if learners possess prerequisite skills to support their achievement of instructional goal	Are we ready to begin moving toward our destination?	Before instruction
Formative	Determine if learners are progressing toward achievement of instructional goal	Are we moving toward our destination?	During instruction
Summative	Determine if learners achieved instructional goal	Did we arrive at our destination?	Following instruction
Diagnostic	Determine why learners did not achieve instructional goal	Why didn't we arrive at our destination?	Following instruction
	Determine why learners are not achieving instructional goal	Why aren't we progressing toward our destination?	During instruction

ficulty learning how to add three-digit numerals with regrouping. Learners who have not yet acquired the ability to write complete sentences will have difficulty learning how to identify and write well-structured paragraphs. Careful preinstructional evaluation is essential for understanding the characteristics of diverse learners who represent varying levels of prior knowledge, different cultural perspectives, and special needs.

From our day-to-day classroom experiences, we often have a good sense of the prerequisite skills and background knowledge that students are bringing to new learning experiences. Nevertheless, we often need additional objective assessment data to help us evaluate our learners' readiness for instruction. We can collect these data by creating opportunities for students to perform the instructional subgoals that we identified through the content analysis process. Recall from Chapter 3 that we express subordinate skills and supporting verbal information as instructional subgoals, with capability verbs and clear content. For preinstructional evaluation, we can then design assessments that permit us to observe whether learners can perform in ways that are consistent with the actions and content of selected instructional subgoals. In Chapter 3 we referred to this type of data collection as preassessment.

For example, according to our procedural analysis for rounding numerals to the nearest ten (see Figure 3.15), learners need to be able to (1) identify one's place digits, (2) compare digits to 5, and (3) count in multiples of ten before we can expect them to acquire the complete intellectual procedure that combines those subordinate skills in a meaningful way. How well can learners actually perform these three subgoals? This is a question that we can answer by creating assessment opportunities for students to demonstrate that they can *identify* one's place digits, *compare* digits to 5, and *count* in multiples of ten.

If preassessment data suggest that learners can indeed perform each of the instructional subgoals, then we can move on to the target instructional goal. If some or all of our learners cannot perform one or more of the instructional subgoals, we first need to design and deliver instruction to help those learners achieve the subordinate skills. Eventually, for these learners, we will return to teaching for our original instructional goals.

Formative Evaluation

Formative evaluation is the process of determining how well learners are progressing toward achievement of an instructional goal (Kemp, Morrison, & Ross, 1994; Ormrod, 2000). After setting clear instructional goals and establishing that learners are ready for instruction, good *design-teachers* monitor their progress as they engage students with instructional activities. They constantly ask, "Are we moving toward our destination?" It is important to ask this question *during* instruction and not wait until our teaching is completed.

If, for example, I take a wrong turn on my way from Pennsylvania to North Carolina, I want to catch my mistake early enough to correct it before I end up in, say, Alabama. Similarly, by constantly collecting formative-assessment data as I am teaching, I place myself in a better position to detect if learners are veering off course. The purpose of formative evaluation, then, is to monitor learners' progress toward achieving the instructional goal, with the intention of changing or adapting our teaching strategy to maximize effectiveness for as many students as possible.

We can use both formal and informal sources of data for formative assessment. *Formal sources* include observations of students as they perform tasks relevant to the target instructional goal. We should build into our instructional strategy ample opportunity for learners to practice recalling new verbal information and applying new skills. By observing learners carefully as they practice, we can make formative evaluation decisions about their progress. *Informal data* also can be rich sources of information about student progress. Such data include the verbal and nonverbal cues that students exhibit during learning:

Effective teachers collect formative assessment data to help them make informed decisions about modifying and adapting their instruction.

facial expressions, attentiveness, restlessness, on-task (or off-task) behavior, questions, comments, and so on.

Depending on the formative assessment data we collect during teaching, we may decide to proceed as planned, slow down, speed up, use more examples, use fewer examples, provide additional practice exercises, provide fewer practice exercises, or, in some extreme cases, abandon our current instructional goals temporarily. Because the instructional strategy that we design is simply our best estimate of the types of learning experiences that may help learners achieve the instructional goals, we need to be prepared to adapt and fine-tune as we implement it.

Summative Evaluation

Summative evaluation is the process of determining how well learners can perform the instructional goals that were the intended focus of our instruction (Kemp et al., 1994; Ormrod, 2000). Through summative evaluation, we attempt to answer the question, "Did we arrive at our destination?" To assist with this important decision, we collect assessment data by having learners perform a set of tasks (you may call it a "test" if you wish) that are consistent with the instructional goals.

Summative evaluation is end-point evaluation; it may occur at the end of a lesson, unit, or course of instruction. Often instructional designers use the term *summative evaluation* to refer to the final evaluation of an instructional product after extensive field testing and refinement (Gagne, Briggs, & Wager, 1992). In the classroom, however, teachers engage in summative evaluation when they reach the end of a segment of teaching so they can judge how well their students learned at that particular time.

We use the results of summative assessment to help us make judgments about the quality of our learners' achievement and the quality of our instruction. Judgments about learners' achievement can help us decide if we should move on to the next set of instructional goals or spend additional classroom time working on the current set of goals. We can also use these judgments to help determine how to communicate students' progress to parents, school administrators, state and community organizations, and the learners themselves. When we apply summative evaluation processes to our learners, it is important to remember that we are also judging the quality of our instruction. When significant numbers of learners are unsuccessful in achieving our instructional goals, we should use this evidence to think about modifying our instructional strategies for those particular learners and for future learners that we will teach.

Summative assessment occurs after students have completed the learning activities we have planned for them. It should not be confused with learning activities that we use in our teaching to help move students toward achievement of our instructional goals. I will illustrate this important point with my educational psychology class. As part of my instructional strategy for helping my students acquire the ability to identify examples of positive and negative reinforcement, I provide definitions and meaningful examples of the concepts in class. Then I give them an opportunity to practice identifying examples of the concepts. Students can work together and use their books or class notes to complete the exercise. Then we review the exercise together in class to provide feedback.

Should I use my students' performance on the exercise as summative assessment data? No! There are several reasons that my doing so could hamper good decision making. First, because students may have received assistance from various sources (book, notes, other students, teacher) to complete the exercise, I have no assurance that each student has acquired the target concepts. Although group and collaborative activities can be valuable learning tools when designed appropriately, they often make evaluation difficult because individual and group achievement are easily confounded. When we substitute group achievement for individual achievement, we commit a profound disservice to those who may not yet have acquired a learned capability for themselves. A commitment to facilitating learning for diverse individuals must be accompanied by a commitment to assessing the capabilities of individual students.

We need to distinguish the activities we use for learning and summative assessment for a second reason: Students will learn from the feedback they receive. For example, one of my educational psychology students might respond incorrectly to many of the practice exercises. The feedback that he receives in class as we review the exercises together may help to correct his misconceptions. On a subsequent assessment opportunity, he may demonstrate perfect performance, reflecting what he learned from the practice-and-feedback experience.

A final reason for separating learning activities from summative assessment activities relates to the effects of time on learning. Often we provide learners with practice and application exercises soon after introducing them to new verbal information or skills so they can work with the new material while it is fresh in their minds. In psychological terms, the material is still active in learners' working memories, resulting in relatively easy recall. Will learners be able to retrieve the material from their long-term memories and use it appropriately two days later? A week later? A month later? We should be careful not to base summative evaluations of learning on short-term performances that do not provide compelling evidence of a long-term acquired capability.

Diagnostic Evaluation

Despite well-designed instruction, we often may find that some learners did not achieve the instructional goals (summative evaluation) or that they are having difficulty achieving the instructional goals (formative evaluation). The purpose of **diagnostic evaluation** is to determine why students are having learning difficulties. The rationale for diagnosing learning problems is the same one that physicians use for diagnosing physical problems. We cannot design an appropriate treatment for the problem unless we understand why the problem is occurring. Of course, this rationale implies that we have a strong desire to help students overcome their learning difficulties through reteaching, or remediation. Hence, the ultimate goal of diagnostic evaluation is to decide how to remediate students' learning difficulties when we become aware of them.

If we become aware of learning difficulties through summative evaluation, then diagnostic assessment will occur after instruction. If we become aware of difficulties through formative evaluation, then diagnostic assessment may occur during instruction. In either case, we need to collect assessment data that help to illuminate the cause of the problem. For some students, learning difficulties may be traced to pervasive, chronic disorders or disabilities such as dyslexia, fetal alcohol syndrome, attention-deficit disorder, or hearing impairments. We should be aware of these types of special needs and constantly build appropriate accommodations into instructional and assessment strategies.

Individual learners who do not possess specific disorders or disabilities may also exhibit learning difficulties from time to time. In fact, I encourage you to think about your own experiences as a learner. Can you think of any specific learning experiences when you just didn't understand at first? Were your temporary difficulties due to a disability or disorder? Your misconceptions, confusions, or difficulties could have been the result of content-related or instruction-related causes.

Content-related causes are rooted in the specific verbal information, skill, or attitude to be acquired. Learners may experience content-related difficulties when they lack important prerequisite skills; do not possess relevant prior knowledge that they can use to make new information meaningful; possess prior misconceptions that conflict with new learning; or possess negative attitudes toward specific knowledge domains. *Instruction-related causes* are rooted in the quality of the instructional events we design. Perhaps in our instruction we have failed to communicate new information or skills clearly to learners. Perhaps we have not used enough meaningful examples to help students connect new information to their own prior knowledge. Perhaps we have not provided students with an adequate number of opportunities to practice retrieving new verbal information or applying new skills.

We collect diagnostic assessment data to help pinpoint the precise content-related or instruction-related causes of a learning difficulty. The assessment strategies used to collect these data will depend on the specific learning outcome that is the focus of instruction and the specific instructional strategies that we are using in the classroom. For example, as we noted in Chapter 3, learners who cannot apply a new principle as an intellectual skill may lack the ability to apply one or more of the principle's subordinate concepts. Therefore, we can collect diagnostic data by asking students to identify new instances of the subordinate concepts.

LET'S SUMMARIZE

All *design-teachers* must make four major types of decisions on a regular basis. Although each type of decision ultimately depends on our informed, professional judgment, we can enhance our evaluations of learners by collecting assessment data that are appropriate for particular types of decisions. Of course, the quality of our decisions will only be as good as the quality of the data that we collect. In the next section, we examine two major qualities that all assessment data must possess to be useful: validity and reliability. However, before we consider validity and reliability, I invite you to interact with Exercise 4.2 in the *Student Exercise Guide* for practice identifying the four major types of instructional decisions and the four corresponding types of assessment data.

Validity and Reliability

I often experience a recurring problem in early January. For some mysterious reason, my clothes begin to feel a bit tighter than usual. Although I would prefer to believe that my clothes shrink every January, the truth of the matter is that all the cookies, pies, and candy that I have consumed during the preceding holiday season have begun to take their toll. When I finally admit to myself that I need to get serious about losing the excess weight, I find myself wondering how many pounds I should try to shed. To make that decision, I need to assess my present weight as *validly* and *reliably* as possible.

Validity and Reliability: Basic Definitions

I can determine my weight by collecting some quantitative assessment data—perhaps the following:

- Measure my height with a meter stick.
- Measure my temperature with a thermometer.
- Measure my visual acuity by visiting an optometrist.

Would you agree with me that the data I obtain from these measurements will help me decide how much weight to lose? I hope not! There is no relationship between height, temperature, and visual acuity and my weight. These measurements clearly would be useless because they are inconsistent with the purpose for which I collected them: to make a decision about how much weight to lose.

Validity   Assessment data that are consistent with the decision-making (evaluation) purpose for which we intend them are *valid* for that purpose. Assessment validity refers to the degree to which data actually match the evaluative decisions for which we want to be able to use them. Assessment data that possess a high degree of validity are those that are highly relevant to the evaluative decision we need to make. Assessment data that possess a low degree of validity are those that are inconsistent with our decision-making goals.

For example, at the end of the motivation unit in my educational psychology class, I have summative evaluation decisions to make concerning my students' abilities to apply concepts and principles related to motivation. If I collect assessment data by giving students twenty physics problems to solve, I will be measuring their ability to apply physics concepts and principles—not the skills that are relevant to the motivation unit's instructional goals. Although the physics problems may yield perfectly good data on these students' physics knowledge, they produce data of low validity for the summative evaluation decision I need to make.

When we design assessment procedures for the purpose of instructional decision making, we need to ensure that the data we collect are as valid as possible. How, for example, can I maximize the validity of my weight-loss data? First and foremost, I need to be sure that I am actually measuring what I intend to measure: weight. I can measure my weight by jumping on some scales. Here are the data I might collect from three different scales:

- Home bathroom scale (197 pounds)
- Scale in a gym (190 pounds)
- Doctor's office scale (194 pounds)

Now that I have improved the validity of my data, I appear to have another assessment problem: Which of the three weights should I trust? I cannot possibly be three different weights all at the same time. Perhaps one of the scales is yielding my actual (or true) weight—or perhaps none is. How can I decide how much weight I should lose if I can't get a consistent, dependable measurement of my present weight?

■ **Reliability**   As you can see, decision making also can be impeded if assessment data are not consistent, dependable, or trustworthy, a characteristic of assessment data known as *reliability*. Reliability refers to the degree to which we can depend on our data to reflect consistently the characteristic we are assessing. Data that possess a high degree of reliability are those that we can trust to provide an accurate reflection of students' actual abilities.

Suppose I design and administer twenty questions to assess my students at the end of the motivation unit. Several days later, I misplace all the students' scores and therefore must ask them to take the test again. I prepare a second form of the test with questions that are different from the first but still related to the same concepts and principles. After the retest, I absent-mindedly lose the scores again, so I have to create a third set of questions. Here are the scores that three students might obtain on each of the three sets of questions:

Student	First Score	Second Score	Third Score
Hector	15	20	17
Tara	20	15	14
Jill	18	16	19

Notice that none of the students' scores is consistent over time, just as none of my three weights was consistent over three different scales. If each form of the test really is assessing my students' achievement of the motivation unit's instructional goals, then the scores should not vary from one form of the test to another because student learning should be stable over time. The fact that the scores do vary suggests that the three tests are measuring something other than what students have learned.

■ **Relationships Between Reliability and Validity**   Unfortunately, I have no way of knowing what that "something" might be. All I know is that basing a summative evaluation decision on any one of the three scores is risky because they do not appear to be reliable indicators of my students' learning. Unreliable assessment data cannot be used for any type of decision making. Thus, when data have a low degree of reliability, they also necessarily have a low degree of validity because we can't be very sure of what exactly we are measuring.

Now let's say that I give my students the twenty physics questions I mentioned earlier. Again, I keep losing the scores and have to give the test three times:

Student	First Score	Second Score	Third Score
Hector	15	14	15
Tara	20	20	19
Jill	18	19	18

For some reason, the physics scores are much more reliable than the motivation scores. However, we already have established the low degree of validity that scores on a physics test would have for summative evaluation of learning for the motivation unit. So no matter how reliable the physics scores are, they still are of no use to me for the decision I need to make.

As you can see, although reliability is a necessary requirement for validity, it does not guarantee validity. In other words, just because we can measure something reliably does not mean we can use those measurements validly for any purpose we want.

I hope that this illustration helps you understand the vital importance of assessment validity and reliability for instructional decision making and their relationships to each other. Now that you have a basic understanding of these two concepts, we will examine each one more closely. Let's look first at strategies we can use to maximize the validity of the assessment data we collect.

Maximizing Assessment Validity

Determining the degree of assessment validity always depends on how we want to be able to use the assessment data we collect. Anything that reduces the match between our data and the evaluation we need to make represents a potential threat to validity. There are two particular sources of mismatch: (1) the content that supports the learned capability and (2) the action or performance that operationalizes the learned capability. As you can see from Table 4.2, we achieve the highest potential validity when both the content and action of learner performance are highly consistent with the learned capability we are attempting to evaluate. Let's examine more closely how content and action inconsistencies can creep into assessments and threaten the validity of data.

Content Consistency Content consistency refers to the match between the specific information, skills, or attitudes that learners demonstrate during assessment and the information, skills, or attitudes that we wish to evaluate. Traditionally, measurement theorists have referred to this aspect of assessment as content validity (Messick, 1995). That is, does the content of the test seem to match the content that learners are to achieve?

Of course, the content that learners actually demonstrate during assessment depends largely on the types of performance opportunities we provide for them. If I provide physics problems for educational psychology students to solve, I will not be able to use the data validly to make decisions about their knowledge of a different content area: motivation. Similarly, if I have students write a short story for the purpose of evaluating their ability to use figures of

Table 4.2
Effects of Content and Action Consistency on Assessment Validity

	Content Consistency	
	High	*Low*
Action Consistency		
High	Highest degree of assessment validity	Lower degree of assessment validity
Low	Lower degree of assessment validity	Lowest degree of assessment validity

Table 4.3
Assessment Strategies for Instructional Goals: Consistent Versus Inconsistent Content

Learning Outcome	Instructional Goal	Assessment Strategy	
		Consistent Content	*Inconsistent Content*
Verbal information	State the characteristics of communities.	On a list of ten statements related to communities, learners place a check mark beside those that are common characteristics of all communities.	On a list of ten statements related to communities, learners place a check mark beside those that describe their local community.
Intellectual skill: Concept	Identify sedimentary rocks.	From an assortment of fifteen different rocks, learners pick out the sedimentary rocks and place them together in a pile.	From an assortment of fifteen different rocks, learners pick out the sedimentary, igneous, and metamorphic rocks and place them in three piles.
Intellectual skill: Rule/principle	Demonstrate the principle of checks and balances.	Learners explain how checks and balances were applied in the confirmation process for Supreme Court Justice David Souter.	Learners explain how Supreme Court Justice David Souter would apply the establishment clause of the First Amendment to the issue of vouchers for private religious schools.
Cognitive strategy	Originate an experiment.	Learners prepare an experiment to test the effects of light, moisture, and temperature on mold growth.	Learners prepare slides for examining mold under a microscope.
Psychomotor skill	Execute a lay-up.	Learners shoot five lay-ups on a basketball court.	Learners dribble a basketball the length of a basketball court five times.
Attitude	Choose to cooperate in small groups.	Learners are placed in groups of five to complete a class project. At the conclusion of the project, each member of the group rates the level of cooperation exhibited by each of the other four members of the group.	Learners are placed in groups of five to complete a class project. At the conclusion of the project, each group submits a self-evaluation statement that describes what they believe they have learned from the experience.

speech and I score the stories primarily on the quality of spelling and punctuation, I will not be able to use those scores to evaluate the target content: figures of speech. Assessment content should match the specific information, skills, or attitudes that are stated clearly in our instructional goals. As Table 4.3 illustrates, it is easy to stray from the target content as we devise concrete assessment procedures for specific instructional goals.

■ **Action Consistency** Action consistency refers to the match between the action described in the instructional goal (or subgoal) and the action that the learner actually performs for the assessment of that goal. As we noted in Chapter 2, each major learning outcome has a typical capability verb (e.g., *state, apply, execute, originate, choose*) that best expresses how learners should demonstrate the outcome. However, when we assess, we must select the specific, concrete actions that students will engage in to demonstrate the learned capability. For example, students could demonstrate the learned capability of stating (*capability verb*) the names of the planets in order from the sun by writing the names in order on a sheet of paper, reciting the names orally, or placing planet models in order. Thus, stating (*capability verb*) in the context of this instructional goal can take the concrete form of writing, reciting, or placing. These are three concrete actions that learners can use to display their capability to state verbal information. Therefore, we refer to them as action verbs. **Action verbs** specify the external concrete actions that learners will engage in to demonstrate their internal learned capabilities (Gagne et al., 1992).

To maximize the validity of our assessment data, we need to ensure that the action verbs we select to operationalize internal learned capabilities are consistent with the learned capabilities we are attempting to evaluate. If, for example, we are assessing our learners' abilities to execute a lay-up in basketball, it would be inappropriate for them to write a paragraph explaining how to perform the skill. Because executing a lay-up is a psychomotor skill, learners should display the target capability by actually shooting lay-ups, not just talking about how to do it. For this instructional goal, *shooting* is an action verb that is more consistent with the acquired psychomotor capability than *writing*. As the example illustrates, selecting effective action verbs for assessment is a thinking process. There are no actions that automatically enhance the validity of our data in all assessment situations. The learned capability, acquired content, and performance context all influence our choice of appropriate actions.

When we select concrete actions, we must also consider appropriate learner response modes (Nitko, 1996). **Response mode** refers to the type of motor activity that learners must be able to produce in an assessment scenario. Every assessment requires learners to produce some type of motor activity to demonstrate internal learning products. Motor activities can be as simple as filling in circles on a computer scan sheet or as complex as singing, drawing, building, or operating a computer. Even giving an oral answer requires the motor activity of producing intelligible speech.

Different learners possess varying degrees of proficiency in producing particular actions. Therefore, we need to ensure that the response modes described by our action verbs are those that learners are capable of performing. For example, a student with cerebral palsy in my educational psychology class may have great difficulty writing words such as *positive* and *negative* in response to reinforcement scenarios, even though she may very well possess the intellectual capability of identifying examples of positive and negative reinforcement. Because of her significant motor impairment, handwritten answers to questions may be an inappropriate response mode for her. In that case, I need to select an alternative action that falls within the student's range of response modes so that her motor difficulties do not confound my evaluation of her achievement of the instructional goal. As an alternative to writing, the student may be able to say, type, or point to the appropriate classifying word.

Response modes are related to a variety of learner characteristics, including developmental level, socioeconomic status, physical capabilities, native language, and cultural background. Detailed analyses of each of these categories of learner differences are well beyond the scope and purpose of this book. However, I encourage you to draw on your existing or emerging knowledge of child development, exceptionalities, cultural diversity, and so on to increase your awareness of individual students' response modes and your ability to adapt to those modes in your assessment procedures. You have both an ethical and legal responsibility to assess students in ways that permit them to demonstrate their knowledge and skills (see AERA, APA, & NCME, 1999).

Strategies for Enhancing Assessment Validity

Now that we have examined how content and action inconsistencies can threaten assessment validity and impede instructional decision making, let's explore some general actions we can take to minimize such threats. We can enhance assessment validity by (1) writing clear instructional goals, (2) preparing assessment blueprints, and (c) asking other people to evaluate our assessments.

■ **Begin with Clear Instructional Goals**   Maximizing the validity of our assessment data is impossible unless we have specified clearly how we eventually want to use the data in decision making. As we noted in Chapter 2, appropriately written instructional goals describe the decisions that we wish to make about our learners' achievement following instruction. A carefully selected capability verb directs our attention to the internal learned capability that learners need to be able to demonstrate. Clearly defined content focuses attention on the specific information, skill, or attitude that learners need to acquire. We can strengthen the validity of our assessment data by monitoring the consistency of our data collection procedures with the capability and content of our instructional goals. This is possible only if we have actually specified our instructional goals.

■ **Prepare Assessment Blueprints**   Carpenters who build houses must satisfy the wishes and specifications of the people who are paying for the construction work. A carpenter does not want to wait until the house is finished to discover that the home buyers wanted four bedrooms instead of three or oak kitchen cabinets rather than maple. To ensure that the building process is consistent with the criteria by which the home buyers will evaluate the finished product, carpenters usually work from a written plan called a blueprint.

Similarly, when we "build" our assessment procedures, we should follow an assessment blueprint to ensure that our data collection strategy will produce data that are as valid as possible. An **assessment blueprint** is a written plan that describes both the content and learner performance to be addressed through assessment procedures (Nitko, 1996; Oosterhof, 1990). Usually this information is organized in the form of a two-dimensional chart, often referred to as a **table of specifications** (Carey, 1994; Hopkins, 1998; Oosterhof, 1990). Although these tables can take a variety of specific forms, we usually structure them by indicating the content areas to be assessed in the left-hand column of the chart and the type of learner performances to be demonstrated across the top row of the chart, as illustrated in Table 4.4.

After we develop the content and performance structure of the blueprint, we are ready to think about the number of performance opportunities (or items) that would be appropriate for each instructional goal. According to Table 4.4, six verbal information items are allocated to instructional goal 1 of Topic A. For instructional goal 3 of Topic C, six opportunities will be provided for learners to apply an intellectual skill. The column and row totals show the number of performance opportunities that we plan to allocate to each topic, instructional goal, and learning outcome.

The blueprint does not automatically guarantee that the data we collect will possess a high degree of validity, just as the blueprint for a house does not guarantee that all of the home buyer's specifications will be achieved. Ultimately the quality of the finished product depends on our skill in translating the plan into concrete actions and materials. We use the blueprint to guide our preparation of specific performance opportunities (or test items) for our learners. Returning to Table 4.4, will the five performance opportunities we develop to assess instructional goal 2 of Topic A yield valid data for evaluating learners' ability to apply an intellectual skill? Although that will depend on *our* skill in developing assessment items (an important topic addressed in the next chapter), our awareness of

Table 4.4
General Structure of an Assessment Blueprint

	Declarative Knowledge	Procedural Knowledge		Attitudinal Knowledge	Total Items
		Motor	Intellectual		
TOPIC A					
Instructional goal 1	6				6
Instructional goal 2			5		5
Instructional goal 3			4		4
Topic A total items					**15**
TOPIC B					
Instructional goal 1			8		8
Instructional goal 2	6				6
Instructional goal 3		3			3
Instructional goal 4				3	3
Topic B total items					**20**
TOPIC C					
Instructional goal 1			5		5
Instructional goal 2	4				4
Instructional goal 3			6		6
Topic C total items					**15**
TOTAL ITEMS	16	3	28	3	50

the evaluative purpose of the items is a crucial first step. The blueprint reminds us of the purpose of each assessment item as we develop it.

We will return to assessment blueprints later in the book in examining principles of unit planning. For now, I hope you understand how the time and effort spent developing a table of specifications prior to assessment can guide your thinking so that assessment validity is strengthened and your decision making is enhanced.

■ **Ask Other People to Evaluate Performance Opportunities** A third general strategy for maximizing assessment validity is to ask other people to evaluate the consistency between our instructional goals and the corresponding performance opportunities. We, of course, already believe that our performance items will yield valid data. However, our subjective personal perceptions are not always accurate (remember the optical illusion earlier in the chapter?). If we can find another person (or persons) to verify the match between our goals and test items, we can use the data generated by those test items more confidently.

People who possess content knowledge, as well as familiarity with the characteristics of learners, will be in the best position to provide this expert judgment. For example, I sometimes ask colleagues in my department to evaluate the classroom assessments I design because they have content knowledge and are familiar with my students. Similarly, you can ask fellow classroom teachers, as well as other education professionals such as administrators, curriculum specialists, and school psychologists, to provide this service for you.

LET'S SUMMARIZE

Whenever we assess students, we need to take steps to maximize the validity of the data we collect so that our decision-making capability is improved. Maximizing validity is a thinking process that can be aided by clear instructional goals, blueprinting, and seeking expert judgments from others. In addition, one significant way that we can enhance the valid use of our data is to be sure they are as reliable as possible. How can we collect assessment data that are trustworthy? Let's turn our attention now to this fundamental question.

Maximizing Assessment Reliability

Earlier in the chapter, I described how three students' scores might change if I were to test them three times. If I take the time to administer three parallel tests to my students, I will be able to see how much fluctuation in scores (i.e., unreliability) is being produced by my assessment procedure. Perhaps if I can test my students, say, ten times, I could average all ten scores to get a fairly reliable estimate of their actual abilities. Unfortunately, however, we do not usually have the luxury of repeated testing in the classroom. We have to acknowledge, therefore, that any single set of assessment data we collect is likely to vary somewhat from learners' actual abilities. In other words, it is virtually impossible to measure the psychological characteristics of people with complete accuracy, so any assessment produces only an estimate of learners' true abilities.

■ **Reliability and Measurement Error**   Suppose that I have some magical way to determine the scores that my students would obtain if I could measure them with complete reliability. Let's call these hypothetical data their *true scores*. Notice in the table that follows that none of Hector's test scores matched his true score. One test score overestimated his true ability, and two scores underestimated his ability. Although two of Tara's scores deviated from her true score, the second one actually hit it. Of course, in a real assessment situation, we have no way of knowing when we accidentally hit a true score because we have no way of knowing with absolute certainty what a student's true score is. For Jill, every test score gave an inflated view of her true ability.

Student	True Score	First Score	Second Score	Third Score
Hector	18	15	20	17
Tara	15	20	15	14
Jill	13	18	16	19

The difference between our learners' true abilities and the estimate of their abilities that we obtain through assessment is called **measurement error** (Hopkins, 1998; Lyman, 1998). Every learner performance is influenced by actual ability (true score) and some degree of measurement error. Measurement error masks learners' true abilities by either inflating or deflating the quality of their performance. If we were measuring only true ability, we would expect learner performance to stay the same over time because true abilities should not change. If learner performance does vary over more than one assessment opportunity, we infer that we are measuring something more (or less) than true ability: measurement error. Assessment reliability increases as the degree of measurement error decreases.

Measurement error occurs when learner performance is influenced by variables that are unrelated to the characteristic we are attempting to assess. For example, Hector may have scored three points below his true score on the first test because he forgot to answer three questions. His forgetfulness is irrelevant to his ability to apply motivation concepts and principles. Tara may have obtained her score of 20 on the first test by guessing five questions correctly. Tara's guessing ability and the low quality of the questions that permitted her to guess correctly are both irrelevant to her achievement of the unit's instructional goals. Of course, I have no way of knowing if forgetfulness, guessing, poorly written test questions, or some other unrelated variables are influencing the test scores, because all I have is a single number for each student.

Although measurement error exerts a random, unpredictable effect on assessment data, that does not mean that we have no control over it. By being aware of some of the common sources of measurement error, we can take steps to minimize its effects. There are five general sources of measurement error: (1) scoring procedures, (2) item sampling, (3) item quality, (4) administration conditions, and (5) learner characteristics (Lyman, 1998).

EFFECTS OF SCORING PROCEDURES ON MEASUREMENT ERROR

Scoring procedure refers to the method used to transform learner performance into a category that reflects the quality of the performance. Often we use numbers (quantitative assessment) to provide these categories. For example, if I develop a twenty-item multiple-choice test to assess my learners' ability to apply motivation concepts, then the number (or percentage) correct can provide a way of classifying or describing their performance on the test. Scores of 19, 17, or 15 correct provide numeric descriptions of learner performance. I can use these numbers to compare my students to a reference point that I believe represents satisfactory achievement of the instructional goals.

Even if I do not quantify learner performance (qualitative assessment), I still must categorize it before I can evaluate it. For example, I might give my students a realistic scenario involving motivation and ask them to write an essay describing how they would apply motivation concepts. I could then place each essay into one of three categories: (1) applies all concepts clearly and accurately, (2) applies some concepts clearly and accurately, or (3) applies few concepts clearly and accurately.

The methods we use to score learner performance may produce measurement error and therefore damage the reliability of our data. Scoring procedures that depend on subjective personal judgments tend to produce greater measurement error than those that are more objective. I can score my twenty-item multiple-choice assessment objectively because I simply have to decide if my students' responses to the items match the predetermined correct answers. There is no personal judgment required for this decision. If I scored the test several times by hand, each student's score would probably be exactly the same with each scoring. In fact, someone with absolutely no knowledge of the content being assessed could score the test with a high degree of reliability. I can even have a computer do the scoring. Common test items that can be scored with a high degree of objectivity include multiple-choice, true-false, matching, sentence-completion, and fill-in-the-blank questions.

Objective scoring is never completely reliable because human error is always a factor. No matter how simple the decision, human beings can always make mistakes. I might lose my place momentarily on the answer key and misscore one or two items, or I might mistake a student's written "a" for a "d." Even a computer can make mistakes. The computer might not detect an answer because the pencil mark is not dark enough, or it might register an errant erasing smudge as a student's response. The possibilities for human and machine error in objective scoring are endless. Therefore, even data that we obtain through objective scoring are vulnerable to some degree of measurement error and thus some degree of unreliability.

Subjective scoring procedures are even more prone to measurement error than objective scoring. Judging learner performance is not necessarily difficult; making judgments *consistently* is extremely difficult. If I were to score my students' essays several times, chances are great that their scores would vary considerably because I would not be able to stay perfectly consistent with myself. After scoring half the essays, I may become fatigued and relax my scoring criteria without even being consciously aware of it. Or I may assign a high score to an essay that has beautiful handwriting, perfect spelling, and perfect punctuation even though the motivation concepts have not been applied well. Conversely, I may score an illegible, poorly written essay lower despite perfectly accurate applications of the concepts being assessed. Sometimes teachers rate learner performance more highly simply because there are other characteristics about the learner that they find appealing. This phenomenon, known as the *halo effect,* influences all of us when we evaluate others (Chase, 1979, 1986).

Common performance opportunities that require greater degrees of scorer subjectivity include short-answer and essay questions because they provide more freedom for learners to demonstrate their knowledge in personal, idiosyncratic ways. No two responses will be exactly the same, so we cannot establish a single correct answer. Performance items also require scorer judgment. **Performance items** provide opportunities for learners to demonstrate their knowledge in the context of a meaningful application activity. For example, a physics teacher might have students design and build model bridges to assess their ability to apply physics principles. A fifth-grade teacher might assess her students' short-story writing ability by having them each develop a "book" of their own stories that they write, illustrate, and "publish." Groups of students in a high school social studies class might design interactive Web pages to demonstrate their understanding of world religions. How well the students' bridges, books, and Web sites reflect their achievement of instructional goals is a decision that depends on each teacher's subjective scoring because these products and performances vary considerably from student to student.

As you can see, both objective and subjective scoring procedures are fraught with opportunities for measurement error to creep into our assessment data. The following general strategies usually are helpful in controlling for scoring-related measurement error:

1. Use objectively scored assessments rather than subjectively scored assessments whenever possible, as long as you do not compromise assessment validity.

2. For objective items, create ways for learners to respond so that you can easily (with minimal judgment) determine whether their responses match a predetermined answer. For example, have students circle the letter of their answer for multiple-choice questions rather than write it. Unclear written answers by some students will make it necessary for you to make some difficult judgments.

3. For subjective assessments, try to control your personal biases, stereotypes, and expectations by scoring blindly. That is, deliberately avoid knowing whose paper or project you are scoring until you are finished.

4. When scoring large numbers of subjective and objective items, avoid fatigue, inattention, and momentary lapses of judgment by taking frequent

breaks or creating conditions in your environment that will help you stay alert (a big cup of coffee works for me) and focused on your task (keep the television set turned off).

5. For subjective and performance assessments, prepare the scoring criteria that you will use in advance. In other words, specify the features of students' responses you are looking for before you start scoring and stick to those features throughout the entire scoring process. In the next chapter we examine principles for developing these types of scoring procedures in greater detail.

EFFECTS OF ITEM SAMPLING ON MEASUREMENT ERROR

Whenever we assess learners, we ask them to perform a limited number of tasks that we have selected from an infinite (or very large) number of possible tasks. For example, my motivation test consists of twenty specific questions that I developed. I could, however, develop many more questions that would be valid for assessing the application of the same motivation concepts and principles. Perhaps my students' performance would be different if I gave them twenty alternate questions from the infinite number of possible questions. If so, the way in which I developed the sample of assessment items introduces some degree of measurement error that decreases the reliability of my data.

The best general strategy for controlling item-sampling measurement error is to ensure that you provide your learners with an adequate number of performance opportunities. Usually the greater the number of items there are (i.e., response opportunities), the greater the reliability is. Let's say I were to assess your foul-shot shooting ability in basketball by giving you one opportunity to shoot from the free-throw line. You miss. But missing one foul shot is hardly a fair representation of your foul-shot ability. (Even Michael Jordan misses one every now and then.) I can control for the possibility that you had an unlucky miss by giving you a second chance. If you miss that one too, I begin to be a bit more confident that perhaps your foul-shot abilities are not very good. However, if you make the second one, I have absolutely no confidence in my data. Which shot truly represents your ability: the miss or the hit? I'll have to give you additional opportunities to find out. Eighteen tries later, you have made fifteen of twenty foul shots. These data strongly suggest that your first miss was simply an aberration. It looks as if you tend to make three of every four foul shots (15/20). The first trial that I gave you happened to be the one in every four you usually miss (5/20).

As you can see, with a small number of performance opportunities, we have less confidence that our sample of items yields performance that is truly representative of learners' abilities. Of course, if their performance is not truly representative of the abilities we are trying to assess, we are collecting measurement error. How many test items or performance opportunities do we need to minimize measurement error? There are no firm answers to this question. Generally the more susceptible the performance is to the effects of random variables such as luck and guessing, the greater the number of items needed to control for those effects.

EFFECTS OF ITEM QUALITY ON MEASUREMENT ERROR

Hundreds of test items will not ensure a high degree of reliability if the items are confusing, misleading, ambiguous, tricky, or too easy. We need to create performance opportunities that allow learners to be successful if, indeed, they have acquired the new knowledge that we are assessing. However, learners who do not possess the target knowledge should *not* be successful with our items. For objective items, this means preparing questions that are clear and unambiguous. Furthermore, we need to write objective items that do not give away the correct answer.

For subjective and performance items, we need to prepare the directions or cues that we will provide to learners to direct their written responses or behaviors. The directions need to provide adequate guidance so that learners understand clearly what they are supposed to do but without providing so much information that we inadvertently help them perform more proficiently than they otherwise would. In the next chapter, we examine some specific principles to help us prepare objective, subjective, and performance items so that reliability is maximized.

EFFECTS OF ADMINISTRATION CONDITIONS ON MEASUREMENT ERROR

We need to consider the effects of variables related to the test items and the environment within which the assessment takes place. For example, an assessment that requires an hour to complete will yield less reliable data if we give students only forty-five minutes. The time-induced stress, anxiety, and frustration may deflate some students' scores in ways that are inconsistent with the knowledge or skill we are trying to assess. A noisy, poorly lit, uncomfortable room (one that is too hot or too cold, for example) may adversely affect how well students can concentrate on the tasks at hand. Scheduling an important assessment right before recess, lunch, or some other favored school activity may make it hard for students to concentrate or may induce some to rush, thus producing random errors that otherwise would not occur.

As you can see, there are many ways in which the overall assessment environment can produce measurement error. It is impossible to predict with certainty the specific administration conditions that will influence assessment reliability. Therefore, in any given assessment situation, we need to anticipate all the possible ways in which environmental variables may potentially contaminate data and then establish appropriate controls to eliminate or minimize the effects of those variables.

Learner Characteristics   Finally, the learners themselves bring to any assessment situation many diverse characteristics that can produce measurement error. Some students are better at guessing than others; some have better intuitions about the answers that teachers are looking for than others. In short, some learners have a higher degree of test-wiseness. **Test-wiseness** is the ability of students to use the features of a test or testing situation to obtain scores that are higher than their true knowledge or ability would produce (Miller, Fagley, & Lane, 1988; Millman, Bishop, & Ebel, 1965).

Additional learner characteristics may influence performance arbitrarily. Some students experience debilitating test anxiety that interferes with their ability to express their knowledge or skill (Sarason, 1980; Snow, Corno, & Jackson, 1996). Other students remain cool, calm, and collected in test situations. Among those who experience test anxiety, some are better able than others to control the negative effects of stress. All learners experience bad days, bad moods, sickness, personal crises, and interpersonal distractions that inject unpredictable degrees of measurement error into their performance.

Although we can do little to prevent these learner characteristics from producing measurement error, we can try to design assessments to minimize their destructive effects on the reliability of our data. For example, if we know that some students have high levels of test anxiety, we should avoid any verbal or nonverbal cues that would exacerbate their stress. For example, when handing out a set of test questions, we would *not* want to say, "Good luck, everyone. You're really going to need it!" Perhaps we can give highly anxious students more time, greater privacy, or other types of supports to help them feel more secure. Of course, we need to be careful that the supports we provide do not threaten assessment validity or introduce new, unanticipated sources of measurement error.

Why Bother with Assessment?

With all the threats to validity and reliability that we have been discussing, you may be wondering whether it is possible to obtain *any* useful information from the assessment process. Certainly assessment is a complicated, difficult, imprecise process because learners are human beings who are complex and multifaceted. Therefore, collecting assessment data that are perfectly valid and reliable is virtually impossible. However, that reality does not excuse us, as *design-teachers*, from developing assessment strategies that produce data that are as valid and reliable as possible. If we stop collecting assessment data because the process is too difficult and the results are not always as trustworthy as we would like, the only alternative is to resort to decision making based on intuition and personal impressions of student learning. We already have seen the dangers of this approach to decision making. Do you remember what happened when you tried to eyeball the two circles in Figure 4.1 at the beginning of the chapter?

Before we leave this chapter, I want you to have the opportunity to practice applying the concepts of validity and reliability. In Exercise 4.3 in the *Student Exercise Guide*, you will find several assessment scenarios that present threats to validity and reliability. Each scenario gives you the opportunity to identify specific threats and suggest actions that you could take to improve the degree of validity and reliability.

LOOKING BACK   LOOKING AHEAD

My primary goal in writing this chapter was to introduce instructional assessment as a thinking process that should contribute to your decision-making ability. Assessment is motivated by the need for trustworthy data to help us make preinstructional, formative, summative, and diagnostic decisions about our learners. When designing any assessment strategy, we need to take steps to ensure that the data we collect are consistent with the decision we need to make (*validity*). We also need to ensure that the data we collect are as dependable, or consistent, as possible (*reliability*). Although the specific steps we take to maximize validity and reliability will vary somewhat with the particular assessment context, we identified some basic threats and strategies that will be common to nearly all assessment situations.

Now that we have laid this important foundation, we are ready to examine specific procedures for maximizing assessment validity and reliability. In the next chapter, we analyze the wide variety of specific assessment procedures that are available to us. Most important, we examine strategies for developing and using these procedures so that the data they produce are as valid and reliable as possible. Before we delve more deeply into the role of assessment in the instructional design process, take a moment to assess yourself. Exercise 4.4 in the *Student Exercise Guide* gives you the opportunity to assess your ability to perform each of this chapter's instructional goals. The results from this self-assessment will help you evaluate your learning from the chapter.

RESOURCES FOR FURTHER REFLECTION AND EXPLORATION

Print Resources

American Educational Research Association, American Psychological Association, & National Council on Measurement in Education. (1999). *Standards for educational and psychological testing.* Washington, DC: American Psychological Association.

A comprehensive summary of the professional guidelines that govern testing practices in educational environments. Standards are relevant to teachers, school administrators, school psychologists, and school counselors.

American Federation of Teachers, National Council on Measurement in Education, & National Education Association. (1990). Standards for teacher competence in educational assessment of students. *Educational Measurement: Issues and Practices, 9,* 30–32.

A statement of professional standards to guide teachers in all aspects of student assessment. Presents specific assessment skills for teachers organized into seven sets of general competencies.

Lyman, H. B. (1998). *Test scores and what they mean* (6th ed.). Boston, MA: Allyn and Bacon.

A no-nonsense, easy-to-read treatment of quantitative assessment concepts. Also includes coverage of basic statistical skills that are useful in interpreting test scores.

Educational Assessment. Mahwah, NJ: Erlbaum.

A scholarly journal that focuses on a wide range of educational assessment issues, including classroom testing practices. Intended audience includes teachers, educational researchers, and school administrators.

World Wide Web Resources

http://ncme.ed.uiuc.edu/

Web site of the National Council on Measurement in Education (NCME). Provides information and links related to educational assessment issues.

http://crest96.cse.ucla.edu/index.htm

Web site of the National Center for Research on Evaluation, Standards, and Student Testing. Provides information, links, and resources related to a wide variety of school assessment issues.

http://ericae.net/

Web site of the ERIC Clearinghouse on Assessment and Evaluation. Provides information on a wide variety of testing issues and resources to promote responsible test use.

Classroom Assessment Strategies

5

When I was mowing the lawn recently, I noticed that one of the front wheels of the lawnmower was wobbling. When I stopped the mower to take a closer look, I found that the nut that held the wheel on the supporting bolt was loose. This looked like an easy problem to solve: just tighten the nut. I opened up my toolbox and examined my tools: a claw hammer, ball-peen hammer, several screwdrivers, a socket set, adjustable wrench, Allen wrenches, vise grips, pipe wrench, an awl (do you know what an awl is?), staple gun, slip-joint pliers, channel-lock pliers, needle-nose pliers, and a set of open-end wrenches—just to name a few.

With all of these wonderful tools available to me, which one should I choose to fix the lawnmower wheel? Clearly I needed a tool that was made to turn a nut on a bolt. That specific need immediately ruled out the hammers, screwdrivers, Allen wrenches, staple gun, and awl. All of the other tools were still viable alternatives because they did have the ability to turn a nut—the desired outcome. However, were they all equally qualified for the job?

I thought about using the socket wrench, but I would have had to find the right size socket, locate the ratchet, place the socket on the ratchet, and make sure the direction was set correctly. That seemed like a lot of work just to tighten a nut. I looked in the toolbox again and spied the vise grips and pliers. Although I could easily clamp the vise grips or pliers on the nut to turn it, they would probably damage the edges with their teeth, possibly making it difficult to tighten it again in the future. The vise grips and pliers could help me achieve the desired outcome efficiently, but they would not produce a quality job.

What about the awl? No, I reminded myself; the awl is not a nut-turning tool (have you found out yet what an awl is?). I needed to stay focused on the task at hand. There were two tools that I had not yet considered: the adjustable wrench and the open-end wrenches. Both would accomplish the nut-turning goal efficiently with-

INSTRUCTIONAL GOALS FOR CHAPTER 5

After reading and thinking about this chapter, you should be able to . . .

1. State and explain the meaning of the term *test item*.

2. Identify and generate examples of cognitive, performance, and attitude assessments.

3. State several specific criteria for selecting test item formats and demonstrate how those criteria apply to specific types of test items.

4. Apply rules for developing objectively scored cognitive test items.

5. Apply rules for developing subjectively scored cognitive test items.

6. Apply rules for developing analytically scored performance items.

7. Apply rules for developing attitude assessment scales.

out marring the edges of the nut. I chose the adjustable wrench so that I would not have to take the time to find the right size open-end wrench, although the extra time would have been minimal. After adjusting the adjustable wrench to fit, I tightened the nut and went back to cutting the grass. I had selected the best tool for the job by considering the *outcome* I needed to achieve, the *efficiency* of each tool available to me, and the *quality* with which each tool would achieve the desired outcome.

What does fixing a lawnmower wheel have to do with classroom assessment? When we assess learners, we need to select the best tools for the job by considering the same three general criteria: outcome, efficiency, and quality. Many useful tools are available to help us collect valid and reliable assessment data. However, all of these tools are not equally effective in producing quality data in all assessment situations. Just as I needed to match my repair tool to the specific task at hand (turning a nut), *design-teachers* need to match their assessment devices to the specific type of assessment data they are attempting to collect.

In this chapter, we examine some common assessment tools and explore criteria for helping us match specific tools to our data collection needs. Then we examine specific rules and procedures for developing and implementing these assessment strategies. We will build on the previous chapter by considering how these rules and procedures help us to maximize assessment validity and reliability. If you still haven't figured out what an awl is, just keep reading; I will keep you in suspense until the end of the chapter. In addition to your being able to describe the function of an awl, some other important outcomes that you should be able to demonstrate by the time you finish with this chapter are listed on the preceding page.

Selecting an Assessment Item Format

Let's say that you have just taught your fifth-grade students how to punctuate compound sentences with commas. Did they achieve the instructional goal? Can they now punctuate compound sentences with commas? This is a question that you can answer by collecting assessment data. But how will you collect the data? Your students' punctuating skill is an *internal* learned capability that resides within the minds of your learners. Therefore, you need a tool to transform the internal capability of punctuating compound sentences into an *external*, observable performance.

You open up your assessment toolbox and see a variety of tools that might help you achieve this transformation. There are open-ended short-answer and essay questions that you might ask about punctuating compound sentences. There are true-false, multiple-choice, matching, and completion questions that might work. You even notice performance assessments that would give your students the opportunity to punctuate compound sentences in the context of a realistic, meaningful writing activity. Which tool should you choose?

This scenario is really quite similar to the lawnmower repair scenario that I described at the beginning of this chapter. Selecting an assessment device is like choosing the best tool for a repair job. We usually refer to an assessment device as a **test item**. A test item is simply a tool for transforming an unobservable, internal learning outcome into an observable, external performance so that we can evaluate the quality of learning that has occurred.

Commonly Used Test Item Formats

From your own school experiences, you know that test items come in several different forms. Which form is the best? This question is just as inappropriate as asking whether a hammer is better than a screwdriver. Neither a hammer nor a screwdriver is inherently better than the other; each is better than the other for *accomplishing specific jobs*. Similarly, there is no test item format that provides the best way to collect assessment data. If the only tool in your toolbox is a hammer, then everything will look like a nail, and you will be tempted to define every repair job as a "hit-it-with-the-hammer" task. Similarly, if you have only one or two preferred test item formats in your assessment toolbox, you might be tempted to bend the evaluation process to fit those particular data collection strategies. Remember that the value and utility of a particular test item format rest in its ability to produce quality data needed for effective decision making, not on any preconceived preference or dislike we may have for that type of item.

■ **Cognitive Test Items**   As you can see in Figure 5.1, there are three major types of test item formats for collecting assessment data: (1) cognitive, (2) attitude, and (3) performance. **Cognitive items** are those that invite the learner to make a relatively simple behavioral response that reflects more complex internal thinking, or cognition. For example, you could assess your fifth graders' sentence punctuating skill by giving them ten compound sentences and having them place a check mark beside each one that was punctuated correctly. To respond to each sentence, students have to apply the rule for punctuating compound sentences as an *intellectual skill.* Writing the check mark is a simple, easy-to-produce, outward manifestation of their internal cognitive work.

I am sure you are familiar with the various forms that cognitive test items can take (Table 5.1 contains examples). We can classify cognitive items as those that are scored objectively and those that require greater subjectivity in scoring (see Figure 5.1). Recall from the previous chapter that objectively scored items have predetermined correct responses that we can simply compare to our learners' specific responses. For subjectively scored items, learner responses can vary considerably, so it is not possible to establish a single correct response. Therefore, subjective judgment is required to determine the quality of each learner's response. There is nothing inherently objective or subjective about

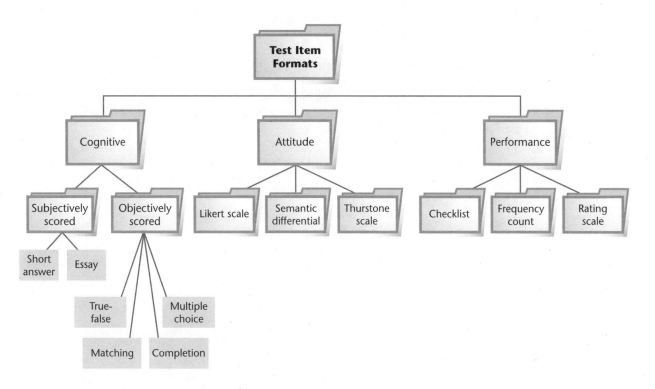

Figure 5.1
Classifying Common Types of Assessment Devices

Table 5.1
Cognitive Test Items

Item Format	Description	Sample Instructional Goal	Examples
OBJECTIVELY SCORED			
True-false	A declarative statement is provided, and the learner indicates whether the statement is accurate by recalling verbal information or by applying an intellectual skill.	State the names of the Union and Confederate states during the U.S. Civil War. (verbal information)	T F 1. Pennsylvania was a Confederate state during the Civil War. T F 2. Georgia was a Union state during the Civil War.
Multiple choice	A question is presented, and a set of alternative answers is provided. The learner selects the best alternative by recalling verbal information or by applying an intellectual skill.	Apply the rule for rounding numerals to the nearest tenth. (intellectual skill–rule)	What is 45.36 rounded to the nearest tenth? a. 50.0 b. 45.30 c. 45.40 d. 46.0
Matching	Two sets of related pieces of information are presented. The learner selects the piece of information from one set that is related to a particular piece of information from the other set by recalling verbal information or by applying an intellectual skill.	State the chemical symbols for elements on the periodic table. (verbal information)	___ oxygen a. Na ___ calcium b. Pb ___ potassium c. O ___ sodium d. K ___ lead e. Ca
Completion	A declarative statement is presented with a piece of critical information omitted. The learner supplies the missing information to complete the statement by recalling verbal information or by applying an intellectual skill.	Classify animals according to major classes of vertebrates. (intellectual skill–concepts)	1. A squirrel is a member of the _____ class of animals. 2. A salamander belongs to the _____ class of animals.
SUBJECTIVELY SCORED			
Short answer	A well-focused question or task is presented. The learner responds orally or in writing to the question by recalling verbal information or by applying an intellectual skill. Each response usually is no more than the length of a typical paragraph.	State the meanings of literary devices, and identify examples of each. (verbal information, intellectual skill–concepts)	In the space provided below, explain the meanings of (a) alliteration, (b) hyperbole, (c) onomatopoeia, (d) metaphor, and (e) simile. Provide one example of each that is different from those presented in class.
Extended essay	An open-ended question or task is presented. The learner responds orally or in writing to the question by recalling verbal information or by applying intellectual skills. Responses usually are several paragraphs or pages in length.	Explain and demonstrate the principle of manifest destiny. (verbal information, intellectual skill–principle)	In the space provided below, explain the principle of manifest destiny. Describe three specific ways in which the principle influenced the westward expansion of the United States. Discuss two ways in which the principle of manifest destiny might influence current U.S. policies and attitudes toward the exploration of space.

cognitive test items. The degree of objectivity and subjectivity is a function of how we score these items.

■ **Performance Test Items**   Returning to Figure 5.1, **performance items** are those that invite the learner to recall verbal information or apply procedural knowledge in the context of a meaningful problem or activity. Performance items often give learners the opportunity to combine declarative and procedural knowledge in complex, integrated ways. For example, a high school English teacher might assess his students' learning about drama by having small groups write, produce, and perform their own plays. A middle school earth science teacher might have her class develop its own "museum of natural history," where fossils, rocks, and minerals are displayed, along with written descriptions and explanations.

When writing performance items, we simply prepare the directions that will guide our learners' performance. Because the performance will be scored subjectively, we also need to devise scoring procedures that will minimize measurement error and maximize reliability. As displayed in Figure 5.1, common scoring procedures are checklists, frequency counts, and rating scales. We will have more to say about developing such procedures later in this chapter.

■ **Attitude Assessments**   Attitude assessments are useful for evaluating learners' feelings toward an attitude object or the probability that they will choose to behave in ways that are consistent with an acquired attitude. Attitude assessments usually take the form of self-report questionnaires that ask people to indicate their level of agreement with opinion statements about the attitude object. Although we can never be absolutely certain of the feelings and behavioral commitments that people profess on these types of self-report measures, the data they produce may help us make better inferences than we would be able to make without them. We examine specific ways to develop attitude assessments later in the chapter.

Criteria for Selecting Test Item Formats

Given the numerous item formats in our assessment toolbox, how do we select the best one for the job? When I selected the adjustable wrench to fix my lawnmower, I considered outcome, efficiency, and quality criteria. These three general criteria apply also when selecting assessment tools. We need to select the item format that will yield the most valid data for the learning outcome we wish to evaluate. Given the many demands on our time and energy as classroom teachers, we will want to collect the data as *efficiently* as we can—without, of course, sacrificing validity. We also want our data to be as reliable (i.e., free from measurement error) as possible. Depending on the learned capability we are attempting to assess, some item formats may control measurement error better than others, improving the *quality* of our data.

I cannot tell you which specific item format will meet these three general criteria in every assessment situation because the "best" assessment devices vary with the instructional goal, evaluation context, learner characteristics, and so on. Nevertheless, there are several specific selection criteria to consider that may help you think systematically about outcome, efficiency, and quality (see Table 5.2). Let's see how each variable applies to the various item format options in our assessment toolbox.

■ **Validity**   The ultimate goal of assessment is to use the data we collect to make inferences about an internal capability. Recall from the previous chapter that validity is the degree to which our inferences are justified from our data. Notice in Table 5.2 that all of the item formats have the potential to produce highly valid data. Whether this potential is realized depends on the specific

Table 5.2
Variables to Consider When Selecting Cognitive and Performance Items

Selection Criteria	OBJECTIVELY SCORED ITEMS				SUBJECTIVELY SCORED ITEMS		
	True-False	Multiple Choice	Completion	Matching	Short Answer	Extended Essay	Performance
Validity	+	+	+	+	+	+	+
Reliability	+	+	+	+	–	–	–
Response production	–	–	–	–	+	+	+
Ease of developing the stimulus	–	–	–	–	+	+	+
Ease of developing scoring criteria	+	+	+	+	–	–	–
Ease of scoring	+	+	+	+	–	–	–
Ease of administering	+	+	+	+	–	–	–
Range of instructional goals	+	+	x	x	–	–	–

Key: + = high; x = moderate; – = low.

learned capability we are assessing. In other words, the assessment device needs to be matched as closely as possible to the internal capability expressed by the instructional goal. For example, we could use a variation of the true-false format to assess learners' achievement of the instructional goal, *punctuate compound sentences*:

> *Directions:* Place a (+) beside each compound sentence that is punctuated correctly. Place a (–) beside each compound sentence that is punctuated incorrectly.
>
> 1. _____ Bob likes vanilla ice cream, but Mary's favorite flavor is strawberry.
> 2. _____ The sun rose high over the ocean, and the sand on the beach became too hot for our feet.
> 3. _____ The large dog frightened us yet we did not turn and run away.

To respond correctly to each question, learners must be able to *apply the rule* for punctuating compound sentences. Hence, we can use the number of questions learners answer correctly to make a fairly valid inference concerning their achievement of the instructional goal.

In contrast, suppose we wanted to assess our students' achievement of this instructional goal: *Prepare and deliver a persuasive speech*. Students' responses to declarative knowledge questions about persuasive speeches would not allow us to infer how well they can actually prepare and deliver a persuasive speech as procedural knowledge. The most valid way to assess for this instructional goal would be to have each student prepare and deliver (as the instructional goal says) a persuasive speech—a performance assessment. In short, we need to select specific item formats that have the best chance of producing data with the highest possible degree of validity. These formats will vary with the specific instructional goal we are attempting to assess. Again we see the critical importance of beginning the instructional design process with clearly specified instructional goals.

■ **Reliability**   Although any poorly written and administered item can produce a high degree of measurement error and, therefore, data with low reliability, certain types of item formats are particularly vulnerable to this difficulty. Notice in Table 5.2 that objectively scored cognitive items tend to control scoring-related measurement error better than subjectively scored cognitive items and performance items. Subjectively scored items and performance items always require scorer judgment to assess the quality of the learner's performance. The bias, inconsistency, and idiosyncratic criteria related to scorer judgment always introduce some degree of measurement error that deflates the reliability of data to some degree.

■ **Response Production**   Whereas some item formats require learners to *produce* a response, others require them to *select* a response from a set of alternatives. Each of these performances places different processing demands on students. To illustrate the differences, look at the two types of item formats that we could use to assess learners' achievement of the following instructional goal: *State the names of the Union and Confederate states during the U.S. Civil War.*

Multiple-Choice Format

> *Which of the following states supported the Union during the U.S. Civil War?*
>
> *a. Pennsylvania*
>
> *b. Oregon*
>
> *c. Maryland*
>
> *d. Alaska*

Short-Answer Format

> *In the space below, list the names of at least five Union and five Confederate states during the U.S. Civil War.*

Both of these assessment items are valid for the instructional goal because they require learners to recall the verbal information that the instructional goal specifies. However, the multiple-choice item provides a set of alternatives from which learners can *select* the correct response. Each of the four state names provided in the question serves as a cue that may help learners activate the verbal information they need. In short, selection items may reduce the need for learners to cue their memories for verbal information and intellectual skills by themselves. In contrast, the short-answer format provides no specific names to serve as retrieval cues, so learners are completely on their own as they *produce* the names of the states and write them on the paper.

■ **Ease of Developing the Stimulus**   Every assessment device presents a stimulus to which learners respond. The **stimulus** is the question or directions given to students to elicit their response or guide their performance. As you can see from Table 5.1, the stimulus may take a variety of forms: a declarative statement to which the learner responds "true" or "false"; a multiple-choice question with four alternatives from which to select a response; an open-ended question that invites an extended essay response. For performance items, the stimulus is the set of directions that will be given to learners, in written or oral form, so they will know what they are supposed to do.

Although preparing stimulus materials that are effective in guiding students' performance always takes some time and effort, the stimuli for some item formats are more easily developed than others. As noted in Table 5.2, developing the stimulus materials for subjectively scored cognitive items and performance items takes less effort and time than for well-written objectively scored cognitive items.

■ **Ease of Developing Scoring Criteria**   The time investment in preparing well-written objectively scored items pays off when we develop the scoring criteria. Because these types of items are designed to have only one correct response, we simply need to indicate clearly what that correct response is. In contrast, subjectively scored items and performance items produce relatively complex responses that can vary from learner to learner, so it is impossible to specify in advance the exact form the performance will take. Therefore, we need to decide in advance which features of the performance are critical to the evaluative decision we need to make and which features are irrelevant. We examine specific procedures for developing these types of scoring criteria later in this chapter.

■ **Ease of Scoring**   As Table 5.2 indicates, objective scoring is significantly faster and easier than subjective scoring. When we score objective items, we simply check to see if student responses match the predetermined responses, with little to no thought or judgment required. (Of course, remember that a lot of thinking and judgment already has gone into developing these items.) In contrast, subjective scoring is slow and laborious because we have to think about the quality of each student's response or performance.

■ **Ease of Administering**   Because all cognitive items can be presented on paper or on a computer screen, we can administer these items to large groups of students. In contrast to objectively scored items, we must administer most performance items individually or in very small groups because we usually need to be able to observe and evaluate the performance as learners are engaged in it. We overcome this limitation if the performance results in a tangible product (e.g., written report, computer program, visual display) that we can score separately from the performance that produced it.

■ **Range of Instructional Goals**   Because students can respond quickly to objectively scored items, we can assess a greater number of instructional goals in a shorter amount of time. Of course, as noted in Table 5.2, completion and matching items may not lend themselves to a wide range of learning outcomes. Although short-answer, extended-essay, and performance items have the potential to provide a richer and more complete picture of students' abilities, the time that it takes to respond to these items prohibits us from addressing a wide variety of instructional goals. If we have a large number of instructional goals to assess and a limited amount of time to administer the assessment, then subjective and performance items may not be the most efficient tools to choose.

LET'S SUMMARIZE

So which test item formats are the best? Now that you are aware of some of the major variables to consider when selecting an assessment tool, I hope you agree with me that this question is impossible to answer. All assessment devices have advantages and disadvantages. When we select specific item formats, we need to do so in a way that maximizes their advantages and minimizes their potential disadvantages. I hope you will not be inclined to exclude any potentially useful formats from your assessment toolbox.

After we think carefully about our assessment options and select the best format for our instructional goals and classroom environment, we still need to prepare the stimulus and, for some formats, also develop the scoring criteria. In the next section, we examine rules and procedures for preparing assessment items so that the data generated from those items are as valid and reliable as possible.

Developing Cognitive Assessment Items

In this section, we examine basic rules and procedures to follow in developing various cognitive item formats so that they produce data that are as valid and reliable as possible. Many books, book chapters, and journal articles provide rules, tips, and guidelines for writing the most common types of test items. I cannot possibly summarize here all that measurement experts have written on this subject. Instead, I present and illustrate some of the guidelines that I think are most important for you to apply in your own item development. I have culled these guidelines from a variety of sources, which I encourage you to consult if you want to further your understanding of test development processes: Carey (1994), Glover and Bruning (1990), Hopkins (1998), Nitko (1996), and Salvia and Ysseldyke (1998).

Guidelines for Developing Objectively Scored Cognitive Items

Objectively scored cognitive items are the most difficult to prepare because the stimulus must cue learners to a single, predetermined correct response without giving them excessive assistance. This balancing act is most difficult to achieve with objective items that have selection formats: multiple choice, true-false, matching, and completion.

■ **Multiple-Choice Items**   Although multiple-choice items are often criticized and maligned, they remain one of the most useful and versatile of all assessment tools. Contrary to popular opinion, well-written multiple-choice items can assess both the recall of verbal information and the application of complex intellectual skills. They also provide excellent control for guessing, cover a large range of instructional goals in a short amount of time, and are very easy to score (Anastasi, 1988; Carey, 1994). Computer software packages that store teachers' multiple-choice questions electronically then permit them to construct tests by choosing questions desired from the item bank. These time-saving programs are readily available and easily accessible (see the resources section at the end of the chapter for specific programs).

Multiple-choice items have two major parts: the *stem* and the *alternatives*. The stem presents the question, and the alternatives provide a set of responses from which the learner selects one answer to the question. For multiple-choice items to function properly, one alternative must be clearly correct and the remaining alternatives (called *foils* or *distracters*) must be reasonable or plausible to ensure that students are actually responding based on their learned capabilities. If students can easily eliminate two or three obviously incorrect distracters, the item fails to assess what they have actually learned. Here are some basic rules for developing effective multiple-choice items:

1. Write the stem as a clearly focused, direct question.
2. Place as much of the problem or question in the stem so that the alternatives do not become excessively long.
3. State redundant information only once in the stem so that words and phrases are not repeated in each of the alternatives.
4. Restrict the number of alternatives to four or five.
5. Create alternatives that are mutually exclusive.
6. Write alternatives that have the same length, sentence structure, and grammatical features. Do not call attention to any particular alternative (either the correct answer or the distracters) by making it obviously different from the others.
7. Make distracters plausible by basing them on misconceptions or errors that students commonly exhibit.
8. Use "none of the above" and "all of the above" sparingly. If they are used as correct answers for some items, be sure to include some items for which these alternatives are not correct.
9. Do not include alternatives that represent combinations of prior alternatives, creating a test of logical thinking ability (e.g., *a* and *b*, *a* or *c*, *a* and *b* or *c*).

Let's see how some of these rules apply to a specific example. Here is a multiple-choice item that I might write to assess your understanding of reliability. Can you identify any rules that are violated?

1. *Reliability*
   a. *is a feature of assessment data that is essential.*
   b. *is a feature of assessment data that is not necessary for valid decision making.*
   c. *is a feature of assessment data that represents the degree to which we can depend on the data to be dependable, consistent, and trustworthy.*
   d. *increases as measurement error increases.*

First, the stem does not provide a clear question (rule 1). Second, more than one statement is true (rule 5) because *a* and *c* are not mutually exclusive. Rule 3 is violated because in the first three alternatives, the same phrase, "is a feature of assessment data that," is repeated. This phrase should be incorporated into the stem so that it is stated only once ("Reliability is a feature of assessment data that . . . "). Finally, notice that *c* is much longer than the other three alternatives and that *d* does not begin with the same phrase as the other three alternatives do (rule 6). I must admit that this is a very poorly written multiple-choice item. Let's see if I can improve it:

2. *Which of the following assessments has the potential to yield the most reliable data?*
   a. *two-question extended-essay test*
   b. *four-question short-answer test*
   c. *fifteen-item true-false test*
   d. *fifty-item multiple-choice test*

Notice first that the stem focuses on a specific question. Although you will select your response, you must apply one or more intellectual skills to do so. Notice also that all of the alternatives possess a similar structure. Your attention was not drawn to any of the three distracters or the correct alternative because of significant differences in length, grammar, or wording. I developed these alternatives so that your selection would be based primarily on your ability to apply reliability principles. That, after all, is the reason for the assessment. By the way, *d* is the correct answer. Can you explain why?

■ **True-False Items**   Effective true-false items are difficult to construct because learners often focus on the form of the statements rather than their content (Hopkins, 1998). True-false items present statements that learners can determine to be correct or incorrect based on their acquired verbal information or an intellectual skill rather than some insignificant, superficial feature. Here are some basic rules to help accomplish this goal:

1. Write items so that the statements are definitely true or false.
2. Avoid using qualifying terms and phrases such as *always, never, often,* or *usually.*
3. Avoid using negatives and double negatives in the statements.
4. Avoid overly complex statements that contain two or more major ideas.
5. Do not write false statements by changing one trivial word or feature of a true statement.
6. Make true statements the same approximate length as false statements.
7. Have approximately equal numbers of true statements and false statements, organized so that there is no discernible pattern of responses (e.g., T T F F T T F F).
8. When appropriate for the types of statements, use responses other than "true" and "false" (e.g., yes-no, right-wrong, correct-incorrect).

Here are some true-false items to assess your understanding of reliability and validity. Have I violated any of the preceding rules?

1. *T   F   Reliability is not unnecessary for valid decision making.*
2. *T   F   Objectively scored test items usually produce more reliable data than subjectively scored test items.*
3. *T   F   True-false items should never be used to assess the application of intellectual skills.*
4. *T   F   Performance items yield more valid data than cognitive test items do.*
5. *T   F   Measurement error is produced by variables that are extraneous to the characteristic being assessed and increases the reliability of assessment data.*

The form of the first item makes it excruciatingly difficult because of the double negative (rule 3). In the second and third items, the qualifiers *usually* and *never* may have tipped you off to the correct answers (rule 2). The fourth item is neither clearly true nor false (rule 1), and the fifth item is a statement that presents two ideas, one true and the other false (rule 4). Does half of the statement's being false make the entire statement false? If you give me a second chance, I will try to improve the five items:

1. *T   F   Reliable data are essential for valid decision making.*
2. *T   F   Subjective items can be scored more reliably than objective items.*
3. *T   F   True-false items can be used to assess the application of intellectual skills.*
4. *T   F   Performance items yield more valid data than cognitive test items do when assessing motor skills.*
5. *T   F   Reliability increases as measurement error increases.*

In addition to fixing each of the five items by applying the particular rule that was violated, I also made sure there were approximately equal numbers of true (1, 3, 4) and false (2, 5) statements so there was no discernible pattern (T F T T F).

■ **Matching**   Matching items are most useful for assessing verbal information and conceptual associations. We structure matching items by developing two columns of information that can be associated on the basis of some underlying concept or set of propositions. The information in one column (usually the left) is the *stem.* The information in the other column (usually the right) are the *responses.* Here are some basic rules for constructing the stems and responses of matching items:

1. Present a list of conceptually similar stimuli in each column.
2. In the directions, clearly explain to learners the basis for matching.
3. Provide unequal numbers of stimuli in the stem and response columns.
4. In the directions, inform learners that they can use any response once, more than once, or not at all.
5. Use numbers to label stimuli in the stem and letters to label responses.
6. Present the stimuli in each column in a logical, organized manner (e.g., alphabetically, chronologically).
7. Limit the length of each column to approximately ten stimuli.

Try the following matching item. Did I break any rules?

Match the following:

1. _____ Verbal information		1. apply
2. _____ Psychomotor skills		2. knowing how to
3. _____ Declarative knowledge		3. identify
4. _____ Rules and principles		4. stable behavior change
5. _____ Cognitive strategies		5. discriminate
6. _____ Procedural knowledge		6. knowing that
7. _____ Attitudes		7. originate
8. _____ Concepts		8. execute
9. _____ Discriminations		9. state
10. _____ Learning		10. choose

I hope you agree with me that this poorly written matching item does not reliably assess your knowledge of learning outcomes and their capability verbs. The first problem is that the directions do not tell you why the stimuli in the two columns are related to each other (rule 2). A second problem is that the item mixes pieces of information from more than one conceptual category (rule 1). Because of the equal numbers of stimuli in each column (rule 3), the set of ten is reduced to nine due to the process of elimination. Further problems with the item include the use of numbers to label both columns (rule 5) and the random arrangement of stimuli in both columns (rule 6). Let's try it again with the following new and improved item:

Match the learning outcomes in Column A with their corresponding capability verbs in Column B. Write the letter of the capability verb beside its learning outcome. You may use each verb in Column B only once.

A	B
1. _____ Attitudes	a. analyze
2. _____ Cognitive strategies	b. apply
3. _____ Concepts	c. choose
4. _____ Discriminations	d. discriminate
5. _____ Psychomotor skills	e. execute
6. _____ Rules and principles	f. evaluate
7. _____ Verbal information	g. identify
	h. originate
	i. practice
	j. state

In the improved version, both columns are organized alphabetically, and the two columns are labeled with numbers and letters to avoid confusion. The directions clearly explain the basis for matching. The item is a more reliable indicator of learning because Column B provides more responses than you actually need, so you have to differentiate carefully between words that are capability verbs and those that are not.

Completion   Let's turn our attention now to an objectively scored item that has a production format. In a completion item, learners write a specific word or phrase from memory that completes a sentence or corresponds to a stimulus. The greatest challenge in writing effective completion items is developing directions and stimuli that cue learners to produce the specific response that is desired, with no possibility for an alternative response that also could be considered correct. Here are some guidelines to help you write effective completion items:

1. Whenever possible, use direct questions rather than incomplete sentences.
2. Place blank lines close to the ends of questions or sentences.
3. Use only one blank line for each item.
4. Make all blank lines the same length.
5. Clearly tell learners the form that their responses should take (e.g., single word, phrase).
6. Avoid providing grammatical cues to correct responses.
7. Ask learners to produce important terms, concepts, and ideas rather than trivial, insignificant information.

Let's see if you can answer the following (poorly written) completion items correctly. More important, see if you can detect any violations of the preceding rules:

1. *_____ is the degree to which our _____ are appropriate based on assessment _____ .*
2. *A statement that describes what learners should be able to do as a result of instruction is an _____ _____ .*

The answers to the first question are "validity," "decisions," and "data," respectively. If you did not produce these three responses, it is probably because there were too many blanks in the question (rule 3), making it nearly impossible to figure out what I was asking you to recall. Furthermore, the blank line at the beginning of the statement provides no meaningful context to help cue your memory (rule 2). The answer to the second item is "instructional goal." I inadvertently provided three extra clues to help you produce this response. First, notice that "an" is a tip-off that the correct response begins with a vowel (only five possibilities here!), violating rule 6. Second, the two lines that are provided let you know that the correct response has two specific words. To make matters worse, the first line is long for the longer word, "instructional," and the second line is short for the shorter word, "goal," violating rule 4. Let's fix the two items:

1. *The degree to which our instructional decisions are appropriate based on the assessment data we have collected is referred to as* _____.

2. *A statement that describes what learners should be able to do as a result of instruction is a(n)* _____.

   OR

   What is a statement called that describes what learners should be able to do as a result of instruction? _____

I improved the first item by using only one blank placed at the end of the sentence. I improved the second item by using "a(n)" rather than "an," removing the vowel cue, and by changing the two blank lines of unequal length to a single line (revised item 2). I also improved the second item by framing it as a direct question, with a blank line provided for the response.

Thus far, we have been examining rules for developing the assessment items that are the most difficult to write. However, the effort we invest in writing these items results in faster, easier, more objective scoring. Now let's take a look at guidelines for developing items that are easier to write but more difficult to score reliably.

Guidelines for Developing Subjectively Scored Cognitive Items

Short-answer and extended-essay items require learners to produce a response to a question or set of directions. Whereas students can usually respond to short-answer questions with a few sentences or a paragraph, extended essays may require several interrelated paragraphs that fill several handwritten (or word-processed) pages. Both types of items also can be adapted to an oral format, provided we have the time to assess students individually.

■ **Writing Short-Answer and Essay Items**   The question or directions must be clear enough to focus learners on the facts they need to state or the skills they need to apply without providing them with unnecessary cues. Furthermore, the stimulus should be constructed in such a way that it helps us evaluate the quality of learners' responses with respect to the learned capabilities we are assessing. Here are some basic guidelines to help you write effective items that meet these criteria:

1. Focus the question on the specific information to be recalled or intellectual skills to be applied.
2. Establish clear limits on the breadth and depth of students' responses.
3. Clearly specify the organizational structure that students' responses should follow.
4. Specify the relative weight in scoring that each part of the response will receive.
5. Use more short-answer questions and fewer extended-essay questions to maximize content sampling.

6. Do not use optional questions.
7. Establish a systematic scoring procedure to maximize scoring reliability.

Let's see how the following essay question measures up to the guidelines:

1. Discuss reliability and validity. (15 points)

The question, I hope you will agree, is terrible. As a student responding to the question, you do not know what specific information concerning reliability and validity you are to discuss (rule 1), and the question does not let you know if you are expected to produce a paragraph, a page, or a book (rule 2). Furthermore, the question does not suggest any kind of organizational structure for you to follow (rule 3), and no scoring procedure is provided (rule 7).

The difficulty for students in responding to this type of ambiguous question eventually translates into a scoring nightmare for the teacher. With no clear expectations, learners are free to write *anything* about the topic, producing such wide variations in their responses that evaluating the quality consistently is extremely difficult. To counter the threats to scoring reliability that are inherent in short-answer and essay questions, we need to construct the question clearly and develop scoring criteria in advance. First, let me clarify the question, and then we will focus on scoring criteria. Here is a new-and-improved version of the question:

1. Demonstrate the importance of reliability and validity to instructional assessment by (a) defining each term in your own words, (b) explaining how the two terms are related to each other, and (c) illustrating how the two terms are related with a concrete classroom assessment scenario. Your example must be different from any used in class or in your textbook, and you need to explain clearly how the features of your scenario illustrate the relationship. Write your responses in the spaces provided below. (15 points)

a. Define the terms validity *and* reliability. *(2 points each)*

validity

reliability

b. Explain the relationship. (4 points)

c. Illustrate relationship with examples and explanations. (7 points)

The revised question leaves nothing to chance. You are now aware of the specific points you must address in your discussion of reliability and validity. Notice how the question also provides explicit guidance for constructing the response. Not only do the extra cues remind you of the specific points you are to address, they will eventually help me find the critical features of learning that are being assessed, saving scoring time and enhancing reliability.

■ **Scoring Short-Answer and Essay Items**   In addition to writing and structuring the question clearly, we also need to establish the scoring criteria for evaluating the quality of student responses. Notice in my revised question that I have decided in advance how the 15 total points will be allocated among the three major components of students' responses. Although this is an important first step, I still must think about each component and specify clearly the features that must be present and how I will assign point values to the quality of those features. For example, I may decide to allocate the 7 points for *part c* as follows:

Feature	Point Values
Concreteness of scenario (1 point possible)	0–general 1–specific
Familiarity of scenario (2 points possible)	0–example from class or book 1–example close to one from class or book 2–example clearly different from class or book
Validity–reliability relationship (3 points possible)	0–principle is not applicable to example 1–validity or reliability is clearly illustrated 2–both validity and reliability are illustrated 3–validity and reliability are interrelated according to principle
Explanations of features (1 point possible)	0–features of situation not related to principle 1–relation of features to principle clearly explained

This scoring scheme will help to ensure that I look for the same features in each student response I evaluate and that I allocate points in a consistent manner across all students. The procedure enhances fairness in evaluation and, most important, improves scoring reliability because it reduces the degree of subjective judgment I need to exercise.

Scoring student responses by comparing them to a set of specific criteria is called **analytical scoring** (Carey, 1994). Recently many educators have begun to refer to analytical scoring procedures as **rubrics** (Popham, 1999). The alternative to analytical scoring is **holistic scoring**, which occurs when we try to assign a single number to reflect the quality of the response as a whole (also called global scoring). For example, if we were to score students' responses to the revised validity-reliability question, we would read each answer and try to put it on a scale from zero to 15. Does that sound difficult? You bet it is! Reducing a complex written response to a single number is exceedingly hard to do consistently from student to student. Therefore, as you would expect, holistic scoring is severely unreliable. Although analytical scoring procedures can help improve the reliability of scores, they do not completely remove the element of subjective judgment that is required for evaluating short-answer and essay responses. We will return to principles of analytical scoring when we examine performance assessments in the next section.

We have been looking at guidelines and principles for constructing a wide variety of cognitive test items so that they yield assessment data that are as valid and reliable as possible. Before moving on to consider the other two categories of assessment tools, performance and attitude items, I invite you to practice applying the guidelines that we have just examined in Exercise 5.1 from your *Student Exercise Guide*.

Developing Performance and Attitude Assessments

To assess some instructional goals, we must do more than ask students questions about their newly acquired verbal information or skills. We often need to create realistic performance opportunities in which they apply new information and skills in complex ways, and sometimes we need to ascertain their level of emotional commitment toward an attitude object. In this section, we explore principles and procedures to help develop effective assessment items for these types of learning outcomes.

Rules and Procedures for Developing Performance Items

Using complex performances for the purpose of evaluating learners often is referred to as "authentic assessment" (Wiggins, 1989). I deliberately avoid the use of this term in our discussion of assessment because it is misleading and divisive. No assessment procedure is "authentic" in the sense that it produces perfectly valid information on internal learning products. Referring to one class of assessment procedures as "authentic," implying that all others are somehow "unauthentic" or artificial, may unnecessarily restrict the data collection processes we choose to implement. As the debate rages over the meaning and appropriateness of the term *authentic assessment* (see Terwilliger, 1997, 1998), I prefer to use a more neutral, descriptive term: *performance assessment.* Furthermore, as Hambleton (1996) notes, this term has been used effectively for quite some time in discussions of psychological and educational testing.

Types of Performance Items   Performance items can take a wide variety of forms, including individual projects, group projects, oral presentations, written essays, experiments, demonstrations, and portfolios (Rudner & Boston, 1994). Performance assessments are often appealing to teachers because they provide a rich variety of response modes that can be matched to the diverse interests, preferences, capabilities, and cultural perspectives of students. However, despite their intuitive appeal, performance assessments are vulnerable to the same types of validity and reliability concerns that plague traditional test items (Hambleton, 1996; Shavelson, Baxter, & Pine, 1992; Swanson, Norman, & Linn, 1995).

Almost any activity that occurs in a somewhat realistic performance context can be considered a performance item if its purpose is to assess the quality of learning that students have achieved. When we design and implement performance items, we must always remember that the ultimate goal is to *evaluate* student learning—not just provide students with an interesting, realistic activity. We need to construct performance items to ensure that students actually recall and apply the information and skills that were the focus of instruction. Furthermore, we need to evaluate students' performance on the basis of how well they recall and apply the information and skills that were the focus of instruction. Regardless of the specific activity, these two issues—construction and evaluation—have significant implications for the procedures used to develop performance items.

Constructing Performance Items   The performance item itself is the set of directions that learners will need to guide their activity. Just as for short-answer and essay questions, the directions need to be written so that students will perform in a way that reflects the learning to be assessed. Therefore, when developing the directions, we must determine the information or skills we will be looking for in the resulting performance and clearly focus students' attention on them. We do not want to be in the position of observing an inadequate performance—one that does not reflect the intended learning outcomes—because the student did not understand clearly what learning outcomes were supposed to be applied to the performance.

When preparing the directions for a performance item, we also need to consider the type of outcome that we intend to evaluate. Some performance items evaluate the quality of the *process* that learners demonstrate. Process evaluation focuses on how well learners produce or engage in specific learned actions. For the instructional goal, *Recite Lincoln's Gettysburg Address,* we would need to be prepared to judge the accuracy with which learners recalled the specific words and the expression they used to deliver the words. Following delivery, there would be no tangible evidence of the performance or any concrete materials that could be examined further.

Some learner performances do lead to tangible, concrete *products* that endure beyond the processes that create them and can be evaluated independently of those processes. Sometimes we can use the quality of a concrete product to infer the quality of the learned processes that created it. For the instructional goal, *Create a set of original sonnets,* we would evaluate students' written sonnets on specified rules of sonnet writing. If students have learned the rules, their learning should be apparent in the quality of the product—their sonnets. We would not have to watch students as they engage in the process of writing sonnets to evaluate their learning of sonnet writing rules.

For some instructional goals, we may need to evaluate both the process and product of a performance. Consider the instructional goal, *Execute basketball foul shots.* It is possible to make a foul shot without using the correct form for the motor skill, and it is possible to exhibit the correct form and not make the shot. Therefore, in addition to judging the accuracy of students' foul shooting by counting the number of shots they make (*product evaluation*), we would also need to evaluate how well students are using the appropriate form as they take each shot (*process evaluation*).

The point of distinguishing between process and product evaluation is so that we can specify in advance the particular aspects of the performance that we intend to evaluate. Then we can develop directions and guidelines for learners that communicate the appropriate expectations. The guidelines that I provided for writing short-answer and essay questions apply equally well to writing directions for performance items. In addition, depending on how complex the performance is, the directions should provide information concerning the following questions that students are likely to have:

1. What materials or equipment may be used?
2. What materials or equipment are available?
3. How much time will be provided for preparation?
4. How much time will be provided for the performance?
5. Who will observe the performance?
6. What types of assistance from others are permissible, if any?

Here is a sample performance item that might be appropriate for you, since you are learning about test item construction. Is the item written appropriately?

Directions: Prepare a test of objectively scored items.

As I think you would agree, the item suffers seriously from a lack of guidance. Probably a number of questions are running through your mind concerning the details of your performance: How many items should the test have? What should the content of the items be? Will I have to develop instructional goals, or will they be provided? Do I need to provide the correct answer for each item? Do I have to hand in a table of specifications along with the test? Does it need to be typed? When is it due? Questions, questions, questions! Let's try writing the item again so that these ambiguities are avoided:

Directions: To demonstrate your ability to apply test construction rules and principles, you need to prepare an objectively scored test. Your test must consist of 20 objectively scored cognitive items, allocated as follows:

1. *Multiple choice (5 items)*
2. *True-false (5 items)*
3. *Completion (5 items)*
4. *Matching (1 item with 5 stimuli in the stem)*

The content of the questions will be taken from a social studies textbook chapter and 15 instructional goals that will be provided to you. Submit your typed test with the correct answers for each item. Label each item with the number of the instructional goal that it is intended to assess. Your test will be evaluated on how well you have applied the rules for writing objectively scored cognitive items and the degree of validity each of your items possesses for its corresponding instructional goal (see accompanying rating sheets). You need to work individually on this project, so see me, not your friends, for answers to any questions you have. I will provide you with 20 minutes of class time on each of the next five days to work on your test. All tests are due at the beginning of class next Friday, October 17.

Because the outcome that will be evaluated in this case is a product (written test items), the revised directions describe in detail the characteristics that the product should have. If in preparing your test you adhere to the guidelines, I should be able to evaluate your product for the evidence of learning I desire. Notice how I deliberately structured the guidelines to ensure that I would be able to evaluate the validity of each item on the test. I explicitly told you to indicate the number of the instructional goal for which each item is intended. This will eliminate a lot of guesswork on my part when scoring the final products, boosting the reliability of the data.

When you write the directions for all the varied performance items you may construct in the future, be sure to apply two critical rules illustrated by the preceding example:

1. Write the directions to ensure that your learners apply the skills you want to evaluate.
2. Write the directions to ensure that you will be able to find clear evidence that your learners have applied the skills you want to evaluate.

Some performance assessments require careful observation, judgment, and record-keeping while students are in action.

■ **Scoring Performance Items**   Writing the directions for performance items is the easy part; scoring students' responses is the hard part! As noted in Figure 5.1, three major types of scoring procedures are available to us, depending on the precise nature of the performance we are assessing: frequency counts, checklists, and rating scales. Each of these scoring tools can help us overcome the hazards of holistic scoring. It is difficult to reduce the quality of a complex performance to a single number without compromising the reliability of the scores. What should we do, for example, if one of our basketball learners makes several foul shots but demonstrates incorrect form? What if a student who executes the form flawlessly misses every single shot? In such cases, we can get a clearer, more reliable assessment by separating the component features that contribute significantly to the quality of the overall performance. As we already have noted, separating the features of a complex performance so that we can evaluate them independently is called *analytical scoring*. Let's see how frequency counts, checklists, and rating scales can function as analytical scoring devices (or rubrics) to enhance scoring reliability.

Frequency counts are most useful when the performance yields an action or product with features that we can easily count. A **frequency count** is simply a record of the number of times we observe a specified feature of the performance. In assessing foul-shooting ability, we might count the number of times the ball goes through the hoop as an index of product quality. In assessing the delivery of a persuasive speech, we might count the number of times the student loses eye contact with the audience, pauses to say "umm," or uses an inappropriate slang expression. As you can see, frequency counts are limited to features of a performance that can be identified objectively. To be counted accurately, the feature is either there or it isn't.

Rarely can an entire complex performance be reduced to the simple frequency count of a single feature. Usually we select component features within the entire process or product to count. In either case, we can improve scoring reliability by clearly writing the feature we are going to count and devising a system for keeping track of the number of times it occurs. For example, a sheet with each student's name and a column to place a tally for each "umm" or slang word would help us obtain a reliable frequency count for speech delivery skills.

When a performance has a number of objectively interpreted features that can be specified clearly, a checklist is the appropriate scoring tool. A **checklist** is a list of critical performance features with an accompanying space to note the presence or absence of each feature. Earlier you saw a performance item for preparing an objectively scored test. Here is a sample checklist that I might use to help me evaluate the quality of the tests my students create for that item:

Yes	*No*	*Feature*
✓		1. 5 multiple-choice items
✓		2. 5 true-false items
✓		3. 5 completion items
✓		4. 1 matching item with 5 stimuli
	✓	5. Correct answers provided for all questions
✓		6. Number of instructional goal provided for all questions
10/12		TOTAL SCORE

The checklist clearly specifies the features that I am looking for in each student's test, helping me to maintain consistency throughout my scoring. The checklist also provides a place for me to indicate in writing whether I actually observe each feature, so I do not have to try to remember which features I do and do not see, also enhancing the consistency of my scoring. Notice that the checklist helps me transform my observations into precise quantitative data to assist with the evaluation process. If each feature in the example is assigned a value of 2 points, then observing five of the six possible features translates into a score of 10 points out of a total of 12 possible points, or 83 percent.

The major limitation of using checklists to score performance items is that they are restricted to easily discernible features that can be judged to be present or not present. Many aspects of learner performance cannot be judged as yes-no, present-absent, adequate-inadequate, satisfactory-unsatisfactory, and so on. What if, for example, I include the following feature in my checklist:

Yes	*No*	*Feature*
		7. All items are valid for their instructional goals

The validity of each item on your test is likely to be a matter of *degree* rather than a feature that is absolutely present or absent. I will need to look at each item and judge how valid it is for its corresponding instructional goal. I can be more precise in my scoring (and therefore more reliable) if I can report varying degrees of quality rather than trying to make an artificial yes-no, black-and-white judgment.

Rating scales are a form of analytical scoring that can help in judging the degree of quality in a set of performance features. A **rating scale** is a list of performance features with an accompanying numeric scale to record each feature's degree of quality. Here is a sample rating scale that would help me evaluate the validity feature (number 7) on the checklist:

Low	*Moderate*	*High*	*Feature*
0	1	2	Validity of multiple-choice item 1
0	1	2	Validity of multiple-choice item 2
0	1	2	Validity of true-false item 1
0	1	2	Validity of true-false item 2

This rating scale would help me place each item on a 3-point scale (from 0 points to 2 points) to indicate the degree of validity (low, moderate, high) I judge it to possess. Notice that the rating scale does not remove the burden of judgment from my scoring. It simply structures and organizes my judgments so that they are more consistent, systematic, and meaningful than they might otherwise be. I still have to make subjective judgments about what "low," "moderate," and "high" mean from item to item and student to student.

One way to ensure that my meaning for these three terms does not change is to build the meanings of the terms into the scale itself. I could analyze each feature into specific aspects of validity and describe the specific criteria that need to be met for certain point values to be assigned. Here is an example:

Item Validity	*Action Consistency*	*Content Consistency*
Multiple-choice item 1	0–no relationship to capability verb 1–somewhat related to capability verb 2–clearly related to capability verb	0–no relationship to content 1–somewhat related to content 2–clearly related to content
True-false item 1	0–no relationship to capability verb 1–somewhat related to capability verb 2–clearly related to capability verb	0–no relationship to content 1–somewhat related to content 2–clearly related to content

Although this rating scale achieves greater precision than the first one, it does not completely remove scorer subjectivity because I still have to judge the meanings of "no relationship," "somewhat related," and "clearly related." An action that I consider to be "somewhat related" could very well be "clearly related" in the eyes of a different scorer.

Now that we have examined three major approaches to analytical scoring, let's put them all together to create a sample scoring sheet that I could use to evaluate the test construction performance item (see Table 5.3). Notice that the sample contains the characteristics of both checklists and rating scales because some features can be evaluated based on their presence or absence, whereas others must be evaluated on the degree of quality they are judged to possess.

■ **The Value of Analytical Scoring**   Rating scales and the other types of analytical scoring are valuable primarily because they help us minimize the degree of measurement error in our scoring. However, analytical scoring procedures can support important aspects of the learning process as well. By developing analytical scoring procedures and sharing them with our students in advance, we empower them to develop their own strategies for achieving the criteria, monitor their progress toward the criteria, and regulate their own goal-directed actions.

A second learning-related benefit of analytical scoring is that we can use such procedures to give students detailed feedback. Because frequency counts, checklists, and rating scales identify the specific features of the performance that we have observed and evaluated, learners can use the data recorded on the forms to determine their own specific strengths and weaknesses. Teachers often can use analytical scoring results to deliver informative feedback efficiently to large numbers of students.

■ **Using Portfolios as Performance Assessment**   Portfolios are a special type of performance assessment that have gained in popularity. A **portfolio** is a collection of concrete pieces of evidence that suggest or demonstrate a student's skills and abilities (Crockett, 1998). A wide variety of specific types of performance evidence can be included in student portfolios: notes, drafts, journal entries, drawings, photographs, audiotapes, videotapes, models, computer disks, ratings and observations by others, interview transcripts, and so on. By collecting such products, students can analyze and reflect on their progress in attaining significant learning outcomes. Teachers can use the products collected in portfolios as performance data for assessment and evaluation purposes.

To serve a useful assessment function, portfolios should possess three critical components (Barton & Collins, 1997):

1. *Purpose.* Teachers must determine the specific learning outcomes (or instructional goals) that the portfolio is to address.

2. *Evidence.* The types of evidence that best relate to the purpose need to be identified. A portfolio is not just a collection of student-generated materials in a manila folder. It is a carefully selected set of materials that will provide clear evidence of learning.

3. *Assessment criteria.* This component refers to clearly established guidelines for translating portfolio materials into valid and reliable data to permit appropriate evaluation decisions. Because of the degree of subjectivity required of teachers as they score or evaluate student portfolios, clear scoring guidelines (i.e., rubrics, rating scales, checklists) must be established.

Assessing a portfolio is just as problematic and challenging as scoring any other type of performance assessment. Although portfolios and other performance assessments may offer a more valid look at student abilities, we cannot automatically assume that they also produce data that are more reliable (White, 1994). In fact, researchers have demonstrated consistently that the reliability levels of portfolio scores are significantly lower than those generally acceptable for sound educational decision making (Baxter, Shavelson, Goldman, & Pine, 1992; Camp, 1993; Linn & Burton, 1994). To enhance the reliability of portfolio assessment data, you should design analytical scoring procedures in the same way that you would develop them for other types of performance assessment.

LET'S SUMMARIZE

Performance assessments can be potentially valuable data collection tools for certain types of learning outcomes. However, for these items to function well, we must select the activities carefully and prepare analytical scoring procedures to enhance scoring reliability. Before we move on to the last major set of assessment tools, attitude assessment, see if you can apply your new performance assessment skills in Exercise 5.2 in the *Student Exercise Guide.*

Assessing Attitudes

Attitudinal learning outcomes are the most challenging internal learning products for teachers to assess. One reason for the difficulty is that attitudes are complex internal states that comprise three variables: emotions, cognitions, and voluntary behavior. Assessing any one of these three components can give some information concerning learners' attitudes but not necessarily the complete picture. Although there are no perfect ways to assess attitudes, we do have some useful tools that can help.

■ **Focusing on Voluntary Behaviors**   The most critical aspect of attitude assessment is voluntary behavior. You may recall from Chapter 3 our analysis of the attitudinal instructional goal, *Choose to plan and implement a personal physical fitness strategy.* After engaging learners in a variety of activities and experiences designed to promote a positive attitude toward personal physical fitness, how would we determine if the instructional goal had in fact been achieved? From the wording of the instructional goal itself, the best possible approach would be to observe whether learners actually developed their own fitness strategies, began eating and exercising in ways that were consistent with their strategies, and stayed committed to carrying out their strategies for a substantial period of time. A student who rushes home after school, creates a written plan by applying fitness rules and principles, and then eats and exercises religiously for the next ten years according to the plan is clearly demonstrating the target attitude.

Table 5.3
Analytical Scoring Procedure for a Performance Item

Test Construction   Name: _____

A. Multiple-Choice Items

0 1   five items presented

0 1   correct answer provided for each item

0 1   number of instructional goal provided for each item

Item Validity:	Action consistency	Content consistency
	0–no relationship to capability verb 1–somewhat related to capability verb 2–clearly related to capability verb	0–no relationship to content 1–somewhat related to content 2–clearly related to content
Item Construction:	0–more than four rule violations 1–four rule violations 2–three rule violations	3–two rule violations 4–one rule violation 5–no rule violations

Total Points = ___ / 12

B. True-False Items

0 1   five items presented

0 1   correct answer provided for each item

0 1   number of instructional goal provided for each item

Item Validity:	Action consistency	Content consistency
	0–no relationship to capability verb 1–somewhat related to capability verb 2–clearly related to capability verb	0–no relationship to content 1–somewhat related to content 2–clearly related to content
Item Construction:	0–more than four rule violations 1–four rule violations 2–three rule violations	3–two rule violations 4–one rule violation 5–no rule violations

Total Points = ___ / 12

Unfortunately, observing students' voluntary behaviors outside the classroom is virtually impossible. We could circumvent the problem by requiring students to develop a plan that they would submit for evaluation in school, creating physical exercise times during the school day, and monitoring what students eat at lunch. However, building these opportunities and requirements into the students' school day would damage the voluntary aspect of their behavior, which is critical for inferring the presence of an attitude. Students must

Table 5.3
Analytical Scoring Procedure for a Performance Item *(continued)*

C. Completetion Items

0 1   five items presented
0 1   correct answer provided for each item
0 1   number of instructional goal provided for each item

Item Validity:	Action consistency	Content consistency
	0–no relationship to capability verb 1–somewhat related to capability verb 2–clearly related to capability verb	0–no relationship to content 1–somewhat related to content 2–clearly related to content
Item Construction:	0–more than four rule violations 1–four rule violations 2–three rule violations	3–two rule violations 4–one rule violation 5–no rule violations

Total Points = ___ / 12

D. Matching Item

0 1   five stimuli presented
0 1   correct answer provided for each item
0 1   number of instructional goal provided for each item

Item Validity:	Action consistency	Content consistency
	0–no relationship to capability verb 1–somewhat related to capability verb 2–clearly related to capability verb	0–no relationship to content 1–somewhat related to content 2–clearly related to content
Item Construction:	0–more than four rule violations 1–four rule violations 2–three rule violations	3–two rule violations 4–one rule violation 5–no rule violations

Total Points = ___ / 12

Total Points Earned =
$$\frac{}{48} = \underline{}\%$$
Total Points Possible =   48

do more than exhibit the behavior described by the instructional goal. They must engage in the behavior for the right reasons and because they really want to do it.

We can assess the verbal information and intellectual skills that support voluntary behavior by applying the tools that we would use to measure any other verbal information or intellectual skill outcomes (see Table 5.4). Objectively scored and subjectively scored cognitive items can help us measure stu-

Table 5.4
Assessing the Components of Attitudes

Attitude Component	Instructional Goal	Assessment Tool
Verbal information	State foods that are high in carbohydrates, protein, and fat.	Cognitive items (objectively scored)
Verbal information	State and explain the health advantages of a strategic approach to personal fitness.	Cognitive items (subjectively scored)
Intellectual skill (rule)	Calculate daily caloric needs.	Cognitive items (objectively scored)
Cognitive strategy	Originate a written diet plan.	Performance item (product focus)
Intellectual skill (rule)	Monitor heart rate during aerobic exercise.	Performance item (process focus)

dents' abilities to recall facts concerning the attitude object and apply intellectual skills that support attitude-related target behaviors. We can even use performance assessments to evaluate supporting intellectual skills or cognitive strategies.

Even if learners can demonstrate all the instructional goals identified in Table 5.4, does that necessarily guarantee that they would _choose to plan and implement a personal physical fitness strategy_ or that they would have a positive emotional commitment to physical fitness? The answer, of course, is no. How, then, can we assess the actual behavioral component and its accompanying emotional commitment? With respect to assessing attitude-related emotion and voluntary behavior, we can take either a direct or indirect approach.

■ **Direct and Indirect Approaches to Attitude Assessment**   For the direct approach, we may be able to identify a voluntary behavior that we can actually observe in the classroom or school setting. After instruction on "kindness," for example, we could systematically record the number of acts of kindness students exhibited toward each other. After attempting to develop positive attitudes toward cooperation, we could place students in cooperative learning groups and observe the quality of their cooperation. Of course, for both of these assessment scenarios, we would need to have developed analytical data collection procedures to enhance the reliability of our observations. A frequency count of kind acts would help us make inferences about students' attitudes toward kindness, and applying a rating scale to students' behaviors while working in cooperative groups would provide data to help us evaluate their attitudes toward cooperation.

Still, it is quite difficult to identify behaviors that we can observe in a school setting. In these circumstances, we may need to take an indirect approach to attitude assessment. Rather than observing directly what learners do, we can ask them how they would behave and how they feel about the attitude object. Clearly this approach is not ideal because we know there often are discrepancies between what people say they would do and what they actually choose to do. Nevertheless, with carefully designed instruments, we can assess learners' feelings and anticipated actions and then use the measurements to make reasonable inferences about how likely they are to engage in the attitude-related target behaviors when opportunities arise.

Instruments that are used for this purpose usually take the form of self-report questionnaires and surveys. Three specific forms that such self-report assessments can take are (1) Thurstone scales, (2) Likert scales, and (3) semantic differential scales. Many fine books describe in great detail procedures for developing each of these types of scales (e.g., Hopkins, 1998; Perloff, 1993; Thorndike, 1997). My goal here is simply to introduce you to the general structure of each type of scale and provide some basic guidance to help you construct them for your own classroom use.

■ **Constructing Thurstone Scales** A Thurstone scale gives learners the opportunity to express their agreement or disagreement with opinion statements about an attitude object. To construct such a scale, we first need to develop statements that would reflect positive or negative feelings toward an attitude object. Then we build in a procedure for students to indicate whether they agree or disagree with each statement.

The sample Thurstone scale in Table 5.5 contains eight statements that are opinions concerning the usefulness of testing in the classroom. The scale contains a mixture of positively (testing is good) and negatively (testing is bad) worded statements. Agreeing with positive statements (numbers 1, 3, 6) and disagreeing with negative statements (numbers 2, 4, 5, 7, 8) would reflect a positive attitude toward the attitude object. I randomly ordered the positive and negative statements to ensure that you would think about each one separately.

How can I use the scale to measure your attitude toward testing? One simple approach would be to count the total number of agreements with positive items and disagreements with negative items. Dividing this number by the total number of statements yields a percentage that reflects the degree of commitment toward the attitude object. So, for example, if you agreed with numbers 1 and 3 and disagreed with numbers 2, 4, 5, and 8, you responded to 75 percent (6/8) of the statements in ways that are consistent with a positive attitude toward classroom testing. From this moderately high level of consistency, I might infer that the probability that you would actually choose to administer well-constructed tests on a regular basis in your own classroom would also be moderately high.

Although very useful, Thurstone scales have the same limitation as frequency counts and checklists because they force people to indicate complete agreement or disagreement, with no middle ground. Sometimes our level of agreement or disagreement is not absolute, but rather a matter of degree. Likert

Table 5.5
A Sample Thurstone Scale for Attitude Assessment

Directions: Read each statement about instructional assessment carefully. Circle **A** if you **agree** with the statement. Circle **D** if you **disagree** with the statement. There are no correct answers.

A	D	1. Teachers should give tests regularly to their students.
A	D	2. Testing creates too much anxiety in students to be useful.
A	D	3. Well-constructed tests can help teachers evaluate their students' learning.
A	D	4. Some learning outcomes cannot be assessed through testing.
A	D	5. Test results cannot be trusted.
A	D	6. Test results can help teachers improve their instruction.
A	D	7. Testing should be abolished.
A	D	8. Student evaluations of their own learning are more useful than test results.

scales overcome this limitation by providing the opportunity to express degrees of agreement or disagreement with attitude statements.

■ **Constructing Likert Scales** Likert scales ask people to express their level of agreement with opinion statements. As with Thurstone scales, we first develop a collection of positive and negative statements concerning the attitude object. Unlike the Thurstone scale, we then provide a range of responses to indicate the strength of agreement or disagreement, as illustrated in Table 5.6. Notice that the statements are exactly the same as those found in the Thurstone scale (Table 5.5). The only difference is that you now have five options from which to select rather than only two. Try this scale. If you find yourself selecting any of the three middle options, you will have demonstrated to yourself their value in uncovering varying shades of commitment.

In most cases, five options are adequate for a Likert scale, although seven levels of agreement can be used if there is a need to increase measurement precision. Likert scales have the potential to yield reliable information when the meaning of each response option is stated clearly, a mixture of positive and negative statements is presented, and the statements appear in random order so that people must think about each statement independently of the others.

To score the responses, each level of agreement can be transformed to a numeric scale. For example, for the Likert scale you just completed, I could set *strongly disagree* equal to 1, *disagree* = 2, *undecided* = 3, *agree* = 4, and *strongly agree* = 5. Now I have a five-point quantitative scale that I can use to compute average responses across all the items. The higher the average response is, the greater is the emotional commitment expressed toward classroom testing. Of course, for negatively worded items, I first need to reverse the direction of the numbers before including them in the average. Strong disagreement with a negative item would be the same as strong agreement with a positive item. For negative items, then, *strongly disagree* = 5, *agree* = 4, and so on. This procedure is referred to as *reverse scoring*. I illustrate the scoring of a Likert scale in Table 5.7.

Table 5.6
A Sample Likert Scale for Attitude Assessment

Directions: Read each statement about instructional assessment carefully. Indicate your level of agreement with each statement by circling the letter(s) that best expresses your personal view:

SD =	Strongly Disagree
D =	Disagree
U =	Undecided
A =	Agree
SA =	Strongly Agree

SD	D	U	A	SA	1. Teachers should give tests regularly to their students.
SD	D	U	A	SA	2. Testing creates too much anxiety in students to be useful.
SD	D	U	A	SA	3. Well-constructed tests can help teachers evaluate their students' learning.
SD	D	U	A	SA	4. Some learning outcomes cannot be assessed through testing.
SD	D	U	A	SA	5. Test results cannot be trusted.
SD	D	U	A	SA	6. Test results can help teachers improve their instruction.
SD	D	U	A	SA	7. Testing should be abolished.
SD	D	U	A	SA	8. Student evaluations of their own learning are more useful than test results.

Table 5.7
Scoring the Results from a Likert Scale

Positive Item Score	Negative Item Score	Scale		
1	5	SD	=	Strongly disagree
2	4	D	=	Disagree
3	3	U	=	Undecided
4	2	A	=	Agree
5	1	SA	=	Strongly agree

Scale					Score	Item
SD	D	U	A	**SA**	5	1. Teachers should give tests regularly to their students.
SD	**D**	U	A	SA	4*	2. Testing creates too much anxiety in students to be useful.
SD	D	U	A	**SA**	5	3. Well-constructed tests can help teachers evaluate their students' learning.
SD	D	**U**	A	SA	3*	4. Some learning outcomes cannot be assessed through testing.
SD	**D**	U	A	SA	4*	5. Test results cannot be trusted.
SD	D	U	A	**SA**	5	6. Test results can help teachers improve their instruction.
SD	D	U	A	SA	5*	7. Testing should be abolished.
SD	**D**	U	A	SA	4*	8. Student evaluations of their own learning are more useful than test results.
			Sum		35	(5 + 4 + 5 + 3 + 4 +5 + 5 + 4 = 35)
			Average		4.38	(35/8 = 4.38)

*reverse scored item

■ **Constructing Semantic Differential Scales**   A third useful approach to attitude assessment is a scale known as the **semantic differential**. The term *semantic differential* refers to the varying degrees of meaning as we move from one word to its extreme opposite. For example, *exciting* and *dull* are two words that represent a semantic differential because they are completely opposite in meaning. Each item on a semantic differential scale presents a pair of these types of bipolar, or opposite, adjectives that could be used to describe an attitude object, along with several degrees of different meaning between them.

Students respond to each item by indicating where their views of the attitude object fall along the continuum of meaning between the two extremes provided. Look at Table 5.8. Show where you would place yourself on each semantic continuum by circling the appropriate number. Notice that I randomly ordered the positive and negative adjectives presented in the word columns. As with Thurstone and Likert scales, random sequencing forces people to think about each pair of adjectives rather than simply circling an entire column of numbers without thinking about the feelings evoked by the adjectives. As for Likert scales, we can derive an overall score by averaging the responses across all the pairs of adjectives, using reverse scoring when necessary to keep all the items on the same scale.

A second way to construct a semantic differential scale is to present each item as a statement about the attitude object that students complete by indicating their position on the continuum between two opposite adjectives (see Table 5.9). With this procedure, we still provide the basic continuum between two opposite adjectives. The only difference is that we also provide a statement

Table 5.8
Illustration of a Semantic Differential Scale

Directions: Circle one of the numbers between each pair of adjectives to indicate your personal feelings toward classroom testing.

Classroom Testing

	1	2	3	4	5	
Bad	1	2	3	4	5	Good
Useful	1	2	3	4	5	Useless
Worthless	1	2	3	4	5	Worthwhile
Productive	1	2	3	4	5	Unproductive
Negative	1	2	3	4	5	Positive
Harmful	1	2	3	4	5	Beneficial
Reliable	1	2	3	4	5	Unreliable
Indefensible	1	2	3	4	5	Defensible

Table 5.9
A Sentence Completion Semantic Differential Scale

Directions: Circle the number that best indicates your personal position on each of the following statements concerning classroom testing.

1. Classroom testing is a process that is

Important	1	2	3	4	5	Unimportant

2. The results teachers obtain from testing their students are

Worthless	1	2	3	4	5	Valuable

3. The time that it takes for teachers to construct and score tests is

Productive	1	2	3	4	5	Unproductive

4. The effects of testing on the quality of teaching and learning are

Negative	1	2	3	4	5	Positive

to place each adjective pair in a meaningful context. The scoring of this scale would be identical to the process I already described for the other type of semantic differential scale.

LET'S SUMMARIZE

In this section we have seen that we can measure even complex performances and attitudes, as long as we construct an appropriate scoring scale. We must admit that none of the approaches to performance and attitude assessment we have described yield perfectly valid and reliable data from which we can draw inferences about learning with absolute confidence. However, in the absence of any other assessment alternative, they are the best procedures we have developed thus far. Before we conclude this chapter on assessment tools, let's look in on our three classroom teachers to see how they are making decisions about the types of assessment items that best fit their evaluation needs.

CASE ANALYSES

Selecting and Preparing Assessment Tools in the Classroom

In Chapters 2 and 3 we observed three teachers as they identified instructional goals, specified instructional content, and applied content analysis procedures. We now return to their classrooms to listen to them think about the types of assessment procedures that have the greatest potential to produce the best possible data for the evaluations of learning they eventually will need to make. As you read and study each case, notice that selecting and constructing assessment items is, above all, a *thinking* process.

TEACHER'S THINKING AND PLANNING

Assessing Principle and Verbal Information Outcomes

Teacher: Ms. Nelson
Grade level: 5
Subject: Science
Instructional Goal (principle): Demonstrate how the rate of cooling influences the size of a mineral crystal.
Instructional Goal (verbal information): State the names of the four major eras in the earth's history and several important characteristics of each.

Assessing a Principle Learning Outcome   How should I find out if my students can perform the instructional goal related to the crystal cooling principle? I need to create opportunities for them to apply the crystal cooling principle. I could take either a performance or a cognitive approach to my assessment strategy. For a performance approach, maybe I could have my students grow crystals under a variety of conditions. Then they would need to apply the principle to explain why some of their crystals are larger than others. I was already planning, however, to use some crystal growing activities to help my students acquire a meaningful understanding of the principle. If they simply repeat the same (or similar) activities, they might be able to explain different crystal sizes from memory rather than by applying the principle as a skill. Besides, the activity of growing the crystals is not what I need to assess. I only need to assess whether they can explain different crystal sizes in terms of different cooling rates.

Rather than taking the time to use performance assessment—especially when the results will have dubious validity—I think a cognitive approach would be ideal. I can create several scenarios involving different crystal sizes and ask my students to apply the principle by explaining in writing how the crystals came to be different sizes. I could also create problems to solve by applying the principle. Again, students would respond in writing to make their explanations and predictions. Because students will be providing open-ended responses to my scenarios, it will not be possible to anticipate exactly what they will say. Therefore, I cannot score their answers objectively and will need to be prepared to implement an analytical scoring procedure. Here is an example of the type of short-answer, subjectively scored cognitive item I could use:

> You and a friend decide to make rock candy by dissolving sugar in boiling water. Your friend wants to make really big sugar crystals, but you would rather make smaller candy crystals. Describe how you and your friend could make rock candy that has both large and small crystals. Make sure you describe exactly *what* you would do and *why* you would do it. (6 points)

To develop the rating scale to enhance my scoring reliability, I need to break down my students' responses into the specific features they need to demonstrate so that I have valid evidence of their applying the principle. Here is a possible analytical scoring scale:

a. Specific actions are described: 0 = no actions

    1 = vague actions

    2 = specific actions

b. Actions related to different cooling rates: 0 = no relationship

    1 = unclear relationship

    2 = clear relationship

c. Relative crystal size accurately predicted: 0 = no predictions

    1 = accurate predictions with no rationale

    2 = accurate predictions with reasons based on cooling rates

How many of these subjective application items will I need? To enhance reliability, I should have more than one, but I don't think I will need more than three, because the potential for careless errors is not great in these types of written responses. Furthermore, students will demonstrate their understanding of the principle by how well they use it in their rationale. So I won't need a lot of items to help me determine if they understand the reasons for their responses.

Assessing a Verbal Information Learning Outcome Now let me see if I can figure out a good assessment strategy for the verbal information goal. For this one, my students need to be able to retrieve the names of the earth's four major eras and several facts about each era. Because I am assessing a lot of factual information here, cognitive items probably would be most useful. If I place the assessment in the context of a more complex performance, it will be more difficult to determine if students can recall the names and propositions on their own.

I can save a lot of time in scoring and make my scoring more objective by using a matching format. I can place the four names on a sheet of paper and randomly list about fifteen facts beneath them—with several extra "facts" that do not belong in any era. Then students can place the letter of the fact under the correct category heading. Scoring will be objective and efficient because I'll just need to look to see if the correct letters are listed in each category. Administration will be efficient because students will not have to write out each fact. There's just one problem, though: This item does not validly assess my students' ability to recall the names of the eras, since I would provide them. Hmmm, how can I fix that problem? I could keep the format just as it is, but leave blank lines for the names of the categories. In that way, students will produce the names of the eras from memory and then select the facts that correspond to each era. Now I have a combination of completion and matching. Here is how the item would look:

Directions: On the blank lines provided, write the names of the earth's four major eras. Then write the letter of each fact that corresponds to an era below its name. Use each fact only once. There may be some facts that you cannot use.

_____ (era name) *facts*	_____ (era name) *facts*	_____ (era name) *facts*	_____ (era name) *facts*
____	____	____	____
____	____	____	____
____	____	____	____
____	____	____	____
____	____	____	____

a. Ferns and evergreens appeared
b. Rocky Mountains formed
c. Bacteria and algae were present
d. Ice ages and glaciers occurred
e. (etc.)

f. Humans appeared
g. Dinosaurs and reptiles dominated
h. Began 4500 million years ago
i. Contains Ordivician period
j. (etc.)

Assessing a Procedural Rule Learning Outcome

Teacher: Mrs. Torres
Grade level: 3
Subject: Mathematics
Instructional Goal: Apply the rules for rounding numbers to the nearest ten and hundred.

When my students apply the rounding algorithm, they will produce a numeral that is rounded either correctly or incorrectly. Therefore, I should be able to use objectively scored cognitive items for assessment. With arithmetic calculations, there is always the chance that students will make careless mistakes, so I need to provide an adequate number of opportunities to decrease the influence of measurement error. Perhaps ten opportunities to round to the nearest ten and ten chances to round to the nearest hundred will be adequate.

Sometimes people can get correct answers for algorithmic procedures, even though they haven't applied the algorithm correctly or do not understand why the algorithm works. Hmmm, how can I be sure that my students understand what they're doing? With a large class, I don't have time for each of the students to explain their actions on twenty exercises. Maybe, though, I can structure the exercises so that students have to *demonstrate* their understanding of the rule. I will have them show an intermediate step in their work, so I can see how they arrive at each answer. When rounding to the nearest ten, they will have to show the next lower and higher multiples of ten. When rounding to the nearest hundred, they will have to show the next lower and higher multiples of one hundred. Then they can apply the rule by writing the multiple to which they would round.

I seem to be describing objectively scored items that fit into the completion category. Although students will have to produce each response rather than select it from given alternatives, each response will be easy to judge as correct or incorrect: Either they write the correct number or they do not. With this item format, I will be able to give many opportunities for students to demonstrate the rounding rule, thereby minimizing measurement error and enhancing the reliability of the results. Furthermore, with the objectivity involved in scoring, I can give a large number of opportunities without committing an excessive amount of time to administration or scoring. Here are some examples of the items:

1. Round each numeral to the nearest *ten.* Write the next lower and higher multiple of ten before you write your answer.

    a. 37 lower multiple = _30_, higher multiple = _40_, rounded numeral = _40_

    b. 72 lower multiple = _____, higher multiple = _____, rounded numeral = _____

    c. 486 lower multiple = _____, higher multiple = _____, rounded numeral = _____

2. Round each numeral to the nearest *hundred.* Write the next lower and higher multiple of one hundred before you write your answer.

    a. 654 lower multiple = _600_, higher multiple = _700_, rounded numeral = _700_

    b. 87 lower multiple = _____, higher multiple = _____, rounded numeral = _____

    c. 283 lower multiple = _____, higher multiple = _____, rounded numeral = _____

Assessing a Cognitive Strategy Learning Outcome

Teacher: Mr. Hoffman
Grade level: 7
Subject: Social studies, learning strategies
Instructional Goal: Originate concept maps for textbook chapters.

I want my students to be able to use concept mapping as a generalizable strategy that they can use to process textbook information. How will I know if their understanding of the strategy does indeed generalize to new textbook chapters? My students should be able to produce an actual concept map for a new, unfamiliar textbook chapter. It wouldn't do any good to have them produce a concept map for a chapter they already have mapped in class. In that case, I wouldn't be certain that they were applying the strategy or just remembering a specific instance as declarative knowledge. The most valid way to assess this outcome therefore would be for me to give my students a new textbook chapter and ask them to create a concept map—a performance assessment.

All I have to do is give them the chapter and tell them what I want them to do. That seems pretty easy. The hard part will be evaluating the quality of their concept maps. Every student's concept map will look a bit different from the others. It is impossible for me to create a "correct" concept map that I can use to score students' maps objectively. How can I be certain that I am applying the appropriate criteria consistently as I look at the maps from my twenty-seven students? I think I should develop a rating scale to enhance the reliability of my scoring. I will use the rating scale to assess the quality of the written product (the concept map) that results when students apply the cognitive strategy. Here are the directions that I plan to give my students, followed by the rating scale I plan to use:

Directions: You need to create a concept map for the chapter handout that will be provided for you. You have four days to complete your concept map. Dur-

ing that time, you will need to read the chapter, take any notes that you want, develop a draft of your map, and create the final form of your map to hand in. Your final concept map needs to be presented neatly on a single sheet of paper that does not have lines. Write your name on the back of your map. This is an independent activity that you need to complete on your own, without help from others. Every day for the next four days, I will provide you with approximately twenty minutes of class time to work on your map. The rating scale that I will use to evaluate your concept map is attached.

To develop the rating scale, I need to identify the specific features of concept maps that must be present in the students' maps and decide how to evaluate the quality of those features. I'll begin this analytical scoring process by making a list of features:

▶ At least three major superordinate concepts from the chapter must appear.

▶ At least two subordinate concepts for each superordinate concept must appear.

▶ Subordinate and superordinate concepts must have valid hierarchical relationships.

▶ Relationships among concepts must be labeled meaningfully and accurately.

▶ At least five cross-links must appear in map.

▶ Each cross-link must represent a meaningful relationship.

▶ Each cross-link must be labeled meaningfully and accurately.

Now I need to decide how I will assign point values to these features. I can simply judge the presence or absence of some features. For example, either there are three superordinate concepts or there are not; either the concepts come from the chapter or they do not. However, I need to judge other features by the degree of quality they represent. For example, the inclusiveness of the superordinate concepts is low, moderate, or high. Here is a partial rating scale that shows how I will rate the superordinate and subordinate concepts students place in their maps:

Superordinate and Subordinate Concepts

A. Three superordinate concepts from chapter at top of map	0–no 1–yes
B. Concepts are inclusive	0–trivial detail 1–moderately inclusive 2–very abstract and inclusive
C. Two concepts from chapter below each superordinate	0–no 1–yes
D. First superordinate concept related hierarchically to two subordinate concepts	0–neither related hierarchically 1–one related hierarchically 2–both related hierarchically
E. Second superordinate concept related hierarchically to two subordinate concepts	0–neither related hierarchically 1–one related hierarchically 2–both related hierarchically
F. Third superordinate concept related hierarchically to two subordinate concepts	0–neither related hierarchically 1–one related hierarchically 2–both related hierarchically

I'll continue with this process until I've accounted for all the features in my list. Adding together the points from each part of the concept map will help me derive a total score that reflects the overall quality of the product. This score will help me evaluate how well my students have acquired the internal cognitive strategy of concept mapping as a generalizable skill.

LOOKING BACK LOOKING AHEAD

In this chapter, I have tried to help you understand that there are no prescribed assessment methods. Just as a number of different tools could be used to perform a repair job, a number of different assessment tools could be used to help us transform internal learning products into external evidence of learning. Our job as *design-teachers* is to match the external evidence we need to evaluate learning with the best assessment tool for the job, considering validity and reliability issues, construction issues, administration and scoring issues, and learner characteristics.

We examined three general classes of assessment items: cognitive, performance, and attitude. We saw that each of these general approaches to assessment has specific advantages, disadvantages, special considerations, and particular learning outcomes for which they are particularly useful. Furthermore, we reviewed specific rules and guidelines for developing such assessments to maximize the validity and reliability of the data they yield.

In the next chapter, the final one on instructional assessment, we will put together the foundational assessment principles from Chapter 4 and the characteristics of specific assessment procedures from this chapter to develop complete assessment strategies, or instructional objectives.

Before we move on to the next chapter, I have two important questions for you. First, can you demonstrate each of the chapter's instructional goals? To find out, try your hand at Exercise 5.3 in the *Student Exercise Guide*. Second, did you find out what an awl is? *Awl*right, *awl*right, I'll tell you: An awl is a pointed metal instrument that is used to make small holes in wood, leather, or metal. Imagine all the hole-punching jobs you can handle more easily and effectively with an awl in your toolbox. Better yet, imagine all the classroom evaluation jobs you can handle validly and reliably with a wide variety of test item tools in your assessment toolbox.

RESOURCES FOR FURTHER REFLECTION AND EXPLORATION

Print Resources

Carey, L. M. (1994). *Measuring and evaluating school learning* (2nd ed.). Boston: Allyn and Bacon.

An excellent book that provides a comprehensive overview of classroom assessment principles and procedures. Provides detailed coverage of item construction, quantitative data analysis, grading, and standardized test interpretation.

Crockett, T. (1998). *The portfolio journey.* Englewood, CO: Teacher Ideas Press.

A practical guide to planning, managing, and assessing portfolios. Provides many useful examples of materials that can be collected in portfolios and possible scoring procedures.

Educational Testing Service. (1995). *Performance assessment: Different needs, difficult answers.* Princeton, NJ: ETS.

An examination of the performance assessment movement, with analyses of relevant assessment issues. Places performance assessment in the context of traditional measurement concerns.

Popham, W. J. (1999). *Classroom assessment: What teachers need to know* (2nd ed.). Boston: Allyn and Bacon.

A down-to-earth book that addresses the classroom assessment concerns of teachers. Provides in-depth chapters on many of the issues covered in this chapter: item construction, performance assessment, portfolio assessment, and attitude assessment.

Portfolio Implementation Guide. Pennsylvania Assessment Through Themes (PATT). Harrisburg, PA: Pennsylvania Department of Education.

A practical guide to using portfolios to support classroom learning and assessment. Provides strategies for using portfolios and demonstrates portfolio formats for specific school subjects.

Software Resources

Prentice Hall Custom Test. (1997). Engineering Software Associates.

Software that helps teachers store a variety of test items and generate tests electronically. Provides capabilities for on-line testing and a grading program for managing data. Available in Windows and Macintosh versions.

Diploma IV. (1990). Brownstone Research Group.

Software that teachers can use to store multiple-choice, true-false, short-answer, and matching questions and to generate classroom tests. Also provides a gradebook program for managing classroom assessment data. Available in IBM PC version.

World Wide Web Resources

http://arc.missouri.edu/

Web site of the Assessment Resource Center (ARC). Provides links to a variety of assessment topics, including performance assessment.

http://www.tappedin.org/pals/

An online, standards-based interactive resource bank of science performance assessment tasks indexed through the National Science Foundation Standards.

http://www.pattonville.k12.mo.us/services/assessment/showme.html

A collection of tasks for performance assessment created by Missouri teachers. Tasks cover all subject areas from kindergarten to high school.

6

Preparing and Using Instructional Objectives

H ave you ever written a résumé for a job search? If so, you may have started by stating your career objective. A career objective describes the specific type of job, occupation, or professional experience you are seeking. Let's assume that your career objective for now is *to obtain a classroom teaching position*. If you are specializing in a specific content area (say, mathematics, chemistry, or English) and prefer to teach adolescents, your objective would be more precise: *to obtain a high school [mathematics, chemistry, English] teaching position*. If you are preparing to teach younger children, your objective would be refined as follows: *to obtain an elementary school teaching position*.

With either of these career objectives, how will you evaluate the success of your job search? If you end up flipping burgers in a fast food restaurant, you will not have achieved your objective. If you land a lucrative upper management position in an advertising company, you might be very happy with your salary, benefits, and work environment, but you will not have met your career objective. The career objective, a clear statement of the outcome you wish to achieve, places limits on how you will evaluate the success of your job-searching efforts.

The objective also creates a clear target that you can use to direct your job-searching decisions. If, for example, your objective is *to obtain an elementary school teaching position,* it would not make sense for you to send your résumé to schools that have openings for high school positions. Nor would it make sense to pursue position openings for secretaries, plumbers, electricians, cab drivers, or radiologists. Furthermore, the types of preparatory experiences you select for yourself should

INSTRUCTIONAL GOALS FOR CHAPTER 6

After reading and thinking about this chapter, you should be able to . . .

1. Identify educational goals, and describe their role in instructional design.

2. Identify instructional goals, and describe their role in instructional design.

3. Identify instructional objectives, and describe their role in instructional design.

4. Demonstrate how educational goals, instructional goals, and instructional objectives relate to each other in the instructional design process.

5. Explain and illustrate how instructional objectives contribute to instructional assessment.

6. Recognize and generate three essential components of instructional objectives: context, performance, and quality.

7. Write instructional objectives that are valid for learning outcomes.

help you attain your career objective. So if your career objective is *to obtain a high school chemistry teaching position,* it would make sense for you to take classes in educational psychology, adolescent psychology, instructional design, and chemistry (lots of chemistry!) and to look for opportunities to interact with high school students through individual tutoring, practicum experiences, camp counseling, and the like. As you can see, a clear career objective helps you select the processes and procedures that you use to attain your goal.

Just as a clear career objective can help guide your job search, a clear instructional objective can help guide your instructional decisions in the classroom. As is true for career objectives, useful instructional objectives describe the outcomes of instruction—not the processes and procedures that will be used to produce those outcomes. The outcomes of instruction are learned capabilities. Instructional objectives therefore describe how learners will demonstrate their learned capabilities—the result of instruction.

This chapter shows you how to prepare and use instructional objectives. Instructional objectives describe assessment strategies and therefore are simply an extension of the assessment principles and procedures we examined in Chapters 4 and 5. Throughout this chapter, I describe how to develop complete assessment strategies by applying principles of validity, reliability, and test item construction. Now that you have a basic understanding of these important assessment principles, you are ready to put them together in the writing of instructional objectives. Before reading further, take a moment to check out the instructional goals for the chapter.

Expressing Educational Outcomes

In the introduction to this chapter, we saw the importance of clearly specifying classroom teaching goals as outcomes rather than processes. Not all educational outcomes are equally useful in guiding our actions as *design-teachers.* I want you to be aware of three major levels of educational outcomes: (1) educational goals, (2) instructional goals, and (3) instructional objectives. I like to think of these three levels as the rings on a target. As you can see from Figure 6.1, educational goals, instructional goals, and instructional objectives represent increasingly precise ways to express educational outcomes, with instructional objectives providing the most precise target—the bull's-eye! Let's take a look at the relationships among these three types of educational outcomes and examine the different degrees of guidance they provide in planning, delivering, and evaluating instruction.

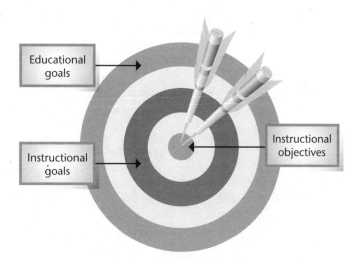

**Figure 6.1
Three Levels of Educational Outcomes**

Educational Goals

Educational goals are the broadest way to express educational outcomes. An **educational goal** is an outcome statement that describes the general characteristics all learners should possess after a significant amount of time engaged with the school curriculum. They describe curriculum-level results and are necessarily broad. Because school curricula reflect cultural values and social norms, educational goals often represent value statements that indicate the kinds of educational outcomes that are important to families, communities, state legislatures, and other groups with a significant interest in education. Lists of educational goals are often found in school district curriculum guides, state-level curriculum guides, statements of national educational priorities, and curricular materials published by professional societies (e.g., National Association of Teachers of Mathematics). Here is a list of outcome statements that would be classified as educational goals:

Students will . . .

1. master basic skills in reading, writing, and mathematics;
2. function in society as productive, contributing citizens;
3. value and respect the earth and its natural resources;
4. understand and describe the components of ecological systems and their functions;
5. develop self-awareness and a sustained commitment to life-long learning.

Notice that the preceding goals are quite vague, either because the verb represents unobservable behavior (*value, respect, understand, develop*) or because the content (reading, writing, mathematics, productive citizens, ecological systems, self-awareness, life-long learning) is too broad to assess. It is impossible to design instruction for these types of goals directly because they are not expressed as learned capabilities. Furthermore, each of these outcomes would be achieved over a long period of time—perhaps throughout a student's entire twelve-year educational experience. Despite their broad nature, educational goals are useful because they point the instructional design process in a general direction and communicate values and expectations that are held by the communities that schools serve.

Instructional Goals

Educational goals are useful to the extent that they provide an organizing framework for more precise instructional goals. An **instructional goal** is a precise statement that describes the learned capability that learners should be able to *demonstrate* as a result of instruction. Instructional goals should be consistent with the broad educational goals of the curriculum and describe learned capabilities that students need to be able to demonstrate through observable performance.

As you can see in Figure 6.2, a single educational goal can be broken down into numerous instructional goals that describe more precise actions and content. The small sample of instructional goals in the figure represents a wide variety of learning outcomes, including intellectual skills (concepts, rules, and principles), verbal information, and attitudes. None of these instructional goals by itself guarantees that the educational goal will be achieved. In fact, it is virtually impossible to determine conclusively whether educational goals are achieved because they are so broad. Instructional goals, however, provide a focus for both teaching and assessment that can help us infer the likelihood that an educational goal has been attained.

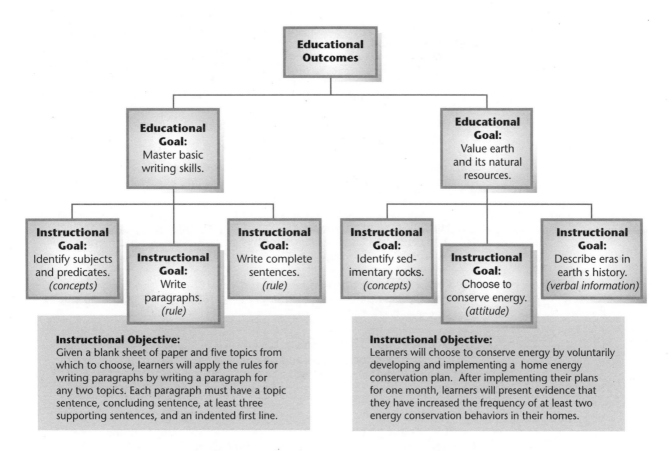

Figure 6.2
Relationships Among Educational Goals, Instructional Goals, and Instructional Objectives

Instructional Objectives

Because instructional goals describe internal learned capabilities, they can be operationalized in any number of specific, external ways. Think for a moment about this instructional goal: *Identify subjects and predicates*. How many ways can learners demonstrate their conceptual knowledge of subjects and predicates? Make a list and then compare it to my list in Table 6.1. Each concrete, external performance listed in the table is a valid way to demonstrate the internal capability (applying concepts) because in each case the learner is classifying parts of sentences as belonging to the "subject" category or the "predicate" category.

Given the various ways to make a learned capability observable, we need an outcome statement that describes our specific assessment intentions—the bull's-eye. An **instructional objective** is an outcome statement that describes specifically the concrete actions that learners will take to demonstrate their achievement of an instructional goal. The detailed level of specification provides a precise target for both teaching and assessment (Gronlund, 1995). Instructional objectives describe precisely how we intend to collect assessment data to verify that learning has occurred. Therefore they are assessment planning tools that reflect the principles of evaluation, measurement, validity, and reliability that we discussed in Chapter 4 and the principles of item selection and construction that we examined in Chapter 5.

Table 6.1
Different Ways to Demonstrate the Ability to Identify Subjects and Predicates

External Performance	Internal Capability
1. From a list of fifteen sentences, students point to subjects and predicates.	Identify subjects and predicates.
2. Students cut apart ten sentences written on strips of paper and sort all the subjects and predicates into two piles.	Identify subjects and predicates.
3. Students underline subjects with a red crayon and predicates with a green crayon for twelve written sentences.	Identify subjects and predicates.
4. For each of ten written sentences, students write the subjects and predicates in columns labeled "subject" and "predicate."	Identify subjects and predicates.
5. Students write complete sentences for each of eight topics, circling the subjects and underlining the predicates of their sentences.	Identify subjects and predicates.

If you return to the model of systematic instructional design presented in Chapter 1 (Figure 1.3), you will notice that *preparing assessment procedures* essentially is equivalent to writing an instructional objective. Notice also that this major phase in the instructional design process occurs before we design and implement the instructional strategy (i.e., how we plan to teach). By specifying the assessment procedure (instructional objective) before preparing instructional plans, we provide a precise outcome target so that we can make the best possible decisions regarding the learning processes needed to hit the target.

Another important reason for preparing instructional objectives before planning and implementing instructional processes is accountability. If an aspiring teacher is unsuccessful in landing a teaching position, he might be able to rationalize the disappointing outcome by saying, "Oh, well, I really wasn't so sure about teaching anyway. Now that I see the bright future in selling insurance, it's clear that this is what I've wanted to do all along." When we do not hit a target we set for ourselves, we can pretend that we were not that serious about the target in the first place (the process of rationalization) or we can try to figure out what is preventing us from hitting the target, make the appropriate adjustments, and take another crack at it.

In our personal lives, we may choose rationalization over goal-directed perseverance. However, as *design-teachers* we are accountable to our students, and rationalizing away their learning difficulties is not an option. By specifying precise objectives in advance, we can hold ourselves accountable to explicit criteria that we will use to judge our learners' performance and our own teaching effectiveness. Ultimately learners benefit from this accountability because the first step in helping students with their difficulties is to recognize and admit that the difficulties exist.

Clear instructional objectives are essential for effective teaching. Although writing instructional objectives is simply an application and extension of the assessment principles we have been examining in this part of the book, there are several specific components of objectives that make them particularly useful. In the next section, we take a closer look at the critical features that all instructional objectives should possess so that they provide useful guidance for teaching and assessment.

Developing Instructional Objectives

Over the years, writing instructional objectives has become a much more complicated and confusing process than it needs to be. Two reasons for the confusion are the different terminology and formats that instructional design experts use when talking about objectives. The confusion over terminology and format differences is unnecessary and unproductive because, in the end, an instructional objective is simply a logical, principled plan for collecting assessment data that are as valid and reliable as possible. If we stay focused on this ultimate goal, writing and using objectives become much more meaningful.

Understanding Different Terms

Instructional objectives sprang on the educational scene during the heyday of the behavioral psychology movement (approximately 1930s through 1960s). Behavioral psychologists such as B. F. Skinner advocated the use of behavioral objectives because they specified clearly the exact behaviors students would be expected to exhibit to demonstrate learning. Unfortunately, behaviorists tended to define learning as a simple association between an environmental stimulus and an overt response on the part of the learner. Not much attention was given to the internal process of learner understanding. Thanks to the cognitive revolution of the past thirty years (Di Vesta, 1987; Mandler, 1996; Wittrock, 1979), we now know much more about how meaningful learning occurs and no longer try to get learners to produce superficial behavioral responses to stimuli. However, the behavioral emphasis on overt, observable performance to evaluate learning is still right on target. Even if we view learning as a constructive, internal process based on meaningful understanding, we still need outward evidence that learning and understanding have occurred.

A behavioral objective is exactly the same as an instructional objective. And sometimes we also refer to instructional objectives as performance objectives. Do not let the language throw you: *instructional objective, behavioral objective,* and *performance objective* all refer to the same idea. I prefer the term *instructional objective* because it reminds us that the objective describes the target of instruction and the goal of instruction is to get meaningful learning to happen.

Understanding Different Formats

The second source of confusion regarding instructional objectives is format. How should we develop and write instructional objectives? What are the key ingredients that they should possess? The answers to these two questions depend on which instructional designer you ask. Robert Mager (1962), for example, says that an instructional objective has three basic components: (1) the learner's behavior, (2) the conditions under which the learner will perform the behavior, and (3) the criteria that will be used to judge the quality of the learner's behavior.

According to the Instructional Development Institutes that were created in the 1970s to assist public schools with instructional design applications, instructional objectives have four parts: (1) the *audience* for whom the instruction is intended, (2) the *behavior* that the audience will exhibit following instruction, (3) the *conditions* within which the behavior will occur, and (4) the *degree* of quality the behavior needs to possess (Seels & Glasgow, 1998). Notice that the first letter of each of the key words (audience, behavior, conditions, degree) forms a handy mnemonic device to help you remember them: ABCD.

Robert Gagne, Leslie Briggs, and Walter Wager (1992) developed yet another format that has five basic components. An instructional objective, they say, needs to indicate (1) the assessment situation the learner will experience, (2) a learned capability verb, (3) the object, or content, of the learned capability, (4) an action verb that describes how the learner will demonstrate the learned capability, and (5) any tools, constraints, or special conditions that will influence how the action is produced or evaluated.

So who is right? Actually, everyone is right because essentially they are all saying the same thing. Before getting bogged down with the specific components suggested by each of the three preceding formats, let's think logically about this issue. Remembering that the ultimate purpose of an instructional objective is to formulate a plan for collecting assessment data to verify learning, let's determine what really needs to be specified in any sensible data collection strategy.

First, it is clear that learners are going to have to *do* something to produce the data. If students do not perform some sort of behavior, we have nothing to observe. We can describe learner performance in two ways. The first way is as a learned capability, using verbs that are consistent with the major learning outcomes (e.g., *state, identify, apply, originate, execute, choose*). However, when learners demonstrate an inner learned capability, they exhibit an external behavior that requires bodily action. We cannot produce any kind of observable behavior without moving some part of our bodies. Therefore, the second way to describe performance is to indicate clearly the specific bodily action that students will use to display the learned capability. Look again at Table 6.1. Notice that several bodily actions (point, sort, underline, write, circle) can be used to demonstrate the internal capability of identifying examples of subjects and predicates.

Second, people produce actions in real time and space—in a real environmental context. Therefore, we should describe how learner performance will be situated in that context. Furthermore, there may be specific types of materials, objects, and other resources that learners may need to produce the necessary actions in that context. Refer again to Table 6.1. Students cannot point to subjects and predicates unless they have something to point at, and before they can underline subjects and predicates with red and green crayons, we need to provide the sentences as well as the crayons. In short, we have to ensure that the necessary context conditions are met for students to produce the appropriate actions.

To generate the third critical feature of an assessment strategy, we need to remember what the ultimate purpose of assessment is: evaluation. Eventually we need to interpret the data and make a decision regarding the quality of learning and teaching that has transpired. To hold ourselves accountable, we should make explicit the quality of the performance from which we are expecting to infer that learning has occurred. In other words, we should build quality control criteria into the assessment strategy.

We have just identified the three essential ingredients of any assessment strategy and, therefore, any instructional objective:

1. What performance (both capability and action) learners will demonstrate

2. The context in which the performance will occur

3. The expected quality of the performance

If it appears that I have just suggested yet another instructional objective format, look again (and see Table 6.2). The *performance* component is consistent with Mager's "behavior," the "behavior" in the ABCD format, and Gagne et al.'s "capability verb with content" and "action verb." The *context* component is similar to Mager's "conditions," ABCD's "conditions," and Gagne et

Table 6.2
Components of Instructional Objectives: A Comparison of Formats

	Mager Format	**ABCD Format**	**Gagne et al. Format**
PERFORMANCE	Behavior	Behavior	Capability verb Action verb
CONTEXT	Conditions	Conditions	Tools Constraints Special conditions
QUALITY	Criteria	Degree	Constraints

al.'s "tools, constraints, or special conditions." The *quality* component means the same thing as Mager's "criteria," ABCD's "degree," and Gagne et al.'s "constraints." The only feature I have left out is ABCD's "audience." In classroom teaching situations, it is pretty clear who our learners are, but if you like the "audience" component, go ahead and throw it in.

I am not at all rigid about components or terminology because I do not want you to get sidetracked from the primary goal of instructional objective writing: developing a summative assessment plan that has the potential to produce the most valid and reliable data possible. Any statement that clearly and thoroughly describes how you intend to collect assessment data will function as an instructional objective as long as you address, at a minimum, these three variables:

1. *Performance:* What will learners *do*?
2. *Context:* In what kind of *environment* will they do it?
3. *Quality:* How *well* do they have to do it?

If you do your best to answer these three questions meaningfully and thoroughly, you will create an instructional objective: a useful target for your teaching and your students' learning. Now that we have created a workable format for ourselves, let's zoom in for a closer look at each essential ingredient of an instructional objective.

Performance: What Will Learners Do?

Imagine that you are preparing an instructional system to help your fifth-grade students achieve the following instructional goal: *Learners will be able to apply the rule for measuring angles with a protractor.* After you have engaged your students in the learning process, how will you collect evidence that they have achieved the learning outcome you intended? The answer is fairly obvious: You need to provide your students with an opportunity to perform the outcome described by this instructional goal. You can begin constructing your instructional objective by essentially restating your instructional goal, which includes an appropriate *capability verb* and the object, or *content*, of the capability:

▶ Learners will be able to *apply* [capability verb] the rule for *measuring angles with a protractor* [content].

Although it may seem redundant and unnecessary to repeat the instructional goal in the objective, I think it is very useful to do so for two reasons. First, the instructional goal serves as yet another reminder that outward behavior per se is not what we desire. The external action that learners demonstrate during assessment needs to be the result of an acquired internal capability. By restating the internal capability and content, we stay focused on the reason for the assessment procedure. Second, in building on the instructional goal to add the details of the assessment procedure, we need to make sure that everything we specify helps us make a valid inference regarding the achievement of that goal. Restating the capability verb and content within the objective builds in a control feature that helps ensure the internal consistency of the entire assessment procedure.

Returning now to the objective for assessing protractor skills, in addition to restating the capability verb and content, you need to decide on the bodily action that will make the internal skill observable. What will students do in real time and space? Will they verbalize, point, write, sort, underline, circle, shade, match, sing, paint, draw, build, jump, kick, whistle, wink, or wiggle their ears? These seemingly trivial outward behaviors are windows through which you must observe your students' learning. You have to pick one. For demonstrating protractor skills, it would make sense for your students to write the measurements of angles. Now you can expand your objective by including *write* as the action verb:

▶ Learners will demonstrate the ability to apply the rule for measuring angles with a protractor by *writing the measurements of angles in degrees*.

Notice the form that the action verb takes in the objective we are building. The word *by* follows the capability. Then the action verb in the form *–ing* follows. To create this useful format, begin with the capability and then ask yourself this question: *By doing what?* Here are some examples:

Capability	Question	Action
1. *Identify* sedimentary rocks.	By doing what?	By *sorting* rocks into sedimentary and nonsedimentary piles
2. *Apply* the rule for finding the mean of a set of numbers.	By doing what?	By *calculating* and *writing* the mean of a set of numbers
3. *State* the major phases of photosynthesis.	By doing what?	By *writing* and *explaining* the sequence of phases in photosynthesis
4. *Demonstrate* the principle of food chains.	By doing what?	By *drawing* an example of a food chain
5. *Apply* the scientific method.	By doing what?	By *designing, implementing,* and *reporting* an original experiment

Context: Under What Conditions Will Learners Perform?

For learners to perform the actions that we specify, we often need to supply them with information, materials, or other resources. For example, students cannot sort rocks unless they have rocks to sort. To calculate and write the mean of a set of numbers, students need to have a set of numbers with which to work. Examples such as these illustrate the need for us to specify the context within which the action will occur. Even when the action is somewhat open-ended and does not require specific materials (see examples 3, 4, and 5 above), learners still need to be provided with some type of direction so they will know

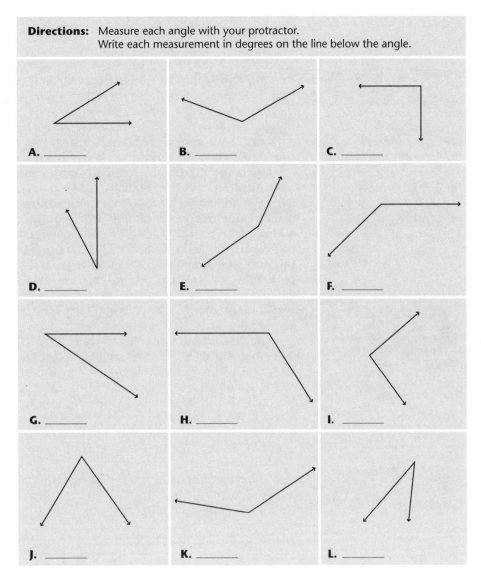

Directions: Measure each angle with your protractor.
Write each measurement in degrees on the line below the angle.

A. _____   B. _____   C. _____

D. _____   E. _____   F. _____

G. _____   H. _____   I. _____

J. _____   K. _____   L. _____

**Figure 6.3
Sample Items for Assessing Protractor Skills**

what they are supposed to do. This type of information also falls within the context component of the instructional objective.

Let's return to the protractor skills objective. For learners to be able to write the measurements of angles (action), you obviously will need to provide them with angles to measure. Probably the most efficient way to do this is to create a sheet of angles, as illustrated in Figure 6.3. The context component of your objective therefore should clearly describe the sheet of angles. How many angles will there be? What types of angles will be represented? How many of each type of angle will there be? In what spatial orientation will the angles be presented? Where will students write their measurements? Here is the context you might develop to address these questions:

▶ Learners will demonstrate the ability to apply the rule for measuring angles with a protractor by writing the measurements of angles in degrees. Learners will be given a sheet with twelve line drawings of angles and a protractor. Five of the angles will be acute, five will be obtuse, and two will be right angles. All of the angles will be presented on the sheet in a variety of positions (vertex left, right, up, down), and a line will be provided beneath each angle for learners to write their measurements.

The detailed context is necessary to help you produce assessment data that are as valid and reliable as possible. Giving students angles that they will actually measure with a protractor enhances the *validity* of the results. A less valid alternative would be to give them pictures of angles that have a protractor already in position, so all students have to do is read the measurement. This approach will yield less valid results because students do not have to position the protractor themselves. Having numerous opportunities (twelve) to perform the skill enhances the *reliability* of the results. Whereas chance variables may cause students to measure a single angle correctly or incorrectly, it is unlikely that those variables would exert the same influence across twelve trials.

Specifying the number of acute, obtuse, and right angles and indicating the variety of spatial orientations will help to ensure that students are generalizing the skill across a number of specific instances, enhancing your ability to make valid inferences regarding their acquisition of procedural knowledge. If all the angles on the sheet are acute, you will have no evidence that students can generalize their protractor skills to obtuse and right angles. Similarly, if all the angles are presented with one horizontal ray and the vertex to the left (e.g., see item A in Figure 6.3), you will have no evidence that students can manipulate the protractor correctly when they encounter angles that have a different spatial orientation. Thus, your ability to make valid inferences about the generalizability of the skill will be impeded.

Why include the line below each angle? This is a *reliability* issue. When you score the sheet, you will be able to look at the numbers written on the lines and compare them objectively to the predetermined correct measurements. Each line is a prompt, or cue, to students that they must write the measurement. If a student measures one or more angles correctly but carelessly neglects to write the measurements, then measurement error will deflate the score. The blank lines under the angles do not eliminate the possibility of student carelessness (nothing does, of course), but they at least help to minimize its damaging effects.

I explained the rationale for the context component of the protractor objective in depth because I want you to understand that this is a *thinking* process. By thinking carefully about the context features of assessment, you have the opportunity to anticipate possible threats to validity and reliability and take steps to help control for them. A second reason to think carefully about the assessment context is so you can be prepared with all the materials and resources learners will need to perform. For example, given the context of the protractor objective, you now know that you will need to develop the twelve-item sheet according to your specifications and have enough protractors on hand for all students.

A third reason to specify the context clearly is to help ensure that you provide learning activities and practice opportunities that are as consistent as possible with the way you eventually will assess your students. With the clear action and context of your objective, you can create practice sheets that are highly similar to the assessment. This type of appropriate practice is essential to guard against the possibility that learners could perform poorly on the assessment simply because they are unfamiliar with its format, damaging the reliability of the resulting data.

I cannot possibly describe all the assessment contexts that you will need to use in your classroom. I do, however, want to alert you to three general categories of context conditions that may help you think about possibilities when writing objectives: cues, resources, and complexity (Dick & Carey, 1996).

■ **Describing Cues to Stimulate Performance**   Regardless of the specific action learners are to perform, they must have some cue or stimulus to direct their activity. That is, they need to know what they are to do and how they are to do it. Furthermore, to respond to most types of cognitive assessment formats, students need to experience an item or set of items. This aspect of the context answers the question, "What will we provide to prompt the performance?" For subjectively scored cognitive assessments and performance assessments, the context should describe the directions that students will be given, as illustrated by the following example:

▶ Given three topics from which to choose and directions to write a paragraph that has at least three supporting sentences, learners will apply paragraph writing rules by writing a paragraph.

For objectively scored cognitive assessments, the context should describe the items to which students will respond, as illustrated by the following examples:

▶ Given fifteen pairs of common fractions with unlike denominators, learners will demonstrate the rule for adding fractions with unlike denominators by converting them to equivalent fractions with common denominators, writing the sums, and reducing to lowest terms.

▶ Given six sets of pictures of vertebrate animals with one representative from each of the five vertebrate animal classes, learners will identify examples of mammals, amphibians, reptiles, birds, and fish by writing the number of each picture beneath the appropriate heading on a sheet of paper.

In these two examples I have specified clearly the number of response opportunities that students will have. Recall from the discussion of reliability in Chapter 4 that the effects of measurement error generally decrease as the number of responses increases. We need to decide how many responses will be required to make confident inferences about students' learning and then prepare the assessment accordingly.

Notice also that the context of each objective indicates the nature of the stimulus items. Here we are ensuring that the items are valid for the instructional goal to be evaluated. Even if we plan to use assessment items that are found in a textbook, workbook, computer program, or some other instructional resource, we should still take the time to describe the items to ensure they are valid for our assessment purposes. The following objective, for example, would not describe the assessment context adequately:

▶ Given workbook page 67, students will demonstrate the ability to apply the rules for forming singular and plural possessives by completing the exercises.

The context of this objective is inadequate because it provides no description of the stimuli to which students will respond. How can we be certain that each exercise on the workbook page does in fact require students to apply a rule? In this case, the fact that the assessment items are found on a particular workbook page is far less important than what is actually on the workbook page. Here is a better way to write this objective:

▶ Given twenty sentences that contain either a singular (ten items) or plural (ten items) possessive situation (see *Literacy Activities Workbook*, page 67), learners will apply the rules for forming singular and plural possessives by writing the correct possessive form of the noun on a line that follows each sentence.

One mistake that inexperienced writers of instructional objectives often make is to describe the classroom instructional process (or teaching activities) as the cue to prompt assessment performance, as illustrated by the following *nonexample:*

▶ Given a videotape and class discussion on endangered plants and animals of the world's rain forests, students will state three plants and three animals that are in danger of extinction by drawing pictures of them in a rain forest environment.

Including the videotape and class discussion in the context does not contribute to the objective because they are elements of the instructional (or teaching) process. Of course, some type of instructional activity has occurred. This fact always is recognized implicitly in any objective. It is understood that the assessment will occur following some set of instructional activities, so it is unnecessary (and potentially misleading) to include them in the objective.

■ **Describing Resources to Enable Performance** In addition to the stimulus items to which students will respond, we may also need to specify additional resources that they will need to enable their performance. For example, for students to measure the twelve angles described in the protractor objective, they will need to have protractors in their hands. The specific types of essential resources you need to include in the context of your instructional objectives vary widely with the exact nature of the task to be performed. Here are some common categories of resources that could be relevant to your assessment contexts:

▶ Data summary materials such as tables, charts, and graphs

▶ Written materials such as reports, stories, book chapters, and poems

▶ Physical objects such as Bunsen burners, Cuisenaire rods, rocks, thermometers, and soccer balls

▶ Reference materials such as encyclopedias, web pages, compact discs, tape recordings, and dictionaries

■ **Describing Complexity of Context to Restrict Performance** A final element to consider for the context component is the scope or complexity of the performance environment. Depending on the characteristics of the learners and the potential complexity of the content they have acquired, we may deliberately choose to restrict the range of stimuli we present. For example, if your students are in third grade and just beginning to learn about angles and protractors, you might restrict the scope of the protractor objective by specifying that students will measure only acute and right angles. In that case, you would target only acute and right angles in your instruction and make sure that no obtuse angles appear for summative assessment. If we are assessing young learners' paragraph writing skills, we might provide them with three possible topics from which to choose. We might also provide them with a sheet that structures their actions by providing lines for the topic sentence, three supporting sentences, and a concluding sentence (see Figure 6.4).

Quality: How Will Learner Performance Be Evaluated?

Your protractor objective is almost complete. There is just one more important question to ask: How good does the performance have to be? Do all twelve measurements have to be correct for you to infer that students have mastered the skill of measuring angles with a protractor? What about small discrepancies between students' measurements and your "correct" measurements? If you say an angle is 34 degrees and a student says it is 35 degrees, is the response incorrect? What about a difference of 3 degrees or 5 degrees from the correct measurement? What if students forget to include the degree symbol (°)? Does it matter? Should it matter?

These are the types of questions that you must consider to establish *quality* criteria. When you anticipate and address quality issues thoughtfully, you deliberately place controls on how you will interpret your assessment data. In the absence of clear, predetermined standards, you may be vulnerable to interpreting your data in ways that mask your students' learning difficulties. Using your

Topic: _____

Topic Sentence: _____
_____
_____

Supporting Sentence: _____
_____
_____

Supporting Sentence: _____
_____
_____

Supporting Sentence: _____
_____
_____

Concluding Sentence: _____
_____
_____

Figure 6.4
Structuring a
Paragraph-Writing
Task for Assessment

best reasoned, professional judgment, you need to establish quality criteria and then hold yourself accountable to them. Here once again is the first part of the protractor skills objective:

▶ Learners will demonstrate the ability to apply the rule for measuring angles with a protractor by writing the measurements of angles in degrees. Learners will be given a sheet with twelve line drawings of angles and a protractor. Five of the angles will be acute, five will be obtuse, and two will be right angles. All of the angles will be presented on the sheet in a variety of positions (vertex left, right, up, down), and a line will be provided beneath each angle for learners to write their measurements . . .

And here are two ways to conclude the objective. Notice how the quality component could vary according to your professional judgment:

▶ Ten of the twelve measurements must fall within three degrees above or below the correct measurement, and at least half of the measurements must include the degree symbol.

OR

▶ All twelve measurements must be correct, deviating no more than one degree above or below the correct measurement. The degree symbol must be included for all twelve measurements.

These two divergent examples of quality criteria demonstrate that there is no official way to describe evaluation standards. Different ways of expressing quality criteria are appropriate for different context conditions, performances, and learners. The following five approaches to describing quality criteria

Before teachers can evaluate their students' performance of learning outcomes, they must think carefully about the quality criteria they will apply.

should serve you well in writing nearly all instructional objectives (Mager, 1962; Smith & Ragan, 1993):

1. Accuracy or precision
2. Number of correct responses or errors
3. Time limits
4. Consistency with an established or stated standard
5. Concrete consequences or outcomes

■ **Accuracy or Precision**   Describing quality criteria in terms of accuracy or precision is appropriate when you expect learners to vary naturally in how closely their responses approximate an ideal, or perfect, response. The two protractor objectives demonstrate the use of accuracy criteria. Each angle on the sheet has a single ideal measurement. However, it is reasonable to expect that even learners who have mastered protractor skills may deviate a bit (measurement error again) from each predetermined measurement. How much natural deviation will you tolerate? How much deviation is too much? Perhaps you will tolerate angle measurements that fall within a range of 6 degrees around the ideal answer, as in the first objective. Perhaps your learners are older and better able to manipulate the protractor with greater precision, so you will tolerate only a 2-degree range of accuracy, as in the second objective.

■ **Number of Correct Responses or Errors**   When students have multiple opportunities to produce objectively scored responses, it may be appropriate for you to use the number of correct responses to describe quality. If you provide twelve performance opportunities, as in the protractor objective, you may wish to state the quality criteria as the number correct out of twelve. Of course, you can express the same information by indicating the number incorrect out of twelve. When learners have numerous opportunities to perform a class of responses, you can express the number correct or incorrect as a percentage. Thus, for the first protractor objective, you could state the criteria as 83 percent (10/12), and you could state the criteria for the second objective as 100 percent (12/12).

In these examples, you can see how quality considerations go hand in hand with decisions about context. If the context of assessment does not provide for multiple opportunities to make objectively scored responses, it makes no sense to describe quality in terms of number or percentage correct. It makes no sense, for example, to say that learners will state a definition with 100 percent accuracy, demonstrate an attitude with 85 percent correct, or explain the application of a principle with 90 percent proficiency. Another common mistake that beginning teachers make is to express quality criteria as percentages that are mathematically impossible given the total number of possible responses. For example, it is mathematically impossible to achieve 95 percent correct on a ten-item assessment task. I raise these issues to remind you that establishing quality standards is a meaningful *thinking* process. To be useful, your quality criteria need to make sense in the context of your assessment procedure.

Time Limits   Some types of skills and verbal information are most useful when learners can recall them quickly or even automatically, without having to think consciously about them (e.g., basic math facts, spelling rules, keyboarding skills). Therefore, when assessing such learning outcomes, you may need to include time limits as part of your quality criteria. You also may need to place time limits on some higher-level skills as well, if it seems reasonable to do so. For example, you might be more confident in students' abilities to calculate and interpret descriptive statistics for a set of data if they can apply those skills successfully in one hour rather than needing half the school day to accomplish the task. Here are some additional examples of how you can use time limits to help express quality criteria:

▶ Write the multiplication facts for factors 1 through 5 in less than 10 minutes.
▶ Produce (write, save, and print) a word-processed paragraph in 30 minutes.
▶ Find and correct all the comma errors in a story in no more than 20 minutes.

Notice that the time limit enhances the quality component for each of the three objectives, but it would need to be supplemented with further standards concerning accuracy. We probably would not be satisfied with students' writing only half the multiplication facts for factors 1 through 5 correctly—even if they did it really quickly. Similarly, a word-processed paragraph produced within 30 minutes would not be acceptable if the paragraph is full of typographical errors.

Consistency with an Established or Stated Standard   If you were to write the definitions of *evaluation, assessment,* and *measurement* and illustrate each concept with an example, how would I establish meaningful evaluation standards? In this case, "correctness" is a slippery idea that depends on my subjective judgment. As described in Chapter 5, I can enhance the reliability of my subjective judgments by developing an analytical scoring procedure (or rubric) that specifies the features that must be present in your definitions and examples.

I can identify the critical features in one of two ways. I could simply say that the features of your definitions must be the same as those presented in Chapter 4, in which case I would be relying on an established standard to derive my evaluation criteria. Established standards can be drawn from textbook material, specific materials presented to students in class, curriculum guides, or any other relevant instructional resource. Alternatively, I could derive quality criteria by summarizing the specific features that each of your definitions must demonstrate:

Criterion	Features
Evaluation	Determining worth or value Requires subjective judgment
Assessment	Data collection process Purpose is to help with evaluation Data can be quantitative or qualitative
Measurement	Type of assessment Data expressed quantitatively (with numbers) Test is a measurement scale

I could also specify that the examples must be clearly different from any used in Chapter 4 or in class and that they clearly exemplify each of the features stated above. In this case, I would be using a stated standard to express my evaluation criteria. In other words, I would be creating the qualitative features that responses must exemplify and stating those features in my instructional objective. As you can see from the example, you will need to employ stated and established standards most frequently when developing objectives that describe subjectively scored cognitive items and performance items.

■ **Concrete Consequences or Outcomes**   Sometimes you can evaluate the quality of a performance by determining whether an appropriate consequence or outcome—one that is consistent with the learned capability—has occurred. For example, after teaching your students the value of cooperation (an attitudinal outcome), you might look for evidence that they are applying the attitude by how well they work together in cooperative learning groups. If your students are choosing to work cooperatively, there should be fewer instances of interpersonal friction and dissatisfaction with individuals who are not "pulling their weight" than would otherwise be the case. Alternatively, there should be more frequent instances of interpersonal harmony, and groups should produce better quality work than would otherwise be the case. Of course, you still will eventually have to specify what you mean by "interpersonal friction," "interpersonal harmony," "quality work," and so on. Some types of consequences are much easier to operationalize, as, for example, the outcome that you would expect after teaching your students the procedural rule for printing a document on a computer system: The document should actually come out of the printer. If the document does not come out of the printer, it is obvious that the learner has not applied the rule correctly.

LET'S SUMMARIZE

When developing the quality component of your instructional objectives, you have a variety of approaches from which to choose. I have described five categories to help you become aware of several options. Because the context and performance components vary, your quality criteria must vary accordingly so that they make sense and provide a useful way to evaluate learning. Thus far in this section on performance quality, we have been examining different options for expressing meaningful criteria. How we decide on the level of quality that is appropriate for learners is a much more difficult question. Let's tackle it in the next section.

Determining Mastery Criteria

When we establish quality criteria for an instructional objective, we are really indicating the level of performance that we will use to decide which students have mastered the learning outcome and which students have not. It is useful to think of quality criteria as the threshold that learners must cross for us to infer that they have indeed achieved mastery. But what is mastery, and where exactly is the threshold? As with so much else of the instructional design process, I cannot give absolute answers to these questions, only principles to help guide your thinking about them. There are three general sets of principles to consider when establishing mastery criteria:

1. Those related to learner characteristics
2. Those related to characteristics of the task to be performed
3. The consequences of misclassifying learners

Learner Characteristics   Often the social, emotional, physical, and cognitive characteristics of learners place constraints on the mastery levels that are appropriate to set for them. Variables that are related to these domains of functioning may exert an influence that masks learners' true abilities. In other words, learners may have mastered a particular learning outcome even though various personal characteristics may prevent them from demonstrating the outcome perfectly.

Let's return to the protractor objective to illustrate this principle. Would it be reasonable to expect third-grade children to measure all twelve angles correctly, with absolutely no deviation from the correct measurement? Using a protractor requires a degree of physical dexterity that some third graders may not yet possess. Furthermore, across a dozen items, it is quite likely that some students may have attention or memory lapses that interfere with performance. For third graders, then, the criteria for demonstrating newly acquired protractor skills should be somewhat less demanding than those set for older students.

Task Characteristics   In general, the greater the task complexity, the greater the chance for random variables (measurement error) to influence learner performance. With greater degrees of measurement error, it is less reasonable to expect perfect performance. The goal, of course, is to find the point at which student difficulty is more attributable to lack of mastery than it is to the possible effects of measurement error.

Take, for example, the case of three-digit long division. The application of this algorithm requires careful attention to the details of each step in a multistep procedure. Numerals must be lined up carefully, multiplication and subtraction algorithms must be applied correctly, and basic math facts must be recalled accurately. If you have forgotten how complex the algorithm is, give it a try: divide 4,556,708 by 358 by hand. As you can see, there are lots of places where you can go wrong and make careless mistakes, even though you can apply the algorithm correctly. If we expect 100 percent accuracy on a large number of long-division exercises, we may be placing learners in a nearly impossible position to demonstrate the skill. This principle applies to any multifaceted, complex performance. In contrast, if students are to write a definition for the concept of de facto segregation, describe three examples, and explain how the examples satisfy the concept's critical features, we can establish a higher level of quality because there is less chance that random variables (chance, guessing, careless mistakes, etc.) will confound the performance.

■ **Consequences of Misclassification**   A third perspective to use in establishing mastery criteria is to think about the consequences of making a mistake in classifying learners as achieving (or not achieving) mastery. As Table 6.3 illustrates, four types of results can occur when we evaluate student learning. Two of these results are correct classifications. When students who possess the learned capability meet our quality criteria, we correctly classify them as achieving mastery (cell A). When those who have not acquired the learned capability fall short of our quality criteria, we correctly classify them as not achieving mastery (cell D).

Assessment data, however, can also lead to two types of errors. *False-positive errors* occur when learners who do not possess the desired learned capability are somehow able to achieve our mastery criteria. We commit *false-negative errors* when learners who really do possess the desired learned capability are somehow unable to achieve our mastery criteria. We increase the probability of committing false-positive errors when we set mastery criteria too low. We increase the probability of committing false-negative errors by setting mastery criteria too high. Which outcome is worse: to err by "setting the bar" too low (more false positives) or by "raising the bar" too high (more false negatives)? I believe that false-positive errors are significantly more dangerous than false negatives. Let me explain why.

After placing students in the nonmastery category, we should do everything within our power to find out why they had difficulty (*diagnosis*) so we can prepare and deliver additional instruction (*remediation*). Through the diagnosis process, we may discover that a nonmastery student is more capable than the original assessment data indicated (the false-negative error). Therefore, even if we err on the side of setting the mastery criteria too high, the diagnosis and remediation processes will serve as additional checkpoints. Setting quality criteria too high actually provides a service to learners–as long as we follow up and look at individual performance more closely.

In contrast, once we place learners in the mastery category, we are not likely to investigate their abilities further. Therefore, students who have not achieved the instructional goal may go undetected because they managed to meet the mastery criteria (the false-positive error). We may eventually discover

Table 6.3
Mastery Decisions: Four Possible Outcomes

		Does Learner Performance Meet Standard?	
		Yes (mastery decision)	No (nonmastery decision)
Does Learner Actually Possess Learned Capability?	Yes	(A) Correct Decision: MASTERY	(B) Error: FALSE NEGATIVE
	No	(C) Error: FALSE POSITIVE	(D) Correct Decision: NONMASTERY

the misclassification if students have difficulty in a related learning area that depends on the prerequisite skill that was not mastered. Clearly, the better approach is not to let students slip through in the first place by setting the criteria too low. By setting the quality criteria higher rather than lower, we can help to ensure that false-positive students do not escape notice and provide them with the diagnosis and remediation they need.

Beyond the general goal of decreasing the risk of false-positive classification errors, we also need to consider the potential consequences of making such mistakes. Some types of classification errors have more serious consequences than others and therefore should be minimized by setting quality criteria higher rather than lower. For example, if students fail to master a fundamental basic skill that lays the foundation for learning more complex skills later, misclassifying them as achieving mastery (false positive) does them a serious disservice, jeopardizing their future learning success. Therefore, it would be better to raise the bar—setting the criteria higher—even if the higher criteria increase the probability of committing false-negative errors for some learners. Learned capabilities that have significant implications for personal health and well-being also require higher mastery criteria because of the serious consequences of believing that students possess the capabilities when they in fact do not. Such examples could include fire safety skills, attitudes toward drug abuse, and conflict management skills.

■ **Summary and a Final Word on Form**   There are no formulas for establishing the level of quality required for achieving mastery. The best we can do is to set the mastery threshold by thinking carefully about relevant learner characteristics, the complexity of the task, and the consequences of making classification errors. As long as we make consistent efforts to diagnose and remediate when learners do not achieve mastery, we should err somewhat on the side of setting quality criteria too high rather than too low.

Before leaving this section, I need to make one final point concerning the form of instructional objectives. As long as you include the essential ingredients of context, performance, and quality in your objectives, you can write them in any form that is comfortable for you. You can write them using one sentence, two sentences, or a dozen sentences. You can write them in chart or outline form. There is no official formula. Look, for example, at these different ways you could write the protractor objective that we developed:

Example 1: Several Sentences

▶ Learners will demonstrate the ability to apply the rule for measuring angles with a protractor by writing the measurements of angles in degrees. Learners will be given a sheet with twelve line drawings of angles and a protractor. Five of the angles will be acute, five will be obtuse, and two will be right angles. All of the angles will be presented on the sheet in a variety of positions (vertex left, right, up, down), and a line will be provided beneath each angle for learners to write their measurements. Ten of the twelve measurements must fall within 3 degrees above or below the correct measurement, and at least half of the measurements must include the degree symbol.

Example 2: One Sentence

▶ Given a sheet with twelve line drawings of angles (five acute, five obtuse, and two right) presented in a variety of positions (vertex left, right, up, down) with a blank line for each and a protractor, learners will demonstrate the ability to apply the rule for measuring angles by writing ten of the twelve measurements of the angles within 3 degrees above or below the correct measurement, including the degree symbol for at least six measurements.

Example 3: Chart Form

Context	• Twelve line drawings of angles on a sheet • Five acute, five obtuse, two right • Various positions: vertex left, right, up, down • Blank line for each angle • Provide a protractor
Performance	• Apply rule for measuring angles with a protractor • Write measurement of each angle on line provided
Quality	• Ten of twelve must be correct • Must be within 3 degrees above or below to be correct • At least half must include degree symbol

Now that we have thoroughly explored the major components of instructional objectives, it is time for you to get into action. Exercise 6.1 in the *Student Exercise Guide* gives you the opportunity to practice identifying the components of instructional objectives, and Exercise 6.2 gives you the opportunity to evaluate several instructional objectives. Check out these exercises, and then move on to the next section, where we will analyze instructional objectives for each of the major learning outcomes.

Instructional Objectives for Learning Outcomes

No matter how elegant and well written instructional objectives are, they will be useless if the assessment data they produce do not help us make valid inferences about the learned capabilities we are trying to evaluate. Therefore, it is essential to prepare instructional objectives that are consistent with our instructional goals and valid for our intended learning outcomes. In the last section of this chapter, I want to show you how you can write meaningful instructional objectives that correspond to each of the five major learning outcomes: verbal information, intellectual skills, cognitive strategies, motor skills, and attitudes.

To illustrate objectives for some of these learning outcomes, we will return to our three case analysis teachers: Ms. Nelson, Mr. Hoffman, and Mrs. Torres. In the preceding chapter, we observed these teachers as they selected and prepared assessment items for their instructional goals. The teachers should have prepared written instructional objectives from which they developed these assessment items because the purpose of an instructional objective is to describe how we intend to assess learners. However, I chose to introduce you to the various types of assessment items (Chapter 5) before showing you how to develop instructional objectives because I wanted you to be aware of all the data collection tools that are available to you when you prepare an assessment strategy. So now let's examine the instructional objectives that the teachers would have written to guide the development of their assessment procedures.

Instructional Objectives for Verbal Information Outcomes

Recall from Chapter 5 that Ms. Nelson decided to use a combination of completion and matching formats to assess her verbal information instructional goal: *State the names of the four major eras in the earth's history and several important characteristics of each.* (You can refer back to Chapter 5 to review the specific assessment item and Ms. Nelson's rationale for developing it.) To help her develop the item, Ms. Nelson could have written the following instructional objective:

▶ *Context:* Learners will be provided with an organizational chart that has four columns with a blank line at the top of each column. Beneath the chart will be twenty-five facts, lettered *a* through *y*. Sixteen of the facts will be characteristics of the four major eras in the earth's history, with four facts corresponding to each of the four eras. The remaining nine facts will not correspond to any of the four eras.

▶ *Performance*: Learners will state the names of the four major eras in the earth's history [capability] by writing each of them [action] at the top of the four columns. Learners will state important characteristics of each era [capability] by writing the letters of the facts [action] in each of the appropriate columns.

▶ *Quality:* All four era names must be written on the blank lines, but the names do not need to be spelled perfectly. The letters of fourteen of the sixteen characteristics must be placed in the correct columns. The letters of no more than two of the nine distracters can be placed in a column.

Let's evaluate the quality of Ms. Nelson's instructional objective from the dual perspectives of validity and reliability. First, is the assessment strategy described by the objective likely to produce data that she can use validly to make inferences about her students' acquisition of verbal information? That is, if her students do meet the quality criteria, can she validly infer that it is because they are recalling verbal information they have stored in long-term memory? Part of Ms. Nelson's instructional goal says that students should be able to state the names of the four major eras in the earth's history. Clearly, the students will have to retrieve the names of the four eras from long-term memory before they can write them on the lines, so writing the names does seem to be a valid way to express acquired verbal information.

The second part of the instructional goal says that students should be able to state several important characteristics of each era. However, because of the selection format of the matching task, Ms. Nelson cannot be certain that her students are actually retrieving the characteristics of each era from long-term memory. Therefore, she increases the validity of the item by including a substantial number of distracters. Students now must do more than match each characteristic with its corresponding era; they must first decide if the statement is a characteristic of *any* of the four eras. To make this decision, they need to search their long-term memories for the proposition and then continue searching for evidence that the proposition is associated with one of the four eras.

How does Ms. Nelson's objective maximize assessment reliability? First, because the item that the objective describes can be scored objectively (completion, matching), scoring reliability is enhanced. Second, she provides multiple opportunities (sixteen) for learners to retrieve the relevant propositions from long-term memory, because, as we noted in Chapter 4, assessment reliability generally increases as the number of performance opportunities increases. Ms. Nelson also enhances the reliability of her data by structuring the task clearly. She provides blank lines to cue students to write the era names and columns to help them remember to associate the names with specific characteristics. Even if students cannot remember one or more era names, they still can cluster characteristics together in the appropriate columns and leave the "name" lines blank.

Ms. Nelson's assessment strategy, as described by the instructional objective, does appear to be quite valid for her verbal information instructional goal. Here are two additional verbal information instructional objectives. Notice how the critical components of each objective are valid for assessing a verbal information learning outcome.

▶ *Instructional goal: Learners will be able to state the names, locations, and uses of major skeletal muscles of the human body.*

▶ *Instructional objective:* Learners will be given the following four muscle categories written on a sheet of paper: flexors, extensors, abductors, adductors. Learners will state the names, locations, and uses of major skeletal muscles of the human body by writing this information under each heading. For each category, learners must write the names of at least two upper body and two lower body muscles. Learners will indicate the location of each muscle by placing a number (1 through 16) in a circle on a drawing of the human body. Fourteen of sixteen muscle names must be spelled correctly and placed within the appropriate categories. Fourteen of sixteen numbers must be placed in the correct circles.

▶ *Instructional goal: Learners will be able to state the preamble to the U.S. Constitution.*

▶ *Instructional objective:* Learners will demonstrate the ability to state the preamble to the U.S. Constitution by reciting it orally when directed to do so. Each learner will meet individually with the teacher to recite the preamble. To have the recitation judged acceptable, each learner should make no more than three minor word substitutions and no more than two minor word sequence errors. No major clauses or sentences may be omitted.

Instructional Objectives for Intellectual Skill Outcomes: Concepts

You may recall from Chapter 2 that Ms. Nelson also developed some intellectual skill instructional goals for her fifth-grade geology unit. Among these goals was one that represented the acquisition of concepts: *Learners will be able to identify sedimentary, igneous, and metamorphic rocks.* How might she assess her learners' achievement of this instructional goal? Here is a possible instructional objective:

▶ Given a set of fifteen rock samples that have not been used during instruction (four metamorphic, five igneous, and six sedimentary) and three containers labeled according to the three rock categories, learners will demonstrate the ability to identify sedimentary, igneous, and metamorphic rocks by sorting the rocks into the three labeled containers. To demonstrate mastery, learners must place twelve of the fifteen rocks in the correct container.

Will this assessment strategy produce valid data that Ms. Nelson can use to infer that her learners have acquired three new concepts? The evidence of concept acquisition is the ability to classify *new* instances as members and nonmembers of the concept category. Notice how the objective maintains the integrity of this requirement by indicating that the rock samples to be classified need to be new instances with which learners are unfamiliar. If instead Ms. Nelson had students classify rock samples that she had used during her teaching, and they did so correctly, she would be able to make inferences about the verbal information that students could recall but not how well they could generalize the three concepts as skills. Having students classify new rock samples will be more difficult for them and will require extra effort for Ms. Nelson to prepare, but Ms. Nelson is serious about evaluating her students' achievement of her instructional goal.

Notice also that Ms. Nelson does not collect assessment data by asking her students to list some names of sedimentary, igneous, and metamorphic rocks. Again, it is possible for a learner to remember and state as verbal information that limestone is sedimentary, granite is igneous, and schist is metamorphic without being able to generalize the three concepts to actual rocks that they experience. Furthermore, the instructional goal does not indicate that learning the names of specific types of sedimentary, igneous, and metamorphic rocks is essential—only that students are able to recognize examples of each category based on their critical features.

How does Ms. Nelson maximize assessment reliability in the objective? Because the classification of each rock sample is either correct or incorrect, scorer-related measurement error is minimized. Notice, however, that students have a 33 percent probability of correctly classifying each rock through guessing. Ms. Nelson controls for the high probability of a false-positive error by increasing the number of response opportunities to fifteen. Although students have a one-in-three chance of guessing the correct classification of each individual rock sample, the probability of guessing correctly on all fifteen is extremely low.

As illustrated by Ms. Nelson's objective, the key to assessing concept acquisition is to provide an adequate number of new instances that learners can categorize as examples or nonexamples. Here are two additional instructional objectives that meet these criteria:

▶ *Instructional goal: Learners will be able to identify common and proper nouns.*

▶ *Instructional objective:* Given a written story that contains fifteen common nouns and five proper nouns, learners will demonstrate the ability to identify common and proper nouns by underlining each proper noun and circling each common noun. Thirteen of the fifteen common nouns must be circled, and four of the five proper nouns must be underlined. No more than one of each type of noun can be underlined or circled inappropriately (e.g., common noun that is underlined, proper noun that is circled).

▶ *Instructional goal: Learners will be able to recognize instances of racial prejudice.*

▶ *Instructional objective:* Students will be given three short newspaper or magazine articles that describe conflicts between people of different ethnic or racial background. Two of the conflicts will be based on racial prejudice; the third will not. Students will demonstrate the ability to recognize instances of racial prejudice by writing an analysis of each conflict. Each analysis must state clearly whether the conflict is based on racial prejudice. Students must classify all three scenarios correctly. For the two positive instances, students' written analyses must clearly show how specific features of the conflicts relate to the defining features of racial prejudice. For the negative instance, students must clearly show how specific features of the conflict are inconsistent with the defining features of racial prejudice.

Instructional Objectives for Rules, Principles, and Cognitive Strategies

In Chapter 5, Mrs. Torres developed an assessment strategy for the following instructional goal: *Learners will apply the rules for rounding numbers to the nearest ten and hundred.* Here is an instructional objective that describes how she will assess this rule learning outcome:

▶ *Context:* Twenty two-digit and three-digit numerals will be provided with instructions to round each to the nearest ten or nearest hundred (ten each). Each numeral to be rounded will have blank lines for the next lower multiple, the next higher multiple, and the multiple to which the numeral is rounded.

▶ *Performance:* Learners will apply the rules for rounding numbers to the nearest ten and hundred (capability). They will write the next higher multiple of ten or one hundred and the next lower multiple on the lines provided. They will write the numeral rounded to the nearest ten or hundred on the lines provided.

▶ *Quality:* 90 percent of each set of numerals must be rounded correctly. To be considered correct, both the lower and higher multiple also must be written correctly.

Is this objective valid for its corresponding instructional goal? According to the goal, students need to be able to apply rules as intellectual skills. According to the instructional objective, students will be given numerous opportunities to apply the rules they should have acquired. It will be impossible for Mrs.

Torres's students to write the correct numerals on the lines consistently if they cannot apply the rounding rules. Therefore, the objective does appear to be valid for assessing achievement of the intended instructional goal. Mrs. Torres enhances the validity of the assessment data by requiring students to show essential steps along the way—not just the final result—to ensure that they are actually applying the rule.

With respect to reliability, Mrs. Torres has minimized scorer-related measurement error by constructing objectively scored items. Providing the blank lines also will reduce measurement error by reminding students that they are to write three numerals for each item. Finally, providing twenty items greatly minimizes the possible effects of guessing or other random variables.

To illustrate writing an instructional objective for a principle, let's return to one of Ms. Nelson's instructional goals: *Learners will be able to demonstrate how the rate of cooling influences the size of a mineral crystal.* Here is Ms. Nelson's corresponding instructional objective:

▶ Given three written problem scenarios that involve crystal growth, learners will demonstrate how the rate of cooling influences the size of a mineral crystal by writing predictions and explanations that are consistent with the cooling rate principle. Each of the three written responses must (1) describe specific actions to be taken in the problem scenario, (2) demonstrate clear relationships among actions and cooling rates, and (3) accurately predict crystal size.

As you know, we apply principles as intellectual skills by using them to help us solve new problems. Because Ms. Nelson's objective contains realistic problem scenarios to which students will apply the target principle, her assessment strategy appears to be valid for her instructional goal. Students will not be able to write predictions and explanations for the unfamiliar problems unless they can apply the cooling principle as an intellectual skill.

Because students' written responses to the three scenarios can vary, Ms. Nelson will not be able to score them objectively. In Chapter 5, I illustrated an analytical scoring system that she could develop to maximize reliability. Notice how the instructional objective describes the structure of the scoring system so that the guidelines are available to her when she develops the actual rating scale (or rubric).

Instructional objectives for cognitive strategies are very similar to objectives for rules and principles. As for rules and principles, we assess the learning of cognitive strategies by giving learners new opportunities to apply them. Let's return to Mr. Hoffman's cognitive strategy instructional goal: *Learners will be able to originate concept maps for textbook chapters.* Here is the instructional objective from which he derived the assessment procedure described in Chapter 5:

▶ I will provide students with a twenty-page chapter from a seventh-grade social studies textbook. The chapter will be one that they have never seen before. Students will demonstrate the ability to originate concept maps by producing a written concept map for the chapter provided. Students have four days to complete their concept maps, with twenty minutes of class time provided each day. To be acceptable, students' concept maps must contain at least three major superordinate concepts from the chapter, with at least two subordinate concepts for each superordinate concept from the chapter. Relationships among concepts must be hierarchical and labeled meaningfully and accurately. At least five cross-links must be included. Each cross-link must represent a meaningful relationship and must be labeled meaningfully and accurately. I will develop an analytical scoring instrument that focuses on the criteria just described.

Is Mr. Hoffman's instructional objective valid for his instructional goal? Yes! Students will, in fact, be evaluated on how well they can create their own concept maps for an unfamiliar textbook chapter. By providing an unfamiliar chapter, Mr. Hoffman can be assured that students are producing their concept maps by generalizing the cognitive strategy as an intellectual skill rather than simply reproducing a map from memory that they already have seen. Furthermore, by applying an analytical scoring instrument, Mr. Hoffman has greater assurance that his students created their concept maps by engaging in the necessary cognitive processes. That, after all, is what concept mapping is supposed to help learners do. Of course, the analytical scoring instrument for this performance assessment also will help to enhance the reliability of Mr. Hoffman's scoring.

Instructional Objectives for Motor Skill Outcomes

The key to writing valid instructional objectives for motor skill instructional goals is to ensure that learners have the opportunity to make a motor response. A second key is thoughtfully preparing criteria for evaluating the quality of students' physical movements. Let's illustrate these two points by examining an objective that could be written for the following instructional goal: *Learners will be able to execute the procedure for making a circle with a compass.*

▶ Learners will be given a compass and a sheet with eight points and circle diameters in centimeters. Learners will demonstrate the ability to execute the procedure for making a circle with a compass by constructing a circle for each of the eight points with the diameter indicated. For seven of the eight circles, the beginning and end of the lines must meet. For seven of the eight circles, the diameters can be no more than 2 millimeters larger or smaller than the diameters indicated on the sheet.

Notice first that the performance indicated in the objective is valid for the capability expressed by the instructional goal. Learners will not describe or talk about how to use a compass. They will not answer questions about how they would use a compass. They will actually get compasses in their hands and make circles with them. This performance definitely will require them to execute the acquired motor skill. As for reliability, notice that students will have several opportunities to demonstrate the skill. Notice also that the objective specifies how we will judge the quality of the performance—in this case, a product outcome. By checking to see that the lines meet and that the diameters are not off by more than 2 millimeters, we can infer that students have applied the appropriate process in making the circles.

Instructional Objectives for Attitude Outcomes

Recall that we can take either a direct or indirect approach to attitude assessment. When we take a direct approach, we need to ensure that learners have the opportunity to demonstrate voluntary behaviors that are consistent with the attitude. Suppose, for example, we need to assess students' acquisition of the following attitudinal goal: *Learners will choose to listen to classical music.* What we want to know is if learners have developed an appreciation (or positive attitude) for classical music. Although this appreciation could be operationalized in different ways, we have decided to look for evidence that learners would choose to *listen* to it, given the opportunity to choose voluntarily to do so. Here is an instructional objective that describes how the choice will be provided:

▶ Learners will demonstrate a positive attitude toward classical music by choosing to listen to classical symphonies. They will voluntarily go to the school library during free time, select a recording of a classical symphony, listen to at least one movement, and complete a personal reaction form. On the reaction form, students will indicate the name of the composer and the name of the symphony and write a one-paragraph reaction that describes features of the music that they heard. Students will be provided access to library recordings during their free time (e.g., lunch, recess, study time). During the school year, students will submit three reaction forms.

This instructional objective describes the circumstances that we might create in a school environment to elicit the target voluntary behavior. We would have to make students aware that the library recordings are available to them. We would also have to make sure they know how to complete the reaction forms. However, in setting up the conditions of the assessment, we would need to be very careful that students do not get the impression that they are *required* to listen and complete the forms. I know what you are thinking: If we don't require them to listen, they probably won't. Well, that may be true, but at least they will be listening because they have a positive attitude toward classical music, which is what we are trying to assess. If we force students to listen to three symphonies, we cannot be certain that they are demonstrating a positive attitude toward classical music. Because the objective describes a situation that allows us to observe voluntary behavior consistent with the target attitude object, it is valid for the instructional goal.

Another potential limitation of this assessment strategy is that students may find the reaction form too burdensome, which may inhibit their willingness to engage in the target behavior. The reaction forms are a critical part of the assessment strategy because they will help us monitor the number of students who are listening to classical symphonies. However, the form should require a minimal amount of effort for students to complete. Students who do possess a positive attitude toward listening to classical music may choose not to demonstrate it if they perceive the reaction form as too much work.

As you can see, creating the optimal conditions for assessing attitudes directly is tricky business. Assessing attitudes indirectly is much easier, although the data do not permit completely confident inferences about learners' attitude-related behaviors. Here is an example of an objective that illustrates an indirect approach:

▶ *Instructional goal: Learners will choose not to abuse alcohol.*

▶ *Instructional objective:* Learners will demonstrate a negative attitude toward alcohol abuse by choosing not to abuse alcohol. Learners will indicate the likelihood that they would not abuse alcohol by responding to a twenty-item questionnaire. Each item will be in the form of a five-point Likert scale. Students must respond with "4" or "5" to at least fifteen of the statements that are consistent with a negative attitude toward alcohol abuse.

For this objective, we do not have to be concerned about creating the optimal conditions for students to demonstrate an attitude-related behavior. We do, however, need to prepare an assessment instrument that will yield valid, reliable data from which to make inferences regarding students' actual behaviors. Although the objective appears to be valid for its instructional goal, the critical test will be the degree to which each of the Likert items elicits valid, reliable responses from students.

LET'S SUMMARIZE

In this section, I have demonstrated that we can write instructional objectives for any type of learning outcome. I have also demonstrated the variety of forms that instructional objectives can take. As long as the context, performance, and quality of assessment are included, your instructional objectives can take any form you wish. I hope that this last section has demonstrated the degree of thinking that goes into the process of preparing instructional objectives. As you think through the context, performance, and quality components of your objectives, you need to do so in ways that maximize both the validity and reliability of the data that eventually will be produced. Before we leave this chapter, I invite you to try your hand at writing valid instructional objectives for the instructional goals you will find in Exercise 6.3 in the *Student Exercise Guide*.

LOOKING BACK   LOOKING AHEAD

In this chapter we have seen that educational outcomes can be stated at three different levels of specificity: educational goal, instructional goals, and instructional objectives. Although each type of outcome is useful to the instructional design process, instructional objectives describe the results of classroom instruction with the greatest degree of clarity and precision.

The primary purpose of writing instructional objectives is to transform instructional goals into detailed plans for collecting assessment data. To function adequately, these detailed plans need to include a minimum of three components: (1) context, (2) performance, and (3) quality. By specifying these critical features of assessment before teaching, we hold ourselves accountable to the instructional goals that we intend for our learners to achieve. In other words, instructional objectives function as specific hypotheses that we can test following instruction to collect concrete evidence of our teaching effectiveness.

A second purpose for writing instructional objectives is to guide instructional planning. With a clear, concrete career objective, you can make good decisions about the kinds of experiences and credentials you will need to achieve that objective. Similarly, with a clear, concrete instructional objective, you will be in the best position to make good decisions about the kinds of learning activities and materials your learners will need to achieve the objective. As illustrated by the Zook family camping trip in Chapter 1, a successful journey depends primarily on beginning with a clear destination. Instructional objectives are the clear destinations that are essential for planning the remainder of the instructional journey. I encourage you to check your understanding of instructional objectives by completing Exercise 6.4 in the *Student Exercise Guide*.

Now that we have explored assessment issues that are relevant to establishing our teaching destinations (What will we do when we get there?), we are ready to address the third fundamental question of trip planning and instructional planning: How will we get there? We take up this question in the next part of the book.

RESOURCES FOR FURTHER REFLECTION AND EXPLORATION

Print Resources

Gronlund, N. E. (1995). *How to write and use instructional objectives* (5th ed.). Englewood Cliffs, NJ: Merrill.

A classic work written by a highly regarded expert in the field of educational assessment. Provides detailed practical guidance in writing and using objectives for intellectual, affective, and performance learning outcomes.

Mager, R. F. (1962). *Preparing instructional objectives*. Palo Alto, CA: Fearon Publishers.

Another classic work. The process of writing instructional objectives is presented in a lively, engaging programmed-instruction format. A highly influential book that remains essential for teachers.

How Will We Get There?
Developing Instructional Strategies for Learning Goals

Part Three

With a clear destination (instructional goal) and assessment strategy (instructional objective), we are now ready to begin thinking about the third key instructional planning question: How do we get there? In other words, what kinds of teaching activities will we design to promote the learning outcomes described by our instructional goals? With the wide variety of teaching methods, materials, activities, and resources that are available to us, how do we determine the teaching techniques that will be most effective for our learners? In the next part of the book, we will address this question by exploring the learning processes and teaching strategies associated with the learning outcomes that are most common in school classrooms: verbal information (Chapter 7), concepts (Chapter 8), rules, principles, and cognitive strategies (Chapter 9). After developing an understanding of the learning requirements for these specific outcomes, we will examine a general strategy for sequencing instructional events (Chapter 10) and explore procedures for planning larger units of instruction (Chapter 11).

7

Instructional Strategies for Verbal Information Outcomes

I f you have ever played on a sports team, you understand the importance of entering an athletic contest with a game plan. Coaches whose teams win consistently are good at developing an effective game plan before each game begins. A game plan outlines the general approach that the team will take to play successfully against its opponent. For a plan to be effective, the coach must first analyze the characteristics of the opposing team. In other words, before thinking about what her own team will do, the coach must be able to understand and anticipate what the other team is likely to do.

Several aspects of a coach's game plan are relevant to the instructional design processes that we discuss in the next several chapters. First, a game plan is a general strategy that influences the details of all the specific actions the team will take during the game. It establishes general expectations and provides a sense of direction to maximize the potential success of the team. Second, the game plan is derived from an understanding of the other team's characteristics. The coach carefully takes into consideration the way the other team plays and then plans accordingly, avoiding actions that allow the other team to use its strengths and deliberately trying to exploit the other team's weaknesses.

Whether the game plan leads to victory ultimately depends on how well it actually matches what the other team does on the field—the third principle. The

INSTRUCTIONAL GOALS FOR CHAPTER 7

After reading and thinking about this chapter, you should be able to . . .

1. Differentiate between the internal and external conditions of learning.

2. Identify the three major components of an instructional strategy.

3. Describe the characteristics and functions of the major components of the human information processing system: memory structures, control processes, and executive control.

4. Demonstrate how verbal information is acquired according to the information processing system.

5. Explain and demonstrate the effects of elaboration and organization processes on learning.

6. Describe and apply highlighting strategies, schema activation strategies, generative learning activities, mnemonic devices, organization strategies, and practice to support verbal information learning.

7. Design instructional strategies to support verbal information learning.

coach develops the plan by *thinking* about the strengths and weaknesses of the other team. Ultimately, however, the quality of the plan must be evaluated by looking at observable evidence—the score. Finally, if the team wins the game, should the same game plan be used for the next game? Not necessarily. Every team is different, and a game plan that is effective against one team may not work at all against a different one.

In the next several chapters we will be exploring the essential ingredients of effective instructional plans. As we have noted repeatedly throughout the book thus far, different learning outcomes require different types of instructional goals, content analysis procedures, and assessment procedures. Now we shall see that different learning outcomes also require different approaches to instruction—different game plans, if you will. If we want to design a potentially effective instructional game plan, we have to do just what athletic coaches do: first understand the characteristics and learning processes of the learners who are on the playing field with us. In this chapter, we examine the basic components of instructional plans in general and then look specifically at instructional plans for verbal information learning. Before we get to the details, take a look at the instructional goals (part of my game plan) that I want you to achieve through reading this chapter.

Internal and External Conditions of Learning

When athletic coaches design a game plan, they do not then declare their team the winner just because they have a plan. The outcome of an athletic contest ultimately depends on how both teams interact with each other on the playing field. Similarly, whenever we design an instructional plan and implement it, we obviously cannot declare that learners have necessarily achieved our instructional goals.

Instructional Events and Learning Processes

The **instruction** that we plan and deliver is simply a set of events that we design to support the learning process. Learning is something that happens *inside* the minds of learners; instruction is something that happens *outside* learners. Instruction has the best chance of being effective (i.e., learners achieve the instructional goals) when the outside events match what needs to happen within learners' minds—just like a coach's game plan.

Think about all the specific events that occur externally to learners when they are experiencing instruction. Try to replay in your mind some instructional episodes that you have experienced. Make a list, and then compare it to the list I provide in Table 7.1. I have organized my list according to four major variables that we might use to classify the types of instructional events that occur in school classrooms every day: communications, media, materials and equipment, and activities. As you can see from the list, classroom teachers have a large smorgasbord of instructional events from which to choose when teaching. Which ones work? Which ones do not work? My answer to these two questions might surprise you: *All* of them work—and *none* of them works.

Asking which instructional events are effective is like asking which game plan will work. The game plan that is most closely matched to the strengths and weaknesses of the other team has the greatest potential to be effective. Similarly, the instructional events that are designed to match students' internal learning needs have the greatest potential to be effective (Grabowski,

Table 7.1
Major Categories of Classroom Instructional Events

Category	Examples
1. Communications	Teacher to student Student to teacher Student to student Verbal Nonverbal
2. Media	Chalkboard Overhead projector Filmstrip 16-mm film Videotape Tape recording Computer
3. Materials and equipment	Textbook Workbook Worksheets Handouts Maps Cuisenaire rods Place-value blocks Fossil specimens Flashcards Scissors Construction paper Markers
4. Activities	Expository explanation Large group discussion Small group discussion Cooperative groups Peer tutoring Field trip Game Independent seatwork Homework Classroom practice

1996). The quality of learners' internal processing ultimately has a direct impact on achieving the learning outcome. The external events of instruction have, at best, only an indirect impact on learning, as you can see in Figure 7.1.

Internal and External Conditions of Learning

When we develop an instructional game plan, we need to consider both internal learning processes and external instructional events. Gagne (1985) refers to instructional events as the external conditions of learning. The **external conditions of learning** describe the experiences that learners will have during the learning process. These conditions refer to the characteristics of the learning environment that are external to, or outside, learners. They include the com-

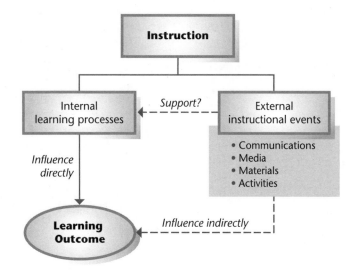

**Figure 7.1
Relationships Among
Internal Learning
Processes, External In-
structional Events, and
Learning**

munications, media, materials and equipment, and learning activities that students will experience directly. These are the only conditions of learning that teachers can control.

In contrast, the **internal conditions of learning** describe aspects of learners that influence how they process information and construct meaning. These conditions include the ways in which learners acquire new propositions, skills, and attitudes within their own minds, as well as the myriad of individual differences that they bring with them into the classroom: interests, motivations, prior knowledge, cultural perspectives, learning strategies, and so on. Unfortunately, no teacher can control or manipulate the internal conditions of learning directly (see Figure 7.1).

Effective instruction is possible when we orchestrate the external conditions of learning to match the internal conditions of learning. Notice that the emphasis is on what our *learners* need to be successful, not on the activities and materials that *we* might like or prefer. How do we know what our learners need to be successful? What are the internal conditions of learning for specific instructional goals?

Conditions of Learning for Major Learning Outcomes

At first glance, it may appear that every instructional goal would have its own unique internal conditions of learning and therefore its own unique external conditions, or teaching methods. Fortunately, however, the situation is not that complex. To illustrate this point, look at the twelve instructional goals listed below. Are these goals completely different, or can you find some ways to group them?

Choose to recycle.
Recognize cumulus clouds.
State the names of the planets in
   order from the sun.
Identify proper nouns.
Dribble a basketball.
Choose to listen to others
   without interrupting.

Name the capitals of the fifty states.
Choose to refrain from alcohol
   abuse.
Execute a tennis serve.
Describe the reactions in
   photosynthesis.
Classify groups of people as
   communities.
Swim the backstroke.

I hope you quickly recognized that these instructional goals fit into four major learning outcomes: verbal information, concepts, attitudes, and psy-

Table 7.2
Instructional Goals Grouped by Learning Outcome

Verbal Information	Concepts	Attitudes	Psychomotor Skills
State the names of the planets in order from the sun.	Recognize cumulus clouds.	Choose to recycle.	Dribble a basketball.
Name the capitals of the fifty states.	Identify proper nouns.	Choose to listen to others without interrupting.	Execute a tennis serve.
Describe the sequence of reactions in photosynthesis.	Classify groups of people as communities.	Choose to refrain from alcohol abuse.	Swim the backstroke.

chomotor skills (see Table 7.2). Each cluster of instructional goals represents a different type of learning outcome. Within each cluster, the internal conditions of learning for each of the three instructional goals are actually the same. However, the internal conditions of learning across the four learning outcomes are different (Gagne, 1985; Ragan & Smith, 1996).

For example, although the specific content, or concept, is different in each of these instructional goals (cumulus cloud, proper noun, community), the internal learning processes needed to achieve each goal are not different. Regardless of the specific content, people acquire a new concept by becoming aware of the critical features of the category and applying those features as broadly as possible to new instances (in the next chapter we look at this principle in much greater detail). These are the internal conditions of concept learning. The only thing that changes is the specific content on which the internal conditions of learning operate.

Now what about differences across learning outcomes? Here we find that the internal conditions of learning do vary. For example, the internal conditions of learning that govern how learners acquire the ability to identify proper nouns and serve tennis balls are different. Students can learn to identify proper nouns without necessarily moving any skeletal muscles; it's an intellectual skill. However, to learn how to execute a tennis serve as a psychomotor skill, learners have to get tennis racquets in their hands and swing them at tennis balls. This activity obviously requires them to move lots of skeletal muscles in coordinated ways.

The internal conditions of learning for each of the major learning outcomes generalize across an infinite number of specific content areas. This focus on internal learning processes rather than external teaching methods has several advantages. First, by applying your knowledge of internal learning processes, you are empowered to develop your own specific teaching methods and materials tailored to the particular characteristics of your learners. You will not need to be dependent on a textbook, curriculum kit, teaching magazine, or activity book to provide methods and materials for you. You will be able to explain the reasons for your teaching methods, and you will not be gullible to the latest fads and bandwagons that plague the field of education. Furthermore, you will experience the excitement of bringing your own personal creativity to teaching. As long as you are supporting your learners' processing needs, you can use a variety of approaches that may differ from those other teachers use.

The Instructional Strategy: The Teacher's Game Plan

The game plan that a teacher prepares, called an **instructional strategy**, describes the external teaching events that we plan to use to support our learners' internal learning processes so they will be able to achieve our instructional goals. A well-designed instructional strategy should focus on three key elements of the teaching-learning process (Dick & Carey, 1996): information, engagement, and practice.

■ **Information**   The information to describe in an instructional strategy includes the specific content that learners need to think about: definitions, explanations, examples, nonexamples, illustrations, demonstrations, and so on. This is the content that we think our learners need to process in order to acquire the target capability. Because the ultimate goal is for learners to process this information, we need to think about ways of expressing it that are as meaningful as possible to them. By "expressing it," I am not suggesting that teachers always need to verbalize information for learners. I simply mean that we need to be clear about the declarative statement of a proposition, rule, principle, concept definition, cognitive strategy, or motor skill that we want learners to represent in their own memories. How we deliver that statement to learners is the focus of the second element, engagement.

■ **Engagement**   Teachers mediate information for their learners. That is, they create ways for learners to experience information in a manner that will influence their internal learning processes. Engagement refers to the procedures that we will use to help learners experience content in active, meaningful ways. Will we write the content on a poster and hang it in the classroom for use in a small group activity? Will learners read the content for themselves in a book? Will they discuss it with other students? Will they construct the content for themselves in a guided discovery activity? Will students apply the content as they experience a computer simulation? These are the types of questions we address in the engagement component of an instructional strategy.

Three specific engagement considerations are media, learning activities, and motivation and attention. Instructional media are simply the means by which we communicate information to learners (Gentry, 1994; Heinich, Molenda, & Russell, 1989). When you think of instructional media, technological gadgets like VCRs, computers, and CD players probably come to mind. These are indeed examples of instructional media. However, do not overlook tools that are less technologically sophisticated, like overhead projectors, filmstrips, tape recordings, televisions, cameras, posters, books, and even chalkboards. In fact, you, as a teacher, are a potentially powerful instructional medium. We should select and use instructional media not just because they are technologically advanced or readily available but to support our learners' internal processing needs (Hooper & Hannafin, 1991).

Communicating information by means of some type of instructional medium usually is not enough to produce learning. You and I have received lots of visual and auditory messages over the years that we cannot remember five minutes later. That students see or hear information does not mean they will necessarily learn anything from it—even if they see it on a computer screen or hear it on a compact disc. They will learn from information they receive only to the extent that they actively construct meaning from it (Cooper, 1993; Duffy & Jonassen, 1991). That is, they have to *do* something to the information to internalize it as their own. A **learning activity** is an action or event in which learners actively participate to increase the probability that they will process information in ways that are appropriate for the learning outcome they are to acquire.

Classroom teachers have a large number of learning activities from which to choose. Table 7.1 contains only a partial list of some of the major types of activities that are available to you to engage your learners with content. Using your own creativity, ingenuity, and knowledge of internal learning processes, you can think of many, many more. The activity itself, however, does not produce learning. Discussions, cooperative groups, peer tutoring, and field trips do not magically produce learned capabilities. Only when we design these types of activities to support the internal conditions of learning do they have the potential to help students learn.

A third critical ingredient in engaging learners is their level of attention and motivation. Have you ever found yourself daydreaming as you were sitting in a class or reading a book? You may have discovered that you could not recall anything that was said or that you read during the previous fifteen minutes. As we will see later in this chapter, the first essential requirement of meaningful learning is that learners pay attention to the information. When learners pay **attention**, it means that they are directing their senses toward a source of information so that they will be able to receive it most effectively—that is, to be able to think about it further (Ormrod, 1995).

Usually the stimuli that we choose to attend to in the environment depend on our motivational state. **Motivation** is an extremely complex construct to understand; let's define it simply as an internal state that stimulates, focuses, and maintains our thinking and behavior (Maehr & Meyer, 1997). Succinctly stated, motivation is the reason we do what we do. Although motivation in itself does not guarantee learning, students usually learn best when they have some motivation for doing so. Therefore, you should consider carefully the kinds of media, materials, and learning activities that are as attention getting and motivating as possible for your particular learners.

■ **Practice**   The third critical component of an instructional strategy is practice: the opportunity for learners to perform the capability described by an instructional goal prior to performing it for summative assessment purposes. Practice is a significant, essential part of the learning process for three reasons. First, the outward actions that students perform when practicing have the potential to help them become more active participants in the learning process, thus strengthening the quality of their learning. Second, through practice, students have the opportunity to receive informative, corrective feedback on the quality of their learning. Third, teachers can use student practice to collect assessment data for the purpose of making formative evaluation decisions. Whenever students practice, we have the opportunity to observe their performance, evaluate their progress, and make appropriate adjustments.

Practice is essential for acquiring any learned capability. Usually we recognize the necessity of practice for the acquisition of motor skills. Intuitively, it is easy to see that swinging a golf club, dribbling a basketball, and dancing a waltz are skills that cannot be acquired unless learners have the chance to swing, dribble, and dance. The same principle applies to acquiring intellectual skills (including cognitive strategies), verbal information, and the cognitive and behavioral components of attitudes.

LET'S SUMMARIZE

Information, engagement, and practice are three critical elements in any instructional strategy. Although we have examined them separately, you will want to consider the three variables simultaneously in your instructional planning, as illustrated in Figure 7.2. By thinking carefully about each variable, you will be able to walk into your classroom with a well-prepared game plan that

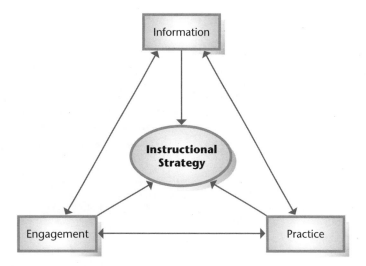

**Figure 7.2
Three Integrated Components of an Instructional Strategy**

has a great deal of potential to help students learn. Of course, as you already know, the most effective instructional plans are based on an understanding of the internal conditions of learning. What are the internal conditions of learning for various learning outcomes? How can we develop external instructional events to match those internal conditions? For the remainder of this chapter, let's try to answer these two questions for one particular learning outcome: verbal information.

Verbal Information: Internal Conditions of Learning

How does new information from a teacher, book, videotape, computer program, or field trip move from a learner's external environment to internal memory so that it can be retrieved when needed and stated in some useful way? As noted in Figure 7.3, these questions are best answered by understanding the internal learning processes that directly influence verbal information learning.

Learners Are Information Processors

Over the past thirty years, educational psychologists have made great progress in understanding learning from a cognitive perspective (Di Vesta, 1987, 1989). The research evidence is now quite compelling: How well people remember information depends mostly on how well they process it at the time of learning. What does it mean for people to process information? Maybe you have experienced processing food with a food processor. A carrot goes into one end of the food processor, the processor does something to the carrot, and the carrot ends up sliced, shredded, or chopped. The food processor transforms, or changes, the carrot into a different state by acting on it in some way.

Similarly, when learners process information, they receive it and act on it mentally to change its form so that it remains firmly lodged in memory. When that happens, we have learning, and the evidence for that learning is the learner's ability to recall, state, or apply the information in some meaningful way.

Information processing depends on more than the input that learners receive from the environment; it depends as well on the prior knowledge and thinking that learners bring to the process. The ultimate result of the learning process, then, is a *construction*—a form of knowledge created by each individ-

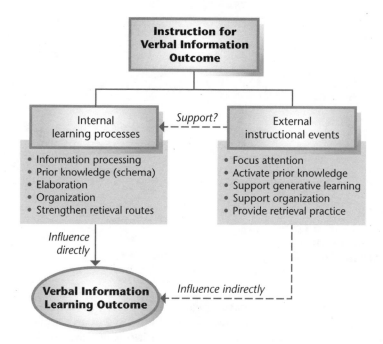

Figure 7.3
Internal and External Conditions of Learning for Verbal Information

ual learner. As learners apply their own knowledge, experience, and thinking to the processing of new information, they make it meaningful to themselves. As they make new information meaningful, they transform it into forms that are increasingly durable, stable, and memorable.

An Information Processing Model of Learning

Although each individual learner is capable of constructing different meanings for information because of their own prior knowledge and skills, knowledge construction processes operate across different learners in similar ways. The Information Processing Model depicted in Figure 7.4 summarizes the major types of cognitive processes that are at work internally when learning happens. Let's briefly review the three major components of the model: (1) memory structures, (2) control processes, and (3) executive control.

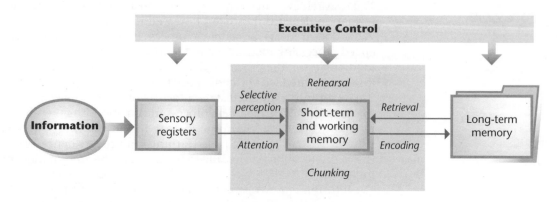

Figure 7.4
An Information Processing Model of Learning

■ **Memory Structures** The new information that learners receive from the environment can exist in three different states, depending on what they do to it: (1) sensory registers, (2) short-term memory, and (3) long-term memory.

When learners receive information through one or more of their five senses (see, hear, smell, taste, touch), it resides very briefly in the memory structure known as the **sensory registers**. Information takes this form when the learner's sense receptors are stimulated by sights, sounds, smells, tastes, and touches. If the learner processes these sensory stimuli further, they are transformed into a state known as **short-term memory**. Short-term memory holds information in the form of sounds, images, or words—the knowledge that we are consciously thinking about at any given moment. Although this representation is more durable than that of the sensory registers, it is limited in two significant ways. First, we can hold a very limited amount of information in this form. According to research evidence, most adults can hold only about seven unrelated pieces of information, give or take two or three (Miller, 1956). This amount, however, can vary somewhat depending on the specific circumstances of the situation (Anderson, 1990; Carlson, 1997).

Second, we can hold that small amount of information for only ten to twenty seconds unless we process it further. So if we stop thinking about information in its short-term memory form, we lose it, and it is no longer available to us for further processing. Losing information from short-term memory is similar to losing a document when power is cut off from a computer. If you haven't saved the document to a floppy disk or to the hard drive, it is lost for good. We use some of our limited short-term memory space to perform mental operations such as planning, problem solving, skill application, and decision making. The part of short-term memory we use for these "thinking" activities is known as **working memory**. Working memory is where the action is.

The most durable knowledge state is known as **long-term memory**. In contrast to short-term memory, this memory structure is not limited by either time or space. The amount of information that we can store in long-term memory is limitless. Furthermore, if we have stored the information well, we will be able to remember it for long periods of time (perhaps our entire lives) without constantly having to think about it. I can still remember my family's telephone number from the house we lived in nearly thirty years ago. Sometimes, however, I can't remember the name of a new acquaintance only three minutes after being introduced. Why doesn't all the information we encounter get stored in long-term memory? The answer is that learning doesn't always happen because we don't *process* all the information we encounter in the same way. Let's look now at the *control processes* that are responsible for learning.

■ **Control Processes** The **control processes** of the information processing model are the mental actions that transform information from one memory structure to another (Gagne, 1985; Ormrod, 1995). As you can see in Figure 7.4, attention and selective perception are two control processes that "move" information from the sensory registers to short-term memory. As we already have noted, attention is the process of directing our senses toward a source of information. Attention prepares the learner to receive information into the processing system. **Selective perception** occurs when we find meaning in a piece of sensory information. Of course, assigning meaning means that we are *thinking* about that piece of information, and thinking happens in working memory. It is important to note that we are selective about assigning meaning to sensory stimuli. This means that we pick and choose what we are going to invest time and effort in thinking about. We have to be selective because short-term memory is very limited in size.

As you can see in Figure 7.4, two control processes help us maintain information in short-term memory. **Rehearsal** is the process of repeating information. We can rehearse information by verbalizing it over and over to ourselves, either out loud or inside our heads. We can also rehearse information by continuing to look at, smell, listen to, or touch it. As long as we are rehearsing information, we are thinking about it, and as long as we are thinking about it, we are maintaining it actively in short-term memory.

Chunking is the process of finding meaningful patterns in new information. A meaningful relationship among two or more pieces of information forms a pattern that helps conserve space in short-term memory. For example, can you find any meaningful relationships among the following twelve objects?

hammer	leg	banana	dog
mouse	horse	nose	foot
apple	wrench	saw	grape

You probably noticed easily that the objects are members of four broader concepts: tool, animal, fruit, body part. By using the concepts to cluster the objects into four meaningful groups of three, you can reduce the short-term memory load from twelve discrete items to four meaningful chunks. Remembering the twelve items now is much easier because you can rely on the knowledge of tools, animals, fruits, and body parts that you already have stored in long-term memory.

Although chunking and rehearsal represent a greater depth of processing than attention and selective perception, they are still not enough to transform information into the state of long-term memory. We can encounter an object or event repeatedly and still not learn anything from the rehearsal. For example, you have seen hundreds, perhaps thousands, of pennies in your lifetime. From that repeated exposure, can you recall the direction that Lincoln's head faces? If not, don't feel bad; most people find this question difficult to answer (Nickerson & Adams, 1979).

As the penny question illustrates, being exposed to information is not the same as learning it. Transforming new information into the durable, stable state of long-term memory requires the deepest and most meaningful type of processing. **Encoding** is the control process that transforms information from working memory to long-term memory. Encoding is a *thinking* process in which the learner constructs a meaningful connection between a new piece of information and an idea that already is stored in long-term memory.

For information to be stored in long-term memory, the learner must encode it so that it is meaningfully related to the existing knowledge base. If this transformation occurs, the learner should be able to find the proposition later. **Retrieval** is the control process that transforms information back from its propositional state in long-term memory to working memory where the learner can either think about it further or demonstrate it in some observable way such as stating or applying.

To summarize, according to the Information Processing Model, as we process information with increasing depth and meaningfulness, it is transformed from the sensory registers to short-term memory, and eventually to long-term memory. This gradual transformation depends on the ways in which we apply the control processes of attention, selective perception, chunking, rehearsal, encoding, and retrieval to act on information. What, however, determines how the control processes operate on information? That is, what controls the control processes? To answer this question, we turn to the third major component of the model, executive control.

■ **Executive Control**   When you sit down to work at a computer, what determines the flow of information between the various components of the system: keyboard or mouse, central processing unit, floppy disk or hard drive, printer, and so on? *You* do! The commands you give the computer depend on what *you* want to accomplish. If your goal is to write and print a letter, you enter the information and then tell the computer to send it to the printer. If you want to be able to come back to the letter and use it in the future, you tell the computer to store it on a disk or on the hard drive. In the same way that you and your goals control information flow in a computer system, **executive control** manages the control processes that are responsible for information flow during learning (Gredler, 1997), as noted in Figure 7.4.

Executive control takes two general forms. First, our personal goals, interests, motivations, aspirations, and attitudes influence what we select to process and how deeply we process it. Executive control also can take the form of specific cognitive strategies (Graham, 1997). Recall from Chapter 2 that we defined cognitive strategies as plans that we apply to manage our thinking and behavior during problem solving or learning. Cognitive learning strategies such as note taking, outlining, concept mapping, summarizing, and so on help us deploy our built-in control processes in a more systematic, effective manner than we might otherwise. We can acquire cognitive strategies through personal experiences (e.g., a student might develop her own note-taking system when she reads a book) or through formal learning experiences (e.g., deliberately teaching students how to construct concept maps).

LET'S SUMMARIZE

The Information Processing Model provides a powerful perspective on the internal conditions of learning: both in general and for the learning of verbal information. Encoding is the key cognitive process that produces learning because it transforms information into the durable state known as long-term memory. As we have seen, encoding happens when learners construct meaning by relating new, incoming information to ideas they already have stored in long-term memory. To understand the encoding process fully, we need to take a closer look at the nature of long-term memory, yet another critical aspect of the internal conditions of learning noted in Figure 7.3.

Schemas: The Building Blocks of Long-Term Memory

No one really knows for sure what long-term memory is like. The best evidence we have at this point strongly suggests that long-term memory is something like a gigantic web of ideas and images that are all interconnected in meaningful ways. You can easily demonstrate this for yourself by daydreaming for a few minutes. Start with a familiar topic, say, "river." What is the very next idea or picture that pops into your short-term memory? Write it down. What is the next? The next? If you daydream like this for only five minutes, you will easily fill up a sheet of paper. Everything you wrote down came from your long-term memory. You were able to fetch it back into short-term memory and state it because it was already meaningfully connected to the other ideas.

You have just illustrated for yourself that knowledge in long-term memory takes the form of numerous ideas that are connected meaningfully to each other—what cognitive psychologists refer to as a **semantic network** (Anderson, 1990). Figure 7.5 shows you what a hypothetical semantic network might look like. The word *network* reflects the interconnectedness of the ideas; the word *semantic* reflects the fact that each connection is based on some kind of meaning that you have constructed. Once knowledge is interconnected in a semantic network, getting it back out—that is, retrieving it back into short-term memory so we can do something with it—is simply a matter of activating the connections that lead to the piece of information we need. Cognitive psychologists refer to this process as **spreading activation** (Anderson, 1990): Thinking about one piece of information activates a related idea, which, in turn, activates related ideas, which in turn . . . you get the idea.

Executive control influences the spreading activation process. We are most likely to constrain spreading activation to the ideas that are most relevant to

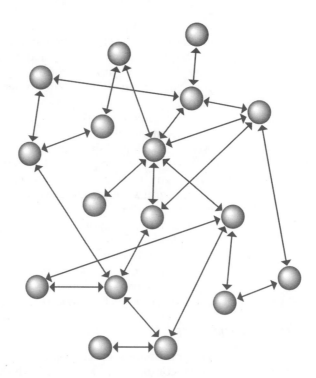

**Figure 7.5
Hypothetical Example of
a Semantic Network**

our interests, motivations, or immediate goals. So for a particular individual, thinking about rivers might activate related ideas like water, boat, fish, and lure or ideas like flood, bridge, levee, and storm. As Figure 7.6 illustrates, both sets of ideas are available in the semantic network, but their activation depends on whether the person is thinking about rivers in the context of an occupation (civil engineer) or a hobby (fishing).

We do not store information in long-term memory by throwing it in randomly. The huge semantic network that comprises all of our stored knowledge is organized by meaningful units that are called **schemas:** organized units of knowledge that consist of general categories (or variables) and the relationships between them (Anderson, 1990; Ormrod, 1995; Rumelhart & Ortony, 1977). For example, within your vast semantic network, you probably have a schema for the concept of "dog." Within your dog schema, you probably have stored some general features that are common to all dogs as you have experienced them (see Figure 7.7): species, four legs, furry, tail, bark. You also have more detailed information such as facts and images about specific dogs related meaningfully to each general variable. Your schema for dog is a subset of even larger schemas. Your dog schema probably resides within a general schema for "animals," which in turn resides within a general schema for "living things" (see Figure 7.7). This type of hierarchical organization appears to be a common feature of schemas.

Cognitive psychologists are still trying to figure out exactly how schemas are organized within semantic networks. Schemas have neither clear boundaries nor consistent structure. For our purposes, it is more useful to concentrate on how schemas function in the learning process. Here, the research evidence is quite compelling. Schemas—whatever their actual structure—have a profound impact on every aspect of the learning process (see Schoenfeld, Smith, & Arcavi, 1993; Winn & Snyder, 1996). We tend to interpret new information in ways that are consistent with our preexisting schemas. Our schemas influence how well we comprehend and remember new information. In general, the better that new information fits into a preexisting schema, the easier it is to understand it and encode it in a way that makes retrieval possible (Anderson,

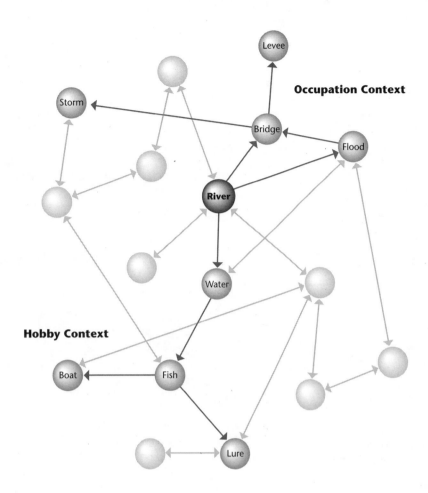

Figure 7.6
Effects of Spreading Activation on Information Retrieval

Reynolds, Schallert, & Goetz, 1977; Bransford & Johnson, 1972; Martin & Halverson, 1981; Saxe, 1988).

From the perspective of schema theory, learning is something like a chemical reaction. When two different chemicals react with each other, they create a new chemical. Both of the original chemicals contribute something to the reaction and the new product. However, the reaction will never occur unless both chemicals get into the same test tube. When meaningful learning happens, two units of information have to react with each other. Both the incoming new information and the preexisting knowledge (or schema) contribute something to the learner's construction of meaning, but the construction cannot happen until both are activated together in the learner's "test tube"—working memory. To transform verbal information into the state of long-term memory, learners have to bring something to the learning process. They need to add knowledge from their own schemas. Another term for this adding-on process is *elaboration*, another internal condition of learning (see Figure 7.3).

Meaningful Encoding: Elaboration Processes

Elaboration occurs when learners enrich new information by adding extra information from their own semantic networks (Anderson, 1990; Wittrock, 1979). In other words, as learners actively use their own schemas to think about a new proposition, it becomes linked meaningfully to that activated schema. The link that the learner constructs then becomes a potential retrieval route for spreading activation. If the learner does not construct a meaningful link, then retrieval is impossible because there is no way for the process of spreading activation to "find" it.

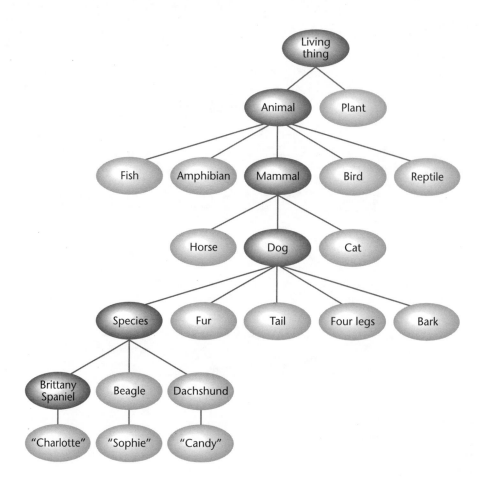

Figure 7.7
Organizational Structure of Schemas

Let me illustrate the critical importance of elaboration with Figure 7.8. In the left-hand portion of the diagram, you see a semantic network (or schema) and a proposition (X-Y). Notice that there are no meaningful connections between any of the concepts in the schema and either the concept X or Y. This may represent a situation in which a learner is rehearsing a fact in working memory but is not really thinking about the meaning of the fact. Now let's assume that the student starts thinking about the X-Y proposition. He may think, "Hmmm. X appears to me to be an example of concept A." The student has now elaborated on the new proposition by adding some information from his own schema. In doing so, he has generated a new link between A and X. Now the encoding process has begun, and a retrieval route has been created for spreading activation, as you can see in the lower portion of Figure 7.8.

Let's suppose that the learner continues to think about the proposition and realizes that concept H is similar to concept X—another link! He thinks some more, constructing relationships that link F to X and Y to D and H, *elaborations* that create several more retrieval routes for spreading activation. Now he can remember the proposition even more easily because there are lots of ways to find it. By wrapping a new idea with meaning, the learner creates the pathways that will be needed to remember and state that idea (Stein & Bransford, 1979; Stein et al., 1982).

Let's go back to Lincoln's head on the penny. If you couldn't remember which way Lincoln faces, perhaps your curiosity got to you, and you looked at a penny. You then saw that Lincoln's head faces to the right. How could you elaborate on this proposition if you wanted to be sure to remember it? Here are two possibilities:

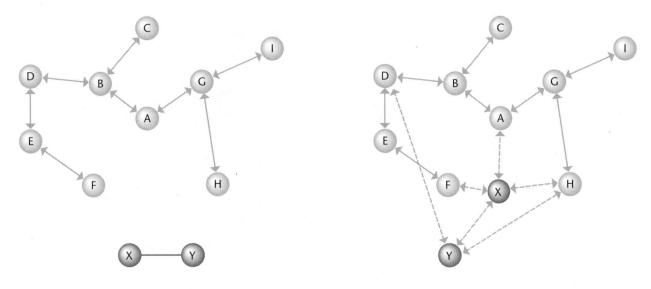

Figure 7.8
Effects of Elaboration on a Semantic Network

1. Lincoln was on the *right* side of the slavery issue. He looked to what was *right* for the country as he looks to the *right* on the penny.

2. Lincoln was a Republican president, and Republicans usually are on the *right* of the political spectrum. As a Republican, Lincoln faces to the *right* of the political spectrum and also to the *right* on the penny.

These statements are examples of *verbal elaboration*. **Verbal elaborations** are additional ideas that learners construct by means of words that they might say out loud or to themselves. It is essential for *learners* to create verbal elaborations for them to be most effective (Wittrock, 1990; Gagne, Weidemann, Bell, & Anders, 1984). Simply giving statements like the two above for students to rehearse does not guarantee that they will be activating their own schemas. Furthermore, learners may not know that Lincoln was a Republican president. When learners construct their own verbal elaborations, we have greater confidence that they have actually activated and used some part of their semantic network that is meaningful to them. This, of course, means that two different learners may elaborate on the same piece of information in very different ways.

Sometimes we can elaborate on propositions by creating visual images in our minds. When we create **image elaborations**, we add on to the information to be learned by creating mental pictures that combine the new information with some visual image that is already part of a schema (Clark & Paivio, 1991). For example, to help you remember that reptiles, fish, and amphibians are all cold-blooded animals, you might create in your mind a picture of a snake, fish, and frog sitting in a refrigerator shivering. In addition to verbal and image elaborations, students can elaborate on new propositions by creating analogies for themselves, summarizing ideas in their own words, or setting information to rhymes or music. Each of these elaborations adds something new to information from learners' prior knowledge.

Meaningful Encoding: Organization Processes

Sometimes we can encode new information by relating it to an organizational structure that exists in our semantic network. When learners *organize* verbal information, they place specific ideas into meaningful units and construct relationships among those units (Gagne, Yekovich, & Yekovich, 1993). The relationships within and between units provide retrieval routes for spreading activation.

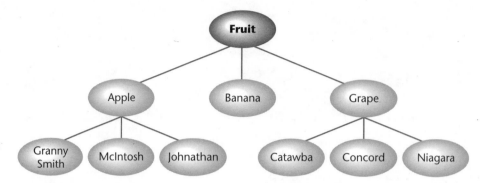

Figure 7.9
Organizing Information Within a Semantic Network

Let's illustrate the organization process with the list of tools, fruits, animals, and body parts you saw earlier. You were able to chunk the twelve objects into those four groups because you already possessed the four superordinate concepts in your semantic network. What if you had some specific apples and grapes to remember also? As illustrated in Figure 7.9, you could relate McIntosh, Granny Smith, and Jonathan together within the superordinate concept of apple. Concord, Niagara, and Catawba are three specific types of grapes that you could organize within the superordinate concept of grape.

How does thinking about subordinate-superordinate relationships within a set of propositions help us encode them? The superordinate concepts that we use to organize information come from our schemas. Because schemas are stored in memory, they already have many meaningful links within them and to other parts of the semantic network. These organizational links then provide retrieval routes for spreading activation (McDaniel & Einstein, 1989).

LET'S SUMMARIZE

In this section, we have been exploring the internal conditions of learning that are relevant to verbal information learning outcomes. As summarized in Figure 7.3, we identified several key features that influence how learners acquire verbal information: information processing, prior knowledge, elaboration, organization, and strengthening retrieval routes. Thus far, we have been silent about how we as *design-teachers* actually teach for verbal information learning outcomes. We have focused exclusively on understanding what our learners need to do—just like a coach develops a game plan by first studying the other team's characteristics. Ultimately, as Figure 7.3 reminds you, learners themselves have to engage in the cognitive processes described in this section. We can't do the processing for them, but we can help. In the next section, we examine some ways that we can help—the *external* conditions of learning.

Verbal Information: External Conditions of Learning

Now that we have a better understanding of what learners need to do to acquire verbal information, we can develop a game plan to help support those processes. As Figure 7.3 illustrates, we need to help learners process verbal information by matching *our* external actions as closely as possible to *their* internal processing needs. Let's examine some specific strategies we can use to accomplish this goal. I have organized them according to the following general processes highlighted in Figure 7.3: attention, activating prior knowledge, elaboration, organization, and practice.

Helping Learners Attend to Verbal Information

Before learners can encode verbal information, they must be aware of it. That is, they must focus their attention on it so that it can be transformed into the working memory state. For names and labels, learners must be aware of both the name or label and the object, event, or idea to which it refers. For propositions, learners must be aware of the words or phrases that communicate a meaningful idea. For organized propositions, learners must be aware of the words, phrases, and sentences that communicate a set of meaningful ideas.

How can we help students attend to specific symbols, words, phrases, and sentences that are used to communicate verbal information? Clearly the specific strategies we might use will depend on the media we select to engage learners. For example, how we call attention to verbal information that appears in a book will be somewhat different from how we call attention to verbal information that is spoken by a peer or teacher, presented on a computer screen, or viewed on an overhead transparency. Nevertheless, despite these superficial media differences, we can use three general types of instructional events to support learners' attention processes: (1) highlighting strategies, (2) questioning strategies, and (3) distinctiveness strategies.

Highlighting Strategies   **Highlighting** refers to emphasizing a message so that it stands out from surrounding information that is not as important or relevant. We can highlight words and phrases in text by underlining, shading, coloring, changing font size or style, boldfacing, italicizing, or animating—to name a few of the most common techniques (see Glynn, 1978; Rickards, 1980). We also can cue learners' attention by pointing to information, increasing or decreasing the loudness of the message, or repeating the information. One simple way to highlight information is to pull it out from its written or spoken context and list it clearly.

With all of these strategies, our goal is the same: to make sure learners look at, hear, smell, taste, or touch the verbal information we want them to acquire. For example, I am sure that by now you have noticed that I have been using **boldface type** throughout this book to call your attention to key terms and their meanings. At the beginning of each chapter, I call your attention to the chapter's instructional goals by listing them. As a further example, if you were designing a computer-based lesson to help your students learn the names of selected skeletal muscles, you could present an image on the screen that showed the body's major muscles, with their names listed on either side of the image. When students click on a specific muscle or the name of a muscle, that muscle is highlighted by turning blue and a line appears connecting it to its name, which also is highlighted by turning blue. Then the muscle contracts, calling attention to the part of the body it is responsible for moving. In this example, the highlighting strategy would help learners attend to muscle names, locations, and functions. The specific techniques you select to highlight verbal information are limited only by your own ingenuity and creativity.

Questioning Strategies   Another way to support attention is to provide questions or orienting activities that alert learners to the important pieces of verbal information you want them to process further. When questions are used in this way, we refer to them as **adjunct questions** because they are added on (i.e., adjunct) to the information to be learned (Burton, Niles, Lalik, & Reed, 1986; Rothkopf, 1966, 1970). Notice that the first sentence of the paragraph preceding the section on highlighting strategies begins with an adjunct question (How can we help students attend . . . ?). The question raises an issue for you to think about and causes you to anticipate an answer. If you were more attentive to the propositions communicated by the next several sentences than you otherwise would have been, the adjunct question did its job.

The key to using adjunct questions is to get students to think about the information related to the question—not just to sprinkle in some extra questions. One way to increase the probability that students are attending to the information suggested by an adjunct question is to have them produce a meaningful, concrete response, through writing, speaking, or some other appropriate action. Usually the act of speaking or writing forces us to think consciously about the information about which we are talking or writing (Ericsson & Simon, 1980), so to some degree we have to be paying attention to it.

We can use adjunct questions effectively by placing them before the information to be learned, by embedding them throughout the information, or by placing them at the end:

Preceding New Information

▶ The computer program you are about to run will introduce you to the names of some of the major skeletal muscles in your body. *Do you know the name of the muscle that straightens your knee?* Watch for it as you navigate the program and write it in your workbook when you find it.

Embedded Within Information

▶ Your body has many flexors and extensors to move different parts. Flexors bring bones closer together at joints that bend. Extensors straighten joints out again. *Why do you think your body needs both flexors and extensors?* Remember, your muscles can only contract, so if one muscle bends a joint when it contracts, another muscle needs to straighten it back out when it contracts.

Following Information

▶ Now that you have finished this section on flexors and extensors, *how many muscle names can you remember?* Try to list as many muscle names as you can. Beside each name on your list, write "F" if it is a flexor and "E" if it is an extensor. Click on the program's Feedback section to see how well you did.

■ **Distinctiveness Strategies** We make information distinctive for learners when we help them separate propositions that could interfere with each other

By organizing information in a table, chart, or concept map, students can recognize how ideas are related to each other and how they are distinct from each other.

Table 7.3
An Empty Cluster Analysis Chart to Promote Distinctiveness

Muscle Function	Muscle Name	Location	Use
Flexors			
Upper body			
Lower body			
Extensors			
Upper body			
Lower body			
Abductors			
Upper body			
Lower body			
Adductors			
Upper body			
Lower body			

(Gagne, Briggs, & Wager, 1992). For example, muscle names, locations, and functions could easily be confused because many of them are so similar. To help learners attend to critical differences among similar muscles, we could provide an organizational scheme (e.g., table, diagram, concept map) that shows how muscles differ according to some important variables such as function, location, and use. Does this process sound familiar? We created such an organizational scheme when we performed a cluster analysis in Chapter 3 (see Table 3.3).

We can use a cluster analysis chart to promote distinctiveness during learning. For example, we might give students a blank chart and have them fill in the information as they encounter it in the context of a textbook chapter, computer program, or some other learning activity (see Table 7.3). Not only will the table help them attend to specific features that make each muscle distinct and different from others, it will also serve as a type of adjunct question to guide their attention. Furthermore, by having students themselves fill in the chart, we increase the probability that they are actually attending to the specific propositions they need to acquire.

Helping Learners Activate Prior Knowledge

Even if you are successful in getting your learners to attend to verbal information, that does not necessarily mean they will learn it. Learning depends on encoding, and encoding depends on how well students construct their own links between new information and prior knowledge in working memory. How can we help learners activate their prior knowledge to working memory? Here we have at least four general types of external instructional events: (1) direct cues and reminders, (2) instructional analogies, (3) advance organizers, and (4) concrete experiences.

■ **Direct Cues and Reminders**   One of the easiest ways to stimulate learners to recall prior knowledge is simply to tell them to do so. For example, before engaging students with verbal information about their skeletal muscles, you might say, "Take a few minutes to think about all the different parts of your body that you have moved so far today." To ensure that students start activating their prior knowledge, you might ask each of them to make a list of five movements they have made so far and the specific parts of the body that have moved. The same types of cues can be embedded into written text, instructional videotapes, computer software, and any other medium in the form of adjunct questions.

Regardless of the specific form, whenever you prompt learners to recall relevant prior knowledge, you should have them *do* something that is well defined and observable to help ensure that they have actually engaged in the necessary thinking. By giving students a specific task to perform, you can focus their thinking on the knowledge that will be relevant to the new information and see the evidence that they have thought about it. Making lists, writing summaries, answering adjunct questions, drawing diagrams, and role-playing past experiences are all potentially effective strategies for helping learners activate relevant prior knowledge.

■ **Instructional Analogies**   Sometimes learners' prior knowledge can be related analogically to new information. **Analogies** are relational comparisons between two knowledge areas that seem to be outwardly dissimilar. Previously in this chapter, for example, I compared information processing to food processing. Although information processing and food processing look very different on the outside, both areas share similar relationships:

▶ A new substance enters the system from the environment.

▶ The system operates on the substance to transform, or change, it.

▶ The resulting substance is still the original material, but in a different form.

With this analogy, I tried to help you understand these important aspects of human information processing by having you think about how they operate in an object that probably is already familiar to you. The new, less familiar information is called the analogy's *target domain* (e.g., information processing) and the familiar prior knowledge is call the *base domain* (e.g., food processing).

As Figure 7.10 illustrates, the purpose of an instructional analogy is to help learners understand the target domain by **mapping** (or transferring) the meaningful relationships they already have stored in the base domain (Gentner, 1983; Holland, Holyoak, & Nisbett, 1986). As learners map relationships, they need to disregard the actual features of the specific base domain objects. So, for example, you would not want to map your knowledge of what food processors look like to your understanding of information processing. Although the relational processes are similar, we obviously do not have electronic gadgets with spinning metal blades inside our heads to operate on information! Here are some commonly used instructional analogies:

Base Domain	Target Domain
1. Solar system	1. Structure of an atom
2. Hard-boiled egg	2. Layers of the earth
3. Factory	3. Structure and function of a cell
4. Computer	4. Information processing system
5. Balance beam	5. Average (arithmetic mean)

Although many research studies have demonstrated the effectiveness of providing instructional analogies for learners (Bromage & Mayer, 1981; Glynn & Britton, 1984; Royer & Cable, 1976), we should use them carefully. First, we have to be sure that learners do in fact understand the key relationships within the base domain to map. Then we have to make sure that they map only the appropriate relationships to the target domain, not everything they know about the base. When learners map inappropriate relationships and object features, they may create misconceptions for themselves (Zook, 1991; Zook, 1993; Zook & Di Vesta, 1989; Zook & Maier, 1994).

■ **Advance Organizers**   Sometimes we need to help learners construct a relevant schema before processing new information. Advance organizers are instructional tools that can help us accomplish this goal. David Ausubel developed the use of advance organizers in the early 1960s as a way to help learners integrate new information with prior knowledge. According to Ausubel (1960, 1968), an **advance organizer** is a carefully prepared body of information that provides learners with concepts, principles, and other general ideas that they can use to bring structure, organization, and understanding to the specific, detailed information they are about to learn. To serve this organizing function, learners need to process the material before they are engaged with the new information—hence the term *advance* organizer.

I have used several advance organizers throughout this book. Turn back to the first chapter and find the section titled, "Basic Principles of Instructional Design." Before I presented specific information on instructional design principles, I described the process of planning a camping trip. I used a trip planning

**Figure 7.10
Instructional Analogies:
Mapping Base Domain
Relationships to a
Target Domain**

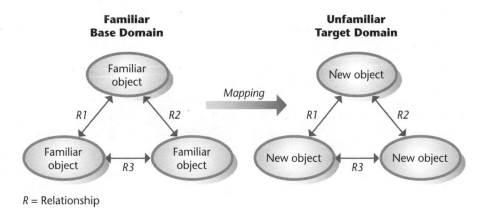

R = Relationship

scenario to help you construct a schema that possessed several major principles of trip planning that are also relevant to instructional design:

▶ To begin planning a trip, you need to decide on a clear destination.

▶ Different destinations result in different strategies to help you arrive at your destination.

▶ Three interrelated questions must be addressed when planning a trip: (1) Where are we going? (2) What will we do when we get there? and (3) How will we get there?

After engaging you with the camping trip scenario and highlighting these major organizing principles of trip planning, I used the remainder of the chapter to explain how the same principles could be applied to the instructional design process. Throughout the remainder of the chapter, I frequently illustrated specific points by referring you back to the camping scenario. I designed the camping trip information to serve as an advance organizer for the first chapter, and I designed the first chapter to serve as an advance organizer for the entire book. At the beginning of every subsequent chapter in this book, I have presented an advance organizer to you (see Table 7.4).

To be effective in activating learners' prior knowledge, an advance organizer should engage learners with actual content in ways that make sense to them. The advance organizer should make learners aware of the major organizing concepts or principles that they eventually will be applying when they process the new information. Simple reminders about relevant pieces of information, asking students to summarize information they already have learned, or giving students an outline to follow are *not* examples of advance organizers (Mayer, 1979; Corkill, 1992). The processing of the advance organizer itself should be a meaningful learning experience that engages students with actual content to be learned (Joyce & Weil, 1986). In general, research evidence sug-

Table 7.4
Advance Organizers Used to Introduce the Chapters in This Book

Chapter	Advance Organizer	Chapter Topic
2	Teaching without a book or curriculum guide.	Establishing instructional goals and learning outcomes.
3	Acquiring basic skills in learning to play the violin.	Using content analysis procedures to identify prerequisite knowledge and skills.
4	Consequences of eliminating tests from classroom teaching.	Importance of assessment in classroom teaching and learning.
5	Selecting the best tool to fix the wheel on a lawnmower.	Matching specific assessment strategies to the decisions that need to be made.
6	Identifying career objectives as a guide in job-seeking activities and using them to evaluate the success of the activities.	Writing and using instructional objectives to guide teaching and assessment.
7	Developing an athletic game plan.	Developing an instructional strategy based on the internal conditions of learning.

gests that advance organizers help learners understand and recall new information (Corkill, 1992). Some studies have even demonstrated that well-designed advance organizers can contribute to students' creative thinking and problem solving (Mayer, 1989a).

We can develop two types of advance organizers to help support learners: expository and comparative organizers. *Expository* organizers present the underlying concepts and principles for unfamiliar material in terms that are familiar to learners (Joyce & Weil, 1986). For example, before engaging students with several specific examples of flexor and extensor muscle names, locations, and uses, you could demonstrate how flexors and extensors work together in teams by having the students flex and extend different body parts (e.g., leg, forearm, wrist) and placing their hands on the muscles that are contracting. As students feel for themselves the fact that the muscle that flexes the joint is different from the muscle that straightens the joint, you can emphasize organizing concepts and principles such as the following:

- Skeletal muscles can produce only one kind of movement by contracting.
- Every joint has a team of flexors and extensors to bend and straighten it.
- When the flexor contracts, the extensor relaxes; when the extensor contracts, the flexor relaxes.

Comparative organizers help learners develop a meaningful understanding of organizing concepts and principles by showing them how those ideas operate in a somewhat different domain (Joyce & Weil, 1986). My camping trip scenario in Chapter 1 is an example of a comparative organizer because I invited you to understand several organizing principles by comparing how those ideas operate within two different domains: camping trips and instructional design. A comparative organizer for flexor and extensor muscle teams could be the movement of a screen door. The spring or hydraulic pulls on a screen door can only *close* the door by contracting. To *open* the door, another force needs to be applied. Again, you would need to engage your learners actively and meaningfully with this organizer for it to be potentially useful to them. Because comparative organizers encourage learners to think about similar conceptual relationships within two different domains, they often take the form of instructional analogies. Numerous research studies have documented the effectiveness of using analogies as advance organizers (see Mayer, 1989a; Zook, 1991).

■ **Concrete Experiences** Personal experiences are powerful contributors to our schemas. Before engaging students with abstract, detailed new information about a topic, we may need to provide them with opportunities for direct, concrete experiences that they can then use as a meaningful schema (De Corte, Greer, & Verschaffel, 1996). For example, before having students read about fossils, you could take them on a fossil collecting field trip. Before engaging students with detailed information about muscles, you could let them experiment with their own muscles and examine the muscles of an animal—say, a chicken leg and thigh from the grocery store. The most meaningful, concrete forms of information should always come before we engage students with more abstract, symbolic forms so that they have a schema to aid understanding.

Although helping learners activate their prior knowledge through the strategies we have just examined is an important part of the learning process, it does not guarantee encoding. Students still must construct meaningful connections between that prior knowledge and the new propositions to be acquired. Let's take a look at some specific instructional events that we can use to support the encoding process.

Helping Learners Encode Information: Supporting Generative Learning

Encoding happens when learners use their prior knowledge to elaborate on new information. Encoding is a generative process (Osborne & Wittrock, 1983; Wittrock, 1974, 1990). When learners elaborate in meaningful ways, they *generate,* or construct, connections between new information and their knowledge base, enhancing understanding and memory. We can support the encoding process by helping learners apply several different types of generative learning strategies, including verbal elaboration, imagery, self-generated analogies, self-summarization, and self-questioning (Grabowski, 1996). As Wittrock (1979) points out, each of these generative activities requires active mental work on the part of the learner:

> Cognitive models [of learning], ironically, are also practical. One of their most delightful and important implications for instruction is their inexpensive, easy-to-learn classroom teaching techniques. Images, thoughts, and verbal elaborations are precious but inexpensive. Unlike teaching machines, they are easy to construct, transport, and change. They need very little maintenance, never rust, and last usually as long as you need them. Their supply is infinite, and they cannot be consumed. The more of them you try to give away, the more of them you have. But there is one catch. You have to generate them yourself. (p. 10)

■ **Verbal Elaboration and Imagery** We can support verbal elaboration by suggesting possible ways for learners to elaborate on propositions (Di Vesta & Peverly, 1984; Johnsey, Morrison, & Ross, 1992; Simpson, Olejnik, Tam, & Supattathum, 1994). The key here is for us to guide their elaborations without doing the elaborating for them. Similarly, we can support the use of imagery by suggesting ideas for specific mental pictures learners can generate for themselves (McDaniel & Einstein, 1986). For example, instructional materials could ask students to explain how flexors and extensors work together when they bend their elbows, wrists, and knees. Each of these joints is already familiar to them. By generating the explanations, students will have the opportunity to link their emerging understanding of flexors and extensors to this prior knowledge. For imagery, the instructional materials might ask students to visualize a screen door closing to illustrate the effect that a flexing muscle has on a joint.

We can often encourage verbal and imagery elaborations by asking adjunct questions that focus students' thinking. For example, to encourage elaboration on muscle information, you might ask students what they think would happen if suddenly all of their extensor muscles stopped working. You could have some fun with this by asking them to picture what they might end up looking like and drawing pictures to illustrate. You could also ask students to respond to "why" questions to support elaboration: Why are the triceps located on the back of the upper arm? Why are our bones surrounded by muscles? By answering these types of questions, learners are encouraged to use their schemas to generate connections between muscles and their features. This strategy is called **elaborative interrogation** (Pressley et al., 1992; Willoughby, Wood, & Khan, 1994; Willoughby, Wood, Desmarais, Sims, & Kalra, 1997).

How students construct their verbal elaborations and visual images is less important than that they all *do* it. The activity could be an individual exercise, in class or at home, or a small group activity. Students could produce their verbal elaborations by saying them out loud to a friend, a small group, or the whole class. They could write them on pieces of paper or type them on a computer screen. Regardless of the specific, superficial method used, it is imperative for the students themselves to engage in the generative activity.

■ **Self-Generated Analogies** In addition to creating analogies for learners to help them activate relevant schemas, we can also encourage them to generate their own analogies (Hooper, Sales, & Rysavy, 1994; Linden & Wittrock, 1981; Wittrock & Alesandrini, 1990). To produce a self-generated analogy, learners must use their emerging understanding of the target domain to cue, or activate, a familiar base domain that shares a similar relational structure. For example, the instructional materials might present the screen door analogy and then ask learners to think of some other familiar objects that function in a similar way to flexor and extensor muscle teams.

■ **Self-Summaries and Self-Questioning**   Constructing a meaningful *self-summary* is a generative process because learners must engage in two thinking processes. First, they must boil down a larger set of information to a smaller set that contains the most important general ideas, encouraging learners to construct their own understanding of the information. Then they must translate those meaningful ideas into their own words, whose meanings are already stored in long-term memory. Self-summarizing often enhances understanding and retention of ideas (Dole, Duffy, Roehler, & Pearson, 1991; King, 1992a, 1992b; Wittrock & Alesandrini, 1990).

Self-questioning is a strategy in which learners not only answer questions about new information; they also ask the questions. In Table 7.5, you will see several types of questions that students can learn to ask themselves. With careful instruction in asking and answering these types of questions, learners can engage in generative processes that enhance both their comprehension and recall of new information (Dole et al., 1991; King, 1992a, 1992b). The self-questioning strategy may be particularly helpful for students who already have experienced learning difficulties (King, 1992a).

Keep in mind that the generative learning strategies we have just examined are simply general possibilities. If you have the gist of what generative learning processes are all about, you can certainly create your own variations of these strategies—perhaps some that are completely new. Writing a story, producing a play, drawing a picture, constructing a model, and role playing are all potentially effective generative activities. As you teach in your own classroom, I encourage you to think of many more.

Manufacturing Meaning: Using Mnemonic Devices

Some types of new information are difficult to relate to prior knowledge in any meaningful way. For example, there is no meaningful reason why the muscle located on the side of the thigh that flexes the thigh is named the "sartorius." Although Pearl Harbor was bombed on December 7, 1941, there is no meaningful link between the event and the date. The names of the first five planets in order from the sun are Mercury, Venus, Earth, Mars, and Jupiter. Why do the planets have those particular names, and why couldn't the order of the names be Venus, Jupiter, Mars, Mercury, Earth?

Names, symbols, dates, ordered lists, and other types of verbal information that are somewhat arbitrary can be difficult for students to remember because meaningful encoding is nearly impossible. For these types of verbal information learning, you may need to help your learners create, or manufacture, their own meaning. Often regarded as "memory tricks," **mnemonic devices** are actually cognitive strategies that help learners manufacture artificial links between new information and their prior knowledge. Many types of mnemonic devices exist, and I cannot possibly describe all of them here (see Baine, 1986; McDaniel & Pressley, 1987). However, let's look at three major categories of mnemonics that may be useful to you and your learners: (1) rhymes, (2) words, and (3) images.

■ **Rhyme-Based Mnemonics**   Putting information into a rhyme makes it easier to remember. For example, you probably use a rhyme to help you remember the number of days in each month (thirty days hath September . . .) and to

Table 7.5
General Types of Questions to Use in a Self-Questioning Strategy

Question Type	Example
1. Explain why (or how) . . .	Explain why elaboration facilitates learning.
2. What is the main idea of . . . ?	What is the main idea of the section on advance organizers?
3. How would you use . . . to . . . ?	How would you use imagery to remember the names of skeletal muscles?
4. What is a new example of . . . ?	What is a new example of a verbal elaboration?
5. What do you think would happen if . . . ?	What do you think would happen if a teacher tried to teach without an instructional strategy?
6. What is the difference between . . . and . . . ?	What is the difference between short-term memory and working memory?
7. How are . . . and . . . similar?	How are learners and computer systems similar?
8. What conclusions can you draw about . . . ?	What conclusions can you draw about the learner's active involvement in the learning process?
9. How does . . . affect . . . ?	How does a learner's prior knowledge affect attention and selective perception?
10. What are the strengths and weaknesses of . . . ?	What are the strengths and weaknesses of using imagery elaborations?
11. What is the best . . . and why?	What is the best way to encode information into long-term memory? Why?
12. How is . . . related to . . . that we studied earlier?	How are concept maps related to the cluster analyses that we studied earlier?

Source: King (1992).

help you spell words like *believe* and *receive* (*i* before *e*, except after *c* . . .). Putting information into a rhyme and then setting the rhyme to a catchy musical tune is even more helpful. By using rhythm, rhyme, and melody, very young children are able to remember an arbitrary sequence of twenty-six letters. You can create rhymes and songs to help your students remember verbal information or, better yet, have them use their creativity to generate their own.

■ **Word-Based Mnemonics**　Sometimes we can put pieces of arbitrary information together in ways that create familiar words that are more memorable to us. For example, the first letters of the names of the Great Lakes can be put together to make the word HOMES: Huron, Ontario, Michigan, Erie, Superior. Words whose letters are the first letters of other words to be remembered are called **acronyms**. Have you ever used the familiar acronym FOIL to help you multiply algebraic expressions such as $(3x + 5)(4y + 2)$? The acronym helps you remember which terms to multiply: First, Outer, Inner, Last.

A second word-based mnemonic device is the **acrostic**. To create an acrostic, take the first letters of the words you want to remember and use them as the first letters of words that form a meaningful, memorable sentence. A useful acrostic to remember the names of the nine planets of the solar system in order is: <u>M</u>y <u>v</u>ery <u>e</u>ducated <u>m</u>other just <u>s</u>erved <u>u</u>s <u>n</u>ine <u>p</u>izzas. Here is another acrostic that learners can use to remember the levels of a classification taxonomy in biology:

<u>K</u>ingdom	<u>K</u>ing	<u>F</u>amily	<u>F</u>or
<u>P</u>hylum	<u>Ph</u>illip	<u>G</u>enus	<u>G</u>reat
<u>C</u>lass	<u>C</u>ame	<u>Sp</u>ecies	<u>Sp</u>aghetti
<u>O</u>rder	<u>O</u>ver		

■ **Image-Based Mnemonics**   For image-based mnemonics to work, learners need to create mental pictures of the ideas to be remembered interacting with something that is familiar to them. Specific types of image-based mnemonics include the method of loci, peg-word systems, and the keyword method.

Briefly, to use the **method of loci** (*loci* is a Latin word for places), you walk through a familiar area (e.g., the rooms of your house) and visualize a piece of information interacting with an object that appears there. When you want to recall the items, just take a mental walk back through the area. As you visualize objects, they will cue your memory for the pieces of information you already linked to them.

To use a **peg-word** system, you first memorize a list of words that will serve as "pegs" to "hang" information on in your memory. Here is an example:

One is a bun.	Six is a stick.
Two is a shoe.	Seven is heaven.
Three is a tree.	Eight is a gate.
Four is a door.	Nine is a line.
Five is a hive.	Ten is a hen.

Because of the rhyming, these pegs are not difficult to remember. To remember the specific position of a word in a list, just create a picture of the object interacting with the peg object. For example, if the third item on your list is "class" (from the earlier taxonomy example), you could visualize all the students in a *class* sitting up in a *tree*. At the time of recall, you can retrieve the information by thinking, "three is a tree." When you visualize "tree," you should also see a *class* sitting in the tree.

To use the **keyword method**, you first need to create a "keyword" that sounds similar to the piece of information to be encoded (Levin, 1996). For example, you could use the keyword, <u>sard</u>ine, for the <u>sart</u>orius muscle because of the similar beginning sound. Then, to remember that the <u>sart</u>orius is the muscle located on the side of your thigh, you might picture your thigh with a long <u>sard</u>ine in the place where the sartorius muscle would be located. To remember the location of the gluteus maximus, you could create a picture of yourself sitting down in a large (maximus) bucket of glue (gluteus)—get the picture?

In addition to being extremely effective for remembering arbitrary pieces of verbal information, mnemonic images can be a lot of fun for students as well—especially if you encourage them to create their own. Furthermore, some recent research evidence suggests that mnemonic encoding can also support higher-level thinking as well as memory (Levin, 1996; Levin & Levin, 1990). Mnemonics are effective not because they are fun but because they stimulate learners to generate relationships between arbitrary pieces of verbal information to be remembered and meaningful aspects of their long-term memories (Levin, 1996). Mnemonics work because they actively involve learners in the encoding process.

Helping Learners Encode Information: Supporting Organization

As noted in Figure 7.3, another way to support learners' encoding processes is to help them organize new information. Three general external events can help us support learners' organization processes: (1) outlines, charts, and tables, (2) concept maps, and (3) schematic diagrams.

■ **Outlines, Charts, and Tables**   Outlines, charts, and tables are useful for helping learners think about the superordinate-subordinate relationships that appear within a set of propositions. As they encounter specific pieces of verbal information, they can "place" those ideas within an organizing group of related ideas, which, in turn, will be related to a higher-level idea. For example, you can find the organizational structure that I am using to write this section of the chapter in Table 7.6.

The organizational links provided by an outline will not contribute to encoding unless learners actively process them. If you want to support your learners by providing them with an outline before they experience new information, they need to think about the categories and relationships contained within the outline. To ensure that students really are thinking about categories and relationships, you could have them construct their own outlines (McDaniel & Einstein, 1989), assuming, of course, that they already have learned the cognitive strategy of outlining. Another possibility is to provide your students with a partial outline that they can complete as they encounter and think about specific pieces of information (see Table 7.7). By asking themselves, "How does this new piece of information fit into the organizational structure?" learners are actively constructing the organizational relationships that eventually will guide their retrieval processes.

Charts and tables are simply variations on the outlining theme. Any information that can be outlined also can be placed into an organized chart or table. As with an outline, we could also create a partial table—one that contains only the major superordinate categories—and have students fill it in as they process specific propositions and think about where they would fit in the structure (for example, see Table 7.3).

Table 7.6
Outline for a Chapter Section

I. External Conditions of Learning for Verbal Information

A. Attention and selective perception
   1. Highlighting strategies
   2. Adjunct questions
   3. Distinctiveness strategies

B. Schema activation
   1. Direct cues and reminders
   2. Analogies
   3. Advance organizers
   4. Concrete experiences

C. Encoding: Supporting generative learning processes
   1. Verbal elaboration and imagery
   2. Self-generated analogies
   3. Self-summarization and self-questioning

D. Manufacturing meaning: Using mnemonic devices
   1. Rhyme based
   2. Word based
   3. Image based

E. Encoding: Supporting organization
   1. Outlines, charts, tables
   2. Concept maps
   3. Schematic diagrams

F. Provide practice
   1. Retrieval versus rehearsal
   2. Massed versus distributed practice

Table 7.7
Partial Outline for a Chapter Section

I. External Conditions of Learning for Verbal Information

A. Attention and selective perception
1. _____
2. _____
3. _____

B. Schema activation
1. _____
2. _____
3. _____
4. _____

C. Encoding: Supporting generative learning processes
1. _____
2. _____
3. _____

D. Manufacturing meaning: Using mnemonic devices
1. _____
2. _____
3. _____

E. Encoding: Supporting organization
1. _____
2. _____
3. _____

F. Provide practice
1. _____
2. _____

■ **Concept Maps**   A concept map is a visual form of an outline. As with an outline, it helps learners construct the superordinate-subordinate relationships among major concepts and ideas (Lambiotte, Dansereau, Cross, & Reynolds, 1989; Novak & Gowin, 1984). Notice in Figure 7.11, for example, that *memory structures* is the superordinate concept that is used for the subordinate concepts of *sensory registers, working memory,* and *long-term memory*. After constructing these types of hierarchical relationships, learners begin to establish cross-links among ideas. For example, notice that chunking *maintains information in* working memory. By finding and labeling relationships across the map, learners further elaborate on ideas and create rich, meaningful internal connections (Mayer & Greeno, 1972) that serve as retrieval routes for spreading activation.

Notice also that some of the relationships learners construct connect new ideas to familiar ideas that are already stored in long-term memory. When learners realize that *executive control* is like a *manager,* they forge an *external connection* (Mayer & Greeno, 1972) to a related idea outside the schema that is being acquired. Such external connections eventually will assist learners in creative thinking and problem solving (Mayer, 1989a).

You can use concept mapping to support learners' organizational processes by providing maps for your learners and designing activities to help them process the relationships depicted. Better yet, teach students how to construct their own concept maps. Through the mapping process, they will have to identify major concepts and really think about how those concepts are related meaningfully to other concepts (Heinze-Fry & Novak, 1990; Okebukola, 1990).

■ **Schematic Diagrams**   A final way to support learners' organization of information is to create a picture that shows them how a system of interrelated ideas interacts—a **schematic diagram**. Figures 7.1, 7.2, 7.3, and 7.4 are examples of schematic diagrams. Each of these diagrams comprises general concepts that are related to each other by actions, processes, or other types of meaningful relationships. These diagrams are intended to do more than simply show superordinate-subordinate relationships. They are intended to help you think about how the system of ideas works or operates (Mayer, 1989b). Of course,

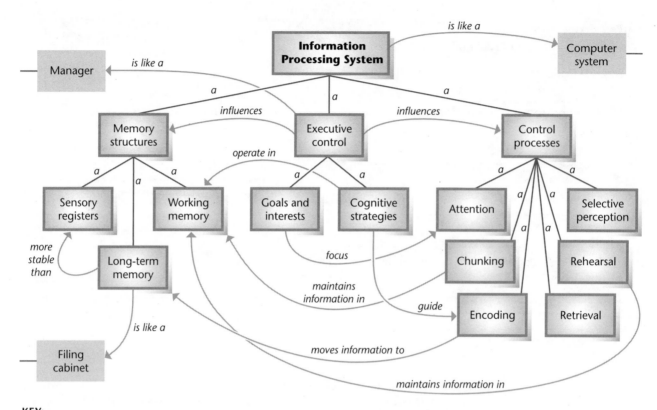

Figure 7.11
Concept Mapping for Information Processing System

these schematic diagrams will be useful to you only to the extent that you actively process the ideas and relationships that are represented (Mayer, 1999; Mayer & Gallini, 1990; Mayer & Sims, 1994). As for outlines and concept maps, one way to enhance learner processing is to have students generate their own schematic diagrams based on their emerging understanding of a set of organized propositions (Clark & Paivio, 1991).

Practice: Helping Learners Construct and Strengthen Retrieval Routes

As noted in Figure 7.3, a final external event that we can employ to support learners is providing practice opportunities. To be effective, learners need to practice retrieving propositions, not just rehearsing them (Gagne, 1985). In other words, the practice opportunity should be designed so that students have to search their own long-term memories to find the information and activate it to working memory, where it can be used or stated in a meaningful way. By retrieving and using verbal information in a wide variety of contexts and situations, learners have multiple opportunities to continue elaborating on the information, thereby constructing even more retrieval routes and strengthening those that already exist.

When you design practice opportunities, you should try to spread them out over several sessions rather than massing them all in one or two really long sessions (Bahrick, Bahrick, Bahrick, & Bahrick, 1993; Bahrick & Phelps, 1987; Toppino, Kasserman, & Mracek, 1991). This is the well-known learning principle often referred to as **distributed practice**. For example, students who spend fifteen minutes a day for six days practicing the retrieval of muscle names, locations, and uses will remember those propositions much more effectively than students who practice in a single hour-and-a-half marathon session. Once the propositions are activated in the marathon session, they are simply rehearsed in working memory for the duration of the time period. However, when practice is distributed, learners retrieve the propositions from long-term memory several different times. Each new retrieval has the potential to add rich new elaborations, especially if the practice occurs within a variety of meaningful contexts and situations.

How could you vary the context for retrieving muscle names? Students could practice retrieval by playing a memory game like "concentration"; labeling a blank diagram of the human body; building a model of the human body and labeling the muscles; keeping a log of their movements for certain time intervals and naming the muscles they use; or answering questions about moving or injuring different body parts. The possibilities are endless.

LET'S SUMMARIZE

In this section, we have examined external learning events that are consistent with the internal processes of learning for acquiring verbal information. Because your students need to construct meaningful elaborations to encode propositions in long-term memory, you should help them attend and perceive new propositions, activate relevant prior knowledge, elaborate meaningfully, and construct an organizational structure. Furthermore, you should provide practice opportunities to support their need to strengthen retrieval routes. Before we conclude this chapter, let's look in on one of our case analysis teachers, Ms. Nelson, as she designs an instructional game plan by applying her understanding of the internal conditions of learning for verbal information.

CASE ANALYSIS

Designing an Instructional Strategy for Verbal Information Learning

Ms. Nelson already has decided "where she is going" and "what her students will do when they get there." Here are the verbal information instructional goal and instructional objective that describe her destination:

- *Instructional goal:* Learners will be able to state the names of the four major eras in the earth's history and several important characteristics of each.

- *Instructional objective:* Learners will be provided with an organizational chart that has four columns with a blank line at the top of each column. Beneath the chart will be twenty-five facts, lettered *a* through *y*. Sixteen of the facts will be characteristics of the four major eras in the earth's history, with four facts corresponding to each of the four eras. The remaining nine facts will not correspond to any of the four eras. Learners will state the names of the four major eras in the earth's history by writing each of them at the top of the four columns. Learners will state important characteristics of each era by writing the letters of the facts in each of the appropriate columns. All four era names must be written on the blank lines, but the names do not need to be spelled perfectly. The letters of fourteen of the sixteen characteristics must be placed in the correct columns. The letters of no more than two of the nine distracters can be placed in a column.

Now Ms. Nelson must answer the question, "How will we get there?" How will she help her fifth-grade students acquire the verbal information they need to be able to state as evidence of their learning? She designs her instructional strategy by creating external instructional events that she believes will support her students' internal conditions of learning. Let's analyze Ms. Nelson's instructional strategy by examining how she thinks about the three critical elements of an instructional strategy that we identified earlier in the chapter: information, engagement, and practice (see Figure 7.2).

Information: What Do My Students Need to Process?

The answer to this question is easy because I already have carefully identified and analyzed the content that my students need to acquire. To make sure that I stay focused on this content, I will state it again clearly:

- The names of the four major eras in the earth's history are Precambrian, Paleozoic, Mesozoic, and Cenozoic.
- Through the cluster analysis process, I have organized the specific features of each era according to the following categories: meaning of term, beginning time, names of subperiods, earth features, plant life, and animal life [see Table 7.8].

Engagement: How Will My Students Process the Information?

Now I need to plan learning activities and materials that I believe will help my students process the propositions they need to encode into long-term memory. I will develop some of these materials and activities by using my own knowledge of information processing and my own creativity. I will also take a look at the teacher's edition of the science textbook, some science reference books that I have collected, and multimedia catalogs from the school library. I also may be able to find some teaching resources by searching the Internet.

Creating an Advance Organizer   To begin my instructional strategy, I will engage my students with an advance organizer. By acquiring some major organizing principles, my students will have a schema that they can apply to all the facts I want them to encode in long-term memory. Here are two major organizing principles that my students should understand:

1. The earth's living and nonliving features have changed over time.
2. The earth's plant and animal life has changed in response to changes in the earth's geologic features.

Changes in geologic time happen too slowly for students to experience. Therefore I will create somewhat of an analogy by having them think about the changes they would experience if they traveled from one state, Colorado, to another state, Florida. I will show them pictures of typical Colorado and Florida terrain, emphasizing the Rocky Mountain features of Colorado and the tropical Everglades region of Florida. Then we will make a list of plant and animal features that are common to each state, using pictures to prompt students for ideas:

	Colorado	Florida
Plant life	Evergreen forests, pines, spruces, firs	Swamp grasses, palm trees
Animal life	Elk, mule deer, mountain goats	Alligators, lizards, snakes

I will use the pictures and the lists to demonstrate to students that different parts of the country have different geologic features and climates, which, in turn, influence the types of plants and animals that are found there. I will relate this point to the two organizing principles, using the analogy that traveling to different parts of the country is like traveling through different time periods in the earth's history.

Providing Meaningful Prior Experiences   Some of the features of the four eras will be somewhat new and strange to my students. For example, if they

Table 7.8
Cluster Analysis for Facts about Earth's History

	Precambrian Era	Paleozoic Era	Mesozoic Era	Cenozoic Era
Meaning		Ancient life	Middle life	Recent life
Beginning time	4500 million years ago	600 million years ago	225 million years ago	65 million years ago
Periods	• Hadean • Archean • Proterozoic	• Cambrian • Ordivician • Silurian • Devonian • Carboniferous • Permian	• Triassic • Jurassic • Cretaceous	• Tertiary • Quarternary
Earth features	• Crust increased • Large oceans formed	• Appalachian Mountains formed • Shallow seas covered land • Forests of fern plants (produced coal)	• Inland seas dried up • Rocky Mountains formed near end	• Volcano activity • Recurring ice ages (glaciation)
Plant life	• Algae • Simple one-celled organisms	• Ferns • Evergreens	• Flowering plants • Plants with seeds	• Present-day plants
Animal life	• Bacteria • Simple one-celled organisms	• Invertebrates: trilobites, snails, insects, jellyfish • Vertebrates: fish, amphibians, reptiles	• Dinosaurs and other reptiles dominated • Turtles, crocodiles, snakes, lizards • Early mammals	• Mammal populations increased • Larger mammals appeared • Humans appeared

read or hear about a woolly mammoth, glacier, or trilobites, will they understand what the terms mean? Obviously I can't bring my students in contact
with real mammoths, glaciers, and trilobites; the next best thing could be an
instructional CD or videotape that provides some realistic visual images of
these types of prehistoric creatures. By checking some multimedia catalogs, I
found a CD-ROM titled, *The History of the Earth: Over the Eons* (AIMS Multimedia). The program provides a basic overview of the earth's geologic and bi-
ologic features from the Precambrian era to the present. I will set up the CD
on the class computer and have pairs of students work together. To support
students' attention and active processing, I will give each pair a checklist of
specific geologic features, plants, and animals to identify and describe as they
use the CD.

Helping Students Attend to New Information   Now that I have prepared
my students with some schema activation strategies, I think they should be
ready to process the specific propositions to be learned. I will have them read
the earth history chapter in their textbook. To help students attend to the
specific propositions they need to encode, I will give them the cluster analysis
chart [Table 7.8] with empty cells. As they read, they will need to look for the
information that fits within each cell of the chart and write it. Not only will
this activity help my students begin processing the verbal information they
need to learn, they also will be learning how to read expository text in an active, strategic way. After all students are finished reading and filling in their
charts, I will have them break into small groups to check the completeness
and accuracy of each others' information.

Helping Students Elaborate on New Information: Adjunct Questions   To
help students begin elaborating on the verbal information, I will ask each
small group to develop written answers to several adjunct questions. Some of
the questions will ask students to elaborate on information by restating it
meaningfully in their own words:

1. Briefly explain how the Appalachian Mountains formed during the Paleozoic era.
2. Describe the types of animals that dominated the earth during the Mesozoic era.

Some of the questions will employ the elaborative interrogation strategy:

1. Why did dinosaurs flourish during the Mesozoic era?
2. Why have mammals flourished during the Cenozoic era?
3. Why did aquatic animals dominate during the Paleozoic era?

Helping Students Elaborate on Information: Imagery   To help students
construct meaningful images for the verbal information, I will have them create a bulletin board mural. Four teams of students will create a mural for each
of the four eras. Each mural needs to present all of its era's propositions in an
integrated, visual form. When finished, each group will present and explain
its mural to the rest of the class—a further opportunity for verbal elaboration.
As each group is presenting its mural, the rest of the class will be checking off
the information represented on their information charts.

In addition to creating the murals, I will have each student create three illustrated time lines to show changes across the four eras. The three time
lines will represent changes in geologic features, plant life, and animal life.
Students will need to present the changes accurately on their time lines and
draw pictures to illustrate. Creating the murals and time lines will be generative learning activities.

Helping Learners Elaborate on Information: Mnemonics   My students are not going to find some of this verbal information very meaningful. For example, the arbitrary names of the eras and the names of the subperiods will be difficult for students to relate to their schemas. Perhaps an acrostic could help them remember the periods of the Paleozoic era. Rather than just giving students an acrostic, I will guide them in constructing their own:

Cambrian	C _____
Ordivician	O _____
Silurian	S _____
Devonian	D _____
Carboniferous	C _____
Permian	P _____

Practice: How Will My Students Strengthen Their Learning?

I need to create some opportunities for my students to practice retrieving the information. I will design several different types of retrieval activities so students can have *distributed practice* over several days in varied contexts. One possible activity is to give my students another blank cluster analysis chart for them to fill in from memory. For any cells that give them difficulty, they can check the murals, time lines, textbook, or CD-ROM. I will have students mark these difficult propositions so they can come back to them and elaborate on them further.

For a second practice activity, I will create a game called "journey through time." The game board will be a segmented path that moves through each of the four major eras [see Figure 7.12]. To move along in their "journey through time," each team will have several questions to answer for each era. Students will have to retrieve the propositions to be learned to answer the questions. To win, a team must be the first to move all the way through the Cenozoic era.

As a third practice activity, I will have students pretend that they are paleontologists. I will give them a sheet that lists various objects that a paleontologist might discover (e.g., a fern fossil, dinosaur footprints, rock deposited by a glacier). From the description of the objects, students will need to estimate the era that the object came from and approximately how old it would be. Students will have to retrieve propositions for each era to solve the problems.

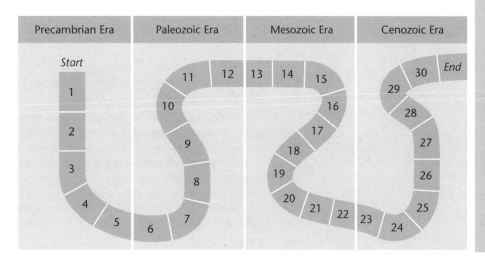

Figure 7.12
A Learning Game:
"Journey Through Time"

For further practice in a different context, I could have students imagine that they are able to travel back in time and visit each of the four eras. They will write a story about the adventures they would have during their visit to each era. Students will have to include evidence of specific geologic, plant, and animal features that are relevant for each era. As students write their stories, they will practice retrieving the propositions they are to learn, a generative activity that will create even more meaningful retrieval routes.

Finally, I want to make sure that my students are able to practice in a way that is consistent with my summative assessment activity. The assessment activity I have planned calls for students to place specific facts within the appropriate era column [see instructional objective]. Therefore, I will give them blank charts with four columns and have them write the names of the four eras in order at the top of each column. Then I will give students a few minutes to write down everything they can remember about each era. I will give them verbal cues to think about geologic features, plant life, and so on. When they are finished, each student will trade charts with another student, and they will use their previously completed cluster analysis charts to check each others' recall.

By monitoring all of these distributed practice activities, I will be able to conduct formative assessment. By the time all of the practice activities are completed, I should be able to identify any propositions that are still giving students difficulties. I can then provide additional elaboration exercises for those students. When I am finished with the practice phase, there will be only one more question left to ask: Did we get there? To help me answer that evaluation question, I will collect assessment data in the way that I have already described in my instructional objective.

LET'S SUMMARIZE

We now have come full circle in the instructional design process. Ms. Nelson has created a complete, integrated instructional system comprising an instructional goal, content to be learned, an instructional objective, and an instructional strategy. She will evaluate the quality of her instructional system by determining whether her students are able to demonstrate the instructional goal: the final destination for her instructional journey. Although Ms. Nelson's varied learning activities seem to be creative, innovative, and interesting, their ultimate value depends on convincing assessment evidence that her students actually can state the verbal information that they were to acquire.

LOOKING BACK LOOKING AHEAD

In this chapter, we began to explore the internal and external conditions of learning for different types of learning outcomes. An instructional strategy is a plan that describes the external, outward events that we will eventually implement to try to influence our learners' internal processing of information. Just as an effective game plan is based on characteristics of the other team, an instructional strategy must be matched carefully to students' internal learning needs. Even when we believe that we have accomplished such a match, we still need to collect valid and reliable assessment data to be sure we have reached our instructional goals.

We also analyzed the internal conditions of learning for acquiring verbal information. In general, the ability to recall propositions is a function of how well learners have processed the information. We used the Information Processing Model to organize our understanding of how learners need to process information to produce learning. Finally, we reviewed some of the specific instructional strategies that we can use to help learners acquire verbal information. Strategies such as advance organizers, adjunct questions, mnemonics, and concept mapping are powerful instructional tools with the potential to support learners' internal processing needs.

In the next chapter, we extend the discussion of the internal and external conditions of learning to intellectual skill outcomes. Before moving on, however, there are still some parts of my game plan for the chapter that we need to finish. Now that you have watched Ms. Nelson develop an instructional strategy, I want you to give it a try. Exercise 7.1 in the *Student Exercise Guide* will give you an opportunity to design the information, engagement, and practice components of instructional strategies for several verbal information instructional goals. Exercise 7.2 provides an opportunity for you to demonstrate each of the chapter's instructional goals. While you work on these exercises, I'll be working on my game plan for the next chapter.

RESOURCES FOR FURTHER REFLECTION AND EXPLORATION

Print Resources

Bruning, R. H., Schraw, G. J., & Ronning, R. R. (1999). *Cognitive psychology and instruction* (3rd ed.). Upper Saddle River, NJ: Merrill.

An excellent book that presents a cognitive perspective on teaching and learning. The first part of the book provides an overview of information processing theory and implications for instruction. The four chapters in this part focus on topics relevant to verbal information learning: sensory, short-term, and working memory (Chapter 2), long-term memory (Chapter 3), encoding processes (Chapter 4), and retrieval processes (Chapter 5).

Grabowski, B. L. (1996). Generative learning: Past, present, and future. In D. H. Jonassen (Ed.), *Handbook of research for educational communication and technology* (pp. 897–918). New York: Macmillan.

Presents the theoretical foundations of Wittrock's model of generative learning and provides summaries of research studies that have validated the model. A good overview of the many generative learning activities that are available to teachers and students.

Mayer, R. E. (1997). Multimedia learning: Are we asking the right questions? *Educational Psychologist, 32,* 1–19.

Presents a view of multimedia learning from the perspective of generative learning. The author reviews several research studies that demonstrate the effects of selection, organization, and integration cognitive processes on learning verbal and visual information.

Mayer, R. E. (1992). Schema theory: Thinking as an effort after meaning. In *Thinking, problem solving, cognition* (2nd ed.). New York: Freeman.

Provides a fine overview of schema theory, including the effects of schemas on understanding and memory.

CD-ROM Resources

Alaska: The Wildlife

An interactive CD-ROM that engages students with information about Alaska's wildlife. Movies, slides, music, and narration are used effectively to help learners process information. An excellent example of instructional strategies to help make verbal information meaningful to students. A quick tour is available online at **http://www.gowild.org/**.

American History Inspirer: The Civil War

A CD-ROM that engages students with information related to the U.S. Civil War. Provides examples of generative learning activities that can be incorporated into multimedia technology. Windows or Macintosh. Available from Educational Software Institute (**www.edsoft.com**).

World Wide Web Resources

http://www.csu.edu.au/education/library.html

Web site of the Education Virtual Library. Provides links to a wide variety of instructional resources for classroom teachers: books, databases, tutorials, software, and educational technology.

http://www.nhm.ac.uk/

Web site of the Natural History Museum in London. Provides good web-based examples of strategies for making museum information meaningful, including live video of the museum's leafcutter ant colony (antcam). Click on the site's interactive section for excellent examples of generative strategies for engaging learners with information related to fossils, dinosaurs, eclipses, and other topics.

8

Instructional Strategies for Concept-Learning Outcomes

For the past few years, I have coached my daughters' softball team. Because the girls on the team are only ages seven, eight, and nine, they have a lot to learn about the game. Obviously, I work with them to develop the motor skills of throwing, catching, and hitting. However, playing softball also requires a lot of thinking and decision making. For example, suppose there is a runner on first base and the ball is hit to the shortstop. The runner runs to second base as the shortstop throws the ball to the second baseman. How should the second baseman make the out? Should she tag the base or the runner? What if the ball is hit to the first baseman, who first steps on first base to make the out on the batter and then throws to second base to try to get the other runner? Should the second baseman tag the base or tag the runner? What if there is a runner on second base and no runner on first base when the ball is hit to the shortstop? When the shortstop throws to the third baseman, should she tag the base or the runner? Decisions, decisions, decisions!

To help the girls on my softball team make these kinds of decisions, I need to teach them the appropriate rules:

- If the play is a force-out, either the base or the runner may be tagged.

- If the play is not a force-out, the runner must be tagged.

According to these two rules, all the girls need to do is figure out whether they have a force-out situation. If they do, they can tag the base or the runner—whichever is easier. If they do not, then they have no choice: they have to tag the runner. But how will they recognize if they are in a force-out situation? Here are the conditions that must be met for a force-out:

INSTRUCTIONAL GOALS FOR CHAPTER 8

After reading and thinking about this chapter, you should be able to . . .

1. Explain and demonstrate the if-then structure of productions for intellectual skills.

2. State the names of three stages of skill learning, and describe the major learning processes for each stage.

3. Describe and demonstrate the internal and external conditions of learning for concepts.

4. Apply the three stages of skill acquisition to design an instructional strategy to support concept learning.

5. Apply the divergent example strategy and the matched example and nonexample strategy to support concept generalization and discrimination.

Table 8.1
Applying Tagging Rules in Softball

Situation	Action	Reason
Runner on first base; ball hit to shortstop; runner runs to second base; shortstop throws ball to second baseman.	Tag base or runner.	Situation is a force-out: The runner has to run to second base.
Runner on first base; ball hit to first baseman; runner runs to second base; first baseman steps on first, then throws to second baseman.	Tag runner.	Situation is a non-force-out: After the first baseman gets the out at first, the runner no longer has to run to second.
Runner on second base; ball hit to shortstop; runner runs to third base; shortstop throws ball to third baseman.	Tag runner.	Situation is a non-force-out: The runner on second base does not have to run to third.

An out is a force-out if the runner must run to the next base because another runner is running to the base she is occupying.

So which of the situations I presented above are examples of force-outs according to this definition, and how should the tagging rules be applied? If you aren't sure, check out Table 8.1 for some help. Most important, notice what the girls on my team need to learn to do to tag correctly. First, they need to learn how to identify examples and nonexamples of force-outs. Then they need to learn how to apply the tagging rules when the force-out conditions are met and when they are not met.

As the coach, I now have a fairly complex teaching situation on my hands. I need to teach my players how to recognize all the different ways that force- and non-force-out situations can occur—a *concept-learning goal.* Then I need to teach the girls how to decide on the appropriate tagging procedure for the two situations—a *rule-learning goal.* In both cases, my players need to be able to do more than just explain the tagging rules and state the definitions of force-outs and non-force-outs. They have to be able to apply them as procedural knowledge—as *intellectual skills.*

Teaching students how to apply intellectual skills in the classroom is exactly like teaching softball players how to apply intellectual skills on the softball field. We need to design instruction to help them understand the conditions for recognizing examples of concepts and for applying rules and principles. Most important, we need to prepare them to apply (or transfer) their intellectual skills beyond the classroom in the real-world situations they will encounter for the rest of their lives.

These are indeed challenging tasks for us as classroom *design-teachers.* However, just as we are able to rely on our understanding of the internal conditions of learning to design instructional strategies for verbal information outcomes, we can look to the internal conditions of learning for guidance in designing strategies to support intellectual skill outcomes. That is what the next two chapters are all about. In this chapter, we explore general skill learning processes and then focus on the conditions of learning for a specific type of intellectual skill: concepts. Before we begin, I invite you to check out our instructional goals for the chapter.

Intellectual Skills: General Learning Processes

Intellectual skills are critically important learning outcomes. We frequently design classroom instruction for intellectual skill outcomes because these skills have the power to help our students become effective thinkers, problem solvers, and decision makers. You already know that there are different levels of intellectual skill that are related hierarchically to each other: discriminations, concepts, rules, and principles. You can even consider cognitive strategies as high-level intellectual skills that influence how we apply other skills in problem-solving situations. In later sections of this chapter and in the next chapter, we will explore the internal and external conditions of learning that are unique to these different types of intellectual skills. We begin, however, by analyzing the general characteristics and learning processes that are common to all intellectual skills.

Representing Procedural Knowledge

Recall that intellectual skill outcomes are examples of procedural (how-to) knowledge. As we noted in Chapter 2, many cognitive psychologists think of procedural knowledge as sets of conditions and actions (Anderson, 1993, 1996; Gilhooly & Green, 1989). In other words, we produce some type of action when the conditions for producing that action are satisfied. As a softball coach, I want my players to be able to decide whether to tag the base or the runner (*action*). To make the decision, they need to know when each type of tag is appropriate (conditions).

■ **Productions: Units of Procedural Knowledge** The condition-action sequences we store in memory are called **productions**. In a production, conditions are represented by an *if* component that describes when an action should be produced. The action is represented by a *then* component. Here is an example of a production for the tagging rule:

> **IF**   Goal is to get base runner out
> *And* situation is not a force-out
> *And* if ball is in possession
>
> **THEN**   Decide to tag runner
> *And* touch runner with ball

Notice that the *if* part of the production is crucial because it tells the player when to apply the action. I do not want my players just to know how to touch a runner with a ball. I want them to be able to do it at the right time—in the appropriate situation.

Do we really store if-then statements like these in long-term memory? Probably not. The truth is that we really do not know exactly how any knowledge is stored in long-term memory. Nevertheless, the production format seems to be a very good model, or approximation, of what is happening inside our heads when we apply skills because it is usually consistent with how people actually perform (Anderson, 1993). In other words, regardless of whether we really have if-then productions stored in our heads, we tend to act as if we do. Therefore, the production format is useful for thinking about how to help learners acquire new skills.

The intellectual skills we teach most frequently in school classrooms are concepts, rules, principles, and cognitive strategies. How does the production form of procedural knowledge help us understand the internal conditions of learning for each of these types of skills? For *concepts,* identifying instances as examples and nonexamples is the *action* part of the production. The *conditions* are the defining features that must be present for any instance to be classified as a member of the concept category. Let's suppose we are teaching a class of high school English students to recognize the literary genre known as satire, in which human actions or thought are ridiculed although the writing style appears to be serious. Here is a possible production for applying the concept of satire as a skill:

> **IF**   Goal is to classify genre of piece of writing
> *And* ridicule is displayed

And the object of ridicule is human action or thought
And the writing style appears to be serious

THEN Identify piece of writing as satire
And say, "satire"

The defining features of the concept appear as conditions (*if*) that need to be met for the action (*then*) part of the production to occur. According to this production format, students need to identify pieces of writing as examples of satire in the presence of the defining features, or conditions. Just memorizing the definition of "satire" as declarative knowledge, or verbal information, is not adequate to produce the skill. Learners must associate the features of the definition—the conditions—with the appropriate action.

For *rules* and *principles*, the action is applying relationships among concepts. The conditions are the concepts that are found within the rule or principle. Look again at the production for the softball tagging rule. Notice that the conditions (*if*) are actually concepts that players have to be able to recognize: base runner, out, force-out, possession, ball. In a game situation, each one of these concepts needs to be identified for the tagging action to occur, as illustrated in the top portion of Figure 8.1. If any one of the concepts is not present in the situation, the action will not occur, and perhaps even a different action will be executed, as illustrated in the bottom portion of Figure 8.1.

■ **Production Systems: Condition-Action Rules for Complex Skills** Many intellectual skills are too complex to represent with a single production. For such skills, learners acquire sets of related productions called **production systems** (Anderson, 1983; Gagne, Yekovich, & Yekovich, 1993). In a production system,

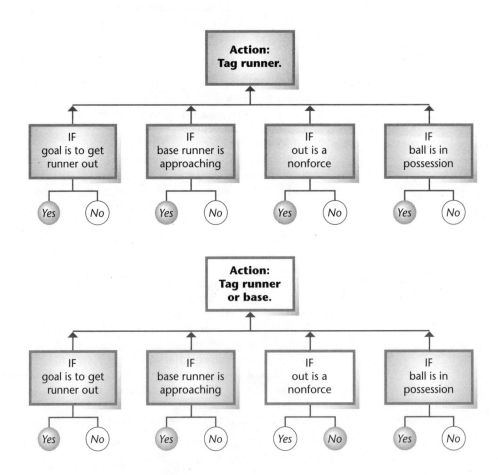

**Figure 8.1
Concepts: The Conditions for Applying the Tagging Rule**

individual productions are connected because the outcome (or action) of one production helps to satisfy the conditions of another production. For example, applying the tagging rule correctly depends on recognizing force-outs and non-force-outs. Therefore, the production for identifying force-outs creates an action that provides critical information for the tagging production. Here is a production system that shows how these two individual productions work together:

	IF	Goal is to get base runner out
P1	**THEN**	Set subgoal of identifying type of out as force-out or non-force-out
	IF	Subgoal is to identify type of out as force-out or non-force-out
		And base runner must advance
P2	**THEN**	Identify out as force-out
		And create proposition that out is a force-out
	IF	Base runner is advancing toward base
		And there is a force-out situation
		And ball is in possession
P3	**THEN**	Decide to tag base or runner
		And step on base or touch runner with ball

In this simple production system, three individual productions are related to each other in two important ways:

1. All three productions are focused on achieving an overall goal (getting the base runner out).

2. The actions of earlier productions establish the conditions for later productions in the system.

Thus, the action of P1 (creating a subgoal) satisfies one of the conditions of P2, and the action of P2 (identifying the situation as a force-out) satisfies one of the conditions of P3.

Cognitive psychologists eventually may find a better way to represent complex intellectual skills than production systems. For now, however, the evidence strongly suggests that production systems are useful ways to understand the nature of intellectual skills because human behavior is very consistent with them. For your work as a *design-teacher*, it is not essential to create productions and production systems for the intellectual skills you want your students to learn. My primary goal in introducing you to these theoretical ideas is to demonstrate and emphasize the conditionalized nature of procedural knowledge. **Conditionalized knowledge** is knowledge that is stored in memory along with the conditions and constraints of its use (Glaser, 1984). Our learners will be able to use their procedural knowledge in productive ways only to the extent that they have the conditions and constraints of that knowledge stored along with specific actions. In other words, they will know what to do and, most important, when to do it.

To illustrate this point, a few days ago I was helping my daughter, Anna, with her third-grade math homework. She was working on a set of problems involving time-related skills. One of the problems went something like this: "A European clockmaker constructed a wooden clock in 1753. The clock ran until the year 1800. How many years did the clock keep time?" At first Anna did not recognize this problem as a subtraction situation. So although she knew how to apply the rule (or algorithm) for subtracting 1753 from 1800, she did not know that she should use it.

This situation requires the understanding of subtraction as a *concept*, not just an algorithm. When learners like Anna acquire the ability to recognize subtraction situations conceptually, they are also developing the conditions and constraints that they will need to decide when to apply the subtraction algorithm. How do learners acquire conditionalized procedural knowledge? Let's tackle that important question in the next section.

Acquiring Conditionalized Procedural Knowledge

According to Anderson's theory of skill acquisition, learners progress according to three general stages: cognitive, associative, and autonomous (Anderson, 1983, 1990; Colley & Beech, 1989; Gagne et al., 1993). As we examine each of these three general stages of skill learning, I will illustrate them with the softball tagging rule for which we already have created a production system. I am deliberately choosing not to use a typical school-learned intellectual skill at this point because I want you to understand that these three stages apply to the learning of all intellectual skills.

■ **Cognitive Stage of Skill Learning**   During the **cognitive stage**, learners acquire a basic cognitive understanding, or representation, of what they are to do and when they are to do it. This early understanding of the conditions and actions is in more of a declarative knowledge form than a procedural form. For this reason, the cognitive stage is also referred to as the *declarative stage* (Anderson, 1983, 1990). At this stage, learners usually can verbalize, or talk about, the conditions and actions associated with the skill. In fact, they usually rely on being able to verbalize the components of a skill to help guide their actions. We might say that the skill at this point is not a skill at all, but merely a set of propositions—verbal information—that helps to control what learners do. As learners consciously state the conditions and actions to themselves (either silently or out loud), the information is occupying a great deal of space in working memory.

In the cognitive stage of learning the tagging rule, my softball players would understand the conditions and actions of the individual productions as verbal information, so they would be able to recall and state those propositions—although without necessarily being able to use them to produce an appropriate action. In an actual tagging situation, a girl might think to herself,

> Okay here comes the runner. What do I do if I get the ball? Should I tag the base or the runner? Let's see; it depends on whether it's a force-out. Does the runner have to run? Yes, I think she does, because the batter who just hit the ball is running to first. So the runner who was on first—the one coming toward me now—has to run to second. Since this is a force-out, I can either step on the base or touch the runner with the ball. But first I have to have the ball. Hey, hurry up and throw it to me!

This girl knows on a declarative level what to do. However, she is not at a point in her learning where she can apply the skill without talking herself through the situation. By the time she finishes thinking through all the conditions and actions declaratively, the runner may be standing safely on second base!

■ **Associative Stage of Skill Learning**   During the **associative stage**, learners begin to change their declarative representation to a procedural representation. According to Anderson (1983, 1990), two processes are responsible for this change. During the **composition process**, two or more individual productions become associated into one complex procedure. This happens as the actions produced by one production satisfy the conditions for other productions. The composition process occurs as learners begin to perform the actions (*then*) in the presence of the appropriate conditions (*if*).

The second major process, **proceduralization**, occurs as learners rely less and less on the cues provided by the declarative knowledge they acquired in the cognitive stage. The associations being formed among productions begin to control learner actions rather than conscious statements of verbal information. As declarative cues drop out, learners can perform the skill by executing the production system with increasing speed and efficiency, without having to think as much about it. The less we have to devote conscious thinking and attention when we perform a skill, the more **automatic** it becomes. Hence, skill automaticity begins to develop during the associative stage.

At the associative stage, the softball player I described earlier might be thinking something like the following: "Here comes the runner. It's a force. Step on the bag!" Without having to think consciously and deliberately about all the specific features of the situation, the player produces the action (stepping on the bag) because she has quickly used her conceptual skills to classify the situation as a force-out. Satisfying that condition then leads automatically to applying the appropriate tag. This quick, efficient, accurate performance will be possible only if the player has had many practice opportunities to perform the actions of the individual productions in the context of the complete production system.

Autonomous Stage of Skill Learning   In the **autonomous stage** learners continue to refine the skill. The associations that were formed during the associative stage continue to be strengthened through performance, and declarative cues continue to drop out, resulting in even greater automaticity. In a sense, learners continue to fine-tune the skill. For this reason, some psychologists also refer to this stage as the *tuning stage* (Fitts & Posner, 1967). The autonomous stage actually is a gradual continuation of the associative stage; there is no clear boundary between the two stages.

If we keep practicing and performing a skill, we continue to improve in speed and accuracy, although often the improvements are so small we have a hard time recognizing them. Another way in which learners continue to improve in the tuning stage is the ability to make increasingly complex judgments about when, where, and how to apply the skill in different situations. To illustrate what happens in the autonomous stage, let's return to softball. As the third baseman practices making the out at third base by stepping on the bag when a ground ball is hit to the infield with runners on first and second bases, she will get better and better at executing the correct action in game situations in which a runner on second is forced to move to third on a batted ball to the infield. However, if after an outfielder catches a fly ball and the second-base runner tries to advance to third, she may decide (correctly) to apply the tag to the *runner* instead of the base because of the non-force-out situation.

If the player has never practiced this specific scenario, how does she know what to do? By recognizing the situation as a non-force-out, the conditions for the "tag-the-runner" action are met. The player's ability to apply the concept of "non-force-out" as a skill and the association of that production with the tagging production makes the correct action possible. As this scenario illustrates, conceptual understanding is a key element in helping learners decide when to apply their skills (Mayer, 1987, 1992).

LET'S SUMMARIZE

In this introductory section, we have laid a powerful foundation for our thinking about designing instructional strategies for all types of intellectual skills. From the production system perspective, we see that skill learning requires learners to create connections among conditions and actions through their own performance. We see also that learners progress through three general phases of skill learning as their knowledge of the skill is transformed from declarative to procedural form through their own performance. In the remainder of this chapter, we examine how these general internal conditions apply to our thinking about the external conditions of learning for one specific type of intellectual skill: concepts.

Concepts: Internal Conditions of Learning

How do people learn concepts as intellectual skills? How can we design instructional strategies to help people learn concepts as skills? The answers to these two questions, we learned in the previous chapter, depend on the internal conditions of learning. As Figure 8.2 illustrates, our understanding of learners' internal knowledge and processing needs should help us design external instructional events to support those needs. Although a great deal of theorizing and research has been done on concept formation (see Mayer, 1992; Ormrod, 1995; Smith, 1995), not all of that information is equally relevant to classroom instructional design. In this section, I highlight the aspects of concept learning that I believe are most useful when we deliberately work to help others acquire new concepts in the classroom.

Regardless of the specific content, several internal conditions are common to all concept-learning situations (Gagne, 1985). You already know that concept learning involves acquiring a mental category that we can use to classify members (examples) and nonmembers (nonexamples) of the group (Margolis, 1994). Basically, then, learners must be able to apply the membership criteria to any new instance they encounter. However, the ability to apply the membership criteria means that learners must possess each of these features as concepts also. Figure 8.3 presents this view of concept learning in visual form for a specific concept, "noun."

Prerequisite Concepts and Discriminations

Notice in Figure 8.3 that learners will be able to identify any word as a noun only when they can recognize words (a describing feature) and each of the following three defining features: persons, places, things. So before they can acquire the target concept, learners must already possess several prerequisite concepts that they can apply as intellectual skills. That is, they have to be able to distinguish between words and nonwords, persons and nonpersons, places and nonplaces, and things and nonthings.

If we have performed a thorough hierarchical analysis of the target concept, we will have a good idea of what the necessary prerequisite concepts are.

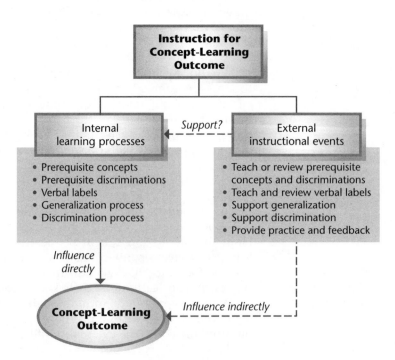

**Figure 8.2
Internal and External
Conditions of Learning
for Concepts**

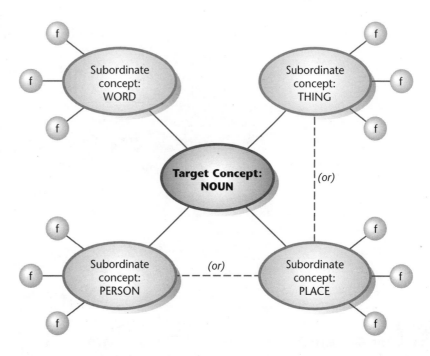

**Figure 8.3
Subordinate Concepts
for the Concept of Noun**

Target concept: A noun is a word that names a person, place, or thing.
Subordinate concepts: word, person, place, thing
f = features of subordinate concepts

Notice, however, in Figure 8.3 that each of these prerequisite concepts has its own set of describing and defining features. Therefore, learners must be able to apply each of those features as skills as well. (Perhaps we could call them *pre*-prerequisite skill.) I am not suggesting that we will necessarily have to teach our learners all of these prerequisite (and *pre*-prerequisite) concepts before providing instruction for the target concept. I simply want you to recognize that the conditions in a concept production are concepts themselves with their own condition-action productions. Learners who do not possess those productions will have difficulty acquiring the target production for the target concept.

In addition to prerequisite concepts, learners also may need to be able to apply prerequisite discriminations. Recall from Chapter 2 that a discrimination is an intellectual skill that enables us to tell the difference between two perceptual stimuli such as sights, sounds, tastes, smells, and touches. Prerequisite discriminations are most relevant to concept learning when the target concepts are concrete concepts—those whose defining features are perceptual stimuli. How easy would it be to learn to recognize basic shapes like squares, triangles, and circles if you could not see any differences between them or could not tell the difference between a straight line and a curved line? As you can see, discriminations are critical prerequisite skills for learning concrete concepts. However, as I noted for prerequisite concepts, recognizing that learners need to possess certain discrimination skills does not necessarily mean that we will have to teach those skills to them.

Verbal Labels for Prerequisite Concepts

People can possess a concept without necessarily having a verbal label, or word, to name the category. To prove this point to yourself, compare the group of positive instances (examples) in Figure 8.4 to the negative instances (nonexamples). When you think you've figured out the defining features of the category, try to classify the new instances at the bottom. If you classified A and D

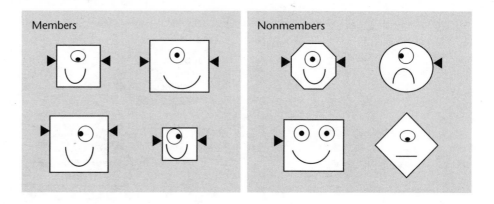

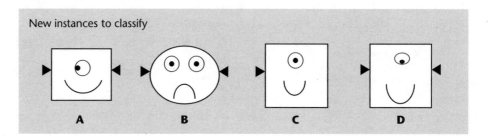

**Figure 8.4
What is the Concept
Category?**

as examples, you are correct. You have just acquired a concept for classifying one-eyed, two-eared, smiling squares. Notice that although you can recognize members of the category, you do not yet have a specific name for these strange-looking things. The *concept* is the act of classifying; the *name* is simply a label (verbal information) we attach to the category so we can talk and think about the concept more efficiently.

Learners who already possess the internal condition of verbal labels for the target concept's defining features (see Figure 8.2) may be able to learn the concept more easily than those who do not. When your learners are acquiring a new concept, you probably will be calling their attention to the subordinate concepts that make up the describing and defining features by using the word labels for those concepts. This will occur regardless of the specific media or learning activities you use to engage your learners. For example, if your students hear that a noun is a word that names a person, place, or thing, that statement will be meaningless to them unless they already know the concepts to which the word labels "person," "place," and "thing" refer.

The Generalization Process

The **generalization process** is a critical internal learning process (see Figure 8.2) that determines how well learners eventually will be able to apply, or transfer, a concept (Merrill & Tennyson, 1977; Woolley & Tennyson, 1972). Through the generalization process, learners acquire the ability to recognize all possible examples of the concept, even if the examples are quite different. In other words, students come to understand that as long as instances have the critical features of the concept, they can differ quite a bit on the irrelevant features—those that do not matter.

To illustrate, let's see how well your own personal concept of "mammal" generalizes. Table 8.2 lists eighteen instances. I want you to classify each one as a mammal or a nonmammal. Think of an example of a concept as a hit and a nonexample as a miss, so circle the "H" for each instance that you believe is a hit and the "M" for any that are misses. Then circle one of the numbers to express how confident you are in your response. Circle the 0 if you are completely uncertain (that is, you are guessing), 3 if you are absolutely confident,

Table 8.2
Identifying Examples and Nonexamples of the Concept "Mammal"

Directions: If the instance is an example of a mammal, circle H for "hit." If the instance is not an example of a mammal, circle M for "miss." Circle the number that represents how much confidence you have in your classification: 0 = no confidence (guessing), 1 = low confidence, 2 = moderate confidence, 3 = very high confidence (absolutely certain).

H	M	0	1	2	3	1. Rabbit
H	M	0	1	2	3	2. Snake
H	M	0	1	2	3	3. Butterfly
H	M	0	1	2	3	4. Hamster
H	M	0	1	2	3	5. Seal
H	M	0	1	2	3	6. Owl
H	M	0	1	2	3	7. Human
H	M	0	1	2	3	8. Frog
H	M	0	1	2	3	9. Rock
H	M	0	1	2	3	10. Dog
H	M	0	1	2	3	11. Bacteria
H	M	0	1	2	3	12. Penguin
H	M	0	1	2	3	13. Mouse
H	M	0	1	2	3	14. Cat
H	M	0	1	2	3	15. Earthworm
H	M	0	1	2	3	16. Tarantula
H	M	0	1	2	3	17. Manatee
H	M	0	1	2	3	18. Bat

and 1 or 2 for levels of certainty between those two extremes. Go ahead, take a few minutes to do this adjunct activity—*without* reaching for a dictionary or biology book. I want you to use your existing understanding of the mammal concept to make your classifications.

When you are finished with your own classifications, you may look at the data that I collected from some of my own students for the mammal exercise in Figure 8.5. Within the circle are all the instances that belong in the mammal category. They all meet the membership criteria: warm-blooded, hairy animals that give birth to live young and nurse them with milk. All the instances outside the circle are nonexamples because they violate at least one of these criteria. Look at your own responses. Are there any surprises for you? Below each instance you will see two numbers. The first number is the percentage of students who classified the instance correctly; the second number is the average confidence level. So, for example, 90 percent of the students correctly identified hamsters as mammals (10 percent incorrectly identified them as nonmammals) and they were reasonably confident (2.45 out of 3.0) in their classifications.

Notice that within the circle, there is a range of correct classifications, from a high of 93 percent for humans, dogs, cats, and rabbits to a low of 45 percent for bats. The confidence level is also much higher for humans (2.9), dogs (2.6), cats (2.75), and rabbits (2.4) than for bats (only 1.8). These data demonstrate that some mammals are much easier to classify than others. The easiest examples to classify are those that are most similar to the *prototypical* mammal. A **prototype** is an example of a concept category that possesses the most typical, or common, values of the critical features (Rosch, 1975; Rosch & Mervis, 1975; Smith, 1995). For example, when you think of hairy animals, those with thick, furry coats usually come to mind: rabbits, cats, dogs. When you think of animals nursing their young, you easily think of humans, dogs, and cats. I like to refer to these obvious, easy examples as *near hits* because they are closest to the concept prototype.

At the outer edge of the circle, however, are examples that are further from the prototypical mammal. They definitely belong in the category because they meet all the criteria; however, the ways in which they meet the criteria are more atypical or unusual. For example, it is hard to imagine hair on a seal because their bodies look so sleek. It is even harder to consider mother bats nursing baby bats (bat milk?)! I like to refer to these types of examples on the fringes of a concept category as *far hits*. Learners should be able to generalize concept features to the very edge of the category so that they can identify both the near hits and the far hits, as well as all the examples in between.

When learners cannot generalize a concept to all possible examples, they demonstrate a type of misconception called **undergeneralization**. An undergeneralized concept of mammal, for example, may result in students' not recognizing that bats and seals are mammals because one lives in the ocean rather than on land and the other can fly. In production system terms, learners who undergeneralize have too many unnecessary conditions that have to be satisfied before the action (identifying the instance as an example) can occur. If learners believe that all mammals live on land (an irrelevant feature), they will not be able to generalize the concept to aquatic mammals such as seals, whales, and dolphins because those instances do not satisfy the production's extra "land-dwelling condition." If they add an extra "nonflying" condition to the production, they will not generalize the concept to mammals, such as bats, that do fly.

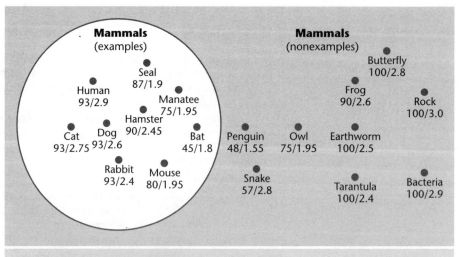

How to Interpret the Numbers
The first number below each instance is the percentage of people who classified the instance correctly as an example or nonexample. The second number is the average confidence level that people expressed for each classification (maximum = 3.0).

Example
Hamster: 90% of the people surveyed correctly classified hamsters as mammals; their average confidence level was 2.45 out of 3.0.

**Figure 8.5
Ranges of Generalization and Discrimination for the Concept of "Mammal"**

Is it a fish or a mammal? Will this boy be able to generalize his concept of mammal to classify this killer whale correctly?

From a production perspective, then, the generalization learning process occurs as learners eliminate any unnecessary conditions that are related to irrelevant features (Gilhooly & Green, 1989). How do students accomplish this process? First, they must produce the identifying action for a variety of positive instances that have different values for the critical features. For example, as learners identify dogs, seals, humans, and bats as mammals, they will see the full range of values that their hair and nursing of young can take. Second, learners themselves must identify positive instances that have obviously different values for the irrelevant features. For example, as learners identify both mice and whales as mammals, they eliminate size as a condition from the production. If small size is a condition, then a whale cannot be a mammal; if large size is a condition, then a mouse cannot possibly be a mammal. Whales and mice both cannot be mammals if size is a defining feature.

LET'S SUMMARIZE

Generalization is the learning process that helps people apply a concept as broadly as possible to all possible positive instances. As illustrated in Figure 8.6, learners can generalize a concept when they are able to recognize the full range of possible values that its subordinate concepts can take. In other words, the ability to generalize the prerequisite concepts (A, B, and C in Figure 8.6) makes it possible to generalize the target concept. In turn, generalizing the prerequisite concepts depends on the ability to generalize each of their features (A1, A2, and A3 in Figure 8.6) as broadly as possible.

The Discrimination Process

When our students acquire concepts, we certainly want them to be able to generalize those categories as far as possible. Sometimes, however, people try to generalize concepts too far, resulting in another type of misconception: **overgeneralization.**

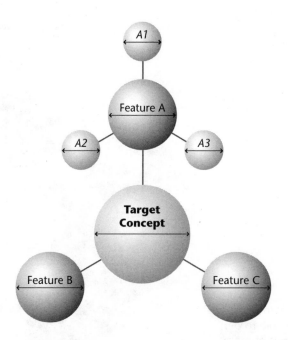

Figure 8.6
Concept Generalization

Let's turn our attention now to a second critical internal learning process that can prevent overgeneralization from happening: discrimination (see Figure 8.2). Notice in Figure 8.5 that only 48 percent of my students classified penguins correctly as nonmammals and only 57 percent classified snakes correctly. That means that penguins and snakes were identified incorrectly as mammals by a large number of students (52 percent, 43 percent). When people include instances in a concept category that do not belong, they are overgeneralizing the concept.

Some instances are easy to exclude from a concept category. As you can see, my students had no difficulty at all in classifying butterflies, bacteria, and earthworms as nonexamples with a high level of confidence. I like to refer to these types of obvious nonexamples as *far misses* because they aren't even close to having any of the necessary criteria. Other nonexamples, however, can be trickier to identify—like penguins and snakes (at least for some people). I like to refer to the tricky negative instances as *near misses* because they may actually possess one or more of the critical features (e.g., penguins are warm-blooded animals) or they may have a feature that looks like a critical feature (e.g., the wet feathers of penguins may look like wet fur).

Learners overgeneralize concepts when their productions are missing one or more necessary conditions. For example, learners who overgeneralize the concept of mammal to birds may not have the hair condition or the live-birth condition firmly represented in the production. Through the **discrimination process**, learners add necessary conditions to their productions, just the opposite of what happens during the generalization process (Gilhooly & Green, 1989; Gagne et al., 1993). Generalization occurs as learners delete unnecessary conditions; discrimination occurs as learners add necessary conditions. Discrimination occurs as learners themselves make appropriate responses to nonexamples, especially those that are near misses (Merrill & Tennyson, 1977).

Generalization and discrimination are two sides of the concept-learning coin. Whereas the generalization process *expands* a concept, the discrimination process *restricts* it. Both internal learning processes are vital to ensure that students do not acquire misconceptions. Now that we know a bit more about what needs to happen within our learners during concept learning, let's see what we can do on the outside to help support these learning processes.

Concepts: External Conditions of Learning

As noted in Figure 8.2, all of the external conditions of concept learning that we will consider in this section are related to our understanding of the internal conditions of concept learning. I have culled these external instructional events from numerous research studies and theoretical perspectives on concept learning (see Gagne, 1985; Merrill & Tennyson, 1977; Tennyson & Cocchiarella, 1986; Tennyson & Park, 1980). These perspectives consistently describe concept acquisition as a process of learning how to recognize and apply critical features. Although a great deal of evidence suggests that we eventually store many concepts in memory as generalized examples, or prototypes (see Ormrod, 1995; Smith, 1995), novice learners still need to process critical features to help them construct these generalizations. Whereas concept prototypes seem to be most useful for classifying instances that are fairly typical (near hits) and obvious nonexamples (far misses), critical features provide the most guidance when learners encounter ambiguous, less obvious instances (far hits, near misses) that require some degree of careful thinking and analysis (Andre, 1986).

Both prototypical examples and critical features seem to be important elements of effective instruction for concept learning (Tennyson & Cocchiarella, 1986). Let's look at how we can use our knowledge of prototypes and critical features to support concept learning. We will organize our discussion of instructional events according to the three major stages of skill acquisition that we reviewed earlier in the chapter: cognitive, associative, and autonomous.

Concept Learning: The Cognitive Stage

During the cognitive phase, our learners need to begin forming a declarative representation of the necessary conditions and the appropriate action associated with the concept to be learned. Because learners should be able to demonstrate their declarative knowledge by stating it, we are really trying to help them acquire the concept as verbal information at this point. Thus, all of the strategies for supporting verbal information learning that we examined in Chapter 7 are also relevant here. We should use a variety of attention, elaboration, organization, and distinctiveness strategies to help students acquire a meaningful understanding of the concept's critical features so they can store them as propositions in long-term memory.

We begin the concept-learning process by helping students become aware of the concept's critical features (conditions) and demonstrating that any instances that possess those features can be classified (action) as examples. Regardless of the instructional media or specific learning activities we select, learners need to find out what the critical features of the concept are. In information processing terms, we need to help focus students' attention and selective perception on the concept's describing and defining features.

We can take either of two general approaches to accomplish this goal: deductive or inductive (see Figure 8.7). With a **deductive** teaching approach, learners are presented with a generalization such as a concept definition, rule, or principle and then provided specific examples to make the generalization meaningful. In contrast, with an **inductive** teaching approach, we engage learners with specific examples of a concept, rule, or principle and then help them construct an appropriate generalization. Sometimes this approach is referred to as **guided discovery**. General teaching models such as Hilda Taba's Inductive Thinking Model and Richard Suchman's Inquiry Training Model use an inductive approach to the teaching-learning process (see Joyce & Weil, 1986). Both deductive and inductive approaches can be equally effective, as long as we keep in mind our primary goal in using them: Our learners must develop a meaningful awareness of the concept's critical features.

The examples that we select for learners to process in this early stage should be those that are most effective in helping them understand the con-

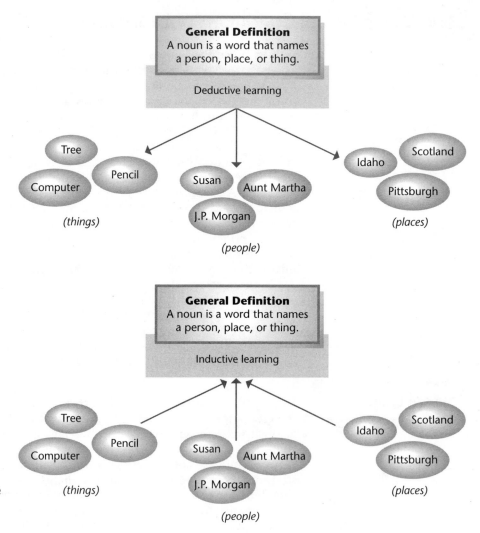

Figure 8.7
Deduction and Inductive Concept Learning Processes

cept's critical features. Usually these examples will be the prototypical ones—the near hits. The set of near hits should be as similar as possible to help students focus easily on the concept's critical features and abstract a prototypical representation (Leemkuil, 1990; Ranzijn, 1991). For example, to promote conceptual understanding of mammals during the cognitive stage, learners should process such obvious examples as rabbits, dogs, cats, and hamsters. Furthermore, to maximize the effectiveness of the near hits that students process, we may first need to review (or even teach) the prerequisite concepts and their verbal labels (see Figure 8.2) that represent those critical features so that the examples make sense—that is, so learners can see why the examples fit the category. Knowing, for example, that a noun is a word that names a person and then seeing that "Aunt Martha" qualifies as a noun will not be helpful unless students can already apply the concept of "person" to Aunt Martha.

Another way to strengthen the effectiveness of examples in the cognitive stage is to make them as obvious and distinctive as possible, even if we have to exaggerate the features a bit to get students to pay attention to them. To accomplish this goal, it is often useful to create prototypical examples that have obvious, easily recognized features. For example, to help students become aware of the defining features of most adult insects (three body parts, six legs, two antennae, two pairs of wings), I might engage them with a simplified line drawing, such as the one in Figure 8.8. Learners who use this prototypical

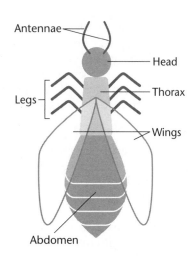

**Figure 8.8
Line Drawing of a
Prototypical Insect**

drawing will find it easy to focus on each of the defining features because the example does not represent any particular insect. Therefore, there are no irrelevant details, such as size or color, to distract them from the critical features.

A third way to maximize the effectiveness of examples in the cognitive phase is by making sure they are reasonably familiar to learners. Stating that a *collared peccary* is an example of a mammal probably would not be useful to learners at any level because most people would not know what that animal looks like. Learners cannot possibly use an example to instantiate a concept's critical features when they have no meaningful representation in long-term memory for the example.

Finally, we should design instructional materials and activities to show learners explicitly the connections between specific examples and a concept's critical features. For example, to help students understand why certain words are nouns, I (or my students) might organize them in a chart that clearly relates them to the critical features, as illustrated in Table 8.3. A chart like this one helps learners clearly see why an example is a member of a concept category, especially if they are actively involved in constructing the chart. As another example, look at how the labels in Figure 8.8 help learners connect this prototypical example to each of the concept's defining features.

**Table 8.3
Chart Showing How Nouns Are Related to Critical Features: Person, Place, Thing**

A Noun Is a Word That Names a Person	A Noun Is a Word That Names a Place	A Noun Is a Word That Names a Thing
Joe	Alabama	house
George Washington	Switzerland	car
Grandma	Sacramento	computer
Uncle Pete	Chicago	picture
Queen Elizabeth	Grand Canyon	paper clip
Marilyn Monroe	Shenandoah National Park	tree
boy	Globe Mills, Pennsylvania	shoe
girl	Sahara Desert	brick
child	Arctic Circle	community

Even if we do a superb job of focusing students' attention on the concept's critical features so that they encode them meaningfully in long-term memory, does that guarantee they will be able to recognize examples and nonexamples of the concept? As you and I know, just being able to state a concept definition does not mean that we can apply it. Learning to apply the concept is the focus of the second stage of skill learning: the associative stage.

Concept Learning: The Associative Stage

In the associative stage, learners need to start producing the action in the presence of the necessary conditions. In simple terms, this means that we have to provide opportunities for learners to practice identifying instances as examples and nonexamples. Not until they try to identify instances themselves will they begin changing their knowledge of the concept from declarative to procedural form. In their classic study of concept learning, Bruner, Goodnow, and Austin (1956) discovered that concept formation is an active process in which people make and test hypotheses concerning the concept's critical features. During the associative stage, learners need practice opportunities to nurture this type of active cognitive involvement. We should structure practice opportunities to promote the internal generalization and discrimination processes we described earlier in this chapter and provide informative feedback.

■ **Supporting Concept Generalization** Recall from the previous section that generalization and discrimination are two critical internal processes for skill learning. As learners begin proceduralizing their knowledge in the associative phase, we need to design instructional events to support both processes. The best way to support the generalization process is to make sure that learners practice applying the concept's critical features to divergent examples (Driscoll & Tessmer, 1985; Gagne, 1985). **Divergent examples** are positive instances that differ from one another because they have different values for the irrelevant features (Merrill & Tennyson, 1977; Ranzijn, 1991). Divergent examples should include both near and far hits. Divergent examples for the concept of "noun" would be both long and short words (*egg, elephant*), capitalized and uncapitalized words (*Mozart, motorcycle*), and words that begin with both vowels and consonants (*tree, asparagus*) because word length, capitalization, and beginning letter are all irrelevant features; they do not matter.

What would happen if our learners do not practice applying their productions to divergent examples? Look at the three columns of examples below and see if you can anticipate a possible misconception that learners could acquire for each concept:

Insect	Squaring	Community
Praying mantis	4×4	Jamestown, VA
Katydid	3×3	Mazeppa, PA
Grasshopper	7×7	Baltimore, MD
Aphid	9×9	Your town or city

Color is an irrelevant feature of insects. However, these four examples are all green, encouraging learners to add an unnecessary condition (greenness) to their productions. This extra condition will make it difficult for them to generalize the concept to insects that are not green (e.g., a ladybug is not an insect). Squaring happens when a quantity is multiplied by itself. The quantity can be any size—not just a single digit. Furthermore, the quantity does not even have to be expressed with numbers. If learners process only the single-digit examples of squaring, they may have difficulty generalizing the concept to other instances of squaring such as 35×35, $(6\times)(6\times)$, or $(a + b)(a + b)$. All of the examples of communities are the geographic locations of towns or cities. However, groups of people who work together to achieve common goals may not necessarily live in close geographic proximity to each other. Given these similar examples, learners may have difficulty identifying their families, school classrooms, religious organizations, or athletic teams as valid examples of communities. As you can see, when we fail to engage learners with divergent examples, we risk the possibility that they will develop undergeneralized concepts, which will greatly restrict transfer (Ranzijn, 1991; Tennyson & Park, 1980). Divergent examples help learners delete unnecessary conditions from their developing productions.

Divergent examples also help learners by showing them the range of possible values the relevant features can take. Mammals are animals that have hair, a defining feature. However, mammal hair is not all the same. It can be thick and furry (cats, rabbits), sleek and shiny (otters, seals), or sparse and bristly (elephants, pigs). If the only examples of mammals that learners process are cats, rabbits, guinea pigs, and dogs (all near hits), they are likely to include the overly restrictive condition "has thick, furry hair" in their productions rather than the appropriate condition, "has hair." By engaging learners with less prototypical examples that exemplify a wide range of possible values for each of the describing and defining features (far hits), we help them abstract those features as concepts that can vary quite a bit, thereby supporting the generalization process.

■ **Supporting Concept Discrimination**   In addition to broadening the concept through generalization, learners need to restrict the concept through the discrimination process. That is, they need to have all the necessary conditions in their productions that will enable them to exclude nonexamples from the concept category. How can we help them accomplish this goal? The best way to support discrimination is by making sure that learners apply their productions to nonexamples (Bourne, 1982; Houtz, Moore, & Davis, 1972; Merrill & Tennyson, 1977; Tennyson & Park, 1980). In other words, students can learn what a concept *is* by seeing what it is *not*.

The most useful nonexamples to support discrimination are those that are somewhat close to belonging in the category—the near misses. Engaging learners with the obvious far misses will not help them very much because those instances are likely to have none (or very few) of the concept's describing and defining features. So, for example, engaging students with rocks and bacteria as nonexamples of mammal is not going to help them refine the concept. After all, rocks and bacteria aren't even animals. But what about other animals—especially those that are warm-blooded and hairy looking? Birds are much more useful nonexamples than rocks and bacteria because they are warm-blooded and sometimes hairy-looking animals.

However, just because learners process near-miss nonexamples does not necessarily mean they will pay attention to the critical features that are violated. A student who finds out that a penguin is not a mammal may mistakenly believe that it is a nonexample because it is black and white, swims in water, or has flippers. These characteristics of penguins are actually irrelevant to the concept of mammal: zebras are black and white, seals swim in water, and dolphins have flippers.

By engaging learners simultaneously with both nonexamples and examples, we can increase the likelihood that they will pay attention to the critical features that the nonexamples do not possess. To be most effective, we should use nonexamples together with matched examples. **Matched examples and**

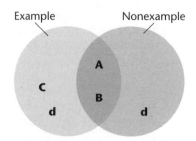

A = A critical feature shared by both examples and nonexamples

B = A critical feature shared by both examples and nonexamples

C = A critical feature found only in examples

d = An irrelevant feature shared by both examples and nonexamples

Figure 8.9
Using Matched Examples and Nonexamples to Promote Concept Discrimination

nonexamples are pairs of examples and nonexamples that are as similar as possible with respect to the features that do not matter—the irrelevant features (Gagne et al., 1993; Merrill & Tennyson, 1977). Of course, the examples and nonexamples will differ with respect to one or more features that do matter.

Figure 8.9 illustrates the value of using matched examples and nonexamples in instruction to promote discrimination. Here, the nonexample is a near miss because it shares two critical features (A and B) with concept members. Suppose that learners are actively involved in classifying the nonexample as an example (overgeneralization) and then receive feedback that they are incorrect. How will they understand the reason for being incorrect? If a nonexample has an irrelevant feature (d) that the example does not have, learners may be tempted to believe that this is the feature that makes the instance a nonmember rather than the critical feature that really matters (C). However, if we make sure that the example also possesses the irrelevant feature (d), then learners cannot possibly consider d to be the disqualifying feature. Their attention should focus on C, thus strengthening C as a necessary condition in the production.

Let's look at an illustration. Suppose that you planned to use fish as nonexamples for the concept of mammal. Students may believe that fish (salmon, tuna) are not mammals because they swim in water—an irrelevant feature. To prevent this misconception from occurring, you could have students analyze a fish and a fishlike mammal—say, a dolphin. Because both tuna and dolphins swim in the water, they are matched on that irrelevant feature, and students will be less likely to add "swims in water" as a critical feature. They also have a similar appearance and body structure, helping students focus their attention on the critical features that really matter: live birth, hair (yes, dolphins do have hair), and warm blood.

■ **Providing Informative Feedback**   Throughout the associative stage, as students are actively involved in identifying instances as examples or nonexamples, they will need to find out if they have applied the critical features correctly by receiving informative feedback. **Informative feedback** is information that learners receive following an action that tells them (1) whether their performance was appropriate and (2) why the performance was appropriate or inappropriate (see Balzer, Doherty, & O'Connor, 1989; Lhyle & Kulhavy, 1987). When students simply find out that a classification is incorrect, they may not be able to determine easily for themselves which unnecessary features they should delete or which necessary features they should add. When students make undergeneralization errors, the instructional materials need to focus their attention on the irrelevant features that must be eliminated as production conditions. When students make overgeneralization errors, we need to focus their attention on the describing and defining features that must be added as production conditions.

LET'S SUMMARIZE

In the associative phase of concept learning, learners have to begin proceduralizing their declarative representation by identifying concept examples in the presence of the critical features. In this way, the necessary conditions become associated with the appropriate action. As students practice classifying instances, we want to try to prevent misconceptions from occurring. Engaging learners with divergent examples (both near and far hits) will help prevent the misconception of undergeneralization. Engaging them with nonexamples (near misses) matched with examples will help prevent the misconception of overgeneralization.

As you can see, we need to design instructional materials and activities that bring learners into contact with appropriate examples and nonexamples, carefully structuring the near hits, far hits, and near misses that learners process. For this reason, I want you to try Exercise 8.1 in the *Student Exercise Guide*. In this exercise, you will extend the concept analysis you completed in Exercise 3.3 by creating a set of useful examples and nonexamples for a concept-learning instructional strategy.

Concept Learning: The Autonomous Stage

The autonomous stage of concept learning is a continuation of the associative stage. Learners need to continue to apply the concept to strengthen the condition-action associations in their productions. They also need to continue to broaden the concept through the generalization process and to make finer and finer discriminations. How can we help support these learning needs?

Clearly, an essential instructional event must be additional practice opportunities. To be effective in developing automaticity and transfer, practice opportunities should have four characteristics:

1. *The opportunities should be valid for the learning outcome.* That is, students should continue identifying, classifying, or categorizing examples and nonexamples of the concept because that is the action they will be expected to perform at the time of summative assessment.

2. *The practice opportunities should be distributed over a longer period of time, rather than massed in a shorter time period* (Gagne et al., 1993). As we saw with verbal information practice, every time learners must retrieve and apply a production from long-term memory, connections to the semantic network are added and strengthened.

3. *Provide informative feedback so learners can monitor their own progress and fine-tune their own productions.* As students practice, they need confirmation that they are applying the skill correctly or incorrectly.

4. *Practice opportunities should be presented in varied contexts.* This will promote transfer to a wide variety of real-world situations when students are long gone from the classroom environment (Cox, 1997; Voss, 1987).

Students should also have the opportunity to use their newly learned concepts as tools to help them function in a variety of generative tasks. Tessmer, Wilson, and Driscoll (1990) suggest four types of tasks that we can use to extend learners' conceptual knowledge: (1) using newly learned concepts in conversation and writing, (2) applying them in simulations and role playing, (3) making inferences about characteristics that are not critical features (e.g., in what kinds of environments are mammals best suited to live?), and (4) making inferences about how they relate to other concepts (e.g., how are mammal hair, reptile scales, and bird feathers similar and different?). By employing such concept-extending activities, we can help learners develop well-elaborated and functional concepts that are richly intertwined with their preexisting schemas.

Thus far, we have been examining the external conditions of concept learning in general terms. There is no single way to apply these conditions in every concept-learning situation. To help bring the external conditions to life, let's watch as one of our case analysis teachers, Ms. Nelson, designs an instructional strategy to help her fifth-graders acquire three new concepts.

CASE ANALYSIS

Designing an Instructional Strategy for Concept Learning

As part of her geology unit, Ms. Nelson wants students to be able to recognize examples of three major types of rocks: sedimentary, igneous, and metamorphic. Therefore, she wants her students to acquire each type of rock as a concept. From Chapter 6, here are Ms. Nelson's instructional goal and instructional objective for this learning outcome:

- *Instructional Goal: Learners will be able to identify sedimentary, igneous, and metamorphic rocks.*

- *Instructional Objective:* Given a set of fifteen rock samples that have not been used during instruction (four metamorphic, five igneous, six sedimentary) and three containers labeled according to the three rock categories, learners will demonstrate the ability to identify sedimentary, igneous, and metamorphic rocks by sorting the rocks into the three labeled containers. To demonstrate mastery, learners must place twelve of the fifteen rocks in the correct container.

To design an instructional strategy to help her students achieve the instructional goal, Ms. Nelson focuses on the three critical elements we highlighted in the previous chapter: information, engagement, and practice. Let's listen as she thinks about each of these elements.

Information: What Do My Students Need to Process?

During the cognitive stage, my students need to become aware of the describing and defining features of sedimentary, igneous, and metamorphic rocks. What are the features they need to know about? Here are the age-appropriate critical features that I want my students to acquire so that they can identify the most common examples of each:

▶ *Sedimentary:* Rock that forms from sediments (mud, sand, gravel, shells) that settle out of water and are cemented together. Common features are layering, water marks (ripples, mud cracks), fossil evidence, and dull appearance. Common examples: limestone, sandstone, shale, conglomerate, breccia, mudstone.

▶ *Igneous:* Rock that forms when melted rock (magma) from the earth's mantle forces its way into the earth's crust and cools. Common features are crystals in a random pattern, glassy or glossy, spongelike, no banding or layering. Common examples: granite, obsidian, basalt, gabbro, pumice.

▶ *Metamorphic:* Rock that forms when either sedimentary or igneous rocks are changed from heat or pressure. Common features are wavy lines, well-formed crystals, banded or flaky layers. Common examples: slate, marble, schist, gneiss.

Engagement: How Will My Students Process the Information?

Because skill learning happens in three general stages, I'm going to design learning activities so that they support the internal processes that are critical at each phase. I'll begin by thinking about how to engage my students at the cognitive stage.

Engaging Students at the Cognitive Stage   I will begin helping students become aware of each rock's major features with an inductive activity. Working in groups of five, students will try to place a collection of rock samples into categories. After each group has developed its categories, we will analyze the features the students used. I will guide the activity so that we eventually arrive at the three major rock classes. By using this inductive approach, students will begin to hypothesize actively about the features that may be relevant to rock classification.

After helping students sort their rocks into the three major classes, we will make a class chart in the form of a concept map that states the names and major features of each, promoting organization and distinctiveness [see Figure 8.10]. Then I will have students examine two or three prototypical examples (near hits) for each type: sandstone (sedimentary), granite (igneous), and gneiss (metamorphic). I will also show students color transparencies of these rocks on the overhead projector. As students examine each sample with magnifying glasses, I will explicitly point out the critical features on the transparencies. For example, as they look at the sandstone, I will direct their attention to the dull color, the sand grains, and the layering. As they look at the granite, I will direct their attention to the glossy surfaces of the mineral particles and the random arrangement of the mineral grains.

My students will gain a better understanding of the critical features for each rock type if they acquire some meaningful verbal information to explain

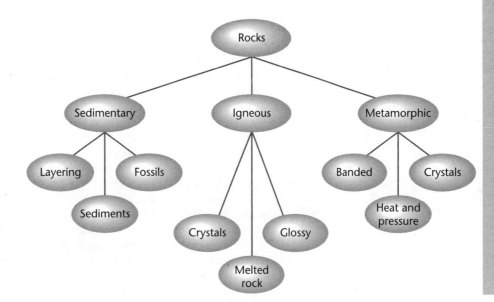

**Figure 8.10
Concept Map for Three
Types of Rocks and
Their Features**

how each forms. We will do an activity to demonstrate the composition and layering of sedimentary rocks. We will place different types of sediments (sand, soil, fine gravel, coarse gravel) into a large glass jar, add water, thoroughly shake it, and let it sit undisturbed overnight. The next day, students will be able to see different sediment layers that were formed as materials of different weights settled out at different rates. I will use the results in the jar to illustrate the layering feature of sedimentary rocks.

To illustrate igneous rock formation, we can boil a saturated solution of sugar water and grow sugar crystals on a string that is suspended in the solution. The hot solution will be like hot, molten magma that cools in the earth's crust, forming crystals. Crystal faces are common features of igneous rocks. To help students understand how volcanic igneous rocks like pumice and basalt are formed, I will have them watch a videotape that shows how lava from volcanoes hardens to form rock.

To illustrate *metamorphic* rock formation, I will melt flowers of sulfur in a test tube. When they have melted, I will pour the liquid sulfur into a jar of cold water. When students examine the sulfur, they will notice that it has become rubbery. Within a short time, they will notice that crystals are forming. As they continue to examine the sulfur with a magnifying glass, they will see that the crystals themselves change in appearance. The changing appearance of the sulfur will help students understand how igneous and sedimentary rocks change into metamorphic rocks.

Engaging Students at the Associative Stage Once my students have a meaningful awareness of each rock's features, it's time for them to start proceduralizing their declarative knowledge. Students will work together in small groups to sort rock specimens into the three categories. We will repeat the activity several times, with each group having a different set of specimens to sort. To promote generalization, each set will have a wide variety (divergent examples) of rocks that fit into each category. The rocks will differ with respect to irrelevant features such as size, shape, and color. To support the generalization process further, I will cut out photographs from field guides for students to practice sorting. The field guides will present an even greater range of divergent examples than the rock specimens.

Every time students classify a rock as belonging to one of the three categories, they also will be discriminating it from the other two remaining categories. Some rocks may pose special challenges because they appear to have some of the characteristics of another category. Therefore, to provide further support for my students' discrimination processes, I will engage them deliberately with several of these "near-miss" rocks.

Metamorphic rocks often have features that make them look as if they could be sedimentary rocks. For example, students may mistake the parallel bands of gneiss for layers of sedimentary rock. To help students discriminate gneiss from the sedimentary category, I will show them a sample of gneiss and a sample of sandstone that are similar to each other in size, shape, and coloration (irrelevant features). Each sample will have a banded, layered appearance. The gneiss sample will be a nonexample of the sedimentary category, and the sandstone will be a matched example. By matching the samples closely, I will focus my students' attention on the crystalline mineral grains in the gneiss—features that are not usually found in sedimentary rocks.

To help students refine their productions, I will have them study the two samples and make preliminary classifications (predictions) so they will be producing an action. Then I will use a magnifying glass to direct their attention to the mineral grains in the gneiss sample and help them reclassify it (again, they produce the action) as a sedimentary rock. Following a similar strategy, I will guide students in processing several pairs of potentially confusing rocks using matched examples and nonexamples: gneiss (metamorphic) and granite (igneous), shale (sedimentary) and slate (metamorphic), and diorite (igneous) and sandstone (sedimentary).

Engaging Students at the Autonomous Stage   To provide further experience in applying the three rock concepts, I will take my class on a field trip to local rock outcrops, where they will be able to collect their own samples of each type of rock. These natural sites will help to promote transfer because they will provide new specimens in varied, naturally occurring contexts. At each natural site, I will first have students try to classify the rock as sedimentary, igneous, or metamorphic and provide a justification. Then I will either confirm or challenge their predictions, focusing on the critical features that are present in the outcrops.

Back in the classroom, students will develop their own individual rock collections using the specimens they collected on the trip. They can also bring rocks from home. Of course, their collections will be organized according to the three major categories, so each specimen will be a further opportunity to practice generalizing and discriminating the three concepts.

Practice: How Will My Students Strengthen Their Learning?

Throughout these engagement activities, students will have many opportunities to practice applying the three rock concepts as skills. I do want to make sure, however, that they have an opportunity to practice in a way that is similar to the summative assessment I have planned for them. Using my instructional objective as a guide, I will prepare three sets of rocks for students to sort into three containers. I will number each rock and provide an answer key so students can receive immediate informative feedback. After students work with each set, they should be ready to apply the rock concepts to a new set of instances, as described in the instructional objective.

LET'S SUMMARIZE

You have just watched Ms. Nelson design an instructional strategy to help her learners acquire three concepts as procedural knowledge. She developed the external information, engagement, and practice elements of her strategy to support her students' internal learning needs. Will her strategy work? Neither we nor Ms. Nelson can answer this question until students actually demonstrate whether they can identify sedimentary, igneous, and metamorphic rocks, as assessed by the procedure described in Ms. Nelson's instructional objective.

LOOKING BACK LOOKING AHEAD

In this chapter, we examined the general internal learning processes that we must support to help learners acquire new intellectual skills such as concepts, rules, principles, and cognitive strategies. We identified three general stages of skill acquisition—cognitive, associative, and autonomous—that can structure and guide the planning of instructional events. Finally, we took an in-depth look at the internal processes that are at work during concept learning. We then used those internal conditions of learning to guide our thinking about the instructional events that we can design to help students learn new concepts as procedural knowledge.

Now that you are aware of the basic internal and external conditions of concept learning, I invite you to begin proceduralizing your knowledge by completing Exercise 8.2 in the *Student Exercise Guide*. This exercise gives you an opportunity to design an instructional strategy for teaching a concept. Also, you will want to monitor your achievement of the chapter's instructional goals by completing Exercise 8.3. When you have your own concept-learning productions firmly in place, you will be ready to tackle the next level of intellectual skill: rules and principles.

RESOURCES FOR FURTHER REFLECTION AND EXPLORATION

Print Resources

Gagne, E. D., Yekovich, C. W., & Yekovich, F. R. (1993). *The cognitive psychology of school learning* (2nd ed.). New York: HarperCollins.

An excellent overview of Anderson's ACT theory and its implications for classroom teaching. Three chapters are particularly relevant to our discussion of skill learning and concept acquisition: "Representing Procedural Knowledge" (Chapter 6), "Acquisition of Schemas: Schema Formation and Refinement" (Chapter 8), and "Acquisition of Procedural Knowledge" (Chapter 9).

Joyce, B., & Weil, M. (1985). *Models of teaching* (3rd ed.). Englewood Cliffs, NJ: Prentice-Hall.

A highly regarded book that presents a comprehensive overview of many different teaching models that have been developed over the years. Of particular relevance to the discussion of concept learning are chapters that describe a Concept Attainment Model of Teaching (Chapter 2), Hilda Taba's Inductive Thinking Model (Chapter 3), and Richard Suchman's Inquiry Training Model (Chapter 4).

Novak, J. D., & Musonda, D. (1991). A twelve-year longitudinal study of science concept learning. *American Educational Research Journal, 28,* 117–153.

A research study that incorporates many instructional practices relevant to concept learning and assessment. Demonstrates how concept maps can be used to help learners develop conceptual understanding and to assess conceptual understanding and misconceptions.

Ormrod, J. E. (1995). *Human learning* (2nd ed.). Englewood Cliffs, NJ: Merrill.

A fine book that presents current theories of human learning in an engaging style. An entire chapter on concept learning (Chapter 14) presents theoretical principles and useful recommendations for concept teaching in the classroom.

Tennyson, R. D., & Park, O. (1980). The teaching of concepts: A review of instructional design research literature. *Review of Educational Research, 50,* 55–70.

A comprehensive summary of research on concept teaching and learning with many useful research-based principles on the use of examples and nonexamples to promote concept generalization and discrimination.

World Wide Web Resources

http://act.psy.cmu.edu/

Web site for the ACT research group at Carnegie Mellon University. Provides in-depth information on John R. Anderson's ACT theory of cognition and knowledge acquisition. Links to research papers, software, and tutorials for learning more about the theory.

http://ww2010.atmos.uiuc.edu/(Gh)/guides/mtr/home.rxml

Web site for the Online Meteorology Guide, a collection of web-based instructional modules that use text, colorful diagrams, animations, computer simulations, and audio and video to introduce basic concepts related to weather. Good examples of concept-learning principles applied to teaching materials.

http://ecedweb.unomaha.edu/teach.htm

Web site for Economics Education. Provides numerous links to useful instructional materials. Also provides lists of fundamental economics concepts appropriate for students of different age levels and online materials and lesson plans for teaching economics concepts.

9

Instructional Strategies for Rule, Principle, and Cognitive Strategy Learning Outcomes

This morning when I awoke, it was snowing—our first snowfall of the winter. Driving to work over the winding, snow-covered country roads that I usually travel was an adventure. I did eventually make it to the university safely, but there were a couple of hair-raising moments along the way. For example, as I descended a fairly steep hill, I stepped on the brake to slow down a bit and felt the car begin to slide out of control. I had to think fast about how to react. Fortunately, I remembered two rules that applied to the situation:

- When sliding on snow or ice, pump the brakes gently.
- When sliding on snow or ice, steer into the slide.

These two rules are easy to remember and talk about but very difficult to apply when your car is sliding out of control because the first impulse is to slam on the brakes to stop the skid and to steer away from the direction in which you're skidding. Fortunately, I resisted my natural impulses and actually followed the two rules, gaining control of the car and allowing me to sit in my office writing these words rather than digging my car out of a ditch—or worse.

This driving experience reminded me once again of the important role that intellectual skills play in our lives, both in and out of school. Although I eventually made the motor responses of steering and pumping the brakes to solve my sliding

---

INSTRUCTIONAL GOALS FOR CHAPTER 9

After reading and thinking about this chapter, you should be able to . . .

1. Describe and demonstrate the internal and external conditions of learning for rules and principles.

2. Apply the three stages of skill acquisition to design an instructional strategy to support rule and principle learning.

3. Apply the divergent example strategy to support rule and principle generalization.

4. Apply the matched example and nonexample strategy to support rule and principle discrimination.

5. Describe and apply the internal and external conditions of learning to design an instructional strategy to support cognitive strategy learning.

problem, it was the two rules that I applied as *intellectual* skills—as procedural knowledge—that helped me figure out what to do. How did I acquire these two rules as skills? I first *heard* the rules as verbal information many years ago when I was learning to drive. They didn't become skills for me, though, until I actually started to *use* them, transforming my declarative knowledge to procedural knowledge. Through several sliding experiences on icy and snow-covered roads, I have learned that the rules do indeed work because I have tried them in various sliding situations and have been able to observe their positive effects (practice with examples). The times when I didn't apply the rules, I learned of their importance the hard way (practice with nonexamples).

As illustrated by my driving example, our students will learn to apply rules as intellectual skills only to the extent that they have the opportunity to proceduralize the declarative statements of rules that they encounter in textbooks, computer programs, and other instructional materials. They also need to apply the rules as condition-action productions to a wide variety of examples and nonexamples to promote generalization and discrimination. This sounds a lot like the territory we covered in the last chapter on concept learning, doesn't it?

In this chapter, we explore instructional strategies that can help students acquire rules, principles, and cognitive strategies as skills that they can apply to a wide variety of thinking and problem-solving tasks. You will see that this approach to designing instruction for these intellectual skill outcomes has a lot in common with our approach to concept teaching. Before sliding into the chapter, please pump your brakes gently and steer into the instructional goals that will be our focus.

Rules and Principles: Internal Conditions of Learning

When we apply concepts as intellectual skills, we use the concepts' features to classify instances as examples and nonexamples. When we apply rules and principles, we use concept relationships to produce a new mental action that helps us solve a problem, explain a situation, or make a prediction (Gagne, 1985; Ormrod, 1995). As illustrated in Figure 9.1, before we can help a student learn how to produce such mental actions, we need to understand their internal learning needs.

Look closely at the last sentence of the preceding paragraph. Do you notice anything strange, unusual, or incorrect? If not, here is a clue: " . . . before we can help a *student* learn how to produce these mental actions, we need to understand *their* internal learning needs."

The words *student* and *their* are related to each other. *Their* is a pronoun that refers back to its antecedent, *student*. The problem is that *their* is a plural pronoun and *student* is a singular antecedent. As it is written, the sentence violates a rule: *When the word that a pronoun refers to (the antecedent) is singular, use a singular pronoun. When the antecedent is plural, use a plural pronoun.*

If you caught the error in the sentence, you did so because you were able to apply this rule as procedural knowledge. Can you now apply the rule to fix the sentence? To correct the problem of antecedent-pronoun agreement, you can change the plural pronoun (*their*) to a singular pronoun (*his, her, his or her*), or you can change the singular antecedent (*student*) to a plural noun (*students*) so it matches the plural pronoun (*their*):

▶ Before we can help a *student* learn how to produce such mental actions, we need to understand *her* internal learning needs. [*Student* and *her* are both singular.]

▶ Before we can help *students* learn how to produce such mental actions, we need to understand *their* internal learning needs. [*Students* and *their* are both plural.]

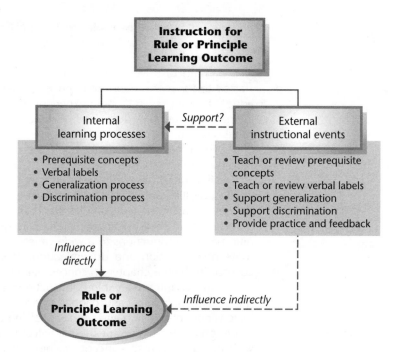

**Figure 9.1
Internal and External
Conditions of Learning
for Rules and Principles**

Rules and principles are powerful intellectual skills because they guide our thinking and behavior in an infinite number of specific situations. Rules and principles generalize to large numbers of new instances because they are made up of concepts that themselves generalize to an infinite number of specific instances. As illustrated in Figure 9.2, the pronoun-antecedent rule comprises two major concepts (pronoun, antecedent) that are related by a third concept, number agreement. An infinite number of antecedents can be either singular or plural; an infinite number of sentences can have singular or plural pronouns. Therefore, pronouns can agree (and disagree) with their antecedents in number in an infinite number of ways.

When learners acquire rules and principles as procedural knowledge, they develop productions that direct their actions when certain conditions are met (Anderson, 1993, 1996; Singley & Anderson, 1989). So if you are writing a sentence and need to use a pronoun (condition) and if the antecedent of the pronoun is singular (another condition), then you need to select a singular pronoun (action). Notice that the production's conditions are the *concepts* that make up the rule, and the action is guided by the concept *relationship*. For learners to acquire these types of productions, three internal conditions of learning are critical: prerequisite concepts and the dual learning processes of generalization and discrimination (see Figure 9.1). Let's examine each.

Prerequisite Concepts

Before learners can construct productions for applying rules and principles, they need to possess the concepts that comprise these higher-level skills (Gagne, 1985; Gagne & Driscoll, 1988; Ormrod, 1995). Furthermore, learners must be able to apply these subordinate concepts as skills. A student who cannot recognize singular and plural antecedents, for example, will not be able to apply the pronoun-antecedent rule successfully. A student who cannot identify pronouns will have difficulty recognizing when the rule is applicable. In short, for the subordinate concepts to function as conditions in a learner's production, the learner must already have productions for those concepts.

Recall from the preceding chapter that we can acquire concepts as skills without necessarily learning their verbal labels. To acquire a new rule or princi-

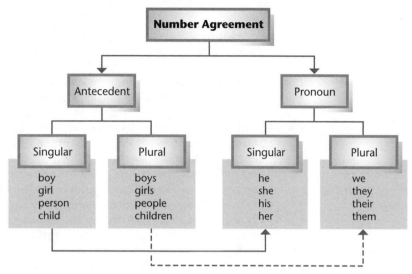

Rule: Pronouns must agree in number with their antecedents.
If the antecedent is singular, the pronoun also must be singular.
If the antecedent is plural, the pronoun also must be plural.

**Figure 9.2
Rules and Principles
Generalize because their
Subordinate Concepts
Generalize**

Examples: The *child* lost *her* toys.
The *child* lost *his* toys.
The *children* lost *their* toys.

ple, learners must possess the concepts that comprise the rule or principle, but they do not necessarily have to know particular verbal labels for the concepts. For example, students would not have to know that the word a pronoun refers to is called its "antecedent." Students could very easily learn the following "antecedent-free" version of the pronoun-antecedent rule: *When the word a pronoun refers to is singular, the pronoun also must be singular. When the word a pronoun refers to is plural, the pronoun also must be plural.*

During the learning process, however, it is usually more efficient to refer to concepts by one-word verbal labels. If learners are going to process the rule with the verbal label *antecedent*, then they will need to know that *antecedent* is the word to which a pronoun refers. Of course, they also will need to be able to apply this concept—that is, identify examples and nonexamples of antecedents. If learners are going to process the rule without the word *antecedent*, they still need to understand the meaning of other verbal labels such as "the word a pronoun refers to."

The Generalization Process

Similar to concept learning, **generalization** is the learning process that helps students apply a rule or principle as broadly as possible to all possible situations where it is applicable. If you can evaluate and correct each of the following sentences, you are demonstrating the ability to generalize the pronoun-antecedent rule:

▶ *All the boys in the class lined up to get his picture taken.*

▶ *Family vacations are valuable experiences. It gives family members the opportunity to learn and have fun. It provides a set of common memories.*

▶ *After the dogs escaped from the kennel, they ran across the street.*

To evaluate and correct (if necessary) each of these sentences, you need to be able to apply the rule despite a number of irrelevant features. The specific antecedent (boys, vacations, dogs) does not matter. The specific pronoun (his, it, they) does not matter. Nor do the gist, length, number, and complexity of the sentences matter. Furthermore, it would not matter if these sentences appeared in a book, a newspaper article, or a letter. It would not even matter if the sentences were spoken rather than written.

During the generalization process, then, learners acquire the ability to produce the appropriate action in situations that vary as widely as the concepts that comprise the rule or principle. For generalization to occur, learners must produce the action themselves in a number of situations that vary with respect to irrelevant features. As learners produce the same rule-governed action in different situations, they delete unnecessary conditions from their developing productions (Gagne, Yekovich, & Yekovich, 1993; Gilhooly & Green, 1989). Sound familiar? As we saw in Chapter 8, this is exactly the same way that concept generalization occurs.

When learners fail to delete unnecessary conditions, undergeneralization can result. For example, students who do not experience the antecedent and pronoun in separate sentences (e.g., the second example above) may acquire the misconception that the pronoun-antecedent rule applies only when the pronoun and antecedent appear within the same sentence. Just as concepts have prototypical examples (near hits) and unusual examples (far hits), rules and principles usually can be applied in prototypical ways to prototypical situations. They can also be applied in less obvious ways to more unusual situations. For learners to generalize a rule or principle from the near-hit situations to the far-hit situations, they need to produce the action in a wide variety of possible situations.

The Discrimination Process

When learners apply a rule or principle too broadly, they are overgeneralizing it. A common type of rule overgeneralization occurs when young children try to apply the rule for forming past tense to irregular verbs that are exceptions to the rule:

Regular Verbs		Irregular Verbs	
Verb	*Past Tense*	*Verb*	*Past Tense*
Walk	Walked	Fall	Falled (fell)
Decide	Decided	Think	Thinked (thought)
Carry	Carried	Break	Breaked (broke)

Young children make these kinds of language errors because they have heard enough examples to begin inducing an efficient rule for forming past tense (just add —*ed*), but they have not yet experienced enough nonexamples, or exceptions, to limit the rule to regular verbs.

As in concept learning, the **discrimination** process is necessary for learners to restrict rules and principles to the situations where they really do apply. Some nonexample situations will be rather obvious (far misses). Others will be trickier because one or more of the rule's subordinate concepts may be present in the situation. Do you remember the landscaping problem I told you about in Chapter 2? I used the Pythagorean theorem, a mathematical principle, to help me determine the length of a side in a right triangle. However, what if I needed to figure out how much fertilizer to use to prepare the soil within the triangle for planting shrubs and flowers? Because this is a right-triangle situation (concept), I might be tempted to try to apply the Pythagorean theorem (a near miss) rather than the rule for computing the *area* of a right triangle.

Learners discriminate the application of a rule or principle when they add necessary conditions to their productions (Gilhooly & Green, 1989; Gagne et al., 1993; Singley & Anderson, 1989). Discrimination occurs, then, as learners attempt to apply a rule or principle incorrectly to an inappropriate instance. They produce the action (or attempt to produce it) but eventually discover that the action does not help them achieve their thinking or problem-solving goals. If they can figure out what condition was not satisfied (i.e., why the rule or principle was not applicable), that condition can be added to the developing production so the mistake is less likely to happen again.

LET'S SUMMARIZE

The internal conditions for rule and principle learning are remarkably similar to those for concept learning (see Figure 9.1). Learners must possess prerequisite concepts and their verbal labels (if the labels will be used in instruction). They should apply the rule or principle to a wide variety of examples to develop skill generalization, and they should apply the rule or principle to nonexamples to develop skill discrimination. Will the external conditions of rule and principle learning also be similar to those for concept learning? Let's find out in the next section.

Learning Rules and Principles: External Conditions

As you can see in Figure 9.1, the external conditions for supporting rule and principle learning are very similar to those for supporting concept learning. As in our examination of concept learning, let's organize our analysis of rule and principle instruction according to the three general phases of skill acquisition: cognitive, associative, autonomous.

Rule and Principle Learning: The Cognitive Stage

The goal of instruction in the cognitive stage is to help learners acquire a meaningful declarative representation of the rule or principle to be learned. Regardless of the specific instructional media or activities we use to communicate with learners, we need to help them become aware of the concepts and concept relationships that are described by the rule or principle.

Similar to concept teaching, we can take either of two approaches to helping learners acquire the rule or principle as verbal information. With a **deductive** approach, we use learning activities and materials to communicate the rule or principle to learners and then engage them with specific examples to make it meaningful (Mayer, 1987; Smith & Ragan, 1993). For example, we might begin a lesson by telling students that all the angles in a triangle add up to 180 degrees and then demonstrate the principle by measuring the angles of several triangles and adding them together.

With an **inductive** approach (sometimes referred to as discovery learning or inquiry), we engage learners with specific application examples and then help them figure out the general rule or principle (Hammer, 1995, 1997; Joyce & Weil, 1986; Mayer, 1987; Smith & Ragan, 1993). For example, we could begin a lesson by having students draw several triangles, measure each of the angles, and look for relationships among them. Through questioning and prompts, students eventually would discover that the angles always add up to 180 degrees. Deductive and inductive approaches to introducing learners to new skills seem to be equally effective, as long as they achieve the primary goal of the cognitive stage: meaningful awareness of the concepts and concept relationships that comprise the rule or principle.

Of course, a necessary condition for this meaningful awareness is learner knowledge of prerequisite concepts and their verbal labels. If we have completed a thorough hierarchical content analysis (see Chapter 3), we should already be aware of the subordinate concepts our learners must be able to apply before they can acquire the target rule or principle. If we have reason to believe that our learners do not possess these prerequisite skills, we will need to design instruction for them, applying our knowledge of concept-learning principles (see Chapter 8). So, for example, if my learners do not yet know how to identify singular and plural pronouns, I would need to teach them those concepts (along with appropriate verbal labels) before continuing with instruction on the pronoun-antecedent agreement rule. Even if we do not have to teach students prerequisite concepts directly, we probably will need to help them activate these subordinate skills into working memory so they are ready to be combined into the new rule or principle.

Perhaps the most important element of instruction in the cognitive stage is the use of examples to help make the rule or principle meaningful to learners so that they do not just memorize verbal information by rote (Chinn & Brewer, 1993; Griffin, Case, & Capodilupo, 1995; Mayer, 1987). Students need to see meaningful examples of the rules and principles during instruction to help focus their attention on the critical concepts rather than superficial, irrelevant features that are always present in realistic application situations (Butterfield, Slocum, & Nelson, 1993). Students themselves often are able to provide meaningful examples of cognitive skills if they are encouraged to demonstrate their intuitive understanding or invent their own procedures before presenting them with a formal rule, algorithm, or principle. When students have the opportunity to begin the learning process by using the skills they already understand, they can then map their prior intuitive understanding to the skill to be acquired, reducing the likelihood that they will simply memorize rules and principles as abstract, meaningless declarative statements (Hiebert & Wearne, 1996; Kamii & Dominick, 1998). Although providing students with opportunities to experiment with new skills is time-consuming, the payoff is often greater interest, understanding, and transfer.

As for concepts, the most useful examples that we can provide at this stage are those that clearly demonstrate how the rule or principle is applied—the near hits. These prototypical examples should be as obvious and easy to understand as possible. We should even exaggerate them to ensure that learners are focusing their attention on the key concepts and relationships. To illustrate, in the case of pronoun-antecedent agreement, we might use the following near-hit examples to help learners become aware of the rule in a meaningful way:

- The *children* put on *their* coats.
- *Dogs* are good pets because *they* are loyal and friendly.
- The *boy* lost *his* book.
- Did you see the *girl* who broke *her* leg?

In each of these four simple sentences, it is highly unlikely that students would even be tempted to use the wrong pronoun, so that makes it easier for them to focus their attention on the rule. *Children* and *dogs* are obviously plural; *boy* and *girl* are obviously singular.

How can we be sure that learners clearly see how the examples illustrate the rule? Look at Figure 9.3 for some ideas. Through the use of attention-directing strategies such as highlighting, shading, lines, and labels, these examples clearly show learners how the rule works and how the rule's concepts are related to each other. Notice that both the pronoun and the antecedent are shaded and labeled in each sentence, and an arrow points from each pronoun to its antecedent. Of course, the specific ways in which we help learners see how examples relate to a rule or principle depend on our media choices, learner characteristics, and the content itself. There is no single way to accomplish this goal for all types of rules and principles.

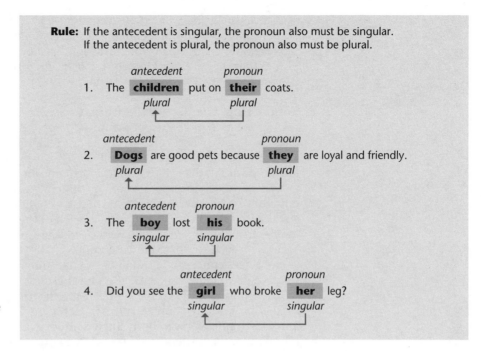

**Figure 9.3
Using Examples to Make
Learners Aware of a
Rule or Principle**

Rule and Principle Learning: The Associative Stage

After the declarative foundation has been laid, learners are ready to begin proceduralizing their knowledge. This means that *they* have to start producing an action that is consistent with the rule or principle. Providing exercises such as the following would give learners an opportunity to produce an appropriate action in the presence of the necessary conditions:

Directions: For each sentence, circle the pronoun in parentheses that agrees with its antecedent.

Joe rode (his, their) bicycle to school.

A person who works hard will create opportunities for (herself, themselves).

The bird flew from (its, their) perch when we approached.

In this early phase of action production, it is important for learners to keep reminding themselves of the rule so that they are producing the action for the right reasons. In other words, they need to think consciously about the rule so that both the conditions and actions are active simultaneously in working memory, where they will become associated (Gray & Orasanu, 1987). We could modify the three sentences in the preceding exercise to ensure that learners select the appropriate pronoun because they are actually applying the rule—not just because it sounds right—by having them identify the antecedent and indicate whether it is singular or plural:

Directions: In each sentence, circle the pronoun's antecedent. Circle **S** if the antecedent is singular and **P** if it is plural. Then circle the pronoun that agrees with the antecedent.

S   P   Joe rode (his, their) bicycle to school.

S   P   A person who works hard will create opportunities for (herself, themselves).

S   P   The bird flew from (its, their) perch when we approached.

Another way to encourage the association process is to have learners verbalize their actions and the reasons (or conditions) for them as they apply a skill. Eventually we want these verbal cues to drop out as the production becomes composed and proceduralized. In the early part of the association stage, however, having learners talk meaningfully about what they are doing helps to ensure that they are thinking consciously about the condition-action sequence (Gagne & Smith, 1962; Zook & Di Vesta, 1989).

■ **Supporting the Generalization Process**   During the association stage, learners need to have the opportunity to apply the skill in a wide variety of situations that vary according to irrelevant features (Cheng, Holyoak, Nisbett, & Oliver, 1986; Schmidt & Bjork, 1992). This is exactly the same **divergent example** strategy that we use to support concept generalization. The divergent examples we use to promote rule or principle generalization should be different from each other in two ways. First, we should use a wide variety of instances that stretch the boundaries of each of the subordinate concepts. For example, instances for the antecedent-pronoun rule should demonstrate a wide variety of each of the following subordinate concepts: singular antecedents (subordinate concept), plural antecedents (subordinate concept), singular pronouns (subordinate concept), and plural pronouns (subordinate concept).

A second type of divergence relates to the irrelevant features that are found in the application context (White, 1993). As I noted earlier, the pronoun-antecedent rule works in both single sentences and multiple sentences. It doesn't matter if the sentences are found in a book, newspaper article, or essay that you have written yourself. It doesn't matter how long or complex the sentences are. Learners need to practice applying the pronoun-antecedent rule with divergent examples that vary widely with respect to these types of irrelevant context features to avoid undergeneralizing the rule.

To promote the greatest possible degree of generalization, we should eventually engage learners with far hits, or less prototypical situations. For rule and principle learning, the far hits are instances in which it is more difficult to recognize that the skill is applicable or to apply the skill accurately. For the pronoun-antecedent rule, a good example of a far hit would be a sentence such as the following:

Everybody completed (his, her, their) assignment on time.

Does the rule apply to this sentence? Yes! Although *everybody* is itself a pronoun, in this sentence it also functions as an antecedent that happens to be singular. Therefore, the singular pronoun *his* or *her* is correct.

This type of sentence is a very difficult instance for many people because we also want to try to avoid sexist language whenever possible. Although using either *his* or *her* is technically correct, these words unnecessarily exclude members of one sex (unless, of course, we are actually describing a specific situation in which all the students do happen to be boys or girls). A common solution that people often use to deal with this difficulty is to use the pronoun *their* because it is not gender specific. However, using the *plural* pronoun *their* violates the rule.

■ **Supporting the Discrimination Process**   Using the plural pronoun "their" with a singular antecedent is a good example of a near miss in which the rule is overgeneralized or applied incorrectly. We need to support learners' discrimination processes to protect them from overgeneralization errors. Having learners apply the rule to far misses probably will not help them discriminate the use of the rule because these nonexamples are so obviously incorrect:

Joe *rode* their *bicycle to school.*

The birds *flew from* its *perch when we approached.*

Similar to concept teaching, the best instances to use to support the discrimination process are those that are likely to give our learners the most difficulty, not those that are easiest. We can identify difficult, near-miss nonexamples by asking ourselves two questions:

▶ What are some situations in which students might be tempted to think the rule or principle applies but it doesn't?

▶ What are some of the typical errors students might make in applying the rule or principle?

Eventually, perhaps long after students leave our classrooms, they *will* encounter these types of tricky, less obvious situations. Although we cannot prepare our students for all the specific situations they will encounter for the rest of their lives, we can prepare them to apply their procedural knowledge appropriately to some of the most challenging instances they are likely to experience.

The best way to engage students with challenging nonexamples is by matching them carefully to examples. Does this approach sound familiar? Matching near-miss nonexamples of concepts to examples helps to focus learner attention on the critical features that are violated. Similarly, we can match near-miss nonexamples of rules and principles to examples to help focus attention on critical features that are violated. As for concepts, we should try to match nonexamples with examples on the basis of irrelevant features. Let's see how this **matched example and nonexample** strategy might work for the pronoun-antecedent rule:

Nonexample: Everybody *completed* their *assignment on time.*

Example 1: Everybody *completed* his *assignment on time.*

Example 2: Everybody *completed* her *assignment on time.*

Example 3: Everybody *completed* his *or* her *assignment on time.*

Example 4: All *of the students completed* their *assignments on time.*

Notice how the four examples (the correct instances) and the nonexample (the incorrect instance) are matched perfectly on irrelevant features. They all have the same subjects, predicates, ideas, length, complexity, and so on. The antecedent is singular in each case. In fact, the only difference between the nonexample and the first two examples is a single word: the pronoun. With this close matching, it will be much easier for learners to focus on the critical variable that makes the nonexample incorrect: the plural pronoun. Notice that the fourth example demonstrates a way to apply the rule correctly (*students* and *their* are both plural) while avoiding both sexist language and the awkwardness of using *his or her*. This set of matched nonexamples and examples would support discrimination of the rule by helping learners add (or strengthen) a necessary condition to their productions, recognizing that *everybody* is a singular pronoun.

■ **Providing Practice and Feedback**   As you can see, to support learners' generalization and discrimination processes, we need to engage them with appropriate instances. However, that does not mean that our students are just sitting there passively looking at sets of examples and nonexamples that we create for them. It is essential to use the divergent example and matched example and nonexample strategies in ways that actively engage learners. That is, learners need to be actively involved in producing the appropriate action for each of the instances, and then they need to receive informative feedback that will help them focus on the conditions to add or delete (Anderson & Singley, 1989; Anderson, 1993). By using examples and nonexamples as active practice opportunities, we promote proceduralization, composition, and the development of automaticity because students are using their emerging productions (Phye, 1986). The ways in which you engage your learners with examples and nonexamples so that they become active practice opportunities are limited only by your own energy, initiative, and creativity.

Now that you have a better understanding of the value of examples and nonexamples in rule and principle learning, I want you to practice developing your own sets of instances to support rule and principle learning. In Exercise 9.1 in the *Student Exercise Guide*, you have the opportunity to develop divergent examples and matched examples and nonexamples for several rules and principles.

Rule and Principle Learning: The Autonomous Stage

As you know from Chapter 8, the goal of the autonomous stage is to continue strengthening the associations that were developed in the preceding stage. To accomplish this goal, learners need further opportunities for practice and informative feedback (Ericsson, Krampe, & Tesch-Romer, 1993; Phye, 1986). Presenting practice opportunities in a wide variety of interesting, realistic contexts will help to increase the probability that students will be able to transfer the skill outside the classroom (Cox, 1997; Reimann & Schult, 1996; Ross, 1988). These practice opportunities will be particularly effective if students themselves have to decide which rule or principle is applicable. In other words, they have to evaluate the situation and then decide for themselves which rule or principle to activate.

A common problem with the design of many instructional materials is that practice exercises are often provided immediately following the introduction of a new skill. For example, a language arts book might present an explanation of the pronoun-antecedent rule on one page, followed by practice exercises on the next page. With this format, it is obvious to students what rule they need to apply, so they never have to figure out for themselves what language rule to retrieve from memory. Because of the obvious cues provided in the materials, they already know what the relevant rule is going to be, and all they have to do is apply it correctly. Students who can apply the pronoun-antecedent rule perfectly in a set of twenty practice exercises may completely ignore the rule in their own writing because they have to activate the rule themselves. The rule therefore must be stored in memory along with the conditions under which it should be applied (Glaser, 1984).

How can we help our learners activate rules and principles themselves? In the autonomous stage, we can provide varied practice opportunities in which the relevance of the target rule or principle is not obvious or apparent (Perkins & Salomon, 1987; Voss, 1987). For example, in mathematics we could provide students with sets of realistic problems that involve all four operations (add, subtract, multiply, divide). Then the students have to determine which operation (or combination) is relevant to each problem, as well as apply each operation (or rule) correctly. This type of practice is even more effective when it is spread out over a long period of time, a strategy known as **distributed practice** (Phye, 1986).

Finally, some rules and principles are so basic in learning and problem solving that we may desire students to acquire a high degree of automaticity. When skills become automatic, they take up very little mental space in working memory when we execute them, thus freeing up a greater amount of space for thinking, decision making, and so on (Case, 1991; Resnick, 1989). For example, automatic sentence punctuation rules free up working memory space for writers to focus on the meaning they are trying to communicate. Automatic algorithms for adding numbers or telling time free up working memory space for thinking about mathematical problems. So in the autonomous stage, we may have students practice in ways that increase their speed and accuracy. Often students can be motivated to improve their speed in applying a skill by competing with themselves and monitoring their own individual progress (speed and error rate).

Often students enjoy competing against each other in learning games. Speed drills and learning games can be effective strategies for promoting skill

Learning games provide excellent opportunities for students to practice newly acquired skills, as long as the stress of competition does not interfere with their performance.

automaticity during the autonomous stage. However, if we try to use such strategies too early in the learning process (during the cognitive and associative stages), stress and anxiety may interfere with learning by overloading the limited processing space of working memory. The well-known Yerkes-Dodson (1908) principle reminds us that most people perform best when they experience moderate levels of stress and arousal. When we overload students with too much competitive stress (e.g., before new skills approach automaticity), their performance can be severely impeded (Eysenck, 1992).

LET'S SUMMARIZE

As you can see from Figure 9.1, the external conditions of learning for rule and principle learning are very similar to those we identified for concept learning. When designing an instructional strategy to promote rule or principle learning, we need to focus on prerequisite concepts and their verbal labels, generalization, and discrimination. Most important, we need to provide ample opportunities for practice and informative feedback if we really want students to be able to apply the rules and principles as skills.

Now that we have identified both the internal and external conditions of learning for rules and principles, let's put them to use with some real classroom *design-teaching* examples. Let's look in on Mrs. Torres and Ms. Nelson as they design instructional strategies for teaching rules and principles as intellectual skills.

CASE ANALYSIS

Designing an Instructional Strategy for Rule Learning

Mrs. Torres needs to design an instructional strategy to help her third-grade students acquire rules for rounding to the nearest ten and hundred as intellectual skills. Here are the instructional goal and objective that she has developed thus far (see Chapters 2 and 6):

Instructional Goal: Learners will be able to apply the rules for rounding numbers to the nearest ten and hundred.

Instructional Objective: Twenty two-digit and three-digit numerals will be provided with instructions to round each to the nearest ten or nearest hundred (ten each). Each numeral to be rounded will have blank lines for the next lower multiple, the next higher multiple, and the multiple to which the numeral is rounded. Learners will apply the rules for rounding numbers to the nearest ten and hundred. They will first write the next higher multiple of ten or one hundred and the next lower multiple on the lines provided. They will then write the numeral rounded to the nearest ten or hundred on the lines provided. Learners must round 90 percent of each set of numerals correctly. To be considered correct, both the lower and higher multiple also must be written correctly.

To design an instructional strategy to help her students achieve this clear destination, Mrs. Torres focuses her thinking on three critical issues (see Chapter 7): information, engagement, and practice.

Information: What Do My Students Need to Process?

Ultimately I want my students to be able to round to both the nearest ten and hundred. Since rounding to the nearest hundred is simply an extension of the rule for rounding to the nearest ten, I think I will focus first on the rule for rounding to the nearest ten. Let's see, when I completed my content analysis [see Chapter 3], I stated that rule clearly as a three-step procedure:

1. Identify the digit in the one's place.
2. Compare the one's place digit to five.
3. If the digit is less than five, round down to the next lower multiple of ten. If the digit is five or greater, round up to the next higher multiple of ten.

As a result of my instruction, students need to transform these steps into a production. How can I engage them with the information so that this transformation occurs?

Engagement: How Will My Students Process the Information?

My students need to engage in three levels of processing as they acquire the skill of rounding to the nearest ten: cognitive, associative, and autonomous. I'll begin by first thinking about the instructional materials and activities that may help them at the cognitive stage.

Engaging Students at the Cognitive Stage   First, I need to be sure my students can apply the key subordinate concepts found in the rule: ten's place, one's place, digit, multiple of ten, higher, lower. These are basic concepts that students acquired last year in second grade. Furthermore, I devoted some time at the beginning of the year to reviewing them. On an earlier assessment, all my students demonstrated the ability to identify digits in the one's and ten's places and the ability to recognize multiples of ten. This concrete evidence suggests that I can move on confidently to the target rule for rounding.

To prepare students for understanding the rounding rule, I will begin with an advance organizer to help them construct an understanding of rounding principles inductively. I will fill two measuring cups level-full with sand and ask students to tell me how many cups of sand I have (two). Then I will place a very small amount of sand in a third cup and ask how many cups of sand there are (still two). I will emphasize that two full cups with a little of a third cup is closer to two cups than it is to three cups. Then I will fill the third cup almost level full and ask students again how many cups of sand I have. Now we have almost three, so by imagining a little more sand in the third cup, we would have three cups. The quantity of sand is closer to three full cups than to two full cups.

I will then return to two full cups with a very small amount in the third. I will begin increasing the amount of sand gradually, each time guiding students to agree that the amount is still closer to two cups than three. When the third cup is exactly half full, I will emphasize the dilemma to students: Now we're closer to neither two nor three; we're exactly halfway between them! At this point, I will let students propose a solution. Do they think we should adjust the quantity down or up? Which seems more useful? Eventually I will inform them that the usual convention is to adjust the quantity up. After this discussion, I will continue to add to the sand in the third cup, showing students that after we pass the halfway point, we continue to get closer and closer to the next full cup.

By the conclusion of this inductive advance organizer activity, I will have helped students understand the essential features of rounding on a meaningful declarative level:

1. Rounding means that we adjust amounts to make them easier to think and talk about. We make these adjustments by adding a little more to a quantity or by taking away a little extra to bring us to a unit that is easy to use.

2. When we have less than half of the unit, we adjust down to the next lower unit.

3. When we have more than half of the unit, we adjust up to the next higher unit.

4. When we have exactly half of the unit, we agree to adjust up to the next higher unit.

Now we will move to an activity with base-ten blocks. The purpose of the activity is to continue developing students' declarative understanding of the rounding process. Each student will have seven rods [a rod is one group of ten] and nine small cubes [a cube is equivalent to one; ten cubes make one rod]. I will have students place three rods on the left and the other four on their right [as illustrated in Figure 9.4]. As students perform these actions at their seats, I will model the same actions by placing blocks on an overhead projector, so their images appear on a screen. I will write "30" beneath the three rods in green and "40" beneath the four rods in blue. Next I will have students add one cube to the three rods and ask what number the blocks represent. I will write "31" in red beside the cube [see Figure 9.4].

I will then ask students to judge whether 31 is closer to 30 or 40 by looking at the blocks. I will help them see that they are only one cube away from 30 but nine cubes away from 40. So if we wanted to round 31 to the nearest ten (or rod), we would round down to 30. I will draw an arrow from 31 back to 30 to call their attention to this outcome [see Figure 9.4]. Similar to the sand activity, I will gradually increase the cubes until reaching the halfway point: 35. For each instance, I will encourage students to hold a rod up to the cubes to see if the halfway point has been reached. From 35 to 39, I will draw the arrow to 40 to demonstrate rounding up to the nearest ten.

We will repeat this activity several more times, using other multiples of ten: 50 to 60, 10 to 20, and 80 to 90. As we work through each set of instances, I will call on students—individuals and whole class—to verbalize the critical conditions of the production—number in the one's place, next lower multiple of ten, next higher multiple of ten—and the appropriate action

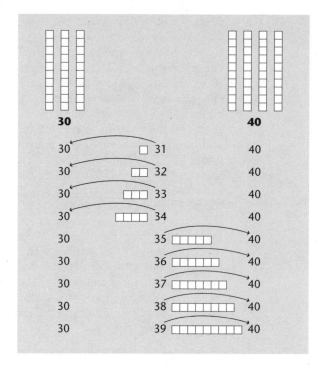

Figure 9.4
Using Base-Ten Blocks to Demonstrate the Rule for Rounding to the Nearest Ten

(round up to next higher multiple, round down to next lower multiple) to ensure that they are active simultaneously in their working memories.

After working with the base-ten blocks, we will move to a number-line representation of rounding [see Figure 9.5]. I will model the use of the number line on the overhead projector while students work with their own number lines at their seats. Together we will examine pairs of numbers that fall between two multiples of ten. For example, students will mark the locations of 54 and 57 on their number lines. Since 54 is below the halfway point (55), we round it back to the next lower multiple of ten (50). Since 57 is above the halfway point (55), we round it up to the next higher multiple of ten (60).

Through these three conceptual learning activities—measuring cups, base-ten blocks, and number line—students should be able to encode the rounding rule as meaningful verbal information, the goal of the cognitive stage. By the end of the cognitive phase, they should be able to remember the

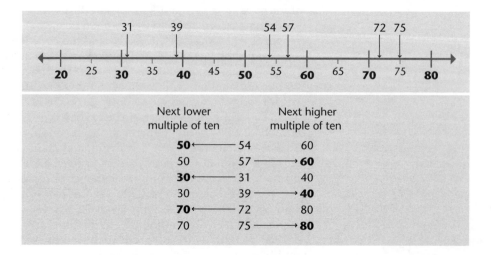

Figure 9.5
Using a Number Line to Demonstrate the Rule for Rounding to the Nearest Ten

rule and state it in a meaningful way. To collect formative assessment data, I will have students either write an explanation of how to round or explain the procedure to me individually. When I have evidence that all my students understand the rule as declarative knowledge, it will be time to begin proceduralizing it.

Engaging Students at the Associative Stage Thus far, I have been demonstrating the rounding rule to help my students understand how the rule works. Now *they* need to begin associating the conditions with the appropriate actions. To begin the association process, I will provide a set of numerals for students to round using their base-ten blocks: 29, 43, 78, 67, 51. For each numeral, students will have to write the next lower and higher multiple of ten on either side of the numeral, represent the number with base-ten blocks, and then select the appropriate multiple of ten. After students complete each number, I will call on an individual to come to the overhead projector to demonstrate and explain for everyone. This will provide additional modeling of the rounding process as well as informative feedback.

After the block activity, we will move to the number line. Again, I will provide a set of numerals to round. For each numeral, students will write the lower and higher multiples of ten, indicate the numeral's location on the number line, and then select the appropriate multiple. To provide informative feedback, I will call on individuals to come to the overhead projector to model and explain.

To promote generalization, I will begin expanding the types of instances to which students apply the rule with divergent examples. Let's see, we've been working only with two-digit numerals thus far. Now students should apply the rule to more difficult instances, such as one-digit and three-digit numerals. Single-digit numerals will be challenging because the higher multiple of ten is ten, and the lower multiple is zero. I will guide students through some one-digit examples with the number line to help them see that zero and ten are the multiples of ten to consider. Three-digit numerals will be challenging because students need to focus on the ten's place and ignore the hundred's place. Thus, the lower and higher multiples of ten for 547 are 540 and 550. Again, a number line representation should help students determine these multiples of ten. To promote generalization, the number line examples will vary on irrelevant features such as the number of digits in the number and the specific digits in the ten's and one's places.

As students apply the rounding rule to this variety of examples, I will also create divergence by presenting the instances in a variety of meaningful application contexts such as the following:

- A museum has a special price for groups of students. For every ten students, the museum will reduce the admission price of $5.00 by $1.00. To determine the amount of the discount, the museum will either round down or round up to the nearest group of 10. How much of a discount will the museum give for the following numbers of students: 31, 57, 8, 125, 374, 4?

- A caterer knows that one pie usually is enough for approximately 10 people. How many pies should the caterer prepare for the following numbers of people: 29, 5, 14, 71, 268?

In these divergent examples, my students can practice applying their productions with conditions that vary on irrelevant features such as the size of the number (one, two, or three digits) and the quantities to which the numbers refer (money, pies).

To promote discrimination, I need to anticipate some of the difficult instances and the errors students are likely to make. I think that three-digit numerals that have zero in the ten's place (302, 604) may be difficult to round down because the next lower multiple of ten also happens to be a multiple of one hundred. Students may be tempted to reduce the number all the way down to nine tens rather than zero tens. Also, numerals that have nine in the ten's place (98, 397, 996) may be difficult to round up because the next higher multiple of ten requires increasing the digit in the hundred's place by one. Students may be tempted to jump up to one ten and leave the hundred's place digit alone.

To help my students become aware of these types of errors, I will engage them with nonexamples matched with examples, such as the following:

INCORRECT:	290	←	**302**	310
CORRECT:	300	←	**302**	310
INCORRECT:	390		**397**	→	410
CORRECT:	390		**397**	→	400

I will engage students with these pairs of examples and matched nonexamples by giving students several of them on a sheet and challenging them to indicate which one is correct and which one is incorrect. Then we will review them together to make sure students are focusing on the error in each nonexample.

Engaging Students at the Autonomous Stage   Rounding is a basic mathematical skill that will help students estimate quantities in problem-solving situations. Therefore, I want my students to develop the skill to a high level of automaticity. This will take a lot more additional time and practice. One approach is to provide periodic practice sheets [distributed practice] with numerals to be rounded to the nearest ten and hundred so students have to remember which rule to apply to each instance. Continuing to provide a variety of realistic problems such as the ones I used in the associative stage should also be helpful, as long as some problems require rounding and some do not.

Finally, a game such as "The Price Is Right" could be fun for students to practice their rounding skills. Students can "bid" on magazine pictures of items that have prices marked on them (to the nearest whole dollar). They can win a point for their team by bidding on the items that will come closest to a predetermined dollar amount. Since they will have to combine the amounts of the individual items in their heads, they will need to apply their rounding skills.

Practice: How Will My Students Strengthen Their Learning?

Throughout the associative and autonomous stages, students will be practicing their developing rounding skills, so I have already addressed this part of the instructional strategy. However, I do need to ensure that students have the opportunity to practice in a way that is consistent with the summative assessment. Therefore, I will need to create one or two practice sheets that are similar to the one I described in my instructional objective. When I assess students, they will already be familiar with that particular performance format.

LET'S SUMMARIZE

You have just watched Mrs. Torres design an instructional strategy to help her learners acquire a rule as procedural knowledge. She developed the external information, engagement, and practice elements of her strategy to support her students' internal learning needs (see Figure 9.1). Although the strategy looks appropriate and potentially effective, she will have to wait for her summative assessment data to make the final determination.

Before we move on to analyze an instructional strategy for principle learning, I invite you to use Exercise 9.2 in the *Student Exercise Guide* as an opportunity to practice designing an instructional strategy to support rule learning.

CASE ANALYSIS

Designing an Instructional Strategy for Principle Learning

Although both rules and principles represent concept relationships, they enable us to produce different types of actions. Ms. Nelson, our fifth-grade science teacher, will demonstrate how to develop an instructional strategy to help learners acquire a principle as procedural knowledge. She wants her students to understand a principle that governs the size of the mineral crystals that are found in igneous rocks. This is what she wants her students to be able to do to demonstrate their understanding:

> *Instructional Goal: Learners will be able to demonstrate how the rate of cooling influences the size of a mineral crystal.*
>
> *Instructional Objective:* Given three written problem scenarios that involve crystal growth, learners will demonstrate how the rate of cooling influences the size of a mineral crystal by writing predictions and explanations that are consistent with the cooling rate principle. Each of the three written responses must (1) describe specific actions to be taken in the problem scenario, (2) demonstrate clear relationships among actions and cooling rates, and (3) accurately predict crystal size.

Now let's listen as Ms. Nelson designs an instructional strategy to help her students reach this learning destination by thinking about the critical elements of information, engagement, and practice.

Information: What Do My Students Need to Process?

When I completed the content analysis for the principle [see Chapter 3], I stated it as clearly as I could: *When solutions cool quickly, they produce smaller mineral crystals; when they cool slowly, larger mineral crystals form.* I do not want my students to memorize this particular sentence—that's not principle learning—so having another way to express the principle on a declarative level would be useful. Here's another possibility: *The faster a solution cools, the smaller the mineral crystals that are formed; the slower a solution cools, the larger the mineral crystals.*

My content analysis for this principle yielded several subordinate concepts: solution, mineral, crystal, cooling, quick/fast, slow, small, and large. I will proceed with teaching for the target principle because earlier in my geology unit, I taught students how to recognize minerals and crystals. I did not teach them directly about solutions. However, from prior everyday experiences with dissolving substances in liquid (e.g., Kool-Aid in water, sugar in iced tea) my students already possess the concept of solution, although they may not be able to state the verbal label, *solution*.

Engagement: How Will My Students Process the Information?

Before my students can apply the principle as an intellectual skill, they need to have a meaningful awareness of it. I'll begin helping them develop that declarative representation by creating instructional events at the cognitive stage.

Engaging Students at the Cognitive Stage   Science principles often lend themselves well to inductive, inquiry, or discovery approaches. Engaging in inquiry processes gives students the opportunity to apply aspects of the scientific method, a cognitive strategy that I've been helping students develop throughout the entire school year. To start things off, I could present my students with two samples of granite that differ in the size of their mineral grains. Because scientific inquiry begins with the processes of observing, theorizing, and hypothesizing, that's what I'll ask my students to do, using the following guiding questions:

- Look closely at these two rock samples. What types of rock do you think they might be? Why? (Igneous, because the mineral grains are apparent and they do not have a banded or layered appearance.)
- How are the two igneous rocks similar? (Both have white, pink, and black mineral crystals.)
- How are the two igneous rocks different? (The mineral crystals in one rock are larger than the mineral crystals in the other.)
- If both are igneous rocks that appear to have the same minerals, why would the crystals of one be larger than the other? What are some possible reasons?

The final question will invite students to begin theorizing about the reason for differences in crystal size. I will get students actively involved by inviting them to brainstorm possible answers to the question. Then we will evaluate each of the possibilities together. Through further questioning and analogies (e.g., a twenty-year-old person is larger than a ten-year-old person because of more time to grow), I will lead my students to theorize that the different crystal sizes are possibly related to the conditions under which the two samples of hot magma cooled beneath the earth's surface.

The next step in the scientific method is to formulate and test hypotheses to verify the theoretical explanation. The students and I will try to answer the following empirical question: Does the rate of cooling affect the size of a crystal? Through questioning, I will lead students to the following hypothesis: When solutions cool slowly, crystals have more time to grow, so they grow larger; when solutions cool quickly, crystals have less time to grow, so they do not grow as large.

We will test the hypothesis by designing and implementing an experiment together. We will prepare a supersaturated solution of sugar water and pour equal amounts in three containers. After suspending a string in each solution, we will place one in a warm place (near the classroom heater), one in a moderately cool place (on a cool windowsill), and the third in a very cold place (in a refrigerator). Of course, the three solutions will cool at different rates (our independent variable).

For several days, we will observe changes in the solutions, including the sugar crystals that begin to form on the strings. After several days of observation, we will examine the three crystal samples with hand lenses. Students will describe similarities (e.g., crystal shape) and differences (e.g., crystal size) that they observe in the three samples. They should observe that the solution near the heater produced the largest crystals, the one in the refrigerator yielded the smallest crystals, and the one on the windowsill produced crystals in between these two sizes.

Using the results of our experiment, I will help students induce the target principle: *Solutions that cool slowly produce larger crystals than those that cool quickly.* Because students have observed the principle at work, they should have a meaningful understanding of it. We can now return to the two igneous rock samples and predict which one was formed from slowly cooling solutions of magma and which from quickly cooling solutions. Students can think further about the kinds of conditions that would create slow and quick cooling: deep in the earth versus closer to earth's surface; beneath the earth's crust versus exposure to air; no contact with water versus contact with water; warm climate versus cold climate.

Engaging Students at the Associative Stage   I do not want students to be able to predict crystal sizes for just granite samples and sugar crystals. To promote generalization, they need to apply the principle to some divergent examples that vary on irrelevant features, such as the specific type of igneous rock, crystal shape, type of solution, and specific cooling conditions. For this principle, cooling rate speed is the only relevant variable. For each instance, students need to begin associating the principle's conditions with appropriate actions by actually making a prediction or constructing an explanation themselves.

To accomplish this goal, I will have five groups of students work cooperatively to repeat the cooling experiment with five different substances (one substance per group): borax, alum, photographic fixer, salt, and saltpeter. The crystals formed by these substances will have different shapes and colors—all irrelevant features for the principle to be learned. All the students will predict the sizes of all five crystals under the three cooling rate conditions. Then each group will present its results, and students can check their predictions, thus receiving informative feedback. Each student will write a report that explains the group's hypotheses, procedures, and findings. This process will ensure that each student is associating the principle's concepts with the action of predicting crystal size.

To promote generalization further, I will provide groups of students with igneous rock samples (e.g., granite, gabbro, diorite) that differ with respect to irrelevant features such as color, size, weight, and shape. Students will arrange the rocks from fastest-cooling to slowest-cooling magma based on their crystal sizes. Each group will then present and explain its results to the rest of the class for feedback.

To promote discrimination, I need to anticipate some errors that students might make when they attempt to apply the principle. Two possible errors come to mind. First, students may try to apply the principle inappropriately to the sizes of "cut" gem stones. Two quartz crystals may differ in size because of the way they have been cut rather than the rate of cooling. To emphasize this point, I will engage students with several uncut quartz crystals (examples) and several cut and polished quartz crystals of various sizes (matched nonexamples). To encourage students to apply their productions, I will first ask them to predict which crystals formed from slower and faster cooling. When they include some of the cut specimens, I will point out that the sizes of those crystals resulted from *unnatural* processes (i.e., they have been cut by humans), so the principle cannot be applied to make predictions about cooling rate unless the crystals are still in their natural form.

A second error may occur if students focus on the overall size of the rock sample rather than the size of the mineral grains that comprise the rock sample. To prevent this error, I will engage my students with two pieces of granite that are matched with respect to their color and mineral grains. However, one piece will be small with large crystals, and the other will be large with small crystals. After giving students an opportunity to make predictions about the cooling rates of the two samples, I will point out that the overall size of the rock does not matter—only the size of the crystals that are found within the rock. The matched samples should help focus students' attention on the critical feature of crystal size, not the overall size of the rock.

Engaging Students at the Autonomous Stage   Unlike basic math skills such as adding, subtracting, and rounding, the cooling rate principle is not really a basic skill that needs to be applied automatically. Nevertheless, I should try to continue to provide application opportunities to strengthen the associations my students constructed during the previous stage and to help them construct additional connections to other schemas. A wonderful opportunity for such strengthening will occur when I take students on the rock collecting field trip [described in Chapter 8]. While examining outcrops of igneous rocks, I will ask students to offer predictions about how quickly those rocks cooled. Of course, they will have to apply the target principle to create their predictions and explanations. Furthermore, when students develop their rock collections, I will have them arrange their igneous specimens in a way that demonstrates different rates of cooling according to crystal size—another application opportunity.

Practice: How Will My Students Strengthen Their Learning?

Throughout the associative and autonomous stages, students will be applying their emerging productions in numerous practice opportunities. They will not just be watching passively as I show them rock samples and tell them how to apply the principle. One final type of practice that I need to provide as part of my instructional strategy should be consistent with the summative assessment procedure, as described by my instructional objective. Therefore, I will create several realistic problems to solve by applying the cooling rate principle [see the scenario presented in Chapter 5]. Students can individually create solutions to the problems and then work together in groups to evaluate those solutions and to obtain informative feedback.

I will monitor the students individually and as they work in groups to obtain formative assessment data. If my formative assessment data suggest that students are applying the principle appropriately and that they are comfortable with the format of the problems, I will be ready to proceed with the summative assessment, as described by my objective.

LET'S SUMMARIZE

Ms. Nelson has just designed a potentially effective instructional strategy to help her students acquire a science principle as an intellectual skill that they will be able to apply as procedural knowledge. She designed her strategy by using two sets of guiding ideas. First, she specified the information, engagement, and practice that would be necessary for learning the skill. Second, she used her understanding of the cognitive, associative, and autonomous stages of skill learning to guide her thinking about how to engage learners with the principle. Ms. Nelson's external instructional events appear to match the internal conditions of principle learning quite well. As always, however, the proof will be in the summative assessment data she collects.

Now I want *you* to start proceduralizing your understanding of the conditions of learning for principles. Similar to the previous exercise, Exercise 9.3 in the *Student Exercise Guide* gives you an opportunity to design an instructional strategy for a principle. Give it a try before you move on to the final section of this chapter.

CASE ANALYSIS

Designing an Instructional Strategy for Cognitive Strategy Learning

Cognitive strategies are one final type of intellectual ability that we often try to help our learners acquire. Recall from Chapter 2 that cognitive strategies are like big, complex rules that guide our thinking and problem-solving actions. Because cognitive strategies are large rules, their internal conditions of learning are very similar to those for rules and principles (see Figure 9.6). The only difference is that cognitive strategies have subordinate rules and principles that learners must be able to apply, as well as subordinate concepts that comprise the rules and principles (Gagne, 1985).

Rather than repeating much of what we already have noted regarding the internal and external conditions for concept learning and rule and principle learning, let's go right to the process of designing an instructional strategy for cognitive strategy learning. One of our case analysis teachers, Mr. Hoffman, will demonstrate the process for us. Recall that Mr. Hoffman wants his seventh-grade social studies students to learn concept-mapping skills to enable them to become more active, strategic readers. Here are his instructional goal (from Chapter 2) and objective (from Chapter 6) for this cognitive strategy learning outcome:

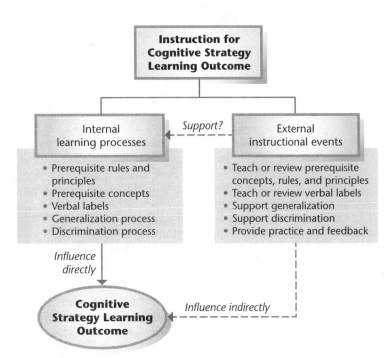

Figure 9.6
Internal and External Conditions of Learning for Cognitive Strategies

Instructional Goal: Learners will be able to originate concept maps for textbook chapters.

Instructional Objective: I will provide students with a twenty-page chapter from a seventh-grade social studies textbook. The chapter will be one that they have never seen before. Students will demonstrate the ability to originate concept maps by producing a written concept map for the chapter provided. Students have four days to complete their concept maps, with twenty minutes of class time provided each day. To be acceptable, students' concept maps must contain at least three major superordinate concepts from the chapter, with at least two subordinate concepts for each superordinate concept from the chapter. Relationships among concepts must be hierarchical and labeled meaningfully and accurately. At least five cross-links must be included. Each cross-link must represent a meaningful relationship and must be labeled meaningfully and accurately. I will develop an analytical scoring instrument that focuses on the criteria just described.

Information: What Do My Students Need to Process?

In my content analysis [see Figure 3.16], I described concept mapping as a four-step procedure:

1. Read chapter and list major concepts.
2. Order concepts from most inclusive to least inclusive.
3. Arrange concepts in a hierarchical diagram.
4. Create cross-links.

These are simply the four general phases in the process of concept mapping. To carry out each phase, the students must apply a number of rules, principles, and concepts as skills [see Figure 3.16]. My students already have learned how to create outlines, so I think they should be able to distinguish between major concepts and minor details. However, inclusiveness, hierarchical diagramming, and cross-links are three subordinate concepts that I probably will need to help them acquire as I teach the concept mapping procedure.

Engagement: How Will My Students Process the Information?

Because I want my students to be able to create, or originate, their own concept maps, I need to engage them with the concept mapping strategy in a way that helps them acquire the strategy as procedural knowledge. Therefore, I will need to develop activities and materials to support learning at each of the three stages of procedural knowledge acquisition.

Engaging Students at the Cognitive Stage At this stage, students need to become aware of the critical features of concept maps and the basic steps in the procedure to create them. Here are brief descriptions of some activities to achieve this goal:

- After students read a chapter in their social studies book, ask them if they would like to see a "picture" of the chapter. Place a concept map for the chapter on the overhead projector. Using colored markers, point out the major parts of the map: general concepts (green), specific concepts (blue), hierarchical links (red), and cross-links (purple). Students shade each component on their own copies of the map.

- Explain the purpose of the map. Concept mapping is a tool that helps us think about the ideas we read. Creating a concept map helps us understand and remember information we read. To illustrate this point, give students time to review the chapter to find all the concepts on the map. For each concept and link they find in the chapter, they write the page numbers where they found the information.

- Model the process of creating the concept map. Go through the chapter with students, and make a list of all the major concepts found. Order the concepts from general (most inclusive) to specific (least inclusive). Using the overhead projector, place concepts in a hierarchical diagram, calling on students to participate in deciding where to place specific concepts. Use the same colors as described earlier when placing features on the map to call students' attention to the major parts. As concepts are placed on the map hierarchically, have students generate words that describe the relationships among the concepts and write them on the map with connecting lines. Finally, prompt students to generate cross-links and place them on the map. Emphasize and demonstrate that cross-links are often created by thinking about relationships that are not explicitly stated in the material.

- Summarize the steps in the strategy by writing them on a poster and hanging it in the room.

Engaging Students at the Associative Stage   Following along as I create a concept map is not the same as students' originating their own maps. So now my students need the chance to begin proceduralizing the strategy for themselves. Here are brief descriptions of some activities to help achieve this goal:

- To promote generalization, hand out three different concept maps (different content, structure, etc.) and have students color-code the four major parts. Provide feedback by showing the color-coded maps on the overhead projector.

- To promote discrimination, hand out a map that has been constructed incorrectly (e.g., with nonhierarchical relationships or meaningless labels), and have students try to identify and correct the errors. Then provide a correct model (matched example) for the same map. Use the nonexample and matched example to focus students' attention on features their maps must possess.

- Give students a list of concepts from a chapter they have already read. Have students work in groups to decide which concepts are most inclusive and which are least inclusive. Have them list subordinate concepts beneath superordinate concepts. Come together as a whole class to review lists and receive feedback.

- Have students return to groups to arrange concepts hierarchically. They also will construct and label links. Come together as a whole class to review maps and receive feedback. Have a model map on the overhead projector to which students can compare their own maps.

- Students return to groups to work on constructing cross-links. Come together as a whole class for feedback with a model on the overhead projector.

- Have students work in groups to create a concept map for another chapter they already have read. Photocopy each group's map on an overhead transparency. Together as a class, evaluate and provide feedback. Irrelevant differences among the groups' maps will help to promote generalization.

Engaging Students at the Autonomous Stage   A cognitive strategy is most useful when students can use it somewhat automatically so that the strategy itself does not take mental resources away from the thinking processes the strategy is supposed to influence. Also, students should be able to use the strategy under a wide variety of learning situations. Here are some activities to support these goals during the autonomous stage:

- Give students opportunities for distributed practice throughout the remainder of the school year by applying the concept mapping strategy to each chapter they read.

- Students will trade concept maps and give each other feedback. Students also will receive feedback from a model map for each chapter that I will present on the overhead projector.

- Learners usually are motivated to use a strategy on their own when they see the benefits. Therefore, after each chapter test, students will write personal reflections on the effectiveness of the concept mapping strategy in helping them remember and apply ideas.

- Toward the end of the year, I will ask students to produce two concept maps for materials they are reading in other classes and have them write personal reflections on the usefulness of the strategy when they are tested in those classes. This activity should help strengthen students' ability to transfer the strategy beyond social studies textbooks.

Practice: How Will My Students Strengthen Their Learning?

Throughout the associative and autonomous stages, students will be practicing their concept mapping skills. The practice that they receive when concept mapping their social studies chapters is very consistent with the summative assessment described by my instructional objective. I will use the last chapter students map to provide summative assessment data.

LET'S SUMMARIZE

Mr. Hoffman designed an instructional strategy for cognitive strategy learning in the same way that Ms. Nelson and Mrs. Torres designed instructional strategies for concept, rule, and principle learning. By thinking carefully about his learners' internal processing needs, he was able to create external learning activities and materials to support those needs. Before we leave this chapter, it is critical for you to understand that the instructional strategies these three teachers created are not the only ways to teach about rocks, rounding, crystal size, and concept mapping. I offer them to you as examples of the types of learning activities that *design-teachers* can create when they understand the internal learning processes of their students. You or another teacher could start with the same instructional goals and, using your understanding of the internal and external conditions of learning, as well as your own creativity, design different activities and materials that could be equally effective.

LOOKING BACK LOOKING AHEAD

In this chapter, we have explored the kind of thinking that *design-teachers* need to employ to create instruction for rules, principles, and cognitive strategies as intellectual skills. Students acquire usable, transferable skills when they change their initial declarative representations to procedural knowledge. For this transformation to occur, students themselves must get into action by applying the skill. Distributed practice with a wide variety of examples and nonexamples will promote the generalization and discrimination processes that are critical for conditionalized knowledge to develop. In short, if we truly want our students to be able to transfer their skills beyond the classroom, we need to design careful instruction for this purpose rather than leaving it to chance.

The major goal of this chapter was not to provide specific examples of teaching activities for you to imitate. The goal was to empower you to think for yourself when you have an intellectual skill outcome to help your learners achieve. In the next chapter, I hope to continue to empower your thinking about instructional design by examining some of the most useful instructional sequences we can use to structure classroom lessons. But first, take a moment to check your achievement of the chapter's instructional goals by completing Exercise 9.4 in the *Student Exercise Guide*.

RESOURCES FOR FURTHER REFLECTION AND EXPLORATION

Print Resources

Gagne, R. M., Briggs, L. J., & Wager, W. W. (1992). *Principles of instructional design* (4th ed.). New York: Harcourt Brace Jovanovich.

> Chapter 4 ("Varieties of Learning: Intellectual Skills and Strategies") presents an excellent overview of the internal and external conditions of learning that are relevant to concepts, rules, principles, and cognitive strategies.

Griffin, S., Case, R., & Capodilupo, A. (1995). Teaching for understanding: The importance of the central conceptual structures in the elementary mathematics curriculum. In A. McKeough, J. Lupart, & A. Marini (Eds.), *Teaching for transfer: Fostering generalization in learning* (pp. 123–151). Mahwah, NJ: Erlbaum.

> This chapter presents an approach to helping children acquire meaningful mathematics rules and principles. The authors describe the theoretical foundations of the Rightstart Mathematics Module and then present the results of evaluation studies to support this approach to mathematics instruction.

Hammer, D. (1997). Discovery learning and discovery teaching. *Cognition and Instruction, 15,* 485–529.

> An article that presents theoretical issues involved in teaching from an inductive, or discovery, perspective. The author describes his own classroom experiences with discovery teaching and learning.

Mayer, R. E. (1987). The elusive search for teachable aspects of problem solving. In J. A. Glover & R. R. Ronning (Eds.), *Historical foundations of educational psychology* (pp. 327–347). New York: Plenum Press.

> An excellent chapter that summarizes what we know about teaching concepts, rules, and principles to promote students' problem-solving and thinking abilities.

Morrow, L. J., & Kenney, M. J. (Eds.). (1998). *The teaching and learning of algorithms in school mathematics.* Reston, VA: National Council of Teachers of Mathematics.

> Rules in the form of algorithms are often taught in mathematics classrooms. This excellent book provides many fine essays that describe learning and teaching processes that are relevant to algorithm acquisition. A must-read for mathematics teachers.

World Wide Web and CD-ROM Resources

http://www.onlineclass.com/Physics/PhysicsSub.html

> Web site of Physics Park: Building Rides Online. This is an online classroom that gives students the opportunity to learn physics principles while solving interesting, realistic problems such as building amusement park rides.

http://www.dole5aday.com/

Web site of the Dole Food Company. The link for educators provides lesson plans and activities related to teaching children rules and principles of good nutrition. Lesson plans are included for language arts, mathematics, social studies, and science. A companion CD-ROM is available through the site.

http://clearinghouse.k12.ca.us/

Web site of the California Instructional Technology Clearinghouse. The site provides reviews of high-quality instructional technology resources. A good site to use when searching for technology-based resources to support the teaching and learning of intellectual skills.

Prejudice: Decisions; Environment: Decisions; Thinking Like a Scientist

Three CD-ROM resources that demonstrate how technology can support meaningful rule, principle, and cognitive strategy instruction. Each CD-ROM presents meaningful simulations that engage students with opportunities to apply cognitive skills and receive feedback. All three are available for Macintosh or Windows environments and are available from Educational Software Institute, 4213 South 94th Street, Omaha, NE 68127.

Sequencing Instructional Events

10

For the past several years, I have been fixing up an old house. Because I have done much of the work myself, I have learned a lot of useful skills such as shingling a roof, dry-walling a room, hanging wallpaper, wiring light switches, soldering copper pipes, and replacing water faucets. As I have acquired these new skills, I also have learned a very important principle of house renovation: The order in which I apply the skills matters a lot. For example, I can't put new shingles on a roof until I have replaced the plywood sheeting that goes under them, and I can't install a new water faucet until the copper pipes that carry the water are soldered in place. If I perform any of these actions out of sequence, I can end up with a real mess. Imagine what would happen if I spent hours wallpapering a room before running electrical wiring through a wall to a new light switch. All that careful wallpapering work would be ruined when I cut open the wall for the wiring.

From experience, I have learned that house renovation work usually progresses in three general stages. First, I need to *prepare* the work area. If I am going to renovate a bedroom, for example, I may need to strip off all the old wallpaper, tear down old plaster walls, and take up the old carpet. During the second stage, I can start the *construction* process: building or installing new structures such as hanging dry-wall, painting the ceiling, wallpapering, and laying down new carpet. Finally, I will need to put on some *finishing touches*. In a bedroom, finishing touches might include setting finishing nails and filling the holes, putting new knobs on closet doors, or installing a new light fixture. When I design a home improvement project, I usually make my plans according to these three general stages. By breaking

INSTRUCTIONAL GOALS FOR CHAPTER 10

After reading and thinking about this chapter, you should be able to . . .

1. Describe the purpose and features of an instructional sequence.

2. Explain and demonstrate the general goals and features of the preinstructional, instructional, and postinstructional phases of instruction.

3. Explain how learner characteristics, instructional media, and learning outcomes influence the planning of external instructional events.

4. Describe and apply strategies for supporting cognitive processes related to learner attention, expectancy, and prior knowledge activation.

5. Identify and apply strategies related to Keller's ARCS model of motivation.

6. Describe and apply strategies for supporting cognitive processes related to learner selective perception and encoding.

7. Describe and apply strategies for supporting cognitive processes related to learner responding, reinforcement, and transfer.

down a big project into these three phases, I can think strategically about the specific actions, materials, and resources I will need.

When *design-teachers* create their instructional plans, they also have many important variables to consider: the specific actions, materials, and resources they will use to help their learners achieve instructional goals. Just as all the elements of a home improvement project should be sequenced carefully, teachers should carefully sequence all the elements of instruction they intend to use to support learning.

In this chapter, you will discover that we can make decisions about instructional sequencing by thinking about the internal learning needs of our students. These learning needs often correspond to the three general stages of home improvement: preparation, construction, and finishing touches. If you are wondering how the stages of instruction could possibly be similar to fixing up an old house, I invite you to read on. But first, take a moment to think about our instructional goals for the chapter.

An Introduction to Instructional Sequencing

Imagine that you are about to walk into a classroom full of eager students. Your mission is to engage your learners with a forty-five-minute lesson so that they learn something. Have you prepared your instructional goal and instructional objective? Great! Have you thoroughly analyzed the content you want your students to acquire? Wonderful! Do you have a good selection of examples, non-examples, and learning activities to engage your students? Super! What about instructional technology? Are you planning to use any neat gadgets like overhead projectors, VCRs, computers, or Internet connections? You are? I'm impressed. It certainly looks as if you have all the bases covered.

May I ask you one more question before you step into the classroom? What exactly are you going to *do* with all that stuff? How will you orchestrate all those resources to get learning to happen? What will you and your students actually do for, say, the first two minutes of your lesson? What about the next five minutes? In addition to time, you also have a number of instructional resources to allocate. Which activity will you use first? Second? Third? Will you begin with a whole class discussion, cooperative group discovery activity, or a dazzling multimedia presentation?

These are common, routine questions that all classroom teachers face every day. All teachers need to make decisions about how they will use the instructional time and the instructional space available to them. Let's define **instructional time** simply as the amount of time teachers have available to engage their learners with learning activities and materials. Let's define **instructional space** as the set of physical resources at our disposal to support student learning. Instructional space can include everything within the classroom environment, other parts of the school building such as a library or computer lab, or even the home and community environment. All learning takes place in real time and space. How will we manage the time and space available to us and our students to produce learning?

What Is an Instructional Sequence?

An **instructional sequence** is a general series of events that teachers use to manage instructional time and space to maximize the probability that learning will occur. Just as I can increase the quality of a home improvement project by following a certain general sequence of steps (preparation, construction, finishing touches), we can increase the probability that students will achieve our instructional goals if we order instructional events in a particular sequence. An instructional sequence provides a useful structure to guide our thinking about instructional events, not a rigid recipe to follow in a mechanical, nonthinking way.

On what basis should we make instructional sequencing decisions? Let me address this question by examining how I should make house renovation decisions. Why should I install new electrical wiring before hanging wallpaper? The structure of the wall dictates the sequence. The wiring is hidden inside the wall, and the wallpaper covers the outside. If I paper the wall first, I will ruin the papering when I cut openings in the wall to get to the electrical wires. As you can see, the structure of the building helps me determine the ideal sequence of renovation events. By sequencing my actions according to building structure, I can maximize efficiency, minimize effort, and enhance the overall quality of the job. Because the ultimate goal of instruction is to facilitate learning, we should rely on the structure of the learning process to inform our instructional sequencing decisions. In other words, we rely once again on the internal conditions of learning to guide our thinking about external instructional events.

In the previous three chapters, we saw that the internal conditions of learning vary for different learning outcomes such as verbal information, concepts, rules, principles, and cognitive strategies. To develop a useful instructional sequence, we need to focus on the internal conditions of learning that are *common* to all types of learning outcomes. Regardless of the specific learning outcome and content to be acquired, the learning process usually progresses in an orderly, predictable sequence. That sequence is described quite well by current information processing models of learning (see Chapter 7 for a review).

Information processing theory describes the general structure of cognitive learning processes. According to Robert Gagne (1985), to maximize the effectiveness of instructional events, we should design and sequence them in ways that are sensitive to this structure. Let's take a look at the sequence of instructional events that Gagne recommends based on information processing models of learning.

Gagne's Events of Instruction

According to Gagne (1985), there are eight fundamental instructional events—eight basic actions that teachers should engage in to help their students learn (Driscoll, 1994; Gagne, Briggs, & Wager, 1992). You will see these eight external instructional events listed in the third column of Table 10.1 in the order that Gagne recommends. Why does Gagne identify these particular external events in this particular order? The answer to this question is found in the first column of the table. Here we see eight *internal* learning processes in the general order in which they are likely to operate within our students, as suggested by information processing theory.

When we design and implement an instructional sequence using these eight instructional events, we are not merely creating eight sets of learning activities. Rather, we are creating instructional experiences that should actually influence students' internal learning processes. No instructional event, or learning activity, produces learning directly. Only students' internal processing of information produces learning. Therefore, any sequence of instructional events that we design will be effective only to the extent that each event actually supports one or more specific cognitive processes within our learners.

Although Gagne presents his model of instructional events as a sequence, you should not interpret it as a rigid, unvarying set of steps. Learning is not that simple. The order of internal processes and external events provides a general approach to designing and sequencing learning activities and materials. Rather than viewing Gagne's sequence as a set of discrete, rigidly ordered steps, I prefer to organize the eight learning processes and instructional events into three general phases: preinstructional, instructional, and postinstructional (see Table

Table 10.1
Robert Gagne's Events of Instruction

Internal Learning Process	Influence?	External Instructional Event
PREINSTRUCTIONAL PHASE: PREPARATION		
1. Attention: Alertness	←	1. Gaining learner attention
2. Expectancy	←	2. Establishing learning goals; supporting learner motivation
3. Retrieval to working memory	←	3. Stimulating learner recall of prior knowledge
INSTRUCTIONAL PHASE: CONSTRUCTION		
4. Selective perception	←	4. Engaging learner with information to be processed
5. Encoding: Storage in long-term memory	←	5. Providing guidance and support for encoding processes
POSTINSTRUCTIONAL PHASE: FINISHING TOUCHES		
6. Responding	←	6. Providing performance opportunities
7. Reinforcement	←	7. Assessing performance and providing feedback
8. Cueing retrieval	←	8. Supporting long-term retention and transfer

10.1 and Figure 10.1). These three phases are similar to the three stages of a home improvement project: preparation, construction, and finishing touches.

The purpose of the **preinstructional phase** is to prepare learners to process the content they need to acquire. Before I can wallpaper a room, I need to prepare the walls by stripping old wallpaper and patching holes in the plaster. How do we prepare our students for learning? According to Gagne, we prepare students by helping them (1) pay attention, (2) develop personal expectancies for their learning, and (3) retrieve relevant prior knowledge to working memory (see Figure 10.1).

After preparing the walls, I can hang the new wallpaper. Similarly, the purpose of the **instructional phase** is to help learners construct a meaningful representation of the new information they are to acquire—whether it be declarative, procedural or affective. From an information processing perspective, learners construct new knowledge by (4) selectively perceiving and (5) encoding it (see Figure 10.1). During the instructional phase, we engage learners by bringing them into direct contact with the facts, skills, or emotions to be learned.

My home improvement project is not complete until I put the finishing touches on it. For example, after hanging the new wallpaper, I can then install light fixtures, replace plates on electrical outlets, and hang pictures. Similarly, instruction is not complete until we help learners put the finishing touches on the learning process. The purpose of the **postinstructional phase** is to help learners put on these finishing touches by strengthening and extending the new knowledge they have constructed. According to Gagne, learners must (6) make overt responses based on their new knowledge, (7) cue retrieval of information to make those responses, and (8) receive reinforcement on the quality of their performance (see Figure 10.1).

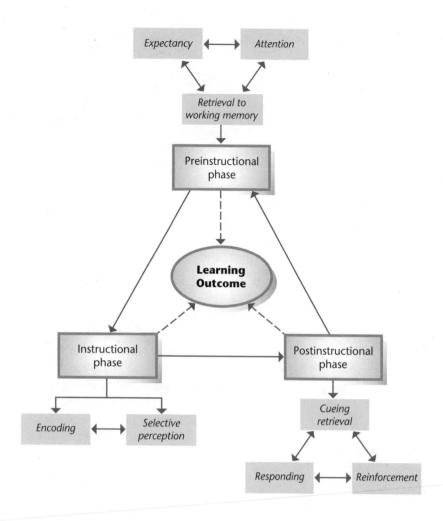

**Figure 10.1
Gagne's Instructional
Events: An Interactive
Model**

Notice in Figure 10.1 that the specific learning processes comprising each general phase are not presented in a two-step or three-step sequence. Rather, these elements interact in complex nonsequential ways, as the double-headed arrows linking them suggest. Notice also that the three general instructional phases do not occur in an unalterable, rigid sequence. For example, the learning processes that are particularly critical to prepare learners during the preinstructional phase may need to be revisited during the remaining two phases. At any phase in the instructional sequence, you may need to return to earlier learning processes.

Planning External Instructional Events

The internal learning processes that Gagne outlines do not occur in a vacuum. As Figure 10.2 illustrates, external instructional events also need to be sensitive to at least three additional interacting variables: (1) learner characteristics, (2) instructional media, and (3) learning outcome.

■ **Learner Characteristics** Thus far, we have focused primarily on the general processing characteristics that all learners have in common. However, there are many characteristics that produce diversity between learners (Snow, 1997). Smith and Ragan (1993) outline three main categories of learner characteristics that we should consider when designing instruction: (1) cognitive, (2)

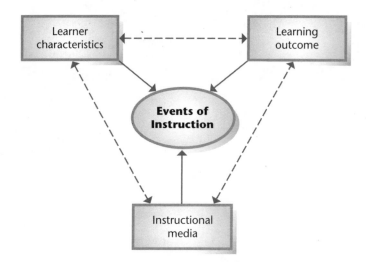

**Figure 10.2
Variables That Influence
the Design of Instruc-
tional Events**

psychosocial, and (3) physical. Smith and Ragan suggest several variables that
are related to each of these categories (see Table 10.2):

▶ *Cognitive characteristics.* Features of learners that influence the ways in which
they interpret or process information

▶ *Psychosocial characteristics.* Features that influence learners' attitudes, interests, motivations, and social relationships.

▶ *Physical characteristics.* Learner features that are produced by natural biological variation among individuals or maturational processes.

Listing the many ways that learners might differ from each other is easy,
but adapting instruction to those differences is immensely challenging. All

**Table 10.2
Cognitive, Psychosocial, and Physical Learner Characteristics**

Cognitive Characteristics	Psychosocial Characteristics	Physical Characteristics
1. General intellectual aptitude (i.e., intelligence)	1. Personal interests	1. Sensory perception abilities (e.g., visual and auditory acuity)
2. Specific aptitudes for particular knowledge domains	2. Motivation to learn	2. General health
3. Cognitive development level	3. Attitude toward learning and subject matter to be learned	3. Specific physical impairments (e.g., cerebral palsy, spina bifida)
4. Language development level	4. Academic self-concept (i.e., self-efficacy)	4. Age
5. Reading ability	5. Anxiety levels	
6. Visual literacy (i.e., ability to interpret graphic information)	6. Peer relationships	
7. Learning strategies and preferred processing styles	7. Role models	
8. General world knowledge	8. Social learning preferences (e.g., cooperation versus competition; independent versus group)	
9. Specific prior knowledge of content domain	9. Moral development level	
	10. Socioeconomic background	
	11. Racial or ethnic background	

learners differ from each other, and all deviate from the average. For any given instructional goal or set of learning materials, specific students may have difficulties because of their unique cognitive, psychosocial, or physical characteristics (Snow, 1997). Recently, for example, my daughter Anna was having trouble with a math problem in which she was supposed to estimate the length of a city block in meters. The problem was difficult for Anna because she had no conception of the length of a city block. You see, we live in a very small rural village. (We don't even have sidewalks in our village, let alone city blocks.) The same problem could be much easier for a child whose urban experiences have provided the general world knowledge (a cognitive characteristic) necessary to understand it.

Depending on the specific nature of learner differences, we may need to be prepared to adjust our instructional goals, assessment strategies, or instructional strategies for individual learners or groups of learners. However, even when we make such adjustments, the basic systematic instructional design process that we have been exploring in this book does not need to change.

◼ **Instructional Media**   A second variable that will always influence the design process is the instructional media that we have selected to communicate with our learners. Different media have different features that create strengths and limitations in specific instructional situations. An instructional videotape, for example, is a wonderful medium for demonstrating movement, but if you want to show your students the spelling of a specific vocabulary word that is used on the tape, you will need to pause the video and switch momentarily to another medium, such as the chalkboard, flipchart, or overhead projector. If you want your learners to interact with the information they are experiencing on the videotape, you will need to provide a workbook or handout (perhaps a partial outline or concept map) to accompany it. Alternatively, you could find an interactive CD-ROM or web site that promotes the kind of cognitive interaction your learners need.

Clearly the instructional media that we choose to use place limits and constraints on how we design external instructional events. They also open up a range of possibilities for our external events. Similar to the point made in an earlier chapter about assessment formats, no instructional medium is superior to all others for every learning situation (Clark & Salomon, 1986). Usually teachers need to orchestrate several media within a single instructional system to support learning. In a single lesson, a teacher may engage learners with books and other print materials, a filmstrip, the chalkboard, concrete objects, and computers. Of critical importance is not the specific media but how we will use those media resources to support the internal conditions of learning.

◼ **Learning Outcome**   The intended learning outcome reflected in the instructional goal also influences how we design external instructional events. We need to apply each of Gagne's eight instructional events in ways that make the most sense for our target learning outcomes. If, for example, the target learning outcome is a concept, we need to design each instructional event with that particular outcome in mind. We are not going to try to get our learners' attention (Gagne's first instructional event) just for the sake of getting their attention. We need to try to capture and maintain attention in ways that help them focus on the critical features of the concept to be learned.

LET'S SUMMARIZE

Gagne's proposed instructional sequence is a dynamic, fluid model of interacting elements that can help us think strategically about instructional time and space. When we combine Gagne's sequence with our knowledge of information processing, learner characteristics, media capabilities, and learning outcomes, we have a powerful structure to help us solve the problem of planning instruction to support learning. Now let's zoom in for a closer look at each of the three general instructional phases and their specific internal learning processes and external instructional events.

Preparation: Planning for the Preinstructional Phase

Our goal in planning preinstructional events is to help learners engage in the cognitive processes that will prepare them to receive and act on declarative, procedural, or affective information. From an information processing perspective, there are three such processes: (1) attention, (2) expectancy, and (3) retrieval to working memory (see Table 10.1). Although these three processes are more interactive and integrated than isolated and sequential, let's separate them here so we can get a clear understanding of each.

Attention: The Gateway to Learning

Attention is the gateway to learning. If learners do not attend to new information, regardless of the media or learning activity used to engage them with it, that information will never make it to working memory. If information never moves into the state of working memory, learners cannot construct meaningful links to their preexisting knowledge in long-term memory.

In general, attending to information means that learners must direct their senses toward the source of that information (Bruning, Schraw, & Ronning, 1999). Depending on the exact nature of the content to process, learners will need to activate at least one of their five senses. They will need to look, listen, taste, smell, or touch. If the source of information is a computer screen, learners must look at the screen. If sounds accompany the images on the computer screen, learners must listen to those sounds. If the source of information is another person who is demonstrating a new skill, learners must look at and perhaps listen to that model. If the source of information is a set of materials with different textures, then learners must touch those materials.

Although Gagne presents attention as the first cognitive process in which learners need to engage, attention is not a one-time activity. If your mind has ever wandered—while watching a movie, observing a sporting event, listening to a speech, or reading a book (not this one, I hope!)—then you have experienced the need to reactivate your attention periodically. It is difficult for all of us to maintain a high level of attention and alertness over long periods of time, even when we are highly interested in the task. Therefore, when planning external instructional events to support our learners' attention needs, we should think about how to try to capture their attention initially and also make provisions for helping them reactivate their attention regularly.

As you can see from Table 10.1, Gagne recommends simply that we attempt to *gain learner attention* as the first external instructional event. The specific attention-getting strategies we build into our learning activities and materials will be as varied as our learners, instructional media, instructional goals, and our own creativity. I cannot possibly tell you how to support your learners' attention needs in all your future classroom teaching. Let me share with you, however, six general categories of attention-getting strategies to give you a sense of the possibilities that are available. These six categories come from Keller's (1983, 1987) recommendations for enhancing learner motivation.

■ **Using Variability to Support Attention**   Have you ever wondered why television commercials are often louder than the programs they interrupt? The advertisers are trying to get your attention by changing the intensity of the sound. If, as you are reading this book, a friend accidentally drops a glass of water on the floor, you probably will turn away from the book and focus your attention on the sudden sound of shattering glass. What do these two examples tell us about human attention? We tend to turn our attention to aspects of our environments that change, especially if the change is sudden, extreme, or unexpected (Driscoll, 1994).

We can capitalize on this principle by building variety and change into our instructional sequences. There are numerous external variables that we can change to support attention, depending on the specific medium we are using to communicate with students. Here are some examples to show you the range of possibilities:

▶ When using *visual* media (e.g., overhead projector, computer, videotape), vary images by using movement, scene changes, and color changes.

▶ When using *print* media, vary the appearance of words, phrases, and sentences by changing font styles, font sizes, and colors. Also use italicizing, boldfacing, underlining, and shading to call attention to specific pieces of information.

▶ When using *auditory* media, vary sounds by changing loudness, using background music, and including sound effects that support the content to be learned.

▶ When using the human *voice* to communicate with students, vary voice quality by inflection, accent, speed, pauses, and loudness.

Classroom attention-getting possibilities are endless. When you, as the teacher, are the primary instructional medium, you can even vary aspects of your appearance to gain learner attention. For example, for one of my instructional design classes, I walk into the classroom in full fly-fishing garb, complete with hip-waders, fishing vest, hat, net, and fly rod. Because I (and most other professors) normally do not dress like this for class, students usually sit up and take notice. I do not pull this stunt, however, just for the sake of doing something different to startle students. I dress like this on the day that we explore principles of motor skill learning, using fly rod casting to demonstrate motor skill learning because it is a skill that is usually new to students. So not only does my dramatically changed appearance help to capture attention and interest, it also relates to the focus of *instruction*. This is a principle that I encourage you to apply as you explore various techniques to help your learners attend: Use attention-getting strategies that are relevant to the instructional goal to be achieved. Otherwise, students can be easily distracted by irrelevant, seductive details of the learning environment that actually impede their learning (Garner, 1992; Garner, Gillingham, & White, 1989; Garner, Alexander, Gillingham, Kulikowich, & Brown, 1991; Mayer, 1997a).

In addition to varying the sensory stimuli our learners experience, we can also try to vary the types of learning activities we use to engage them. In general, humans tend to lose interest in an activity the longer they engage in that activity. Students can easily lose interest in the most dynamic speaker, computer software, or instructional video if they get an overdose of that particular medium. We can guard against habituation by including a number of different learning activities within a single instructional sequence so that students are not just listening, watching, discussing, experimenting, writing, or playing a game during the entire instructional episode.

■ **Using Humor to Support Attention** Building humor into instructional events has a positive impact on learner attention and interest (Powell & Andresen, 1985). There are many ways to incorporate humor into teaching, including jokes, riddles, puns, and funny anecdotes. You can even clip cartoons from magazines and newspapers and share them with learners. Humor is best used when it relates to the instructional goal at hand. For example, I use the

THE FAR SIDE By GARY LARSON

Professor Gallagher and his controversial technique of simultaneously confronting the fear of heights, snakes and the dark.

Figure 10.3
Using Humor to Illustrate a Classical Conditioning Concept
THE FAR SIDE copyright 1986 FARWORKS, INC. All Rights Reserved. Used by permission.

cartoon shown in Figure 10.3 in my educational psychology class when we examine the use of "flooding" as a procedure to extinguish classically conditioned phobias. The cartoon is not just funny and attention getting. It also distinctively illustrates the principle of flooding I want my students to understand, albeit in an extreme, bizarre way.

■ **Using Concreteness to Support Attention** Teachers often use the term *concrete* to refer to instructional materials, but what exactly does "concreteness" mean, and why is "concreteness" attention getting? To answer these questions, think about concrete—yes, the hard stuff of sidewalks, driveways, and cinder-block walls. When something made of concrete is available in your environment, you easily know it. You can see it and feel it. It is solid, firm, and not easily dismissed or pushed aside. That is the nature of concrete learning materials. Concrete instructional events are those that engage learner senses directly with information. They often, though not necessarily, involve students in bodily movements or direct physical contact with objects and materials. This direct sensory stimulation usually creates greater meaningfulness for learners.

Concrete materials support attention because they give learners something solid and meaningful to process directly. You can enhance the concreteness of the learning materials you design by using real objects and experiences, providing meaningful and realistic examples of ideas, and providing visual representations of information. Throughout this book, for example, I have consistently attempted to help you pay attention to information by illustrating ideas with visual diagrams, personal stories, meaningful examples (both teaching and nonteaching), and realistic classroom case studies—all examples of concrete instructional events.

■ **Using Cognitive Conflict to Support Attention** Cognitive conflict (also called **cognitive dissonance**) is the mental discomfort we feel when we experience two ideas or events that are contradictory or discrepant (Berlyne, 1960; Festinger, 1957; West & Pines, 1985). In his theory of cognitive development, Piaget (1983) refers to this phenomenon as **disequilibrium**—a state of intellectual imbalance. As humans, we have a natural tendency to try to resolve the discrepancies we encounter. As we actively work to resolve the conflict or dissonance, we have a heightened attentiveness to additional information or experiences that can help us account for the discrepancy or restructure our own thinking to eliminate it.

Teachers can capitalize on cognitive conflict as an attention-getting device by creating discrepant events for their students (Nussbaum & Novick, 1982; Posner, Strike, Hewson, & Gertzog, 1982). For example (notice that I am concretizing), as part of a unit on weather, my seventh-grade students were learning about air pressure. Before class, I put a small amount of water in a large metal container that I had borrowed from the school secretary and placed it on a hot plate. As students entered the classroom, the water was boiling. Without saying anything about the container, I nonchalantly turned off the hot plate, screwed the cap on the container, and started talking with the students about an unrelated topic. Within a few minutes, the container started to collapse. As expected, this event captured my students' attention. To heighten the dissonance, I pretended that I was upset because the secretary wanted the container back. This *really* captured the students' attention because teachers aren't supposed to be surprised by things that happen in their classrooms.

This event created cognitive conflict for my students because a can was being crushed before their very eyes, yet there was no visible force that they could see doing the crushing. Furthermore, their teacher's feigned surprise and uncertainty created dissonance because teachers are supposed to know everything and *never* make mistakes. Naturally, the students wanted to know why the can had collapsed. So together we developed hypotheses about the source of the pressure that crushed the can, eventually arriving at the principle that air does indeed exert pressure. The point that I want to emphasize here is that for the remainder of the class period, I had a group of seventh-graders who were rapt with attention because their own curiosity had been aroused and they were naturally motivated to resolve the sense of disequilibrium they were experiencing.

■ **Using Inquiry to Support Attention** Cognitive dissonance can be an extraordinarily powerful attention-getting tool. An additional advantage of creating cognitive conflict is that it then sets the stage for learners to be active problem solvers as they restructure their prior schemas (Dole & Sinatra, 1998; Vosniadou & Brewer, 1987). When learners are actively involved in hypothesizing, testing hypotheses, seeking information, and drawing conclusions, they are much more likely to be attentive. When learners have the opportunity to inquire about problems and issues that are relevant to their own personal interests, they may be able to attend to new information more effectively.

■ **Using Active Participation to Support Attention** Our learners' minds are most likely to wander when we fail to provide them with anything to do but sit and listen. Participating in activities such as games, role playing, simulations, interactive computer programs, and group projects forces learners to attend. Even when we are delivering whole class instruction in a direct, expository manner, we can build student participation into our instructional strategy. For example, students can work along at their seats as we demonstrate the application of a mathematics rule on the overhead projector. They can complete a partial outline as they watch an instructional videotape. Students can respond to questions by giving a thumbs-up sign for "yes" and a thumbs-down sign for "no." A learning game in which only one student responds at a time can be modified so that all students first write their answers before a single individual responds. The possibilities are numerous.

LET'S SUMMARIZE

As you can see, teachers have a variety of attention-getting and attention-maintaining strategies from which to choose. However, none of these strategies is guaranteed to work all the time for all learners. You, as a *design-teacher*, must remember that your ultimate goal is to influence your learners' internal attention processes, not just to implement one or more of these external strategies. Regardless of the strategies you use, you will need to monitor your students consistently for evidence that their attention is indeed being supported as you intend.

Expectancy: Establishing a Reason for Learning

According to Gagne (1985), a second important consideration during the pre-instructional phase is supporting students' expectancies. In general, **expectancy** refers to learners' awareness and understanding of the learning outcome they are attempting to achieve. From an information processing perspective, expectancy influences executive control, which helps learners engage in goal-directed, strategic learning processes for themselves. Recall that executive control is the component of the information processing model that manages the control processes.

Learner expectancy has two components—one cognitive and one affective. The cognitive component is learners' knowledge of the capability they are to achieve. In other words, they have an understanding of *what* they are going to learn. The affective component is learners' motivation for achieving the new capability. In other words, they understand *why* they are going to learn. To support expectancy, Gagne recommends that we consider both components by (1) informing learners of the instructional objective and (2) activating learner motivation. Let's examine the cognitive aspect of expectancy first.

■ **Informing Learners of Objectives** At this point in the instructional design process, you already know what your instructional goal and instructional objective are. *You* know exactly where you're going. But what about your *learners*? Do they have any goals or objectives? They sure do! Here are some possibilities (I'm concretizing again):

- Figure out what will be on the next test.
- Flirt with a member of the opposite sex.
- Work out a solution to a personal problem.

- Eat candy without the teacher's noticing.
- Stay awake.
- Take a nap.
- Have a good time with friends.
- Get notes for later rehearsal.

Unfortunately, none of these personal, idiosyncratic goals is very compatible with the instructional goal (or goals) that you may have for your students. Although some students may very well share your instructional goals, many students probably will not. For this reason, you should take deliberate steps to try to get as many students as possible to adopt the learning goals that you have for them.

Just as we become better instructional decision makers when we express learning outcomes as performance capabilities, our learners will become better information processors when they understand the performance they should be able to exhibit as a result of learning. In other words, we need to help students understand what they eventually will be able to do to demonstrate their learning. To achieve this understanding, we could simply show students the instructional goal or, better yet, the instructional objective, since it conveys a lot of detailed information about how they eventually will be assessed. Keep in mind, however, that we express instructional goals and objectives so that they are meaningful to *us*. Our learners probably will not find the words equally meaningful, and if the words do not have meaning, executive control will not be influenced. For example, if tenth-grade students in a geometry class simply hear (or see) that they are going to learn how to *apply the Pythagorean theorem to find the lengths of the sides of right triangles* (the instructional goal), they may not necessarily have the conceptual understanding to know what that performance will actually look like. What are right triangles? What is the Pythagorean theorem? What is the length of a side? Communicating the full-blown objective as the teacher has written it isn't likely to help much either: *Given ten line drawings of right triangles on a sheet of paper with the lengths of two sides provided and the length of one side missing, learners will . . .*

Can't you just see the eyes of students glazing over as they read this objective or listen to a teacher recite it? To influence executive control, learners must have a meaningful representation of the goal or objective. So we often need to show learners what the learned capability will be in a way that makes sense to them. For example, the teacher could begin the instructional sequence by posing a problem such as the following (see Figure 10.4):

> *A civil engineer is planning to build a new street in a city. The new street will connect the intersection of 5th Street and Main with the intersection of 1st Street and Pine. The engineer needs to know the length of the new diagonal street (in blocks) so she can estimate the materials and time needed to build it. Can you determine the length of the new street in blocks without measuring it?*

The teacher could place students in groups to devise solutions to the problem. After giving the groups some time to work, the teacher could lead a discussion of the strategies they have tried and then inform students that there is a simple mathematical way to find the length of the street without measuring. Placing the street figure on an overhead projector, the teacher outlines the right triangle that is formed by Main Street, 1st Street, and the new diagonal street with a thick, dark line and says something like this:

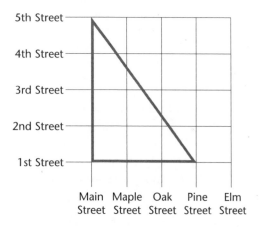

**Figure 10.4
Introducing the
Pythagorean Theorem
with a Realistic Problem**

We already know the length of the 1st Street side of the right triangle [highlight with a green marker] and the Main Street side of the right triangle [highlight in blue]. There is just one missing side: the new street [highlight in red]. Centuries ago, a Greek mathematician named Pythagoras discovered that if you know the lengths of any two sides of a right triangle—like 1st Street and Main Street—you can always find the length of the third side. By the time we're finished exploring Pythagoras's discovery, you will be able to find the length of a missing side for any right triangle as long as you know the lengths of at least two sides.

In this scenario, the teacher has helped students understand what they will eventually be able to do by first allowing them to experience limitations in their current knowledge base. It is but a single illustration of how you can creatively inform students of the learning objective in a way that has meaning for them.

Informing learners of the instructional goal empowers them to participate in managing their own learning. Learners who are aware of instructional goals or objectives achieve more than learners who are not (Duchastel, 1979; Klauer, 1984; Spears & Calvin, 1982), although they may learn less information that is incidental, or not as relevant, to the objectives (Klauer, 1984). However, given our emphasis on designing instruction for specific learning outcomes, this seems like a reasonable, and perhaps even desirable, trade-off.

Activating Learner Motivation   Just because learners know what they are supposed to learn, that does not necessarily mean they will *want* to learn it. Why, for example, should students care that they will be able to apply the Pythagorean theorem? Because they might need this skill in a subsequent math class? Because it will be on the test? Caring about learning is a motivational issue. As we noted in Chapter 7, **motivation** is the hidden force that directs and energizes our behavior. Ideally, learners should be as motivated as possible to achieve the intended instructional goals because the learning process probably is going to require some degree of mental effort, persistence, and on-task behavior on their part.

Using Keller's ARCS Model to Support Motivation   There are numerous psychological theories of motivation that we can draw on to help us support our learners. Reviewing all of these theoretical perspectives is well beyond the scope of this book. Fortunately, however, Keller (1983, 1987) has developed a useful model of motivation variables for supporting learner motivation in a systematic way. Keller's ARCS model identifies four major categories of motivation strategies: Attention, Relevance, Confidence, and Satisfaction (see Table 10.3).

One basic aspect of motivation is attention. Attention-getting instructional events generally are more motivating to learners than those that are not. Because we examined Keller's six recommendations for gaining learner attention earlier in this section, we will not review them again here.

Relevance strategies support motivation by helping students understand how the new information or learned capability relates to them. Learners should be more motivated to persevere on learning tasks when they perceive that the material they are learning has some degree of personal value (Brophy, 1999; Cordova & Lepper, 1996). Keller recommends several general strategies to promote relevance:

▶ *Experience.* Show learners how new information relates to their prior skills, interests, or past experiences.

▶ *Present worth.* Help learners see how new information can be valuable or useful in a problem or task they are working on.

▶ *Future usefulness.* Show learners how new learning may benefit them in the future by supporting their personal aspirations and goals.

Table 10.3
Summary of Keller's ARCS Model of Motivation

A	R	C	S
Attention	Relevance	Confidence	Satisfaction
1. Variability	1. Experience	1. Learning require-ments	1. Natural conse-quences
2. Humor	2. Present worth	2. Difficulty	2. Unexpected re-wards
3. Concreteness	3. Future usefulness	3. Expectations	3. Positive outcomes
4. Cognitive conflict	4. Need matching	4. Attributions	4. Avoiding negative influences
5. Inquiry	5. Modeling	5. Self-confidence	5. Scheduling of rein-forcements
6. Participation	6. Choice		

▶ *Need matching.* Structure instructional events so that they are relevant to students' needs for achievement, risk taking, autonomy, or social interaction.

▶ *Modeling.* Use models to demonstrate the value of the learned capability or exhibit enthusiasm for the learning process (don't forget that the teacher can be a model).

▶ *Choice.* Encourage students to participate in creating their own relevance by giving them some degree of choice in what and how they learn.

How will we know what types of experiences, aspirations, interests, needs, models, and choices will be most relevant to our learners? We can best design relevance strategies by carefully considering as many learner characteristics as possible: cognitive, psychosocial, and physical. Because individual learners are quite diverse with respect to Keller's relevance variables, we should be prepared to build a variety of relevance strategies into our instructional events.

Confidence strategies support learner motivation by helping students construct positive expectations for themselves. Generally people are more motivated to participate in an activity when they are confident that they have a reasonable chance of success as a result of their efforts. Learner expectations for success at a learning task often are referred to as **self-efficacy** (Bandura, 1977, 1982). Research results consistently demonstrate that high levels of self-efficacy are positively related to higher degrees of motivation, learning, and achievement (Schunk, 1991; Wigfield & Karpathian, 1991).

Supporting learner self-efficacy requires more than just "cheerleading"— that is, simply telling students that they are capable and should feel good about their abilities. Learners develop a sense of self-efficacy when they experience evidence of their abilities and potential for success (Kohn, 1994) and then attribute success to their own effort or ability (Graham, 1991; Weiner, 1979, 1985). According to Keller, to support self-efficacy—that is, confidence—we should design learning events to provide clear, positive cues to students about their own capabilities and potential for success (see Table 10.3):

▶ *Learning requirements.* Make students aware of learning goals and assessment criteria, and provide opportunities for self-evaluation.

▶ *Difficulty.* Sequence instruction so that learners encounter easier material before difficult material.

▶ *Expectations.* Help students set realistic goals for themselves.

▶ *Attributions.* Encourage students to attribute (or explain) their degree of learning success to their own effort.

▶ *Self-confidence.* Gradually provide opportunities for students to perform realistic, challenging tasks with increasing degrees of independence.

Satisfaction strategies support motivation by influencing the types of consequences students experience as they are engaged in learning activities. Some learners may experience satisfaction simply because they have mastered a new skill. Other learners may need greater motivational support through the careful application of operant conditioning techniques such as positive reinforcement, shaping, and the Premack principle (Ackerman, 1972; Alberto & Troutman, 1982; Skinner, 1953). Keller recommends five general satisfaction strategies:

▶ *Natural consequences.* Provide consequences that are intrinsic to the learning outcome (e.g., let students apply a new skill in a realistic context).

▶ *Unexpected rewards.* Reinforce on-task learning behavior by providing positive reinforcers; use unexpected rewards (e.g., surprising students with extra recess time) for tasks that students already find interesting and expected rewards (e.g., telling students ahead of time that they can earn extra recess time) for tasks students find less interesting.

▶ *Positive outcomes.* Provide positive personal reactions (e.g., verbal praise, personal attention) to learner effort and achievement.

▶ *Avoiding negative influences.* Avoid actions that students may find aversive, such as coercion, threats, ridicule, sarcasm, and embarrassment.

▶ *Scheduling of reinforcements.* Adjust the timing of reinforcements as learners progress; use more frequent reinforcement in early stages of learning and gradually change to a variable schedule.

LET'S SUMMARIZE

Gagne suggests that we support expectancy by making students aware of learning objectives and activating their motivation to learn. As you have seen, Keller's ARCS model provides a varied and theoretically sound perspective on supporting learner motivation. I must caution you again, however, that none of Keller's suggested strategies magically works with all learners in all learning situations. After designing and implementing any of the expectancy strategies we have reviewed in this section, you will need to monitor your learners frequently to ensure that their executive control processes have indeed been influenced by your efforts. Furthermore, you may need to support your students' expectancy needs throughout the instructional sequence—not just at the beginning of the learning process.

Retrieval to Working Memory: What Do Learners Already Know?

Meaningful learning happens when learners are able to generate connections between new information (facts, skills, or attitudes) and the prior knowledge that already resides in their long-term memory (Gagne, Yekovich, & Yekovich, 1993; Mayer, 1999). Because the part of the information processing system where this mental construction activity occurs is working memory, learners will be in the best position to construct meaningful links when they have activated relevant prior knowledge from long-term memory to working memory. Therefore, Gagne's (1985) third instructional event is to help learners recall relevant prior knowledge.

By emphasizing the need to stimulate the retrieval of prior knowledge to working memory, Gagne is not implying that learners, left to their own devices, will fail to activate any relevant schemas by themselves. In fact, humans automatically call on the schemas they have stored in long-term memory to help them interpret any situation they encounter—whether the situation is new or familiar (see Gentner & Gentner, 1983; LaZansky, Spencer, & Johnston, 1987; Rumelhart, 1991). Schema activation is not a mental activity that we can turn on and off with a switch. This is not to say, however, that learners will always activate the most relevant or useful prior knowledge to support their learning. That's where we can help. To help learners activate the most useful prior knowledge to working memory, we need to address two fundamental questions: (1) What type of knowledge do learners need to activate? and (2) How can we support the activation process? Let's tackle the knowledge question first.

■ **Relevant Prior Knowledge and Learning Outcomes**   First, the content area described by the instructional goal provides a general knowledge domain that will be relevant to the new information. If, for example, learners are to *apply predator-prey relationships in a desert ecosystem* (instructional goal), then helping them activate their general knowledge (or schema) of animals that live in a desert ecosystem, as well as the common features of desert ecosystems, could be useful.

The learning outcome represented by the instructional goal provides a second source of information regarding the prior knowledge learners will need to activate. From the preceding two chapters, you know that each learning outcome has prerequisite knowledge that is particularly relevant to the learning process:

Verbal information:	Schema, superordinate concepts
Intellectual skills—concepts:	Subordinate concepts, discriminations, verbal labels
Intellectual skills—rules and principles:	Subordinate concepts, verbal labels
Cognitive strategies:	Subordinate rules, principles, concepts, verbal labels

By using the content analysis procedures we examined in Chapter 3, you should be able to identify the declarative, procedural, and affective knowledge your learners will need to retrieve to working memory to facilitate their construction of new knowledge.

■ **Supporting Retrieval to Working Memory**   After identifying prior knowledge that learners need to retrieve to working memory, we then must decide how best to support the retrieval process. Of course, if we cannot be certain that learners do possess the critical prior knowledge that we have identified, we should first prepare appropriate instructional events to help them acquire that knowledge. If we are certain that learners do possess the critical prior knowledge, then we can build into our instruction a variety of knowledge-activation procedures:

▶ *Verbal reminders.* Statements given to learners verbally or through print about relevant prior knowledge can help them activate it to working memory. *Example:* Before presenting information about predator-prey relationships in a desert ecosystem, the teacher or instructional materials could state, "Let's think about all the plants, animals, and nonliving features that you would find in a desert ecosystem."

▶ *Questioning.* Build questions into the instructional materials that require learners to activate relevant prior knowledge. To ensure activation to working memory, have all students respond actively to the questions. *Example:* "What are some animals that you would find living in the desert? On a blank sheet of paper, try to list as many as you can."

▶ *Teacher-generated review.* Before presenting new information, the teacher or instructional materials can provide a summary of relevant prior knowledge for learners. Such a summary can be given to learners orally or in written form. Outlines, concept maps, tables, and other organizational tools can be useful in summarizing information for learners. *Example:* The teacher places a concept map for desert ecosystems on the overhead projector and reviews it with students, directing their attention to three major superordinate categories: animals, plants, and nonliving features.

▶ *Learner-generated review.* Before experiencing new information, learners themselves can construct a summary or review of relevant prior knowledge. Students can be encouraged to state information orally or in written form. They can be encouraged to create outlines, concept maps, tables, figures, or other visual representations. *Example:* Organize students in small groups, and have each group create its own concept map for desert ecosystems.

▶ *Analogies.* Suggest an analogy to learners that encourages them to compare the relationships within a new target domain to relationships within a familiar base domain (see Chapter 7 for a review of instructional analogies). On the surface, the two domains may not appear to be similar, but on a deeper level they share a common relational structure. *Example:* Have students compare the mean (or average) of a set of numbers to the fulcrum of a balance beam (or seesaw).

▶ *Advance organizers.* Engage learners with higher-level concepts or principles with which they are already familiar before engaging them with the new information (see Chapter 7 for a review of advance organizers). When learners activate these superordinate structures, they become available to subsume new information during the learning process. *Example:* Before learning about food web relationships in a desert ecosystem, students identify relationships among themselves (e.g., John and José play on the same baseball team; Margie and Samantha walk to school together). For each relationship, the two students identified hold opposite ends of a piece of yarn that connects them. Eventually everyone in the entire class will be interconnected in a relational web, illustrating the interconnectedness of a food web.

Before we leave this section, there are two important points to note concerning retrieval to working memory. First, we should design knowledge-activation events throughout the instructional sequence, not just for use at the beginning of a lesson. Although it certainly makes sense to activate prior knowledge early in the learning process, it is unlikely that students will be able to activate all the information they will need in the knowledge construction process, especially given the limited capacity of working memory.

Second, we must remember that learners of all ages often possess misconceptions that can interfere with learning. When learners activate their prior knowledge, they may actually be retrieving incorrect or inappropriate information to working memory, increasing the likelihood that the new knowledge they construct also will be incorrect or flawed (Bishop & Anderson, 1990; Eaton, Anderson, & Smith, 1984). As we support working memory retrieval, we need to monitor students' prior knowledge carefully to identify and remediate potential misconceptions (Vosniadou & Brewer, 1987). Often it is useful to remediate misconceptions by confronting students with ideas or experiences that directly conflict with their current views (Chinn & Brewer, 1993), another useful way to apply cognitive dissonance in instruction.

LET'S SUMMARIZE

We have been examining the first three critical learning processes that Gagne (1985) identifies: attention, expectancy, and retrieval to working memory (see

Table 10.1). We can support these internal learning processes by designing external events to help students pay attention, establish learning goals for themselves, activate their motivation, and stimulate their recall of prior knowledge. Although we have described these preparation events separately, they can be integrated within an instructional sequence, as suggested by Figure 10.1. Before we move on to the instructional phase, let's see how one of our case analysis teachers, Ms. Nelson, plans to incorporate integrated preinstructional events into her classroom teaching.

CASE ANALYSIS

Planning Preinstructional Events

Before we analyze Ms. Nelson's preinstructional events, you should review the instructional planning she has accomplished thus far. Take a few minutes now to review the instructional strategy for her verbal information goal (Chapter 7), concept goal (Chapter 8), and principle goal (Chapter 9). Due to the nature of Ms. Nelson's three instructional goals, we cannot illustrate all the specific preinstructional strategies we have just reviewed. However, as you will see, she does plan to incorporate many of these strategies. Let's listen as Ms. Nelson thinks out loud about how she will attempt to support learner attention, expectancy, and retrieval to working memory.

Supporting Learner Attention

For my verbal information lesson [names and features of the earth's geologic eras], I will apply Keller's variability strategy by designing a wide variety of learning activities, including an introductory advance organizer, multimedia computer software, reading from the textbook, completing a cluster analysis chart, group mural project, and the "journey through time" game. I will apply the concreteness strategy by showing students pictures of Florida and Colorado, engaging them with visual images of prehistoric animals from a CD-ROM, and having them create murals of the four eras. I will build participation strategies into the instructional sequence by having students interact with the CD-ROM; complete the partial cluster analysis chart as they read; respond to adjunct questions; create a mural; develop a mnemonic to remember the names of the periods of the Paleozoic era; play the "journey through time" game; pretend to be paleontologists; and write stories about traveling through time.

For my concept lesson (sedimentary, igneous, metamorphic rocks), I will again apply the variability strategy by using a variety of learning activities that are full of concrete experiences: sorting rock samples, growing sugar crystals, melting sulfur, demonstrating sedimentary layering in a glass jar, taking a rock collecting field trip, and creating rock collections. Keller's inquiry strategy can be found throughout the sequence. The initial guided discovery activity gives students the opportunity to begin asking questions and hypothesizing about the common features of rocks. They will continue to have inquiry experiences through the demonstrations of crystal formation, sedimentary layering, and sulfur metamorphosis. As these activities are completed, I will be asking students to formulate and defend hypotheses (i.e., what do you think will happen and why?), observe results, and draw conclusions.

In my principle lesson (cooling rate and crystal size), I will begin with an inquiry activity that also helps to create cognitive conflict (how can the same type of rock have mineral crystals of different sizes?). I will then use a concrete application of the scientific method—that is, an experiment—to help students collect data to resolve the dissonance. Students will continue participating actively with concrete objects by experimenting further with crystal formation and observing crystal size directly on the field trip.

Supporting Learner Expectancy

After using an advance organizer to help students understand that the earth's geologic and climate features have changed over time, I will ask them if they know the names of any of the four eras and any of their specific features. I will summarize their responses with a chart on the chalkboard (similar to Table 7.8). After a few minutes of allowing students to try out their prior knowledge, I will tell them that eventually they will be able to complete the entire chart by themselves. To motivate students to want to learn this information, I will let them know that later in the unit, they will be taking a fossil collecting field trip. To identify the fossils they will be collecting, they will need to be able to remember the names of the four periods and their features: Keller's future usefulness strategy.

For my concept lesson, I plan to inform students of the goal at the end of the initial inductive activity. After guiding students to create the three rock categories, I will tell them that all rocks are members of these three basic categories and that they will be expected to classify any new rock they encounter as a member of the sedimentary, igneous, or metamorphic category. I will again use the upcoming field trip and the opportunity for students to create their own rock collections as a motivational tool (future usefulness, natural consequences). I will also use experience as a motivational strategy by encouraging students to bring in rocks they find around their own homes to classify.

To support learner expectancy for the principle lesson, I will inform students of the instructional goal after they have the opportunity to hypothesize about the reasons for different crystal sizes. I will tell them that they will learn why crystals grow to different sizes. Then, anytime they see crystals in rocks, *they* will be able to explain why some crystals are larger than others. By beginning the lesson with a problem to solve (why are some crystals larger than others?), I can capitalize on the motivational strategy of present worth. Also, I plan to model my own personal enthusiasm for the principle by making verbal comments that communicate my genuine interest in the content. Later in the lesson, when students work in groups to generalize the principle to different types of crystals, I will allow each group to choose its members and the specific type of crystals they want to grow (Keller's choice strategy).

Supporting Prior Knowledge Activation

For the verbal information lesson, I plan to use an advance organizer, in the form of an analogy, to activate learner prior knowledge. I will help my students think about the different climates, plants, and animals of two states with which they are familiar. Then students can relate the idea of geologic time periods to differences between those states. Before students process information about the Mesozoic era, I will play a clip from the movie *Jurassic Park*, a film with which students probably will be familiar, to help them activate their prior knowledge of the dinosaurs and other reptiles that dominated the earth during this period.

To activate prior knowledge relevant to sedimentary rock formation, I will ask students to recall the meaning of "sediment" from a previous lesson. Students will write the word on a sheet of paper and then list all the specific sediments that can possibly be deposited in water (questioning, learner-generated review). To get students thinking about the pressure that transforms sediments into sedimentary rock, I will ask them to write one or two sentences that describe what it feels like to dive under water several feet (questioning).

To help my students activate their prior knowledge of mineral crystals, I will give them a partial concept map to complete (learner-generated review). The map will organize the major types of mineral crystals and their shapes. Completing the map will help my students activate their crystal schemas so they will be prepared to learn about the cooling rate principle.

LET'S SUMMARIZE

The preceding selected strategies provide some concrete examples of preinstructional events. As these examples have illustrated, attention, expectancy, and retrieval are three interrelated internal processes that we can support through integrated external events. As you have seen, a single learning activity can be designed to support more than one internal learning process. Now that you have a good understanding of preinstructional learning events, I invite you to begin proceduralizing your knowledge by completing Exercise 10.1 in the *Student Exercise Guide*.

Construction: Planning for the Instructional Phase

Our primary goal in planning events at the instructional phase is to help learners engage in the cognitive processes that will help them construct their own meaningful representations of declarative, procedural, or affective information. From an information processing perspective, there are two key internal processes that our instructional events need to support: selective perception and encoding (see Table 10.1). As in the previous section, we will separate these two processes in order to focus on the unique characteristics of each.

Selective Perception: Focusing on the Meaning That Matters

Have you ever watched a movie with your friends and afterward discovered that each of you noticed and remembered different details? Each of you watched exactly the same movie, yet you selected different bits of information to process. Why? Because each of you brought different expectations, background knowledge, interests, and goals to the experience. These different personal characteristics influenced the details that each of you perceived as relevant or important.

The same thing happens when a group of learners experience instruction. Because of differences in learners' cognitive, psychosocial, and physical characteristics, individual students select different elements of the instructional environment to think about, the control process known as **selective perception** (Bruning et al., 1999; Ormrod, 1995). Learners are always selective about what they process in working memory because they cannot possibly think meaningfully about everything that is available in their sensory environments.

The key question for us, then, is how we can increase the likelihood that learners will selectively perceive the critical features of the instructional environment that are most relevant to the content they are to learn. This is not a simple question of how to get learner attention (Gagne, 1985). Learners can be paying attention to a colorful, animated computer screen (as opposed to looking out the window) and still not focus their thinking on the most critical information relevant to the instructional goal. To help students move beyond a general sense of attentiveness and focus in on the critical content features to process, we need to think first about the information that is most critical to learners' achievement of the intended learning outcome. Then we can identify external support strategies.

■ **Selective Perception and Learning Outcomes**   As you saw in the previous three chapters, different types of knowledge have different key features that learners must process. These are features that learners absolutely must selectively perceive from the instructional environment to facilitate the learning targeted by the instructional goal:

Learning Outcome	Critical Content Features
Verbal information:	Proposition(s)
Concepts:	Describing and defining features
Rules:	Concepts, concept relationships, sequence of actions
Principles:	Concepts and concept relationships
Cognitive strategies:	Rules, principles, concepts, sequence of actions

Of all the sights, sounds, tastes, touches, and smells learners may select from the environment for processing, they absolutely must think about the content features that are most relevant to attaining the target instructional goal. Although we cannot control what learners think about, we can certainly structure learning activities and materials to increase the probability that they are thinking about the meaning that matters most to the target learning outcome.

■ **Selective Perception and Learner Schemas: A Developmental Perspective**   For learners to assign meaning to new information, the information must be potentially meaningful to them (Mayer, 1987, 1999). For information to be potentially meaningful, learners must be able to relate it to a schema they already possess. Therefore, one important way to support learners' selective perception is to present critical content in a manner that is consistent with their present schemas, or levels of understanding.

Consider, for example, the mathematical rule for calculating the area of a rectangle: *The area of a rectangle is found by multiplying the length by the width.* Would this rule be meaningful to third-grade children? That depends on how we engage them with it. If we present the rule in an abstract, symbolic, algebraic form such as $A = l \times w$, young children are not likely to find much meaning in it because they have not yet begun to represent concrete quantities with abstract symbols.

But what if we were to engage students with a concrete representation of the rule? We could show them rectangles that are divided into unit squares (perhaps by outlining the floor tiles in the classroom with masking tape) and help them understand that the area within each rectangle can be found by adding up all the unit squares inside it (see Figure 10.5). We could help them understand that adding up all the unit squares is easier if we multiply (e.g., the width of three occurs five times—$3 \times 5 = 15$).

Notice in this example that the essential content to be learned—how to calculate the area of a rectangle—does not change. What does change is how we adapt the content to fit learners' levels of understanding. In other words,

When teachers mediate the learning process by providing guidance and support, they encourage learning within Vygotsky's zone of proximal development.

we *mediate* the learning experience so that there is an optimal match between the learner and the content to be learned. **Mediated learning experiences** are those in which teachers transform both the content and learner thinking to maximize the degree of meaning that learners can construct from instructional activities and materials (Kozulin & Presseisen, 1995). For example, notice that we transformed the symbolic formula for calculating the area of a rectangle into a concrete representation (content transformation), and we transformed learner thinking by having students add up the unit squares in sets that correspond to the rectangle's length and width (learner transformation). When teachers transform both content and learner thinking, they create a common ground on which learners and content can interact in meaningful ways (Karpov & Bransford, 1995).

According to Vygotsky (1978), mediated learning experiences occur within the learner's zone of proximal development. The **zone of proximal development** is the difference between what learners can accomplish by themselves and what they are capable of achieving with the assistance of a knowledgeable adult or peer who performs a mediating role (Tudge, 1990; Vygotsky, 1978). Vygotsky's zone of proximal development reminds us that new learning emerges out of learners' prior knowledge and understanding. Learners are ready to ac-

Figure 10.5
Concrete Representation of a Mathematical Rule

What is the area of a rectangle that has a length of 5 units and a width of 3 units?

5

5

$$\text{Area} = 3 + 3 + 3 + 3 + 3$$
$$= 5 \times 3$$
$$= 15$$

3

3

quire new knowledge that is nearest, or closest, to the knowledge they already possess. It is our job as *design-teachers* to mediate the learning process within this "construction zone" (Newman, Griffin, & Cole, 1989) so that learners experience new content within their individual zones of proximal development.

Vygotsky's instructional principles are echoed by two other important developmental theorists, Jean Piaget and Jerome Bruner. According to both Piaget and Bruner, the ways in which learners act on and represent the world change with age and experience. In Piaget's view, learners progress through four general stages of cognitive development: (1) sensorimotor, (2) preoperational, (3) concrete operational, and (4) formal operational (Inhelder & Piaget, 1958; Lunzer, 1986; Phillips, 1975). At each of these stages, learners possess certain schemes, or action patterns, that they use to interpret the world and solve problems (Case, 1993). According to Piaget, learners actively construct meaningful representations of the world around them when they can assimilate new experiences into the schemes they currently possess. In general, learner schemes tend to progress from physical actions (sensorimotor intelligence), to concrete mental representation (preoperational and concrete operational), to abstract, symbolic thought (formal operational).

Similarly, in Bruner's (1960, 1966) view, learners progress through three general stages of cognitive development: (1) enactive, (2) iconic, and (3) symbolic (Mayer, 1987). Each of these terms describes a predominant way of representing knowledge. **Enactive representation** refers to understanding the world through direct physical contact and bodily movement. **Iconic representation** refers to using pictures or visual images to represent ideas. **Symbolic representation** is the ability to use abstract symbols such as numbers, letters, words, and formulas to stand for ideas. Bruner asserts that even young learners can understand powerful, complex ideas when those ideas are presented in a representational mode that is consistent with their current developmental levels.

One of my favorite examples to illustrate the power of Bruner's assertion is the Pythagorean theorem. At a *symbolic* level, learners can experience this mathematical principle as $a^2 + b^2 = c^2$. Could the principle be transformed to a different representational mode so that younger learners can experience it in a meaningful way? An *iconic* (or visual) form of the Pythagorean theorem is provided in Figure 10.6. When you put the two smaller squares together, they equal the same area as the big square. Notice that we have not changed the meaning of the principle—only the way in which it is represented. We can even transform the principle to the *enactive* level. Students can draw a right triangle, cut out the two smaller squares, and fit them both inside the largest square—exactly what the Pythagorean theorem says should happen—try it for yourself! Bruner asserts that learners have the best chance of understanding symbolic ideas only after they have constructed iconic or enactive (or both) representations of them.

What do the developmental perspectives of Vygotsky, Piaget, and Bruner have to do with selective perception and engaging learners with information? Succinctly stated, we need to engage learners with new declarative, procedural, and affective information in ways that are meaningful for *them*. Learners are not likely to select information for further processing if it does not make any sense to them. To ensure that information is potentially meaningful to learners, we need to transform it to fit their developmental levels and prior schemas.

■ **Strategies to Support Selective Perception**   Beyond ensuring an optimal match between new information and learner schemas, we can use several specific strategies to help support learner selective perception. Keep in mind that these are simply possibilities. The specific strategies you use will always depend on learner characteristics, instructional media, and the target learning outcome. In the following list of strategies, you will notice some that we already examined in Chapters 7, 8, and 9 so you already should have an understanding of how they can be applied to specific learning outcomes.

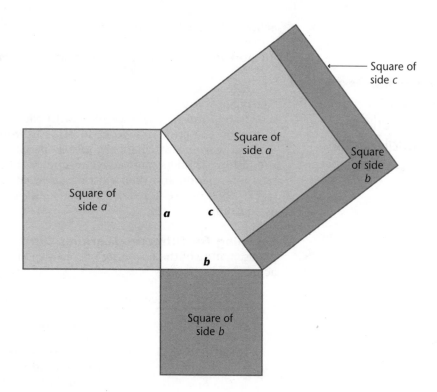

Figure 10.6
An Iconic Representation of the Pythagorean Theorem

▶ *Verbal communication.* Tell learners, orally or in writing, exactly where they need to focus their attention.

▶ *Highlighting.* Call attention to key words, phrases, or ideas by underlining, italicizing, boldfacing, enlarging, coloring, or animating them.

▶ *Controlled presentation.* Ease the burden on learners' working memories by reducing the amount of new information they have to select for processing. Limit the amount of information that learners experience at one time on a page of text, overhead transparency, or computer screen.

▶ *Organizational chunking.* Ease the burden on learners' working memories by engaging them with information that already has been organized into meaningful chunks, or patterns. For verbal information learning, cluster analysis charts can help provide the superordinate concepts for such chunks.

▶ *Repetition.* Focus learner attention on critical content features by having them experience those features repeatedly—and ideally in more than one sensory modality (i.e., see it, hear it, touch it).

▶ *Simplified drawings.* Help learners perceive the most important content features by representing them in simple drawings that eliminate distracting irrelevant features.

▶ *Exaggerated examples.* Use obvious examples early in the instructional sequence to illustrate content features so learners do not have to expend working memory resources to figure out how the examples instantiate the critical features.

▶ *Signals.* Give learners clear signals so they know in advance what content features to select. If learners need to process four major steps to apply a rule, let them know that there are four steps they should anticipate.

LET'S SUMMARIZE

In this section, we have been exploring strategies to help learners selectively perceive the content features that they must process in working memory to achieve the target learning outcome. Now we turn to the next critical learning process: the process of transforming information that is active in working memory to the durable state known as long-term memory.

Encoding: Constructing Personal Meaning

Getting people together in the same room does not guarantee that they will interact and form new relationships with each other. Similarly, getting new information and prior knowledge together in working memory does not guarantee that learning will happen. Just as people need to interact to make new friendships, learners must actively generate meaningful relationships between new information and their existing knowledge base (Gagne et al., 1993; Wittrock, 1992). As we noted in Chapter 7, this critical learning process is known as encoding.

■ **Encoding for Different Learning Outcomes** As you already know, the precise nature of the encoding process depends on the learning outcome to be achieved:

Learning Outcome	Encoding Process
Verbal information:	Meaningful elaboration (verbal, image) and organization
Concepts:	Generalization and discrimination of defining and describing features
Rules:	Generalization and discrimination of concepts and concept relationships
Principles:	Generalization and discrimination of concepts and concept relationships
Cognitive strategies:	Generalization and discrimination of rules and principles

As we noted in Chapter 7, learners encode declarative knowledge by generating meaningful connections to their own organized schemas by means of elaboration and organization processes (Bruning et al., 1999; Gagne et al., 1993). Strategies for guiding students' encoding processes include verbal elaboration, image elaboration, self-generated analogies, self-summaries, self-questioning, mnemonic devices, outlines, concept maps, and schematic diagrams (see Chapter 7). Learners encode procedural knowledge by producing a set of actions when certain conceptual conditions are satisfied (Anderson, 1993, 1996). By thinking about the necessary conditions and producing the appropriate action themselves, learners transform information from a verbal or declarative representation to a procedural representation, or production (see Chapters 8 and 9).

■ **Supporting Encoding Through Learning Strategies** As you can see, the key to encoding is getting learners to act on new information in meaningful ways. Sometimes students are able to accomplish active knowledge construction processes on their own, with little or no assistance from us, by applying learning strategies. A **learning strategy** is a particular action plan, method, or set of steps that people use to control their own learning processes.

Although nearly all learners pick up some basic learning strategies informally throughout their school years, very few develop the ability to deploy a wide variety of strategies effectively in diverse learning situations—that is, unless they are taught to do so. Furthermore, the learning strategies that students induce for themselves often are less effective and efficient than they could be. For example, many middle school, high school, and even college students use rote rehearsal to help them remember information. But even after hours of rote rehearsal, students still are not likely to be able to retrieve the information when needed and use it meaningfully.

Usually learners benefit when we build learning strategies right into an instructional sequence. Various types of learning strategies have been developed and evaluated (see Weinstein & Mayer, 1986; Pressley, 1990), and it is well beyond the scope of this book to review all of them. Let me simply remind you of the major types of learning strategies that are available to support learner encoding and encourage you to incorporate them into your classroom teaching. Most learning strategies can be classified as those that support the encoding process through elaboration or organization:

Elaboration Strategies		Organization Strategies
Verbal elaboration	Analogy	Outlining
Imagery	Mnemonics	Categorizing
Summarization	Generative	Concept mapping
Self-questioning	Note taking	Schematic diagramming

In addition to these independent strategies, students also can be taught to engage in peer-mediated learning strategies—for example, by discussing new material with others, questioning each other, modeling skills, and providing feedback (King, 1997; Maheady, 1996). These strategies provide a systematic structure to promote meaningful social interactions that support learning.

Incorporating learning strategies into instructional sequences benefits learners in two important ways. First, learning strategies help students actively encode the information and skills they are to acquire. Second, learners have the opportunity to learn how to apply the learning strategies themselves so that they become more autonomous in their own learning and less dependent on us to manage their learning processes for them. Students can "learn how to learn" while simultaneously achieving content-related instructional goals (West, Farmer, & Wolff, 1991).

Learning strategies are examples of the broader learning outcome that we have been referring to as *cognitive strategies*. Therefore, integrating learning strategy instruction with content-related instruction requires us to apply the principles of intellectual skill learning that we reviewed in Chapter 9. Students first need to develop a declarative representation (what to do) of the strategy, followed by procedural knowledge (how to do it). Finally, learners need to acquire conditional knowledge of the strategy (when to do it) (Glaser, 1984). When learners possess conditional knowledge, they have a good sense of when a particular learning strategy could be appropriate, the degree of success they can expect from applying it, and metacognitive understanding of how it can influence their learning processes (Jones, Palincsar, Ogle, & Carr, 1987; Paris & Cunningham, 1996; Zimmerman, 1998).

Teaching students how to apply learning strategies seems to be most effective when all three types of knowledge are emphasized through instruction, exactly the point we made in Chapters 8 and 9. Furthermore, students tend to benefit the most from learning strategy instruction when they are taught in the context of subject matter learning. In other words, when strategy instruction is integrated into content instruction, learners are better able to generalize the strategies to new content domains and learning settings (Jones et al., 1987; Pressley, 1990). So, for example, if you want your social studies students to engage in generative note-taking to support their encoding of verbal information presented in an instructional videotape, you should teach them deliberately and explicitly how to engage in generative note-taking in your social studies class rather than in a separate study skills class.

LET'S SUMMARIZE

Careful planning for the instructional phase is critical, for it is at this stage in the learning sequence that students are engaged with the critical content that they must selectively perceive and actively encode into long-term memory. The particular external ways in which we support learners' internal selective perception and encoding processes will vary depending on the learning outcomes we are attempting to achieve.

Now that you have a sense of the internal and external conditions of learning that are relevant to the instructional phase, let's analyze two classroom teaching examples.

CASE ANALYSIS

Planning Instructional Events for a Verbal Information Goal

Ms. Nelson has invited us to listen to her think out loud as she plans her instructional events for verbal information learning. You should review the planning that she has already done in Chapter 7 before reading the case analysis.

TEACHER'S THINKING AND PLANNING

For my verbal information instructional goal [state the names of the four major eras in the earth's history and several important characteristics of each], students will first encounter the propositions they are to learn by reading them in their textbook. To help them selectively perceive the specific propositions that are relevant to the instructional goal, I will give them an empty cluster analysis chart [see Table 7.8] to complete. Each empty cell will represent a specific proposition or set of propositions for students to find as they read. The chart will help students assign meaning to the propositions because they will already understand the superordinate conceptual categories that provide the organizational structure.

By reading and writing the target propositions, my students are likely to be thinking about them—that is, they will be active in working memory. Now what can I do to help them move the information from working memory to long-term memory? I will use the following external events [described in Chapter 7] to support my students' encoding processes:

- Cluster analysis chart to support organization
- Adjunct questions to encourage meaningful verbal elaboration—not just verbatim recall of specific propositions
- Elaborative interrogation to support verbal elaboration
- Student-constructed murals and time lines to support imagery elaboration
- Mnemonics to support elaboration on era and subperiod names

To help my students become strategic, self-regulated learners, I will continue teaching them how to use elaborative interrogation and verbal mnemonics as learning strategies. I have been working with students all year on these two learning strategies, so this verbal information instructional sequence provides yet another opportunity for them to see how these strategies affect their learning of domain-specific content.

CASE ANALYSIS

Planning Instructional Events for an Intellectual Skill Goal

Now let's listen to Mrs. Torres think out loud as she plans her instructional events for intellectual skill learning. You should review the planning that Mrs. Torres has already done in Chapter 9 before reading the case analysis.

TEACHER'S THINKING AND PLANNING

For my intellectual skill instructional goal (apply the rule for rounding numbers to the nearest ten), I will introduce students to the rule by demonstrating it for them with meaningful materials such as base-ten blocks and number lines [see Figures 9.4 and 9.5], using the following actions to influence their selective perception of the rule's critical features:

- Maintaining the same multiples of ten for each set of examples
- Writing both the next lower and next higher multiples of ten for each number and using arrows to point to the rounded multiple
- Using boldface multiples of ten on the number line and column headings for the next lower and next higher multiples of ten
- Providing visual images (blocks, number line) that clearly show each element of the rule: number to be rounded, next lower multiple of ten, next higher multiple of ten

After students are thinking consciously about how the rounding rule works, they need to begin encoding it into long-term memory as a production. The key to encoding a skill as procedural knowledge is for learners themselves to produce the appropriate actions under the right conditions. I will try to support learner encoding with the following external events [described in Chapter 9]:

- Providing several two-digit numbers for students to round using their base-ten blocks
- Providing several two-digit numbers for students to round using a number line
- Providing one- and three-digit numbers for students to round to promote generalization
- Providing meaningful scenarios in which number rounding occurs
- Providing difficult instances (e.g., zero in ten's place) for students to round to promote discrimination

During each of the preceding activities, I will help my students think meaningfully about what they are doing and why they are doing it so they are not just memorizing a set of steps as verbal information. I will require them to demonstrate their rounding with base-ten blocks and number lines. I also will require them to explain verbally to me and each other why they are making specific rounding decisions.

LET'S SUMMARIZE

The specific instructional events that Ms. Nelson and Mrs. Torres have just described are not the only ways to teach geologic history and rounding, of course. They represent the attempts of two different teachers to support their learners' internal processing needs. Other teachers can design quite different external events to support learner selective perception and encoding. The specific learning materials and activities are not as important as our understanding of the internal learning processes we are trying to influence.

We have prepared our learners (the preinstructional phase) and have supported their construction of meaning (the instructional phase). In the next section, we examine the third and final general instructional phase, the finishing touches. Before you read on, however, I encourage you to apply what you've learned about the instructional phase by interacting with Exercise 10.2 in the *Student Exercise Guide*.

Finishing Touches: Planning for the Postinstructional Phase

Have you ever sat in a class in which you understood everything perfectly, only to find that when you tried to do some homework problems or exercises on your own, you were stuck? I think nearly all of us have had that unfortunate experience at one time or another. Why does it happen? How can everything make perfect sense in the classroom and hours later be so confusing? We don't have the complete answer to that question yet. However, we do know that the ability to apply newly encoded knowledge outside the classroom is usually difficult to achieve (Mayer, 1987). I believe that learners often have difficulty applying what they have learned beyond the classroom because we as teachers often fail to support this critical part of the learning process adequately.

Let's return for a moment to my house renovation analogy. Just as there are numerous finishing touches that complete a room renovation project (e.g., filling nail holes, installing light fixtures), there are finishing touches that complete and strengthen the learning process. These learning events usually occur after the construction phase. Therefore, I use the term *postinstructional phase* to categorize them. This phase still is part of an instructional sequence; however, it occurs after learners have constructed an initial encoding.

Gagne (1985) identifies three component learning events that are critical to the postinstructional phase (see Table 10.1): (1) responding, (2) reinforcement, and (3) cueing retrieval. Let's explore the meaning of these three internal learning processes and some external strategies to support them.

Responding: Applying New Skills and Recalling New Facts

The real test of the quality of learner encoding is the retrieval process. Retrieval is the control process that searches long-term memory for information and activates it back into working memory, where it can be used to generate some type of overt behavior or response. Learners need opportunities to make overt responses because such performances require them to retrieve newly encoded information. We can best support this internal need by designing external performance opportunities that encourage learners to retrieve freshly encoded propositions and productions. Usually, we refer to these types of activities as *practice*.

■ **Practice for Learning Outcomes** Just getting learners to engage in any kind of outward performance or activity is not the goal of this learning phase. Students need deliberate practice opportunities that encourage them to retrieve the target propositions and productions that are relevant to the instructional goals to be achieved (Ericsson, Krampe, & Tesch-Romer, 1993). If learners can state a proposition or apply a production without having to retrieve it from their own long-term memories, then practice will provide little benefit. Furthermore, practice opportunities must be consistent with the target learning outcome if they are to support achieving the intended instructional goal (Yelon, 1996):

Instructional Goal	Practice Activity
State verbal information:	State propositions as meaningful ideas.
Apply a concept:	Use concept features to identify new examples and nonexamples.
Apply a rule:	Apply concepts and their relationships to new examples and nonexamples.
Apply a principle:	Apply concepts and their relationships to new examples and nonexamples.
Apply a cognitive strategy:	Apply rules and principles to new examples and nonexamples.

How do practice opportunities strengthen learning? As we noted in Chapter 7, every time learners retrieve newly encoded propositions, they have the chance to engage in further generative learning processes that strengthen existing retrieval routes and create new ones. The more retrieval routes learners create, the greater is the probability that they will be able to recall a proposition in the future. As we noted in Chapters 8 and 9, learners need performance opportunities to proceduralize skills during the associative stage of skill acquisition. Every time learners retrieve and apply a newly encoded production, they strengthen associations among multiple conditions and also among conditions and actions.

■ **Principles of Effective Practice**   In earlier chapters, we examined many specific features of practice opportunities for verbal information and intellectual skill learning outcomes. Furthermore, the effects of practice on learning in general have been well documented (see Annett, 1989; Ericsson et al., 1993; Yelon, 1996). Therefore, let's look at four general principles that you can apply to a wide variety of practice situations to maximize their effectiveness.

PRACTICE PRINCIPLE 1: STRUCTURE PRACTICE TO REQUIRE INDIVIDUAL OVERT RESPONSES BASED ON RETRIEVAL OF TARGET CONTENT

Practice can take a wide variety of forms, depending on the learning outcome, learner characteristics, available resources, and so on. Despite these surface differences, all practice should make it possible for learners to make their internal cognitive responses external and observable. When learners must actually make an overt response such as speaking, writing, drawing, pointing, or constructing, we increase the probability that they are indeed retrieving newly encoded information to working memory. Only when information is activated to working memory do learners have the opportunity to elaborate on it further.

Suppose, for example, that you tell your students to study a list of ten new vocabulary words. What will they actually do? How can you be sure that each student is retrieving the meanings of the words from long-term memory? Just because students are sitting quietly and looking at the words does not mean they are engaged in meaningful processing of the words' meanings. You can structure this practice opportunity better by giving each student the chance to make an overt response. Perhaps you can provide a sheet with all the words written in one column and space for students to write (an overt response) the meanings in another column. Perhaps you can pair up your students and have them take turns verbalizing (an overt response) the meanings of the words to each other. Perhaps your students can type the appropriate vocabulary word when the definition appears on a computer screen. The specific practice possibilities are endless, but individual learners will benefit only if they are actively retrieving information and making meaningful responses.

PRACTICE PRINCIPLE 2: STRUCTURE PRACTICE ACTIVITIES TO PROMOTE INCREASING INDEPENDENCE

Learners are rarely able to retrieve and use newly encoded information all by themselves, especially if the content is fairly complex. Research evidence suggests that effective teachers—those who consistently produce higher achievement gains with their students—routinely guide their students in the early stages of practice and gradually help them gain independence (Brophy, 1986; Emmer, Evertson, Clements, & Worsham, 1997; Evertson, Emmer, Clements, & Worsham, 1997; Leinhardt & Greeno, 1986). When your students begin practicing, you should guide them to ensure they are recalling ideas and performing skills correctly. For example, before students write fifteen compound sentences by joining two independent clauses, you could demonstrate again how to apply the skill by doing the first practice exercise with them on the overhead projector. You can involve students by calling on them to tell you what to do (e.g., Do I need a coordinating conjunction? Where does it go? Where should I place the comma?) and by having them follow along on their own papers. When students continue on their own, you should circulate throughout the room and monitor their progress carefully.

This type of carefully guided and closely monitored practice is important for two reasons—one cognitive and the other affective. First, when applying newly encoded productions, learners are likely to make errors. If these errors go undetected, they may easily become part of an automatic production. Once a production becomes automatic, it is much more difficult to change because it is not easy to think consciously about it (Gagne et al., 1993). From an affective perspective, we want learners to stay on task and persevere over many practice activities. If they experience stress, frustration, and other negative emotions early in the postinstructional phase, they may be less motivated to want to continue practicing (Stodolsky, Salk, & Glaessner, 1991; Wigfield & Meece, 1988). We can help prevent these negative emotional reactions by guiding learners carefully so that they experience success early in the practice process.

PRACTICE PRINCIPLE 3: STRUCTURE PRACTICE ACTIVITIES FROM EASY TO DIFFICULT

In earlier chapters, we noted that some skill applications are fairly obvious (e.g., a cat is a mammal) and others are more difficult (e.g., a seal is a mammal). Every skill can be applied to a wide range of specific instances that vary in complexity and difficulty. We certainly want to promote generalization and discrimination by providing practice opportunities that vary across this wide range of possible complexity. In fact, we should design practice activities that encourage learners to make mistakes so that they can confront their misconceptions and faulty productions (Smith & Ragan, 1993). However, we should begin practice with easier instances and gradually move to those that are more complex and difficult.

The reasons for moving from easy to difficult practice instances are similar to those given for providing guided practice. First, with easy instances, learners have a higher probability of proceduralizing skills correctly, avoiding errors that will be difficult to correct later. Second, with easy instances, learners will gain confidence and a sense of self-efficacy that will help motivate them to continue practicing (Bandura, 1982; Pintrich & De Groot, 1990; Zimmerman & Kitsantas, 1999).

PRACTICE PRINCIPLE 4: DESIGN A VARIETY OF PRACTICE FORMATS THAT PROMOTE LEARNER GENERATIVITY

Theoretically, you could have your students practice stating a set of facts by having them recite the propositions verbatim every day for a week: "Okay, class. Let's all say the steps in the rock cycle together. Ready? Go!" There are two big problems with this approach. First, just having learners repeat material verbatim gives them little opportunity to elaborate on it further; it's not a generative activity. The second problem is that for many students it's just downright boring.

Some verbal information (e.g., basic math facts) and intellectual skills (e.g., outlining) require a lot of practice for learners to retrieve and use them effectively and automatically. Therefore, it is really important to design practice opportunities that help keep learners actively engaged, interested, and motivated to keep working. Everything we noted earlier in this chapter about supporting learner attention, interest, and motivation in the preinstructional phase continues to be relevant in the postinstructional phase.

Returning to Keller's (1983, 1987) ARCS model, we should design practice activities that are sensitive to attention, relevance, confidence, and satisfaction variables. For example, it is amazing how enthusiastically students will practice a skill when it is presented in a game format. Students who lose interest and concentration when practicing with paper-and-pencil exercises may persevere for hours when they can respond in the context of a lively computer-based drill program (Kinzie, 1990; Malone, 1981; Rieber, 1992). We should try to support learner motivation by providing practice opportunities in a variety of forms that are likely to appeal to learner interests: worksheets, workbooks, oral recitation, games, learning centers, projects; computer simulations, and so on.

As we vary practice formats to support learner interest, we should also vary the practice context to promote learner generativity. By practice context, I am referring to the set of conceptual ideas that surround the practice event and probably will be activated simultaneously with the content to be learned. Look, for example, at Figure 10.7. If the target skill is the ability to compute percentages, you could have your students practice in a variety of ways—for example:

▶ Computing batting averages in baseball (*context A*)

▶ Calculating the percentages of racial and ethnic minorities in their school, community, or state (*context B*)

▶ Determining the percentages of vehicle colors, makes, and models in the teachers' parking lot (*context C*)

▶ Computing the percentages of fat, protein, and carbohydrate calories in various foods (*context D*)

By giving students meaningful, authentic problems to solve in each of these contexts, they generate meaningful links to a number of different schemas in long-term memory. In addition to promoting generativity, a variety of practice contexts can support learner motivation by demonstrating how newly learned knowledge may be relevant to personal interests, aspirations, or present needs (Keller, 1987).

Reinforcement: Confirmation of Learning

No doubt you have heard the expression, "Practice makes perfect." Although the statement intuitively sounds correct, it is actually not quite accurate. Declarative and procedural knowledge will not become perfect with practice unless learners are practicing perfectly. Only *perfect* practice makes perfect! Learners are not likely to be practicing perfectly, especially in the early stages

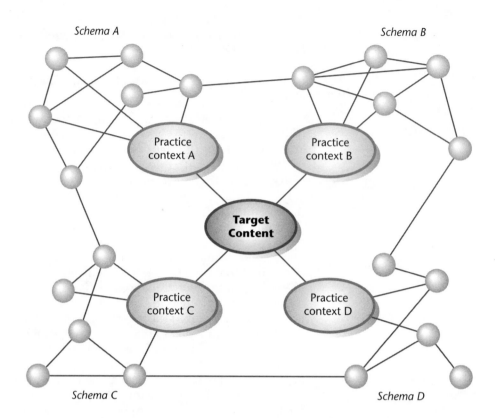

Schema A　　　　　　　　　　　　　　　*Schema B*

Practice context A

Practice context B

Target Content

Practice context C

Practice context D

Schema C　　　　　　　　　　　　　　　*Schema D*

**Figure 10.7
Varying Practice
Contexts to Promote
Generativity**

of responding, unless they are receiving guidance concerning the quality of their performance.

According to Gagne (1985), learners need to experience reinforcement at this stage of instruction to provide correction and confirmation (see Table 10.1). *Reinforcement* is a slippery term that we can define in two somewhat different ways. From a *behavioral* perspective, reinforcement is a stimulus, event, or outcome that occurs following a response that increases the likelihood that the learner will produce the same (or a similar) response in the future. In the classroom, these types of reinforcements can take a variety of forms: gold stars, smiley faces, pieces of candy, extra recess time, letter grades, or verbal praise from a teacher. Although such reinforcers often motivate learners to engage in certain learning activities, they have limited utility for influencing internal learning processes because they ignore meaningfulness, understanding, and learner generativity—critical cognitive aspects of learning.

From a *cognitive* perspective, reinforcement is meaningful information that learners can use to guide and regulate their own learning processes, not just external consequences that strengthen stimulus-response associations (Bangert-Drowns, Kulik, Kulik, & Morgan, 1991). The term used to describe the cognitive function of reinforcement is **feedback**. Although feedback can be defined in several different ways (see Mory, 1996), for our purposes, let's define it simply as any communication provided to learners to inform them of the quality of their performance and to help them improve the quality of their learning. In earlier chapters, we referred to these communications as *informative* feedback. What kinds of information do students need to improve their learning? The answer to this question depends, as we have seen throughout this book, on the nature of the learned capability they are trying to achieve.

■ **Feedback for Different Learning Outcomes** By thinking about the unique features of each learning outcome, we can get a good sense of the information we need to communicate to our learners through feedback. Let's characterize these features by expressing them as questions that students might ask about their *own* performance:

Learning Outcome	Feedback Information
Verbal information:	Did I state the proposition(s) accurately? Did I state the proposition(s) meaningfully?
Intellectual skill— Concept:	Did I classify new examples and nonexamples correctly? What irrelevant features did I overgeneralize? What critical features did I undergeneralize?
Intellectual skill— Rule:	Did I apply the procedure or concept relationships accurately and meaningfully? Did I apply the rule when it was relevant? What subordinate concepts did I overgeneralize? What subordinate concepts did I undergeneralize?
Intellectual skill— Principle:	Did I apply the concept relationships accurately and meaningfully? Did I apply the principle when it was relevant? How meaningful was my explanation or prediction? What subordinate concepts did I overgeneralize? What subordinate concepts did I undergeneralize?
Cognitive strategy:	Did I apply the strategy accurately to new situations? How well does my new product reflect the strategy? What subordinate rules, principles, or concepts did I apply incorrectly? How did the strategy enhance my learning or problem solving?

As you can see from this range of questions, informative feedback can vary considerably. Sometimes learners need confirmation that a specific response is correct or incorrect. For example, after stating the names of the thirteen original U.S. colonies from memory, learners need to know if the thirteen names they have stated match the names of the actual thirteen colonies. Either they stated them correctly or they didn't. Often, however, student responses are more complex and open-ended, requiring more elaborated feedback than simply "correct" or "incorrect." For example, after explaining and demonstrating how the nitrogen cycle operates in a forest ecosystem (application of a principle), learners will need to find out how well they applied the principle's concepts and relationships to the specific features of a forest environment—not just whether they did or didn't. Students will need to find out if they are explaining what happens in the forest ecosystem in a meaningful way—that is, in a way that demonstrates that they understand what they are talking about.

I cannot possibly tell you what kind of feedback information to convey in every learning situation. Instead, I want you to recognize that *you* can determine the basic information your learners will need by thinking carefully about the demands of the learning outcome they are to achieve, as I just illustrated. Following this analysis, you can think about the most effective ways to make that information available to your students.

■ **Delivering Feedback: Sources and Strategies**   The sources of feedback are quite varied. Any medium that has the capacity to communicate the necessary information to learners can serve effectively as a source of feedback. For example, textbooks and workbooks can communicate feedback by providing answer keys. Instructional videotapes can be designed to provide on-screen feedback after learners have made oral or written responses. Computers can be programmed to prompt students for a response, evaluate the student's response against a set of predetermined options, and then tailor the feedback information to students' needs (e.g., "Yes, you are correct," "No, try again," or "Incorrect again; return to this section for a review before you try to answer again"). Computers can easily keep records of the number of correct and incorrect answers and the time it takes for students to respond. Some computer software even has the capacity to find patterns in students' incorrect responses and communicate useful diagnostic information to them so they can correct their errors.

Probably the richest source of feedback is you, the teacher. As useful and flexible as some computer-based media are, they are no match for your ability to tailor feedback to the needs and characteristics of your individual learners. In fact, for some types of practice performances, you (or another knowledgeable person) *must* be the source of feedback. No answer key, computer program, or videotape can give adequate feedback to students on how well they have written a poem, constructed a rock collection, cooperated with others in a group, or designed an original science experiment. For some types of performances, you may choose to elaborate personally on information provided through another feedback medium. For example, after students check an answer key to find out if their responses to math exercises are correct, you may need to look at the procedures that particular students are using to help them diagnose any errors they may be making. Remember also that learners can often provide useful feedback to each other.

■ **Principles of Effective Feedback**   Rather than trying to describe all the specific forms that feedback can take, let's step back and focus on some key general principles that can guide you in designing feedback that is as effective as possible. Numerous research studies have investigated the characteristics of effective feedback. (For excellent reviews of these studies, see Bangert-Drowns et al., 1991, and Mory, 1996.) Following are several principles of effective feedback that are supported by empirical research.

FEEDBACK PRINCIPLE 1: SUPPORT LEARNER MINDFULNESS

This principle means that feedback is most effective when students process it in a meaningful way (Salomon & Globerson, 1987). All of the strategies that we identified earlier in the chapter for focusing learners on critical content features are also useful in focusing learners on feedback information. One particular way to decrease mindfulness is to allow learners to have access to corrective feedback before they make their own responses, a situation that is called *presearch availability* (Kulhavy, 1977). For example, if students can find correct answers to practice exercises in an answer key, they may simply copy the answers they find rather than engaging in their own retrieval and elaboration processes.

One excellent way to increase the amount of effort students invest in processing feedback is to make sure they find out about incorrect or inadequate responses when they think they have responded correctly. When learners experience this discrepancy (a good example of cognitive dissonance), they are more likely to think actively about the meaning of the feedback they receive (Kulhavy & Stock, 1989). This principle fits nicely with Keller's (1983, 1987) present-worth strategy for supporting relevance.

FEEDBACK PRINCIPLE 2: PROVIDE FEEDBACK AS QUICKLY AS POSSIBLE

Although some research studies have yielded conflicting results on the most effective timing of feedback, most of the empirical evidence suggests that immediate feedback, especially during the early stages of practice, is more useful to learners than delayed feedback (see Kulik & Kulik, 1988). Some research suggests that as learners gain proficiency, feedback should be increasingly delayed so that they can develop the ability to detect their own errors and apply their own guidance strategies (Schmidt, Young, Swinnen, & Shapiro, 1989).

FEEDBACK PRINCIPLE 3: PROVIDE AS MUCH INFORMATION AS POSSIBLE WITHOUT OVERLOADING LEARNERS

The complexity of the feedback to learners can vary from simply telling them they are correct or incorrect to more elaborated forms, such as informing them of the correct response (when their response is incorrect) and providing specific suggestions for improvement (Dempsey, Driscoll, & Swindell, 1993). Research evidence strongly suggests that more complex forms of feedback are more effective in supporting learning than simple right-wrong feedback (see Bangert-Drowns et al., 1991). However, just as we can overload learners' working memories with too much information during the instructional phase, we can also overload them with too much feedback information. We should control the amount of feedback information learners receive so that they can selectively perceive it and process it mindfully, focusing on the most critical aspects of the performance and not all the minute details (Sweller & Chandler, 1994).

FEEDBACK PRINCIPLE 4: USE FEEDBACK TO SUPPORT LEARNER MOTIVATION

In addition to its informative function, feedback can support learning indirectly by influencing student motivation. Feedback often influences motivation by giving students implicit cues concerning their own abilities. When feedback focuses students on their individual progress and the degree of personal effort they are expending on a learning task, they have greater incentive to continue participating in the learning process. In contrast, when feedback consistently calls attention to students' lack of ability or inferior performance in comparison to others, they may have less incentive to continue trying (Maehr & Midgley, 1991).

A teacher who says to a student, "You only missed five today—that's two fewer than yesterday. Let's look at your answers and try to figure out where you went wrong," is helping the learner to think about her own progress and suggesting that it is possible for her to find her mistakes, correct them, and learn from them. In contrast, a teacher who says, "You missed five today—that's more than anyone else in the class. Everyone else is catching on but you're still having trouble," is encouraging the learner to define his learning success (or failure) only in relation to how others perform. In this case, competition with other students may be damaging to motivation if the individual has come to believe that he does not possess the same level of ability or intelligence as others and that his ability is not likely to change in the future (Dweck, 1986).

We should be particularly careful in our use of praise feedback. Researchers have discovered that students often use praise statements to make judgments about their own abilities (see Hoska, 1993). For example, if you give learners a lot of praise after they successfully complete a relatively easy task, they may believe that you think they have low ability. If you give little praise after they successfully complete a difficult task, they may believe that you think they have high ability, diminishing the necessity of their own personal effort.

Students who are successful at a learning task will increase their expectations for continued success and then strive to meet those expectations if they attribute their success to their own level of ability or effort. Even when students are not successful, they will raise their expectations for the future if they believe the failure was caused by their own lack of effort—a factor they can control and change in the future. From the perspective of Weiner's (1979, 1985) attribution theory, we should provide feedback to learners that helps them attribute their successes and failures to appropriate causal variables. A teacher who says to a student, "I know you're doing the best you can; math is hard for you," is encouraging the student to attribute his difficulties to low math ability. This type of attribution offers little hope for future success because learners usually perceive their abilities as being relatively stable and unchanging. In contrast, a teacher who says, "You missed quite a few of these exercises, but I think it's because you waited until the last minute and then rushed through them, making careless mistakes," is encouraging the student to attribute her difficulties to her own behavior—something she can control and change. Ethnic minority students may be more likely than nonminority students to attribute their difficulties to personal effort because they often receive feedback statements that convey sympathy rather than high expectations (Graham, 1988).

As you can see, it is important to think carefully about both the content of our feedback (*what* information learners receive) and the style of delivery (*how* information is communicated). Well-designed and -delivered feedback can be an effective tool in strengthening new knowledge and encouraging learner self-efficacy and motivation. Will the new knowledge be available to learners forever into the future? Will they be able to use it flexibly and creatively in a wide variety of new situations? The answers to these questions depend on the internal and external learning processes that occur during the final learning event. Let's look at that event now.

Cueing Retrieval: Teaching for Transfer

Transfer is the ultimate goal of all classroom teaching. Teachers do not want their students to be able to retrieve and apply the knowledge they acquire only in the context of the classroom in which they learn it. **Transfer** is a general term that refers to the degree to which learners can apply their knowledge to new tasks, problems, or situations (Mayer, 1987). *Near transfer* occurs when students apply their knowledge in situations that are highly similar to the context in which the knowledge was originally acquired. For example, when students apply the algorithm for multiplying two-digit numerals on a worksheet that has twenty two-digit multiplication exercises on it, they are exhibiting near transfer of the rule.

Far transfer occurs when students apply their knowledge in new situations that are highly dissimilar to the original learning context in which it was acquired. When a girl uses the two-digit multiplication algorithm while at her grandparents' farm to determine how many linear feet of lumber will be needed to construct a fence that has fifteen 12-foot sections ($12 \times 15 = 180$), she is exhibiting far transfer of the multiplication algorithm. Notice that the girl uses the intellectual skill outside the school classroom and that she must recognize herself that the multiplication algorithm is applicable; no teacher is telling her to use it.

How do we prepare learners to engage in this type of far transfer? There are no easy answers to this question (Detterman, 1993; Larkin, 1989; Mayer, 1987). It is simply impossible to anticipate all the specific problems, tasks, and experiences our learners will encounter for the rest of their lives. That is not to say, however, that we must leave transfer to chance. Although we cannot guarantee that learners will be able to use everything they learn in the future, we can increase the probability that they will be able to use their knowledge in some new situations.

■ **Transfer for Different Learning Outcomes** Supporting learners' transfer needs depends first on understanding how the internal processing needs vary for different learning outcomes:

Learning Outcome	Internal Processes for Far Transfer
Verbal information:	Generate numerous meaningful relations between propositions and many varied schemas.
Concept:	Generate numerous meaningful relations between concept features and many varied schemas.
Rule:	Generate numerous meaningful relations between subordinate concepts and concept relationships and many varied schemas.
Principle:	Generate numerous meaningful relations between subordinate concepts and concept relationships and many varied schemas.
Cognitive strategy:	Generate numerous meaningful relations between subordinate rules, principles, and concepts and many varied schemas.

Do you see a pattern in this list of processing needs? For each outcome, the probability of far transfer depends on how well learners have generated meaningful connections between the critical content features and their own schemas. The greater the number of meaningful connections learners generate for themselves to a variety of schemas, the greater the number of retrieval routes that will be available to them in the future, a basic information processing principle that we discussed at length in Chapter 7.

■ **Effects of Situated Cognition on Transfer**   Unfortunately, rather than generating a wide variety of meaningful retrieval routes, learners usually establish a somewhat limited number of nonmeaningful retrieval cues. These cues often reflect irrelevant surface features of either the social or physical environment in which learning takes place. For example, students may understand two-digit multiplication as something to do when they are in a school classroom (physical environment) and their teacher (social environment) gives them a worksheet with exercises (physical environment) that look like this: 45 × 67 = _____, rather than linking the algorithm to a meaningful conceptual understanding of multiplication situations.

Learners always link new propositions and productions to the social and physical contexts in which they are learned. This common phenomenon is called **situated cognition** (Derry & Lesgold, 1996; Detterman, 1993; Greeno, Smith, & Moore, 1993). Unfortunately, the everyday, real-world situations in which students will eventually need to retrieve and apply their knowledge is usually very different from the classroom environment in which their knowledge is situated. Learners will have difficulty transferring their classroom-situated knowledge unless they are able to situate that knowledge in a wide variety of real-world contexts.

■ **Supporting Retention and Transfer**   How can we help learners decontextualize (or resituate) their newly learned propositions and productions? Gagne's final instructional event really is a continuation of the practice (responding) and feedback (reinforcement) events we have just reviewed. Eventually the practice opportunities we provide for learners should encourage them to cue their own retrieval of new propositions and productions in a wide variety of new contexts and situations. Let me suggest four general principles to help you achieve this goal.

RETENTION AND TRANSFER PRINCIPLE 1: HELP LEARNERS DECONTEXTUALIZE KNOWLEDGE BY PROVIDING VARIED PRACTICE AND APPLICATION OPPORTUNITIES

The best way to overcome the dangers of situated cognition is to be sure learners experience new knowledge in the widest possible range of application contexts

(Collins, Brown, & Newman, 1989; Perkins & Salomon, 1989; Salomon & Perkins, 1989). We need to design practice opportunities that demonstrate to learners how new propositions and productions are related to a wide variety of social and physical environments, as well as a wide variety of specific content domains, so they can abstract transferable schemas (Dansereau, 1995; Reed, 1993).

For example, students who are learning the rule for pronoun-antecedent agreement (see Chapter 9) can practice applying the rule in a wide variety of application contexts: story writing, report writing, letter writing, newspaper article writing, and so on. Some of the practice activities can occur at home rather than at school. The activities can be designed for paper and pencil or for computer-based communication (e.g., e-mail, Internet). Students can practice applying the rule as they write about science, social studies, mathematics, or other topics. By retrieving and using new knowledge in a wide variety of contexts that have different features, learners are more likely to break the cues that tie it exclusively to a particular subject domain or the classroom environment.

RETENTION AND TRANSFER PRINCIPLE 2: STRENGTHEN LEARNING BY PROVIDING SPACED REVIEW AND PRACTICE ACTIVITIES

Returning to newly learned knowledge regularly over a long period of time has a positive effect on retention and transfer. As we noted in earlier chapters, practice that is distributed in short segments over a long period of time is more effective than practice that is massed in one long session. Having students, for example, continue to practice the pronoun-antecedent rule (again, in varied contexts) every few weeks (perhaps in combination with other language skills) would strengthen the skill because learners would retrieve it from long-term memory and elaborate on it many times.

RETENTION AND TRANSFER PRINCIPLE 3: INCORPORATE REALISTIC DEMANDS THAT AFFECT PERFORMANCE INTO PRACTICE ACTIVITIES

As learners engage in distributed practice in varied contexts, they should begin to experience as much authenticity as possible. That is, we should design application situations that begin to approximate some of the demands and constraints that may be placed on them outside the classroom (Collins et al., 1989; De Corte, Greer, & Verschaffel, 1996). For example, rather than simply giving students sets of data for them to practice calculating various descriptive statistics (e.g., means, standard deviations), we could have them design a simple research study in which they would collect their own data to address a realistic empirical question. This type of **authentic learning activity** will help students connect their statistics skills to meaningful situations in which those skills are applicable. Other examples of realistic demands may include time constraints (especially for skills that should become automatic), competition, natural consequences, observation by others, and evaluation by others.

RETENTION AND TRANSFER PRINCIPLE 4: EMPHASIZE CONCEPTUAL UNDERSTANDING AS KNOWLEDGE IS RETRIEVED AND APPLIED

A great deal of research evidence strongly suggests that conceptual understanding is a critical key to problem solving and transfer (Mayer, 1987, 1989a, 1997b). Students are not likely to be able to transfer facts and skills that they have learned through rote memorization. Studies of experts in various content domains demonstrate that they possess extensive domain-specific knowledge that is organized around meaningful concepts and principles (Chi, Feltovich, & Glaser, 1981; Larkin, McDermott, Simon, & Simon, 1980).

Therefore, practice opportunities should encourage students to cue their own knowledge retrieval based on their conceptual classification of the situation presented to them. In other words, the practice activities we design at the cueing retrieval phase should not spell out for students exactly what propositions or productions are relevant, forcing students to attend to the relevant conceptual cues provided in the situation. If necessary, we can guide students by focusing their attention on the context features that represent the critical features of meaningful concepts, rules, or principles. Suppose, for example, that your students are refining their ability to apply the principle, *distance = rate x time,* by solving some realistic word problems that also include a variety of other mathematical formulas, equations, and operations. Your students must decide for themselves whether the "distance" principle is relevant to each situation. To guide them in making this decision, you might prompt their thinking with a set of conceptual questions:

- Is an object moving from one location to another?
- Do you know how fast the object is moving?
- Do you know how far the object is traveling?
- Do you know how much time the object spends traveling?

LET'S SUMMARIZE

Although transfer is not easy to achieve with learners, that reality should not deter us from trying to achieve it. By teaching for conceptual understanding and providing frequent, varied application opportunities over a long period of time, we can increase the probability that students will transfer their knowledge beyond the classroom walls. ". . . what is typically viewed as a failure of knowledge to transfer is actually a failure to teach the conceptual knowledge in the first place" (Bereiter, 1995, p. 28). In short, if we want students to be able to demonstrate transfer outside the classroom, we need to design numerous transfer opportunities for them inside the classroom.

A Brief Word About Summative Assessment

How does summative assessment—the process of collecting data to help us decide if learners have achieved the intended learning outcome (see Chapter 4)—fit into the sequence of instructional events we have just described? If each of the three instructional phases we have just described is critical in moving learners increasingly closer to the intended learning outcome, it makes sense to wait until all of the instructional events are completed before collecting summative assessment data.

By analogy, we wouldn't evaluate the quality of a room renovation until all the finishing touches have been completed (e.g., while installing a light fixture, I might tear the wallpaper or scratch the paint). Neither should we evaluate the quality of learning until students have had ample opportunity to profit from all of the instructional events and resources that we have designed to support their internal learning processes. This does not mean that we should wait until the very end of instruction to collect information about how learners are progressing. We should be collecting data throughout the instructional sequence to inform our decision making while teaching, a process that we referred to earlier in the book as formative assessment.

During the postinstructional phase, when learners are performing and receiving feedback, we have opportunities to collect, analyze, and use formative assessment data because students will be making outward responses that we can observe and evaluate. After using the results of formative assessment to enhance the effectiveness of our external conditions of learning, we will eventually try to answer the summative evaluation question: Did learners achieve the intended instructional goal as described by the instructional objective? When we are ready to address this question—better yet, when our learners are ready—we apply the assessment strategy described by the instructional objective.

Planning Postinstructional Events for a Verbal Information Goal

Before we conclude our discussion of instructional events, let's check in on two of our case analysis teachers as they design external events for the postinstructional phase. Before reading the following case, you should review Ms. Nelson's detailed planning in Chapter 7. Listen now as Ms. Nelson thinks out loud about her verbal information goal: *Learners will be able to state the names of the four major eras in the earth's history and several important characteristics of each.*

For the postinstructional phase, I need to give my students opportunities to practice retrieving the propositions they will have just encoded. I have a variety of practice activities for them [see Chapter 7]:

- Completing a blank cluster analysis chart with the appropriate propositions
- Playing the game "journey through time"
- Solving paleontologist problems by recalling the appropriate propositions
- Writing stories about time travel that include the target propositions
- Writing facts about each era in the appropriate column of a table (consistent with the summative assessment performance)

Because the activities take several different forms (chart, game, problem solving) and will occur in different contexts (game, paleontologist role play, story writing), they should help students link the propositions to a variety of schemas. Also, the authentic nature of the paleontologist problems and story writing should reduce the possibility that students will acquire situated propositions that are linked solely to the classroom context.

Will each of these activities give all individual students the opportunity to retrieve the target propositions and respond actively? For all but one of these activities, each student will be able to respond actively in writing. When we play the "journey through time" game, only one student on a team can respond at once. Let's see, how can I structure the game so that all students are responding to each question? I've got it! Each student will answer the question individually on a sheet of paper. Then I will call on an individual from a team to answer. If the person answers incorrectly, then I will call randomly on anyone from the other team. Although not every student will be called on each time, each one has the opportunity to respond actively to all the questions.

Now what about feedback? After students complete their cluster analysis charts individually, I will have them pair up with partners to check each other's information. The partners can refer back to their textbook or any other resources in the classroom if they need help. During the game, students will receive immediate feedback on the correctness of each response. To provide feedback on the paleontology problems, I will conduct a discussion with the whole class. It will be interesting for students to hear others' solutions to the problems and give feedback to each other on how well they think the propositions have been used. Of course, I will be available to guide the discussion if the students cannot agree among themselves. To provide feedback for the time-travel stories, I'll have students engage in peer editing. Each member of a team will identify specific facts in the other student's story and indicate whether the fact is correctly represented and makes sense within the context of the story. I will also collect, read, and provide written comments on the stories after they have been revised.

Planning Postinstructional Events for a Cognitive Strategy Goal

Now let's listen as Mr. Hoffman designs postinstructional events for his cognitive strategy instructional goal: *Learners will be able to originate concept maps for textbook chapters.* You should first review Mr. Hoffman's instructional strategy described in Chapter 9.

After students encode the basic production system for creating concept maps, they will practice the strategy a lot. In fact, they will practice regularly during the entire school year on every chapter in their social studies textbook. This spaced, distributed practice should really strengthen the strategy and enhance its transferability. To reduce the effects of situated cognition on strategy transfer, I will have students create two concept maps for chapters they are reading in subjects other than social studies. This will help them link the strategy to several subject domains and limit the possibility that they are situating the strategy within the superficial features of my particular classroom and the content of seventh-grade social studies.

Every time my students construct a concept map for a chapter, they will receive informative feedback. Students will trade maps with a partner, who will make written comments about the concepts and relations represented in the map. Then I will display a model map on the overhead projector and ask students to write several specific ways in which their maps differ from the model. Students also will receive informative feedback on the value of concept mapping. After each chapter test, students will describe how their maps helped them remember and apply ideas, relating the quality of their maps to the quality of their assessment performance.

LET'S SUMMARIZE

Ms. Nelson and Mr. Hoffman demonstrate contrasting external events for the postinstructional phase. That should not surprise you because each is focusing on a different type of learning outcome. Furthermore, each teacher's personal creativity influences the selection and design of specific external events. Both teachers' external events have the potential to be effective because they are designed with their learners' internal processing needs in mind. Now that you have an understanding of the internal and external learning events associated with the postinstructional phase, I invite you to create some of your own finishing touches in Exercise 10.3 in the *Student Exercise Guide*. Then check your achievement of the chapter's instructional goals by completing Exercise 10.4.

LOOKING BACK   LOOKING AHEAD

In this chapter, we examined a general sequence of instructional events that can help guide instructional planning. This instructional sequence is potentially effective because it is firmly grounded in the flow of cognitive processes as described by information processing theory. Every external element of the sequence is designed to support a particular internal processing need. A well-designed sequence of in-structional events should first *prepare* learners for the new information they are about to process. Then it should engage them with the information they are to learn so that they actively *construct* meaningful representations of it through the encoding process. Finally, it should provide ample opportunity for learners to *strengthen* their newly acquired representations through active practice and appli-cation experiences.

The sequence provides a good reminder to us that when we teach, we are not just doing external activities with our students. Everything we do with students in the classroom should be focused on supporting the internal processes that they need to engage in to facilitate learning. From this perspective, then, any specific teaching method, material, or activity simply becomes one possible instructional technique out of a very large number (perhaps even an infinite number) of poten-tially effective instructional techniques.

I hope you feel empowered by this approach to designing instruction. You should feel empowered to create and implement your own unique teaching meth-ods based on your firm grasp of internal learning processes. The sequence we have examined in this chapter is not intended to be applied rigidly as a magic recipe. Its potential effectiveness will be realized only as you mindfully create learning experi-ences to support your learners' internal conditions of learning and then monitor those experiences carefully to ensure that your learners are indeed engaged in the types of cognitive processes you intend.

Thus far, we have focused on principles to guide our thinking about individual instructional goals and lessons. In real classrooms, however, *design-teachers* usually plan and implement instruction for larger sets of related instructional goals. How do we plan for units of instruction? Let's take up that important question in the next chapter.

RESOURCES FOR FURTHER REFLECTION AND EXPLORATION

Print Resources

Eby, J. W., & Kujawa, E. (1994). *Reflective planning, teaching, and evaluation: K–12.* New York: Merrill.

Chapter 10 of this book, "Developing a Repertoire of Teaching Strategies," provides an excellent summary of the wide variety of specific teaching strategies available to you. The authors discuss such teaching strategies as discovery, role playing, computer-aided instruction, audio-video technology, learning centers, and many others. All of the strategies described can be in-corporated into the general instructional sequence examined in this chapter.

Hannafin, M. J., Hannafin, K. M., Hooper, S. R., Rieber, L. P., & Kini, A. S. (1996). Research on and research with emerging technologies. In D. H. Jonassen (Ed.), *Handbook of research for educational communications and tech-nology* (pp. 378–402). New York: Macmillan.

This chapter provides an extensive review of the use of computer technology to promote learning. The authors evaluate the effectiveness of computer technology and review research findings that relate to instructional se-quence variables such as orienting learners, supporting encoding, providing practice and feedback, and supporting motivation.

Keller, J. M. (1987). Development and use of the ARCS model of instructional design. *Journal of Instructional Development, 10,* 2–10.

An article in which Keller describes the basic features of his model and pre-sents the results of field testing within in-service teacher education pro-grams.

Mayer, R. E. (1997). Multimedia learning: Are we asking the right questions? *Educational Psychologist, 32,* 1–19.

An in-depth summary of individual differences and their influence on the

Richard Mayer is one of the foremost authorities on meaningful learning. In this article, he discusses strategies for using multimedia presentations to support meaningful learning of complex information such as how scientific systems work. The article is a must-read for anyone who wants to use multimedia technology in the classroom effectively.

Snow, R. E. (1997). Individual differences. In R. D. Tennyson, F. Schott, N. Seel, & S. Dijkstra (Eds.), *Instructional design: International perspectives* (Vol. 1, pp. 215–241). Mahwah, NJ: Erlbaum.

An in-depth summary of individual differences and their influence on the instructional design process. The author discusses strategies for adapting to learner differences in a variety of instructional environments.

Yelon, S. L. (1996). *Powerful principles of instruction.* White Plains, NY: Longman.

An excellent book that summarizes research-based principles of teaching that are relevant to all components of a well-designed instructional sequence. Major topics include teaching for meaningfulness, organizing essential content, supporting learner motivation, using learning aids, and providing practice.

World Wide Web Resources

http://mdk12.org/

Web site for school improvement in the state of Maryland. Follow the links to *Best Practices, Good Instruction, Project BETTER,* and *Thinking and Learning.* Here you will find numerous links to a wide variety of topics relevant to designing and sequencing instructional events: activating prior knowledge, advance organizers, inquiry approaches, intrinsic motivation, student-generated summaries, and so on. For each topic, research findings are summarized, and specific teaching suggestions are offered.

http://www.indiana.edu/~idtheory/home.html

Web site for instructional design theories operated by Charles Reigeluth, an authority on instructional design theory and practice. The site provides links to numerous topics and learning modules related to instructional design.

http://www.Learn2.com

Web site devoted to providing access to online tutorials, online courses, instructional CDs, and instructional videos. Check out the Learn2's. These are numerous online tutorials on every imaginable topic and skill such as how to wash a dog, how to brush your teeth, and preparing for a job interview. On-line courses provide learning opportunities for a variety of computer and business topics. A very interesting site that can provide lots of examples of instructional events.

11

Designing Instructional Units

love to travel. Here are a few of the places I would like to visit someday:

Boston, Massachusetts   Cape Hatteras Lighthouse, North Carolina
Outer Banks, North Carolina   Madison River, Montana
Cape Cod, Massachusetts   Grand Canyon, Colorado
Bennington, Vermont   Acadia National Park, Maine

If I had a few weeks to do nothing but travel, I would first like to see all the historical sites in Boston (see Figure 11.1, site 1). After being in a big city environment, it might be nice to head for the Outer Banks of North Carolina (site 2). Then I'd like to spend a few days on Cape Cod (site 3). Then a week of fly-fishing on the Madison River in Montana (site 4) would be fun. I'd come back to North Carolina for a visit to the Cape Hatteras Lighthouse (site 5), followed by a visit to Bennington (site 6). From Bennington, I'd head out to the Grand Canyon (site 7) and then back east to Acadia National Park in Maine (site 8).

As I look at my map, I see that my disorganized travel routes zigzag across the country. While I am in Boston, it would make more sense to visit nearby northeastern sites like Cape Cod, Bennington, and Acadia instead of traveling hundreds of miles south to the Outer Banks and then coming back to Cape Cod. While I'm out west in Montana, it would make sense to visit the Grand Canyon rather than coming all the way back east to Acadia National Park in Maine. Furthermore, all my destinations can be clustered together into three major geographic areas: Northeast,

INSTRUCTIONAL GOALS FOR CHAPTER 11

After reading and thinking about this chapter, you should be able to . . .

1. State the definition of an instructional unit, and explain several benefits of unit planning.

2. Describe and develop the major components of an instructional unit.

3. Demonstrate the interrelationships among unit topics, educational goals, instructional goals, and instructional objectives.

4. Develop organizing themes for instructional units.

5. Describe the purpose and features of a unit block plan.

6. Identify instructional resources to support instructional objectives, instructional goals, and educational goals within instructional units.

7. Develop culminating learning activities for instructional units.

8. Describe the features of thematic units, and explain their value to the curriculum.

9. Describe and apply procedures for planning thematic units.

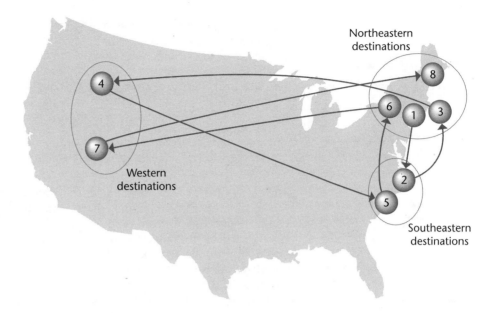

**Figure 11.1
Itinerary of a Disor-
ganized Traveler**

Southeast, and West. If I concentrate on one cluster at a time, I can use my time and resources much more efficiently. I can minimize wasted time and energy, thereby maximizing the number of sites I can visit. If I focus on one geographic area at a time, I might even be able to see more sites than I had originally planned. Identifying the three geographic areas may also help me think about the order in which to visit them. For example, I may want to visit the southeastern sites early in the summer before it gets too hot and the northeastern sites later in the summer to escape the heat.

As you can see, it is easier to reach multiple travel destinations when they are grouped together in coordinated, organized sets. Similarly, it is easier to reach multiple learning outcomes in the classroom when we group those outcomes into organized sets, or units. Classroom teachers who do not plan units of instruction may end up zigzagging through the school year, from one topic to another and from one activity to another, without thinking about how the topics and activities relate (or should relate) to one another.

In this chapter, I introduce you to the basic principles and procedures you will need to design organized units of instruction. Before continuing, examine the instructional goals that I want you to achieve through your interaction with the chapter.

A Rationale for Unit Planning

What exactly is an instructional unit? As you might guess, different curriculum experts have different answers to this question. I like the clear definition offered by Ellis, Mackey, and Glenn (1988): "A **unit** is a teaching sequence of several weeks' duration in which instruction is based on a central or organizing theme" (p. 81). Unit plans are tools that *design-teachers* use to help them think about achieving groups of related learning outcomes during particular time intervals throughout the school year. Teachers design unit plans for four reasons:

▶ To identify groups of related instructional goals

▶ To prepare appropriate resources to help their learners achieve those goals

▶ To develop appropriate sequences of instructional goals

▶ To prepare assessment procedures

Benefits of Designing Instructional Units

How does unit planning strengthen the quality of learning and instruction within a classroom? Let's address that question with a somewhat extreme nonexample. Suppose a teacher had no unit plan in mind when teaching science. On Monday, the students learn about magnets. On Tuesday, they learn about photosynthesis. On Wednesday, they make fossil molds and casts. On Thursday, they learn about animals that live in a tundra ecosystem. To end the week, they look at plant cells under a microscope.

Although each of the week's science activities may be effective in supporting a specific learning outcome, there is no discernable relationship among each of the five learning outcomes. This deficiency creates two problems. First, it is very difficult for students to elaborate deeply on verbal information and proceduralize intellectual skills with a single, isolated activity that occurs in a relatively short period of time. When teachers plan units of instruction, they can integrate daily learning activities with consistent themes and unifying ideas that help learners generate meaningful connections over a longer period of time (Posner & Rudnitsky, 1997; Van Patten, Chao, & Reigeluth, 1986).

The second problem is that these isolated learning outcomes do not support each other. The learning outcome achieved on one day does not necessarily prepare students to achieve the learning outcome scheduled for the following day. Returning to the travel analogy, suppose I wish to learn about the Revolutionary War by visiting some of New England's historical sites. After visiting sites in Boston, I should continue on to related destinations such as Lexington and Concord, Massachusetts, and Bennington, Vermont, rather than taking a long side trip to the Outer Banks of North Carolina. The Outer Banks is a fine place to visit, but it has nothing to do with my overall goal of learning about the Revolutionary War. The side trip would disrupt my flow of thought about the Revolutionary War and make it more difficult to perceive meaningful relationships among Boston, Lexington, Concord, and Bennington.

Relationships among learning outcomes are particularly critical in content domains that have well-defined skill hierarchies (Van Patten et al., 1986; Shuell, 1996). In mathematics, for example, learning to add common fractions with different denominators depends on acquiring several subskills first:

▶ Recognizing numerators and denominators

▶ Finding least common multiples

▶ Generating equivalent fractions

▶ Reducing fractions to lowest terms

Including all of these component skills within a single unit of instruction helps learners achieve the final goal of adding fractions. Imagine how difficult it would be for students if the daily sequence of mathematics outcomes were as follows: factoring numbers, identifying geometric shapes, rounding to the nearest hundred, dividing by three-digit divisors, reducing fractions to lowest terms, converting percentages to decimals, calculating the volume of a rectangular solid, and adding fractions. In this case, zigzagging randomly through the mathematics curriculum reduces learning efficiency and effectiveness because the sequence of instructional goals is not grounded in a meaningful learning hierarchy.

As you can see, planning units of instruction helps to maximize both *processing depth* and *learning structure* in the learning process. A third major benefit of unit planning is that it enhances *time management*. With a finite number of school days each year, limited time for each subject, and numerous learning goals to achieve, teachers must be effective time managers. By breaking down the school year into several unit topics and allocating several weeks to each unit, we can ensure that we will have enough time to address each important topic and its associated learning goals throughout the school year. By identifying clear instructional goals for each unit and creating an approximate timetable for achieving those goals, we ensure enough time to address the learning outcomes that we believe are important.

To summarize, instructional units are long-term planning tools that we design to maximize our short-term decision-making capabilities in the classroom. Well-designed units help teachers translate large amounts of material into daily lessons, make decisions about teaching activities, and gather potentially useful teaching materials (Muth & Alvermann, 1999). As Posner and Rudnitsky (1997) emphasize, unit plans help us make important instructional decisions within a broader, meaningful framework:

> One of the most important benefits of unit planning is that teachers have a "bigger picture" on which to base their decisions and actions. Unit plans form the bridge between the curriculum and daily lesson plans. Lesson plans should not reflect day-to-day planning but should be part of a long-term planning effort. Having thought about the unit as a whole, teachers can plan and teach with greater flexibility. Pace is more easily adjusted, "teachable moments" are more readily recognized and taken advantage of, misconceptions are more apparent, and enrichment can be better conceived. Perhaps most importantly, the themes or ideas underlying a unit can be appropriately emphasized in every lesson. (p. 122)

Major Components of Instructional Units

To realize the three major benefits of processing depth, learning structure, and time management, instructional units should incorporate several critical components (see Frazee & Rudnitski, 1995; Lorber, 1996). There is no official recipe or form that all unit plans must follow. However, to design a useful instructional unit, you should try to address the following questions as thoroughly and thoughtfully as possible:

▶ What is the *central theme or topic* of my unit?

▶ What are the broad *educational goals* to be addressed through my unit?

▶ What are the specific *instructional goals* to be addressed through my unit?

▶ What is the *essential content* that my learners will need to acquire to achieve the instructional goals?

▶ What are the broad *organizing themes* that I will use to bring unity and coherence to the set of instructional goals?

▶ What are the *instructional objectives* that I will use to assess my learners' achievement of each instructional goal?

▶ How will I *evaluate learning for the unit* as a whole?

▶ How will I *organize and sequence my instructional goals* throughout the unit?

▶ How will I *allocate time* to each instructional goal or to clusters of related instructional goals?

▶ What are the *learning activities and resources* that will help my learners achieve each instructional goal?

I certainly hope that these questions sound familiar. We have already focused extensively on instructional goals, essential content, instructional objectives, and designing learning activities. Now, in unit planning, we consider several instructional goals simultaneously in a systematic, coordinated way.

Let's take a closer look at how we can use these ten questions to guide the unit planning process.

Designing a Unit Plan

The degree of unit planning that you will engage in as a classroom teacher will vary on a continuum. At one extreme end of the continuum, you may be provided with curriculum guides, textbooks, teaching modules, or other instructional materials in which every unit component has been designed for you. Even if this is the case, you will have a better understanding of each unit's structure and rationale if you have learned how to design complete instructional units yourself. Furthermore, you will have a firm foundation of skill and confidence that you can draw on if you need to restructure or modify a unit to match your particular teaching style or the characteristics of your specific learners. At the other extreme end of the continuum, you may be provided virtually no guidance in your instructional planning, or you may be required to teach a topic for which your school has no textbook, curriculum guide, or organizing materials. In each of these situations, you will need to possess the skills and confidence necessary to plan and deliver your own instructional units.

In reality, the extreme ends of the continuum are rare. Although most schools provide a substantial degree of guidance through curriculum guides and textbooks, classroom teachers often have the autonomy and flexibility to engage in much of their own planning. Regardless of where you find yourself on the continuum, I believe that you will enhance your teaching effectiveness and bolster your professional confidence if you have the ability to design your own instructional units. Let's look now at some of the important decisions you will need to make in the unit planning process.

Selecting a Central Theme or Topic

The first step in designing an instructional unit is to identify a central theme or topic. The unit topic usually is a broad concept to which you can relate many other concepts, rules, principles, verbal information, motor skills, and attitudes. At this point, you probably will have a number of specific instructional goals, facts, skills, learning activities, and so on that you are thinking about addressing or implementing in your unit. What is the one major superordinate concept or theme that would encompass all those detailed ideas? To identify the unit topic, ask yourself this simple question: What do I want my students to learn about? Then answer the question with a single word or a brief phrase:

Question: I want my students to learn about . . .	Unit Topic
Fractions.	Fractions
Magnets.	Magnets
The use of literary devices.	Literary devices
The role of technology in society.	Society and technology
Using mnemonic strategies as study aids.	Mnemonic strategies

Individual unit topics should fit into a logical sequence of topics for the entire school year, with an estimate of the amount of time that will be needed for each, as illustrated in Table 11.1. Unit topics that appear earlier in the sequence should provide preliminary information and prerequisite skills for unit topics that appear later in the sequence. Notice in Table 11.1, for example, that units on fractions and decimals will provide many of the subordinate skills that students eventually will need for the ratio and percentage unit.

Table 11.1
Sample Sequences of Unit Topics for the School Year

	4th Grade Math	6th Grade Science	9th Grade English	2nd Grade Social Studies
1	Numeral Systems (3)	Matter (4)	Short Stories (5)	How We Learn (4)
2	Addition and Subtraction (4)	Energy (4)	Nonfiction Living Biographies (5)	Living in Communities (5)
3	Multiplication and Division (4)	Earth's Crust (5)	Nonfiction: Autobiographies (5)	Working in Communities (4)
4	Fractions (5)	Solar System (5)	Mythology (5)	Communities of Long Ago (6)
5	Geometry (4)	Weather and Climate (4)	The Novel (6)	Maps of Communities (3)
6	Decimals: Addition and Subtraction (4)	Body Systems (5)	Poetry (5)	Communities Around the World (6)
7	Decimals: Multiplication and Division (4)	Planet and Animal Reproduction (5)	Theater and Drama (5)	Our Country (4)
8	Measurement and Data Analysis (4)	Ecosystems (4)		Countries Around the World (4)
9	Ratio and Percent (4)			

Note: Numbers in parentheses represent number of weeks estimated for unit, assuming approximately 36 weeks in a typical school year.

Identifying Educational Goals and Instructional Goals

Now that you have a central unit topic to provide focus, what exactly do you want to accomplish by engaging your learners with that topic? Just as we begin the lesson planning process by identifying a clear destination, we also begin the unit planning process by determining the goals to be accomplished through the unit. Eventually, when we implement the unit, our learners will experience a collection of learning activities and materials. However, a well-designed unit must be more than a collection of activities. As Eby and Kujawa (1994) caution, the learning activities must help students achieve intended learning outcomes:

> Less reflective teachers often focus almost entirely on learning activities and materials when planning a unit. They may skip the planning of goals and outcomes in their eagerness to plan fun or practical learning activities. Their units may be nothing more than a loosely organized collection of games and worksheets, with no planned outcomes or concept development. As an evaluation, they put together a test or do a project with no real consideration for whether it measures important goals. (p. 118)

Because instructional units represent large chunks of domain-specific learning, it can be difficult to identify all of the specific instructional goals that

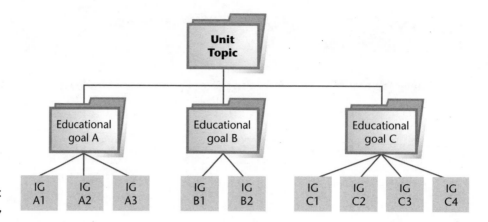

**Figure 11.2
Consistency Among Unit
Topic, Educational Goals,
and Instructional Goals
in a Unit Plan**

IG = Instructional Goal

you want your learners to achieve. Therefore, identifying broader educational goals for the unit can be a useful first step. Recall from Chapter 6 that **educational goals** describe the general characteristics that all learners should possess after a prescribed amount of time engaged with the school curriculum. The time interval could be an entire twelve-year school experience, nine months of a school year, or several weeks of an instructional unit. The educational goals we specify for a unit describe the types of general knowledge, understanding, insights, and values that learners should take with them from the entire unit. Of course, the educational goals should be consistent with the unit's content topic, as indicated in Figure 11.2. For example, here are two sets of educational goals that correspond to two unit topics in the domains of mathematics and social studies:

Mathematics	**Social Studies**
Unit Topic: Geometry	**Unit Topic: Native Americans**

Educational Goals: Learners will . . .

1. Understand and apply basic geometric concepts and principles.
2. Develop an awareness of basic geometric shapes and their properties.
3. Apply problem-solving strategies.
4. Appreciate the value of geometry in everyday life.

Educational Goals: Learners will . . .

1. Understand why European explorers were not the first "Americans."
2. Understand the origins of Native American people.
3. Increase their appreciation for cultural diversity in the United States.
4. Understand and value the common characteristics that all humans share.
5. Understand how environmental conditions influence cultural characteristics.
6. Appreciate the advanced societies developed by some Native American groups.

Some of the educational goals that you specify will be unit-level goals, and others will be curriculum-level goals. **Unit-level educational goals** are those that are closely related to the unit topic and are most likely to be addressed within that particular unit. For example, *Understand and apply basic geometric* *concepts and principles* is a goal that you would address primarily in the context of a geometry unit rather than other mathematics units such as place value, fractions, and decimals. Similarly, *Understand the origins of Native American people* is a goal that would be best achieved in the context of a social studies unit on Native Americans rather than other unit topics such as the U.S. Civil War, South American cultures, or world religions.

In contrast, **curriculum-level educational goals** are those that transcend specific unit topics. They are broad enough to generalize to a wide variety of unit topics and content domains. For example, *Apply problem-solving strategies* is a broad goal that you could emphasize in a variety of mathematics units—not just geometry. Furthermore, you may even be able to support this educational goal in the context of science or social studies units. Similarly, *Increase appreciation for cultural diversity in the United States* is a goal that you could address throughout the entire social studies curriculum—not just in a unit on Native Americans.

Specifying both unit-level and curriculum-level goals is important at the beginning of the unit planning process. Unit-level goals help provide focus for the particular domain-specific learning outcomes you want your learners to achieve. Curriculum-level goals help ensure that your unit is contributing significantly to the broader school curriculum. Furthermore, they will provide a means for helping learners see connections among different content domains and unit topics.

After you identify your unit's educational goals, you can begin to transform them into instructional goals. As illustrated in Figure 11.2, each instructional goal should represent a learned capability that is clearly related to one or more educational goals. You will need to use your professional judgment to establish the relationships between your educational and instructional goals. To help with the process, ask yourself the following question: If my learners acquire a specific learned capability (i.e., achieve a particular instructional goal), will they be closer to possessing the characteristic described by the educational goal? If the answer is yes, the instructional goal probably is valid for the educational goal. Let's look at an example. For the educational goal, *Understand and apply basic geometric concepts and principles,* which of the following learned capabilities do you think would be relevant?

1. State the definitions of line, point, line segment, ray, and angle.
2. Identify examples of lines, points, line segments, rays, and angles.
3. Recognize parallel and perpendicular lines.
4. Measure acute and obtuse angles with a protractor.
5. Name vocations and careers in which geometry skills are useful.
6. Prove that the line that bisects the angle formed by the two equal sides in an isosceles triangle is perpendicular to the third side of the triangle.

The first four instructional goals are clearly relevant to the educational goal because the content of each goal represents some understanding or application of a basic geometric concept or principle. What about the last two goals? The fifth goal has nothing to do with basic geometric concepts and principles. It is quite possible for students to name some vocations and careers that draw on geometry skills without being able to apply any basic geometry skills themselves. Should this instructional goal be removed from the unit? Not necessarily. The goal may be quite appropriate for the unit; it just doesn't fit into the unit in the context of this particular *educational* goal. It seems to be related more closely to the fourth geometry goal, *Appreciate the value of geometry in everyday life.* The sixth instructional goal is a judgment call. Although the content clearly represents understanding and application of geometry, the principle to be applied does not appear to be basic for a fourth-grade level. This goal may be more appropriate for a geometry unit in a middle school or high school mathematics class.

How do we identify the set of potential instructional goals to consider for each educational goal? Teachers often find it useful to apply a webbing or concept-mapping process to help brainstorm learned capabilities (see Martinello & Cook, 1994). Begin thinking about topics that you can cluster meaningfully within each of your educational goals. Then record your thinking on a large sheet of paper, using connecting lines to show how subtopics are related to educational goals and to each other, as I have demonstrated for you in Figure 11.3.

Notice that this thinking process produces a diagram that looks like a web or concept map. You can use your web as a heuristic tool to make yourself aware of all the possible subtopics that are related to your unit's central theme. Seeing this big picture should help you decide which subtopics to include and which to exclude so that the unit is manageable for the amount of time you have designated for it. Of course, for the subtopics you do decide to include in your unit, you will need to write clear instructional goals that are appropriate for the particular learning outcomes you have in mind, as I have illustrated in Figure 11.3. Now try Exercise 11.1 in the *Student Exercise Guide*, an opportunity to practice developing instructional goals that are valid for educational goals.

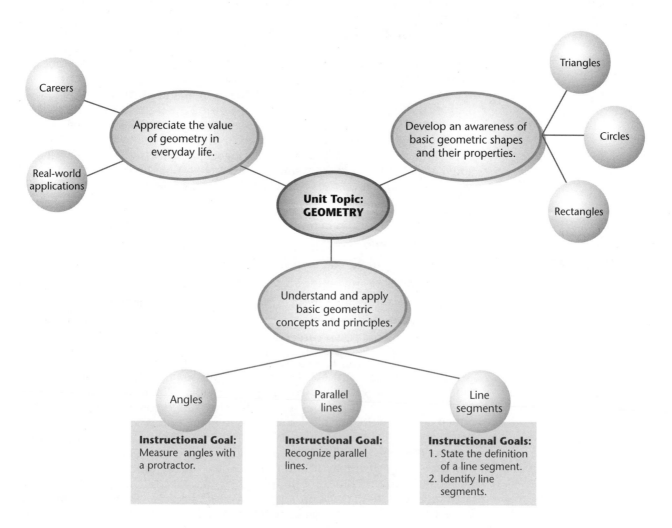

Figure 11.3
Using Concept Mapping to Identify Potential Instructional Goals

Identifying Organizing Themes

Our primary concern in planning an instructional unit is to develop learning opportunities that our students can experience as a coherent, unified, interconnected whole. We can develop our students' abilities to perceive, understand, and appreciate this coherence by identifying and communicating major organizing themes that tie different subtopics and instructional goals together. An **organizing unit theme** is a very broad generalization that can be related to a wide variety of specific declarative, procedural, or affective content knowledge.

Let me share with you an example of an organizing theme from my own teaching. The central topic of one of the units in my Educational Psychology class is "learner characteristics and individual differences." I try to bring coherence to the unit by using the following organizing theme: *Human traits and abilities are always a product of a complex interaction between our biological makeup (our nature) and our experiences with the environment (our nurture).* To establish this theme, I begin the unit with a videotape that presents compelling research evidence for both sides of the famous nature versus nurture debate, and I present the results of twin studies that illustrate the effects of both nature and nurture on individual differences.

For the remainder of the unit, we examine such subtopics as aptitude by treatment interactions, principles of physical growth and development, cognitive development, personal and social development, and exceptionalities. As we work on the instructional goals for each of these subtopics, I constantly point out how the subtopics relate to the nature-nurture issue. Thus, each subtopic becomes a vehicle for achieving specific instructional goals as well as an opportunity to illustrate, apply, and explore the organizing theme. Although I already have developed the unit's subtopics and instructional goals to fit together, the organizing theme helps students perceive that coherence more readily. In Exercise 11.2 in the *Student Exercise Guide,* you will find opportunities to develop organizing themes for unit topics and sets of instructional goals.

Selecting and Analyzing Essential Content

A critical part of any unit plan is determining the content that learners will need to acquire. What are the actual propositions, concepts, rules, principles, cognitive strategies, motor skills, and attitudes that students must learn so that they will be able to demonstrate the unit's instructional goals? The procedures for identifying and analyzing essential content are exactly the same as those described in our discussion of content analysis (see Chapter 3). The only difference is that you are now determining the content for multiple instructional goals rather than a single goal. The results of each content analysis provide further information for you in determining the unit's goal structure. The instructional goals that you have identified thus far are simply preliminary goals. Your content analyses probably will reveal additional instructional goals that you should include in the unit.

For example, when you study the results of your hierarchical analyses, you may notice one or more subordinate skills that your learners do not yet possess or for which you believe they will need some review. Similarly, your procedural analyses may yield one or more component skills that you had previously neglected. You should write additional instructional goals for these subordinate skills and plan to include them in the unit. Sometimes the same prerequisite skill reappears in several different hierarchical analyses. When this happens, it may suggest to you that the skill is an important basic skill that helps to lay a solid foundation for many of the unit's higher-level instructional goals. Therefore, if your learners have not yet acquired the skill, you should include it as an instructional goal in the unit plan, and you should plan to place your instruction for it early in the unit.

When you develop a cluster analysis for verbal information, you need to induce a set of superordinate concepts to organize groups of specific propositions. Sometimes the superordinate concepts are already familiar to learners and do not need to be taught to them. If, however, the organizing concepts are relatively new to your students, you should write instructional goals for them and include them in the unit. Recall the cluster analysis that we created in Chapter 3 for skeletal muscles. We induced four superordinate concepts to help organize clusters of muscle names: flexor, extensor, abductor, and adductor (see Table 3.3). Before these concepts can function as meaningful organizers, learners must understand them. If students do not already understand these concepts, then we should write instructional goals for them (e.g., *Learners will be able to classify muscles as flexors, extensors, abductors, and adductors*) and include the goals in the unit. Now when students learn about muscle names, they will have at least two instructional goals to achieve:

1. The *procedural* knowledge necessary to identify four major types of muscles.
2. The *declarative* knowledge necessary to state specific muscle names.

Determining the essential content and instructional goals for a unit is a messy, nonlinear, unpredictable thinking process that takes time, effort, and perseverance. You should not expect to be able to accomplish this aspect of unit planning by following a prescribed recipe or applying a simple algorithm. The process requires your understanding of the learning outcomes described in Chapter 2, thorough application of the content analysis tools described in Chapter 3, and, above all, careful professional judgment.

The result of your thinking should be a unit goal structure that resembles the general form illustrated in Figure 11.4. Notice that each of the four preliminary instructional goals (A1, A2, B1, B2) is clearly referenced to two broader educational goals (A and B). For each instructional goal, we identify the primary content that students need to acquire. For instructional goal A1, learners need to acquire a principle; for goal A2, they need to acquire a set of propositions; for goal B1, a concept, and for goal B2, a rule. The content analyses for these four instructional goals yield four additional instructional goals to include in the unit. For example, the hierarchical analysis for the principle (goal A1) produced an important subordinate concept that learners do not yet possess. The subordinate concept is represented by the additional instructional goal A1.1. As a result of the thinking process illustrated in Figure 11.4, the unit now has two educational goals and eight instructional goals rather than just four.

Preparing Assessment Procedures

Now that you have clearly specified all of your instructional goals for the unit, you need to plan for assessment. How will you eventually collect assessment data to evaluate your learners' success in achieving the instructional goals? Thus, for each instructional goal, you need to write a precise instructional objective that thoroughly describes learner performance, the context of the performance, and the expected quality of the performance (see Chapter 6). You should be able to trace each of your unit's objectives back to one of your instructional goals, as illustrated in Figure 11.4. Often, however, it makes sense to combine two or more instructional goals into a single objective for the purpose of assessment. For example, here are two closely related instructional goals:

▶ *Learners will identify metaphors.*

▶ *Learners will identify similes.*

Because these learning outcomes are so closely related, we may choose to assess them simultaneously. Furthermore, assessing for the two concepts together will help us find out if learners are likely to confuse the two types of figures of speech. Here is a single objective that combines the two instructional goals:

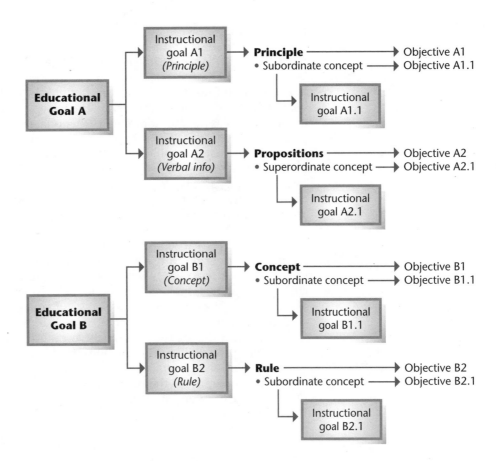

Figure 11.4
Unit Plan Structure:
Goals, Content,
Objectives

▶ *Learners will be provided with a short story that contains five metaphors and five similes. Learners will demonstrate the ability to identify metaphors and similes by writing specific examples on a sheet of paper. The sheet of paper will be organized in two columns, labeled "metaphors" and "similes." Learners must place nine of the ten metaphors and similes in the appropriate column to demonstrate mastery of the concepts.*

Notice that the objective clearly relates to and is equally valid for both instructional goals. Combining too many instructional goals for assessment can be dangerous because the performance we describe may be less valid for one or more of the goals. Furthermore, reliability may suffer because we may have to decrease the number of performance opportunities to compensate for the larger number of goals to evaluate. If you do combine two or more instructional goals in a single objective, make sure that you do not sacrifice the validity or reliability of your assessment data.

When you begin teaching your unit, you will engage in summative assessment by implementing the data collection strategies described by your instructional objectives. Assessment will proceed as your instruction proceeds. However, it is also useful to build an additional form of assessment into the unit. **Unit-level assessment** is a data collection process implemented at the conclusion of the unit. The purpose of unit-level assessment (often referred to as a unit test) is to provide a final check on the learning that should have occurred through the entire unit. Therefore, the test items should represent as many of the unit's instructional goals as possible.

Testing for multiple instructional goals creates three sticky problems. First, we need to ensure that all of the instructional goals are indeed *represented* in the unit test. The best approach to this problem is to create an assessment blueprint or table of specifications that shows each instructional goal to be addressed by the test and the number of items that will be allocated to each goal (see Chapter 4). Second, *reliability* for each instructional goal will be threatened because we will have to use a small number of items for each goal. Imagine the length of a unit test if we try to use 10 items for each of, say, 15 instructional goals, which would mean 150 items! The general principle here is to try to use as many items as possible for each instructional goal while keeping the test to a manageable length. The third problem is a threat to *validity*. Because a unit's instructional goals probably will reflect a variety of learning outcomes, it may be impossible to use a single test format to assess validly for all of them. Some instructional goals may lend themselves better to a paper-and-pencil cognitive format, whereas other goals may require a performance format (see Chapter 5). To solve this problem, we may need to consider developing two or more subtests: one with cognitive items and the other with performance items.

Unit projects can sometimes be used as unit-level performance assessments. If you decide to use a project for the purpose of performance assessment, however, you need to design the project so that it clearly addresses a specific set of instructional goals to protect assessment validity. If you decide to use a group project for performance assessment, you need to design it so that you will be able to collect evidence of each individual learner's performance consistent with the instructional goals you want to be able to evaluate.

Despite the validity and reliability problems with unit-level assessment, unit tests can serve several useful functions. The data they yield can provide further confirmation of the data that you already have collected through the summative assessment strategies described by your instructional objectives. The data also can provide a general sense of the effectiveness of the instructional strategies you have used throughout the unit. Because the unit test occurs some time after instruction for specific instructional goals and the summative assessment described by the objectives, the data may provide a better sense of what learning outcomes students have really retained. By preparing for the unit test and participating in it, learners are provided with yet another opportunity to engage with the material through opportunities for elaborative, spaced review (Dempster, 1991). Finally, unit tests may serve a motivational function for students. When learners know that they eventually will be tested, they tend to process information more effectively and learn more (Doyle, 1983; Paris, Lawton, Turner, & Roth, 1991). Thus, in addition to helping teachers make important evaluative decisions, testing actually seems to help promote learning.

Sequencing Goals and Allocating Time

Up to this point, we have focused primarily on decisions related to establishing clear destinations and assessment strategies for units. Now we need to turn our attention to two practical questions:

1. In what order will we address the unit's instructional goals?
2. How will we fit all the goals into the time allotted for the unit?

Clustering Instructional Goals   Within the unit itself, we want to make sure that we group and sequence instructional goals in a meaningful way. Whereas instructional units prevent us from zigzagging randomly across the curriculum, goal clustering and sequencing prevent us from zigzagging randomly within each unit. **Goal clustering** refers to grouping instructional goals together on the basis of shared features or useful teaching-learning relationships. In a sense, goal clustering produces several "subunits" within the unit. Posner and Rudnitsky (1997) suggest five possible categories that we can use to cluster instructional goals: world related, concept related, inquiry related, learning related, and utilization related.

World-related clustering is based on the temporal (time), spatial, and physical similarities that objects, ideas, and events share. For example, *Calculate the area of a rectangle* and *Calculate the area of a square* (a special type of rectangle), two mathematics instructional goals, could be clustered together on a world-related basis because rectangles and squares have many physical similarities. Furthermore, the area of a square is spatially very similar to the area of a nonsquare rectangle. We can use *concept-related clustering* to group instructional goals that reflect subordinate and superordinate concept relationships. For example, within a science unit on geology, we could cluster the goals, *Identify limestone*, *Recognize sandstone*, and *Identify shale*, because limestone, sandstone, and shale are all examples of a broader superordinate concept—sedimentary rocks.

Inquiry-related clustering is based on the processes that humans use to produce knowledge: observing, theorizing, hypothesizing, analyzing data, and drawing conclusions. A science teacher might cluster instructional goals such as *Apply the energy pyramid to a pond ecosystem* and *Demonstrate how food webs operate within a pond ecosystem* because data collection and analysis learning activities could be used to engage students with the relevant skills. Students could take a field trip to a pond, where they collect data relevant to each instructional goal. Back in the classroom, the teacher helps students analyze their data and induce the target principles (energy pyramid, food webs). While students are learning principles related to ecosystems, they are also learning to think like scientists.

When clustering goals on a *learning-related* basis, we search for characteristics of the goals that may influence the quality of student learning. For example, Posner and Rudnitsky suggest we consider learning-related variables such as prior familiarity, interest, content difficulty, and prerequisites. In most cases, clustering on the basis of familiarity, interest, and content difficulty is not easy because students usually vary quite a bit with respect to these variables. Furthermore, these variables typically influence learning indirectly rather than directly. Prerequisites, however, can have a direct and powerful impact on learning (a principle that educational psychologists have known about for quite a long time), particularly in hierarchically structured domains such as mathematics, English grammar, foreign languages, and psychomotor skills (Gagne & Paradise, 1962; White & Gagne, 1974, 1978; Ragan & Smith, 1996).

The most useful tools for learning-related clustering are hierarchical content analysis diagrams (see Chapter 3). If we see from a hierarchical analysis diagram that a major skill in the unit depends on three prerequisite subordinate skills, then we may wish to cluster those three subordinate skills together for the purpose of instruction. Clustering the three subordinate skills may be even more critical to student learning if we see that they are prerequisites for other higher-level skills in the unit. For example, the instructional goals *Identify numerators and denominators*, *Generate equivalent fractions*, and *Reduce fractions to lowest terms* all represent skills that are prerequisite to the higher-level skill of adding common fractions with unequal denominators. Therefore, we can support student learning by clustering them together and sequencing them *before* the higher-level skill for which they are prerequisites.

The final clustering category, *utilization related*, reflects how learners are likely to use the content they acquire in the future. If a set of instructional goals represents a procedure in the form of a rule, cognitive strategy, or motor skill, then those goals probably should be grouped together for teaching. Of course, our procedural content analysis diagrams will be helpful in identifying such sets of instructional goals. For example, in a high school unit on personal finance, we may identify major steps in a procedure to plan a personal budget. Clustering the instructional goals for each of these steps would make sense because someday, in real time, students will implement the steps in an integrated way.

I must emphasize here that goal clustering is a *thinking* process. Posner and Rudnitsky's five clustering categories are simply conceptual tools that may help you think more clearly about how your unit's instructional goals may be related to each other. If, in the process of goal clustering, you can create alternative organizational categories that you believe will support your teaching, you should go ahead and use them. The primary goal is to organize and sequence the unit's instructional goals in ways that eventually will help you teach and your students learn.

■ **Developing a Block Plan**   As an additional thinking strategy, teachers often find it useful to create a road map for the unit by creating a block plan (Ellis et al., 1988). A unit **block plan** is a simple chart that shows the day-to-day sequence of instructional goals and the approximate amount of time that you plan to allocate to each one. Look at the sample block plan provided in Table 11.2. Notice that the unit is expected to take approximately five weeks to teach. During this time period, the teacher will provide instruction designed for five clusters of instructional goals (A–E). Each cell in the block plan indicates the specific instructional goal (or goals) to be addressed on a particular day, with an accompanying estimate of the amount of time that will be needed.

Table 11.2
Structure of a Unit Block Plan

Monday	Tuesday	Wednesday	Thursday	Friday
1 Introduction: Organizing Theme (45)	2 **Cluster A** Goal A-1 (45)	3 **Cluster A** Goal A-2 (45)	4 **Cluster A** Goal A-2 (45)	5 **Cluster A** Goal A-3 (45)
6 **Cluster B** Goals B-1, B-2 (45)	7 **Cluster B** Goals B-3, B-4 (45)	8 **Cluster B** Goal B-5 (15) Goal B-6 (30)	9 **Cluster C** Goal C-1 (45)	10 **Cluster C** Goal C-2 (45)
11 **Cluster C** Goal C-3 (45)	12 **Cluster C** Goal C-3 (45)	13 **Cluster C** Goal C-3 (15) Goal C-4 (30)	14 **Cluster C** Goal C-4 (45)	15 **Cluster C** Goal C-4 (45)
16 **Cluster D** Goal D-1 (45)	17 **Cluster D** Goal D-2 (45)	18 **Cluster D** Goal D-3 (45)	19 **Cluster E** Goal E-1 (45)	20 **Cluster E** Goal E-2 (45)
21 **Cluster E** Goal E-2 (45)	22 Culminating Activity (45)	23 Culminating Activity (45)	24 Culminating Activity (45)	25 Unit Review (45)
26 End-of-Unit Assessment (60)				

Note: Numbers in parentheses indicate number of minutes estimated for instruction.

How should you allocate time to instructional goals? Estimating the amount of time that your instructional events require is an ability that you will acquire with experience. Even after many years of teaching, I am often surprised at how badly I have underestimated or overestimated the amount of time an activity will take in the classroom. As you gain that experience, also keep in mind the following factors when you estimate instructional time:

▶ Learners need adequate time for meaningful elaboration.

▶ Learners need adequate time to proceduralize knowledge.

▶ Learners need adequate time for assessment.

By creating a block plan, you force yourself to make tentative decisions about the instructional goals to include in the unit, how you will sequence the goals, and how much instructional time you will allocate to each. The block plan then provides a general planning structure that you can use to create detailed lesson plans for the instructional goals. You should not view a block plan as a rigid, inflexible daily sequence that constrains you, but rather as a fluid, dynamic structure that enhances your instructional decision making.

Selecting Learning Activities and Resources

The final consideration in designing a unit plan is how to facilitate learning that is consistent with the instructional goals and objectives. Eventually you will design detailed instructional strategies that include descriptions of specific external learning events. At this point, however, you can simply describe activities, materials, and resources that you believe may be useful for each instructional goal. When you are ready to design detailed lesson plans, you will have a large collection of possible resources from which to draw.

What types of instructional events should you collect for this part of the unit plan? You should try to identify any resources that you believe will support learning. Some of the resources you identify will be learning activities such as games, demonstrations, simulations, discussions, projects, field trips, role playing, and practice opportunities. Some resources will be learning materials such as books, workbooks, magazines, handouts, concrete manipulatives, equipment, posters, films, videotapes, computer software, audio recordings, and guest speakers. You can find learning activities and materials in a wide variety of sources: teacher editions of textbooks, media catalogs, Internet web sites, libraries, popular magazines for adults and children, activity books for teachers, conversations with other teachers, workshops, conferences, and so on. Remember also that *you* are a rich source of instructional resources. You have the knowledge and ability to create ideas for your own learning activities and materials.

■ **Organizing Instructional Resources** As you identify various instructional resources, you should organize them according to the instructional goals and objectives they are likely to support. I suggest you use a format similar to the one provided in Table 11.3. This format encourages you to think in advance about how you intend to use your instructional resources to promote learning. This does not mean that you cannot change your mind later. It simply helps to ensure that you are developing instructional resources to help achieve your intended learning outcomes, rather than just creating a list of activities and materials that may be related in some way to your unit topic. The format ensures some degree of internal consistency and coherence among your instructional goals, objectives, and resources.

The planning format in Table 11.3 also encourages you to think about the specific role your resources may play in the skill-learning process. For skill acquisition instructional goals, you should classify your learning activities and materials according to the specific stage of skill learning they would support (see Chapter 8 for a review). For example, a classroom demonstration activity may work well for the cognitive stage of skill learning; a fast-paced game may help support the autonomous stage. By preclassifying your resources according to these three stages, you can (1) ensure that you have identified enough activities and materials to support all the critical stages of skill learning and (2) readily incorporate them into the detailed lesson plans that you will design later. If your instructional goal represents a verbal information learning outcome, then your resources would fit into the cognitive level.

■ **Planning Culminating Activities**   As you identify instructional resources, you may also want to try to develop one or more culminating activities for the unit. A **culminating activity** is a learning activity that gives students the opportunity to apply all (or many) of the capabilities they have acquired in an integrated way. Culminating activities cap off a unit by giving students a chance to use their newly learned capabilities in the context of complex, meaningful, and authentic tasks (Zemelman, Daniels, & Hyde, 1998). Notice in our sample block plan (Table 11.2) that three class sessions (22, 23, and 24) are devoted to a culminating activity to end the unit.

Culminating activities encourage learners to elaborate further on newly acquired verbal information and intellectual skills, creating additional links within and between different schemas in long-term memory. They also help students situate their learning in authentic contexts and tasks, thus enhancing future transfer (Collins, 1991; Resnick, 1987). For example, a culminating activity for a science unit on plant and animal classification could be a class trip to a zoo and botanical garden. Students could work together in teams to find examples of specific plant and animal classes. As a culminating activity for a social studies unit on the U.S. federal government, you could organize the class into the three branches of government and have them function appropriately to handle classroom issues.

With some creativity, ambition, and careful planning on your part, you can design one or more culminating activities for nearly any unit topic. Re-

Culminating activities give students realistic, integrated opportunities to apply the facts, skills, and attitudes they have acquired in an instructional unit.

Table 11.3
A Suggested Format for Organizing Instructional Resources in a Unit Plan

Grade	Subject	Unit Topic
Instructional Goal:	*What is the learned capability students should be able to <u>demonstrate</u> following instruction?*	
Instructional Objective:	*How will students demonstrate the learned capability for the purpose of <u>assessment</u>?*	
Instructional Resources:	*What are the learning activities and materials that may help students <u>achieve</u> the instructional goal (as assessed by the instructional objective)?*	
Cognitive Stage:	1. 2. 3. 4. 5.	
Associative Stage:	1. 2. 3. 4. 5.	
Autonomous Stage:	1. 2. 3. 4. 5.	

member, however, that a culminating activity is not just an interesting project related in some tangential way to the unit topic. To function as effective *learning* experiences, culminating activities need to give students opportunities to apply the capabilities that are expressed in your instructional goals.

LET'S SUMMARIZE

In this section, we have examined a set of decisions, procedures, and thinking processes that can help us design units of instruction. Well-designed unit plans are thinking tools that help us integrate content, goals, assessments, and instructional resources. They put us in the best possible position to design detailed lesson plans, and they help to ensure that we don't try to travel from Boston to North Carolina by way of Montana!

Now that you have a basic orientation to unit planning processes, let's look into Ms. Nelson's fifth-grade classroom as she develops her science unit on geology.

CASE ANALYSIS

Unit Planning in the Classroom

Throughout this book, we have been observing Ms. Nelson as she implements each aspect of the instructional design process. In our final case analysis, we will watch as she designs a science unit by applying the processes described in the preceding section. Let's listen in as she thinks aloud.

Selecting a Central Theme or Topic

As a result of teaching my unit, I want my students to learn about geology, so that's the topic of my unit. More specifically, I want my students to learn about rocks, minerals, fossils, and the earth's geologic history. Through each of these subtopics, I want my fifth graders to understand that our earth is a dynamic, changing planet. I want them to understand that the solid components of our earth can help tell the story of how the earth has changed over time. To convey this theme, I'll give my unit a catchy title: *Geology: The Stories Rocks Tell.*

Identifying Educational Goals and Preliminary Instructional Goals

Now that I have a topic focus, what are the educational goals that I want to achieve through that topic? Here are several: Learners will . . .

1. Understand how the earth's plant and animal life has changed over time as a result of changing geologic conditions.
2. Understand the processes that form rocks and minerals.
3. Understand how rocks and minerals are related to each other.
4. Be familiar with common rocks, minerals, and fossils.
5. Understand how fossils reveal earth changes.
6. Value the earth as a dynamic, complex, changing place.
7. Develop scientific research skills.

It looks as if my first six goals are unit-level educational goals because they are very closely related to the unit topic, *Geology: Stories Rocks Tell.* The last goal, however, is a curriculum-level goal because I am working on it throughout the entire school year across the entire fifth-grade science curriculum. As we study each science unit topic this year, I will be trying to develop students' scientific research and thinking skills.

All of my educational goals are helpful because they point me in some general directions. However, they are much too broad to guide my classroom instruction. So what will my instructional goals be? To ensure that I move students toward the seven educational goals, I need to make sure that each of my instructional goals is clearly related to one or more of my educational goals. To help me in this thinking process, I'll develop a chart that shows each educational goal and its corresponding instructional goals [see Table 11.4].

Identifying Organizing Themes   Although I have identified seventeen preliminary instructional goals, I want my students to experience the unit as a unified whole. As we work on each instructional goal, I want students to be thinking about how the earth is a constantly changing place. I also want them to see how rocks, minerals, and fossils tell the story of how the earth has changed over time. I will try to use each lesson to illustrate one or both of these generalizations in addition to using each lesson to help students achieve specific instructional goals. These ideas will become my primary organizing themes for the unit:

- Earth is a constantly changing place.
- Rocks, minerals, and fossils tell stories of how the earth has changed over time.

Selecting and Analyzing Essential Content

Now what content will I expect my students to acquire? I can address that question by analyzing each of the seventeen preliminary instructional goals. Each instructional goal describes content that learners need to acquire. By using cluster analysis, procedural analysis, and hierarchical analysis, I can organize that content and break it down into subordinate prerequisite skills. For example, I'll perform a cluster analysis for the verbal information goals, 1a and 1b [see Table 3.5] and a hierarchical analysis for the intellectual skill goal, 2d [see Figure 3.12].

Do these analyses suggest any additional instructional goals for the unit? The cluster analysis did not yield any superordinate concepts that students will need to learn because I believe they already understand the basic concepts of beginning time, time period, earth features, plant life, and animal life sufficiently well to use them to help organize the verbal information they need to acquire. On the other hand, my hierarchical analysis of the cooling rate principle produced two subordinate concepts that I believe are important for students to learn before they can apply the cooling rate principle: mineral and crystal. Therefore, I'll write two additional instructional goals representing these concepts and label them to show how they are related to instructional goal 2d:

- *Learners will classify substances as minerals* (instructional goal 2d.1).
- *Learners will classify solids as crystals* (instructional goal 2d.2).

Of course, I should also analyze the content for these two new instructional goals. [For a hierarchical analysis of the concept of crystal, see Figure 3.13.] As I study the diagram, I notice three major prerequisite concepts: (1) identify surfaces, (2) identify three-dimensional solids, and (3) identify angles. I believe my students already possess these skills because we addressed them earlier in a geometry unit. So although I'll emphasize these subordinate concepts when I teach the concept of *crystal*, I'm not going to create any additional instructional goals for them.

Table 11.4
Educational Goals and Preliminary Instructional Goals for a Unit Plan

Educational Goals	*Instructional Goals*
1. Understand how the earth's plant and animal life has changed over time as a result of changing geologic conditions.	1a. State the names of the four major eras in the earth's history and several important characteristics of each. (verbal information) 1b. Describe the plant and animal life associated with each of the four geologic eras. (verbal information) 1c. Demonstrate how earth's geologic features influence plant and animal life. (principle)
2. Understand the processes that form rocks and minerals.	2a. Explain how sedimentary, igneous, and metamorphic rocks are formed. (verbal information) 2b. Identify examples of sedimentary, igneous and metamorphic rocks. (concepts) 2c. Identify common shapes of mineral crystals. (concepts) 2d. Demonstrate how the rate of cooling influences the size of a mineral crystal. (principle)
3. Understand how rocks and minerals are related to each other.	3a. State the names of minerals that are found in common sedimentary, igneous, and metamorphic rocks. (verbal information) 3b. Apply the rock cycle. (principle)
4. Be familiar with common rocks, minerals, and fossils.	4a. State the three types of rock and describe how each is formed. (verbal information) 4b. Identify examples of limestone, sandstone, shale, granite, pumice, slate, and schist. (concepts) 4c. Identify examples of quartz, azurite, garnet, feldspar, and mica. (concepts) 4d. Identify examples of brachiopods, gastropods, crinoids, and trilobites. (concepts)
5. Understand how fossils reveal earth changes.	5a. Demonstrate how fossils are formed in sedimentary rock. (principle) 5b. Describe the conditions under which common fossils were formed. (verbal information)
6. Value the earth as a dynamic, complex, changing place.	All instructional goals.
7. Develop scientific research skills. Observation: Experimentation:	7a. Classify rocks, minerals, and fossils. (concepts) 7b. Design an experiment to test the strengths of sedimentary, igneous, and metamorphic rocks. (cognitive strategy)

Preparing Assessment Procedures

As part of my instruction for each of the unit's instructional goals, I'll need a summative assessment strategy. So I need to write an instructional objective that is valid for each instructional goal. Here, for example, are three of my instructional objectives, with each clearly referenced to its corresponding instructional goal [from Table 11.4]:

- *Instructional Objective for Instructional Goals 1a and 1b:* Learners will be provided with an organizational chart that has four columns with a blank line at the top of each column. Beneath the chart will be twenty-five facts, lettered *a* through *y*. Sixteen of the facts will be characteristics of the four major eras in the earth's history, with four facts corresponding to each of the four eras. The remaining nine facts will not correspond to any of the four eras. Learners will state the names of the four major eras in the earth's history by writing each of them at the top of the four columns. Learners will state important characteristics of each era by writing the letters of the facts in each of the appropriate columns. All four era names must be written on the blank lines, but the names do not need to be spelled perfectly. The letters of fourteen of the sixteen characteristics must be placed in the correct columns. The letters of no more than two of the nine distracters can be placed in a column.

- *Instructional Objective for Instructional Goal 2b:* Given a set of fifteen rock samples that have not been used during instruction (four metamorphic, five igneous, six sedimentary) and three containers labeled according to the three rock categories, learners will demonstrate the ability to identify sedimentary, igneous, and metamorphic rocks by sorting the rocks into the three labeled containers. To demonstrate mastery, learners must place twelve of the fifteen rocks in the correct container.

- *Instructional Objective for Instructional Goal 2d:* Given three written problem scenarios about crystal growth, learners will demonstrate how the rate of cooling influences the size of a mineral crystal by writing predictions and explanations that are consistent with the cooling rate principle. Each of the three written responses must (1) describe specific actions to be taken in the problem scenario, (2) demonstrate clear relationships among actions and cooling rates, and (3) accurately predict crystal size.

In addition to all of my instructional objectives, I should have an end-of-unit assessment that focuses on as many of the instructional goals as possible. To guide my preparation of the unit test and enhance assessment validity, I'll first prepare a test blueprint [see Chapter 4] that shows how I will allocate test items to each of the instructional goals [see Table 11.5]. Now I need to write the items according to the specifications of the blueprint. I'll use a combination of objectively and subjectively scored cognitive items. For example, here are two sample test questions that are valid for their respective instructional goals:

Instructional Goals 1a and 1b
Which of the following animals did NOT exist during the Paleozoic era?

a. dinosaurs

b. snails

c. fish

d. insects

Table 11.5
Blueprint for a Geology Unit Test

	Verbal Information	Intellectual Skill	Total Items
Earth History			**7**
1a	5	-	5
1b			
1c	-	2	2
Rocks			**14**
2a	2	-	2
2b	-	3	3
3a	2	-	2
3b	-	3	3
4a	2	-	2
4b	-	2	2
Minerals			**8**
2c	-	2	2
2d	-	2	2
2d.1	-	1	1
2d.2	-	1	1
4c	-	2	2
Fossils			**6**
4d	-	2	2
5a	-	2	2
5b	2	-	2
Research Skills			**5**
6a	-	2	2
6b	-	3	3
Total	**13**	**27**	**40**

Instructional Goal 2d
A geologist finds two samples of a mineral that look like this:

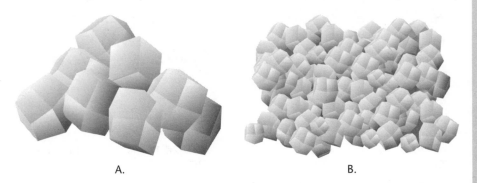

A.   B.

The geologist wonders why the sizes of the crystals are different in the two samples. Help the geologist by explaining why sample A's crystals are larger than sample B's crystals.

Sequencing Goals and Allocating Time

Now that I've established the goals and assessments for the unit, I need to start thinking about how I'm going to cluster and sequence the goals in my teaching. As I study my nineteen instructional goals, I see some logical group-ings [see Table 11.6]. Now what about sequencing the clusters and the goals? I think it makes sense to begin the unit with the earth history cluster so that I can establish my organizing theme and give students a perspective on the earth's features that helped to produce certain rocks, minerals, and fossils. Since rocks are made up of minerals, I should focus on the mineral cluster next, followed by the rock and fossil clusters. Since fossils are found in sedi-mentary rock, it makes sense for students to understand rock concepts before we move on to fossils.

To sequence the goals within each cluster, I'll refer back to my content analysis charts for guidance. For example, *crystal* is a subordinate concept for understanding the superordinate concept of mineral, so it makes sense to ad-dress instructional goal 2d.2 before 2c and 2d.1:

- *Classify solids as crystals* (instructional goal 2d.2).
- *Identify common shapes of mineral crystals* (instructional goal 2c).
- *Classify substances as minerals* (instructional goal 2d.1).

Using my content analyses and professional judgment, I'll now create a block plan that shows visually how I intend to sequence my instructional

Table 11.6
Clusters of Instructional Goals for a Geology Unit

Cluster	Instructional Goals
(A)—Earth History	1a, 1b, 1c
(B)—Minerals	2d.2, 2c, 2d.1, 2d, 4c, 6a
(C)—Rocks	4a, 2a, 3a, 2b, 4b, 6b, 3b, 6a
(D)—Fossils	5a, 5b, 4d, 6a

Table 11.7
Block Plan for a Geology Unit

Monday	Tuesday	Wednesday	Thursday	Friday
1 Introduction: Organizing Theme (30)	2 Organizing Theme Continued (30)	3 **Cluster A** Goals 1a & 1b (30)	4 **Cluster A** Goals 1a & 1b (30)	5 **Cluster A** Goals 1a & 1b (30)
6 Cluster B Goal 2d.2 (30)	7 Cluster B Goal 2c (30)	8 Cluster B Goal 2d.1 (30)	9 Cluster B Goal 2d (60)	10 Cluster B Goal 4c (30)
11 Cluster B Goal 6a (30)	12 **Cluster C** Goals 4a & 2a (30)	13 **Cluster C** Goals 3a & 2b (30)	14 **Cluster C** Goals 3a & 2b (30)	15 **Cluster C** Goal 4b (30)
16 **Cluster C** Goal 6b (30)	17 **Cluster C** Goal 3b (30)	18 **Cluster C** Goal 6a (30)	19 Cluster D Goal 5a (30)	20 Cluster D Goal 5a (30)
21 Cluster D Goal 5a (30)	22 Cluster D Goal 5b (30)	23 Cluster D Goal 5b (30)	24 Cluster D Goal 5b (30)	25 Field Trip Goals 4a, 4c, 4d (all day)
26 Culminating Activity (45)	27 Culminating Activity (45)	28 Culminating Activity (45)	29 Unit Review (45)	30 End-of-Unit Test (45)

Note: Numbers in parentheses indicate number of minutes estimated for instruction.

goals and how much time I think I will need to provide instruction for each of them [see Table 11.7]. The block plan eventually will be a valuable tool in helping me to sequence my daily lessons appropriately. It also will help ensure that I address all of the instructional goals within the overall time frame of the unit. I love fossils. Without a block plan, I could easily get carried away and spend half the unit on fossils, cutting short the time I'll need for all the other important topics.

Selecting Learning Activities and Resources

Finally, I need to identify learning activities and materials that I can use to help my students achieve each of the instructional goals. Actually, I've had some ideas for learning activities in mind since I started planning this unit. Now that I've established my goal structure, I'll be able to make better decisions about how to use them to address specific instructional goals. To come up with additional ideas, I'll check the school library, the school's curriculum guide, multimedia catalogs, the Internet, and science textbooks. I know a professor who teaches in the geology department at a nearby university. I think I'll talk with her about some teaching ideas, as well as the possibility of borrowing some of the specimens from the department's rock, mineral, and fossil collections. Since I have a firm understanding of the internal conditions of learning for various learning outcomes, I know that I can use my own creativity to generate ideas for activities and materials too. As I'm collecting and creating my instructional resources, I'll organize them by instructional goal and objective [see Tables 11.8 and 11.9] to ensure that they have the potential to contribute to the unit's learning goals.

Table 11.8
Identifying Instructional Resources for a Verbal Information Instructional Goal

Grade	Subject	Unit Topic
Instructional Goal:	*What is the learned capability students should be able to <u>demonstrate</u> following instruction? Learners will be able to . . .* • state the names of the four major eras in the earth's history and several important characteristics of each. (1a) • describe the plant and animal life associated with each of the four geologic eras. (1b)	
Instructional Objective:	*How will students demonstrate the learned capability for the purpose of <u>assessment</u>?* Learners will be provided with an organizational chart that has four columns with a blank line at the top of each column. Beneath the chart will be twenty-five facts, lettered a–y. Sixteen of the facts will be characteristics of the four major eras in the earth's history, with four facts corresponding to each of the four eras. The remaining nine facts will not correspond to any of the four eras. Learners will state the names of the four major eras in the earth's history [capability] by writing each of them [action] at the top of the four columns. Learners will state important characteristics of each era [capability] by writing the letters of the facts [action] in each of the appropriate columns. All four era names must be written on the blank lines, but the names do not need to be spelled perfectly. The letters of fourteen of the sixteen characteristics must be placed in the correct columns. The letters of no more than two of the nine distracters can be placed in a column.	
Instructional Resources:	*What are the learning activities and materials that may help students <u>achieve</u> the instructional goal (as assessed by the instructional objective)?*	
*Cognitive Stage:	<u>Engagement with Information</u> 1. Advance organizer: pictures of Florida and Colorado. 2. CD-ROM: History of the Earth—Over the Eons; students view in pairs with checklist. 3. Read chapter 3 in textbook, provide blank cluster analysis chart for students to complete. 4. Adjunct questions for students to complete following reading, with focus on elaboration. 5. Students work in groups to create bulletin board murals to represent each era. When complete, each group presents and explains its mural to class. 6. Students create three illustrated time lines: plants, animals, geologic features. <u>Practice Retrieving Information</u> 1. Students complete cluster analysis chart from memory. 2. Team game: Journey Through Time. 3. Paleontologist role-playing activity to determine ages of objects. 4. Students write stories about traveling back in time to the four eras. 5. To prepare for summative assessment: students complete charts with four columns (as described in objective), check against their cluster analysis charts.	

*For verbal information instructional goals, instruction focuses only on the <u>cognitive</u> stage, developing meaningful declarative knowledge. The <u>associative</u> and <u>autonomous</u> stages apply only to skill learning.

Table 11.9
Identifying Instructional Resources for an Intellectual Skill Instructional Goal

Grade	Subject	Unit Topic
Instructional Goal:	What is the learned capability students should be able to <u>demonstrate</u> following instruction? Learners will be able to . . . • Identify examples of sedimentary, igneous, and metamorphic rocks. (2b)	
Instructional Objective:	How will students demonstrate the learned capability for the purpose of <u>assessment</u>? Given a set of fifteen rock samples that have not been used during instruction (four metamorphic, five igneous, six sedimentary) and three containers labeled according to the three rock categories, learners will demonstrate the ability to identify sedimentary, igneous, and metamorphic rocks by sorting the rocks into the three labeled containers. To demonstrate mastery, learners must place twelve of the fifteen rocks in the correct container.	
Instructional Resources:	What are the learning activities and materials that may help students <u>achieve</u> the instructional goal (as assessed by the instructional objective)?	
Cognitive Stage:	1. Students attempt to classify rocks, use to induce three categories. 2. Create class concept map for rock categories and their features. 3. Provide prototypical specimens for students to observe with magnifying glasses. Direct attention to critical features. 4. Sedimentary rock formation activity: sediments in a jar of water. 5. Igneous rock formation activity: growing crystals from hot solution. 6. Videotape of volcano eruptions to show pumice and basalt. 7. Metamorphic rock formation activity: melt sulfur and pour into water.	
Associative Stage:	1. In small groups, students sort rock specimens and photos from field guides into three categories. Vary on irrelevant features. 2. Analyze example and matched nonexample pairs (e.g., gneiss & sandstone) with magnifying glass to promote discrimination. Students offer their own hypotheses first.	
Autonomous Stage:	1. Take students on a rock collecting field trip. 2. Students bring rock specimens from home. 3. Students develop their own rock collections organized according to three categories.	

Now what about a culminating activity—something to tie the entire unit together in an authentic way that actively engages my students? Students are going to be creating wall murals of the geologic eras and collecting rocks, minerals, and fossils. They could bring all of these activities together by creating their own museum of natural history. I'll have students work in groups to create displays for the museum. Some students will be classifying and labeling rocks, minerals, and fossils; some can prepare a concrete model of the rock cycle; and others can produce displays of the earth's geologic eras. There is an empty room just down the hall that we may be able to use to house our museum. After we create the displays for the museum, we can invite students and teachers from the rest of the school—and maybe even from other schools—to visit. We can invite parents to visit the museum too.

When others visit our museum, my students will need to be prepared to explain each of the exhibits. Through this verbal activity, they can talk about the content of the unit in meaningful ways to others—a good elaboration opportunity. Although specific groups of students will produce each exhibit, I'll rotate the explanation tasks so all the students get a chance to elaborate on all the unit's subtopics. When the unit begins, I'll let students know about our ultimate goal of creating a natural history museum. This should help give them some purpose and motivation as they learn about various topics and go out on the field trips to collect specimens.

Although the natural history museum sounds like a great idea, I need to make sure that it reflects as many of the unit's instructional goals as possible. Just to double-check, I'm going to go down over my list of instructional goals and indicate briefly which goals will be supported by the museum activity. Looking at my checklist [see Table 11.10], it looks as if the museum activity does in fact relate to most of my instructional goals. Therefore, I will go ahead and plan to implement it. I'm really excited about this authentic project, and I think my students will be too.

Table 11.10
A Checklist to Establish the Validity of a Culminating Activity for a Geology Unit

Does the natural history museum culminating activity provide opportunities for students to demonstrate each of the unit's instructional goals?

✔ = yes

— = no

✔	State the names of the four major eras in the earth's history and several important characteristics of each. (verbal information)
✔	Describe the plant and animal life associated with each of the four geologic eras. (verbal information)
✔	Demonstrate how earth's geologic features influence plant and animal life. (principle)
✔	Explain how sedimentary, igneous, and metamorphic rocks are formed. (verbal information)
✔	Identify examples of sedimentary, igneous, and metamorphic rocks. (concepts)
—	Identify common shapes of mineral crystals. (concepts)
—	Demonstrate how the rate of cooling influences the size of a mineral crystal. (principle)
✔	State the names of minerals that are found in common sedimentary, igneous, and metamorphic rocks. (verbal information)
✔	Apply the rock cycle. (principle)
✔	Demonstrate how fossils are formed in sedimentary rock. (principle)
✔	Describe the conditions under which common fossils were formed. (verbal information)
✔	Classify rocks, minerals, and fossils. (concepts)
—	Design an experiment to test the strengths of sedimentary, igneous, and metamorphic rocks. (cognitive strategy)

LET'S SUMMARIZE

By following the unit planning process outlined in this chapter, Ms. Nelson was able to design a unit that promises to provide meaningful learning opportunities for her students. She developed a rich list of instructional resources, including a culminating activity, that should be interesting and motivating to her learners. It all looks great on paper, but will students learn anything from it? Fortunately, Ms. Nelson's instructional goals and objectives for the learning activities are clearly defined, so she does not have to speculate about this critical question. The assessment data that she collects will tell her how effective the unit is in helping students achieve each of the instructional goals. She can use these data to make decisions about remediation as she teaches the unit. She can also use the data to fine-tune the unit as she teaches it from year to year. The unit planning process produced a starting point to help Ms. Nelson structure her day-to-day teaching in the classroom. That is exactly the purpose of a unit plan: to provide a general planning structure that guides daily instructional decision making.

Ms. Nelson demonstrated how to design a unit for a topic (geology) in a single subject area (science). Often, however, teachers design units that integrate two or more school subjects. Does our unit planning process apply to these types of units? Let's check it out in the next section.

Designing Thematic Units

Schools are one of the few places where people experience the world in categories. School curricula carve up the world into subjects such as mathematics, science, language, social studies, and so on. Although these subject distinctions make teaching more efficient, and perhaps more effective, they may suggest to our learners an artificial, fragmented compartmentalization that, in reality, does not exist (Boyer, 1995; Fogarty, 1991). Whereas the real world that students experience daily is a seamless tapestry of interconnected sights, sounds, events, and ideas that transcend and integrate traditional content domains, typical school curricula, even at the college level, often put up boundaries and parameters around school-learned subjects. For example, math class is from 9:00 to 10:00; English from 10:00 to 11:00; and science is something we think about only from 11:00 to 12:00.

Students themselves often prefer to keep their knowledge in neat, discrete categories and may resist integrating ideas across the curriculum. This point was illustrated to me very powerfully a few years ago when I was teaching a graduate-level course in testing and measurement. After introducing the class to z-scores (a basic statistical concept), several students asked me to explain how z-scores in my course would be different from the z-scores they had learned about in a previous course on research methods. My answer stunned them: There is no difference! Although z-scores can be put to different uses in the contexts of educational testing and educational research, the statistic itself is fundamentally the same in its meaning and computation in both contexts. My response was met with skepticism and resistance from the students. They seemed to be asking, "How can it possibly be the same thing if we learned about it in two different classes?"

Using Thematic Units to Support a Seamless Curriculum

How can we overcome these types of misconceptions and naive expectations in our classroom teaching? How can we create a seamless curriculum that minimizes artificial distinctions among academic disciplines and students' real-world experiences? One powerful approach to the problem is to design instructional units that deliberately show learners how different domains are interconnected and integrated. Such plans are often referred to as *thematic units*: "A **thematic unit** is a method of organizing instructional time and materials around a topic which lends itself naturally to the integration of curriculum content areas" (Eisele, 1990, p. 49). In other words, a central theme, or topic, can be used as a subject matter vehicle for achieving a variety of instructional goals in different content domains.

The most important feature of a thematic unit is its focus on integrating subject matter from different academic disciplines. In fact, some educators use the term *integrative unit* (e.g., Zemelman et al., 1998). For example, *snow* could be used as the integrating topic for a thematic unit that connects science, mathematics, social studies, and language arts. How can a simple concept like snow integrate four different academic disciplines? The theme or topic can promote content-based integration by providing a common conceptual context to which different disciplines can be applied (see Figure 11.5). Students can learn about snow as they study weather (science), measurement and data analysis (mathematics), culture and environment (social studies), and writing poetry (language arts).

The theme also can provide process-based integration by providing a common context for learning activities that address two or more instructional goals from different content domains. For example, as students calculate and graph the average yearly snowfall in various environments, they may be working toward mathematics instructional goals (*Apply the rule for calculating a mean; Construct and interpret a bar graph*) as well as social studies goals (*Describe how environmental features vary for people of different cultures; Demonstrate how different environmental conditions influence different cultures*). Students may use the topic of snow as a focus for writing different types of poems in language arts or reading.

Elementary teachers usually have an advantage over secondary teachers in planning thematic units. Elementary teachers often have responsibility for teaching all subjects in a self-contained classroom (the same teacher has the same students for the entire school day) in which they can schedule subjects with some flexibility. In contrast, most secondary teachers have responsibility for teaching a single subject to different groups of students whom they see for a short period of time every day (Fogarty, 1991; Zemelman et al., 1998). Clearly teachers must work within the organizational constraints imposed by their schools. However, secondary teachers may be able to create additional oppor-

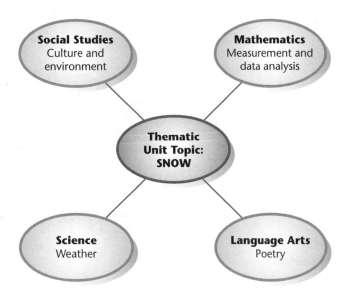

**Figure 11.5
Content Integration in a
Thematic Unit**

tunities for thematic units through team teaching with other teachers who teach different subjects. Schools can support the possibility of thematic team teaching by allocating larger amounts of time to classes, a process known as block scheduling (Canady & Rettig, 1995a, 1995b).

Planning a Thematic Unit

Effective thematic units require a great deal of careful planning and preparation. A thematic unit is more than a collection of activities that all seem to relate in some way to a central topic. In addition to making connections between different content areas, a thematic unit also must help students achieve important learning outcomes within each content area. Those outcomes must be identified and sequenced appropriately to support student learning.

◼ **Identifying an Integrating Theme**   The first step in designing a thematic unit is to identify a unifying topic or theme that has the potential to connect different subjects. A good way to identify such a topic is by mapping out your anticipated sequence of unit topics for the school year and then searching for common themes and time frames (Maurer, 1994). Look, for example, at Figure 11.6. Here we see that a teacher—let's call him Mr. Hendricks—has roughly mapped out his anticipated unit topics for four subjects by month. He wonders how to tie together units in measurement, weather, environment and culture, and poetry. Since these units will occur during the winter and he teaches in a northern climate, he begins to think about winter-like themes: cold, snow, winter sports, and so on. Mr. Hendricks begins to try out these potential themes with each of the four unit topics, asking himself if there are at least some applications that he can make to each theme. Through this process, he

Figure 11.6
Identifying Thematic Unit Topics

	Mathematics	**Science**	**Social Studies**	**Language Arts**
September	Unit A	Unit A	Unit A	Unit A
October	Unit B	**Unit B**	Unit B	Unit B
November	Unit C	Unit C	Unit C	Unit C
December	Unit D	Unit D	**Unit D**	Unit D
January	Unit E *Measurement and data analysis*	Unit E *Weather*	Unit E *Environment and culture*	Unit E *Poetry*
February	**Unit F**	Unit F	Unit F	Unit F
March	Unit G	Unit G	Unit G	Unit G
April	Unit H	Unit H	Unit H	Unit H
May	Unit I	Unit I	Unit I	Unit I

discovers that there are aspects of snow that he can weave into each of the four units. He therefore selects *snow* as the central theme.

As you can see, there is no magic formula for creating the topic for a thematic unit; it is a thinking process. You can almost always find ways to connect one subject area to the rest of the curriculum (see Kleiman, 1991, for numerous ways to link mathematics to other subjects). As you analyze your chart, you may find an integrating theme for unit topics that you do not plan to be teaching simultaneously. For example, math topic F in Figure 11.6 could be linked with science topic B and social studies topic D, but these units probably will not overlap in time. If altering the sequence of unit topics does not impede learning in each subject, you may be able to shift the topics around a bit to ensure that you will be addressing them at approximately the same time, thus making thematic integration possible. If, for example, math unit F must wait until students acquire the prerequisite skills related to units A, B, C, D, and E, then you may be able to move science unit B and social studies unit D to later in the school year.

■ **Identifying Goals, Content, and Objectives**   After you identify your unifying theme and the unit topics to integrate, you need to specify educational goals, instructional goals, essential content, and instructional objectives as described in the previous section. You may think it strange that we would still want to analyze each unit topic separately if our ultimate goal is to integrate them. Actually, the goal of integration makes content analysis for each unit topic even more critical. Let me illustrate this point with a simple example. Suppose Mr. Hendricks designs a snow-related lesson in which learners will construct bar graphs of average yearly snowfall amounts for various cities around the world. Before students can apply their data analysis skills to snow-related information, they need to possess those skills. Furthermore, they need to have acquired any necessary prerequisite skills (e.g., reading tables, rounding, adding, dividing). These are exactly the types of critical capabilities that are revealed through careful content analysis. In short, before you can integrate units *across* different school subjects, you need to know where you are headed *within* each of those domains.

■ **Identifying Instructional Resources**   As you continue your planning by clustering and sequencing instructional goals, you can be on the lookout for thematically based groupings. Furthermore, you can look for ways to combine instructional objectives that relate to the overall theme. The primary opportunity for content integration occurs when you begin to identify learning activities and materials. To guide your thinking, you can adapt the format I provided earlier (see Table 11.3) in two ways. First, you can specify two or more instructional goals and objectives from different subjects, making sure to note clearly how each one fits into its individual unit. For example, Mr. Hendricks could write the following in the instructional goal section of Table 11.3: Learners will be able to . . .

▶ *Calculate the arithmetic mean for a set of data expressed in decimal form* (math goal 2b).

▶ *Describe patterns in average yearly snowfall for cities in different climates around the world* (social studies goal 1c).

Mr. Hendricks has decided to address these two instructional goals simultaneously. He can now develop an assessment strategy (instructional objective) that validly combines the two instructional goals, or he can prepare two separate objectives. Most important, he now needs to identify learning materials and activities. In this situation, he has a golden opportunity to enhance motivation for learning how to calculate averages by having students apply the skill

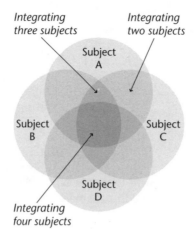

**Figure 11.7
Thematic Unit Instructional Goals: Possible Connections for Four Content Domains**

in a meaningful, relevant context (remember Keller's ARCS model from Chapter 10): trying to figure out how climate and snowfall influence human cultures around the world. He also has a wonderful opportunity to have students practice calculating and interpreting means with authentic, meaningful data rather than artificial sets of numbers that have been contrived just for the sake of providing practice.

Will Mr. Hendricks be able to integrate every instructional goal with one or more goals from the other three subjects? Probably not. Some aspects of each individual unit may be nearly impossible to connect to another content domain. Nevertheless, with some careful thought, creativity, and perseverance, he may be able to connect two, three, or even all four subjects (see Figure 11.7). An ideal way to connect all four subjects is to create a culminating activity for the thematic unit. Just as the culminating activity for a subject-specific unit encourages students to generate connections among the facts and skills they have acquired, the culminating activity for a thematic unit gives students the opportunity to generate further connections between different academic subjects. For example, Mr. Hendricks's students could record snowfall data for their community (*mathematics, science*), analyze the data by calculating average accumulations and water content (*mathematics*), and write a report of their findings to publish in the local newspaper (*language arts*).

LET'S SUMMARIZE

Thematic instructional units are powerful teaching devices for tearing down the walls that artificially compartmentalize school-learned knowledge. Effective thematic teaching first requires careful attention to content structure and instructional goals within each subject domain we wish to integrate. Then we need to think creatively and innovatively about instructional strategies that will help learners achieve those instructional goals in the context of the integrating theme of the unit. As you can imagine, planning and teaching thematic units requires a lot of extra effort. However, if our students come away from their learning experiences with more integrated, seamless knowledge, the extra effort will have been worthwhile.

LOOKING BACK   LOOKING AHEAD

In this chapter we have placed the instructional design process into the context of creating units of instruction. By designing instructional units, we avoid the temptation to zigzag ineffectively and inefficiently across the curriculum by specifying coherent, unified sets of instructional goals. To design an instructional unit, we need to consider the educational goals to be achieved through the unit, as well as the more precise instructional goals that specify the actual learning outcomes that students are to acquire. Once we have specified instructional goals, we can move on to write instructional objectives and identify and analyze essential content. These are exactly the same design procedures that we apply when dealing with a single instructional goal. The only difference in unit planning is that we are focusing on a number of instructional goals simultaneously rather than just one, providing opportunities for integration and coherence within the unit. Thematic instructional units provide all the benefits of unit planning. In addition, thematic units also help us engage students with the school curriculum in ways that encourage them to make connections between different content domains.

This is the final chapter in which we explore the nuts-and-bolts procedures that are relevant to applying instructional design principles to classroom teaching. Before leaving this chapter, check your achievement of the instructional goals by completing Exercise 11.3. In the next, and final, chapter, we take a few steps back to look at classroom instructional design in the broader context of schooling and classroom teaching. I address some of the questions and concerns that you may have about *design-teaching* in a real school classroom and give you some practical advice on how to make the systems approach to instructional design work for you and your learners. This may be the most important chapter that we spend together.

RESOURCES FOR FURTHER REFLECTION AND EXPLORATION

Print Resources

Allen, D. D., & Piersma, M. L. (1995). *Developing thematic units*. Albany, NY: Delmar.

An entire book devoted to designing thematic units. The book emphasizes the use of reading and literature themes as central topics around which to organize other school subjects. The authors present specific examples of potential organizing themes for primary and intermediate children along with specific suggested teaching resources for each.

Boyer, E. L. (1995). *The basic school: A community for learning*. Princeton, NJ: The Carnegie Foundation for the Advancement of Teaching.

A prominent educator describes his vision for elementary schooling. Among other recommendations, the author advocates a thematic, integrated curriculum built on the centrality of language and eight "core commonalities": the life cycle, the use of symbols, membership in groups, a sense of time and space, response to the aesthetic, connections to nature, producing and consuming, and living with purpose.

Educational Leadership, 49, October 1991.

An entire issue devoted to curriculum integration and thematic teaching. Articles present theoretical perspectives on thematic curricula as well as specific examples of integrated teaching in school subjects.

Kohl, H. (1984). *Growing minds: On becoming a teacher.* New York: Harper & Row.

A fascinating book in which a well-known educator traces his own intellectual journey as a classroom teacher. Although the entire book is full of thoughtful observations and insights, Kohl presents some particularly stimulating ideas on thematic teaching and content organization in the third part. A must-read for all beginning teachers.

Martinello, M. L., & Cook, G. E. (1994). *Interdisciplinary inquiry in teaching and learning.* New York: Merrill.

A book that explores issues and principles related to integrated, thematic teaching in schools. Chapter 4, "Webbing and Questioning," provides useful explanations and examples of using webbing techniques to identify cross-content connections in thematic units.

Maurer, R. E. (1994). *Designing interdisciplinary curriculum in middle, junior high, and high schools.* Boston, MA: Allyn and Bacon.

An entire book devoted to the topic of designing integrated and thematic school curricula. The book includes numerous integrated curriculum models from award-winning middle, junior high, and high schools across the country.

Zemelman, S., Daniels, H., & Hyde, A. (1998). *Best practice: New standards for teaching and learning in America's schools* (2nd ed.). Portsmouth, NH: Heinemann.

A book that describes exemplary school programs across the United States in the areas of reading, writing, science, social studies, and the arts. Chapter 8, "Classroom Structures for Best Practice," provides useful information on two topics relevant to our discussion of unit planning: integrative units and authentic experiences.

World Wide Web Resources

http://www.census.gov/cgi-bin/gazetteer

Web site that provides access to information from the U.S. Census Bureau. Information can be obtained for any location in the United States on population statistics, maps, latitude and longitude, bodies of water, and other topics. A valuable source of data for research projects in social studies units or thematic units.

http://netvet.wustl.edu/e-zoo.htm

Web site of the Electronic Zoo. The zoo provides numerous links to information about major classes of animals. For example, the marine mammals link provides access to links to the Center for Whale Studies, Biological Sciences Database from California Polytechnic State University, Dolphin Alliance, European Cetacean Organization, and Friends of the Sea Otter, to name just a few. A valuable resource for obtaining resources for science units related to animals and a rich source of integration ideas for thematic units involving animal themes.

http://www.discovery.com/

Web site of the Discovery Channel. Provides information on a wide variety of topics related to science and social studies. A good source of information, materials, and learning activities to incorporate into science and social studies units.

http://www.ccaa.edu/~kalmesm/edu402/Presentations/unitplan/

Web site of Concordia College that focuses on the teaching of social studies. Fundamentals of unit planning are presented. Topics include unit types, building a resource unit, teacher functions, and student performances.

http://www.sasked.gov.sk.ca/docs/ela/ela_plan.html

Web site that provides information related to unit planning processes: *English language arts: A curriculum guide for the elementary level.* (1992). Regina, SK: Saskatchewan Education. Includes a useful unit planning checklist and an interesting case study of a fourth-grade teacher's yearly unit planning.

Points of Departure
Personalizing the Instructional Design Process

Throughout this book, we have been exploring an ideal, well-defined systems model of instructional design. Although the model has great potential to help you structure your classroom teaching, your teaching effectiveness ultimately will depend on your ability to make the model work within the complex classroom environment with real students, time constraints, classroom management difficulties, and numerous other challenges. The instructional design process simply does not occur in a context-free vacuum. You undoubtedly will encounter obstacles, detours, forks in the road, flat tires, and alternative routes. So now that we have reached the end of our instructional design journey, we need to consider the most important question of all: Where are *you* going with your knowledge of instructional design? How will *you* make it work in the classroom? In this final chapter, we think together about using the systems model as a point of departure—a stepping-off point from which you can personalize the instructional design process and make it your own.

12

Instructional Design in the Classroom

Have you ever learned a new hobby? Several years ago, I began learning how to be a fly-fisherman. I read books and magazine articles, watched instructional videotapes and television programs, and talked with other fly-fishing men and women and asked them a lot of questions. Each of these resources provided me with useful facts, concepts, rules, principles, strategies, tips, and techniques for catching fish with artificial flies. Armed with this knowledge, I would head out to my favorite trout streams with high hopes.

I discovered, however, that the rules, strategies, and techniques didn't always work as well as the books, magazines, videos, CD-ROMs, and people said they would. The real stream was always a lot more complicated than the situations described by my instructional resources. There usually were a number of variables that I had to think about simultaneously: type of stream, water level, water temperature, type of fly, size of fly, line length, line size, casting style, weather conditions, time of day, and so on. My learning resources usually would analyze only one or two variables at a time. They never were able to deal with all possible variables simultaneously.

No book, magazine, or videotape can possibly demonstrate how to fish every stream under every possible combination of conditions. Does that mean the rules, principles, and strategies are worthless? Not at all. The knowledge in my head is just the starting point for becoming a successful fly-fisherman. When standing knee-deep in a cold trout stream, I find myself thinking about many of the principles that I believe are relevant to the situation. However, I also find myself relying increasingly on my own experience and judgment to put the principles together in each specific situation.

At this point in our discussion of the instructional design process, you may be wondering whether all the rules, principles, and strategies we have been considering will work in a complex classroom environment. When you try to apply them to your classroom teaching, will you discover, as I did in fly-fishing, that reality is much more complex than theory? Yes, of course, you will. No book, including this

INSTRUCTIONAL GOALS FOR CHAPTER 12

After reading and thinking about this chapter, you should be able to . . .

1. Summarize the major components of a systems approach to instructional design.

2. Describe three general impediments to classroom design teaching.

3. Explain the value of instructional design for learners and the teaching profession.

4. Explain how teachers can resolve potential discrepancies between systematic instructional design and the realities of classroom teaching.

one, can tell you precisely how to be an effective *design-teacher* in every possible classroom teaching situation. There are too many unpredictable variables that influence the teaching-learning process. Does this mean that spending the preceding eleven chapters together has been a waste of our time? I certainly hope not!

In this final chapter, I explore some of the challenges and questions you will confront as you attempt to function as a *design-teacher* within the complex classroom environment. Rather than offering you additional procedures and principles, my primary goal in this concluding chapter is to help you think about the instructional design process within the broader context of classroom teaching and schooling. I believe that you can apply systematic instructional design effectively in your classroom. Check out the instructional goals for the chapter and read on.

Systematic Instructional Design: A Classroom Perspective

Throughout this book, we have been exploring instructional design as a systematic process. This means that every aspect of our instructional decision making relates in some meaningful way to other aspects of instruction. No decision or action takes place in a vacuum; they all must work together to help move learners toward achieving an instructional goal: the final destination. Figure 12.1 summarizes the systems model that we have used to organize our thinking about instructional design. As you know by now, it is impossible to design an instructional strategy until you know how you are planning to assess your learners. Designing an appropriate assessment strategy depends on the learning outcome your students should be able to demonstrate. Demonstrating that outcome depends on how well they acquire certain facts, skills, or attitudes—the content of instruction. Returning to the three trip planning questions we identified in Chapter 1, before you can plan how to get somewhere (*instructional strategy*), you have to specify where you are going (*instructional goal and content*) and what you want to be able to do when you get there (*assessment*).

It all sounds logical on paper, but even inexperienced classroom teachers know that the teaching-learning process is not that simple. As an aspiring teacher, you probably have some reservations about applying the model in a real classroom. I want you to pause here for a few moments and think about your reservations. Think back over the entire design process, and make a list of some specific concerns you have about applying our systems model in a real classroom with real students.

Impediments to Design-Teaching

I suspect that the concerns on your list fall into three major categories: classroom-level variables, school-level variables, and personal variables. Let's look closely at each set of concerns that may create impediments to classroom *design-teaching*.

Classroom-Level Impediments to *Design-Teaching* Two major impediments to design-teaching are time and learner variability. *Time* is a critical classroom variable (Shulman, 1983). Teachers never have enough daily classroom time with their students. When they are not actively involved with students, there is always lots more to do: photocopying, grading papers, phone calls to parents, conferences with other school personnel, school forms to complete, meetings to attend, personal business, and on and on it goes.

Careful, systematic instructional design, however, requires a lot of time. To be a *design-teacher*, you need to invest large quantities of time in the planning process: identifying instructional goals, analyzing content, preparing assessments, and designing instructional events. You also need a lot of instructional time with your students to provide the types of meaningful learning activities

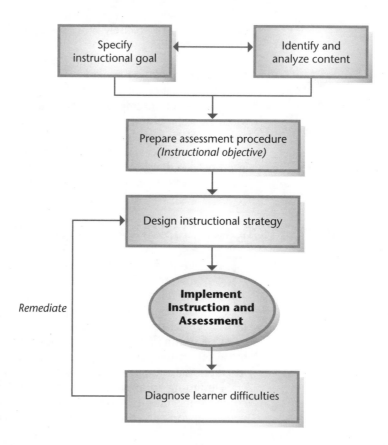

**Figure 12.1
A General Systems
Model of Instructional
Design**

necessary to achieve your learning outcomes (Alexander, Entwisle, & Dauber, 1993; Brophy, 1988; Wittrock, 1986). As a *design-teacher*, you cannot just "cover" the textbook. Quality assessment also takes a lot of time—not only to design but to implement and interpret.

Unfortunately, I don't have the power to create more hours in the day for you. I do, however, have some suggestions for coping with the time demands of *design-teaching*. First, you should realize that you already are devoting significant amounts of time to planning, instruction, and assessment. You may simply need to refocus your energies on instructional design principles and procedures rather than carving out a lot of additional time. Second, remember that you probably will be teaching similar subjects and students from year to year. So the time investment that you make during your first two or three years of teaching will pay huge dividends in subsequent years. You will be able to revise and modify instructional systems that you already have created rather than starting from scratch every year. Third, you will find that the design process will become increasingly automatic and efficient for you the more you engage in it, just as any other intellectual skill or strategy would.

A second major classroom-level impediment is *learner variability*. You always will find that there are differences among your learners, even if you teach a specialized subject to a homogeneously grouped class. Learners always vary in prior knowledge, aptitude, motivation, cultural backgrounds, and so on (Garcia, 1992, 1994; Ladson-Billings, 1994, 1995; Murrell & Diez, 1997). You may encounter some learners who vary significantly from the group average due to specific disabilities. In addition to requiring more classroom time, such students may need individualized learning goals and activities tailored to their unique needs and characteristics.

Our systems model does not force individual learners into a rigid mold. Instead, the order and structure that the model brings to your decision making should free you to devote more thought to the individual differences of your learners. At every point in the design process, you can exercise your professional judgment concerning the need for possible modifications for individual learners. For example, you may choose to prepare alternative instructional goals for some of your learners. If so, you can still apply the design process by focusing on the internal conditions of learning for those particular outcomes. You can modify content, assessments, and learning activities for individual students as well, a point that I have emphasized throughout earlier chapters.

■ **School-Level Impediments to *Design-Teaching***   School-level impediments are variables that reflect the organizational structure of the school. Teachers usually have little control over such variables as grade-level organization, subject differentiation within the curriculum, time periods allotted for instruction in specific subjects, and class size. To illustrate a potential dilemma, consider a high school teacher who is required to "cover" the entire social studies book during the school year. To get through the whole book, she must sacrifice many generative learning activities because they are too time-consuming. In other words, she must sacrifice her students' depth of processing for breadth of coverage. Consider a first-grade teacher who has some children who already have mastered much of the first-grade curriculum and are ready for skills that are taught in second and third grades. Because of the children's ages, they must continue to plod through the first-grade materials, working on instructional goals that are not appropriate for them.

In cases such as these, school-level policies or organizational structures are preventing classroom teachers from designing instruction with maximum effectiveness. How should *design-teachers* handle such impediments? First, by cultivating the habits of mind associated with systematic instructional design, you will be in a good position to participate actively in school-level policy and curriculum decisions (see Clandinin & Connelly, 1992). Through your influence, perhaps schools can become more supportive of focused, meaningful, goal-oriented instruction. Second, you may be able to find creative ways to minimize the negative impact of school-level impediments. For example, the social studies teacher who needs to cover the entire book may choose to consolidate three book chapters into a single unit that addresses learning outcomes common to all three. Third, you may simply need to recognize the impediments and exercise your best professional judgment in working within—rather than struggling against—the constraints they impose.

■ **Personal Impediments to *Design-Teaching***   Some of the most serious impediments to *design-teaching* may emerge from your own knowledge and attitudes. Effective instructional design requires in-depth knowledge of subject matter, learner characteristics, assessment, internal learning processes, and external instructional strategies (Calderhead, 1996; Shulman, 1986; Stein, Baxter, & Leinhardt, 1990). If your knowledge base is deficient in any of these areas, you may have difficulty applying a systems model of instructional design in your classroom. As a professional educator, you need to monitor your own knowledge base and actively seek opportunities and resources to expand it as needed.

A second personal impediment you may experience is your own attitude toward the instructional design process. Goal-directed *design-teaching* requires effort, persistence, careful thinking, and hard work. You may not always be able or willing to invest the effort necessary to function as a *design-teacher*. At times, you may be tempted to fill the school day with unfocused activities because it is much less demanding. Keeping your students occupied with interesting activities is not difficult. Ensuring that your students are really *learning* something from those activities requires constant thinking, planning, assessment, and reflection.

A third personal impediment may be your own reaction to accountability. When you do not specify instructional goals, you can avoid holding yourself accountable for your students' learning. In the absence of clear instructional goals, you can create assessments to evaluate any student performance you choose. You can easily manufacture assessment results to give yourself the false illusion of effective teaching. In contrast, when you focus right from the start on precise learning outcomes and design assessment strategies that are valid for those outcomes, you force yourself to judge your teaching effectiveness by looking objectively at how well your learners achieve the instructional goals. If you have reservations about your ability to design effective instructional strategies to achieve precise learning outcomes, you may be reluctant to build this type of accountability into your teaching.

So Why Be a Design-Teacher?

With all the classroom, school, and personal impediments we have just noted, you may be wondering if it is possible or even desirable to be a classroom *design-teacher*. I believe it is both possible and desirable for two reasons. First, as teachers, we are ultimately responsible for our students' learning. By taking a systematic approach to instructional design, we maximize the probability that individual learners will achieve important learning outcomes. Most important, through careful, valid assessment procedures, we are able to detect when students have *not* learned. Only then will we be in a position to diagnose their learning difficulties and provide additional learning opportunities (remediation). In short, bringing *all* our students to a high level of achievement first requires that we define clearly what that level of achievement will be. At a time when teachers are dealing with greater degrees of learner diversity than ever before, it is absolutely essential to focus on clear learning goals so that no student misses out on the opportunity to acquire the knowledge that will be critical to adult success and fulfillment.

Second, we are also responsible to the teaching profession. Traditionally, teachers have not been held in very high esteem by the public they serve, and many people are reluctant to grant professional status to teachers. There are many complex reasons for this state of affairs (e.g., see Doyle, 1992; Freedman, Jackson, & Boles, 1983; Goodlad, 1990), and I cannot review them here. I do,

Instructional design skills empower teachers to make the independent decisions and judgments that are characteristic of professionals.

however, believe that the professional status of teachers will improve only to the extent that teachers themselves think and behave as professionals.

The hallmark of professionalism is the ability to think, make independent judgments, and solve problems autonomously (Doyle, 1992; Goodlad, 1990). In this book, I have tried to empower you with a general strategy to structure your thinking about the primary problem that all teachers face: how to facilitate student learning. When teachers rely on curriculum kits, prepackaged instructional modules, teachers' guides, and multimedia software to tell them how to teach in their classrooms or, worse, to teach for them, they give up a significant degree of professional autonomy. If teaching is simply the act of implementing activities and materials that others have created, then almost anyone can be a good teacher, and there is no compelling reason to believe that teaching is a profession.

I believe that teachers who understand learning processes well enough to design and evaluate instructional resources for themselves are more likely to be respected as professionals than those who do not. Furthermore, as a *design-teacher* you will have the ability to evaluate the many teaching fads and innovations that come and go. By staying focused on learning goals and internal learning processes, you will be able to resist the temptation to jump on the latest bandwagon. You will always be able to justify your teaching decisions and actions from a sound psychological perspective. You will be able to gather valid assessment data to demonstrate the effectiveness of the instructional strategies that you design. When you do incorporate new techniques and innovations into your teaching, you will have appropriate reasons for doing so, and, most important, you will have the ability to assess their actual impact on learning.

Now that we have identified some general reasons for classroom *design-teaching*, I want to address some specific questions and concerns that you may have about the instructional design process.

Questions, Answers, and Points of Departure

In the preceding chapters, we examined the major components of a general strategy to guide the instructional design process. As you begin implementing the strategy in your own classroom, you will continue to refine your thinking about instructional design. In many ways, we have not reached the end of the instructional design process, although we are nearing the end of this book. We are only at the beginning, because every day of *design-teaching* brings new opportunities, challenges, issues, and questions to resolve. Each of these challenges represents a point of departure—an opportunity for you to extend your thinking about instructional design and make the systems approach work for you in your classroom with your students. Let's examine briefly some of these points of departure. I will frame each point as a question that you may be asking or that you may eventually be asking about systematic instructional design.

Question: We have described the instructional design process as a step-by-step procedure. How can the process always be this neat, logical, and linear in a complex classroom environment? The instructional design process is not always a linear, step-by-step procedure (see Derry & Lesgold, 1996). In fact, research evidence suggests that many effective and experienced teachers do not even follow a systems model in their planning (Young, Reiser, & Dick, 1998; Moallem, 1998). I have presented it in an idealistic linear form to draw your attention to the key relationships among all the components of an instructional system. For either a beginning or experienced teacher who may have little prior familiarity with instructional design principles, the systems model provides a high degree of structure to guide your initial planning efforts (Dick,

1996). Once you have mastered each of these components and relationships, you will be in the best position to modify and adapt the model in nonlinear ways that also may have the potential to produce effective instruction.

You may, for example, select a concept for your learners to acquire before you think about the instructional goal to be achieved. There is nothing wrong with determining content before identifying instructional goals—as long as you realize that your eventual instructional goal must be valid for the content to be learned. Sometimes you will find or create learning activities that you think will work well with your learners before you have considered the instructional goals or content the activities are to support. Again, this "out-of-order" thinking is acceptable as long as you do eventually back up and specify your instructional goals.

Researchers have discovered that teachers' planning processes are not always orderly and linear (Clark & Yinger, 1987; McCutcheon, 1980). Classroom teachers plan both "preactively" and "postactively" (see Calderhead, 1996; Clark & Peterson, 1986). In other words, they think in advance about how they are going to teach, and they analyze their interactions with students after teaching. Furthermore, teachers continue to think and plan interactively, that is, as they are engaged in teaching. In short, teachers think and plan constantly, and they do not necessarily engage in these cognitive processes in the same order all the time. This reality is all the more reason for teachers to use the structure provided by a systems model of instructional design.

Whether you are planning before, during, or after your classroom interactions with students, our systems model provides an ideal context for you to consider the implications of your thoughts. If, for example, in the middle of implementing a learning activity you think of an additional follow-up activity (interactive planning), your systems orientation should lead you to evaluate the proposed activity by prompting the following types of questions: (1) Is the activity valid for my instructional goals? (2) Is the activity valid for the content my learners are to acquire? (3) Is the activity valid for the summative assessment I have planned? and (4) Will the activity support my students' internal learning processes for the learned capability they are to achieve? Reflecting on such questions should help ensure that the ideas that emerge from your nonlinear thinking have the maximum potential for effectiveness.

Question: Systematic instructional design seems to be a scientific, sterile, matter-of-fact approach to classroom teaching. Isn't teaching more of an art than an exact science? Where do teacher creativity, personality, and intuition fit into the system?　Effective teaching ultimately is an artful blend of skill, judgment, intuition, creativity, and content knowledge. However, each of these aspects of teaching can—and should—be informed by scientific research on the teaching-learning process. Accomplished musicians, artists, and writers achieve their extraordinary creative abilities largely because of years spent studying principles of music, art, and writing (Hayes, 1985). As a musician, I know that I can be more creative and intuitive because I have studied music theory. Understanding the chord structures of various musical styles guides me when I improvise with a piano or trumpet. What may look like raw creativity on the outside really is an extension of my understanding and mastery of basic musical concepts and principles.

Similarly, your understanding and mastery of our systems approach to instructional design will provide a springboard for your own creative teaching. As long as you understand and apply principles of content analysis, assessment, and learning, you are certainly free to bring your own personal creative energies to your classroom teaching. In fact, you have no choice but to bring your own personal touch to teaching. Our systems model does not dictate exactly what you should do in your classroom; it simply provides a structured way for you to plan and evaluate your actions and decisions.

Question: With the emphasis on clear instructional goals and carefully designed instructional strategies, this book seems to be promoting an expository, direct-instruction approach to teaching. Can teachers use other models of teaching within an instructional design framework?   Absolutely. In fact, throughout this book I have emphasized repeatedly that there is no single, sure-fire way to teach. Just because we focus on clear instructional goals and content to be achieved, that does not mean that all teaching should be direct and expository in nature. As we noted in Chapters 8, 9, and 10, inductive (i.e., inquiry, discovery) teaching models are also consistent with our systems model. However, regardless of the teaching methods that you use with your students, you need to know what learning outcomes you are trying to achieve, how you will assess those outcomes, and the underlying learning processes that your methods must support. These fundamental instructional issues apply equally to the wide variety of specific teaching models that have been developed over the years: discussion, cooperative learning, analogies, simulations, role-playing, Socratic dialogue, research projects, creative writing, learning centers, computer-assisted instruction, and on and on.

Excellent overviews of the many varied approaches to teaching are available (Eby & Kujawa, 1994; Gunter, Estes, & Schwab, 1990; Joyce & Weil, 1986; Rosenshine & Stevens, 1986). I encourage you to learn about as many of them as possible, including their theoretical foundations and the types of learning processes they can support. However, for maximum effectiveness, I also encourage you to use our systems model to help you make decisions about when and how to use the teaching strategies in your repertoire.

Question: Effective classroom teaching is more than just designing instruction, isn't it? What about classroom management, interacting with students, classroom climate, and other skills that teachers need?   I agree that instructional design is only one aspect of classroom teaching. Even the best-designed instructional systems will be ineffective if you lack the skills to implement them. In this book, I have not tried to examine every variable that contributes to effective classroom teaching—only the instructional design aspect. As an aspiring teacher, you need to acquire and constantly sharpen your abilities to manage the classroom, interact with students, and establish an appropriate classroom climate. Each of these aspects of interactive classroom teaching has been investigated extensively, and you can easily find many fine books and articles that address these issues (Brophy, 1986; Orlich, Harder, Callahan, Kauchak, & Gibson, 1994; Shuell, 1996).

You should recognize, however, that we actually *have* been dealing with classroom management issues. Classroom management is simply the process of creating an environment that maximizes the opportunity for learning. Teachers maintain order, discipline students, establish routines and procedures, and enforce rules to create an organized structure within which learning goals can more easily be achieved (Emmer, Evertson, Clements, & Worsham, 1997; Evertson, Emmer, Clements, & Worsham, 1997). Effective classroom management functions to reduce the complexity of the classroom environment, thereby freeing teachers to think about solving the problem of facilitating learning.

When you design your instruction carefully and focus on achieving your instructional goals in the classroom, you establish a task-oriented focus that helps maintain classroom order (Doyle, 1986). If your students are highly engaged with well-designed instructional materials and activities, they will be far less likely to behave inappropriately and disruptively in the classroom. One of the most effective forms of classroom management is well-designed, goal-directed instruction.

Question: How can teachers specify precise instructional goals for all their students to achieve when there are so many individual differences among students? What about learners who bring special needs and exceptionalities to the classroom? As I indicated earlier in this chapter, one of the impediments to *design-teaching* is learner variability. There are two ways to think about this important issue. First, you may need to make adjustments and accommodations at several points in the instructional design process for individual students or groups of students who have specific learning needs or special abilities. For example, you may need to establish differentiated instructional goals or summative assessment procedures and criteria. You almost certainly will need to devise learning activities and materials that are sensitive to individual differences.

Making these types of accommodations, however, does not change the systematic nature of the instructional design process. For example, after establishing an alternative instructional goal for a child in your class who has Down syndrome, you (and the child) still will benefit from following the systems strategy to ensure that goals, content, assessment, and instruction are aligned appropriately. Our systems model is powerful enough to generalize across all types of learners and subject matter. *You* will need to identify and understand the characteristics of each of your individual learners so you can make appropriate adjustments and adaptations.

The second way to think about the variability issue is to view your students' prospects for learning with optimism. I urge you not to underestimate the power of well-designed instruction to facilitate learning for students who have learning difficulties and other special needs. By establishing clear instructional goals and focusing on the internal learning processes necessary to achieve those goals, you may be able to help your learners achieve levels of success that otherwise would be impossible (Leinhardt & Bickel, 1987).

Question: The emphasis on students' achieving clear instructional goals seems unrealistic. What happens when some learners do not meet our objectives? The answer to this question can be found in Figure 12.1: diagnose and remediate. Diagnosis is the process of trying to find out why students are having difficulty. Remediation is the process of designing alternative learning experiences (i.e., reteaching) to overcome the difficulty based on the diagnosis. Even with the most carefully designed instruction, some learners may need additional help to achieve target objectives. If it is important for students to achieve the instructional goals we have specified, then we should hold ourselves accountable for helping them succeed. If the goals are not important enough to make the extra effort to diagnose and remediate, then perhaps we should not have specified them in the first place.

I recognize that school-level and classroom-level structures often do not support the amount of time and effort required for teachers to diagnose and remediate effectively with individual learners. This represents a tension and challenge in teaching with which you will wrestle constantly. I encourage you to search for creative mechanisms to support remediation such as peer tutoring, parental assistance, and the use of instructional technology. Although you may never be able to do all the diagnosis and remediation with individuals as you would like, do not let that stop you from doing as much as you can within your teaching situation.

Question: We've talked a lot about aiming for clear instructional goals and objectives as evidence of learning, but this book has been silent on the issue of grading. How should teachers translate assessment data into grades? I have deliberately avoided the complex topic of grading in this book. Grading is the process of communicating evaluation information to learners, families, schools, employers, and other school constituencies. In contrast, we have focused exclusively on learning outcomes and learning processes. As a *design-teacher*, I want you to focus your energies on supporting learning in the minds of your students rather than on their earning grades. How you choose (or are required) to communicate the degree of achievement your learners demonstrate is a secondary consideration.

Because grading is an evaluative process, it always requires subjective judgment. As a result, there are no perfect grading systems. You can find discussions of grading procedures in nearly any educational psychology or measurement textbook (Carey, 1994; Gage & Berliner, 1998; Lorber, 1996). I encourage you to investigate the various models of grading that exist and select (or design) the approach that best matches your personal philosophy on the purpose of grades. Regardless of the grading model you select, you will certainly enhance the quality of your grading system by collecting assessment data that are as valid and reliable as possible—a major contribution of our systems approach.

Question: This book is full of examples of instructional goals, but these goals are not necessarily found in all school curricula. How do teachers and schools make decisions about what goals to include in their curricula?   Every specific example in this book is intended to illustrate a particular concept or principle related to the instructional design process. I do not intend for teachers and schools to imitate the examples. Furthermore, the examples do not prescribe the specific instructional goals or subject matter that should be found in school classrooms. These types of curricular decisions must be made by teachers, schools, and the communities they serve. The instructional design process does not specify the goals and content that schools believe are important for learners to achieve. The instructional design process can help you figure out how to help your learners achieve those goals once they are established. If you understand the design principles we have examined in this book, you can apply our systems model of instructional design to any instructional goals within any content domain.

Question: In this book, we have focused on a single model of instructional design. Is this the only approach to instructional design that is available? Are there alternative ways to think about instructional design?   The single model of instructional design that we have explored in this book is a generalized combination of various design models that are grounded in the assumption that different learning outcomes require different learning conditions. Although different theorists have proposed numerous systems models and different ways to think about instructional design processes from this conditions-based perspective (see Edmonds, Branch, & Mukherjee, 1994; Ragan & Smith, 1996; Seels & Glasgow, 1998), they all seem to share the basic fundamental components we have examined (Dick, 1996). Rather than trying to familiarize you superficially with a wide variety of approaches to instructional design, I have tried to develop your in-depth understanding of a generalized systems model that you should be able to apply broadly and powerfully to any number of different classroom teaching contexts.

There certainly are alternative ways to think about instructional design and apply it to classroom teaching. Now that you have a firm grasp of the approach described in this book, I encourage you to expand and extend your knowledge of instructional design by exploring alternative conceptions and models presented by other theorists. As you read and think about alternative views, I believe you will find much in common with our systems model. You also will encounter some discrepancies between our systems model and other views. When this happens, you will need to analyze the points of disagreement and resolve them in ways that are consistent with your emerging knowledge base, research evidence, and classroom teaching experiences.

The field of instructional design is like any other area of human inquiry in that it is constantly evolving (Derry & Lesgold, 1996; Dick, 1996; Duffy & Cunningham, 1996). As theorists continue to modify and adapt their views of instructional design to fit new theoretical assumptions and research evidence, you may wish to revise your own thinking about designing classroom instruction. Trying to apply the ideas of a dynamic, constantly changing field to a complex endeavor such as classroom teaching can be enormously frustrating. However, the possibility that some ideas may change in the future does not negate their potential utility for today. You do not need to wait for the perfect instructional design model. I encourage you to begin now to apply what we do know about designing effective instruction for classroom teaching and learning.

LOOKING BACK LOOKING AHEAD

In this closing chapter, I have tried to anticipate some of the difficulties and challenges that you will encounter as you apply a systems approach to instructional design in your classroom teaching. Although you will face various classroom, school-level, and personal obstacles, I believe you will find the systems approach to be both highly effective and professionally rewarding.

We have now come to the end of our instructional design journey. Throughout this book, we have addressed three fundamental design questions and their interrelationships:

- Where are we going?
- What will we do when we get there?
- How will we get there?

As you enter (or continue in) the exciting and complex world of classroom teaching, I hope you will constantly ask yourself these three critical questions and use them to guide your thinking about instructional design. I also hope you will use these questions and our systems model as points of departure as you look ahead to personalizing the instructional design process and making it your own. You have a wonderful *design-teaching* journey ahead of you. Have fun, and enjoy the trip!

RESOURCES FOR FURTHER REFLECTION AND EXPLORATION

Print Resources

Banks, J. A. (1999). *An introduction to multicultural education.* Boston: Allyn and Bacon.

A book that provides an orientation to multicultural issues in teaching. The author demonstrates how specific teaching strategies and materials can be created or adapted to promote learning for students of diverse cultural backgrounds and to promote multicultural understanding among all students.

Calderhead, J. (1996). Teachers: Beliefs and knowledge. In D. C. Berliner & R. C. Calfee (Eds.), *Handbook of educational psychology* (pp. 709–725). New York: Macmillan.

The authors explore the effects of teacher beliefs and knowledge on their classroom teaching activities. A useful overview of the ways in which teachers' knowledge and thought processes play important roles in the effectiveness of any approach to classroom instructional design.

Dick, W. (1996). The Dick and Carey Model: Will it survive the decade? *Educational Technology Research and Development, 44,* 55–63.

A fascinating article in which Walter Dick, a long-time advocate of systems approaches to instructional design, traces the development of the well-known Dick and Carey Model and contrasts its assumptions to those of current constructivist models. Despite changing views of teaching and learning, Dick argues that systems models will remain relevant and useful to instructional designers.

Garcia, E. E. (1999). *Student cultural diversity: Understanding and meeting the challenge (2nd ed.).* Boston: Houghton Mifflin.

Explores the ways in which children learn to think and communicate within their homes, communities, and school environments by analyzing the social, cognitive, and communicative roots of diversity. Provides practical classroom applications for dealing with student diversity.

Goodlad, J. I. (1990). The occupation of teaching in schools. In J. I. Goodlad, R. Soder, & K. A. Sirotnik (Eds.), *The moral dimensions of teaching* (pp. 3–34). San Francisco: Jossey-Bass.

A thought-provoking chapter that examines the professional status of teaching. The author traces the historical roots of the problem and suggests some concrete solutions, urging educators to focus on the complexity of classroom decision making and problem solving as the only legitimate claim to professional status for teachers.

Glossary

Acronym. A mnemonic device in which words are created from the first letters of the words to be remembered.

Acrostic. A mnemonic device in which the first letters of a set of words to be remembered are used as the first letters of words that form a meaningful, memorable sentence.

Action consistency. The match between the action described in an instructional goal (or subgoal) and the action that learners perform during the assessment of that goal.

Action verb. A verb that specifies the external concrete action that learners will engage in to demonstrate their internal learned capabilities.

Adjunct questions. Questions or orienting activities embedded within instructional materials to call attention to important ideas and help learners process information actively.

Advance organizer. A carefully prepared body of information that provides learners with concepts, principles, and other general ideas that they can use to bring structure, organization, and understanding to the specific, detailed information they are about to learn.

Affect. A psychological term that refers to feelings and emotions.

Affective knowledge. Emotional knowledge that influences what people choose to do.

Algorithm. A series of specific steps to take to reach a specific problem-solving goal; a procedural rule.

Analogy. A relational comparison between two knowledge areas that seem to be dissimilar in outward appearance or characteristics.

Analytical scoring. Scoring student responses by comparing them to a set of specific criteria.

Assessment. The process of collecting information for the purpose of making decisions or evaluation.

Assessment blueprint. A general plan that describes the content and learner performance to be addressed through an assessment procedure, or test.

Associative stage. The second general stage of skill learning during which learners begin to change their declarative representation to a procedural representation by associating the production's conditions with their own actions. See also *cognitive stage* and *autonomous stage.*

Attention. The process of directing one's senses toward a source of information so that it can be received most effectively.

Attitude. An internal state that influences an individual's personal action choices.

Attitude assessment. A test item used to evaluate learners' feelings toward an attitude object or the probability that they will choose to behave in ways that are consistent with an acquired attitude.

Attitude system. The combination and interaction of behaviors, cognitions, and emotions related to an attitude object.

Authentic learning activities. Learning activities that give students the opportunity to apply new knowledge to meaningful, realistic situations.

Automatic. Performing a skill without devoting conscious thinking and attention.

Autonomous stage. The third general stage of skill acquisition during which learners continue to refine their performance of the skill, further strengthening condition-action associations and eliminating declarative cues. See also *cognitive stage* and *associative stage.*

Block plan. A chart that shows the day-to-day sequence of instructional goals within an instructional unit and the approximate amount of time to be allocated to each.

Capability verb. A verb used in an instructional goal to describe a performance that is consistent with the internal product of learning to be acquired through instruction.

Checklist. An analytical scoring device that provides a list of performance features with an accompanying space to note the presence or absence of each feature.

Chunking. A control process of the information processing system that occurs when meaningful patterns are found in new information.

Cluster analysis. A content analysis procedure for organizing isolated pieces of factual information into groupings (or clusters) of information that represent meaningful subordinate and superordinate relationships.

Cognitive conflict. A state of mental discomfort produced when people experience two ideas or events that are contradictory or discrepant; also referred to as *cognitive dissonance*.

Cognitive dissonance.   A state of mental discomfort produced when people experience two ideas or events that are contradictory or discrepant; also referred to as *cognitive conflict*.

Cognitive item.   A test item to which learners make a relatively simple behavioral response that reflects more complex internal cognitive processes.

Cognitive stage.   The first general stage of skill learning during which learners acquire a declarative representation of a production's conditions and actions. See also *associative stage* and *autonomous stage*.

Cognitive strategy.   A mental plan applied to manage thinking processes and behavior during problem-solving or learning tasks.

Composition process.   A process that occurs during the associative stage of skill learning by which two or more individual productions become integrated into one complex procedure.

Concept.   A type of intellectual skill that enables the categorization of objects or events that share common features.

Concrete concept.   A classification category whose common features can be easily perceived through one or more of the five senses.

Conditionalized knowledge.   Knowledge that is stored in memory along with the conditions and constraints of its use.

Content analysis.   The principles and procedures that instructional designers use to break down declarative, procedural, or affective knowledge into its component, or supporting, parts and specify how those parts are related to each other.

Content consistency.   The match between the specific information, skills, or attitudes that learners demonstrate during assessment and the information, skills, or attitudes that are to be evaluated.

Control processes.   Mental actions that occur within the information processing system to transform information from one memory structure to another.

Correlational concept features.   Irrelevant concept features that are frequently associated with members of the category but technically are not required for membership.

Culminating activity.   A learning activity that gives students the opportunity to apply many or all of a unit's instructional goals in an integrated way.

Curriculum-level educational goals.   Educational goals that generalize to a wide variety of specific unit topics and content domains.

Declarative knowledge.   Factual information stored in long-term memory so that it can be recalled and stated when desired.

Deductive teaching.   Presenting learners with a generalization such as a concept definition, rule, or principle and then providing specific examples to make the generalization meaningful.

Defined concept.   An abstract classification category whose common features cannot be easily perceived through sight, sound, smell, taste, or touch.

Defining concept features.   Relevant concept features that restrict concept membership only to positive instances.

Describing concept features.   Relevant concept features that do not necessarily distinguish examples from nonexamples.

Design.   Actions, processes, or procedures that are intended to accomplish a particular outcome or goal.

Design-teacher.   A teacher who focuses on clear learning goals to guide specific decisions, actions, and interactions with learners in the classroom.

Diagnosis.   Collecting data for the purpose of identifying the causes of a learning difficulty.

Diagnostic evaluation.   The process of determining why learners are having difficulty achieving an instructional goal.

Discrimination.   A type of intellectual skill that enables the detection differences between perceptual stimuli.

Discrimination process.   The learning process by which learners acquire the ability to recognize instances to which a skill does not apply.

Disequilibrium.   A state of intellectual imbalance created when new experiences cannot be explained by existing knowledge. See also *cognitive dissonance; cognitive conflict*.

Distributed practice.   Using a greater number of practice sessions that are shorter in duration.

Divergent examples.   Positive instances of a concept, rule, or principle that differ from one another because they have different values for the irrelevant features.

Domain-specific.   Knowledge that can be applied within a well-defined content area.

Educational goal.   A broad outcome statement that describes the general characteristics all learners should possess after a significant amount of time engaged with the school curriculum.

Elaboration.   A generative learning process that occurs when learners enrich new information by adding extra information from their own semantic networks.

Elaborative interrogation.   A learning strategy in which learners elaborate on new information by asking and answering "why" questions about the information.

Enactive representation.   J. S. Bruner's first level of knowledge acquisition; understanding the world through direct physical contact and bodily movement. See also *iconic representation* and *symbolic representation*.

Encoding.   A control process of the information processing system that occurs when information is transformed from working memory to long-term memory.

Evaluation.   The process of making judgments about the value, importance, quality, or worth of the characteristics observed in people.

Executive control.   A component of the information processing system that manages the control processes that are responsible for information flow during learning.

Expectancy.   Learners' awareness and understanding of the learning outcome they are attempting to achieve.

External conditions of learning.   The communications, media, materials, equipment, and learning activities that students experience directly and that teachers can manipulate to support learning indirectly.

External processes of learning.   Interactions with objects, people, events, and ideas from the environment that produce learning.

External products of learning.   The ability to perform new capabilities as outward manifestations of learning.

Facts.   Ideas stored in long-term memory that can be recalled and stated as complete sentences.

Feedback.   Any communication provided to learners to inform them of the quality of their performance and help them improve the quality of their learning.

Formative evaluation.   The process of determining how well learners are progressing toward achievement of an instructional goal.

Frequency count.   An analytical scoring device in which the number of times a specified feature of a student's performance is observed and recorded.

Generalization process.   The learning process by which learners acquire the ability to apply a skill broadly to all positive instances.

Global scoring.   See *holistic scoring.*

Goal clustering.   The process of grouping instructional goals together on the basis of shared features or useful teaching-learning relationships.

Guided discovery.   Engaging learners with specific examples of a concept, rule, or principle and then helping them construct an appropriate generalization; an alternative term for *inductive teaching.*

Heuristic.   A domain-general plan that helps problem solvers coordinate declarative and procedural knowledge to achieve a goal.

Hierarchical analysis.   A content analysis procedure for identifying subordinate, prerequisite skills that learners need to possess before they are ready to acquire a higher-level skill.

Higher-order rule.   A combination of rules and principles that are sequenced and applied as intellectual skills to guide problem-solving thinking and behavior.

Highlighting.   The process of emphasizing a message so that it stands out from surrounding information that is not as important or relevant.

Holistic scoring.   Scoring student responses by assigning a single number to reflect the quality of the entire response or performance.

Iconic representation.   J. S. Bruner's second level of knowledge acquisition: using pictures or visual images to represent ideas. See also *enactive representation* and *symbolic representation.*

Image elaboration.   A mental picture that learners create by combining new information with visual images that are already part of their schemas.

Inclusion.   The effort to provide learning experiences for children with special needs in regular classrooms with their normally functioning peers.

Inductive teaching.   Engaging learners with specific examples of a concept, rule, or principle and then helping them construct an appropriate generalization. See also *guided discovery.*

Informative feedback.   Information that learners receive following an action that tells them whether their performance was appropriate and why the performance was appropriate or inappropriate.

Instruction.   A set of events external to learners that are intended to support their internal learning processes.

Instructional designer.   A person who carefully and thoughtfully creates learning experiences for others.

Instructional goal.   A statement that describes the capability learners should be able to demonstrate following, or as a result of, instruction.

Instructional objective.   A detailed description of how data will be collected to provide evidence that learners have achieved an instructional goal.

Instructional phase.   The second general stage in an instructional sequence in which the primary goal is to help learners construct a meaningful representation of the new information they are to acquire. See also *preinstructional phase* and *postinstructional phase.*

Instructional sequence. A general series of events that teachers use to manage instructional time and space to maximize the probability that learning will occur.

Instructional space. The set of physical resources that teachers can use to support student learning.

Instructional strategy. A sequence of learning activities, materials, and resources developed to help learners achieve an instructional goal.

Instructional subgoal. An instructional goal that describes a learned capability for a subordinate (or prerequisite) skill.

Instructional system. A set of interrelated components that work together to produce a specified learning outcome.

Instructional time. The amount of time teachers have available to engage their learners with learning activities and materials.

Intellectual skills. Generalizations that are symbolized mentally and used to interact with the environment.

Internal conditions of learning. The inner characteristics and learning processes that influence directly how students achieve learning outcomes.

Internal processes of learning. Constructive mental actions, hidden from direct observation, that learners employ to perceive, interpret, and think about their experiences with the environment.

Internal products of learning. Forms of knowledge that learners construct from their internal learning processes and represent mentally (e.g, factual information, skills, attitudes).

Irrelevant concept features. The features of concept instances that vary from example to example and, therefore, have no bearing on membership in the concept category.

Keyword method. A mnemonic device in which learners create a visual image of an idea that sounds like a key part of a word to be remembered interacting with the word's meaning.

Labels. Names or symbols associated with objects or events so that they can be referred to more easily.

Learning. A relatively stable change in outward capability that is constructed internally from experiences with the world.

Learning activity. An action or event in which learners actively participate to increase the probability that they will process information in ways

that are appropriate for the learning outcome they are to acquire.

Learning outcome. A set of learned capabilities that have common learning processes, teaching strategies, and assessment procedures.

Learning strategy. A cognitive plan that helps the learner manage the flow of new information so that it can be stored effectively in long-term memory.

Likert scale. An attitude assessment device that asks people to express their level of agreement with opinion statements about an attitude object.

Long-term memory. A memory structure of the information processing system that holds an infinite amount of information for very long periods of time.

Mapping. The process of transferring relationships from the base domain of an analogy to the target domain.

Matched examples and nonexamples. Pairs of examples and nonexamples that are as similar as possible with respect to irrelevant features; used to promote skill discrimination.

Measurement. The process of assigning numbers to learner characteristics so that the numbers indicate the degree to which the characteristics are present.

Measurement error. The difference between learners' true abilities and the estimate of their abilities that is obtained through assessment.

Mediated learning experiences. Teaching-learning episodes in which teachers transform both the content and learner thinking to maximize the degree of meaning learners can construct from instructional activities and materials.

Method of loci. A mnemonic device in which ideas to be remembered are associated visually with objects located in a familiar area, such as the rooms in one's house.

Mnemonic devices. Cognitive strategies that help learners manufacture artificial links between new information and their prior knowledge.

Motivation. An internal state that stimulates, focuses, and maintains thinking and behavior.

Motor skill. A series of smooth, coordinated, well-timed muscular movements that are performed to accomplish a goal.

Objective data. Observations that two or more different people are likely to interpret in the same way.

Organized facts. A collection of propositions that are related to each other in a meaningful way.

Organizing unit theme. A very broad generalization that can be related to a wide variety of declarative, procedural, or affective content knowledge within an instructional unit.

Overgeneralization. A type of misconception that occurs when learners apply a skill too broadly to negative instances or nonexamples.

Part-skill. A subordinate skill found in a sequence of steps that make up a more complex intellectual or motor procedure.

Peg-word system. A mnemonic device in which learners create visual images of ideas to be remembered interacting with concrete objects that already have been memorized.

Performance item. A test item in which learners recall verbal information or apply procedural knowledge in the context of a meaningful problem or activity.

Physical characteristics. Features of learners that are produced by natural biological variation between individuals or maturational processes.

Portfolio. A collection of concrete pieces of evidence that suggest or demonstrate a student's skills and abilities.

Postinstructional phase. The third general stage in an instructional sequence in which the primary goal is to help learners strengthen and extend newly acquired knowledge. See also *preinstructional phase* and *instructional phase*.

Preassessment. The process of collecting data prior to instruction to evaluate learners' preexisting knowledge and skills.

Preinstructional evaluation. The process of determining learner readiness for instruction.

Preinstructional phase. The first general stage in an instructional sequence in which the primary goal is to prepare learners to process the content they need to acquire. See also *instructional phase* and *postinstructional phase*.

Prerequisite skills. Lower-level skills that make possible the learning of higher-level skills; also referred to as *subordinate skills*.

Principle. A type of intellectual skill that expresses regular concept relationships and enables understanding, explaining, and predicting in thinking or problem-solving situations.

Problem. Any situation in which a goal (or goals) has been identified but with no clear set of procedures for achieving it.

Problem representation. The initial understanding of a problem that people construct in their minds.

Problem solving. A type of intellectual skill in which thinking processes and actions reduce the distance between a given state and a goal to be achieved.

Procedural analysis. A content analysis procedure for identifying and sequencing the series of mental or physical steps required to perform a procedural rule, cognitive strategy, or motor skill.

Procedural knowledge. Skills and strategies that can be used to perform mental and physical tasks.

Procedural rule. A series of specific steps to take to reach a specific problem-solving goal; an algorithm.

Proceduralization. A process that occurs during the associative stage of skill learning as the associations being formed among productions begin to control learner actions rather than the conscious declarative cues acquired during the cognitive stage.

Production. The form in which procedural knowledge is represented in long-term memory; a rule that triggers an action (either mental or physical) when certain conditions are met.

Production system. A set of individual productions that are connected because the outcome of one production helps to satisfy the conditions of another production.

Proposition. A complete idea unit that can be judged to be either true or false.

Prototype. An example of a concept category that possesses the most typical, or common, values of the critical features; the most common examples of a concept.

Psychomotor skill. An alternative term for motor skill; emphasizes the cognitive skills that support skilled muscular movement.

Psychosocial characteristics. Features of learners that influence their attitudes, interests, motivations, and social relationships.

Qualitative assessment. The process of collecting data that are not expressed numerically.

Quantitative assessment. The process of collecting data that are expressed numerically.

Rating scale. An analytical scoring device that provides a list of performance features with an accompanying numeric scale to record each feature's degree of quality.

Rehearsal. A control process of the information processing system that occurs when information is repeated while in the state of short-term memory.

Relevant concept features. The features that all positive instances of a concept possess. Their presence is essential for membership in the concept category.

Reliability. The degree to which assessment data are free from measurement error so that they provide a dependable, trustworthy estimate of learner ability.

Remediation. The process of planning and implementing an alternative instructional strategy to overcome a learning difficulty that has been diagnosed.

Response mode. The type of motor activity that learners must be able to produce to respond to an assessment opportunity.

Retrieval. A control process of the information processing system that occurs when information is transformed from its long-term memory state to working memory.

Rubric. A scoring guide; an alternative term for *analytical scoring procedure.*

Rule. A type of intellectual skill that expresses regular concept relationships and guides thinking or problem-solving behavior.

Schema. An organized network of ideas that are related to each other and stored in long-term memory.

Schematic diagram. A visual representation that shows how a system of interrelated ideas or concepts interacts.

Selective perception. A control process of the information processing system that occurs when meaning is assigned to a piece of sensory information.

Self-efficacy. Beliefs that learners have about how successfully they will perform particular tasks; perceived expectations for success.

Semantic differential. An attitude assessment device that presents pairs of bipolar, or opposite, adjectives that could be used to describe an attitude object, along with several degrees of different meaning between them. Students respond to each item by indicating where their views of the attitude object fall along the continuum of meaning between the two extremes provided.

Semantic network. The web of interconnected propositions, productions, and images that is stored in long-term memory.

Sensory registers. A memory structure of the information processing system that briefly holds information received from the environment through one or more of the five senses.

Short-term memory. A memory structure of the information processing system that holds information in the form of sounds, images, or words in a conscious state of awareness.

Situated cognition. Linking new knowledge to the superficial social and physical contexts in which it is learned.

Spreading activation. The retrieval process by which thinking about one idea stored in long-term memory triggers related ideas.

Stimulus. The question or directions given to learners to elicit their response or guide their performance during assessment.

Subjective data. Observations that two or more people are likely to interpret differently.

Subordinate skills. Lower-level skills that make possible the learning of higher-level skills; also referred to as *prerequisite skills.*

Summative evaluation. The process of determining how well learners can perform the instructional goals that were the intended focus of instruction.

Symbolic representation. J. S. Bruner's third level of knowledge acquisition: the ability to use abstract symbols such as numbers, letters, words, and formulas to stand for ideas. See also *enactive representation* and *iconic representation.*

Table of specifications. A two-dimensional chart that organizes the information found in an assessment blueprint.

Target goal. The final instructional goal that learners are to achieve through instruction.

Target principle. The final, higher-level principle that learners are to acquire through instruction.

Task analysis. The process of breaking down a learned capability into its component, or supporting, parts and specifying how those parts are related to each other; also referred to as *content analysis.*

Test. An assessment tool designed to collect objective data for use in the evaluation process. A set of questions or tasks for which predetermined types of responses are expected.

Test item. A question or task designed to transform an unobservable, internal learning outcome into an observable, external performance so that learning can be evaluated.

Test-wiseness. The ability of test takers to use the features of a test or testing situation to obtain scores that are higher than their true knowledge or ability would produce.

Thematic unit. Organization of instructional time and materials around a central topic that lends itself naturally to the integration of different curriculum content areas.

Thurstone scale. An attitude assessment device that provides people with the opportunity to express their agreement or disagreement with opinion statements about an attitude object.

Transfer. The degree to which learners can apply their knowledge to new tasks, problems, or situations beyond the original learning environment.

Undergeneralization. A type of misconception that occurs when learners cannot apply a skill to all possible instances.

Unit. A teaching sequence of several weeks' duration in which instruction is based on a central or organizing theme.

Unit-level assessment.   A data collection process implemented at the conclusion of the unit to determine how well the instructional goals have been achieved; a unit test.

Unit-level educational goals.   Educational goals that are closely related to a unit topic and are most likely to be addressed within a particular unit of content.

Validity.   The degree to which assessment data match the evaluative decisions for which they are to be used.

Verbal chain.   A series of words or sentences stored in memory verbatim (word for word).

Verbal elaboration.   An idea that learners add on to new information from their own schemas by means of words that they might say out loud or to themselves.

Verbal information.   Declarative knowledge. Factual information stored in long-term memory so that it can be recalled and stated when needed.

Working memory.   The part of short-term memory that is used to perform mental operations, such as skill application, planning, problem solving, and decision making.

Zone of proximal development.   The difference between the level of understanding that learners can achieve by themselves and what they are capable of achieving with the assistance of a knowledgeable adult or peer who performs a mediating role.

References

Ackerman, J. M. (1972). *Operant conditioning techniques for the classroom teacher.* Glenview, IL: Scott, Foresman.

Alberto, P. A., & Troutman, A. C. (1982). *Applied behavior analysis for teachers.* Columbus: Merrill.

Alexander, K. L., Entwisle, D. R., & Dauber, S. L. (1993). First-grade classroom behavior: Its short- and long-term consequences for school performance. *Child Development, 64,* 801–814.

American Educational Research Association, American Psychological Association, & National Council on Measurement in Education. (1999). *Standards for educational and psychological testing.* Washington, DC: American Psychological Association.

American Federation of Teachers, National Council on Measurement in Education, & National Education Association. (1990). Standards for teacher competence in educational assessment of students. *Educational Measurement: Issues and Practices, 9,* 30–32.

Anastasi, A. (1988). *Psychological testing* (6th ed.). New York: Macmillan.

Anderson, J. R. (1976). *Language, memory, and thought.* Hillsdale, NJ: Erlbaum.

Anderson, J. R. (1980). *Cognitive psychology and its implications.* San Francisco: Freeman.

Anderson, J. R. (1983). *The architecture of cognition.* Cambridge, MA: Harvard University Press.

Anderson, J. R. (1990). *Cognitive psychology and its implications* (3rd ed.). New York: Freeman.

Anderson, J. R. (1993). *Rules of the mind.* Hillsdale, NJ: Erlbaum.

Anderson, J. R. (1995). *Learning and memory: An integrated approach.* New York: Wiley.

Anderson, J. R. (1996). ACT: A simple theory of complex cognition. *American Psychologist, 51,* 355–365.

Anderson, R. C., Reynolds, R. E., Schallert, D. L., & Goetz, E. T. (1977). Frameworks for comprehending discourse. *American Educational Research Journal, 14,* 367–382.

Andre, T. (1986). Problem solving and education. In G. D. Phye & T. Andre (Eds.), *Cognitive classroom learning* (pp. 169–204). New York: Academic Press.

Andrews, J. R., & Goodson, L. A. (1980). A comparative analysis of models of instructional design. *Journal of Instructional Development, 3,* 2–16.

Annett, J. (1989). Training skilled performance. In A. M. Colley & J. R. Beech (Eds.), *Acquisition and performance of cognitive skills.* New York: Wiley.

Ausubel, D. P. (1960). The use of advance organizers in the learning and retention of meaningful verbal learning. *Journal of Educational Psychology, 51,* 26–272.

Ausubel, D. P. (1968). *Educational psychology: A cognitive view.* New York: Holt, Rinehart & Winston.

Bahrick, H. P., & Phelps, E. (1987). Retention of Spanish vocabulary over eight years. *Journal of Experimental Psychology: Learning, Memory, and Cognition, 13,* 344–349.

Bahrick, H. P., Bahrick, L. E., Bahrick, A. S., & Bahrick, P. E. (1993). Maintenance of foreign language vocabulary and the spacing effect. *Psychological Science, 4,* 316–321.

Baine, D. (1986). *Memory and instruction.* Englewood Cliffs, NJ: Educational Technology Publications.

Balzer, W. K., Doherty, M. E., & O'Connor, R. (1989). Effects of cognitive feedback on performance. *Psychological Bulletin, 106,* 410–433.

Bandura, A. (1977). Self-efficacy: Toward a unifying theory of behavioral change. *Psychological Review, 84,* 191–215.

Bandura, A. (1982). Self-efficacy mechanism in human agency. *American Psychologist, 37,* 122–147.

Bangert-Drowns, R. L., Kulik, C. C., Kulik, J. A., & Morgan, M. (1991). The instructional effect of feedback in test-like events. *Review of Educational Research, 61,* 213–238.

Barton, J., & Collins, A. (1997). Starting out: Designing your portfolio. In J. Barton & A. Collins (Eds.), *Portfolio assessment: A handbook for educators* (pp. 1–10). Reading, MA: Addison-Wesley.

Baxter, G., Shavelson, R., Goldman, S., & Pine, J. (1992). Evaluation of procedure-based scoring for hands-on science assessment. *Journal of Educational Measurement, 29,* 1–17.

Bereiter, C. (1995). A dispositional view of transfer. In A. McKeough, J. Lupart, & A. Marini (Eds.), *Teaching for transfer: Fostering generalization in learning* (pp. 21–34). Mahwah, NJ: Erlbaum.

Berlyne, D. E. (1960). *Conflict, arousal, and curiosity.* New York: McGraw-Hill.

Bishop, B. A., & Anderson, C. W. (1990). Student misconceptions of natural selection and its role in evolution. *Journal of Research in Science Teaching, 27,* 415–427.

Boothby, P. R., & Alvermann, D. E. (1984). A classroom training study: The effects of graphic organizer instruction on fourth graders' comprehension. *Reading World, 26,* 325–339.

Bourne, L. E. (1982). Typicality effects in logically defined categories. *Memory and Cognition, 10,* 3–9.

Bousfield, W. A. (1953). The occurrence of clustering in the recall of randomly arranged associates. *Journal of General Psychology, 49,* 229–240.

Boyer, E. L. (1995). *The basic school: A community for learning.* Princeton, NJ: The Carnegie Foundation for the Advancement of Teaching.

Bransford, J. D., & Franks, J. J. (1971). The abstraction of linguistic ideas. *Cognitive Psychology, 2,* 331–350.

Bransford, J. D., & Johnson, M. K. (1972). Contextual prerequisites for understanding: Some investigations of comprehension and recall. *Journal of Verbal Learning and Verbal Behavior, 61,* 717–726.

Bransford, J. D., Vye, N. J., Adams, L. T., & Perfetto, G. A. (1989). Learning skills and the acquisition of knowledge. In A. Lesgold & R. Glaser (Eds.), *Foundations for a psychology of education* (pp. 199–249). Hillsdale, NJ: Erlbaum.

Breckler, S. J. (1984). Empirical validation of affect, behavior, and cognition as distinct components of attitude. *Journal of Personality and Social Psychology, 47,* 1191–1205.

Bromage, B., & Mayer, R. (1981). Relationship between what is remembered and creative problem-solving performance in science learning. *Journal of Educational Psychology, 73,* 451–461.

Brophy, J. (1986). Teacher influences on student achievement. *American Psychologist, 41,* 1069–1077.

Brophy, J. (1988). Research linking teacher behavior to student achievement: Potential implications for instruction of Chapter 1 students. *Educational Psychologist, 23,* 235–286.

Brophy, J. (1999). Toward a model of the value aspects of motivation in education: Developing appreciation for particular learning domains and activities. *Educational Psychologist, 34,* 75–85.

Bruner, J. S. (1960). *The process of education.* Cambridge, MA: Harvard University Press.

Bruner, J. S. (1966). *Toward a theory of instruction.* New York: Norton.

Bruner, J. S. Goodnow, J. J., & Austin, G. A. (1956). *A study of thinking.* New York: Wiley.

Bruning, R. H., Schraw, G., & Ronning, R. R. (1999). *Cognitive psychology and instruction* (3rd ed.). Upper Saddle River, NJ: Merrill.

Burton, J. K., Niles, J. A., Lalik, R. M., & Reed, M. W. (1986). Cognitive capacity engagement during and following interspersed mathemagenic questions. *Journal of Educational Psychology, 78,* 147–152.

Butterfield, E. C., Slocum, T. A., & Nelson, G. D. (1993). Cognitive and behavioral analyses of teaching and transfer: Are they different? In D. K. Detterman & R. J. Sternberg (Eds.), *Transfer on trial: Intelligence, cognition, and instruction* (pp. 192–257). Norwood, NJ: Ablex.

Calderhead, J. (1996). Teachers: Beliefs and knowledge. In D. C. Berliner & R. C. Calfee (Eds.), *Handbook of educational psychology* (pp. 709–725). New York: Macmillan.

Camp, R. (1993). The place of portfolios in our changing views of writing assessment. In R. Bennett & W. Ward (Eds.), *Constructive versus choice in cognitive measurement: Issues in constructed response, performance testing, and portfolio assessment.* Hillsdale, NJ: Erlbaum.

Canady, R. L., & Rettig, M. D. (1995a). The power of innovative scheduling. *Educational Leadership, 53(3),* 4-10.

Canady, R. L., & Rettig, M. D. (1995b). *Block scheduling: A catalyst for change in high schools.* Princeton, NJ: Eye on Education.

Carey, L. M. (1994). *Measuring and evaluating school learning* (2nd ed.). Boston: Allyn and Bacon.

Carey, S. (1985). Are children fundamentally different thinkers and learners from adults? In S. F. Chipman, J. W. Segal, & R. Glaser (Eds.), *Thinking and learning skills* (Vol. 2, pp. 485–517). Hillsdale, NJ: Erlbaum.

Carey, S., & Smith, C. (1993). On understanding the nature of scientific knowledge. *Educational Psychologist, 28,* 235–251.

Carlson, R. A. (1997). *Experienced cognition.* Mahwah, NJ: Erlbaum.

Case, R. (1991). A developmental approach to the design of remedial instruction. In A. McKeough & J. L. Lupart (Eds.), *Toward the practice of theory-based instruction* (pp. 117–147). Hillsdale, NJ: Erlbaum.

Case, R. (1993). Theories of learning and theories of development. *Educational Psychologist, 28,* 219–233.

Chase, C. I. (1979). The impact of achievement expectations and handwriting quality on scoring essay tests. *Journal of Educational Measurement, 16,* 39–42.

Chase, C. I. (1986). Essay test scoring: Interaction of relevant variables. *Journal of Educational Measurement, 23,* 33–41.

Chaskin, R. J., & Rauner, D. M. (1995). Youth and caring. *Phi Delta Kappan, 76,* 667–674.

Cheng, P. W., Holyoak, K. J., Nisbett, R. E., & Oliver, L. M. (1986). Pragmatic versus syntactic approaches to training deductive reasoning. *Cognitive Psychology, 18,* 293–328.

Chi, M. T. H., Feltovich, P. J., & Glaser, R. (1981). Categorization and representation of physics problems by experts and novices. *Cognitive Science, 5,* 121–152.

Chi, M. T. H., Glaser, R., & Farr, M. J. (Eds.). (1988). *The nature of expertise.* Hillsdale, NJ: Erlbaum.

Chinn, C. A., & Brewer, W. F. (1993). The role of anomalous data in knowledge acquisition: A theoretical framework and implications for science instruction. *Review of Educational Research, 63,* 1–49.

Clandinin, D. J., & Connelly, F. M. (1992). Teacher as curriculum maker. In P. W. Jackson (Ed.), *Handbook of research on curriculum* (pp. 363–401). New York: Macmillan.

Clark, C. M., & Peterson, P. L. (1986). Teachers' thought processes. In M. C. Wittrock (Ed.), *Handbook of research on teaching* (3rd ed.) (pp. 255–296). New York: Macmillan.

Clark, C. M., & Yinger, R. J. (1987). Teacher planning. In J. Calderhead (Ed.), *Exploring teachers' thinking* (pp. 84–103). London: Casell.

Clark, J. M., & Paivio, A. (1991). Dual coding theory and education. *Educational Psychology Review, 3,* 149–210.

Clark, R. E., & Salomon, G. (1986). Media in teaching. In M. C. Wittrock (Ed.), *Handbook of research on teaching* (3rd ed.). New York: Macmillan.

Colley, A. M., & Beech, J. R. (1989). Acquiring and performing cognitive skills. In A. M. Colley & J. R. Beech (Eds.), *Acquisition and performance of cognitive skills* (pp. 1–16). New York: Wiley.

Collins, A. (1991). Cognitive apprenticeship and instructional technology. In L. Idol & B. F. Jones (Eds.), *Educational values and cognitive instruction: Implications for education* (pp. 121-138). Hillsdale, NJ: Erlbaum.

Collins, A., Brown, J. S., & Newman, S. E. (1989). Cognitive apprenticeship: Teaching the crafts of reading, writing, and mathematics. In L. B. Resnick (Ed.), *Knowing, learning, and instruction: Essays in honor of Robert Glaser* (pp. 453–494). Hillsdale, NJ: Erlbaum.

Cooper, P. A. (1993). Paradigm shifts in designed instruction: From behaviorism to cognitivism to constructivism. *Educational Technology, 33,* 12–19.

Cordova, D., & Lepper, M. R. (1996). Intrinsic motivation and the process of learning: Beneficial effects of contextualization, personalization, and choice. *Journal of Educational Psychology, 88,* 715–730.

Corkill, A. J. (1992). Advance organizers: Facilitators of recall. *Educational Psychology Review, 4,* 33–67.

Cox, B. D. (1997). The rediscovery of the active learner in adaptive contexts: A developmental-historical analysis of transfer of training. *Educational Psychologist, 32,* 41–55.

Crockett, T. (1998). *The portfolio journey.* Englewood, CO: Teacher Ideas Press.

Cuban, L. (1986). *Teachers and machines.* New York: Teachers College Press.

Dansereau, D. F. (1995). Derived structural schemas and the transfer of knowledge. In A. McKeough, J. Lupart, & A. Marini (Eds.), *Teaching for transfer: Fostering generalization in learning* (pp. 93–121). Mahwah, NJ: Erlbaum.

De Corte, E., Greer, B., & Verschaffel, L. (1996). Mathematics teaching and learning. In D. C. Berliner & R. C. Calfee (Eds.), *Handbook of educational psychology* (pp. 491–549). New York: Macmillan.

Dempsey, J. V., Driscoll, M. P., & Swindell, L. K. (1993). Text-based feedback. In J. V. Dempsey & G. C. Sales (Eds.), *Interactive instruction and feedback* (pp. 21–54). Englewood Cliffs, NJ: Educational Technology.

Dempster, F. N. (1991). Synthesis of research on reviews and tests. *Educational Leadership, 48,* 71–76.

Derry, S., & Lesgold, A. (1996). Toward a situated social practice model for instructional design. In D. C. Berliner & R. C. Calfee (Eds.), *Handbook of educational psychology* (pp. 787–806). New York: Macmillan.

Detterman, D. K. (1993). The case for the prosecution: Transfer as an epiphenomenon. In D. K. Detterman & R. J. Sternberg (Eds.), *Transfer on trial: Intelligence, cognition, and instruction* (pp. 1–24). Norwood, NJ: Ablex.

Di Vesta, F. J. (1987). The cognitive movement and education. In J. A. Glover & R. R. Ronning (Eds.), *Historical foundations of educational psychology* (pp. 203–233). New York: Plenum Press.

Di Vesta, F. J. (1989). Applications of cognitive psychology to education. In M. C. Wittrock & F. Farley (Eds.), *The future of educational psychology.* Hillsdale, NJ: Erlbaum.

Di Vesta, F. J., & Peverly, S. (1984). The effects of encoding variability, processing activity, and rule-examples sequence on the transfer of conceptual rules. *Journal of Educational Psychology, 76,* 108–119.

Dick, W. (1996). The Dick and Carey Model: Will it survive the decade? *Educational Technology Research and Development, 44,* 55–63.

Dick, W. (1997). A model for the systematic design of instruction. In R. D. Tennyson, F. Schott, N. Seel, & S. Dijkstra (Eds.), *Instructional design: International perspective* (Vol. 1, pp. 361–369). Mahwah, NJ: Erlbaum.

Dick, W., & Carey, L. (1996). *The systematic design of instruction* (4th ed.). New York: HarperCollins.

Dick, W., & Reiser, R. A. (1989). *Planning effective instruction.* Englewood Cliffs, NJ: Prentice-Hall.

Dole, J. A., Duffy, G. G., Roehler, L. R., & Pearson, P. D. (1991). Moving from the old to the new: Research on reading comprehension instruction. *Review of Educational Research, 61,* 239–264.

Dole, J. A., & Sinatra, G. M. (1998). Reconceptualizing change in the cognitive construction of knowledge. *Educational Psychologist, 33,* 109–128.

Doll, R. C. (1996). *Curriculum improvement* (9th ed.). Boston: Allyn and Bacon.

Doyle, W. (1983). Academic work. *Review of Educational Research, 53,* 159–199.

Doyle, W. (1986). Classroom organization and management. In M. C. Wittrock (Ed.), *Handbook of research on teaching* (3rd ed.) (pp. 392–431). New York: Macmillan.

Doyle, W. (1992). Curriculum and pedagogy. In P. W. Jackson (Ed.), *Handbook of research on curriculum* (pp. 486-516). New York: Macmillan.

Driscoll, M. P. (1994). *Psychology of learning for instruction*. Boston: Allyn and Bacon.

Driscoll, M. P., & Tessmer, M. A. (1985). The rational set generator: A method for creating concept examples for teaching and training. *Educational Technology, 25*(2), 29–32.

Duchastel, P. (1979). Learning objectives and the organization of prose. *Journal of Educational Psychology, 71,* 100–106.

Duffy, T. M., & Cunningham, D. J. (1996). Constructivism: Implications for the design and delivery of instruction. In D. H. Jonassen (Ed.), *Handbook of research for educational communications and technology* (pp. 170–198). New York: Simon & Schuster.

Duffy, T. M., & Jonassen, D. H. (1991). Constructivism: New implications for instructional technology? *Educational Technology, 31,* 7–12.

Dweck, C. S. (1986). Motivational processes affecting learning. *American Psychologist, 41,* 1040–1048.

Eaton, J. F., Anderson, C. W., & Smith, E. L. (1984). Students' misconceptions interfere with science learning: Case studies of fifth-grade students. *Elementary School Journal, 84,* 365–379.

Eby, J. W., & Kujawa, E. (1994). *Reflective planning, teaching, and evaluation: K–12*. New York: Merrill.

Edmonds, G. S., Branch, R. C., & Mukherjee, P. (1994). A conceptual framework for comparing instructional design models. *Educational Technology Research and Development, 42,* 55–72.

Eisele, B. (1991). *Managing the whole language classroom*. Cypress, CA: Creative Teaching Press.

Elbow, P. (1994). Will the virtues of portfolios blind us to their potential dangers? In L. Black, D. A. Daiker, J. Sommers, & G. Stygall (Eds.), *New directions in portfolio assessment* (pp. 40–55). Portsmouth, NH: Boynton/Cook Publishers.

Ellis, A. K., Mackey, J. A., & Glenn, A. D. (1988). *The school curriculum*. Boston: Allyn and Bacon.

Emmer, E. T., Evertson, C. M., Clements, B. S., & Worsham, M. E. (1997*). Classroom management for secondary teachers* (4th ed.). Boston: Allyn and Bacon.

Ericsson, K. A., Krampe, R. T., & Tesch-Romer, C. (1993). The role of deliberate practice in the acquisition of expert performance. *Psychological Review, 100,* 363–406.

Ericsson, K. A., & Simon, H. A. (1980). Verbal reports as data. *Psychological Review, 87,* 215–251.

Evertson, C. M., Emmer, E. T., Clements, B. S., & Worsham, M. E. (1997). *Classroom management for elementary teachers* (4th ed.). Boston: Allyn and Bacon.

Eysenck, M. W. (1992). *Anxiety: The cognitive perspective*. Hillsdale, NJ: Erlbaum.

Festinger, L. (1957). *A theory of cognitive dissonance*. Evanston, IL: Row, Peterson.

Fitts, P. M., & Posner, M. I. (1967). *Human performance*. Monterey, CA: Brooks-Cole.

Fogarty, R. (1991). Ten ways to integrate curriculum. *Educational Leadership, 49*(2), 61–65.

Frazee, B., & Rudnitski, R. A. (1995). *Integrated teaching methods*. Albany, NY: Delmar.

Freedman, S., Jackson, J., & Boles, K. (1983). Teaching: An imperilled "profession." In L. S. Shulman & G. Sykes (Eds.), *Handbook of teaching and policy* (pp. 261–299). New York: Longman.

Gage, N. L., & Berliner, D. C. (1998). *Educational psychology* (6th ed.). Boston: Houghton Mifflin.

Gagne, E. D., Yekovich, C. W., & Yekovich, F. R. (1993). *The cognitive psychology of school learning* (2nd ed.). New York: HarperCollins.

Gagne, R. M. (1984). Learning outcomes and their effects. *American Psychologist, 39,* 377–385.

Gagne, R. M. (1985). *The conditions of learning* (4th ed.). Philadelphia: Holt, Rinehart and Winston.

Gagne, R. M., & Driscoll, M. P. (1988). *Essentials of learning for instruction* (2nd ed.). Englewood Cliffs, NJ: Prentice-Hall.

Gagne, R. M., & Paradise, N. E. (1961). Abilities and learning sets in knowledge acquisition. *Psychological monographs: General and applied, 74,* whole No. 518.

Gagne, R. M., & Smith, E. A. (1962). A study of the effects of verbalization on problem solving. *Journal of Experimental Psychology, 63,* 12–18.

Gagne, R. M., Briggs, L. J., & Wager, W. W. (1992). *Principles of instructional design* (4th ed.). New York: Harcourt Brace Jovanovich.

Gagne, R. M., Weidemann, C., Bell, M. S., & Anders, T. D. (1984). Training thirteen-year-olds to elaborate while studying text. *Human learning, 3,* 281–294.

Garcia, E. E. (1992). "Hispanic" children: Theoretical, empirical, and related policy issues. *Educational Psychology Review, 4,* 69–93.

Garcia, E. E. (1999). *Student cultural diversity: Understanding and meeting the challenge* (2nd ed.). Boston: Houghton Mifflin.

Garner, R. (1992). Learning from school texts. *Educational Psychologist, 27,* 53–63.

Garner, R., Alexander, P. A., Gillingham, M. G., Kulikowich, J. M., & Brown, R. (1991). Interest and learning from text. *American Educational Research Journal, 28,* 643–660.

Garner, R., Gillingham, M. G., & White, C. S. (1989). Effects of "seductive details" on macroprocessing and microprocessing in adults and children. *Cognition and Instruction, 6,* 41–57.

Gentner, D. (1983). Structure-mapping: A theoretical framework for analogy. *Cognitive Science, 7,* 155–170.

Gentner, D., & Gentner, D. R. (1983). Flowing waters or teeming crowds: Mental models of electricity. In D. Gentner & A. L. Stevens (Eds.), *Mental models* (pp. 99–129). Hillsdale, NJ: Erlbaum.

Gentry, C. G. (1994). *Introduction to instructional development.* Belmont, CA: Wadsworth.

Gilhooly, K. J., & Green, A. J. K. (1989). Learning problem-solving skills. In A. M. Colley & J. R. Beech (Eds.). *Acquisition and performance of cognitive skills* (pp. 85–111). New York: Wiley.

Glaser, R. (1984). Education and thinking: The role of knowledge. *American Psychologist, 39,* 93-104.

Glover, J. A., & Bruning, R. H. (1990). *Educational psychology* (3rd ed.). Glenview, IL: Scott, Foresman.

Glynn, S. M. (1978). Capturing readers' attention by means of typographical cueing strategies. *Educational Technology, 18,* 7–12.

Glynn, S. M., & Britton, B. K. (1984). Supporting readers' comprehension through effective text design. *Educational Technology, 24,* 40–43.

Glynn, S. M., & Di Vesta, F. J. (1977). Outline and hierarchical organization as aids for study and retrieval. *Journal of Educational Psychology, 69,* 89–95.

Goodlad, J. I. (1990). The occupation of teaching in schools. In J. I. Goodlad, R. Soder, & K. A. Sirotnik (Eds.), *The moral dimensions of teaching* (pp. 3–34). San Francisco: Jossey-Bass.

Grabowski, B. L. (1996). Generative learning: Past, present, and future. In D. H. Jonassen (Ed.), *Handbook of research for educational communications and technology* (pp. 897–918). New York: Macmillan.

Graham, S. (1988). Can attribution theory tell us something about motivation in blacks? *Educational Psychologist, 23,* 3–21.

Graham, S. (1991). A review of attribution theory in achievement contexts. *Educational Psychology Review, 3,* 5–39.

Graham, S. (1997). Executive control in the revising of students with learning and writing difficulties. *Journal of Educational Psychology, 89,* 223–234.

Gray, W. D., & Orasanu, J. M. (1987). Transfer of cognitive skills. In S. M. Cormier & J. D. Hagman (Eds.), *Transfer of learning* (pp. 183–215). New York: Academic Press.

Gredler, M. E. (1997). *Learning and instruction* (3rd ed.). Upper Saddle River, NJ: Merrill.

Greeno, J. G., Smith, D. R., & Moore, J. L. (1993). Transfer of situated learning. In D. K. Detterman & R. J. Sternberg (Eds.), *Transfer on trial: Intelligence, cognition, and instruction* (pp. 99–167). Norwood, NJ: Ablex.

Griffin, S., Case, R., & Capodilupo, A. (1995). Teaching for understanding: The importance of the central conceptual structures in the elementary mathematics curriculum. In A. McKeough, J. Lupart, & A. Marini (Eds.), *Teaching for transfer: Fostering generalization in learning* (pp. 123–151). Mahwah, NJ: Erlbaum.

Gronlund, N. E. (1995). *How to write and use instructional objectives* (5th ed.). Englewood Cliffs, NJ: Merrill.

Gunter, M. A., Estes, T. H., & Schwab, J. H. (1990). *Instruction: A models approach.* Boston: Allyn and Bacon.

Hambleton, R. K. (1996). Advances in assessment models, methods, and practices. In D. C. Berliner & R. C. Calfee (Eds.), *Handbook of educational psychology* (pp. 899–925). New York: Macmillan.

Hammer, D. (1995). Student inquiry in a physics class discussion. *Cognition and Instruction, 13,* 401–430.

Hammer, D. (1997). Discovery learning and discovery teaching. *Cognition and Instruction, 15,* 485–529.

Hawk, P. P. (1986). Using graphic organizers to increase achievement in middle school life science. *Science Education, 70,* 81–87.

Hayes, J. R. (1985). Three problems in teaching general skills. In S. Chipman, J. Segal, & R. Glaser (Eds.), *Thinking and learning skills* (pp. 391–406). Hillsdale, NJ: Erlbaum.

Hayes-Roth, B., & Thorndyke, P. W. (1979). Integration of knowledge from text. *Journal of Verbal Learning and Verbal Behavior, 18,* 91–108.

Heinich, R., Molenda, M., & Russell, J. D. (1989). *Instructional media* (3rd ed.). New York: Macmillan.

Heinz-Fry, J. A., & Novak, J. D. (1990). Concept mapping brings long-term movement toward meaningful learning. *Science Education, 74,* 461–472.

Hiebert, J., & Wearne, D. (1996). Instruction, understanding, and skill in multidigit addition and subtraction. *Cognition and Instruction, 14,* 251–283.

Holland, J. H., Holyoak, K. J., Nisbett, R. E., & Thagard, P. R. (1986). *Induction: Processes of inference, learning, and discovery.* Cambridge, MA: MIT Press.

Holley, C. D., Dansereau, D. F., McDonald, B. A., Garland, J. C., & Collins, K. W. (1979). Evaluation of a hierarchical mapping technique as an aid to prose processing. *Contemporary Educational Psychology, 4,* 227–237.

Hooper, S., & Hannafin, M. J. (1991). Psychological perspectives on emerging instructional technologies: A critical analysis. *Educational Psychologist, 26,* 69–95.

Hooper, S., Sales, G., & Rysavy, S. (1994). Generating summaries and analogies in Paris. *Contemporary Educational Psychology, 19,* 53–62.

Hopkins, K. D. (1998). *Educational and psychological measurement and evaluation* (8th ed.). Boston: Allyn and Bacon.

Hoska, D. M. (1993). Motivating learners through CBI feedback: Developing a positive learner perspective. In J. V. Dempsey & G. C. Sales (Eds.), *Interactive instruction and feedback* (pp. 105–132). Englewood Cliffs, NJ: Educational Technology.

Houtz, J. C., Moore, J. W., & Davis, J. K. (1972). Effects of different types of positive and negative instances in learning nondimensional concepts. *Journal of Educational Psychology, 63,* 206–211.

Inhelder, B., & Piaget, J. (1958). *The growth of logical thinking from childhood to adolescence.* New York: Basic Books.

Johnsey, A., Morrison, G. R., & Ross, S. M. (1992). Using elaboration strategies training in computer-based instruction to promote generative learning. *Contemporary Educational Psychology, 17,* 125–135.

Jonassen, D. H., Hannum, W. H., & Tessmer, M. (1989). *Handbook of task analysis procedures.* New York: Praeger.

Jones, B. F., Palincsar, A. S., Ogle, D. S., & Carr, E. G. (1987). Learning and thinking. In B. F. Jones, A. S. Palincsar, D. S. Ogle, & E. G. Carr (Eds.), *Strategic teaching and learning: Cognitive instruction in the content areas* (pp. 3–32). Alexandria, VA: Association for Supervision and Curriculum Development.

Joyce, B., & Weil, M. (1986). *Models of teaching* (3rd ed.). Englewood Cliffs, NJ: Prentice-Hall.

Kamii, C., & Dominick, A. (1998). The harmful effects of algorithms in grades 1–4. In L. J. Morrow & M. J. Kenney (Eds.), *The teaching and learning of algorithms in school mathematics* (pp. 130–140). Reston, VA: National Council of Teachers of Mathematics.

Kamradt, T. F., & Kamradt, E. J. (1999). Structured design for attitudinal instruction. In C. M. Reigeluth (Ed.), *Instructional-design theories and models* (Vol. 2, pp. 563–590). Mahwah, NJ: Erlbaum.

Karpov, Y. V., & Bransford, J. D. (1995). L. S. Vygotsky and the doctrine of empirical and theoretical learning. *Educational Psychologist, 30,* 61–66.

Keller, J. M. (1983). Motivational design of instruction. In C. M. Reigeluth (Ed.), *Instructional-design theories and models.* Hillsdale, NJ: Erlbaum.

Keller, J. M. (1987). Development and use of the ARCS model of motivational design. *Journal of Instructional Development, 10,* 2–11.

Kellogg, R. T. (1995). *Cognitive psychology.* Thousand Oaks, CA: Sage.

Kemp, J. E., Morrison, G. R., & Ross, S. M. (1994). *Designing effective instruction.* New York: Merrill.

King, A. (1992a). Comparison of self-questioning, summarizing, and notetaking-review as strategies for learning from lectures. *American Educational Research Journal, 29,* 303–323.

King, A. (1992b). Facilitating elaborative learning through guided student-generated questioning. *Educational Psychologist, 27,* 111—126.

King, A. (1997). ASK to THINK—TELL WHY: A model of transactive peer tutoring for scaffolding higher level complex learning. *Educational Psychologist, 32,* 221–235.

Kinzie, M. B. (1990). Requirements and benefits of effective interactive instruction: Learner control, self-regulation, and continuing motivation. *Educational Technology Research and Development, 38*(1), 5–21.

Klauer, K. (1984). Intentional and incidental learning with instructional texts: A meta-analysis for 1970–1980. *American Educational Research Journal, 21,* 323–339.

Kleiman, G. M. (1991). Mathematics across the curriculum. *Educational Leadership, 49*(2), 48–51.

Kohn, A. (1994). The truth about self-esteem. *Phi Delta Kappan, 76,* 272–283.

Kozulin, A., & Presseisen, B. Z. (1995). Mediated learning experience and psychological tools: Vygotsky's and Feuerstein's perspectives in a study of student learning. *Educational Psychologist, 30,* 67–75.

Krathwohl, D. R., Bloom, B. S., & Masia, B. B. (1964). *Taxonomy of educational objectives, Handbook II: Affective domain.* New York: McKay.

Kulhavy, R. W. (1977). Feedback in written instruction. *Review of Educational Research, 47,* 211–232.

Kulhavy, R. W., & Stock, W. A. (1989). Feedback in written instruction: The place of response certitude. *Educational Psychology Review, 1,* 279–308.

Kulik, J. A., & Kulik, C-L. C. (1988). Timing of feedback and verbal learning. *Review of Educational Research, 58,* 79–97.

Ladson-Billings, G. (1994). What we can learn from multicultural education research. *Educational Leadership, 51*(8), 22–26.

Ladson-Billings, G. (1995). Toward a theory of culturally relevant pedagogy. *American Educational Research Journal, 32,* 465–491.

Lambiotte, J. G., Dansereau, D. F., Cross, D. R., & Reynolds, S. B. (1989). Multirelational semantic maps. *Educational Psychology Review, 1,* 331–367.

Larkin, J. H. (1989). What kind of knowledge transfers? In L. B. Resnick (Ed.), *Knowing, learning, and instruction: Essays in honor of Robert Glaser* (pp. 283–305). Hillsdale, NJ: Erlbaum.

Larkin, J. H., McDermott, J., Simon, D. P., & Simon, H. A. (1980). Models of competence in solving physics problems. *Cognitive Science, 4,* 317–345.

LaZansky, J., Spencer, F., & Johnston, M. (1987). Reading to learn: Setting students up. In R. J. Tierney, P. L. Anders, & J. N. Mitchell (Eds.), *Understanding readers' understanding: Theory and practice* (pp. 255–281). Hillsdale, NJ: Erlbaum.

Leemkuil, H. H. (1990). Instructional design for teaching concepts: Do the number and dispersion of examples influence the abstraction of a cognitive model of a concept? In S. Dijkstra, B. H. A. M. Van Hout-Wolters, & P. C. Van der Sijde (Eds.), *Research on instructional design* (pp. 123–132). Englewood Cliffs, NJ: Educational Technology Publications.

Leinhardt, G., & Bickel, W. (1987). Instruction's the thing wherein to catch the mind that falls behind. *Educational Psychologist, 22,* 177–207.

Leinhardt, G., & Greeno, J. G. (1986). The cognitive skill of teaching. *Journal of Educational Psychology, 78,* 75-95.

Levin, J. R. (1996). Stalking the wild mnemos: Research that's easy to remember. In G. G. Brannigan (Ed.), *The enlightened educator* (pp. 85–108). New York: McGraw-Hill.

Levin, M. E., & Levin J. R. (1990). Scientific mnemonomies: Methods for maximizing more than memory. *American Educational Research Journal, 27,* 301–321.

Lhyle, K. G., & Kulhavy, R. W. (1987). Feedback processing and error correction. *Journal of Educational Psychology, 79,* 320–322.

Lickona, T. (1999). Character education: The cultivation of virtue. In C. M. Reigeluth (Ed.), *Instructional-design theories and models: A new paradigm of instructional theory* (Vol. 2, pp. 591–612). Mahwah, NJ: Erlbaum.

Linden, M., & Wittrock, M. C. (1981). The teaching of reading comprehension according to the model of generative learning. *Reading Research Quarterly, 17,* 44–57.

Linn, R. L., & Burton, E. (1994). Performance-based assessments: Implications of task specificity. *Educational Measurement: Issues and Practice, 13,* 5–8, 15.

Lorber, M. A. (1996). *Objectives, methods, and evaluation for secondary teaching* (4th ed.). Boston: Allyn and Bacon.

Lunzer, E. (1986). Cognitive development: Learning and the mechanisms of change. In G. D. Phye & T. Andre (Eds.), *Cognitive classroom learning: Understanding, thinking, and problem solving* (pp. 277–316). New York: Academic Press.

Lyman, H. B. (1998). *Test scores and what they mean* (6th ed.). Boston, MA: Allyn and Bacon.

Maehr, M. L., & Meyer, H. A. (1997). Understanding motivation and schooling: Where we've been, where we are, and where we need to go. *Educational Psychology Review, 9,* 371–409.

Maehr, M. L., & Midgley, C. (1991). Enhancing student motivation: A schoolwide approach. *Educational Psychologist, 26,* 399–427.

Mager, R. F. (1984). *Preparing instructional objectives* (2nd ed.). Belmont, CA: Fearon-Pitman.

Maheady, L. (1996). Peer-mediated instruction: I'll get by with a little help from my friends. In G. G. Brannigan (Ed.), *The enlightened educator: Research adventures in the schools* (pp. 206–225). New York: McGraw-Hill.

Malone, T. W. (1981). Toward a theory of intrinsically motivating instruction. *Cognitive Science, 4,* 333–369.

Mandler, G. (1996). The situation of psychology: Landmarks of choice points. *American Journal of Psychology, 109,* 1–35.

Margolis, E. (1994). A reassessment of the shift from the classical theory of concepts to prototype theory. *Cognition, 51,* 73–89.

Marschark, M., Richman, C. L., Yuille, J. C., & Hunt, R. R. (1987). The role of imagery in memory: On shared and distinctive information. *Psychological Bulletin, 102,* 28–41.

Martin, B. L., & Reigeluth, C. M. (1999). Affective education and the affective domain: Implications for instructional-design theories and models. In C. M. Reigeluth (Ed.), *Instructional-design theories and models* (Vol. 2, pp. 485–509). Mahwah, NJ: Erlbaum.

Martin, C. L., & Halverson, C. F. (1981). A schematic processing model of sex typing and stereotyping in children. *Child Development, 52,* 1119–1134.

Martinello, M. L., & Cook, G. E. (1994). *Interdisciplinary inquiry in teaching and learning.* New York: Merrill.

Maurer, R. E. (1994). *Designing interdisciplinary curriculum in middle, junior high, and high schools.* Boston: Allyn and Bacon.

Mayer, R. E. (1979). Can advance organizers influence meaningful learning? *Review of Educational Research, 49,* 371–383.

Mayer, R. E. (1987). The elusive search for teachable aspects of problem solving. In J. A. Glover & R. R. Ronning (Eds.), *Historical foundations of educational psychology* (pp. 327–347). New York: Plenum Press.

Mayer, R. E. (1989a). Models for understanding. *Review of Educational Research, 59,* 43–64.

Mayer, R. E. (1989b). Systematic thinking fostered by illustrations in scientific text. *Journal of Educational Psychology, 81,* 240–246.

Mayer, R. E. (1992). *Thinking, problem solving, cognition* (2nd ed.). New York: Freeman.

Mayer, R. E. (1997a). The role of interest in learning from scientific text and illustrations: On the distinction between emotional interest and cognitive interest. *Journal of Educational Psychology, 89,* 92–102.

Mayer, R. E. (1997b). Multimedia learning: Are we asking the right questions? *Educational Psychologist, 32,* 1–19.

Mayer, R. E. (1999). Designing instruction for constructivist learning. In C. M. Reigeluth (Ed.), *Instructional-design theories and models* (Vol. 2, pp. 141–159). Mahwah, NJ: Erlbaum.

Mayer, R. E., & Gallini, J. (1990). When is an illustration worth ten thousand words? *Journal of Educational Psychology, 82,* 715–727.

Mayer, R. E., & Greeno, J. G. (1972). Structural differences between learning outcomes produced by different instructional methods. *Journal of Educational Psychology, 63,* 165–173.

Mayer, R. E., & Sims, V. (1994). For whom is a picture worth a thousand words? Extensions of a dual-coding theory of multimedia learning. *Journal of Educational Psychology, 86,* 389–401.

McCutcheon, G. (1980). How do elementary school teachers plan? The nature of planning and influences on it. *Elementary School Journal, 81,* 4–23.

McDaniel, M. A., & Einstein, G. O. (1986). Bizarre imagery as an effective memory aid: The importance of distinctiveness. *Journal of Experimental Psychology: Learning, Memory, and Cognition, 12,* 554–565.

McDaniel, M. A., & Einstein, G. O. (1989). Material-appropriate processing: A contextualist approach to reading and studying strategies. *Educational Psychology Review, 1,* 113–145.

McDaniel, M. A., & Pressley, M. (Eds.). (1987). *Imagery and related mnemonic processes.* New York: Springer-Verlag.

Merrill, M. D., & Tennyson, R. D. (1977). *Concept teaching: An instructional design guide.* Englewood Cliffs, NJ: Educational Technology.

Messick, S. (1995). Validity of psychological assessment. *American Psychologist, 50,* 741-749.

Miller, P. M., Fagley, N. S., & Lane, D. S. (1988). Stability of the Gibb experimental test of testwiseness. *Educational and Psychological Measurement, 48,* 1123–1127.

Millman, J., Bishop, C. H., & Ebel, R. L. (1965). An analysis of test-wiseness. *Educational and Psychological Measurement, 25,* 707–726.

Moallem, M. (1998). An expert teacher's thinking and teaching and instructional design models and principles: An ethnographic study. *Educational Technology Research and Development, 46,* 37–64.

Moore, D. W., & Readence, J. E. (1984). A quantitative and qualitative review of graphic organizer research. *Journal of Educational Research, 78,* 11–17.

Mory, E. H. (1996). Feedback research. In D. H. Jonassen (Ed.), *Handbook of research for educational communications and technology* (pp. 919–956). New York: Macmillan.

Murrell, P., & Diez, M. E. (1997). A model program for educating teachers for diversity. In J. E. King, E. R. Hollins, & W. C. Hayman (Eds.), *Preparing teachers for cultural diversity* (pp. 113–128). New York: Teachers College Press.

Muth, K. D., & Alvermann, D. E. (1999). *Teaching and learning in the middle grades* (2nd ed.). Boston: Allyn and Bacon.

National Council for the Social Studies. (1998). *Expectations of excellence: Curriculum standards for social studies.* Washington, DC: National Council for the Social Studies.

National Council of Teachers of Mathematics. (1989). *Curriculum and evaluation standards for school mathematics.* Reston, VA: National Council of Teachers of Mathematics.

National Research Council. (1995). *National science education standards.* Washington, DC: National Academy Press.

Newell, A., & Simon, H. A. (1972). *Human problem solving.* Englewood Cliffs, NJ: Prentice-Hall.

Newman, D., Griffin, P., & Cole, M. (1989). *The construction zone: Working for cognitive change in school.* Cambridge, MA: Cambridge University Press.

Nickerson, R. S., & Adams, M. J. (1979). Long-term memory for a common object. *Cognitive Psychology, 11,* 287–307.

Nitko, A. J. (1996). *Educational assessment of students* (2nd ed.). Englewood Cliffs, NJ: Merrill.

Noddings, N. (1995). Teaching themes of care. *Phi Delta Kappan, 76,* 675–679.

Norman, D. A. (1982). *Learning and memory.* New York: Freeman.

Novak, J. D., & Gowin, D. B. (1984). *Learning how to learn.* New York: Cambridge University Press.

Novak, J. D., & Musonda, D. (1991). A twelve-year longitudinal study of science concept learning. *American Educational Research Journal, 28,* 117–153.

Nussbaum, J., & Novick, S. (1982). Alternative frameworks, conceptual conflict and accommodation: Toward a principled teaching strategy. *Instructional Science, 11,* 183–200.

Okebukola, P. A. (1990). Attaining meaningful learning of concepts in genetics and ecology: An examination of the potency of the concept-mapping technique. *Journal of Research in Science Teaching, 27,* 493–504.

Oliva, P. F. (1997). *Developing the curriculum* (4th ed.). New York: Longman.

Oosterhof, A. C. (1990). *Classroom applications of educational measurement.* Columbus, OH: Merrill.

Orlich, D. C., Harder, R. J., Callahan, R. C., Kauchak, D. P., & Gibson, H. W. (1994). *Teaching strategies* (4th ed.). Lexington, MA: D. C. Heath.

Ormrod, J. E. (1995). *Human learning* (2nd ed.). Englewood Cliffs, NJ: Merrill.

Ormrod, J. E. (2000). *Educational psychology* (3rd ed.). Upper Saddle River, NJ: Merrill.

Osborne, R. J., & Wittrock, M. C. (1983). Learning science: A generative process. *Science Education, 67,* 489–508.

Paris, S. G., & Cunningham, A. E. (1996). Children becoming students. In D. C. Berliner & R. C. Calfee (Eds.), *Handbook of educational psychology* (pp. 117–147). New York: Macmillan.

Paris, S. G., Lawton, T. A., Turner, J. C., & Roth, J. L. (1991). A developmental perspective on standardized achievement testing. *Educational Researcher, 20,* 12–20, 40.

Perkins, D. N., & Salomon, G. (1987). Are cognitive skills context-bound? *Educational Researcher, 18*(1), 16–25.

Perkins, D. N., & Unger, C. (1999). Teaching and learning for understanding. In C. M. Reigeluth (Ed.), *Instructional-design theories and models: A new paradigm of instructional theory* (Vol. 2, pp. 91–113). Mahwah, NJ: Erlbaum.

Perloff, R. M. (1993). The dynamics of persuasion. Hillsdale, NJ: Erlbaum.

Phillips, J. L. (1975). *The origins of intellect: Piaget's theory* (2nd ed.). San Francisco: W. H. Freeman.

Phye, G. D. (1986). Practice and skilled classroom performance. In G. D. Phye & T. Andre (Eds.), *Cognitive classroom learning: Understanding, thinking, and problem solving* (pp. 141–168). New York: Academic Press.

Piaget, J. (1983). Piaget's theory. In W. Kesson (Ed.) & P. H. Mussen (General Ed.), *History, theory, and methods,* Vol.1, *Handbook of child psychology* (pp. 103–128). New York: Wiley.

Pintrich, P., & De Groot, E. (1990). Motivational and self-regulated learning components of classroom academic performance. *Journal of Educational Psychology, 82,* 33–40.

Polya, G. (1957). *How to solve it: A new aspect of mathematical method.* Garden City, NY: Doubleday.

Popham, W. J. (1999). *Classroom assessment: What teachers need to know* (2nd ed.). Boston: Allyn and Bacon.

Posner, G. J., & Rudnitsky, A. N. (1997). *Course design* (5th ed.). New York: Longman.

Posner, G. J., Strike, K. A., Hewson, P. W., & Gertzog, W. A. (1982). Accommodation of a scientific conception: Toward a theory of conceptual change. *Science Education, 66*(2), 211–227.

Powell, J. P., & Andresen, L. W. (1985). Humour and teaching in higher education. *Studies in Higher Education, 10,* 79–90.

Pressley, M. (1990). *Cognitive strategy instruction that really improves children's academic performance.* Cambridge, MA: Brookline Books.

Pressley, M., Wood, E., Woloshyn, V. E., Martin, V., King, A., & Menke, D. (1992). Encouraging mindful use of prior knowledge: Attempting to construct explanatory answers facilitates learning. *Educational Psychologist, 27,* 91–109.

Ragan, T. J., & Smith, P. L. (1996). Conditions-based models for designing instruction. In D. H. Jonassen (Ed.), *Handbook of research for educational communications and technology* (pp. 541–569). New York: Simon & Schuster.

Ranzijn, F. J. (1991). The number of video examples and the dispersion of examples as instructional design variables in teaching concepts. *Journal of Experimental Education, 59,* 320-330.

Reed, S. K. (1993). A schema-based theory of transfer. In D. K. Detterman & R. J. Sternberg (Eds.), *Transfer on trial: Intelligence, cognition, and instruction* (pp. 39–67). Norwood, NJ: Ablex.

Reigeluth, C. M. (1999). The elaboration theory: Guidance for scope and sequence decisions. In C. M. Reigeluth (Ed.), *Instructional-design theories and models: A new paradigm of instructional theory* (Vol. 2, pp. 425–453). Mahwah, NJ: Erlbaum.

Reimann, P., & Schult, T. J. (1996). Turning examples into cases: Acquiring knowledge structures for analogical problem solving. *Educational Psychologist, 31,* 123–132.

Reitman, J. S., & Rueter, H. H. (1980). Organization revealed by recall orders and confirmed by pauses. *Cognitive Psychology, 12,* 554–581.

Resnick, L. B. (1987). Learning in school and out. *Educational Researcher, 16*(9), 13–20.

Resnick, L. B. (1989). Developing mathematical knowledge. *American Psychologist, 44,* 162–169.

Rickards, J. P. (1980). Notetaking, underlining, inserted questions, and organizers in text: Research conclusions and educational implications. *Educational Technology, 20,* 5–11.

Rieber, L. P. (1992). Computer-based microworlds: A bridge between constructivism and direct instruction. *Educational Technology Research and Development, 40*(1), 93–106.

Romiszowski, A. (1999). The development of physical skills: Instruction in the psychomotor domain. In C. M. Reigeluth (Ed.), *Instructional-design theories and models: A new paradigm of instructional theory* (Vol. 2, pp. 457–481). Mahwah, NJ: Erlbaum.

Rosch, E. (1975). Cognitive representations of semantic categories. *Journal of Experimental Psychology, General, 104,* 192–233.

Rosch, E., & Mervis, C. B. (1975). Family resemblances: Studies in the internal structures of categories. *Cognitive Psychology, 7,* 573–605.

Rosenshine, B., & Stevens, R. (1986). Teaching functions. In M. C. Wittrock (Ed.), *Handbook of research on teaching* (3rd ed.) (pp. 376–391). New York: Macmillan.

Ross, J. A. (1988). Controlling variables: A meta-analysis of training studies. *Review of Educational Research, 58,* 405–437.

Rothkopf, E. Z. (1966). Learning from written instructive materials: An exploration of the control of inspection behavior by test-like events. *American Educational Research Journal, 3,* 241–249.

Rothkopf, E. Z. (1970). The concept of mathemagenic activities. *Review of Educational Research, 40,* 325–336.

Rothwell, W. J., & Kazanas, H. C. (1992). *Mastering the instructional design process.* San Francisco: Jossey-Bass.

Royer, J. M., & Cable, G. W. (1976). Illustrations, analogies, and facilitative transfer in prose learning. *Journal of Educational Psychology, 68,* 205–209.

Rudner, L. M., & Boston, C. (1994). Performance assessment. *ERIC Review, 3,* 2–12.

Rumelhart, D. E. (1991). Understanding understanding. In W. Kessen, A. Ortony, & F. Craik (Eds.), *Memories, thoughts, and emotions: Essays in honor of George Mandler* (pp. 257–275). Hillsdale, NJ: Erlbaum.

Rumelhart, D. E., & Ortony, A. (1977). The representation of knowledge in memory. In R. C. Anderson, R. J. Spiro, & W. E. Montague (Eds.), *Schooling and the acquisition of knowledge* (pp. 99–136). Hillsdale, NJ: Erlbaum.

Salomon, G., & Globerson, T. (1987). Skill may not be enough: The role of mindfulness in learning and transfer. *International Journal of Educational Research, 11,* 623–637.

Salomon, G., & Perkins, D. N. (1989). Rocky roads to transfer: Rethinking mechanisms of a neglected phenomenon. *Educational Psychologist, 24,* 113–142.

Salvia, J., & Ysseldyke, J. E. (1998). *Assessment* (7th ed.). Boston: Houghton Mifflin.

Sarason, I. G. (Ed.). (1980). *Test anxiety: Theory, research and applications.* Hillsdale, NJ: Erlbaum.

Saxe, G. B. (1988). Candy selling and math learning. *Educational Researcher, 17*(6), 14–21.

Schmidt, R. A., & Bjork, R. A. (1992). New conceptualizations of practice: Common principles in three paradigms suggest new concepts for training. *Psychological Science, 3,* 207–217.

Schmidt, R. A., Young, D. E., Sinnen, S., & Shapiro, D. C. (1989). Summary knowledge of results for skill acquisition: Support for the guidance hypothesis. *Journal of Experimental Psychology: Learning, Memory, and Cognition, 15,* 352–359.

Schoenfeld, A. H., Smith, J. P., & Arcavi, A. (1993). Learning: The microgenetic analysis of one student's evolving understanding of a complex subject matter domain. In R. Glaser (Ed.), *Advances in instructional psychology* (Vol. 4, pp. 55–176). Hillsdale, NJ: Erlbaum.

Schunk, D. H. (1991). Self-efficacy and academic motivation. *Educational Psychologist, 26,* 207–231.

Seels, B., & Glasgow, Z. (1990). *Exercises in instructional design.* Columbus, OH: Merrill.

Seels, B., & Glasgow, Z. (1998). *Making instructional design decisions* (2nd ed.). Upper Saddle River, NJ: Merrill.

Shank, R. C., & Abelson, R. (1977). *Scripts, plans, goals, and understanding.* Hillsdale, NJ: Erlbaum.

Shavelson, R. J., Baxter, G. P., & Pine, J. (1992). Performance assessments: Political rhetoric and measurement reality. *Educational Researcher, 21,* 22–27.

Shuell, T. J. (1996). Teaching and learning in a classroom context. In D. C. Berliner & R. C. Calfee (Eds.), *Handbook of educational psychology* (pp. 726–764). New York: Macmillan.

Shulman, L. S. (1983). Autonomy and obligation: The remote control of teaching. In L. S. Shulman & G. Sykes (Eds.), *Handbook of teaching and policy* (pp. 484–504). New York: Longman.

Shulman, L. S. (1986). Those who understand: Knowledge growth in teaching. *Educational Researcher, 15,* 4–14.

Simpson, M. L., Olejnik, S., Tam, A. Y., & Supattathum, S. (1994). Elaborative verbal rehearsals and college students' cognitive performance. *Journal of Educational Psychology, 86,* 267–278.

Singley, M. K., & Anderson, J. R. (1989). *The transfer of cognitive skill.* Cambridge, MA: Harvard University Press.

Skinner, B. F. (1953). *Science and human behavior.* New York: Macmillan.

Smith, E. E. (1995). Concepts and categorization. In D. N. Osherson (General Ed.) & E. E. Smith, & D. N. Osherson (Vol. Eds.), *An invitation to cognitive science* (2nd ed.): Vol. 3. *Thinking* (pp. 3-33). Cambridge, MA: MIT Press.

Smith, P. L., & Ragan, T. J. (1993). *Instructional design.* New York: Merrill.

Snow, R. E. (1997). Individual differences. In R. D. Tennyson, F. Schott, N. Seel, & S. Dijkstra (Eds.), *Instructional design: International perspectives* (Vol. 1, pp. 215-241). Mahwah, NJ: Erlbaum.

Snow, R. E., Corno, L., & Jackson, D. (1996). Individual differences in affective and cognitive functions. In D. C. Berliner & R. C. Calfee (Eds.), *Handbook of educational psychology* (pp. 243–310). New York: Macmillan.

Spears, J. O., & Calvin, A. D. (1982). The usefulness of informing students of training objectives. *Performance and Instruction, 21,* 34-36.

Stein, B. S., Baxter, J. A., & Leinhardt, G. (1990). Subject-matter knowledge and elementary instruction: A case from functions and graphing. *American Educational Research Journal, 27,* 639-663.

Stein, B. S., & Bransford, J. D. (1979). Constraints on effective elaboration: Effects of precision and subject generation. *Journal of Verbal Learning and Verbal Behavior, 18,* 769–777.

Stein, B. S., Bransford, J. D., Franks, J. J., Owings, R. A., Vye, N. J., & McGraw, W. (1982). Differences in the precision of self-generated elaborations. *Journal of Experimental Psychology: General, 111,* 399–405.

Stodolsky, S. S., Stalk, S., & Glaessner, B. (1991). Student views about learning math and social studies. *American Educational Research Journal, 28,* 89–116.

Swanson, D. B., Norman, G. R., & Linn, R. L. (1995). Performance-based assessment: Lessons from the health professions. *Educational Researcher, 24,* 5–11, 35.

Sweller, J., & Chandler, P. (1994). Why some material is difficult to learn. *Cognition and Instruction, 12,* 185–233.

Tennyson, R. D. (1997). A system dynamics approach to instructional systems development. In R. D. Tennyson, F. Schott, N. Seel, & S. Dijkstra (Eds.), *Instructional design: International perspective* (Vol. 1, pp. 413–426). Mahwah, NJ: Erlbaum.

Tennyson, R. D., & Cocchiarella, M. J. (1986). An empirically based instructional design theory for teaching concepts. *Review of Educational Research, 56,* 40–71.

Tennyson, R. D., & Park, O. (1980). The teaching of concepts: A review of instructional design research literature. *Review of Educational Research, 50,* 55-70.

Terwilliger, J. S. (1997). Semantics, psychometrics, and assessment reform: A close look at "authentic" assessments. *Educational Researcher, 26*(8), 24–27.

Terwilliger, J. S. (1998). Rejoinder: Response to Wiggins and Newmann. *Educational Researcher, 27*(6), 22–23.

Tessmer, M., Wilson, B., & Driscoll, M. (1990). *Educational Technology Research and Development, 38,* 45–53.

Thorndike, R. M. (1997). *Measurement and evaluation in psychology and education* (6th ed.). Upper Saddle River, NJ: Merrill.

Thorndyke, P. W. (1977). Cognitive structures in comprehension and memory of narrative discourse. *Cognitive Psychology, 9,* 77–110.

Toppino, T. C., Lasserman, J. E., & Mracek, W. A. (1991). The effects of spacing repetitions on the recognition memory of young children and adults. *Journal of Experimental Child Psychology, 51,* 123–138.

Tudge, J. (1990). Vygotsky, the zone of proximal development, and peer collaboration: Implications for classroom practice. In L. C. Moll (Ed.), *Vygotsky and education* (pp. 155–172). New York: Cambridge University Press.

Tulving, E., & Pearlstone, Z. (1966). Availability versus accessibility of information in memory for words. *Journal of Verbal Learning and Verbal Behavior, 5,* 381–391.

Van Patten, J., Chao, C., & Reigeluth, M. (1986). A review of strategies for sequencing and synthesizing instruction. *Review of Educational Research, 56,* 437–471.

Vosniadou, S., & Brewer, W. F. (1987). Theories of knowledge restructuring in development. *Review of Educational Research, 57,* 51–67.

Voss, J. F. (1987). Learning and transfer in subject-matter learning: A problem-solving model. *International Journal of Educational Research, 11,* 607–622.

Vygotsky, L. S. (1978). *Mind in society: The development of higher psychological processes.* Cambridge, MA: Harvard University Press.

Weiner, B. (1979). A theory of motivation for some classroom experiences. *Journal of Educational Psychology, 71,* 3–25.

Weiner, B. (1985). An attributional theory of achievement motivation and emotion. *Psychological Review, 92,* 548–573.

Weinstein, C. E., & Mayer, R. E. (1986). The teaching of learning strategies. In M. Wittrock (Ed.), *Handbook of research on teaching* (3rd ed.) (pp. 315–327). New York: Macmillan.

West, C. K., Farmer, J. A., & Wolff, P. M. (1991). *Instructional design: Implications from cognitive science.* Englewood Cliffs, NJ: Prentice-Hall.

West, L. H. T., & Pines, A. L. (1985). *Cognitive structure and conceptual change.* Orlando, FL: Academic Press.

White, B. Y. (1993). Intermediate causal models: A missing link for successful science education? In R. Glaser (Ed.), *Advances in instructional psychology* (Vol. 4, pp. 177–252). Hillsdale, NJ: Erlbaum.

White, E. M. (1994). Portfolios as an assessment concept. In L. Black, D. A. Daiker, J. Sommers, & G. Stygall (Eds.), *New directions in portfolio assessment* (pp. 25–39). Portsmouth, NH: Boynton/ Cook Publishers.

White, R. T., & Gagne, R. M. (1974). Past and future research on learning hierarchies. *Educational Psychologist, 11,* 19–28.

White, R. T., & Gagne, R. M. (1978). Formative evaluation applied to a learning hierarchy. *Contemporary Educational Psychology, 3,* 87–94.

Wigfield, A., & Karpathian, M. (1991). Who am I and what can I do? Children's self-concepts and motivation in achievement situations. *Educational Psychologist, 26,* 233–261.

Wigfield, A., & Meece, J. L. (1988). Math anxiety in elementary and secondary school students. *Journal of Educational Psychology, 80,* 210–216.

Wiggins, G. P. (1989). A true test: Toward more authentic and equitable performance. *Phi Delta Kappan, 20,* 703–713.

Willoughby, T., Wood, E., Desmarais, S., Sims, S., & Kalra, M. (1997). Mechanisms that facilitate the effectiveness of elaboration strategies. *Journal of Educational Psychology, 89,* 682–685.

Willoughby, T., Wood, E., & Khan, M. (1994). Isolating variables that impact on or detract from the effectiveness of elaboration strategies. *Journal of Educational Psychology, 86,* 279–289.

Winn, W., & Snyder, D. (1996). Cognitive perspectives in psychology. In D. H. Jonassen (Ed.), *Handbook of research for educational communications and technology* (pp. 112–142). New York: Macmillan.

Wittrock, M. C. (1974). Learning as a generative process. *Educational Psychologist, 11,* 87–95.

Wittrock, M. C. (1979). The cognitive movement in instruction. *Educational Researcher, 8,* 511.

Wittrock, M. C. (1986). Students' thought processes. In M. C. Wittrock (Ed.), *Handbook of research on teaching* (3rd ed.) (pp. 297–327). New York: Macmillan.

Wittrock, M. C. (1990). Generative processes of comprehension. *Educational Psychologist, 24,* 345–376.

Wittrock, M. C. (1992). Generative learning processes of the brain. *Educational Psychologist, 27,* 531–541.

Wittrock, M. C., & Alesandrini, K. (1990). Generation of summaries and analogies and analytic and holistic abilities. *American Educational Research Journal, 27,* 489–502.

Woolley, F. R., & Tennyson, R. D. (1972). Conceptual model of classification behavior. *Educational Technology, 12,* 37–39.

Yelon, S. L. (1996). *Powerful principles of instruction.* White Plains, NY: Longman.

Yerkes, R. M., & Dodson, J. D. (1908). The relation of strength of stimulus to rapidity of habit-formation. *Journal of Comparative Neurology and Psychology, 18,* 459–482.

Young, A. C., Reiser, R. A., & Dick, W. (1998). Do *superior* teachers employ systematic instructional planning procedures? A descriptive study. *Educational Technology Research and Development, 46,* 65–78.

Zemelman, S., Daniels, H., & Hyde, A. (1998). *Best practice: New standards for teaching and learning in America's schools* (2nd ed.). Portsmouth, NH: Heinemann.

Zimbardo, P. G., & Leippe, M. R. (1991). *The psychology of attitude change and social influence.* Philadelphia: Temple University Press.

Zimmerman, B. J. (1998). Academic studying and the development of personal skill: A self-regulatory perspective. *Educational Psychologist, 33,* 73–86.

Zimmerman, B. J., & Kitsantas, A. (1999). Acquiring writing revision skill: Shifting from process to outcome self-regulatory goals. *Journal of Educational Psychology, 91,* 241–250.

Zook, K. B. (1991). Effects of analogical processes on learning and misrepresentation. *Educational Psychology Review, 3,* 41–72.

Zook, K. B. (1993). Effects of instructional and learner variables on children's analogically based misrepresentations. *Journal of Experimental Education, 61,* 189-203.

Zook, K. B., & Di Vesta, F. J. (1989). Effects of overt controlled verbalization and goal-specific search on acquisition of procedural knowledge in problem solving. *Journal of Educational Psychology, 81,* 220–225.

Zook, K. B., & Di Vesta, F. J. (1991). Instructional analogies and conceptual misrepresentations. *Journal of Educational Psychology, 83,* 246–252.

Zook, K. B., & Maier, J. M. (1994). Systematic analysis of variables that contribute to the formation of analogical misconceptions. *Journal of Educational Psychology, 86,* 589–600.

Index

ABCD format, for instructional objectives, 171–173
accountability, in teaching, 170
accuracy criteria, 180, 181
acronyms, 222
acrostic mnemonic device, 223
action consistency, in assessment, 118–119, 150
actions, 237–240. *See also* condition-action sequences
action verbs
    and assessment validity, 119
    in instructional goals, 24–26
    see also capability verbs
active participation, as attention-getting strategy, 299–300, 307
activities, instructional, 197, 199, 202
    authentic, 328
    culminating, 350–351, 366
    major types of, 198(table)
    relating to learning outcomes, 339
    selecting and organizing, 349–351, 358–361
adjunct questions, 213–214
administration conditions (assessment)
    ease in, 134, 136
    and measurement error, 126
advance organizers, 217–219, 228–229, 306
affect, 29
    in attitude system, 96, 97, 151
affective knowledge, 28(table), 29, 31
    attitude, 47–48
algorithms, 39
analogies
    for activating prior knowledge, 306
    instructional, 216–217
    self-generated, 220–221, 314, 315
analytical scoring, 144, 148–150, 152–153(table), 154, 160, 190
Anderson, J. R., 240
appreciating, as instructional goal, 23
ARCS model, of motivation, 302–304, 307, 321
assessment
    classroom testing, 106
    diagnostic, 113–114
    formative, 111–112
    preinstructional, 62–63, 110–111
    principles of, 104–106
    in sequence of instructional events, 329
    summative, 112–113, 329, 345
    unit-level, 345–346
    using measurement, 107–109

assessment blueprints, 120–121, 345–346, 356(table)
assessment data
    and action consistency, 118–119
    and content consistency, 117–118
    enhancing validity of, 120–122
    quantitative and qualitative, 107–109
    and relationship between reliability and validity, 116–117
    reliability and measurement error, 122–127
    reliability of, 12–13, 116, 346
    validity of, 12–13, 115–116, 117–119, 346
assessment devices
    attitude, 151–159
    cognitive assessment items, 137–144
    for cognitive strategy learning, 162–164
    common types of, 130–133
    criteria for selecting, 133–136
    performance items, 145–151
    for principle learning, 159–160
    for procedural rule learning, 161–162
    for verbal information learning, 160
    see also attitude assessment; cognitive assessment items; performance assessment; scoring procedures
assessment strategies
    based on learning outcomes, 48–49
    consistent vs. inconsistent content in, 118(table)
    critical elements of, 12
    for instructional units, 344–346, 355–357
    preparing and implementing, 18
    using multiple, 13
    see also instructional objectives
associative stage, of skill learning, 240–241
    for cognitive strategies, 285
    for concepts, 252–255, 258–259
    for rules and principles, 269–272, 277–278, 281–282
attention
    as control process, 204, 205, 206
    defined, 202
    and motivation, 302, 303
    supporting, in preinstructional phase, 292, 293
attention-getting strategies, 268, 296–300, 307–308

active participation, 299–300
cognitive conflict, 299
concreteness, 298–299
humor, 297–298
inquiry, 299
variability, 296–297
for verbal information learning, 213–215, 230
attitude assessment, 133, 151
    assessing components in, 154(table)
    direct and indirect approaches to, 154–155
    instructional objectives for, 191–192
    Likert scales for, 156–157
    semantic differential scales for, 157–158
    Thurstone scales for, 155–156
    and voluntary behaviors, 151–154, 191–192
attitudes
    affective component of, 96
    behavioral component of, 97–98
    cognitive component of, 96–97
    instructional goals for, 31, 47–48, 49, 200
attitude system, 96
attributions, and learner confidence, 304
audience, in instructional objectives, 171, 173
Austin, G. A., 252
Ausubel, David, 217
authentic assessment, 145
authentic learning activity, 328
automatic skill performance, 241, 273
autonomous stage, of skill learning, 240, 241
    for cognitive strategies, 285–286
    for concepts, 255–256, 259
    for rules and principles, 272–273, 278, 282

behavior
    in attitude system, 97–98, 151
    voluntary, and attitude assessment, 151–154, 191–192
behavioral objectives, 171. *See also* instructional objectives
block plan, unit, 348–349, 358(table)
Briggs, Leslie, 172
Bruner, J. S., 252, 312
Bruning, R. H., 137

capacity verbs, for instructional goals, 26, 49(table), 119
  for attitudes, 48
  for cognitive strategies, 42
  for instructional objectives, 173–174
  for intellectual skills, 35–36, 38, 39–41
  for motor skills, 46
  for verbal information, 32–33
Carey, L., 87, 98, 137
charts, 224
checklists, for performance assessment, 148–149
choice, as relevance strategy, 303
chronological relationships, of content, 64, 65. *See also* procedural analysis
chunking strategies, 204, 206, 313
classroom-level impediments, to design teaching, 371–373
classroom management, 377–378
cluster analysis, 65–74
  appropriate use of, 71–72
  case analysis of, 72–74
  determining subordinate-superordinate category relationships, 68–69
  examples of, 67(table), 69(fig), 71(table), 72(fig), 73(table), 229(table)
  inducing superordinate categories, 66–68
  for organizational relationships, 64, 70
  for promoting distinctiveness, 215
  specifying verbal information goal, 66
  value of, 70
  visual format for, 69–70
clustering, instructional goals, 346–348, 357
cognition
  in attitude system, 96–97, 151
  situated, 327
cognitive assessment items, 131–133
  completion, 141–142
  context cues for, 176–177
  essays, 142–144
  matching, 140–141
  multiple choice, 137–139
  objectively scored, 137–142
  for principle learning, 159–160
  for procedural rule learning, 161–162
  short-answer, 142–144
  subjectively scored, 142–144
  true-false, 139–140
  variables to consider when selecting, 134(table)
  for verbal information, 160
cognitive characteristics, of learners, 293–295
cognitive conflict, as attention-getting strategy, 299

cognitive processing, *see* information processing; learning processes, internal
cognitive skills, 34. *See also* intellectual skills
cognitive stage, of skill learning, 240
  for cognitive strategies, 284–285
  for concepts, 249–251, 257–258
  for rules and principles, 267–269, 274–277, 280–281
cognitive strategies, 31, 41–42, 49, 207, 310, 314, 323
  assessing learning of, 162–164
  defined, 41
  far transfer of, 327
  instructional goals for, 42
  instructional objectives for, 190–191
  instructional strategies for, 283–286
  intellectual skills and, 42–45
  internal and external conditions of learning, 283(fig)
  learning strategies as, 41–42, 315
  procedural analysis for, 93–95
communications, instructional, 197, 198, 199, 313
comparative organizers, 219
completion questions, 134, 141–142
complexity, of assessment context, 178
composition process, in skill learning, 240
concept features, 79–82, 249–252
  correlational, 80–81
  identifying, 79–80,
  organizing, 81–82
concept learning, 314, 323
  as aspect of knowledge transfer, 328–329
  discrimination process, 247–248, 253–254
  generalization process, 245–247, 252–253
  if-then productions for, 237–238
  internal and external conditions of, 242(fig)
  prerequisite concepts and discriminations in, 242–243
  and verbal labels, 243–245
  see also concept skills
concept learning instructional strategies
  associative stage of, 252–255, 258–259
  autonomous stage of, 255–256, 259
  case analysis of, 256–259
  cognitive stage of, 249–252, 257–258
  generative tasks, 255–256
  practice opportunities, 255
  providing informative feedback, 254–255
  supporting concept discrimination, 253–254

  supporting concept generalization, 252–253
concept mapping, 41, 257(fig), 314, 315
  assessing learning of, 162–164
  for cluster analysis, 69(fig), 70
  for identifying instructional goals, 342
  as instructional strategy, 225, 226(fig), 283–286
  procedural analysis for, 93–95
concept-related clustering, of goals, 347
concepts, 27, 36–38, 49, 310
  far transfer of, 327
  hierarchical analysis for, 78–82
  and hierarchy of intellectual skills, 42–45
  instructional goals for, 38, 189, 200
  instructional objectives for, 188–189
  relationship to rules and principles, 38
  types of, 36
  see also concept learning
conceptual categories, 244(fig), 246–247, 249
  in cluster analysis, 66–70
concrete concepts, 36
concrete experiences, 219
concreteness strategy, 298–299, 307, 310, 311(fig)
condition-action sequences, 237–238, 240–241, 255
  for complex skills, 238–240
  for learning rules and principles, 269–270
conditionalized knowledge, 239–241, 315
confidence, supporting learner, 303–304
content
  integration in thematic unit, 363
  selecting and analyzing essential, 337, 343–344, 353
content analysis, 11–12, 17, 59
  of attitude instructional goals, 96–98
  cluster analysis, 65–74
  combining procedures for, 95–98
  defined, 61
  for diagnosing learning difficulties, 63–64
  difficulties learning, 98–99
  hierarchical analysis, 74–86
  for instructional decision making, 61–64
procedural analysis, 87–91
  relationship with instructional goals, 17–18
  three approaches to, 64–65
  in unit planning process, 343–344, 365

content consistency, in assessment, 117–118, 150
context, expanding range of learners', 327–328
context, of instructional objectives, 12, 172–173, 174–178
   complexity of, 178
   cues in, 176–178
   resources for, 178
   for rule learning, 189
   for verbal information, 187
control processes, 205–206
   correlational concept features, 80–81
cueing retrieval, in postinstructional phase, 292, 293, 326–329. *See also* transfer
cues
   for activating prior knowledge, 216
   for assessment context, 176–178
   for highlighting information, 213
culminating activities, 350–351, 360–361, 366
curriculum, creating seamless, 362–364
curriculum guides, 62, 338
curriculum-level educational goals, 341
curriculum standards, 50–51

decision making, instructional, 61–64
   major types of, 110–115
   model of, 109(fig)
   role of assessment in, 103–109
declarative knowledge, 27, 28(table), 31
   verbal information as, 29–33
declarative stage, of skill learning, 240, 267, 315. *See also* cognitive stage
deductive teaching approach, 249, 250(fig), 267
defined concepts, 36
defining concept features, 80, 81
describing concept features, 80, 81
design, 3
design-teachers, 5
design-teaching, 5, 7
   assessment strategies in, 12–13
   content analysis in, 11–12
   impediments to, 371–374
   planning instructional strategy, 14–15
   and process-product view of learning, 7–10
   resolving learning difficulties, 15
   using instructional goals, 10–11
   value of, 374–375
   see also systematic instructional design
developmental perspective, on learning, 310–312
diagnosis, of learning difficulties, 15. *See also* learning difficulties

diagnostic assessment, 113–114
Dick, W., 87, 98
difficulty of instruction, and learner confidence, 303
discrimination process
   in concept learning, 247–248, 253–254
   in learning rules and principles, 266–267, 270–271
discrimination skills, 35–36, 49
   in hierarchical analysis, 82
   and hierarchy of intellectual skills, 42–45
   instructional goals for, 35–36
   prerequisite, in concept learning, 243
disequilibrium, 299
distinctiveness strategies, 214–215
distributed practice, 226, 255, 273, 328
divergent examples, 252–253, 270
diverse learners
   analyzing content for, 63, 64
   designing instructional events for, 293–295
   designing relevance strategies for, 303
   diverse instructional goals for, 51–52
   feedback for, 326
   response modes for, 119, 145
   and systematic instructional design, 19–20, 372–373, 378
   see also learners; learner characteristics
domain-specific skill, 40–41
Driscoll, M., 255

Eby, J. W., 339
educational goals, 167, 168, 169
   curriculum-level, 341
   identifying, in unit planning, 339–342, 352–353, 354(table)
   unit-level, 340–341
educational outcomes, 167–171. *See also* instructional objectives
elaboration processes, 315
   as instructional strategy, 220–223, 230–231
   in internal learning, 209–211
elaborative interrogation, 220
Ellis, A. K., 335
enactive representation, 312
encoding, 204
   defined, 206
   for different learning outcomes, 314
   elaboration processes for, 209–211, 220–221
   in instructional phase, 292, 293
   learning strategies for supporting, 314–316
   organization processes for, 211–212
   schema theory of, 207–209
engagement component, of instruc-

tional strategy, 201–202, 203
   for cognitive strategies, 284–286
   for concepts, 257–259
   for rules and principles, 274–278, 280–282
   for verbal information, 228–231
essay questions, 134, 142–144
evaluation, 103–104
   diagnostic, 113–114
   formative, 111–112
   preinstructional, 110–111
   summative, 112–113
   see also assessment
examples, exaggerated, for selective perception, 313
examples, in skill learning
   for concepts, 37–38, 242, 245(table), 249–251
   divergent, 252–253, 270
   matched, 253–254, 271
   for rules and principles, 266, 268–269, 270–271
executive control, 204, 207, 300
expectancy, learner, 300–304, 308
   and activating learner motivation, 302
   and awareness of learning objectives, 300–302
   defined, 300
   and Keller's ARCS model of motivation, 302–304
   in preinstructional phase, 292, 293
experience
   concrete, as teaching strategy, 219
   as relevance strategy, 302
expository organizers, 219
external conditions, of learning, 8–10, 198–199. *See also* instructional events; instructional strategies

facts, 30–32
false-negative evaluation errors, 184
false-positive evaluation errors, 184
far transfer, 326, 327
feedback
   complexity of, 325
   defined, 322
   for different learning outcomes, 322–323
   principles of effective, 324–326
   providing informative, 254–255, 271–273
   sources of, 323–324
   for supporting learner mindfulness, 324
   to support learner motivation, 325–326
   timing of, 324–325
formative assessment, 111–112, 329
frequency counts, in performance assessment, 148, 154
future usefulness, as relevance strategy, 302

Gagne, Robert, 29, 35, 42, 46, 47, 48, 172, 173, 198
    events of instruction, 291–293, 295, 296, 300, 304, 318, 322, 327
    five learning outcomes, 29–48
    hierarchy of intellectual skills, 42–45, 75, 82
generalization process, 34
    in concept learning, 245–247, 252–253
    for learning rules and principles, 265–266, 270
generative learning strategies, 220–221, 255–256, 315
Glenn, A. D., 335
Glover, J. A., 137
goals, see educational goals; instructional goals
goal clustering, 346
Goodnow, J. J., 252
grade levels, instructional goals for different, 25(table)
grading systems, 378–379
guided discovery process, 249

halo effect, 124
Hambleton, R. K., 145
heuristics, 41
hierarchical analysis, 74–86, 242, 343
    analyzing target skill in, 75
    case analysis of, 84–86
    for clustering instructional goals, 347
    for concepts, 78–82
    displaying results of, 76–77
    examples of, 77(fig), 81(fig), 83(fig), 85(fig), 86(fig)
    general process of, 78(fig)
    identifying prerequisite skills in, 75–76
    for learning relationships, 64–65
    for rules and principles, 82–83
hierarchy of intellectual skills, 42–45, 75, 82
higher-order rules, 40, 41, 42
highlighting strategies, 213, 313
holistic scoring, 144
Hopkins, K. D., 137
how-to knowledge, 27. See also procedural knowledge
humor, as attention-getting strategy, 297–298

iconic representation, 312, 313(fig)
if-then structure, of productions, 237–238
image-based mnemonics, 223
image elaborations, 211, 230, 314, 315
imagery, as learning strategy, 220
inclusion, philosophy of, 19
inductive teaching approaches, 249, 250(fig), 267, 377
Inductive Thinking Model, 249

inductive thinking process, 68
information component, of instructional strategy, 201, 203
    for cognitive strategies, 284
    for concepts, 256–257
    for rules and principles, 274, 279–280
    for verbal information, 228
information processing, 203–207
    control processes, 205–206
    executive control, 206–207, 300
    memory structures, 205
    see also learning processes, internal
Information Processing Model, 204–207
informative feedback, 254–255, 271–273
inquiry, as attention-getting strategy, 299
inquiry-related clustering, of goals, 347
Inquiry Training Model, 249
instruction
    based on learning outcomes, 48–50
    defined, 197
instructional design
    basics of, 5–15
    and learning outcomes, 3–5
    systems approach to, 15–20
    see also systematic instructional design
instructional designer, 3
Instructional Development Institutes, 171
instructional events
    as external conditions of learning, 198–199
    Gagne's sequence of, 291–293
    major categories of, 197, 198(table)
    see also instructional sequencing; instructional strategies
instructional goals, 4–5, 16, 17
    action words for describing, 24–26
    analyzing attitudinal, 96–98
    and assessment, 118(table), 120, 134(table), 136
    changing general goals to, 54(table)
    clustering, 346–348
    defined, 10–11, 23–26, 168–169
    deriving from professional standards, 50–51
    deriving from subject matter, 50
    describing learned capabilities with, 10–11
    for diverse learners, 51–52
    to focus classroom teaching, 48–52
    and Gagne's five learning outcomes, 29–48
    and Gagne's hierarchy of intellectual skills, 42–45
    in hierarchical analysis, 77
    identifying, in unit planning, 339–342, 352–353, 354(table)

    and instructional objectives, 12–13, 173–174
    and instructional subgoals, 75
    and learning outcomes, 26–29, 200(table)
    relationship with content analysis, 17–18
    target, 75
    and three types of knowledge, 27–29
    see also learning outcomes
instructional goals, writing, 24–26, 49(table)
    for attitudinal outcomes, 47–48, 192
    for cognitive strategy learning, 42
    for intellectual skill learning, 35–36, 38, 39–41, 189
    for motor skill outcomes, 46
    for verbal information outcomes, 32–33, 187–188
instructional objectives, 18, 167
    for attitudes, 191–192
    components of, 171–173
    context in, 174–178 (see also context)
    defined, 12, 167, 169–171
    determining mastery criteria for, 183–185
    different terms for, 171
    form of, 185–186
    informing learners of, 300–302
    for intellectual skills, 188–189
    and learner characteristics, 183
    for learning outcomes, 186–193
    and misclassification of learner achievements, 184–185
    for motor skills, 191
    performance, 172–174
    preparing, 12–13
    quality component of, 178–182 (see also quality criteria)
    for rules, principles, and cognitive strategies, 189–191
    and task characteristics, 183–184
    for verbal information, 186–188
    see also assessment strategies
instructional phase, of instruction, 291–293
    case analysis of, 316–317
    and encoding process, 314–316
    supporting selective perception, 309–313
instructional planning, see instructional sequencing; instructional strategy
instructional sequencing
    defined, 290–291
    and Gagne's events of instruction, 291–293
    incorporating learning strategies into, 315–316
    instructional phase, 291–293, 309–317

and learner characteristics, 293–294
and learning outcome, 295
and media capabilities, 295
postinstructional phase of, 318–331
preinstructional phase of, 291–293, 296–309
and summative assessment, 329
see also specific phases
instructional space, 290
instructional strategy, 18
    case analysis of, 227–232, 256–259, 273–286
    for concept learning, 249–256
    and content analysis, 63
    deductive and inductive approaches, 249, 250, 267
    defined, 14–15, 201
    engagement component of, 201–202
    information component of, 201
    integrated components of, 203(fig)
    and learning outcomes, 49–51
    practice component of, 202 (*see also* practice)
    for rules and principles, 267–273
    see also concept learning instructional strategies; verbal information instructional strategies
instructional system, 16–19. See also systematic instructional design
instructional subgoal, 75, 87–88
instructional time, 290
instructional units, *see* unit planning process
integrative unit, 363
intellectual skills, 31, 33–41, 49
    chronological and learning relationships of, 64–65
    concepts, 36–38
    discriminations, 35–36
    Gagne's hierarchy of, 42–45
    general learning processes for, 236–241(*see also* concept learning)
    hierarchical analysis of, 74–86
    instructional objectives for, 188–189
    and motor skills, 46
    problem-solving, 40–41
    procedural analysis for, 91–93
    production system perspective on learning, 237–241
    rules and principles, 38–40
    three stages for learning, 240–241
    see also specific skills
internal conditions of learning, 8–10, 198–199. See also learning processes, internal
irrelevant concept features, 79, 80
item-quality measurement error, 125–126
item-sampling measurement error, 125

Keller, J. M., 296, 302–304, 324
Keller's ARCS model, of learner motivation, 302–304, 307, 321
keyword method, 223
knowing, as instructional goal, 23
knowledge
    affective, 28
    conditionalized, 239
    declarative, 27, 28
    procedural, 27–29
Kujawa, E., 339

labels as verbal information, 30
learner(s)
    expectancy, supporting, 300–304, 308
    informing of learning objectives, 300–302
    learning strategies of, 314–316
    misclassifying achievement of, 184–185
    motivation, activating, 302–304, 325–326
    response mode, 119, 145
    supporting selective perception of, 309–313
    variability, as teaching impediment, 372–373, 378
learner characteristics
    and instructional design process, 293–295
    and mastery criteria constraints, 183
    and measurement error, 126–127
    and relevance strategy design, 303
learning
    defined, 7–8
    process and product view of, 7–10
learning activity, 201. See also activities
learning difficulties, diagnosing, 15, 19, 184, 378
    and content analysis, 63–64
    content-related causes, 114
    diagnostic evaluation for, 113–114
    instruction-related causes, 114
learning games, 273
learning outcomes
    activating prior knowledge relevant to, 305
    affective knowledge as, 28, 29
    attitudinal, 47–48
    cognitive strategy, 41–42, 190–191, 310
    content analysis of complex, 95–96
    declarative knowledge as, 27, 28
    defined, 26–27
    identifying relationships among, 336–337
    and instructional design, 4–5, 295
    as instructional goals, 24, 25
    intellectual skill, 33–41, 188–190, 310
    and internal conditions of learning, 199–200

motor skill, 45–47, 191
    practice for, 318–319
    procedural knowledge as, 27–29
    and selective perception, 310
    summary of, 49(table)
    transfer for different, 326–327
    verbal information, 29–33, 186–188, 310
learning processes, internal, 7–10, 199, 204(fig)
    and attention, 296, 300
    cueing retrieval, 326–327
    developmental perspective on, 310–312
    for different learning outcomes, 199–200
    discrimination processes, 247–248, 253–254, 266–267, 270–271
    elaboration processes, 209–211
    encoding, 207–212, 314
    generalization processes, 245–247, 252–253, 265–266, 270
    information processing model, 203–207
    and instructional sequencing, 291–293
    and learner expectancy, 300
    for learning cognitive strategies, 283(fig)
    for learning concepts, 242–248 (*see also* concept learning)
    for learning rules and principles, 263–267
    and motivation, 202, 302–304
    organization processes, 211–212
    production systems, 237–241
    reinforcement, 322
    and retrieval process, 318
    schema and long-term memory in, 207–209, 304–305
    selective perception, 309, 312
    for verbal information, 203–212
learning-related clustering, of goals, 347
learning relationships, of content, 64–65
learning requirements, and learner confidence, 303
learning strategies, 41–42
    for supporting encoding, 314–316
learning structure, and unit planning, 336, 337
Likert scales, 154, 156–157, 192
long-term memory, 70, 204, 206, 207
    defined, 205
    schemas and, 207–209

Mackey, J. A., 335
Mager, Robert, 171, 172, 173
mapping, instructional analogies, 216–217
matched examples, 253–254, 271
matching questions, 134, 140–141, 160

materials and equipment, 197, 198, 199
    selecting and organizing, 349–351, 358–361
    see also media
meaning, constructing, 310–312. *See also* encoding
measurement, 107–109. *See also* assessment
measurement error
    administration conditions and, 126
    item quality and, 125–126
    item sampling and, 125
    learner characteristics and, 126–127, 183
    scoring procedures and, 123–125
    and task characteristics, 183–184
media, instructional, 197, 198, 199, 201
    and instructional design process, 295
    using variety of, 297
    see also materials and equipment
mediated learning experiences, 311
memory structures, 205. *See also* learning processes, internal
mental skills, *see* intellectual skills
method of loci, 223
misconceptions, learner, 306
mnemonic devices, 221–223, 231, 314, 315
modeling, as relevance strategy, 303
motivation
    activating learner, 302
    defined, 202
    Keller's ARCS model of, 302–304
    using feedback to support, 325–326
motor skills
    defined, 46
    instructional goals for, 31, 45–47, 49
    instructional objectives for, 191
    procedural analysis of, 87–91
multiple choice questions, 134, 135, 137–139

National Council for the Social Studies (NCSS), 51
National Council of Teachers of Mathematics (NCTM), 50
natural consequences, and learner motivation, 304
near transfer, 326
need matching, as relevance strategy, 303
negative influences, and learner motivation, 304, 320
Nitko, A. J., 137
nonexamples, in skill learning, 37–38, 242, 245(table), 253–254, 266, 270–271

objective assessment devices, 123–124, 131, 132, 137–142, 161–162
    context clues for, 177
    correct response criteria for, 180–181
objective data, 105
organizational relationships, of content, 64, 65
    and memory retrieval, 70
    see also cluster analysis
organization strategies, 315
    advance organizers, 217–219
    concept maps, 225 (*see also* concept mapping)
    outlines, charts, and tables, 224–225
    for practicing information retrieval, 226–227
    schematic diagrams, 225–226
organized facts, 32
organizing unit theme, 343, 353
outlines, 41, 69, 224–225, 314, 315
overgeneralization, 247–248, 266

participation strategies, for supporting attention, 299–300, 307
part-skills, 87
pedagogical content knowledge, 63
peer-mediated learning strategies, 315
peg-word system, 223
perceptual stimuli, discriminating, 35–36
performance, of instructional objectives, 12, 172–174
    for rule learning, 189
    for verbal information, 187
performance assessment, 124, 133
    analytical scoring procedure for, 150, 152–153(table)
    constructing, 146–147
    scoring, 148–150
    types of, 145–146
    using portfolios as, 150–151
    variables to consider in selecting, 134(table)
performance objectives, 171. *See also* instructional objectives
physical characteristics, of learners, 294–295
Piaget, Jean, 299, 312
Polya, G., 41
portfolios, for performance assessment, 150–151
positive outcomes, and learner motivation, 304
Posner, G. J., 337, 346, 347
postinstructional phase, of instruction, 291–293
    assessment during, 329
    case summary of, 330–331
    practice opportunities, 318–321
    reinforcement strategies, 321–326
    retention and transfer in, 326–329
practice, in instructional strategy, 202, 203

as authentic learning activity, 328
    for cognitive strategy, 286
    for concept learning, 255, 259
    distributed practice, 226, 255, 273, 328
    emphasizing conceptual understanding in, 328–329
    graduating difficulty of, 320–321
    individual overt responses in, 319–320
    for learning outcomes, 318–319
    principles of effective practice, 319–321
    for promoting independence, 320
    for rule and principle learning, 271–273, 278, 282
    variety in, 255, 321, 322(fig)
    for verbal information, 226–227, 231–232
preassessment process, 62–63, 110–111
preinstructional assessment, 110–111
preinstructional phase, of instruction, 291–293
    activating prior knowledge, 304–306
    attention-getting strategies, 296–300
    case analysis of, 307–309
    supporting learners' expectancies, 300–304
prerequisite concepts, *see* subordinate concepts
prerequisite skills, 62. *See also* subordinate skills
presearch availability, 324
present worth, as relevance strategy, 302
principles, 38–40, 49, 310, 323
    assessing learning of, 159–160
    external conditions for learning, 264, 265(fig), 267–273
    far transfer of, 327
    hierarchical analysis for, 82–83
    and hierarchy of intellectual skills, 42–45
    if-then productions for learning, 238
    instructional goals for, 39–40
    instructional objectives for learning, 190
    instructional strategies for learning, 279–282
    internal conditions of learning, 263–267, 314
prior knowledge, 203, 207–209
    elaborating on, 220–221
    and mediated learning, 311–312
    providing meaningful, 219, 229–230
prior knowledge, activating
    and mnemonic devices, 221–223
    in preinstructional phase, 292, 293
    related to learning outcomes, 305

strategies for, 216–219, 305–306, 308–309
see also retrieval, information
problem, 40
problem representation, 60–61
problem-solving, instructional, 60–65
problem-solving skills, 40–41, 49
heuristics, 41
and hierarchy of intellectual skills, 42–45
instructional goals for, 40–41
procedural analysis, 87–95, 343
for chronological relationships, 64
for cognitive strategy, 93–95
displaying results of, 89–91
examples of, 88(table), 90(fig), 91, 92(fig), 94(fig)
identifying major steps in, 87
instructional subgoals in, 87–88
for intellectual skills, 91–93
for motor skills, 87–91
subordinate procedures in, 88–89
proceduralization, 240
procedural knowledge, 27–29, 31
cognitive strategies, 41–42
conditionalized, 239–241, 315
intellectual skills, 33–41
motor skills, 45–47
production format of, 237–240
see also specific skills
procedural rules, 39
assessing learning of, 161–162
process evaluations, in performance assessment, 146
processing depth, and unit planning, 336, 337
process-product view, of learning, 7–10, 14
product evaluation, in performance assessment, 146
productions, 34
defined, 28, 237
if-then structure of, 237–238
in rule and principle learning, 264
production systems, 238–241
and generalization process, 247, 248
professional standards, deriving instructional goals from, 50–51
proposition, 27, 30, 32
and cluster analysis, 71–72
prototype, concept, 246, 249–251
psychomotor skills, 46, 200
psychosocial characteristics, of learners, 294–295

qualitative assessment, 107–108, 123
quality criteria, in instructional objectives, 12, 172–173
accuracy or precision, 180
concrete consequences or outcomes, 182
consistency with stated standards, 181–182

number of correct responses or errors, 180–181
for rule learning, 189
time limits, 181
for verbal information, 187
quantitative assessment, 107–109, 123
questioning strategies, 213–214, 221, 222, 314, 315
for activating prior knowledge, 305

Ragan, T. J., 293–294
rating scales, 148, 149
rehearsal, 204, 205–206
reinforcement
in postinstructional phase, 292, 293, 321–326
timing of, 304
see also feedback
relevance strategies, and learner motivation, 302–303
relevant concept features, 79
reliability, in assessment, 12–13, 116
and analytical scoring, 144, 148–150
and assessment device choice, 134, 135
of instructional objectives, 187, 188–189, 190
of instructional units, 346
and measurement error, 122–127
relationship to validity, 116–117
remediation, 19, 184, 378
repetition, for selective perception, 313
response modes, learner, 119, 145
response production, and assessment device choice, 135
resources
for assessment context, 178
selecting and organizing, 349–351, 358–361
for thematic units, 365–366
responding, in postinstructional phase, 292, 293, 318–319. *See also* practice
retention, strategies for supporting, 327–329
retrieval, information, 204, 208
defined, 206
practicing, 226–227, 319–321
related to learning outcomes, 318–319
and transfer process, 326–329
see also prior knowledge, activating
review
learner-generated, 306
teacher-generated, 306
rewards, and learner motivation, 304
rhyme-based mnemonics, 221–222
rubrics, 144
Rudnitsky, A. N., 337, 346, 347
rules, 38–40, 49, 310, 323
domain-specific, 40–41

external conditions for learning, 264, 265(fig), 267–273
far transfer of, 327
hierarchical analysis for, 82–83
and hierarchy of intellectual skills, 42–45
higher-order, 40, 41
if-then productions for learning, 238
instructional goals for, 39–40
instructional objectives for, 189
instructional strategies for, 273–279
internal conditions for learning, 263–267, 314
procedural, 39, 161–162

Salvia, J., 106, 137
satisfaction strategies, and learner motivation, 304
schemas, 70, 207–209
and developmental perspective on learning, 310–312
organizational structure of, 210(fig)
schematic diagrams, 225–226, 314, 315
school-level impediments, to *design-teaching*, 373
scientific method, 41
scope, in planning instruction, 62
scoring procedures
analytical, 144, 148–150, 154, 160
ease of, 134, 136
for essays and short-answer items, 143–144
holistic, 144
for Likert scales, 156–157
and measurement error, 123–125
number of correct responses criteria in, 180–181
objective, 123–124, 131, 132, 137–142, 161–162
for performance items, 148–150, 151
subjective, 123–124, 131, 132, 142–144
selective perception, 204, 206
defined, 205, 309
and developmental perspectives on learning, 310–312
in instructional phase, 292, 293
and learning outcomes, 310
strategies to support, 312–313
self-confidence, learner, 304
self-efficacy, supporting learner, 303–304
self-generated analogies, 220–221, 314
self-questioning strategy, 221, 222(table), 314, 315
self-summaries, 221, 314, 315
semantic differential scales, 154–155, 157–158
semantic network, 207, 208, 209, 210, 211–212

sensory registers, 205
sensory stimuli, varying, in instruction, 296–297
sequence
 of goals in unit planning, 346–349, 357–358
 in planning instruction, 62
 see also instructional sequencing; procedural analysis
short-answer questions, 134, 135, 142–144, 160
short-term memory, 204, 205, 206
signals, for supporting selective perception, 313
situated cognition, 327
Skinner, B. F., 171
Smith, P. L., 293–294
special needs learners, 19–20. *See also* diverse learners
spreading activation, 207–208, 209, 210, 211–212
SQ3R reading strategy, 42
stimulus
 for assessment context, 176–178
 ease of developing, 134, 135–136
subjective assessment devices, 123–124, 131, 132, 142–144
 context cues for, 177
subjective data, 105
subject matter, deriving goals from, 50
subordinate concepts
 and concept learning, 242–243
 in hierarchical analysis, 75–76, 77, 80, 82–83
 for learning rules and principles, 264–265, 267–268
 verbal labels for, 243–245
subordinate skills, 62
 identifying, in hierarchical analysis, 74–75
 and instructional planning, 62–63
 in procedural analysis, 88–89
subordinate-superordinate relationships, 212, 224, 225
 in cluster analysis, 68–70
Suchman, Richard, 249
summarizing
 for activating prior memory, 306
 as learning strategy, 41, 221, 314, 315
summative assessment, 112–113, 345
 and instructional sequencing, 329
superordinate concept categories, 68–70, 71
symbolic representation, 312
symbols, 30
system, 15–16
systematic instructional design, 15–20, 371
 as cognitive strategy, 41
 diagram of, 16, 17(fig), 372(fig)
 different models of, 379–380
 features of, 16–19

goal-directed focus of, 19–20
 impediments to, 371–374
 questions and concerns about, 375–380
 supporting learner diversity with, 19–20
 value of, 374–375
 see also design-teaching

Taba, Hilda, 249
table of specifications, 120, 121(table), 346
tables, 67(table), 69, 224
target goals, 75
target principle, 75
task analysis, 61. *See also* content analysis
task characteristics, and learner performance, 183–184
technology, 201, 290
 software for assessment, 137
 see also media
Tessmer, M., 255
testing, 106. *See also* assessment
test items
 attitude, 133
 cognitive, 131–133
 defined, 130
 performance, 133
 see also assessment devices; *specific test items*
test-wiseness, of learners, 126
thematic units
 for creating seamless curriculum, 362–364
 goals, content, and objectives for, 365
 instructional resources for, 365–366
 integrating theme for, 364–365
 see also unit planning process
theme, of unit
 organizing, 343, 353
 selecting, 338–339, 352
Thurston scales, 154, 155–156, 157
time, as impediment to *design-teaching*, 371–372
time limits, in assessment, 181
time management, and unit planning, 336–337, 348–349, 358
topic, unit, 338–339, 352
transfer
 defined, 326
 for different learning outcomes, 326–327
 effects of situated cognition on, 327
 strategies for supporting, 327–329
true-false questions, 134, 139–140
tuning stage, in skill learning, 241

undergeneralization, 247, 266
understanding, as instructional goal, 23
unit, 335

unit-level assessment, 345
unit-level educational goals, 340–341
unit planning process
 benefits of, 336–337
 block plan for, 348–349
 case analysis of, 352–362
 central theme of, 338–339
 defined, 335–336
 designing thematic units, 362–366
 identifying educational and instructional goals, 339–342
 identifying organizing themes, 343
 learning activities and resources, 349–351
 major components of, 337
 preparing assessment procedures, 344–346
 sample sequence of topics, 339(table)
 selecting and analyzing essential content, 343–344
 sequencing goals and allocating time, 346–349
 unit goal structure for, 345(fig)
utilization-related clustering, of goals, 347

validity, in assessment, 12–13, 115–116
 action consistency and, 117–118
 and assessment device choice, 133–135
 content consistency and, 117–118
 in performance assessment, 149–150
 of instructional objectives, 187, 190
 of instructional units, 346
 relationship to reliability, 116–117
 strategies for enhancing, 120–122
variability
 as attention-getting strategy, 296–297, 307
 challenges of learner, 372–373, 378
 in instructional practice, 321, 322(fig)
verbal chains, 32
verbal communication, for selective perception, 313
verbal elaborations, 211, 220, 230, 314, 315
verbal information instructional strategies
 for activating prior knowledge, 216–219
 advance organizers, 217–218
 case analysis of, 227–232
 concrete experiences, 219
 cues and reminders, 216
 distinctiveness, 214–215
 for focusing attention, 213–215
 generative, 220–221
 highlighting, 213
 instructional analogies, 216–217

mnemonic devices, 221–223
organization strategies, 224–226
questioning, 213–214
self-generated analogies, 220–221
self-summaries and self-questions, 221
verbal elaboration and imagery, 220
verbal information skills, 29–33, 49, 310, 314, 323
  assessing, 160
  cluster analysis of, 65–70
  external conditions for learning (*see* verbal information instructional strategies)
  facts, 30–32
  far transfer of, 327
  instructional goals for, 32–33, 200
  instructional objectives for, 186–188

instructional resources for learning, 359(table)
internal conditions for learning, 202–212 (*see also* learning process, internal)
labels, 30
and memory structure, 70
organizational relationships of, 64, 65
organized facts, 32
planning instructional events for, 316–317
verbal chains, 32
verbal labels
  and concept formation, 243–245
  in rule and principle learning, 264–265, 267, 268
verbal reminders, for activating prior knowledge, 305

verbs, in instructional goals, 24–26. *See also* capability verbs
Vygotsky, L. S., 311–312

Wager, Walter, 172
Weiner, B., 326
Wilson, B. 255
Wittrock, M. C., 220
word-based mnemonics, 222–223
working memory, 204, 205
  retrieval to, 304–306.
  see also prior knowledge, activating; retrieval, information
world-related clustering, of goals, 347

Yerkes-Dodson principle, 273
Ysseldyke, J. E., 106, 137

zone of proximal development, 311

Appearing in nearly every chapter, extended Case Analyses present realistic examples of teachers applying systematic instructional design principles in the classroom.

LET'S SUMMARIZE

Careful planning for the instructional phase is critical, for it is at this stage in the learning sequence that students are engaged with the critical content that they must selectively perceive and actively encode into long-term memory. The particular external ways in which we support learners' internal selective perception and encoding processes will vary depending on the learning outcomes we are attempting to achieve.

Now that you have a sense of the internal and external conditions of learning that are relevant to the instructional phase of learning, let's analyze two classroom teaching examples.

CASE ANALYSIS

Planning Instructional Events for a Verbal Information Goal

Ms. Nelson has invited us to listen to her think out loud as she plans her instructional events for verbal information learning. You should review the planning that she has already done in Chapter 7 before reading the case analysis.

TEACHER'S THINKING AND PLANNING

For my verbal information instructional goal [state the names of the four major eras in the earth's history and several important characteristics of each], students will first encounter the propositions they are to learn by reading them in their textbook. To help them selectively perceive the specific propositions that are relevant to the instructional goal, I will give them an empty cluster analysis chart [see Table ?] to complete. Each empty cell will represent a specific proposition or set of propositions for students to find as they read. The chart will help students assign meaning to the propositions because they will already understand the superordinate conceptual categories that provide the organizational structure.

By reading and writing the target propositions, my students are likely to be thinking about them—that is, they will be active in working memory. Now what can I do to help them move the information from working memory to long-term memory? I will use the following external events [described in Chapter 7] to support my students' encoding processes:

- Cluster analysis chart to support organization

- meaningful verbal elaboration—not just ~~ons~~
- ~~support~~ verbal elaboration
- ~~time~~ lines to support imagery elaboration
- ~~on~~ era and subperiod names

~~strategic~~, self-regulated learners, I will con~~sider~~ elaborative interrogation and verbal ~~I have~~ been working with students all year ~~with~~ this verbal information instructional se~~quence, opport~~unity for them to see how these strate~~gies relate to s~~pecific content.

CASE ANALYSIS

Planning Instructional Events for an Intellectual Skill Goal

Now let's listen to Mrs. Torres think out loud as she plans her instructional events for intellectual skill learning. You should review the planning that Mrs. Torres has already done in Chapter 9 before reading the case analysis.

TEACHER'S THINKING AND PLANNING

For my intellectual skill instructional goal (apply the rule for rounding numbers to the nearest ten), I will introduce students to the rule by demonstrating it for them with meaningful materials such as base-ten blocks and number lines [see Figures 9.4 and 9.5], using the following actions to influence their selective perception of the rule's critical features:

- Maintaining the same multiples of ten for each set of examples
- Writing both the next lower and next higher multiples of ten for each number and using arrows to point to the rounded multiple
- Using boldface multiples of ten on the number line and column headings for the next lower and next higher multiples of ten
- Providing visual images (blocks, number line) that clearly show each element of the rule: number to be rounded, next lower multiple of ten, next higher multiple of ten

After students are thinking consciously about how the rounding rule works, they need to begin encoding it into long-term memory as a production. The key to encoding a skill as procedural knowledge is for learners themselves to produce the appropriate actions under the right conditions. I will try to support learner encoding with the following external events [described in Chapter 9]:

- Providing several two-digit numbers for students to round using their base-ten blocks
- Providing several two-digit numbers for students to round using a number line
- Providing one- and three-digit numbers for students to round to promote generalization
- Providing meaningful scenarios in which number rounding occurs
- Providing difficult instances (e.g., zero in ten's place) for students to round to promote discrimination

During each of the preceding activities, I will help my students think meaningfully about what they are doing and why they are doing it so they are not just memorizing a set of steps as verbal information. I will require them to demonstrate their rounding with base-ten blocks and number lines. I also will require them to explain verbally to me and each other why they are making specific rounding decisions.